DAWN

Dawn is the first of a series of four Dreiser novels. It deals with the first twenty years of his life.

Dreiser was born in 1871, one of thirteen children. His parents were Germans who had emigrated to the American Middle West in search of their fortune. Dreiser was sent to a Roman Catholic school which he hated, and *Dawn* has a very moving section describing his life there. The family moved to Chicago where Dreiser took a variety of menial jobs — selling papers on street corners, washing dishes in a filthy restaurant, packing goods in a hardware shop. The great turning point in his life comes towards the end of the book when by an incredible stroke of good fortune he enters the State University of Indiana.

Dawn is not only about Dreiser himself but also about the social environment in which he finds himself. He always sees himself against the complex background of his work, education, and social relationships. *Dawn*, as a result, gives a fascinating picture of America at the end of the century.

A HISTORY OF MYSELF

DAWN

BY

THEODORE DREISER

CEDRIC CHIVERS
PORTWAY
BATH

First published 1931
by
Constable & Co. Ltd
This edition published
by
Cedric Chivers Ltd
by arrangement with the copyright holder
at the request of
The London & Home Counties Branch
of
The Library Association
1974

ISBN 0 85997 025 6

Printed in Great Britain by
Redwood Press Ltd, Trowbridge, Wiltshire
Bound by Cedric Chivers Ltd, Bath

DAWN

CHAPTER I

THE average earthling, as I have reason to know, has frequently the greatest hesitation in revealing the net of flesh and emotion and human relationship into which he was born and which conditioned his early efforts at living and too often his subsequent place in life and society. I am free to say here and now that I am in no way troubled by any such thoughts or feelings. In the recital that is about to follow, I think it will be obvious that I am moved only by motives of analysis which are as honest and sympathetic as I hope to make them revealing.

I can feel sorry for him who is so fearful of life and so poorly grounded in an understanding of things that he is terrorised lest someone discover that his uncle was a horse thief or his sister a prostitute or his father a bank-wrecker, but I cannot sympathise with his point of view. What has that to do with me, an individual has a right to ask himself? And if he has sufficient consciousness of individuality, it has nothing to do with him. If he is over-influenced by conditions in which he finds himself, at birth or later, then, of course, they have a great deal to do with him, though it does not follow that they are a cause for shame. It is as necessary at times to cut away from wealth and social tradition or feelings of social superiority or inferiority as it is from poverty and seeming disgrace. The world has been a long time learning this, but it is true. One does not make one's relatives or oneself or the world. The most interesting thing one can do is to observe or rearrange or explain, if possible.

I will not say that this is a true record. It must substantiate itself. It is—as they say in law—*to the best of my knowledge and belief*. I may add, though, that these very sincere impressions and transcriptions are as nearly accurate as memory can guarantee.

Before introducing myself as a member of my family, its character will need some general explanation. My father was German by birth, a native of that region which borders on

Belgium, the Duchy of Luxembourg and France of the Alsace-Lorraine region. Mayen on the Moselle was his birthplace, fifteen miles from Coblentz. He came to America in 1844 to escape conscription and make his fortune—the latter a laudable desire which he was only partially able to fulfil. He was a weaver by trade and presumably with some slight mechanical skill as well as business ability, but of a mind and temperament so circumscribed by his eventually well-nigh fanatical adherence to the Roman Catholic faith as to be entirely unsuited for the humming world of commerce.

It was while working his way from Connecticut and New York to Dayton, Ohio, that not far from Dayton, he met the girl who became my mother. She was the daughter of a prosperous Moravian farmer, of Dunkard or Mennonite faith, who was a unit of the sect that then centred about Bethlehem, Pennsylvania. The world of her rearing must have been a pleasant one, for often I have heard her speak of her parents' prosperity as farmers, of orchard and meadow and great fields of grain, and of some of the primitive conditions and devices of pioneer life that still affected them—neighbours borrowing fire, Indians coming to the door to beg or be sociable, the spinning of wool and cotton on hand looms, the home manufacture of soap, shoes, and furniture.

It became a tradition of our immediate family that as a girl my mother had been possessed of extraordinary beauty. Certainly my father often said as much, and my own earliest recollection of her is of a fair, plump and smiling woman of about forty, to me altogether lovely. She appealed to me as thoughtful, solicitous, wise, and above all, tender and helpful —qualities which evoked in me not so much dependence as love. At sixteen, or when my father met her—as I was told later by him—she was a ravishing country belle, lovely as a garden of roses or a field of wheat, and he fell madly in love with her. Because of his allegiance to the Catholic faith, her parents were bitterly opposed to him. But after he had gone on to Dayton, to connect himself with a new woollen mill there, she, at sixteen, ran away from home to join him and they were married. Her father, the parent of seven or eight children (of whom she was next to the youngest) was so enraged or outraged in his religious sensibilities that he proclaimed his intention of never seeing her again, and to this decision he remained faithful.

8

For a short time after their marriage my father and mother lived in Dayton, then removed to Fort Wayne, Indiana, where was a woollen mill of which he became production manager. Later still they went on to Sullivan, where he built a woollen mill and went into business for himself. For a few years he prospered. Then one spring, just after the surrounding farmers had been persuaded by him (his promise of a quick settlement), to deposit their seasons' fleece in the sheds about his mill, it was destroyed by fire. And no insurance as yet placed upon it. This loss, coupled with his belief that his soul's salvation depended upon his paying dollar for dollar for all that had been destroyed—and that as speedily as possible— all but did for him financially.

Still later, during the process of rebuilding (on borrowed capital), a great beam which was being placed under his architectural direction, fell and struck him on the head and shoulders, destroying the hearing of one ear and bringing on a long and painful brain illness. Simultaneously—as my mother once told me—two individuals, father and son, came to her and asked if they might examine certain papers, telling her this was necessary to the progress of the work in hand. Young and inexperienced as well as fairly impractical and credulous, she handed over various papers—deeds to properties which had nothing to do with the mill as well as some first and second mortgages. The result was that the papers disappeared and were never recovered. Thus, by barefaced robbery and while he was ill—or so I was led to believe—my father lost the remainder of his local wealth.

After this, followed by the death of his first three children (all boys and all taken within three years), my father was never quite himself again. His spirit seemed to be broken. What little commercial flair had previously animated him was dissipated. Indeed, he always seemed to me a man concerned much more with the hereafter than with the now. One needed to know him neither long nor intimately to learn that to him God was a blazing reality, with the Son and Blessed Virgin to the right and left and the Holy Spirit, in the shape of a dove, hovering over all. His faith in the Catholic Church, its Pope and priests, was implicit. He accepted literally the infallibility of the Pope, the Immaculate Conception, the chastity and spirituality of all priests and nuns, transub-

9

stantiation on the altar, forgiveness of sins, communion and the like. Never have I known a man more obsessed by a religious belief. In short, the endless vagaries and complications of mood and conduct which followed upon this succeeded eventually in impressing me as not only fantastic but pathetic. I looked on him as mentally a little weak.

Mention of the death of the first three children recalls a deeply-rooted vein of superstition which was one of the few traits of temperament my father and mother possessed in common and which was the heritage of most of their children. In connection with my own birth, for example, I have heard both of my parents and my eldest sister tell of having seen, at the time my mother was labouring with the birth of me, three maidens (graces, shall we say?), garbed in brightly-coloured costumes, come up the brick walk that led from the street gate to our front door, into the room in which my mother lay, pass about the foot of the bed and finally through a rear door into a small, exitless back yard, from whence they could have escaped only by vanishing into thin air! According to my sister—who still maintains that she saw them—they gave no sign nor made observation of anything, but entered and left most gaily, dancing and laughing, their arms about each other's waists, flowers in their hair! I would like to believe that Fate intended these beauteous apparitions as an august annunciation of my coming and import to this planet, but all things considered, I lack the vainglory as well as sufficient subsequent substantiation.

In like vein, I may add, I have heard my mother relate that just before her meeting with my father, she stood one evening near her home, looking down into a boggy depression—a hollow filled with small trees and dank with pooled water. Of a sudden she saw a number of will-o'-the-wisps or bog-fires, dancing over the water and among the trees, seemingly blown about by feeble breaths of air. Aroused by the spectacle, she counted them and found there were thirteen. By one of those strange vagaries which afflict the imaginative mind, she was moved to identify these lights with the thirteen children to which she subsequently gave birth!

Later, having given birth to three children at the rate of one every fifteen to eighteen months during the first four or five years of her marriage, she was one day filled with an angry rebellion or rage at the cumulative difficulties of wifehood and motherhood. She desired to remain young and free, at least for a time. In this mood, she said, she wished most vehemently that she were dead, or that the children were. Almost instantly —it was evening and she was visiting a brother's farm in northern Indiana—she went to the door and stood looking out at a clearing which surrounded the farmhouse. Out of the woods to the left as she stood there, and out of the gloom of night already gathering, came three lights, bobbing lightly to and fro, processional-wise. They approached very near her—almost intentionally so, it seemed to her—then fluttered on, thistle-down-wise, over a rail fence and into a wood beyond.

"Right away"—I am quoting her—"I knew that those were my three children and that they were going to die!"

And in the space of three years, all *were* dead.

There is a sequel to this which should be added here. As the body of the last of these children was about to be taken from the house, my mother threw herself on her knees beside it and made a solemn promise to God—or Life, or Fate—that if He —or It—would have mercy on her and grant her forgiveness for her rebellious complaint, she would henceforth bear herself as an humble servitor to His or Its will: even though she were given as many as ten children, and the rearing of them proved difficult, she would not complain! Although subsequently, and as if in fulfilment of this mystic bargain, she was given ten children, never did I hear her complain greatly. True, I heard her say once or twice that her life was accursed, or that she wished she were dead, but in the main, she faced life most cheerfully, even gaily, bore with her ills most bravely, and through it all succeeded in drawing her children to her as with hooks of steel. And had she been trained intellectually, I have no doubt she would have directed them into paths and labours eminently satisfactory to herself.

Shortly after the mill debacle in Sullivan, my parents removed to Terre Haute, where I was born on August 27th, 1871, at eight-thirty o'clock in the morning—at which time the three Maytime graces are said to have walked. This house on Ninth Street seems to have been associated in family annals with supernatural occurrences and visitations. There were tales of spirits striding through the rooms, previous to my birth and shortly after moving in, so that my father felt obliged to send for the local priest and have him sprinkle the house with holy water. Although the spirits did not vanish completely, so great was my father's faith that he was less troubled after that. This he personally told me.

Once safely introduced into the world, I proved but a sickly infant. For a time it was thought I could not live. My eldest sister, who was my mother's chief assistant at the time, describes me as puny beyond belief, all ribs and hollow eyes and ailing and whimpering. Perhaps because of this I appear to have seized upon my mother's fancy or affection. But indeed, which of her children did not, poor victim of maternal love that she was! She grieved and grieved over my impending fate, and as she herself later told me, finally resorted to what can only be looked upon as magic or witchcraft.

Opposite us, in an old vine-covered, tree-shaded house falling rapidly into decay, lived an old German woman, a feeble and mysterious recluse who was regarded in the neighbourhood as, if not a witch, at least the possessor of minor supernatural and unhallowed powers. She may have practised illegal medicinal arts, for all I know. At any rate, in cases of illness or great misfortune, she was not infrequently consulted by her neighbours. One night, when the family feared that my death was imminent, my mother, weeping, ordered my eldest sister to run across the street and ask this old woman to come over. But, knowing of my father's strict religious views, she refused. She did say, however: "If your mother wants my help, tell her to take a string and measure your brother from head to toe and from finger-tip to finger-tip. If the arms are as long as the body, bring the string to me."

This was done, and the measurements proving satisfactory, the string was taken to her, whereupon she smiled and sent for my mother.

"Your child will not die," she announced. "But for three nights in succession, you must take him out in the full of the moon. Leave his head and face uncovered, and stand so that the light will fall slant-wise over his forehead and eyes. Then say three times: *'Wass ich hab, nehm ab; wass ich thu, nehm zu!'*"

As a result of this remarkable therapy, I am reported to have improved. In three months I was well.

I report this naïve and peculiar happening precisely as it was told me by my elders.

CHAPTER II

IF asked to describe our family as distinguished from others, I would say that it was of a peculiarly nebulous, emotional, unorganised and traditionless character. Not that in Germany, where my father was born, as well as in Moravia, in Czechoslovakia, whence my mother's parents derived, there were not, as I subsequently learned, evidences of remote, if not necessarily distinguished, connections, but in the ebb and flow of the fortunes of various generations, these had been lost sight of. True enough, throughout my youth I frequently heard my father refer to brothers and sisters, uncles and aunts, as well as a comfortable if somewhat severe German home, in which he was brought up as a stepchild, but as for important ancestors, I never heard him speak of any.

Later on in life I visited his birthplace—Mayen—and found that he sprang from no great or pretentious stock, at least not in recent days. True, among his relatives and connections were some fairly prosperous—one cousin owned stone and coal yards; another, a furniture dealer, had failed for 50,000 marks —but no individuality of great standing. Indeed, I am fairly well satisfied that there were none. The word "Dreiser"—so I have been told—means "barber" in French, and I have heard my father say that there were some Dreisers over the adjacent French border. I never troubled to investigate.

If my mother knew anything of her ancestors, even in America, it was very difficult for her to piece the data together. As a matter of fact, I am sure that she knew nothing about them except that her parents were of Pennsylvania Dutch origin, Mennonites or Dunkards. Her immediate living relatives were plainly honest, energetic, religious farmers. All of her related recollections of them pointed to individuals, male and female, of an industrious and thrifty turn. What accident of physical chemistry compounded the strange, sweet, magnetic, dreamy soul that she was I have often pondered over.

13

Financial misfortune, death and illness do not seem to have deterred my parents from proceeding with the rearing of a family. Passionate individuals both, apparently, they were probably totally ignorant of any means of contraception. Besides, my father's religious code would not have tolerated any such; he would have regarded them as evil and leading directly to hell fire. Indeed, that a man of his iron conventionalism and moral intolerance should have fallen in love with and married a woman of so little moral and social sophistication as my mother is hard to understand, unless it was that he was drawn by a phase of his nature which he would not acknowledge or contemplate. Yet how lucky for the rest of us! For as I think of her now, I know that my mother was beyond or behind so-called good and evil. Neither moral nor immoral, she was non-moral, intellectually, emotionally, temperamentally. A strange, sweet, dreamy woman, who did not know how life was organised; who was quick to forget the miseries of the past and contemplate the comforts of the present, or, those wanting, the possibilities of the future; who travelled romantically a colourful and, to her, for all its ills, beautiful world. She was, after her fashion, a poet who suffers much, yet unfailingly and irresistibly continues to contemplate beauty—her one enduring earthly reward, as I came to know.

Following the first three children who died, there were ten, five boys and five girls, each from seventeen to nineteen months apart. The boys, in their order, were: John Paul, known by everyone as Paul; Marcus Romanus, known as Rome; Alphonse Joachim (Lord, how he did hate that second name!), shortened to Al, and when one of the family wished to taunt him, Jake; myself, Theodore Herman (save the mark!)—to which Albert was also added at some Catholic confirmation proceedings—known as Dorsch, Dorse, Ted, Theo, Dodo and possibly one or two other diminutives; and last but not least, Edward Minerod, always Ed to me and all others, who was my playmate and boon companion from the time I was five until I was sixteen or seventeen and finally left home.

To the girls, for reasons of my own, I shall give fictitious names and disregard the order of their birth. I shall call them Amy, Trina, Eleanor, Ruth and Janet.

What a family! I smile now when I think of them, with their illusions, notions, vanities, quarrels, failures, transgressions,

14

shames—some of them fearful as to what the world might think; others innocent, childlike, impractical; one brother gifted to sing, play, dance, compose; another, if his life could have been controlled, to shine in railroading and traffic management. I have always been sure that Al was intended to be a better writer than I could ever hope to be; that Ruth had the artistic impulses of a Marie Antoinette, also her weaknesses; that Janet was just Janet, simple, affectionate, motherly, not at all ambitious and only mildly practical; Amy, sensual, sensitive, selfish, by no means intelligent, yet convinced always of her superior intelligence; Trina, really intelligent and practical but lacking in warmth and sympathy; and Ed, ambitious and emotional, the actor type but without sufficient luck or daring to forward himself. Paul succeeded admirably as an actor and song writer, and years afterward Ed followed him, but not successfully. Rome drank himself into failure if not death. The girls, all of them, married, but by what devious routes! One, at thirty-seven, was killed by a train; another, at forty, died of cancer. And so it has gone.

I would not go so minutely into this record of my brothers and sisters save that in the earliest days of my unfolding sensory faculties, I was moved by strange impressions in connection with them. Life moved before me then as little more than form, sound, colour, odour. I have often wondered as to the primary condition of the energy or force we call life before it proceeds to construct the piece of machinery that is the human body, by which, through which, in which, it is to function and receive experiences from this earthly state. Sight! What is that? And how comes it to be achieved out of gases, solids, electrons, protons, quantums? And hearing! The ear! How does ultimate energy—atoms, electrons, ergs—go about the work of building an ear? And the senses—touch, smell, the nervous system! And all for what? The very, very temporary enjoyment of such forms, motions, colours, odours, sounds, tastes and feelings as we find here and so soon leave? And without one word as to the meaning of it all; perhaps without ever, anywhere, any least approximation to a repetition of it! A loss here, therefore an eternal loss; yet with no gain, an eternal gain!

Astounding, is it not?

And that strange process going on in the womb, the manufacturing plant of the race, where hearts, muscles, nerves, brains, are fashioned, and so delicately! Some bodies so well-assembled there—brain, muscle, nerve fibre, skin, bone; others so poorly that their owners pule and whine through this life, cursing the day they were born. Some spirits in some wombs have so little to go on, so little to do with, figuring a gestating mother as a base of supplies. What can the spirit of a child encased in the body of a consumptive tenement mother, for instance, find wherewith to build itself? And what the fœtus in a criminal or half-wit? Yet on toils the race-producing force, fumbling like a blind man in a cave, eyeless and feeling dark walls, as though trying to escape into the light and air without, and yet leaving that only to find forces calculated to make short work of the defectives prepared within. Yet we think and speak of a "soul," something (God knows what!) coming with a "spiritual" —whatever that is—as well as physical inheritance—the latter from the race, the former from where or what?

But is it probable? Or is all energy—the ultimate inde-structible energy of the physicist's broken atom—the true spirit of the universe? And is it all-wise? Can it combine and construct itself into any and all form as it chooses? And can it remember? Or does it wish to? Again, this immediate body-building power—is it in the blood and energy of the mother or the father, or an element independent? Or both? Let who can answer, do so!

* * * * * *

Our family, as I was to learn by experience and reflection, had some time before my birth taken on the complexion of poverty and failure, or, at least, seeming failure. My eldest brother Paul, for instance, so charming and helpful a figure in later years, had almost before I was born gotten in with bad boys— due to a troubled home life, I believe—and had forged a note in my father's name. Before this he had been arrested and put in jail with several others on suspicion of robbing a store. This was never proved, but it took considerable money to get him out, money which my father had to borrow. Not long after his release, this same boy (intended by my father for the priesthood!) foolishly smuggled some pepper to a former fellow-prisoner still in the county jail, which pepper this prisoner threw into the eyes of the keeper and thus effected an escape. Although this was merely the sympathetic and foolish action of a boy obviously controlled, and that sympathetically, by stronger, shrewder and more desperate companions, great was the influence necessary to clear Paul of joint responsibility for this crime, even though the man who persuaded him to buy the pepper confessed to having done so.

There are those who dully and naïvely divide the world into evil and good. I wish to present the following complication and paradox for their solution. During one of the most desperate periods of the family's finances, when my father was out of employment, my sister Eleanor, who was then only fifteen or sixteen, met a Colonel Silsby (the name is fictitious), a prominent lawyer and office-holder in Terre Haute. The meeting came about through no less a personage than the family doctor, who met the Colonel outside the family gate one day as he was leaving. Later, seeing her eyeing longingly the hats in a milliner's window at Eastertide, and knowing the family's financial state, this same Colonel asked Eleanor if she wouldn't like to have one.

"Indeed I would!" she replied.

"Then you take this ten dollars and see if you can get one!"

After some persuasion she took the money. And so began a friendship which ended in intimacy and what by some might be deemed seduction. As a matter of fact, I am not sure but that many elements besides the mood of the pursuer contributed. For one thing, my mother, being without moral bias or social training—(I doubt whether her mind had acquired any of the various formulæ or tenets which are supposed to govern correct society)—entered into this arrangement to the extent of permitting the child to keep the money. Afterwards, when misfortune pressed most severely, this man's beneficences were accepted—unknown to my father, of course. When Paul was in jail for the second time, it was this same Colonel Silsby who got him out. (My father, enraged by a line of conduct which to him seemed unforgivable, had decided to let the law take its course.) I seem to remember Paul's return, his lurking in an outhouse so that my father should not see him, and signalling to me to let my mother know he was there. He was, if I recall correctly, dirty, unkempt, prisony. My mother came out, cried, and made some secret arrangement whereby he was sent to the farm of a relative of hers.

In later years, as temperament or chance would have it, it

was Paul who became the truly wonderful son and brother. (MY BROTHER PAUL, of "Twelve Men.") But at the time I mention he was a jail-bird, an outcast, freed and yet homeless, his only friend his mother, and aided by the man who subsequently became my sister's lover.

I can see the moral uptilt of the noses of the dull and religiously regenerate. What a curse to the individual are the moral or social doctrines or taboos of any given day! And what creatures of infinite jest, as well as obstinate and meaningless notions and convictions, we really are! And is the ultimate essence of things like that, too?

CHAPTER III

THE various mental and inward stages of my youth are somewhat clouded or slightly greyed in part by heavy introspective and moralistic inquiries, which seemed a bent with me as they were naturally a mental condition with my father, and, by force of circumstances, with my mother also.

Also America, and especially the Middle West, was at that time miasmatically puritanic as well as patriotic, twin states bred of ignorance and what mental or economic lacks I am not able to discern. At any rate, quite all of the old was bad, all the new good. The enlightenment of the world, as I was to learn by degrees, dated from the Declaration of Independence. The United States of America constituted the greatest country in the world, the strongest and only free one. Catholicism, in our family, was the true religion; some form of Protestantism in all of the homes of our neighbours. The darkness and intolerance in which they were held! An atheist was a criminal. Anyone who doubted that Christ died on the cross to save all men or that men were truly saved thereby, or that there was a specific heaven, a definite hell, and so forth, was a scoundrel, a reprobate, a lost soul. Just how people were to live and die had all been fixed long before. There were no crimes greater than adultery, atheism, and theft. And so it went. I picture this atmosphere because some phases of it were at times so stern and destructive.

My most remote memories—or so they seem—take me back to the house in Twelfth Street, Terre Haute, to which, some time after my birth, our family removed. It was a frame house that stood on the north-west corner of Twelfth and Poplar Streets, a house not unlike thousands of others still to be seen —almost an exact duplicate of the house Lincoln occupied in Springfield at the time he was nominated—with a long, low porch and door in front, a door at one side and at the rear, a yard or measure of ground perhaps one hundred and fifty feet wide and two hundred feet deep, dotted with apple, pear, cherry, and peach trees, and a small kitchen garden bordered on one side by a low row of gooseberry bushes. It may or may not have had charm—early impressions are deceptive—but when is life utterly without charm? The meanest shanty, the back street garret—what vital meaning is here which by some reverse process in art transmutes itself into a rancid, spell-casting glory!

This earliest home of mine presents only faint glimpses of itself, like colours seen through trees or shadows on water. What is hearsay and what direct memory I may not say. I remember a dog, for instance, a courageous, lightsome brindle, that was constantly burying bones and as constantly getting into fights. Somewhere in the profundities of this chiaroscuro there intrudes itself a terrific struggle between Prince (or "Bint," as I called him) and another dog, in which death seemed imminent for one or the other—evidently the stranger, for Bint had to be torn off. I dimly recall yells and screams, an elder sister running with a bucket of water (hot or cold?) and my mother standing in the doorway directing operations.

Again, I have a rather faint memory of us children—my sisters Eleanor and Amy as well as Al and myself—presiding at an obviously cruel, and yet at bottom no more than mischievous, attempt to hang a cat from the limb of an apple tree. I could not have been more than three or four years old at the time, but I recall the cat being strung up and swinging in the wind, ourselves dancing around until we were driven or called off by someone—very likely our mother—and the cat cut down. Again, I recall one of the children falling into a well—I cannot recall which of us.

But most of these earliest memories are probably composed more of hearsay and emotion than of ordinary and common-place reality. And yet they glow with such strong colour! Thus, I am a child of three or four and standing at a gate looking up a road and wondering if the sky actually came down to the street as it seemed to, and whether one looked at it as one might at a curtain, and what was on the other side. Or imagine this same child sitting of an evening watching the trees, the sky, the setting sun, and feeling an intense emotional stir of beauty, so wonderful, so strange, so new, that I recall it even now as if it had been a moving and appealing strain of music.

Also I recall a plague of locusts in these same early years. Previous to this, if I recall aright, my mother had warned me not to go into the cellar, in order obviously to keep me out of mischief there, but made effective or given teeth by the tale of a mythical "cat man" who lurked there and might get me! And now, among the dark green shadows of evening trees, this same "cat man," only come to possess the voice if not the body of the locust or the locust the voice and body of the "cat man," and leaping from one tree to another, as the sound of sawing came from now here, now there. And seeking whom to devour. When two locusts were heard at once, it simply meant that there were two "cat men" or demons lurking to bedevil me! (Tell me, oh, physicists and chemists, why so great a fear, so roiling a sensitivity, in a physical chemism four or five years of age?)

Instantly I was in the house and to my mother's skirts, enfolding her legs in my fright, crying, pressing my face against her body. (Oh, years later, when she was really gone, I knew why I cried!) But when a velvety hand was laid on my cheek, could there be any real danger anywhere? Was I not safe with her? Are not "cat men" afraid of mothers? Since when runneth the memory of man to the contrary?

But how strange the other and various wonders of life! (And how strange, still, for that matter!) And what naïve interpretations I put upon them! Thus, there were the little white cones that grow on fir trees in the spring. Since I wondered concerning them, some pestered person—my mother, probably —had troubled to explain that they were fledgling birds growing toward strength and freedom and would fly away once they were ripe. And true enough, presently they were gone, probably in the night when I was sleeping, as I reasoned. And I had waited and watched so to see, not knowing that the warmth of the sun had given them wings! And now in what far skies were they flying, I wondered? And that sky itself? Was it not a cloth of blue just a little way above the housetops and trees? Readily later, in our Catholic schoolroom, I could believe the fable of the Tower of Babel.

And dreams! I remember dreaming of beautiful red, green, blue, and yellow marbles floating about in the air, and of nickels, dimes and quarters lying everywhere on the ground! What disappointment, what despair, to wake at morn and find that a seeming reality was not! So I came to know of dreams and their sweet futility.

And now it rains, and there is a flash of lightning and a clap of thunder, and somehow and for the first time I am experiencing a storm, the rain beating against the window-panes and making little domes of glass on the walk and quickly-formed pools of water outside.

Or now it is a hot summer day and there is a brilliantly-garbed band coming down the centre of a crowded business street. I am in my father's arms or on his shoulder, to see, and shivering with mingled fear and delight. A giant under a shako, in gilt and gold, is twirling a huge baton. But, oh, the blaze of the sun on red and gold and brass! And the strong, vibrant, metallic tones!

Or again, I am passing the residence of a rich man. On a green sward before the house stands a giant iron stag, its horns spreading enormously. My face is pressed between two iron pickets of the fence, to see. What could so great an animal be? And where did he live?

Or now it is a church, sombre, silent, but with an altar blazing with candles and a bleeding Jesus high on a cross. But the figure is attractive only as a toy or doll might be. And I crave him as a toy, even call out loudly for him to be given me—a great scandal to my father!

Or now and again, it is a railroad yard, with engines and cars, a freight house, a round-house, and all the mysteries and wonders of that. Or a hotel with bright windows.

Again, it is Christmas Day, with snow, and books and toys that display Jack and the Bean Stalk, Little Red Riding Hood, Blue Beard, Mother Goose. How well I remember all! And with what wonder, awe, belief, curiosity, I viewed the black-and-white spotted cow, with a kind of spirited twist to horns and tail, leaping over the moon; the peak-hatted witch, with a sharp nose and chin, riding on her broomstick!

There was a sewing machine I loved to "run," because it was nice to see the wheel go around, dressmaking being meanwhile in progress on the dining-room table. There was also a school to which, at say six, I was led by the hand by my sister Amy, yet terrified and crying: "Amy . . . ah! . . ."

There was . . .

There was . . .

But really now, was there ever?

Or is it all a dream?

I must have been an emotional and sentimental child. I recall, one hot day, playing on the floor of the front room, and about my mother's knees. (I was always a "mother child," hanging to her skirts as much as I was permitted until I was seven or eight years old.) I recall her lounging in a white dressing-sacque, a pair of worn slippers on her feet. In my playful peregrinations I came to her feet and began smoothing her toes. I can hear her now. "See poor mother's shoes? Aren't you sorry she has to wear such torn shoes? See the hole here?" She reached down to show me, and in wonder, and finally pity—evoked by the tone of her voice which so long controlled me—I began to examine, growing more and more sorrowful as I did so. And then finally, a sudden, swelling sense of pity that ended in tears. I smoothed her shoes and cried. I recall her taking me up and holding me affectionately against her breast and smoothing my head. Then feeling still more sorrowful and helpless, I presume, I cried the more. But that was the birth of sympathy and tenderness in me.

At that time there lived across the street from us, in a long, low, red house under green trees, an old woman named Mrs. Stulp—not the "witch lady" who cured me but, like her, German, angular and quite old. She had taken a fancy to me, it appeared, and to assure herself of my return visits, had, among other things, provided me with a little low chair, so small that it would go under the large walnut bed which stood in a corner of her general living and bedroom. Also there were toys to play with—a croquet ball with a yellow band around it, for one thing, and a set of dominoes. Here then, lured by these things, I am sure, I came betimes to play, crawling under her bed for my chair and babbling what infantile inconsequentials any mother may guess. But I vaguely recall the tall, angular, wrinkled old dame, in a knitted hood or lace cap and shawl, who smiled, knitted, and said nice things to me. I also seem to remember that I wore a gingham apron and a small pair of slippers.

But after a time, as I also recall, something happened. The windows of Mrs. Stulp's house were curtained. And now I was taken over and lifted up to look at a sallow crone, finally prostrate with age and infirmity. I recall a street full of vehicles

—buggies, a carriage, a hearse. They took a box out of the house and I never went again to play. Where in eternal substance is Mrs. Stulp, her lace cap, her knitting, her chair?

There was also an old, one-armed watchman, a stocky, great-coated man, who tended a gate at a railroad crossing in Terre Haute, and who passed our house every morning between six-thirty and seven on his way to work and again in the evening between seven-thirty and eight on his way home—a long day. All I recall of him is that he gave me candy, apples and nuts, but also in order to get them, at his command I had to climb up on the fence and reach down into his pockets. Also I seem to remember his grizzled, genial face, brown and kindly, under a wide-brimmed black hat. I also recall a spirit of watchfulness on my part, a lively sense of favours to come, which sent me scampering to the side gate morning and evening, shouting: "Mr. Watchman! Mr. Watchman!" I presume that if my attentions became too lively, he found it convenient to go home by another street.

But the day finally arrived, as with Mrs. Stulp, when Mr. Watchman did not come any more, and since our friendship appeared to have gained the attention as well as sympathy of my elders, I was taken to see him. I remember he lay in a simple coffin set on trestles, which gave it a stark look. He was waxy and still, his features quite as I had known them, but, most interesting of all to my childish mind, there were five-cent pieces on his eyelids! And, by this time, knowing my "nickels" when I saw them, I actually reached for them, only to be told, as you may well guess: "Oh, no, you wouldn't want to take the nickels from poor Mr. Watchman! Poor Mr. Watchman, who used to bring you the candy?" And the import of Mr. Watchman's past favours as well as the mood of the person speaking as instantly caused me to feel that it was all very sad and that what I was doing was very wrong, quite cruel, in fact. It was perhaps my first vivid impression of death.

CHAPTER IV

I HAVE often pondered over the spectacle which our family presented during our occupation of the five or six houses we lived in successively in Terre Haute. Most of the details here narrated came to me by hearsay, but my conclusion is that it must have offered as interesting an example of mental nebulosity and lack of social placement and skill as one would care to find.

I remember a large brick dwelling, said to have stood on Fourteenth Street, where after Twelfth Street, and due to growing financial strain, boarders and roomers were taken in. The individual positions of some of these gave me my earliest, if not quite intelligent, contact with ease and even a species of luxury. For instance, I recall a certain woman—a vulgar, showy creature, probably—who moved about this place in silks, satins and laces, a jewelled and perfumed lady, with a wealth of light yellow hair. She had a little daughter seven or eight years of age and of a related type or mood. In connection with the girl I remember a blue velvet dress she wore; also that none of us could afford so fine a thing. Besides, the contents of the room, or rooms, they occupied must have been superior according to the standards I then had to go by, for looking through the door at a dresser ornamented with silver-backed toilet articles, I remember wishing that I might live in such a room.

But as a boarding house, the place was a failure apparently, since skill in the matter of economy was not among my mother's gifts. So presently there came a smaller house, in Thirteenth Street, where sickness overtook the three youngest of us and enforced idleness on the part of my father compelled my mother to take in washing, go out to clean, do anything and everything which might tend to keep us from starving. It was during this period, as I recall it, that I learned to carry coal, picking it up from between the tracks or stealing it from cars, albeit being occasionally driven away with threats and curses from some ill-natured or officious railroad hand.

Again, I remember a wave of measles or scarlet fever which swept our neighbourhood and to which we three youngest fell victims. And as poor as we were, there was a tall, dark-frocked priest who came and bent over me, anointing my head, feet and hands with holy oil and permitting me to kiss a silver Christ on an ebony cross, which at once I craved as a toy. But the good father—mindful of the property of his church—took it away with him, giving me instead a small blue-and-white china St. Joseph, a mere penny-whistle figure which did not allure me.

What a period! What I have here written is probably no more than accumulated and assorted hearsay, collated and arranged after the facts. What I personally lived through at the time was different—a dour and despondent period which seems to have coloured my life for ever. Young as I was, I sensed somehow the crucifixion that must have been my mother's. I seem to recall long, dreary, grey, cold days; meagre meals, only fried potatoes or fried mush at times. As a child, and at this particular time, I was more than once hungry, but through no want of effort on the part of the woman whose memory I adore.

Life has long since schooled me to its bitter aspects, its grim constructive processes, which I understand and respect well enough, and yet I can never look on crowded tenements or small, shabby cottages in cheap, mean streets, or poorly-clothed children, men, or women, with grimy hands and faces and a weary, troubled or laboured look, without reverting in thought to this particular period of my life and wishing, without quite knowing how, to point out a way by which life might be better organised, wishing that it would not permit the untrained or the inadequate to stew so persistently and helplessly in their own misery—as they still do, though not for ever, may we hope. While I see no change in the ratio of those who must die unfed in the west as well as the east, in Russia at least, is there not a light feebly beginning to glow? I wait to see it flame brightly, illuminating a stubborn, selfish, greedy world.

Up to now I have barely mentioned the second of my two elder brothers, an individual who has always been a problem to me, and still remains so. Rome he was called—short for Marcus

Romanus, a very noble handle for so humble a mid-western boy. Strong and handsome physically if not mentally, he was proving then, as later, a family Nemesis, having early developed into a vainglorious, determined and yet mistaken youth, who seemed to feel that the world was made for him, not he for it. Opposed to him was my father's idea of family organisation: that it should be sustained in unity by the combined efforts of all, and, of course, under his personal and decidedly exacting direction—a truly German thought that did not flourish in this looser western social polity, though it was not for want of endeavour on my father's part. Unfortunately, his method was so interlarded with Catholic dogma, such wholly unyielding directive ritual and precept, as to quite sicken not only his wife but all of his children. It was charged by him, as I later came to know, that my mother's attitude toward all of her children was too easy and yielding. Well, maybe—she was affectionate and forgiving and her knowledge of the ways of life was not great. In Rome's case she seemed to feel that he needed to be dealt with gently rather than critically and dictatorially, as was my father's way.

At any rate, at seventeen or eighteen, Rome had already developed characteristics which were not to profit either himself or those intimately allied with him. Already on occasion he was drinking and gambling. And as bad, if not worse, he had allied himself with a group of loafing—and probably "wise-cracking"—youths who preferred to make their way by their wits rather than by solid if humdrum labour. All that appeared to interest him at that time, as I have heard, or after, in so far as I could see, was chance and adventure. He liked to gamble, and such winnings as he achieved were as recklessly devoted—and this in the face of the dire need of his parents— to a still looser type of adventuring with girls. Self, self, self— he never saw anybody but himself! And worse, his thoughts were streaked with not so much envy as an ironic superiority toward all who prospered—an irony which his adventurings never (to me at least) seemed to warrant. I am judging him by subsequent years of experience.

In connection with him, though, my sister Eleanor once related to me that having one day confided to her mother in Rome's presence that her elderly and wealthy admirer had declared his desire to aid her, Rome waited until she was alone and then proposed that she approach this individual on his behalf. For, as he explained, he knew of a certain combination of lottery numbers shortly to be drawn which would net him thousands. And with fifty dollars he could guarantee to repay her tenfold at the same time that he shared a part of his winnings with his mother. But when Eleanor rejected the scheme with fear as well as irritation, he at once turned on her and denounced her as a cold, heartless, worthless sister. Other girls whom he knew would not act in such a way! Whereupon, as she said, the suggestion did fix itself upon her as a possibility, although at the time she could not bring herself to act upon it.

A little later, though, he was back with another suggestion. It appears that the president of a local lumber company was famed for his generosity. And now if she were to go to him and ask for a loan for her family—to pay the rent, say—he would give it, and without harm to her, since he was religious as well as generous. But this, like the other scheme—although not so objectionable—was fought by Eleanor on the ground of the shame of it. But young Machiavelli proceeded to gloss this over with the statement that everybody knew our family was poor, and how was it to get a start without money? And since this was true enough at the time, as she knew, the matter was put before my mother, who, assailed, wheedled, cajoled and what not else by this driving youth, eventually yielded her own needs as well as his certainty of success being emphasised.

So it was that a day or two later the trip was made, Rome accompanying Eleanor to within a hundred feet of the lumber company office door in order that she might not want for proper encouragement. Once inside the door, as she said, she found herself speechless. Finally, the president himself— attracted by her looks, perhaps—came over and asked her what she wanted. Encouraged by his voice and manner and driven by the force of her brother without, she finally found strength to say what she had been told to say: that she was the daughter of so and so who had once been so and so but was now quite ill and the family about to be evicted for want of rent money. Whereupon, with a "Well, now, isn't that too bad!" and "I'm sorry you had to be the one to ask in this way," this total stranger put his hand in his pocket and drawing out his purse counted out fifty dollars, with which she returned to Rome, who by then had retreated to the next block.

But no particular benefit from this ever flowed to anyone but this young waster, as I understand it. For while he gave a small part of the money to his mother—some fifteen or sixteen dollars—the balance was squandered. And an unfortunate aftermath, as all saw it later, was that this same sister, having thus been inducted into this form of pleading, and other and equally severe conditions descending on the family, found it not so difficult to accept the aid of Colonel Silsby and, of course, return with it to her mother, whose reduced economic condition, as Eleanor put it, was "just too much!"

I have described my father as a religious enthusiast. At that time he was a morose and dour figure, forlorn and despondent, tramping about the house, his hands behind his back and occasionally talking to himself. One of his worst phases was the conviction that there was refuge in religion, more and more self-humiliation before a Creator who revealed Himself only through the forms and ceremonies of the Catholic Church. He believed implicitly that the least neglect or infraction of such forms and ceremonies as were ordered by the Church was sufficient to evoke disfavour or at least neglect on the part of the Universal Ruler. This being true, the rather indifferent religious conduct of his wife and children was sufficient to convince him that they were evil to a degree and in need of driving. Even before this time, my mother had been prone to suspect, and to voice her suspicion, that because of his insistence on the Catholic school as opposed to the public or free school, her children had not been given the proper educational advantages and so were already greatly handicapped in their race for place and position. But none too well grounded in her revolt and still overawed by the ponderous material flummery of the faith she had adopted, she doubted and protested one minute and was the next awed into silence, and even acquiescence, by the uproar that invariably ensued. I rise to testify, for I have heard these arguments with my own ears, almost daily, nightly, or both—what should be said or done for the children when there was so little of any value that was being done for any one of them!

True, as my father once told me, during the period when he was managing the mill of his former rivals in Terre Haute, and before trade misfortune overtook them too, he had urged both of his eldest sons to permit him to teach them the technique of woollen manufacture, since he believed that such manufacture was destined to a future in America. But they would not hear of it, feeling that their interests lay elsewhere. But apart from that, I could never see that he offered any directive suggestions of value.

But in this connection I would like to say that I have no fixed theories as to the best method of educating children. It seems to me an almost inscrutable problem, a system applicable under some conditions being by no means suitable under others. But having had opportunity later to contrast the American public school with the Catholic parochial system, I now regard the first as in the main a real aid to intelligence and freedom of spirit and the second as an outrageous survival of a stultifying mediævalism which should be swept away to its last detail.

The inanity of teaching at this day and date, and as illustrated by the Holy Roman Catechism, the quite lunatic theories and pretensions of that entirely discredited organism to divine inspiration and hence leadership and of putting that unscratched tablet, the mind of a child, into its possession or care! Fie! Faugh! The alleged intelligence of a maundering world! And the brassy insouciance and tongue-in-cheek "authority" with which the alleged "princes of the Church," their factotums or "fathers," step forward not only to receive but to demand the care of the young! No wonder it became the first business of the Russian Communists to rip out root and branch the eastern or Asiatic extension of this same designing and serpentine organisation!

To what end, then, the work of a Galileo, a Newton, a Darwin, a LaMarck, a Huxley, a Faraday, a Tyndall, a Helmholtz, a Jeans, a Millikan, in truth the entire army of distinguished and substantiated students who have laboured and meditated on behalf of reality, if these sacrament and indulgence salesmen are to be allowed to seize upon the child—in the protectory, the orphan asylum, the school and Catholic home —and corrupt its reason with unverifiable dogma or just plain lies? A bishop has a palace while a scientist lacks a laboratory! Churches to St. Joseph, St. Anthony, the Immaculate Conception; monasteries, nunneries, convents, homes and hospitals erected in honour of the same, but also for what profit can be had out of the psychopathic balderdash they represent! Billions in real estate untaxed, and science, whether it conflicts

30

with dogma or not, even called in to help—in the profit-taking but no further!

I often think of the hundreds of thousands of children turned out of the Catholic schools at twelve or thirteen years of age, with not a glimmer of true history or logic, no efficient mechanical training, not a suggestion even of such comparatively simple and yet enormously valuable things as rudimentary botany, chemistry or physics. For in these realms, you see, you come upon strange facts and paradoxes which might endanger an inculcated belief in the infallibility of the Pope, the sanctity of the priests, the importance of the confessional, the presence of a definite hell and a specific heaven. My father died firm in his belief in these dogmas. My mother was troubled by them to the day of her death. They continue, I believe, to influence at least one of my brothers to such an extent that were he to read this he would regard it as blasphemous, my soul in danger of hell.

At any rate, here was I, at six years of age, along with Trina and later my brother Ed, installed in St. Joseph's German Catholic school, an adjunct of St. Joseph's Roman Catholic Church, in Ninth Street in Terre Haute—a pay school, you may be sure, although right around the corner was a free public school where an at least fairly liberal and honest brand of information concerning life was being dispensed. The schoolroom contained forty or fifty hard wooden benches, much scarred, as I recall, by knives and pencils and much bespattered with ink. The other children, mostly of my own age and sex —hardy little jiggers, in the main—may not have been disturbed as much as myself by the meagre and to me forbidding regimen prescribed. (There are temperaments and temperaments, minds and minds!) The floor was bare, the walls covered with blackboards. On a dais which faced us sat—as she then seemed to me—the Nemesis or Gorgon of the place, an outlandish figure of a woman clad in black, with a flaring white hood or bonnet.

Once the business of inducting me into a seat was over, I along with others was called upon to register and apprehend my A, B, C's—a long line of curious-looking German symbols— which were pointed at with a long, thin wand by this hooded figure, herself articulating the letters and ordering us to do the same. Impressed, terrified even, I did so. The remainder of her requests, for that day at least if I recall aright, were principally for silence and order. But the uniform overawed me, as did that of the black-cassocked priest who occasionally on this first day, and almost regularly on every other day thereafter, strutted or prowled amongst us.

Daily we were led into church—attendance at which was compulsory—to hear a mass. At twelve o'clock, after prayers, we were turned out to play and eat until one. If we encountered a priest anywhere, we had to lift our hats and say: "Praised be Jesus Christ!" to which he replied, lifting his hat, "Amen!" And it was our bounden duty, as we soon learned, to appear at mass at least once on Sunday (high mass, preferably) and at Vespers on Sunday afternoon. A number of the boys were selected to do church duty—serve as altar boys, ring the bell or run errands for the priest. At the age of eight or ten we were supposed to begin to go to confession. At twelve, having mastered the Catechism (the rules of the Catholic Church covering our relation to it and God), we were ready for our First Holy Communion. After that our parents could put us to work if they chose. However deficient in other respects our education might be, we were good Catholics, or were supposed to be, and beyond that, what mattered?

But one or two pleasant memories persist in emerging out of my impressions of the little school I attended in Terre Haute. I recall a little primer which contained my A, B, C's, but which also included a few, to me quite enchanting if infantile, pictures —ducks a-voyaging on a pond, a mill wheel with water pouring over it, a windmill with the wind bellying its immense sails; a lighthouse, a ship, a donkey; and, best of all, a German landscape, with a cottage and bird-house in the distance, the sun rising over a pleasant hill, its rays standing out in straight lines, and a young German Hans, books under his arm, making his way cheerfully, instead of ruefully as in my case, to school— the same intended, no doubt, to be an inspiration to recalcitrant American boys!

Also, near our school, was a pond or slough in which in rainy weather it was possible to navigate on a plank or improvised raft. Now from my earliest conscious recollections of natural phenomena, I seem to have been dubious of water. Or at least I had been made fearful by my brother Rome, who once took my brother Al, my sister Trina and myself out in a small rowboat upon the Wabash River, a to me mysterious, ominous and most uncertain body or thing which had motion, and hence life, maybe. I think I must have been overawed by its quantity and movement as well as its difference from solid earth. At any rate, there it was, strange and fearsome. And then when a stern-propelled steamboat, of no doubt minute size but to me enormous, came into view around a bend and after passing, left in its wake a ripple which rocked our small craft, I was panic-stricken. In fact, for some four or five years thereafter I could not view any considerable body of water without having brought back to me most clearly that particular sensation of something that could and might destroy me, and that with almost personal violence.

Despite this fear, however, I soon found myself propelling myself about this very shallow puddle on a plank—my former terror overcome for the time being by the fact that so many others of about my own years were doing the same—and marvelling at my own skill as well as at life itself—water, light, air, boys, schools, homes—at the same time conveniently forgetting that I was forbidden to get myself dirty or wet. The school-bell might ring, the other boys depart, the white-capped sister come to the schoolhouse door to look for any possible straggler, yet here I lingered, when there was water to linger over, often until I knew I was in danger of reproof. Then terrified by the recollection of rules and punishment, running as fast as my legs would carry me, coming up at last breathless, my mind filled with a vague irritation at having to go inside.

CHAPTER V

A SITUATION such as existed here in Terre Haute in connection with our family could only become either somewhat better or fatally worse. In our case, I think "worse" and "better" were finally blended. For my mother, driven by her sufferings, I presume, was forced to think out a more constructive programme. And while this did not lead to any immediate rehabilitation for any one of us, still it did serve to carry over the younger members of the family until such time as they were able to do something for themselves. Her action in this connection, considering her lack of training and her more or less dreamy or mystical character, has always been to me a matter for marvelling.

Her thought, it appeared, was to divide this large family so that its collective weight at any one point should not be too great. At any rate, and along with her husband and older children in counsel, it was decided to leave the four elder girls with their father in Terre Haute, because at that time he was working as manager of a small carpet factory and, with the aid of his four daughters as loom-hands, it would be possible for them, collectively, to earn some thirty-five or forty dollars a week. On this sum they were to live and at the same time lay aside some lesser sums, the same to be sent regularly to my mother, which, along with another resource which had obviously just occurred to her, would enable her to provide for herself and her three youngest. The fourth youngest, Al, was to be sent to a half-sister of my mother's, who with her husband farmed a considerable tract of land near North Manchester, in northern Indiana. Paul already was out of touch with the family, working in his apprentice minstrel world (but unknown to those at home) and my brother Rome had taken flight into the world as a "train butcher." (Popcorn, peanuts, candy! All the latest magazines and papers!)

My mother's first thought was to go with her small brood to

Sullivan, the town in which my father had some years before built and lost his woollen mill. It was a dead place some twenty-five miles from Terre Haute, but there were one or two coal mines there employing a number of men, most of whom boarded around the town. Also still present there as residents were several friends of my parents—people whom they had known in their better days. And now, in her extremity, she had one of my sisters write to one of these, a woman whose husband was connected with the railway at this point and who formerly had done some work for my father. The burden of the letter was that she wished to return to Sullivan, obtain a house with a sizeable piece of ground on which she could plant a garden, and, incidentally, sufficiently near the mines to further the expectation of a boarder or two.

But the reply, when it came, as I later learned, was almost wholly discouraging. It would be hard to make a living there. There were a few houses for rent, but probably not what she wanted. It would be better to come and go over the ground herself.

Coincidentally, my mother chanced to think of another person—a certain Sue Bellette, a French orphan out of Vincennes, Indiana—who was more or less indebted to her. When she first came to my mother for aid, she was working as a seamstress in Terre Haute, and finding my mother kindly, had done her best to attach herself to her as a foster-daughter of sorts, sewing and doing other work for her and her children for the privilege of remaining near her. But some time after that again she had returned to Vincennes and there married one Frank Tinby, captain and engine-man of the principal fire station. Although, as I afterwards learned, my mother had never wholly approved of Sue—looking on her as too wild— Sue had continued to keep in touch with her, looking on her, as she said to me years later, as the only mother she ever had. So now, after the bad news from Sullivan, my mother wrote this Sue for the privilege of coming and bringing her three children for a stay of a few weeks. To this Sue replied—or so she said to me some twelve years later after my mother's death—that she could come and stay for life if she would.

At any rate, it being spring and my mother most anxious to make a new start in life, it was to Vincennes and this woman's home that we four—my mother; Trina, aged ten; myself, eight; and Ed, six—repaired. Curiously enough, I have only the faintest recollection of the railroad trip, although it was my first and must have been an impressive event. At best, and vaguely, I recall a bright, warm day, possibly April or May, certainly the springtime. And, of course, my mother, with Trina and Ed and myself in tow. (That driven, distrait woman!) Also a depot, a train, a noisy railroad yard with engines and cars, and then lesser stations and considerable stretches of woods and fields. Also the great necessity of remaining close to mother. But no more than that. No remembrance of our arrival in Vincennes or how we made our way to our subsequent temporary abode, although many details relating to that place remain clear enough.

One of the things that interests me now as I sit and think about it all is that I have a clear recollection of a visit, just before our leaving Terre Haute, to my father in the new and very small carpet mill with which he had connected himself, although I have no faintest recollection of my sisters at work in the place. Perhaps it was that he was merely making ready, shaping things up. At any rate, I was sent with his lunch, in a small wicker basket. And I recall his showing me about and explaining the various processes—there were about ten machines all told. And just in this connection, I recall his appearance. A spare, brown-eyed man of fifty-five or six, grave and thoughtful, with heavy, overhanging eyebrows and dark reddish-brown hair, who seemed to me, even then, to be doing things beneath our dignity. He was not a large man—perhaps five feet ten—and of a wiry, nervous frame. I remember his hands, long-fingered and wrinkled at the back; also the fact that he was not wearing a beard—an idiosyncrasy in which he indulged from time to time.

At that time he seemed more alive and interested, and if not exactly cheerful, at least less gloomy than at almost any time in the several years preceding. I most clearly recall that for the first time I was conscious of an intellectual as well as affectional interest on his part in me. Some years afterward he told me that as a child I had impressed him as having an abnormally inquiring mind.

I have often wondered why my mother selected her three youngest for this venture. There were seven others, all older, of course, but at least four of them not so old. To be sure, there was the necessity for them to work, if possible, and my father was remaining with them in Terre Haute. But what most likely controlled her was a vagrom thought concerning beginning life anew. Since the mill had burned down some ten years before, she had gone through a valley of misery, a slough of despond, and still remained somewhere within its borders. And with her through that had gone these eldest. But now, possibly the thought of escape was gripping her imagination—a new world, a new life—the tang of a little adventure for herself. Could she but escape, how pleasing to shape three young lives not as yet wholly discoloured by the gloom of failure! I think so. And yet, as is so often the way with vagrom thoughts of so poetic an order, no real plan or method of procedure; at best, the feeblest of economic outlines which meant only hard work for herself. And as time was to prove, no real escape either, but only a colourful day-dream, whose primary sheen was to lessen to a faint if not wholly extinguished glow under the tarnishing power of reality.

CHAPTER VI

HOW valuable is life in any form to all who newly come to it in health and full of wonder, all but startled by that which they behold! New to the moving world about me, I was most sharply arrested and entertained, at times even made fearsome by much that I beheld. Thus, in Vincennes, I saw a strange and, to me, quite exciting American-French town, very different from Terre Haute. Its streets were narrow and winding, the French love of red and white predominating. Also here, as I noted, were those tall French windows to houses and stores, protected at night by solid wooden blinds. And the streets were cobbled, *à la* France. Vincennes—as I did not know then—was settled by the French, but to this hour I do not know when. I know that it was once a French trading station, and like many other places in America had taken its atmosphere from the group of pilgrims that originally settled there. The Wabash, unlike itself at Terre Haute, here flowed a few miles beyond the city and was only to be favourably viewed from a nearby height known as Merom Bluffs. I also recall all of us being driven there one day and that I viewed the river as some wonder that I ought to admire regardless of its direct appeal to my senses.

The Tinbys lived above the fire-house proper, in rooms at the rear of the second floor, some one or two of which we occupied, a lesser part of the much larger suite possessed by the Tinbys. The building itself was three stories high, the front half of its second and all of its third floor being occupied by cots and bunks for the firemen. At any rate, the once harum-scarum Sue Bellette, as I often heard my mother speak of her, was now presumably a quiet housewife. Frank Tinby, as I came to know him, was a young, strong, genial, even frolicking fellow, very proud of his position as captain of this station and driver of its engine. ("Much too good for Sue Bellette!" as one of my sisters commented once in harking back to this period.) He was liberal enough in money matters, as his willingness to permit my mother and her three children to come and stay at his home for some four or five weeks must attest.

But that period was long enough, as it presently appeared, for a form of friction to develop between my mother and her erstwhile protégée, which concerned morality, no less, and resulted in our departure some few weeks later. For as it appears now, my mother, shortly after our arrival, was compelled to awaken to the fact that Sue's morals had not improved any since her marriage, notwithstanding such weighty reasons for improvement (if they are weighty) as a husband and a year-old baby. At any rate, she soon discovered, as she later told me, that the ostensibly marriage-sanctioned world established here in this fire-house was in reality an immoral nest, frequented by various types of women brought in by the firemen. In fact, as it developed, the cots and wall-beds of the forepart of the second floor as well as a third floor or loft, were not infrequently occupied, between midnight and dawn, by other than their rightful occupants. Worse, it appeared that Sue herself was well aware of this; in fact, on genial terms with certain of these tow-headed denizens of the half-world; in short, that there was some sort of pleasure, and possibly even profit, in it for her, if not Tinby. To Tinby's credit, however, it appeared that though before his marriage he had tolerated some such arrangement, at the solicitation of politicians and others who could keep him in his position, he had, after marrying Sue, sought to do away with the custom or live elsewhere, but Sue—so my mother said later—would have none of it. She was of such an animal mood as to enjoy this. I myself, being a restless, early-rising child, one morning saw one of these daughters of desire, a corn-haired blonde, her pink face buried in a curled arm, lying on a bed allotted to one of the firemen serving on the night shift. I also recall a bitter argument between my mother and Sue as to the life being led here and some decision in regard to the same—our certain and moral departure, no less.

But all this must have been some little time after our arrival, since before we again took off, many things occurred which made sharp impressions on me. Outstanding among them were the streets and buildings of this brisk little town, as seen from the fire-house windows. The thrill of slanting threads of rain descending into the streets during a violent thunder-shower; the bobbing of umbrellas on the sidewalks below! And then the bright, clean fire-house itself, always alive with colourful and gleaming equipment, uniformed men, and matched pairs of brown or black or grey horses, each in a tall, red-fenced stall at the rear! And all so orderly and alert, eight or ten of the firemen always on duty or resting aloft. Their red shirts, blue uniforms and brass buttons, great rubber coats and hats and boots ranged near their respective places on the trucks and engines, filled my eyes with wonder.

Although Ed and myself were instructed not to linger below stairs—the danger attendant upon an alarm, when the stall doors automatically opened and the released horses hurried to their positions under suspended harness, being considerable—there was no hope of keeping us out. For downstairs we would go, danger or no danger, and were as much welcomed as though our mother had freely consented. For Tinby, being honestly fond of children, rather liked us around and even troubled to explain many things to me, probably because he found me nosing about in a state of reverence and awe.

But, oh, the wonder of an alarm right here in the fire-house where one chanced to be dwelling! For at the first clang of an electrical gong—already installed in this station in 1879—here were Tinby and his men pulling on their great hats, coats and boots and climbing to their places on the trucks, Tinby the driver of the engine! And the horses running and neighing and champing their bits and striking with their feet, anxious to go, the while their harnesses were thrown and buckled around them! And then out, clanging and scrambling through the streets, with people everywhere pausing to behold them!

Or if it were night when the alarm rang—as not infrequently it was—then what a scampering and calling, the men pulling on their trousers and shirts, and often half-dressed sliding down the brass pole which led from the third to the ground floor! And since a great uproar accompanied all this—even in the streets without, once they were gone—there was really no peace or rest until they returned—a condition of nervous expectancy (at least in my case) bordering on spasm. In fact, life in this place seemed ever to me marvellous, since it appeared, and gloriously, to revolve around this suspended pandemonium. Fortunately, fires in a small town like Vincennes were more a matter of days than of hours apart; otherwise, there would have been no living there at all.

And in connection with this, as I now recall, the first fire I ever witnessed was here. It broke out one night in a great warehouse not much more than eight hundred feet from the station itself, and so violent did it become after a time that its size and fierceness seemed to suggest that we ourselves might once more be made homeless. For even before the engine and other apparatus left, one could see great clouds of smoke issuing from the long, dark building—we invariably hung out the front windows on such occasions, or at least I did—and very shortly afterward, fitful tongues of flame flickering behind hundreds of small panes of glass, coruscating as does sheet lightning during a storm. And then presently a raging furnace there and the little group of this particular station desperately involved. In fact, it was dawn before they returned, soaked and dirty and tired. But with what blusterings and babblings about this and that until once more, about nine or ten o'clock of the same morning, they were all asleep again! But not before the fire-house and its implements were all in shining and perfect order!

Yet presently I learned that these men were by no means the flawless heroes that their facing of danger in a seemingly reckless and sentimental manner seemed to imply. Rather, as I came to know in due course, quite capable of crude and to some, no doubt, decidedly irritating forms of peculation, as when after a fire our hero, Tinby, appeared before us with a clock which he had taken from a burning building and which he presented to his wife with some agreeable comment; and another fireman boldly showing a piece of commonplace statuary which he valued more highly and which he had acquired possibly out of the jaws of death itself—who knows?—but certainly from the house which had burned.

There is, by the way, another Vincennes memory that haunts me, and it is that of the first telephone I ever saw, which was installed in this fire-house while we were there. I was all ears and eyes, dancing around the small group called together by Tinby (who was acting as master of ceremonies), to see, hear and have explained this great new thing, the most amazing of all recent phenomena which but a few months before (not more, surely) had been perfected. Tinby and Sue, my mother, Trina, Ed and myself, four or five of the firemen, and perhaps a few business men of the vicinity swarmed about, all agog. And Tinby himself, very much excited and yet as master of ceremonies self-restrained, permitting first one and then another to listen to something within the box and to say "Hello," or "How are you?" or some related commonplace. I most clearly recall (and with what a thrill at the time) the receiver being put to my ear and while Tinby held the transmitter and called "Hello," a voice inside the box replying, "Hello, hello!" and my thinking how marvellous that anyone could make himself so small as to get in there and yet be able to talk. For I certainly thought that whoever was speaking was in the box—an example of legerdemain which might well overawe anyone!

CHAPTER VII

BUT the charm of this life here was not to endure for long. Not only was summer at hand, but my mother, as I have said, becoming dissatisfied with the moral situation at the fire-house—although I had no real understanding of that at the time—arranged with a friend in Sullivan for some temporary aid there, and presently we were en route to that small and humdrum county seat situated about half-way between Terre Haute and Vincennes and about twenty-five miles from each. No river, no really important industries except a coal mine or two; a round-house, since small trains of soft coal from the mines were made up here and hauled north (not south, since other mines were to the south); an intermittent woollen mill (the one my father had started and lost); and a comparatively new depot, between which and the Sullivan House (some seven or eight "squares" away, as they say in Philadelphia) trundled a shabby, yellow-and-green bus, the business heart boasting this and a few meagre stores. In lieu of a river or lake, one little yellow, ambling stream or creek known as the Busseron (another relic of France), and in one or two places creeping rivulets, tributaries of the Busseron, which now and then in their sylvan windings formed small pools in woods or fields where fish were to be caught—cat, sun, butter, perch and shiners. And then woods and fields. And yokels or farmers driving into town, usually of a Saturday—a but poorly entertained population, yearning, you may be sure, for a wider life, hanging about the few stores and talking. And rattle-trap wooden sidewalks, or none, fortunately in most cases shaded by trees, the mental life of the place—if I may refer to the mind in connection with it—almost non-extant, I am sure.

But since it was summer and the land prosperous enough in an agricultural sense—fields aglow with wheat and corn and rye and clover and sheltering patches of wood at the end of every vista—it seemed pleasing enough. In short, and although we were presently ensconced in an, to me, anachronistic and painful home, it was still friendly enough to my mother and her brood.

This home into which we were first made temporarily welcome was that of one of those hopelessly ignorant and yet materially not uncomfortable families whose psychology and mental manipulation my mother seemed to understand, or if not that, was at least able to call to her aid in a crisis, just as temporarily she had been able to call the Tinby home into service. Yet exactly how she did this has always been a mystery to me, though I do know that in the matter of friendship and that essential diplomacy necessary to its proper functioning, hers was one of the most engaging presences and dispositions it has ever been my lot to encounter. Those wide, intelligent, friendly eyes! A smile that was as winsome and disarming as it was innocent and non-committal. As uninformed as she seemed at times, and at times as recklessly romantic as she was imaginative, still, as I clearly learned in later years, she was a personage or temperament to be reckoned with: strong, patient, understanding, sympathetic, creative, humour-loving, and helpful. And it was varying phases of all of these qualities that drew to her by degrees, and usually permanently, not only her own children but individuals of all walks and shades of temperament and experience.

As I now recall the family with whom we took refuge in Sullivan, I stand in as much awe and pity as disgust. And with no particular charges to make against its individual members as such, or their lacks or errors, but rather against nature itself, which either aimlessly and unwittingly or with intelligence, and hence malice aforethought, devises such things and then leaves them to twist and wallow in the tangle of their own inadequacies.

Thomas Dooney, the father of the family, was in the days when my father had his mill in Sullivan, a humble section-hand on the E. & T. H. (Evansville and Terre Haute Railroad), one of the great army of Irish emigrants that in the forties, fifties, sixties, and even seventies, entered America to find work on the various railroads then building. And a strong and heavy and earnest, if ignorant, mechanism he was, toiling and slaving according to a pattern set him by his forbears for hundreds of years before—a big, red-haired, large-handed-and-footed clod, who at the time we arrived on the scene was no longer a section-hand but a section-boss. Also with a wife, three sons and a daughter, all about as well along in years as our family; and with a dark red wooden house, a garden, a pig pen, a wood pile, etc., etc.; all sustained by the labour of himself, his wife and two eldest sons, both of whom at the time we arrived were apprenticed, and by reason of their father's wish or command, to one of the two local mines.

This Dooney, in addition to being ignorant and a veritable horse or machine for work, was also a priest-ridden Catholic, as much a slave to that world's greatest nostrum vendor as even my father. And that is saying a lot! He was one who had been befriended by my father in earlier days, and it must have been the memory of that, in addition to his knowledge of my father's ardent idolatry of the Church, that commended us to his temporary hospitality. I can see the Dooneys now, on their way to the small wooden Catholic Church—the father tramping heavily and solemnly ahead of his wife and four children, these being presumably not interesting or worthy enough to walk by his side.

Mollie, the only daughter, buxom and red-haired, looked eminently fitted to become the wife of an Irish foreman or a small-town merchant and the mother of a troop of children. None the less, at that time she was already being educated (?) in a convent to the end that she might become a nun! Johnnie, the eldest, a faithful, hard working boy, working in the local coal mine, was caught, shortly before our arrival, in a cave-in and killed, one of eight or ten victims. His body had been recovered and given a rare funeral, as we now heard—all the honours of the Church, as it were! Jimmie, red-haired also, was a more vagrant type and refused to be harnessed, horse-wise, to the cart of the world, and in consequence, as I learned afterwards—not then—was occasionally horribly beaten by his father, who considered a heavy horsehide whip to be of more significance argumentatively than words. This Jimmie in due time developed into a bank robber, and finally, along with three others, killed a man in a robbery at Rensselaer, New York, and was (in 1901 or 1902) electrocuted at Sing Sing under the alias of "Red Sullivan." To the last, except to several who were trying to secure his release (my brother Paul among them), he refused to reveal his true name, though a hint as to his home

45

neighbourhood might have been gathered from the name which he or his underworld associates had tacked on to his sobriquet "Red." But on the morning he was led to the electric chair, he confessed his evil ways, received communion, and so, if we believe the noble religionists, passed, pure and regenerate, into the presence of his Maker!

The Dooney house was a long, low, red frame affair, with little windows and doors which permitted only the scantiest ventilation. Inside, as I recall it now, it was stuffed with rag carpets, sunken-bottomed rush chairs, dilapidated chests of drawers and tables, impossible pictures in frames mouldy and fly-specked—the usual hodge-podge of disorder and misfit which forms the average labourer's conception of connubial association and home ties. (And we sympathise with the fox for his hole; with the bird for its open, wind-blown nest!) I recall the stuffy, musty mattresses and comforters, the "crazy" patchwork quilts of brain-bewildering variety of colour and design; the messy combination kitchen and dining-room, the table, of course, always covered by a red tablecloth dotted with flies. Pigs were in a pen not far from the house. A wood pile, with axe, saw and chopping block, was near at hand. There was a garden, a brown paling fence, a stable for cows or a horse. I felt the general atmosphere to be most unpleasant and longed to be elsewhere.

Fortunately, we were here only some eight or ten days, when my mother, evidently most determined to work out her programme of rehabilitation, found a small white five- or six-room house at the north-east corner of Sullivan, at its outermost edge, and not far from at least one of the mines and the town's one and only railroad yard, to which house in due process we removed our very meagre belongings.

CHAPTER VIII

IF I were asked to indicate any one period of my youth, or even life, of which I might say that it was compounded of innocence, wonder, beauty, little or no trace of the knowledge of good and evil or the broodings thereby entailed, I would fix upon the two or three years spent in the plain little white house that was our abode in Sullivan.

I believe the rent per month was only seven dollars. The whole vicinity, indeed, was shabby and down-at-heels, but not without interest to me. Imagine a wide common, at least three acres in extent, rank with fennel, mullein, golden rod, milkweed, plantain, all of the common outcasts of the vegetable world that flourish where man is most indifferent or neglectful. This ground was unfenced and did not seem to belong to anyone. It was bounded on the east by our house and a large vegetable garden to the north, which we subsequently rented and worked. On the west were the tracks of the one standard gauge railroad of the region, the E. & T. H., a line that ran from Evansville on the south to Terre Haute on the north and transferred passengers or cars at both points. Adjacent to these tracks and this common was a small round-house, with its several chimneys for engines, and just outside it and facing its several doors, a turn-table. To the south of that and on the same side of the track, an immense, unpainted, weather-stained hay press or barn, which always looked as though ready to collapse, yet in which were pressed and baled each season some hundreds, or more likely thousands, of tons of hay brought and bought here every summer by an agency, whether individual, company or railroad I do not know. These bales were pressed by horse power, after which they were loaded into cars and shipped away, to Chicago, I presume. Even now I can see the weary, sweaty horses going their almost endless rounds in the centre of this great, grey, dusty room—which at night I felt to be haunted—and can smell the odour of sweet timothy and hear the squeak of the press and the "Whoa!" and "Giddap!" of the drivers, echoing almost sepulchrally throughout the day.

On the adjoining tracks, daily and nightly, passing north and south, the regular passenger and freight trains plying between Evansville and Terre Haute, as well as some "through" freights and two "through" passenger trains going south as far as Nashville and Memphis and east and north to Indianapolis and Chicago. These last passed north at about eleven o'clock and south at about eight-thirty, at night, and what wonderful things I thought them, lighted with oil lamps and occasionally carrying a parlour or sleeping car! Over half the glory of Sullivan for me was due to the visible arrival and departure of these trains. When, ah, when, would come the day when I should be setting forth on such a train to see the world ? Oh, to be an engineer or a fireman, even a brakeman or conductor!

Before the round-house, freight engines were turned on the turn-table, and as there were the coal mines mentioned and several side tracks—as many as four or five—considerable switching was done, trains of soft coal or freight being made up here. To this day I recall the sight of the firemen crawling beneath the engines parked in this round-house to rake the ashes from the fire-boxes, the engineers in blue jumpers and overalls, their faces, sooty, red, and streaked with oil. Fascinating characters in a great scene staged almost especially for the delectation, if not necessarily the instruction, of the small boys of the town, among whom you may write me down as one, you may be sure.

To the south of this weed-grown square were just two houses, one the shabby, drab home of "the Bowleses," set in a large and ill-kept space of garden (the house still standing when I visited the place thirty years later), the other that of " the Thompsons," an ubiquitous and energetic band of half-breeds —miscegenates of mingled Indian, Negro or gipsy blood, I fancy. Al, or "Blackie," Thompson, who used occasionally to drive one of the teams of the hay press, was a wild and incorrigible creature. Strange to the point of being sinister, he looked to be a mixture of Negro and Indian and was as impulsive, erratic and sly as any animal. Apparently there was no father, only a mother, at the head of this company, and a rag and a bone she certainly was, peaked and dark of face, blowsy and black as to hair, sharp and suspicious as to eye, a strange and mysterious type. There were several younger children as well —one lank and lean and blowsy-haired girl, who ran here and there and occasionally talked with the men in the hay press or the round-house, but who seemed much too wild and unkempt to be of any interest to me—a creature, like her mother, to be avoided. As for the others, all quite young, I do not recall them clearly but all wandered over this common or in the adjoining woods and fields and railroad yard, carrying coal from the cars, stolen fence rails for kindling, corn and potatoes from the fields and anything else they could lay hands on, and apparently without much hindrance as far as I could see. And never in all the time that I knew them did I see them in anything like respectable or presentable clothing.

The Thompson house was also a sight to behold, a mere collection of sheds, brick-red or black or grey, mostly without paint, and strung together after a wandering fashion. They had no horse or cow but kept a small and poorly-tended vegetable garden, a few stolen chickens and about nine bony dogs. When the snow lay thick, one tiny spiral of smoke curling from a thin length of stove-pipe shoved upward from a low tin roof suggested that, like bears or beavers, they had dug in for the winter. At night a somewhat feeble fire might be seen glimmering through the chinks of those windows that were not patched with paper, wood, or tin. I think Blackie Thompson trapped or hunted and so added to the family larder. In summer, their domain was somewhat gayer, what with sunflowers, hollyhocks, various flowering weeds and vines, and their nondescript garden. But as an illustration of not exactly nomad but somewhat wild and predatory life, I think they ranked fairly high.

As to the Bowles family in the other house, "Old Man Bowles" was half-witted. He had been injured in the head during the Civil War and now wandered about singing snatches of songs, stopping people and asking foolish questions, or staring vacantly at them or the sky. Often, since it had been his custom before we came, he came to our well for water, a wooden bucket on each arm. And because we were not unfriendly to him, he would stop and chant strange tunes to my mother, my brother and myself, or stare at the sky, or dance in an angular, ungraceful, jackknife fashion. That he seemed ridiculous, inconsequential, and almost to blame for his silly actions, to

49

two such uninformed innocents as Ed and myself, goes without saying. The ignorant new always laughs at the defeated old.

Among others who dwelt in this neighbourhood, as I now recall, was also a tall, dark girl or woman, Laetitia or "Tish" Herndon by name. She was inordinately fond of her old white-haired and seemingly once strong and intelligent father, with whom she lived in a paintless, rain-beaten hut to the south of us. And again, at the north-east corner of the common, in a low tree-and-vine-shaded cabin of great age, one Mrs. Jonah Hudson, an aged and mumbling crone, whose house was over-run with dirt, dogs, cats and chickens.

Past Mrs. Hudson's place to the north again was a great sunken, rocky field, surrounded by a high rail fence, and occupied, in one of its farthest corners, by a rain-soaked shell of a house or barn which served as the village slaughter-house. And to this, as we soon found, were driven, twice or thrice weekly, by one butcher Spilky and some others for whom he killed, such cows, steers, sheep, hogs, calves and the like as were destined for his market and hence the physical upkeep of such goodly citizens as worshipped God in peace and content in this region and had the price wherewith to pay for the slaughter which he undertook in their behalf. Oh, life! Oh, death! Oh, mysterious, inexplicable forces by whose tolerance we are, and in whose giant keep we move!

I recall him now, a veritable saw-bones of a man, dishevelled, unkempt, not arrestingly intelligent, you may be sure, but energetic and, according to his light, a respectable enough person. But blind of one eye, frizzled as to his grey hair, which stuck out under an old brown felt or straw hat, as the season dictated, and much too enthusiastic or violent, as I saw it, about this business of murder for others. Rattling across the common he could come, along the north and south road which passed our door, in a light, low-bodied spring wagon, in which were piled his knives, cleavers, saws, newly-sharpened and polished, together with various bags and wicker baskets in which were to be deposited the various parts of the carcasses of the late departed ; or sometimes on foot, driving before him the refractory or bellowing animals whom he was about to slay, a whip or goad in his hand, his whole body, eyes, hands, face, vibrating with a kind of restless energy which made him at once ridiculous and sinister. For, mind you, I had never before seen a butcher save in his more or less clean butcher shop, in apron and cap, paper and string to his elbow, his account book in one corner, maybe, and selling parts of things that had once been alive but were now just so many pounds of this or that, and very good to eat into the bargain! But a slaughter-house! These live bleating, squealing, or bellowing creatures—and literally harried to their deaths by their sanctioned murderer! How terribly, horribly different! Why, at the mere thought of these animals being driven across the common and the infernal squeals of greed and anticipation set up by a herd of swine kept near the slaughter-house in order that they might be fattened on the entrails of the approaching cattle, I am haunted by the truth that life is built upon murder and lust, and nothing less! Sweet, tender, flawless universe, indeed!

CHAPTER IX

THE manner in which my mother accepted this place was typical of her extreme poverty and modest resourcefulness. Although she may not have been taken with all that surrounded her, still it must have been of some value as a temporary port. To begin with, it was near Terre Haute—twenty-five miles away—where her husband and four daughters were all working. Whether she had any ready cash, even a small amount, I do not know. I know that on the day we moved in, we had nothing to put in the house save one or two straw-filled mattresses—borrowed from the Dooneys, possibly —three or four quilts and a wooden chair. An iron cooking pot, several pans and buckets, completed the list of our household equipment. There was no stove, no table, no dishes, even, except a few borrowed plates and pans. Yet we came here gaily, or at least I did, and for me it remained to the end a place of charm and delight. For my mother was there, and she seemed happy, at first, anyhow.

I can see her now, smiling cheerfully and rubbing her hands as she surveyed the neat and fairly clean house, with its five or six bare rooms, and the green or blooming fields beyond. For despite the picture of the common to the west which I have set forth, the east was abloom with clover or wheat or corn, and in the not far distance were farm-houses and lovely trees, perhaps as much as twenty acres of them. On these the sunlight of a bright summer morning glowed with an almost personal approving graciousness. There were dark red and pink and white roses in the yard, early and late blooming varieties, for in the southern Indiana region roses linger on until October. And there were flowering vines, trumpet and honeysuckle, sheltering a front and rear porch, as well as a smooth lawn and one or two trees. And somehow I hear her saying—or is it just my fancy?—"See all the nice roses!" and

52

"Aren't the fields about here beautiful now? It's just like the country." And it was.

I recall how on first coming here Ed and I, after viewing the house, went to the wood beyond to gather chips and twigs to build fires in the grates. (There was one in each of the two big living rooms.) Then while mother was busying herself with cleaning windows, floors and woodwork, I went to a grocery store several blocks away for soap, a broom, a loaf of bread and some molasses. I also recall buying a small glass lamp and then doing other things, pulling weeds, maybe. Mostly, though, as I look back, I have an almost ineffable sense of well-being, yet exactly why I cannot say, for our future was certainly not exceptionally bright. It may be that the petty irritations and deprivations of a situation of this kind slough off or fade into inconsequence with the lapse of time. Only the shining moments of delight remain. Who remembers the fading flower? Who forgets the one in full bloom? Not winter, but spring, is celebrated; not pain, but joy!

Come now, let us erect to youth an altar, and against the sapphire sea of time set the scarlet flame of memory! What though the earth be strewn with faded leaves of effort, and in the ground beneath lie broken and forgotten the shreds and remnants of many lives? For youth, like spring, is ever with the world! Bring chalcedony and carnelian for its columns, and of beaten brass let us make its tables! Bring myrtle blooms for memory, and red rose leaves for gratitude, and with these let us strew the ground! Taste now of the sacred cup of joy, brushing aside the odour of dead lips, and sing of new loves and youth and mirth! For, see, it is ever young with the world, and youth and beauty abide where all is change!

The wonder of these days that were spent here, two years in all! From my mother's point of view, it must have been a very difficult period. For there seems to have been scarcely any money to do with. But I can see her now, in her simple dresses always suggestive of that Mennonite world from which she sprang, and so devoid of any suggestion of smartness, only simplicity and faith in some form. But wandering about this humble home, shreds of slippers on her feet, at times the typical Mennonite bonnet pulled over her face, her eyes wide and expressive, bestirring herself about the things which concerned her home and family. A sad woman, at times, no

53

doubt, since never again was she destined to see her dreams fulfilled, yet always making the best of a mean and uncomfortable state. A happy woman, too, at times, in that dreams and simple things satiated her speculative soul.

Has life, the blood stream with its mystic emanations and evocations of bodies and actions and exterior forms, any higher function than merely to be as is here shown? Have we any conceivable destiny other than functioning here as forms or accidental combinations of forces and sensitivities? Is the universe a playground in which this and this alone is achieved— a play of high and low, weak and strong, ruler and slave, poet and clod? If so, how vast a space—how giant the energies devoted to so pathetic a thing! And if not, what else and under what conceivable like or unlike ways? I have never been able to think that there is so much else—anything so much more important. Hence, what there was at this time, as well as what for me followed, was unique, separate, without precedent or subsequent duplication. And hence, this lone woman who was my mother is of strange import to me—a now vivid shadow who once, by reason of mystic impulses in her, was moved to function as guide and mentor to individuals or mechanisms whose bodies had grown out of hers but whose temperaments she little understood.

But essentially to what valuable end? Any? Most of those who were the subject of her care have gone, and after lives in nowise more significant, if more comfortable, than her own. And yet here, in Sullivan, as elsewhere, pathetic and ridiculous figments of earthly blames and shames enmeshed her, yet with no sin to her, poor soul! In the eyes of an ordered society she might already have been looked upon as a failure if not one who had failed as a mother. Yet to me and to all of us, how wonderful! A lamp, a dream, an inspiration, one whose memory even now walks ever on before, making a path of beauty!

CHAPTER X

HAVING found this truly charming little house, it was now my mother's business to find furniture, and after that, boarders, and so an income. But how, I have often wondered? For one thing, I believe that the Dooneys, having some slight standing before the commercial world of Sullivan, commended her and her programme to a local dealer in household utensils, which dealer trusted her with a stove, tables, chairs, a few kitchen utensils and some material out of which she made clean containers for straw. These latter constituted our two beds that summer, and even during a part of the following winter. Also, I believe, there was a rocking-chair for herself. Pending a condition which would permit her to set a table for two or three boarders (I believe eventually there were, by the following spring anyhow, six who ate with us and two who occupied one room), there was an old grocer who had known her years before and who now gave her credit for a small supply of food. Also before any boarders were secured, she arranged with said grocer, furniture dealer and one or two others who could be influenced by them or the Dooneys to do their washing and ironing. And so, shortly after she had placed herself in this house, there appeared this matter of washing and ironing for a living, a labour which must have been ōnerous to a degree and yet which she appeared to undertake with courage and determination, calling upon Trina and myself—since Ed was almost too young—to fetch and carry the wash. (Not an auspicious opening to our lives in Sullivan!)

True, I was too young to know much of social differences or levels. Besides, Sullivan, and especially this portion of it, was scarcely of sufficient means to flaunt luxury in the face of poverty. But even so, I clearly recall that I was sharply aware of what it meant to have less as opposed to more. My mother's occasional comments on her difficulties, as well as my own eye to eye contact with at least seemingly more fortunate or adequate states, were impressive. Certainly many other children did not need to carry coal or wash, as did we. And Trina and myself, as we trudged along with our basket after early dark by back streets, were all too nervous as to who might see us. Ah, who schemed the sorry scheme whereby all conscious creation must suffer so for that which it lacks?

One thing that very much impressed me this first summer and autumn was the fact that neither Ed nor I had shoes to wear. I have not mentioned it thus far, but here, as in Terre Haute and Vincennes, was a Catholic Church, a very small and unimportant affair, visited but once a month by a Catholic priest, who said mass and took dinner with one of his parishioners. And in connection with it—although there were no nuns or separate schoolhouse—a Catholic school—a pay school, you may be sure—conducted by the daughter of a parishioner. And since my mother, in spite of her vague and yet, as I believe, growing doubts as to the value of this form of religious education in so far as her children were concerned, was still mentally overawed by what she had been told these many years, she now and here—and taking in washing for a living—felt morally constrained to send us to this school—though how she proposed to pay and do without our home aid betimes I do not know. None the less, there were the watchful eyes of the Dooneys and the local priest and teacher who in due time came to call.

Hence, and to my personal disgust, into this small school, which was held in the church itself, we were marched, shoes or no shoes! And day after day we went until quite November, when suddenly a very cold day and still no shoes, my brother and I were sent home by this excellent instructor with the word that we were to put on shoes, since it was much too cold to be without them. And this certainly did impress and even humiliate me, for in school were no children without shoes. I have a dim, almost a vanishing, recollection of my mother's face when she heard our story. She had been trying energetically enough, no doubt, and grieving, too, you may be sure, for tenderness and consideration were of the very essence of her being. But shoes cost money, and having no money to spare at the time—insufficient washing and ironing, you may be sure, as well as some hitch in the Terre Haute economic plan—she had been compelled to let us go this long without shoes or stay at home. And now, much to my delight, we were so compelled to remain, for what was one Catholic school less—if not more—to me? But as to her, I cannot say. That she must have grieved and wrung her hands, you may be sure. She was like that. Just the same, for some time thereafter—how long I cannot say—home we remained, for the kindly Catholic Church provided no shoes.

Eventually, though, as I later learned—and possibly on the advice of the Dooneys—one Solomon Goodman, proprietor of the one general dry-goods and clothing store of Sullivan, was approached. And in exchange for future washing and ironing —and a large bundle it was that he provided!—shoes and possibly a few other things were supplied. But after that, a weekly basket of wash to and from the Goodman home—a heavy one. Also we were permitted to resume our education in this local school, where possibly—I do not now recall—we learned to read and spell.

At any rate, in Sullivan it was that I began to read books of sorts: a stray Catholic story or two; that dear Catechism so beloved of the Church; and copies of papers—dailies and weeklies—which betimes found their way into our house. Also here, with the aid of Trina and myself, my mother learned to write. (She had mastered reading long before, but had never learned to write.) And this in the midst of all her labours!

CHAPTER XI

ONE of the reasons for this extreme poverty during our
first winter in Sullivan was that the Terre Haute plan
failed to work. The four girls had found life with their father
under the circumstances all too grim. As I heard after, he
was grudging of every penny and every hour spent in anything
but labour. It must have been that he was so terrified by his
long series of difficulties since the collapse of his mill that he
no longer had any sane judgment of life or its needs. Certainly
these were four girls thrilling, no doubt, with health and energy
and dreams, and yet expected, after working all day, to avoid
any suggestion of social gaiety at night or on Sundays, to keep
house as well as go to mass, and probably Vespers, with him on
Sundays, and to deposit the major part of their earnings in a
general family or expense fund, which must have left them
little enough for anything looking toward personal wear or
entertainment. You can imagine, of course, how long such a
social and economic arrangement would endure. The fact is
that it did not endure for any length of time at all.

According to her own story, Amy proved so inept at weaving
and in addition was so depressed and disgusted by it all that
after two or three weeks she sought other employment. The
wife of a jeweller in Terre Haute, having a three-months-old
baby, took her on as a nurse girl, at, I believe, no wages or no
more than fifty cents a week and her room and board. For a
day or two after leaving home, she did not even trouble to
tell her father where she had gone. Eventually, though, she
went to see one of her sisters, who explained for her, and after
a visit by my father to the jeweller, the new arrangement was
allowed to stand because she refused to return. But it broke
in on the financial plan.

As for the others, Ruth and Janet proved satisfactory enough
from a commercial point of view, the latter developing great
speed and skill. As for Eleanor, almost from the first, her

elderly admirer and patron would not hear of her working in the mill and sought to induce her to quit and enter a private school east of Terre Haute—to which she did resort the following fall. In the meantime, in order to prevent her from working, he offered to pay her more than she was earning, but since she would not accept that, he secured for her a clerkship in a local dry-goods store, for which she was to say she was paid more than she received, allowing him to make up the difference. She accepted this, she said, because she knew she could thereby aid her mother as well as herself. There was also an offer later by this same Colonel Silsby of a better house in a more agreeable portion of Terre Haute, but this, as she said, she did not even dare to mention.

Regularly, though, she continued working, but with plans, as she said, of presently returning to her mother, since life under the dreary rule of her father was almost impossible. There was no least trace of relaxation or gaiety in his viewpoint, his idea being that the girls should find young men who would call at the house, stay until ten-thirty, and after a fourth or fifth visit declare their intentions and become engaged. The result was quarrelling and an almost constant and incurable desire on the part of the girls to be with their mother in Sullivan, where, however, no work was to be had.

My sister Amy, for instance, told me much later in life that her one resource in her misery at being separated from her mother—she was still very young—was to wheel the baby carriage of her charge down to the Terre Haute depot and there inquire about the trains to Sullivan. Finally the station agent, wondering at her frequent presence there, spoke to a freight conductor, who said to her one day: "So you want to go to Sullivan, do you?"

"Yes, sir."

"Why?"

"My mother lives there."

"Why don't she send for you?"

"She hasn't got the money."

"Well, if you want to go, come down to-morrow and I'll take you."

This resulted in her employer, a penurious small-town wife, trading her an old, cast-off dress for the three dollars in wages due her, and thus equipped she arrived one afternoon the following spring in Sullivan. (I can imagine my mother's contemplative eyes and her thoughts!)

By this time, also my sister Ruth had taken flight to another family in Terre Haute, one not so penurious as that of the jeweller. These people came to be quite fond of her, as she said, and later even wanted to adopt her. Because of her mother, though, she would have none of that, and finally secured permission for a visit to Sullivan, and once there, refused, for a time at least, to return.

Janet worked as a waitress in a restaurant, later in a candy store. But all the while she, too, desired to return to her mother, and in the spring following that first dreadful winter, also put in an appearance, but not without provoking difficulties and irritations which presently will be related.

In the meanwhile, the dreary, hard-working period which was being endured by my mother could not have seemed much better than that from which she had sought to escape. At any rate, it was not until the following spring that sufficient means were gathered to buy a fair-sized dining table, with chairs, a bedroom set which made at least one of the bedrooms available for renting, and such dishes and utensils as would make possible a boarding-house table. And next, the planting of a vegetable garden, which under my mother's direction we three youngest carried to a most successful conclusion, thus adding greatly to our economic prosperity. Incidentally, and by degrees, boarders—by the following fall as many as six—and my mother, because of them, enabled to give over the business of washing and ironing—a great relief to Trina and myself, as you may well guess.

CHAPTER XII

THROUGHOUT this entire period—which could not have been less than fifteen months—and regardless of conditions which might have been considered reducing if not wholly depressing to a youth of my years, I was none the less vibrating with an emotional ecstasy in regard to life itself.

Sitting by one of the windows of our living room, and holding in my lap, for love's sake, a small black and yellow mongrel dog, that along with two others had attached itself to us, I used to rock and sing by the hour, enjoying the morning sun. The window at which I sat commanded a view of a wide field of clover, which to me was always a small lake or sea of colour.

There was a brown chicken hawk that perched high on the scarred fork of a riven tree which stood some quarter of a mile distant from our house—a tall trunk ornamented in part with the healing foliage of a climbing vine, and which always appealed to me as some stately sentinel keeping watch over a field of colour. By degrees I came to love this tree and its bird. I dare say I already knew the grimness of the hawk temperament, for I had seen them circling high above a roost of crows or blackbirds, the while their sentries uttered wild or plaintive appeals to their fellows to be on guard or come to their aid. I had seen crows and a hawk, or blackbirds and a hawk—three, four and five of one to a single specimen of the other—fighting desperately under high heaven, the serene blue seeming, to me at least, an antipathetic background for so internecine a struggle. Yet the hawk always seemed to me the most fascinating, if not most respectable, of birds. Grim implement of a great force that willed it regardless of its willing, it, for me, had already taken on both dignity and fascination, the charm as well as the impressiveness of the hypnotic and fateful snake. Captain Kidds of boiling seas of air! Jack Cades of sky-ey alleys and windy lanes! John Silvers and Dick Turpins of leafy bowers and murmuring woodlands! Yet accredited if not sanctified by nature—a part of her immense and inscrutable as well as artful mechanism—an exemplification of her evil in good, good in evil, her love of paradox.

Somewhere in the leafy dells about this simple home, in the thickets which lined the Busseron or the depths of Farmer Beach's sugar camp or Farmer Palmer's wood preserves, there lived a wood dove, or perhaps there were many scattered here and there and seemed but one. How often in later years have I not tried to formulate for myself in words the spirit of these dreamers of the forest, the crystalline liquefaction of the soul of a bird; that quintessence of sound which is not so much sound as dream, and not so much dream as mood, a sigh of nature lonely because of its lorn eternality.

Oh, echoes of the morning! Oh, memories of the youth of the world! Oh, suggestion of ages and æons of forgotten sorrows and forgotten joys! In Sirius, in Beltair, and in Arcturus, in what hot flames of light that still and for ever inundate the world were such perfections as this conceived? Do fading flames poured from the infernal cauldrons of the sun fade at the last into melodies such as these? Then is the creative impulse perfect, its ways ineffable, its spirit song. Though ten thousand plagues beset a fumbling world, this shall answer for its perfection. "I shall set my sign in the heavens!" Say, rather: "In the woodland depths I shall put the song of a bird, and for thee it shall be a covenant and an agreement between thee and me! Lo, I am music, and this is my testimony! I am all colour, and in it shall you find me! I am all ancient sorrows, and lo, they are song! I am forgotten joys, and thus, and thus only, are they remembered! Be thou an ear—mine—and I shall speak to thee of myself and thee!"

But to proceed. From the first, this almost foodless home of ours was an asylum for stray cats and dogs. (Is it not always so?) Hound, and Rover, and Big Tom, the cat, and little Tickles, the kitten, and Snap, my personal pet and companion. Hound was a long, bony bird dog, brown as light chocolate and as depressed and sad-looking as a dog could well be. Life had not done right by him, and his every line seemed to speak of ancient neglects and abuses. His great ears hung about his face curtain-wise and limp, and his tail was so long and thin and stiff that I used to marvel that it could be so. His eyes were large and appealing, and seemed to say: "You wouldn't be mean to me, would you? You couldn't be, could you?" But somehow, after he arrived at our place, though he was dirty and bony and scaly and I don't know what else, he began to perk up and grow more cheerful and to act as though life were quite a bearable affair.

Rover was a splotchy black and white dog of somewhat ungainly design, part hound, part heaven only knows what! More courageous than Hound, he would growl when abused and if annoyed too much, bite. He was already there when Hound arrived on the scene, and at first, thinking that his own discovery of a home was in jeopardy, fought the stranger desperately and constantly. But Hound was not to be driven off. He seemed to sense that here was room for two or more, and would fight back just enough to sustain himself, howling loudly and plaintively until one of us came and properly chastised Rover. And after a time they housed together in a kind of rag-bag harmony under our back porch.

One amusing trick of Hound's related to an occasional desire to get Rover out of a warm corner from which he was unable to oust him physically. He would go to the front yard and come tearing around the corner of the rear porch under which, on a comfortable bed of straw, Rover was lying, and as though in full pursuit of something, raise a mighty uproar, the scheme being to convey to Rover's mind the idea that there was a stranger or intruder at hand. Rover would then dash out of his corner, and Hound would round the house on the second lap and, Rover being out, creep in before he could get back. When the deceived Rover returned and found his crafty rival comfortably ensconced in his bed and even feigning sleep, his rage knew no bounds. On several occasions he even tried to bite him out, but since Hound's yowls brought aid and since while yowling he never budged, the attack was futile. But in time, and much to Hound's chagrin, you may be sure, the trick failed to work. For all his pains he returned only to find the enemy safely curled and in nowise deceived. Then it was that he would droop his tail and slink off as if to say: "Well, there's certainly nothing much to this trick any more."

But as for my pet Snap, he was a little fellow so shabby of coat, so commonplace, that perhaps you would have thought him unfit for association with even such humble children as surely we then were He was brown and black, with a spot of white over one ear and another at the tip of his tail. Because of these he should rightly have been called "Spot," yet Snap was the name I gave him. Why I came to single him out for my own I don't know, but I did. He seemed to me such an intelligent little waif, so amiable and gay—in short, everything that a child's dog should be.

Because of my intense love of nature, I was fond of taking long, solitary walks, and Snap invariably accompanied me. At first my mother could not understand why I wished to be so much alone or why my aloneness should require such exaggerated periods of time, although she never suspected mischief in my case and later told me so. I was just odd, she said, different. But the earth, its surface nature, was then truly a fairyland to me, and I wanted nothing better than to be alone with it. It was a desire and a custom of mine then to arise as early as three or four o'clock in the morning in the summertime, and after looking at the clouds over the fields or watching the sun rise, examine all the wonders of the morning—bejewelled spider webs, striped and tinted morning glories of ravishing form and colour, the yellow trumpet-flowers which covered our porches, our many varieties of roses in full bloom, bluebirds, swallows, wrens—and then stroll away through the clover or timothy to the neighbouring woods or open fields.

Certain aspects of the morning and evening sky; faint shreds of cirrus or stratus clouds; small pools in the woods in which leaves and trees were reflected; the swooping down of the house martins and swallows; the sudden upward rush of a meadow lark; birds' nests in the bushes or trees—these were enough to suffuse me with a rich emotional mood, tremulous, thrilling. Often I would stand, my hands clenched, my body tense, studying any strange and hence to me new thing. I would wonder and question why I too should not be able to rise in the air and fly or float like a bird or a cloud. Indeed, throughout my earliest years I felt as though I had been bereft of this ability by some trick and that I should and must be able to fly if I tried! And so often I would dream of flying. And once I knelt down, and folding my hands as I had been taught, asked God to let me fly. They were always saying that prayers would be answered. But on no material wings did I rise, and noting that, pondered over the futility of prayer as well as the thought that a mistake had been made and that there must be a land somewhere to which I belonged and where I could fly.

Let me add here that this had no relation to any of the woody or plastic angels of the Catholic Church. On the contrary, these were ever indifferent if not exactly abhorrent objects to me, having no least relationship to the ethereal thing that filled my mind. My own sky-ey land was ever remote and, except for wings, intangible, a sea within a sea, a soul of things within the present material presence, maybe.

On these rambles, as I have said, Snap was my invariable companion. His bed was a little soap-box beside the kitchen stove in winter (a new stove which gave me much pleasure because of its nickel trimmings) or out on the back porch in summer. And when I would arise from my pallet (we were too poor, at first, to afford bedsteads), he would invariably get up, cock one ear, look inquiringly over the top of his box, and then jump out. Sometimes he would indulge in a stretch or a yawn before he was quite his brisk self, but soon he was sniffing here and there, interested in the general feel of life.

And what walks! Sometimes in the berry season, I would take a basket and pick wild raspberries or blackberries while Snap would reconnoitre the surrounding world. Whatever his attitude toward me, he was by no means as friendly toward other creatures, and loved especially to chase sheep. Often he would disappear for hours, and return panting and wet. Sometimes it was rabbits or skunks that he sought, there being many of these about. There was also a great black and white bull, with straight horns, which occupied a large stony pasture safely hedged by a high rail fence. Snap would reconnoitre this bull at a safe yet short distance, standing up four-square, one ear up, yap-yapping to irritate the bull, the while Taurus stiffened and shook his huge neck and glared, wondering, no doubt, whether it was worth while to charge. As a rule, though, I could make Snap come away by calling to him sharply, but he was sly and when he thought I was not looking or had forgotten, would return for another argument.

One of my greatest pleasures was to follow Snap's leads or to set him digging at strange holes in the ground. I doubt whether any child ever had a greater curiosity concerning the habitations of animals, crustacea or insects. Everything from wasps' nests to gopher holes fascinated me. Literally, I think I have sat for hours by the banks of some muddy stream or pond, or in our garden where the earth was for some reason watery and full of crawfish burrows, waiting for the crays to appear. Nothing pleased or astounded me more than to surprise one of these creatures coming out of his muddy hole, his soapstone-coloured and so strangely-segmented body, jet-black eyes and swaying antennæ, seeming to indicate personality or a form of intelligence and interest. To think that he should be so different from me, and that he should and could live under the ground! In a trance of thought I would brood over him, having no desire to injure him, but wondering what he knew, thought, how he built his hole, where it led, what it contained, indeed, all about him. And then I wondered why he was at all, and what became of him when he died.

And once in our garden I was scratching about in the ground with a small stick and came to a wet, shiny hole. My curiosity aroused, I went and got a spade and began digging vigorously, and at last unearthed a sub-surface wallow perhaps three or four feet underground, full of thick, muddy water, and in which, to my horror and chill, I saw a salamander, one of the left-over specimens of the older saurian world. I had never seen one before. Its sleek, moist body, lizard-like in form, with wet pink feet and long, thin head, gave me the creeps. In a kind of horror of unlikeness, strangeness, which seems to affect all of us at times, I killed it, squashing its blood and flesh in the mud, and then ran as fast as I could, death and mud-holes and left-over specimens of saurian life completely filling my mind.

In the evening sky at that time, too, was to be seen an immense comet—a red, pellucid affair, with a great, flaring tail. And this was then included in my speculations. I recall now how while hoeing weeds in our garden, I would stop and look up at this great red stranger, sharply outlined against a silver and lemon sea of space, and wonder about it, and how death and mud-holes and this star and myself were all somehow tangled in a strange, beautiful, only semi-tangible and in some of its phases wholly terrifying mystery called life. Like one fumbling in a dark cavern, I also felt blind, yet even so sensing something of the glittering scintillations of a world or universe or mystery which could not be dark.

66

At times I felt quite definitely—as one might look at an immense body of water and have a feeling about it—that I was standing on the shore of something—not a sea, exactly, not anything material, but something immense and inscrutable, like that elusive realm in which at other times I fancied I might fly, greater than a sea perhaps, more timeless, wherefrom these various forms emanated and to which they returned. And since sensations which give rise to ideas are more important than ideas themselves, I may have had hold of something of which we will all be much more definitely conscious later on.

And once I followed a bumble bee, across fields of wheat and bramble, tracking him from flower to flower, watching him work, noting the gold and black of his coat, his eyes, his furry legs. And below a huge wasps' nest under an eave I often sat in the sun for hours, watching the comings and goings of a brilliant and animated band of these insects. I also studied gnats whirling in spirals at evening, and wondered about them. Discovering a bat hanging head down in the old hay press across the common one day, I was moved to speculate as to the strangeness of its life. Fishes in water, wild flowers in fields, the forms of trees, all gave me pause.

I have since regretted that there was no one near who could have told me about these things. For my mind was a clean slate on which many effective things could have been pencilled. I was a polished crystal—accidental, it is true—reflecting all the harmonies, colours, oddities, of my little world. I was a harp on which nature idly strummed her melodies; a flower form into which she blew her endless suggestions of colour; an ear attuned to infinite delicacies of sound; an eye responsive to the faintest shadows of meaning; and yet daily, even hourly, being drilled in the worn-out folderol of the Holy Roman Catholic Church!

But to return to Snap. He left me one summer morning and did not return. I called and called, but he did not come. Even next morning, no Snap! Then I felt it my duty to make a search. Together Ed and I went into the surrounding fields and called, but no Snap! That afternoon I went out into the distant fields alone, and whenever I saw a lone tree which seemed to offer a vantage point of sorts, I stationed myself and called. Anybody hearing me would have known that I was sad. There was a quavering pathos in my voice. "H-y-u-h, Snap! H-y-u-h, Snap!" long and loud I called. But he did not come. After a long time and much conversation with my mother, I concluded that he must have been stolen and that one day if I persisted and when accidentally I chanced to be in the vicinity of the place where he was being held, he would hear my voice and come running. And so, all summer long and late into the fall, I called and called betimes, though ashamed to do so in the presence of others—Ed, for instance, who thought me silly.

But then, one day, an illuminating thing. I was standing at the edge of the cornfield adjoining the woods which contained the slaughter-house. I forget now whether I was merely idling in the shade or whether I was picking up loose wood to take home. Possibly, I was picking some of the corn. Such foraging tactics were naïvely countenanced by my mother at times. But suddenly I heard the report of a gun. With me at the time were Hound and Rover. Coincidental with the gun sound, Hound, who was not more than forty feet away, emitted a yelp and went bounding homeward, yowling as he went. A splattering in the leaves and against the trees indicated bird or buckshot. I looked up, and on the back porch of a distant house across the field, perhaps four acres away, I could see Farmer Palmer or his son Bud holding a gun. He had seen me or the dogs, or both, and perhaps tired of marauders, took this direct way of indicating his displeasure. The loss of an eye or a disfiguring mark might have been his contribution to my life, but that mattered little to him.

Needless to say, I hurried after Hound, to examine his wounds as much as anything. Investigation proved that only the tip of his exceedingly thin tail had been nicked. His obviously shabby life had been spared. Strange to say, there now seeped into my as yet very nebulous mind a suspicion which gradually became a conviction: that thus it was that Snap had been undone. Farmer Palmer or his son had killed him! His sheep or fields had been injured. Thereafter I looked for the skeleton of Snap, whitening like the ox skulls of the abattoir in some distant field, but I never found it.

Peace to his cheerful soul!

CHAPTER XIII

IN addition to this business of washing and ironing for others, then taking in boarders and roomers, my mother also undertook all of the ordinary compulsions of such a family as ours: cleaning, washing, baking, preserving such fruits as she could get for little or nothing—many are the gallons of wild blackberries and raspberries I have picked and brought home to her!—and encouraging us youngsters to rake, hoe, weed and reap a large truck garden, after the ploughing had been done by a hired ploughman. Also she did all the sewing and tailoring for us three children and herself. In so far as I can recall, she made quite everything for us except shoes and hats.

I can see her now, sitting by an open window in summer, from which the fields presented an idyllic view, or near the fire or under a lamp in winter, stitching, stitching, stitching; later when she was able to get a sewing machine, she ran that by the hour. In between were the boarders' as well as our own meals, and at night our final ablutions and prayers. By day, and when school was not holding and it was not too cold, we were given suggestions as to where and how to play, so that we might be kept out of mischief. Naturally, a patient persuasion had to be exercised to make us go to the store, carry fuel wood from the fields or tracks, gather wild berries, keep off the railroad tracks, go to the post office at least once a day, and to school and church when the regular third or fourth Sunday came around.

For a time, as I have recorded, our schooling ceased for want of shoes, and still later in the same first year, for lack of tuition fees, but do you suppose that under such circumstances the free public school was contemplated as a substitute? By my mother possibly, but by my father never! And although he was no longer with us day by day, still, because of his revived contributions and a regular monthly visit around the first of the month (on which occasions he took stock of our religious as well as physical states), we were still not allowed to enter the free public school. It would not do! Irreligion was inculcated there. One was not only in danger but certain of losing one's immortal soul! And as much as my mother must have doubted his practical wisdom in those days, of such was the docility of this genial and uninformed soul that she followed his wishes and instructions in this matter of faith.

And yet with all these drawbacks, ours was a home, full of a kind of sweetness that never since has anywhere been equalled for me, however difficult it must have been for her. And it was but such a little while, as I have said, before the elder children and my father, tortured by their absence from her, began to appear, my father not more than once a month—since the expense of the trip was always a factor with him—the others, Amy, Janet and Ruth, more frequently—as often, in short, as change of position and a growing nostalgia would either permit or demand. Eleanor, as I have said, was attending a convent school, but at the end of the first term she, too, returned to her mother. She did not like it and so would not stay. My brother Al also, as I have recorded, had been sent to an uncle in northern Indiana, whose large and prosperous farm could well include his services, and his presence was thus disposed of for at least two years. But there were frequent letters from him, and at the end of that time he, too, returned.

As for Paul and Rome, they had, as we have seen, taken flight into the world, Rome temporarily to essay the trade of printer and later fireman on a railroad—the latter field of work never afterward completely deserted—Paul to find himself in the realm of the theatre, developing into a really gifted comedian and song-writer, the author of many land-sweeping melodies and their accompanying verses. Just at this time—although unknown to us—he was with a strolling minstrel troupe or travelling street corner cure-all show—Hamlin's Wizard Oil —for which aggregation of boob-ticklers and worthless nostrum vendors he played and sang comic songs (his own earliest compositions among them) to the strains of a small wagon organ.

But as for the presence of the girls in our household, I do not recall that they contributed very much to make this new home self-sustaining. Amy, for instance—a brown-haired, brown-eyed, pink-cheeked, plump creature—I recall being scolded continually by my mother for her idleness and general inefficiency. She preferred to moon about. As she herself explained herself in later years, she was all a-dream, desirous of being with her mother but without any least conception of the problems that confronted either her mother or herself.

"I cannot really say what my thoughts were," she once said to me. "I am fairly well convinced, though, that I was not thinking in any connected way. Probably I wanted to be near mother because it was easier and somehow safer. Before she left Terre Haute I had not been compelled to work, and after she left, I had to go to work. Besides, there was the blood tie. At any rate, once I arrived in Sullivan, I felt my troubles to be over, she would look after me. Of course, that was the reasoning of a child, but I was still very childish, perhaps more so than the others. Maybe I thought that parents were made to take care of children for ever.

"It never occurred to me that there was such a thing as a social scheme or pattern—marriage, home, children, training—to which most people adhered, or sought to. I never understood that until years later. As a matter of fact, I really did not know what was meant by love and men. I felt myself beginning to be drawn to them, but as to consequences in connection with relations with them, I scarcely knew what that meant. My mind did not grasp the meaning of sex and its possible results. That is why I think guardianship of the young up to a certain age by intelligent parents is worth something. Not so much, though—it depends on the parents.

"To illustrate, once mother gave me a dollar to buy a pair of slippers, and I went downtown to get them. In the first shoe store I went into, there was a young drummer standing about, only I didn't know he was a drummer. The clerk was out, and after looking me over, this man came over and said he would wait on me. 'How much did you want to pay for the slippers?' he asked. 'I just have a dollar,' I replied. 'Look at these,' he said, and opened a bag or small trunk in which he carried his samples. I was enraptured. There were eight or ten styles, and they seemed to me beautiful. 'How much are these?' I asked. 'Well, if any of them fit you, you can have them. They're worth four dollars, but I won't charge *you* anything.' He leaned toward me and smiled. Of course, I was grateful and wanted the slippers. Besides, I thought he was handsome. I began to like him. We dilly-dallied over the slippers, and I can't describe the feeling that sprang up between us in this brief time.

71

" 'Oh, but I can't take them!' I said. 'My mother would know.' But he put his hand on my arm and asked where I lived, and said I was beautiful, and wouldn't I run away with him. He said he lived in Ohio, or Pennsylvania—he had a nice home and his mother would love me. He said he would marry me and buy me beautiful dresses, and do you know, then and there I decided to go! It seems almost unbelievable to me now, but so it was, and I believed him. He gave me the shoes and told me to go to a certain corner and wait for him. When he came he paid me more compliments, and then told me where to meet him, at which train, but that I was not to speak to him on the platform; when we were out of Sullivan he would join me. I was so green that I even threw away the dollar mother had given me, for fear she would find it and know that I had not spent it. By some twist of the mind, childish fancy or hypnotism, I thought this was all right. I was to have beautiful clothes and meet his mother. I even thought how she would love me for being his wife!"

The upshot of this was that eight or nine o'clock that evening she met this man on the platform of the local railway. Only as she was stepping on the train, the station agent, who recognised her, called out: "Where are you going, Amy?"

"To Vincennes," she replied, taken aback and not being able to think of another place. She did not even know the direction in which the train was going.

"Well, then, you don't want this train. It's going to Terre Haute."

"But I have to go on this train! I . . ."

"Does your mother know you're going?"

She shook her head.

"Well, then, don't you think you'd better ask your mother first? Don't you know she's going to feel bad about this?"

"He talked to me in such a sweet way," continued my sister, "that I let the train go out. I began to feel that I ought to go home. And it was a long time before I tried to run away again, and then not because I wanted to, really."

My sister Janet was also the cause of considerable worry to my mother at this time. She had become more sophisticated and restless since her short working career in Terre Haute. Chance in her case had operated against her. Her own temperament was probably as much to blame as anything else, although material prosperity and social place would certainly have worked in her favour. At any rate, she was charged by my father with being loose and in need of watching. Bad girl! The endless palaver in regard to that! Whether or not she was, I have no way of knowing. Attractive, her little head buzzing, no doubt, with thoughts of but three things—men, clothes, and the possibilities of combining the twain so as to produce a good time—a dance, a picnic, a patter of conversation—she gave a bad impression to one as strait-laced as my father. Essentially and in the long run, she proved to be one of the best of wives and mothers, sacrificing more for her children than is within the capacity of most women of my ken.

I also talked to this sister once concerning this period of her life, trying to piece out the few general facts which I recalled of her and the others.

"What were you doing?" I asked. "How were you using your time? What were you thinking?"

"Clothes! Clothes and men!" was her reply. "I don't know whether it was because we were poor or because father was so insistent on the Catholic faith, but I was wild for anything that represented the opposite of what I had. Father was always talking about honourable marriage, but I didn't want to get married. I had not met anyone who interested me enough. I don't think I really knew what I wanted, unless it was just passing contact with men or boys, and to go about, be admired for my looks, have everything I saw in the shop windows, and see everything that I thought girls ought to see. I know I hated to go to church, and I wouldn't do it. I despised the idea father had of saving money and going without decent clothes in order to pay old debts. On the other hand, I loved mother, and was sorry for her. When men proposed marriage, I found I didn't like them well enough to marry them, but when they told me I was beautiful and wanted to give me things and take me places, it was a different matter. Where I liked a man, it was easy enough to go with him—it was fun—there wasn't really anything wrong with it that I could see. Aside from the social scheme as people seem to want it, I don't even now see that it was."

At this point I am sure any self-respecting moralist will close this book once and for all!

73

CHAPTER XIV

IN Sullivan were the usual elements which make up an American small town: the many boys and girls who flourished in the local public schools; the graduates who had taken positions here and there inside and outside the town and were coming and going; and the elder citizens of repute, married and unmarried, who made up the solid bulk of the population and conducted its enterprises, such as they were. But of these we knew none; we were on the outskirts of things, socially, materially, and in every other way. Our activities were confined to such chance acquaintances as crossed our path: neighbours, for instance, for whose social condition we younger ones at least had the profoundest contempt. Although we had nothing material ourselves, yet mentally—by reason of natural equipment, I presume, and the retailed tradition of our mother—we felt immensely superior. We did not have anything now, but we would have one day ! Had not our father once owned the mill here ? At the same time, a genial democracy and longing for companionship made us tolerant of certain overtures made by others, although for my part I was always living more or less alone in a world of my own. Nevertheless, young as I was, our social position here was beginning to be very plain to me, along with the avid and in many respects imaginative and life-seeking characteristics of my sisters—things emphasised by talks and quarrels among them and occasional complaints and warnings on the part of my mother.

For, as I have indicated, Amy and Janet now took up with a type of youth not much hampered by the usual safeguards employed by watchful parents. My mother had so little time ! The more carefully-minded of family heads usually look after their children from purely selfish or utilitarian if not religious or ethical points of view. In many cases—most, perhaps—it is not so much a useless preaching or a pale persuasion as a certain iron insistence upon a routine or type of conduct. Poverty having wrecked the spirit or *esprit de corps* of our family, it remained only for the easy and yet natural sympathy of my mother, preyed upon as it was by the natural desires of her children to have something in the form of pleasure, to undo what little opportunity for social, if not virginal, integrity presented itself.

I wish it were possible for those who see life only as an orderly procedure, and from a moralistic or religious point of view, without regard to the law of contrarities which tries every individual growth by its power to survive in conflict with other growths, to consider the case of our family. Here was a group, intelligent enough from one point of view; that is, they differed polarically from the dull clod in having emotion, imagination, a fine capacity (I had almost said "frenzy") for existence. Not one moved untouched by the beauty of life. Not one, as the years went on, failed to respond mentally to superior books, plays, poetic if not necessarily great verse, and the essential drama of life. All could see, to a certain extent, wherein they had failed, and what they had lost. All regretted, in due course of time, the silly physical and tactless social things which had resulted in their discredit locally here and there and for a time. But what would you? Is not the world, in part, at least, compounded of such vain and pointless regrets!

Yet here, the total effect of their efforts to find themselves mentally and socially was, if anything, to reduce rather than improve our already poor local level. I had it from both my sisters Amy and Janet years later that at this time these two struck up a close friendship which set them quite apart from the others and started them gadding about the streets of Sullivan, seeing the sights and making such friends as they might among the well-to-do young men of the town. Amy, as it had proved, did not get on at all with Trina, and Ruth was far too poetic, meditative, elegiac in her mood, to be a boon companion of any of the others. She stayed close to mother, aiding as much as possible. I recall distinctly that Trina considered Amy forward, foolish, man-struck, whereas she herself was cool, moral, proper. Her principal complaint was that Amy painted her lips and cheeks and darkened her brows and lashes and that she was forward with men. Even Ed and I noticed this tendency of Amy's to primp and pose, but we would not have thought much of it, I dare say, had it not been for Trina and Ruth and my mother. With them it was a great scandal, so much so that corrective measures were attempted, but without result. Such temperaments are not to be reformed by threats and scoldings.

One of their flirtations, as I now recall, concerned two strolling tight-rope walkers, if you please, who somewhere in the east, I believe, had encountered my brother Paul, and at his request came to pay the family a visit. (Imagine their satisfaction at finding these good-looking girls on the scene!) Their business in Sullivan was to give an exhibition of tight-rope walking, which same, I, along with most of the population, witnessed, a thick rope being strung from the roof of one of the downtown store buildings to the courthouse and these two balancing and dancing along it, a most hazardous performance! I can see them now, in their vari-coloured fleshings and gorgeous velvet loin cloths. But the thing that was more wonderful to me than even this was that *we* should be privileged to know them! For a great crowd had assembled and a hatful of small coins was taken up. It seemed a world of money to me. Of course, one of them had to become infatuated with Amy and tried, as had the drummer, to induce her to run away with him. Yet she did not. Why I do not know, for I think this home, now that she had passed this much time in it, was held lightly enough in her mind at the time. It must have been that she did not care enough for him.

As for Janet, she also, as it appeared, had soon exhausted the charms of Sullivan, was finding it dull and wished to escape. And finally, for companionship's sake, I am sure, induced Amy to run away with her, filling her mind with the possibility of fine clothes and a comfortable life in a big city. At the time, though, one of Janet's admirers had persuaded her it would be best—happiness in store—and suggested that she bring her sister. I myself remember being asked to assist in their flight by keeping watch of mother's movements while they dressed, packed, and climbed out a side window, bound for a train leaving at nine-thirty that night. And as much as I loved my mother and wished not to injure her in any way, still I did this. Possibly I thought it might not make any difference to her. Or again, it is entirely possible that even a whispered request on the part of one or another of my sisters was sufficient to cause me to aid, without any thinking to speak of, the idea of adventure running high in all of us. And besides, there was no suggestion of any moral or immoral import in all this to me, understanding, as I did, so little of sex.

None the less, there was a slight flaw in the arrangements. Janet had not sufficient money to pay both fares, and so it had been decided that Amy was to secure her ticket from the station agent, he being one of her admirers. But when said agent found that she was seeking to borrow merely in order to leave Sullivan and him, he refused. And in consequence, Amy was compelled to return home alone, while Janet, too immersed in her plans to change, went on, to be gone for a year or more, as it proved. Naturally, Amy came in for a severe lecturing, possibly a light whipping, but against youth of such chemic unreasonableness and force, of what avail are threats, pleas, tears? For ever and ever life goes its chemic way, unmindful of anything save attractions and repulsions. Blood will tell and have its way, the iron, sodium, carbon, hydrogen, of endless suns. Of what else is this seeming composed?

About this time also, another calamity came our way—one that did not tend to lighten my mother's burden in any way, you may be sure. It concerned a girl friend of my sister Eleanor's. My own recollection of the whole affair is rather vague, and the details of it I had from my sister years later, but I remember the girl—Kitty Costigan was her name—and the secrecy attendant upon her presence in our house. It seemed that her constant association with one of the "young bloods" of the town, the son of the bank president, had produced a condition which is honourably supposed to be confined to the marriage state only; in other words, to use the phrase of the day, she was "in a delicate condition," and the very eminent position of her accomplice made it necessary that he should be most guarded in connection with the case. This Kitty worked in the general dry-goods store; had no parents, and apparently no relatives. She lived in a little room in the house of a very religious family, who concerned themselves more with her moral welfare than her physical needs.

According to the story Eleanor told me years later, when young Atco learned of his sweetheart's condition, he gave her a hundred dollars and the address of an old doctor some

77

fifteen miles out of Terre Haute, and forced her to agree to keep his own name concealed. Being in sympathetic accord with him at the time, she did as she was told. But the events which followed contribute one of those pathetic episodes which might well employ the art of the novelist. A girl of eighteen, ignorant in the better technical sense of the word, not lacking in courage, however, and a certain managerial ability, setting forth on this difficult errand! I will try to tell the story in Eleanor's own words, because she was Kitty's confidante and aid during the whole affair, and most deeply troubled herself. In fact, she has never forgotten it.

"When she reached H——" (the town in which the doctor was located), as Eleanor tells it, "she stepped nervously off the train and inquired of the station agent where Dr. Dinsmore (the name is·fictitious) lived. He told her that the doctor had died months before. Imagine her desperation! Her expression must have told the station agent something. Perhaps he had had other inquiries of the kind. 'There's an old woman who lives in the last house out this track,' he volunteered, without other comment. 'It's a yellow house and has green blinds. You can't miss it. She used to be Dr. Dinsmore's nurse. Perhaps you'd like to see her.' Kitty thanked him and went on. There was no train out of the place for two hours. When she reached the house of this old woman, she was scared to death. She had the hundred dollars and feared she might be done away with. The town was so small and dead. The house was old and mouldy and the woods came up to the track opposite. There were no curtains at the windows and the front door looked as though it had never been opened. After she knocked she had to wait a long time before a stout, old, sickly-looking woman came and asked what she wanted. 'I came to see Dr. Dinsmore,' she said. 'Yes, well, he's dead. What did you want with him?' 'Oh,' said Kitty, in despair, 'I have to see someone! The agent told me he was dead but said you had been his nurse and might see me. I have come all the way from Sullivan, and I don't know where else to go.' 'Who sent you here?' asked the old woman, at the same time inviting her in. She went into the stuffy old room, but refused to tell. When the old woman learned she had no relatives, no one to go to, she refused to do anything to help her. She asked how much money she had, how long she had been in that condition, and when told that four menstrual periods had already passed, she sympathised with her and urged her to lie down and rest. But she would do nothing for her. Fear of local censure or punishment perhaps."

Faced with this defeat the girl waited until it was almost dark —it was October—and then returned to the depot, desperate. She did not know anyone to whom she could turn. There was only Eleanor. So she took the next train back to Sullivan and went immediately to our house. And needless to say, it ended by both Eleanor and Kitty taking mother into their confidence. As described by Eleanor to me, my mother was deeply sympathetic and troubled. She had much too much sympathy for the ills of others to face this calmly, let alone coldly. At first, greatly depressed, she urged that Kitty go to the man and force him to marry her, but when persuaded that this was impossible, that, in fact, he had already left town, his whereabouts unknown, she was won over to helping them.

"The end of it all was," continued Eleanor, "that Kitty came into our house to stay until her child was born—under mother's ministrations, of course. It was still-born. When the time came, mother sent for an old doctor she had known for years, and explained the situation, and he agreed to take care of Kitty. When the labour pains came, mother gave her pads of absorbent cotton to stuff into her mouth and dig her nails into, so as not to make an outcry. I remember so well how mother, in that soft, caressing way of hers, took care of this girl. I remember her putting her arms around her, after she first heard the story, and saying to her: 'Well, never mind, I will see you through. You will be all right; don't cry. Perhaps you will be a better girl for it. I hope so, anyhow.'"

My sister's eyes, while narrating this tale, were filled with tears. And so Kitty Costigan, too, was turned into a devotee of the woman who was my mother.

In this connection, though, I have often marvelled at the bungling of the average—in many cases, the exceptional— man in situations of this kind. This girl's lover, while apparently worldly-wise and successful, was obviously a novice in the matter of sex difficulties. Having placed the girl in this un-enviable position, he seemed scarcely to know what to do about it. The bearing of children is simple and commonplace enough, yet where the stigma of the unconventional is involved, all the customary conveniences and easements of the situation disappear and action becomes as difficult and dangerous as in a wild. Among the ultra-sophisticated, it is true, a kind of freemasonry prevails which makes it easy to adjust such things, and in Russia to-day it is among the social conveniences supplied by the government itself. But in Indiana, in 1880 or thereabouts, what a crime! Sex liberty! And the situations in which those who attempted it frequently found themselves!

CHAPTER XV

THE next individual to arrive on the scene was my second oldest brother Rome, who, after having ignored such phases of family life as were offered him from time to time in Terre Haute, had finally drifted into the American world at large, and seen and done . . . what? One could never rightly gather the details from him at any time.

A most supercilious and condescending fellow from his youth up, and without any general, let alone technical, education, as you may well imagine, yet because of a fairly observant and interpretive mind and the best of physical health and strength, inclined to look down upon most of his fellows as inadequate or ill-starred or without that fine experience and ability which he assumed to be his and which would permit them to adjust themselves to life as easily and gracefully as he believed he did. A curious and, in some respects, amazing fellow, handsome, selfish, indifferent, at times cruel, and with all too little of the constructive or organic sense of which he was convinced he possessed so much. And yet ending up relatively comfortably; that is, not actually forsaken, at least —a pensioner of those for whom he had never done anything. (I am in no way angry, merely in a descriptive mood.)

Yet after two years of drifting, here he was back. But to what end? That he might be of any material service to his mother or her family? Never believe it! His one concern, in so far as any and all others went (at least in so far as I was ever able to judge) was their mental and material use to him. And with what an air all that was conveyed! The looks and gestures of command! The demands and orders: for food, drink, service!

And well enough dressed when he arrived, as I recall, even smartly so for his time and region, but already a prey to his one besetting and unshakable vice or weakness—drink. He had learned that, as well as to gamble and beat his way here and there, other men being the "suckers" or undemanding friends that they were. And so he began here well enough, telling fascinating tales of towns and cities he had seen and places he had worked—Texas, New Mexico, Colorado, Chicago—but no money—yet giving me, as well as perhaps the others, a broader notion of the world outside. And presently he was looking up persons whom earlier in our history the family had known here—the Dooneys and others—but with a view only, I am sure, of using them—borrowing money or " showing off," talking about himself and his career. Also making up with the railroad men who frequented the round-house near by, since already he was somewhat experienced in several forms of railroading: firing, switching, train-braking, etc. But soon returning home, and, much to my mother's grief, none the better for liquor, although not actually drunk.

The one agreeable thing about him—if truly agreeable it may be called—was his obvious love of adventure, which readily found a responsive chord in me. For he was a lover of life, its strange exotic, ridiculous and at times fantastic phases and grandeurs; and at times when he was in the right —or perhaps I would better say, an easy and garrulous—mood would picture strange and distant things so graphically that it was as though I myself were there with him. But not to me or any of us younger children, only to his mother, whose temperament, as was the case with the rest of us, appeared to fascinate him, for he was never weary of staying by her side, following her about and talking, talking, talking.

"Why, mamma, you wouldn't believe it! Those peons down there! I can't tell you!" He was talking about Mexico, Arizona, Nevada, California—the Indians, Hopi, Navajo, Blackfeet, their tepees, reservations, costumes, customs. Also of the ranching, mining, gambling life of the extreme south-west and far west. More, he had an extensive collection of photographs of Indian chiefs, their squaws and children, in tribal costumes, together with views of mountains, plains, burros, wild horses, roving bands of cattle, cowboys, saloons. At once on seeing them, my imagination took wing. I wanted to be up and away. Indeed from then on, the trains as they passed to and fro between Evansville and Terre Haute came to have a new meaning. Also the birds, especially when in full flight southward in the fall—great armies of blackbirds, cowbirds, robins, blue jays—going where . . . where? My brain still thrills to *where!*

In short, and as little as I admired or was drawn to him from first to last, I always lingered as near as possible during his easy, graceful narrations, held spellbound along with the others, my mother included, by the pictures he worded. Santa Fé, Albuquerque, Tucson, Mexico City, Chihuahua, San Francisco, Duluth, St. Paul, St. Louis, Chicago, New Orleans, Galveston, Fort Worth! "These yokels around here don't know anything!" he announced one day. "They've never been anywhere!" His handsome young lips curled as he began making suggestions as to where the family ought to go in order to do better economically and socially. One of his most stirring panegyrics, as I now recall it, was devoted to Chicago, then a city of scarcely more than three or four hundred thousand, but obviously already the up-and-coming centre of the middle west, New York's only important rival.

"Why, mamma, you never saw such a place!" (I can hear his voice now.) "That's the place for a family, where they can do something and get along! Not stuck off in a little hole like this! Why, say, there must be four or five hundred thousand people there! And the shops! And the high buildings! And you ought to see the girls and boys going to work in the mornings and coming home at nights! And the horse cars, with their little bells and lights, and packed to the doors with people, hanging on to straps and on to the platforms!" He had been seeing young America grow and was astonished and electrified, filled with the wine of this new mid-west life.

During his stay, which was of a few weeks only—Sullivan being too small and sleepy to claim his attention for long—I was introduced to various phases of the natural life thereabouts which ordinarily might not have reached me so soon. For this brother loved to fish—a charming trait from one point of view, coupled, as it was, with an idyllic love of nature—and to row. He had not been with us more than twenty-four hours before he asked if we had any fishing poles. Finding none to suit him, he actually gave me the money wherewith to buy three of the long bamboo type, and together with Ed and myself— actually commandeered for the purpose—tramped off in search of a place to fish—places we had not discovered but which he knew from having lived here at about our age.

83

Along the Busseron then, for as many as four or five miles, through stretches of wood I had never seen, by strange fields and lanes, we went, encountering silences and pleasances too sweet for words. A very strange and easily irritated young man he seemed to me, though, especially when he had the least liquor in him—which was nearly always. "Sit down!" he would snap angrily at either one of us if we chanced to move while he was fishing. (Not having seen either of us for several years, it might have been supposed that he would be affectionately, or at least humanly, stirred by this renewal of family relations. But not so.) "Can't you keep still, you little brats? Take that pole out of the water, you little snipe! Can't you see I got a bite? If there were any fish, you little fools would chase them away!"

Greatly nonplussed by his attitude were Ed and I, you may be sure. Though previously in contact with him in Terre Haute, we scarcely remembered him, and had it not been for his affectionate attitude toward mother, we would not have believed that he was connected with us at all. Still, since she liked him, he must be all right, was my personal conclusion. True, he was savage and unkind, but, since he was my brother, I felt it my duty to have an affection for him, and—strange insolubility of human relationship—so do I still.

But one day while out on one of these expeditions, we saw two men come out of the woods, one being led by the other, the second man having had his right arm partially blown away by the explosion of his gun. He was white, faint, and suffering. Either Ed or I immediately lent aid by running to a distant farmhouse for help, while Rome stayed with the men. Before either Ed or I—I forget which—returned, a passing farm-wagon had taken up the two men and my brother and carried them to Sullivan. But I recall that I was terribly shocked; it destroyed in me all zest for hunting or even the fields for the time being. It was my first sight of blood—a really serious accident.

But the wonder of that period to me! For despite Rome's irritable temper—which marred, to some extent, my first thrill of fishing—there was the sight of new, still unvisited waters, of red and yellow and green and blue corks floating on slow-moving currents; of dragon-flies glistening like jewels in the sun; of thrilling water-rings made by bobbing corks; and of glistening, wriggling fish—sun, cat, perch, shiners, mud-dogs, eels—pulled out of this or some other insignificant little stream the while I wondered about what lay below its placid surface. If only I had then known some of the many delightful books on natural history! But there were no books in our home and no one to tell me anything about fishes or the chemistry of water or the character of aquatic life in general. Years later I came upon a modest school zoology, also at about the same time "Water Babies," and my mind expanded with a rush. I began to sense dimly how wide, how infinite indeed, in its variety is the world. But here in these still woods, how speedily I might have gathered much that later I came to feel the need of!

CHAPTER XVI

MY sisters, particularly Trina, always described me to myself as a most curious-minded child, hanging about and listening even when I was not wanted—which is probably true enough. Yet it always seemed to me that no one ever wanted me *enough*, unless it was my mother. (Later there were those who wanted me too much, and where I did not "want"!) When not wanted, though, I preferred to play by myself and think and listen, and to this end I invented certain simple games which served my purpose admirably and often made me an unconscious eavesdropper, my presence being scarcely noticed or suspected.

One of these games I can best describe as "train." It consisted of placing half-size cigar boxes in a row, end to end, on the floor of our parlour or living room, and there " switching" or making up a train, with which I travelled from station to station, whistling as I went. A spool on a box at one end made the engine; a larger-sized cigar box at the other end was the caboose. Smaller-sized cigar boxes, without their lids, made the flat cars. With these in groups of fifteen or twenty I was wont to travel to and fro on my knees all morning or afternoon. The wear and tear on my stockings and the seat of my trousers was considerable, as you may guess, and for this I was sometimes scolded. Yet since it tended to quiet and the exact knowledge of my whereabouts, not so much was said.

In summer, of course, I transferred this process to the yard. Here I laid out a series of stations built of twigs along the fence nearest the house, and between these I travelled (the whole length of the yard, by the way, perhaps a hundred and fifty feet), hour after hour. I personally was the engine, cars, conductor, whistle and bell, all in one. To give verisimilitude to the process, in starting and stopping I would revolve my right arm after the fashion of a piston rod, and so clanging, whistling, puffing, calling "All aboard!" and running to and fro, I would while away the hours, with what resulting thoughts in the minds of others I can only guess. Perhaps some may have imagined I was slightly demented.

This love of playing "train" sprang, of course, from watching the switching going on beyond the hay press, the movement of the various trains speeding north and south between Evansville and Terre Haute. I often sat and watched these things, humming a scrap of half-memorised song the while, my mind wandering over all of the realms within the range of my intuitions, my experiences, and what I had learned from others. Ah, those wondrous, silent hours in the sun! The look of the smooth green grass about our house; the flare of the yellow trumpet flowers, each a horn of beauty; the flight of birds; the drifting argosies of clouds; the sound of the wind in the trees; and then those noises of devices made by man! The trains, carrying people away, away! Where did they go? What were they like, those far-off places to which they hurried? I knew of Terre Haute and Vincennes, but then there were Chicago, Denver, Sante Fé, San Francisco—all places to which my brother had been. And I would hear my mother speak of Dayton and Piqua in Ohio; of Beaver Falls and Germantown in Pennsylvania, from whence her parents had come; of Fort Wayne, Warsaw and Silver Lake in the northern part of Indiana, where various members of her family had once and some still lived—a brother or two as well as a sister or two. (I was to see them all in due time, had I only known.) Again, my father had come from Germany, wherever that was! And I had an uncle and aunt in Salem, Oregon, away-away-off west, perhaps farther than any bird could ever fly!

The various characters hereabouts also impressed me, and among them none took higher rank than the Herndons, the poor family living next door to us in a small, unpainted cottage of two rooms, one of them a lean-to or kitchen. In winter, when the snow was heavy on the ground, this cottage seemed the poorest and barest that could be imagined. I have already referred to "Tish" Herndon and her father. "Tish" was an Indian type, as I recall her, piercing black eyes and black hair, and apparently of a fiery, and yet sympathetic, temperament. For often there were quarrels between her and her father, and then loud, agonised sobbings on her part—contrition, as I came to know. For Tish had the reputation of being a "bad

87

woman" and misconducting herself in various and sundry ways—drinking, for one—and so sorrowing her father, who was looked after by her. Occasionally also most noisy and dreadful quarrels between her and a sister who lived on a farm somewhere but came occasionally to visit, bringing her husband and little boy. In between there were long periods during which this girl lived and worked here peaceably enough.

My mother always maintained that Tish Herndon was a good woman at heart, boisterous as she might appear in some of her phases. Often she came to our house to borrow things. And once in the early fall of the second year, as I recall, she reported that there were vast quantities of frost-bitten fruit to be had free of various farmers; it could be used for preserving if gathered quickly enough. Because of this news or "tip," we along with others in the vicinity garnered our share. Also, as my mother said, Tish was generous to a fault, always seeking out those who were ill or in distress and serving them as best she could. I recall that once some scalding hot water having fallen on the back of our dog Rover, she appeared—having heard his yowls, I presume—with a medicinal compound of tar, which she applied and then bound up the wound.

But the thing in connection with this family that fixed itself most definitely in my memory was the death of old Herndon during the second year of our stay in Sullivan, and the amazing grief of this rather ill-reputed daughter. (Death ever seems to take on an abnormal significance in realms of ignorance or wretchedness.) During the old man's illness, my mother, as might be expected, was involved, first in the capacity of aid and counsel to the sufferer, supplying advice, utensils, and even food. Toward the last, etiquette, such as it was in this neighbourhood, seemed to demand that all who were friendly with this family should call and pay their last respects, as it were. And so, on several occasions I was permitted to go as the companion of one of my sisters or my mother, twice when old Herndon was very low and once after he was dead.

The shabby end of man! His immeasurable triviality! As we all saw this old man, he appeared to have been a personage of sorts in his day, certainly very much above the brainless clods by whom he was surrounded. Physically he was of prophetic outline, and mentally, well, I can only say that I heard my mother say he had been a man of means and position.

What she meant by that I cannot say. What I wish to emphasise is this: that as I looked at this old man on my two or three visits, feverish, bony, half unconscious, but with a beautifully modelled head and face, framed in long white hair, there came to me even then a suggestion of the paltry import of our individual lives. He had seen better days, to be sure—who has not?—but here he was in this out-of-the-way corner, in this hut of a house, attended by his daughter, a lone girl of ill repute (and what dark meditations and fears of her own) and a few indifferent or curious neighbours, and dying!

The grass and soil of a finely attuned chemic process have long since absorbed all that was significant or insignificant in connection with old Herndon, and for ever. There remains no trace. Yet I recall that this wretched home was redolent of gloom and the fear of eternal bereavement as well as the pathos of unfulfilled dreams and aspirations. Even I, a child, could gather that much—the sadness of utter annihilation in the face of a desire to persist. All of us went about on tiptoe. The face of Tish Herndon, emaciated and weary, haunted me. And then one afternoon, the end, death! And forthwith such wailings and lamentations as I had never heard before! The eerie, banshee helplessness of it all! It was Tish mourning her dead—the lost affection and past ills and sufferings and despairs of her father.

"He had to die in a little hut, he did! He didn't have enough to eat, he didn't! I know what killed him! Oh, his poor hands, and his poor, poor body!" She threw herself by the bedside, clutching the wretched bedclothes with her tense hands until they led her away weeping, these scrubby counsellors of her defeated state.

And in a day or two, in a pine box and an ordinary express or grocery wagon—no hearse here—but fitted to hold six or eight mourners in addition, and followed by one buggy, this shell of Herndon senior was carted over a long, rough country road to a small weed-grown graveyard in the woods. And here "laid to rest," as they say. But was he? Is changeful, deathless energy ever laid to rest anywhere? We went, my mother and some of us children, out of sympathy. I recall the brown, dead weeds, the open grave, the tumbledown stones here and there.

"God is our life!" said Mrs. Eddy, in passing. But for dissenters let us put it another way: "Life is our God!" Eternal substance holds us all; from that we cannot escape. If we are shabby, so is God, in part. If we are worn and wretched, so is He, in part. If there is sin and shame and evil, they pour to us in the form of sunbeams from on high. We cannot escape them. They are a part of the All-force, of Him, through Him, from Him us all. We cannot escape Him or ourselves, nor He us, with all that we are. That we know.

Then there was old Mrs. Hudson, who suffered an even more unsocial and unremembered death. A faded and crone-like creature she was, in an old brown dress and somewhat Quakerish bonnet, living in the very last house to the north of us and on the extreme north-east edge of the common, where with a few chickens, a cow, some fruit trees, and an exceedingly tiny garden, she kept tryst with what memories! I used to see her, morning and evening, pottering about her branch, vine and weed-grown domain, her possessions seeming to constitute more of a burden than her failing strength was able to cope with. And often I meditated on her, as did my mother, who, although she never visited or intruded upon her, at last sent Ed and me to see if we could arrange for the occasional purchase of eggs and milk from her. This was easy enough, because I do believe that toward the last the old lady had neither the strength nor interest to collect or market her wares. More than that, the occasional bawlings of her cow, perhaps unwatered, unfed, unmilked, and the somewhat doleful and unrewarded assembling of her perhaps two dozen chickens about her side door or front gate, seemed to indicate to my mother as well as myself that all was not always well with her.

And then one evening, my mother, always psychic and moved by intuitions or premonitions—that sixth sense which we have not yet come to accept—was impelled to go over to visit her. I can see her now, arranging for this exceptional visit, putting on a mottled India shawl, and saying to us: "You stay here. I am going over to see Mrs. Hudson for a minute. I have a feeling she may not be well." And true enough, Mrs. Hudson was very ill. For soon mother returned, to call Ruth and Eleanor and to despatch one of us others for a doctor. Water was put on to boil in Mrs. Hudson's dirty kitchen; considerable cleaning-up was done, and later that evening, like soldiers in a good cause, Trina, Amy and myself were picketed in Mrs.

Hudson's house in order to notify mother of any untoward happening. The old lady was out of her mind and dying, and we were in temporary charge of her shabby effects.

In this case there were no relatives to call upon, so far as we could learn. No one seemed to have been intimate with her or concerned as to her welfare. She had lived alone, and now, on the second day after mother's visit, she died alone. It was mother who milked her cow and fed her chickens. No money was found in the house, but since someone in the vicinity reported that once she had professed membership in the Baptist Church and owned this small bit of property, we decided to notify the Baptist minister. Subsequent to that, if I recall aright, a guardianship was claimed by someone connected with the church, and this person undertook to pay the doctor's bill and arrange for the funeral. Throughout all this, there were no visitors to speak of, not even after the minister had been informed. But the funeral cortège, unlike that of old Mr. Herndon—and when it set out for the same tatterdemalion graveyard—consisted of a hearse, one buggy—in which rode the funeral director and a representative of the Baptist Church —and one light open runabout in which my mother and one of my sisters rode, for looks' sake, as it were.

I recall that later my mother was curious as to who was to possess Mrs. Hudson's cow and chickens, since she personally could not afford to buy them. Also as to how it was that although the local Baptist Church was in some way guardian of her affairs—the house and grounds passing into its care— no better funeral or burying ground was provided. Mostly, though, she kept commenting on the fact that "Something kept telling me to go over and see her." As for myself, I recall only the wretched little room, the shabby old bed, and the old lady's gaunt, leathery features and stertorous breathing. Death, as I witnessed it here and in the Herndon home, induced a heavy gloom in me, more dreadful, if anything, than that which came upon me when I saw the cattle mistreated and butchered by Spilky. Those were cattle, but these were creatures like myself. I had seen both of them up and about not long before, and now they were no more, gone, and in the most lonely and forsaken fashion.

Say what you will, poor as was our home, it always seemed radiant with hope and youth and beauty. Birds were in our chimneys and eaves, roses in our garden. Mother was always dreaming of better things to come. But the shabby end of Mrs. Hudson and Mr. Herndon! I think of them to this day with a kind of gloom, or that loneliness that comes at evening when one is alone. At that time I was convinced that I would not want to die quite so bereft. But now . . . well, why not? What difference to the dead whether many or none know or care?

CHAPTER XVII

AFTER the Hudson house had been cleared of its belongings, the Johnson family moved in. It consisted of a buxom, termagant mother of thirty-two or three years of age, yellow-haired, pink-cheeked, blue-eyed, obviously not possessed of much constructive grey matter, and her two children, one a brown, sinister, black-haired, black-eyed boy of twelve, the other a mere child (I forget whether boy or girl) of three or four. No sign of a husband and father all the time they lived there. Various rumours, though—that he was dead, that he was in prison, that he had run away. How like the clouds is rumour! A breath of air, and there you have it; another breath, and it is gone.

I remember that Mrs. Johnson, not long after her appearance in this region, came to our house for something and stopped to talk to mother, and thus the neighbour status was reached. Later, and by degrees, I became aware of "Dock," the son, sitting atop their board fence, dangling his brown legs and calling to me with impish curiosity and innate sociability: "Say, do you people own that house and garden?"

I shook my head.

"I thought not." (Why?) "Don't you ever play ball?"

"Sometimes, me and my brother."

"Why don't you come and play some time? I gotta bat."

"I can't, not now," I replied, recalling my mother's injunction not to take up with any of the neighbours. (Despite our present position, our one-time favourable past would not permit us to look with anything more than a kindly tolerance upon the flotsam and jetsam about us.)

"Aw, come on out this afternoon," he insisted, genially. "Three's enough to play 'one old cat.'"

"Well, maybe," I said, very doubtful of him and his surroundings.

And it was some time before either Ed or I ventured to take

up with Dock, for his very look indicated that he was wily, wilful, savage, and that one could put about as much faith in his friendship as one could in that of a fox or a wolf. Our reasons for finally doing so, even in a tentative way, were, first, fear—it being plain that unless we made a show of friendship we should have an enemy at our very doors—and second, because we could not very well help ourselves. He was always about and he chose to thrust himself upon us whether we would or not.

Like ourselves, the Johnsons were exceedingly poor. Whatever the truth as to her husband, Mrs. Johnson was compelled to take in washing and Dock to "carry coal." I can see him now, a good-sized sack on his young, bent back (a feat which neither Ed nor I could ever accomplish), coming along the railroad track from the none-too-close mine, and yet making a rather cheerful business of that dire necessity. Usually—in summer, at least—his feet were bare and his clothes, summer and winter, ragged, yet he whistled and walked with a defiant roll, pulling his ragged cap over one ear and looking out from between narrowed and defiant lids when he wanted to appear independent or savage. He must have felt considerable contempt for such spindling, house-broken, mothery, well-behaved little boys as Ed and myself. But there we were, joined together as neighbours in a confined and more or less forlorn neighbourhood, and from his or our fate there was no escape.

And together with him and our fate must be included the redoubtable Al Thompson. I have already described the Thompson domicile. But the family! His mother was a tall, thin, worn, ragbag, skeleton-like woman. Cleanliness may be a virtue and a luxury to many. I doubt whether it can be proved to be an absolute necessity. In Al Thompson's case, surely not. A bath? Never! Unless you would call swimming in the creek in summer, bathing. His clothes were rags and patches—a dirty, torn blue or red or grey shirt; long frayed trousers, his one insurance against losing them either a dirty cord or a worn strap slung over one shoulder or around his waist. His ears, eyes, nose, mouth (since he chewed tobacco when he could get it) were gloriously dirty, and his hair usually upstanding like an Indian's feathers. In summer no shoes, his trousers rolled to the knees, revealing a pair of lithe, dirty, brown legs. In winter he donned cracked or decayed

94

boots or gaiters, picked up from some dump, you may be sure.

His mother, as I have said, was a tall, thin, worn, ragbag, skeleton-like woman, in a long black rag of a dress and Shaker bonnet, wandering here and there and betimes shouting or cursing at her beloved son or daughter. (Millie was the daughter's name.) "Now, God damn you, Millie Thompson, if you don't come in hyer and help with these hyer chores now!" For Millie, as I have already said, occasionally wandered forth to chat with some hay-press or railroad hand, attracted, no doubt, by sheer youth and the savagery of her black eyes. And when not Millie, it was the tatterdemalion Al she belaboured: "You, Al! You rotten little whippet! Air you comin' in here when I call ye? Or air I got to come out thar and git ye, ye damn' little loafer!"

And Al, reasonably obedient to her wrath always, would get up from where, perhaps, he was lounging in the sun shooting craps or sitting within the shade of the hay press swapping stories with other boys, and shrugging his none-too-strong shoulders, would remark: "Listen to the damned old . . .! I never have any time to myself!" Yet off he would go, since he was too young to possess the mood or skill to shift for himself in the great world.

Occasionally also one might see him or Millie come dashing out on to the common, a chair being hurled after one or the other and their mother's voice raging and cursing within. Occasionally also there was a man seated on the squeaky, loose-boarded porch. But not always the same man. And for the most part, there was no man present. And at times one heard peals and squeals of strident laughter coming from the wretched interior. And in wintertime the red firelight flickered through their unwashed windows in quite as homey and cheering a way as the glow seen through the French windows of a mansion.

In a sense it was the same with Dock Johnson, who betimes either ignored or raged—and that most violently—at his own none-too-mild-tempered mother.

I recall him now sitting on his front fence one day assailing his mother in his usual picturesque fashion, when she implored him to think of the neighbours.

"Who are yer neighbours, anyway?" he shouted. "A lotta God-damn trash—the Dreisers, the Bowleses, the Thompsons!"

Now had I been a child of a different kidney, I would not only have resented this emotionally (as I did) but physically. But at eight or nine I was still a spindling thing, not much given to defending either my rights or the family honour. On the other hand, I did (or tried to, at least) extract some comfort out of the thought that our family was enormously superior to either the Thompsons or the Johnsons.

Just the same, not only these families but the entire neighbourhood around us constituted a kind of biological specimen board which I studied with the greatest interest. And thus it was that this same Dock Johnson as well as Al Thompson had a kind of value to me as a picturesque and defiant individuality, because they took the probably unsatisfactory details of their state with a brazen vitality which made up in colour and animal ferocity for what it lacked in dignity and charm. I have always thought there is a way of improving everyone a little, if one could just find the way. Individual attention and an attempt to discover the line of keenest appetite would do it. But has the world sufficient resources to give each child individual attention? Dock may readily have landed in the penitentiary a few years later, or he may have seen an opportunity for commercial success (about all that America could offer anyone at that time, or to-day for that matter), and seized it. Be that as it may, here was innate capacity. He was far too incisive, hopeful, high-spirited, to be passed over as nothing at all. Yet he and his mother passed out of our lives the spring before we left Sullivan, and we never saw them again. The possibly mythical husband and father was supposed to have written them to come to Kansas City, as Dock explained at the time, and their ochre-coloured belongings were trundled past our place one morning by a country moving van en route to the local railway station, pots and pans swinging below the wheels. Where they went heaven only knows. To a better state, I trust. But I have always thought that a boy who could thus impress himself on me so vividly that in the lapse of fifty years I have forgotten so few details regarding him must have had considerable force and individuality.

The thing which made him as well as Al Thompson decidedly useful to both Ed and myself at this time was the fact that neither apparently had any false shame about carrying coal. They would even go brazenly across the common to the tracks, sack over back, whereas Ed and myself, struck by the social and financial shame of our state, were inclined to go through the fields by the slaughter-house and so reach the mine in a roundabout way. I must have been the more shamefaced of the two, for Ed used to rebuke me at times for my snivelling desire to avoid publicity. Public opinion, "what will people say," as phrased by my mother and others, exercised a strong influence upon me, and this was one of the times when I felt myself to be if not in the wrong at least in a very unfortunate and hence self-demeaning position. Later in life, when I came to understand the importance of ideas and one's relationship to them, my power to stand my ground, come what might, was not so wavering.

And now in connection with these two boys, let me relate an experience which I may describe as typical in my case. For all my life long, whenever misfortune has pressed me too bitterly, something has turned up to save me, quite accidentally, as it were, and incidentally has appeared to aid in directing the current of my life to a certain extent. Thus, some time before Dock Johnson's departure, there came into being a very strong friendship between him and Al Thompson—typical birds of a feather, I presume. They were, for a period, almost inseparable. Morning, noon and night they might have been seen lolling about this tatterdemalion realm, their shoulders together, occasionally the arm of one over the shoulder of the other, communing and confiding. And by that time, for some perhaps inexplicable but not important reason, both had taken a dislike to Ed and myself. Perhaps it was because we, the only other two youths of this vicinity, kept too much to ourselves, finding joy in less adventurous and strident things than these others and so giving them the impression that we were "saps" or thought ourselves above them.

At any rate, there arose now a feeling of opposition in that quarter, so much so that after a little while it became dangerous for either of us to cross the common alone, either Dock or Al lurking somewhere, or so we feared, to inflict summary punishment for our imagined social sins. So in conference and after due meditation, we decided that we would avoid danger as much as possible by always keeping together. Also that if we were attacked by one alone and could not make good our escape, we would fight together. But now, alas, a new danger arose in the form of this constant companionship of the two. Hitherto we had rarely encountered the two together and Thompson up to this time had been soothingly neutral. But now, and of a sudden, this dark change in that quarter. Johnson no longer smiled in that genial, foxy way which was his when we met anywhere, and Thompson was distant and cold, scowling and even threatening-looking at times. And soon, on the trumped-up excuse that we had said something about him to Thompson, Johnson made open war on us. And Thompson the same.

"Whad'ja wanta tell Al Thompson I said he was a half-nigger for?" Dock demanded of me one day.

"I didn't!" I said.

"You're a liar, you did! I gotta good notion to kick the waddin' outa you! Whad'ja do it for?"

"I didn't, and he never said I did, either. Let him tell me I did."

"You did! You wanta call me a liar!"

A rough pass with his hand completed this declaration. But I, having been backing away ever since the discussion opened, now took to my heels. Lickety-split through the tall weeds I ran and Dock after me, toward my home, only I had to cross the whole wide common before reaching it. But I managed to keep in the lead, putting wings to my heels. Yet as I ran, the sad thought was coming home to me that instead of finding myself a fighter, as already I longed to be, I was proving myself a coward, and this grieved me not a little. If I could only turn and do something! As we neared my home, my sister Trina, more contentious and spirited than myself, seeing my plight, began to threaten Johnson.

"You let my brother alone, you nasty black snipe! Just you go away from here and let him be!"

"Aw, who the hell are you, you little runt?" was his reply to her. "For a cent I'd slap you like I will your big-eared brother when I catch him! (Just wait till I catch you," he called to me in an aside, "I'll fix you, you bastard!) And as for you," he went on to Trina, "I'd just as lief hit you as not!"

I wish I could describe Trina, with her thin, prim, black pigtails, her black, snapping eyes, her thin, defiant legs, a strong element of selfishness in her making her suitable to an occasion of this kind.

"Just you touch me if you dare, you nasty, trashy thing!" she bristled. "Just you lay a finger on me and see what'll happen!"

"Aw, what can you do? You can't do any more than your brother. I can lick the whole damn' family with one hand tied behind me," he boasted, approaching her threateningly.

But now both Amy and Ed had appeared, and this union of forces becoming a little too foreboding, Dock decided to retreat.

"Just you march now!" my sister Amy called, as slowly he began his retreat, yet calling from a comfortable distance: "Why don't you get out the whole damn' family? Where's your mother? I can lick the whole damn' family! I can lick all of you put together!"

We laughed over it afterwards: the recollection of Dock standing proud and contemptuous amid the dog fennel and wild clover, his bare brown legs the colour of the ground. In fact, the Johnsons and the Thompsons were always a source of amusement for us.

But this was not the end by any means. For from thence on either he or Al Thompson or both together were laying for either Ed or myself, or both. In short, for several months thereafter our lives were made miserable by the schemes and snares engineered by these two to catch and trounce us.

The difficulties that stood in the way of this were numerous. Although I had to go to the post office and store regularly, as did Ed and Trina, it was possible to take a roundabout course or get one of the others to accompany me, companionship enough to ward off a single-handed attack at least. And this was most regularly done. Nevertheless, one night, as I was slipping along a quiet residence street behind the local mill that was once my father's (an exact restoration of the one my father built, by the way), and well satisfied that once more I was outwitting my unreasoning and sinister foes, I chanced to look back and to my horror and distress saw that I was being trailed by Johnson. I started to run, hoping by speed to escape at the next corner, when, lo and behold—oh, agony of agonies!—Al Thompson appeared at that end, a lithe, dark sentinel set to guard that exit. For a moment I paused, not knowing what to do. I was "stumped," and worse, convinced that I was in for a terrible beating, when of a sudden a brilliant if not exactly admirable idea occurred to me. I crossed the street and deliberately entered the gate of a small house, of the occupants of which I knew nothing, not even that anyone was at home, so quiet was all in front. But making my way toward the rear (the thought of a savage dog now replacing that of my enemies), I peered cautiously about, only to note an open door, inside of which a middle-aged woman stood ironing clothes. She looked up inquiringly and I nervously explained.

"I just came in here because two boys are following me."

"What do they want?"

"They want to fight with me."

"Well, sit down. They won't bother you here." She looked at me curiously and, I presume, amusedly.

"What's your name?" she asked.

I told her. Then she wanted to know the names of the boys and where they lived, and I told her that. Finally, after remaining there quite a while and my enemies not following, I realised that I had to get to the post office before it closed or at least home to supper, so I asked: "Can I get through this back way into the next street?"

"Yes, if you go through Mrs. Wade's yard. But you'd better look and see that they're not following you first."

I went to the front gate and peeped out, but seeing no one I returned and went out by the alley. I was as fearful as is a mouse of a cat or a cat of a dog. I cut through the next yard and stepped cautiously along the fence to the next corner, intending to beat a hasty retreat if necessary. Fortunately, if they were lurking anywhere they had lost my trail, and so once more I was able to reach the post office in safety and also to return home unharmed. And that was the closest I ever came to single-handed combat with these two, only it made me doubly cautious, as you may well believe.

Vengeance was in store, however, and, oh, what a satisfaction that proved to me! For before any re-encounter had been effected by either of my enemies, a new element was injected into the situation. And one that altered things completely. For—for some reason which I do not now recall—my brother Al returned from the North Manchester farm where he had been apprenticed and took up our troublesome battle for us. He had been away for more than a year and a half and during that time had developed muscle enough to handle a dozen such belligerents. Besides, he was of the very stuff of courage. At once upon explaining the nature of our several ills, he took up our cause, and stirred by his enthusiasm and strength, Ed, Trina and I were quick to unload upon him to the full the conditions now created for us. And it took but little from any of us to set our new David by the ears. What, those snipes and weaklings! Afraid of them! Ho, ho! Also ha, ha! A small, defiant gamecock, his spurs thrilled for the fray. "Just show them to me!" he declared, roundly. "I'll fix 'em! I can lick the both of 'em together! Just wait'll we catch 'em together!"

Oh, immeasurable pleasure then to contrive a re-encounter with Johnson or Thompson, or both together. Nemesis-wise, we lurked about watching for the coming or going of either or both. And it was not so very long before we saw them, ambling across the common almost arm-in-arm. Oh, glory, glory! It was too good to be true! Now would the name and the glory of the house of Dreiser be reclaimed!

Instanter Al was called, of course, and as these two unsuspectingly drew near, we three issued forth: Al, Ed and myself, with Amy and Trina watching from a distance. And not knowing the goodly Al to be our brother, the twain drew nearer to investigate, the while, full of zeal for the impending fray, Al bore down on them like a small, present-day destroyer, decks cleared for action. And to the amazement of both of them, he suddenly and without a word of warning seized Johnson by the shoulder and throat and demanded: "What do you mean by picking on my brothers, you bastard? What are you always hangin' around for, tryin' to hit 'em, hey? What are you doing that for, hey?"

Accompanying these inquiries was sufficient forward energy to propel the contentious but now astounded Dock rapidly and stumblingly backward through the weeds, while his companion gazed after him in troubled amazement. The strangeness and foreboding fever of all this!

"And what about you?" my brother now demanded of Thompson, as Dock Johnson, given one good punch on the jaw, lay prone on the ground and Thompson, near at hand, stared in amazement and growing fear, you may well believe. As for Ed and myself, we were actually dancing with glee. "What do you want around here, anyway?" He approached him as savagely as he had Johnson, only Thompson, now backing and blanching, showed every evidence of contrition and surrender.

A chicken in the mouth of a fox could not have presented a more flustered air.

"I never said anything to them!" explained Al, volubly. "Honest, I never did! Who said I did? Whad'ya want to jump on me for?" The begrieved innocence of Mr. Thompson was a sight to behold. And as for Mr. Johnson, he arose and moved back rapidly to a safe distance. He was utterly dumbfounded at the sudden turn this war had taken.

"And I'll show you!" called my brother after him. "You blackfaced little . . .! Just you lay hands on either of 'em again! I'll cave in your face for you!"

This effective onslaught was accompanied on our part, of course, by cries of: "He's the one, Al!" "Yes, he did!" "Don't you let him lie to ye, Al!" "Hit 'im in the snoot, Al!" and other such friendly bits of encouragement. Also, if you will believe it—so shifty are individuals (and nations) when in danger—Thompson now turned and declared that he had never intended us harm and that it was Johnson who had caused all of the trouble—a change of front which must have astounded Mr. Johnson as much as it did us. In the swift development of this struggle, Thompson had gathered that Al was a dangerous specimen of the genus Dreiser and that it was just as well to placate him here and now.

And so, the situation was adjusted for us. Thereafter, because of the poor showing they had made, the Messrs. Johnson and Thompson manifested only the liveliest interest in and good will toward our welfare. Our stock went up ; they smiled on us. Actually they invited us to carry coal with them, and Johnson made Ed a present of a small knife he found.

Subsequent to this rescue, curiously enough, I have held my brother Al in great respect, not so much because I believed him to be physically undefeatable or because of his mental brilliance (although he gave every evidence of mental sensitivity in many ways) but because of his sheer courage, manifested always in time of danger anywhere. He was never afraid of anyone or anything, in so far as I could see. He was not truculent, but rather genial and chipper, liking to make friends and have a good time. But his outstanding determination to preserve his personal integrity and dignity was never to be lightly imposed upon, a virtue so commendable that it shines like a precious stone.

CHAPTER XVIII

I HAVE always wondered where and how my mother acquired the furniture that made it possible for her to take in boarders and lodgers. I gather that some little furniture that had been put in storage in Terre Haute was released by my father and shipped to her. Also perhaps one of the local furniture dealers for whom she did washing let her have a few things.

At any rate, I recall a late fall day on which a wagon arrived at our small home, bearing several bedsteads, a carpet, a stove, a kitchen table and several chairs, and that thereafter the interior of the house took on an air of comfort such as previously it had not known. I remember, for instance, scuffling over the new carpet and being reprimanded for it. I also recall looking through the front windows one chill evening after returning from a long walk and seeing a bright fire in the larger front room now dubbed a "parlour," being seized with a sense of beauty in regard to it all. For without were the grey and cold of fall, a late October or November evening. In the air was the rustling of dead leaves and grasses, in the sky dusk and the last glow of the early-setting sun. But within, this warmth and light, the flames of a "parlour" stove showing through small mica windows. Ah! And a reddish-brown carpet on the once bare floor, the very floor on which I used to play "freight" with cigar boxes for cars. Home, that's what it meant to me! The comfort of having brothers and sisters, but most of all, my mother within, the one who, for no reason that I was capable of cogitating upon at the time, still sufficed to unite all our cares and desires within the single sanctuary of her heart. Contemplate, if you will, the mystery and poetry of that—the mother bird spreading thinly-feathered wings over weak nestlings.

All my life since I have been sorry for families, and especially those in which there are young children, that have found it necessary to rent rooms or take in boarders. There is something about this economic disruption and invasion of personalities of that blood relation and temperamental unity which should, and no doubt does, characterise the better sort of home, that is distasteful to me. The family is, or should be, as it seems to me, a unit, spiritually and in many other ways. And thus to lay it open to infection from outside sources seems a pity, and parents who can surround their children with all those social safeguards which make for family solidarity and the integrity of its ideals are fortunate. Yet there may be those, too, who can scarcely comprehend the vitiating influence of varying and unstable personalities upon the younger members of a family. Young as I was, though, at this time, I sensed, even though vaguely, something of the truth and force of all this. I resented all along the necessity which compelled us as a family to resort to so many makeshifts to sustain ourselves, the while I sympathised intensely with the efforts and obvious desire of my mother to make a new and better life for herself and her children.

Also at this age I was becoming more and more conscious of the standing, or lack of standing, of our family here as a unit and as individuals. Whenever the elder ones were here, I could not help hearing mother address them in regard to their social ways, begging them to have a sharp eye for the proprieties and not to do anything to make the position of the family any worse than it was. Yet we have seen how thoughtlessly they were approaching the problems not only of their lives but of the family as a unit.

But in this connection I might well ask, who has not experienced the terrors of a small town, where everybody knows the business of everyone else and where no least move can be made without it being written down in the public ledger, the debit and credit accounts of favour and disfavour worked out to the last fraction? Our family as a unit and as individuals, because of the follies heretofore recorded, must have achieved a noisome odour here. Yet as units they were probably not much worse than the average and by no means evil. A more genial and affectionate, if temperamental, crew might not have been found anywhere. Despite all their faults, they were extremely fond of their mother and, after the fashion of each, of each other. Their home meant much to them, even if they did not know how to further it or use it to the best advantage. The unwilled sex lure was the thing that was causing most of the trouble, but that was not their fault. Add to this poverty and mismanagement, or the lack of any managerial ability whatsoever, and you have the whole story. My mother, good soul, was too much concerned with the beauty of life as a spectacle, too much the dreamer, to pay as much attention as she should have, perhaps, to life as a constructive compulsion. Yet she could not help that, either. It was her nature.

And this matter of boarders and roomers would have been well enough had there not been girls about. But from time to time one or another of these appeared on the scene, most likely because of lack of work and inability to find refuge elsewhere. Being lively and susceptible, they were, of course, interesting to men, and though their conduct might have been of the most innocent character, still in a town such as this, even innocent gaiety gave rise to talk. Yet what could be done with girls of that age if one was unable to guard them carefully and prevent all except the imagined ideal contacts?

I have often thought of certain of the characters who came and went in our house as boarders or lodgers. I recall, for instance, a certain Jim Westfall, bachelor or widower, and wanderer like ourselves. He was an engine-driver on the narrow-gauge road here (one of the few such roads I have ever seen). The cars of this line were so small that only two people could crowd into any of its double seats which lined one side, and but one could squeeze into the single seats that lined the other side—a situation which might have been remedied by having seats for three after the English fashion, with an aisle or corridor on the side instead of between.

This Jim Westfall proved to be a gay, generous, warmhearted advocate of my mother's cause, an aid at times in the face of the problems that confronted her. My mother must have been a woman of considerable presence as well as personality, since by that alone, and always instanter, she seemed to inspire respect as well as confidence and affection. Thus, I recall that during the canning season of the summer he was with us, he notified her of an abandoned farm some twenty miles out of Sullivan, where there was a large orchard of pear, peach and cherry trees. According to him, this fruit was for any who chose to take it. And so one day at dawn, Ed and I were scuttled eastward on a small train of flat and box cars to which was attached one passenger coach, and the engineer of which was this same Westfall.

Ah, that lovely ride in the early morning through a beautiful, summery country! Will I ever forget it? The feel of the fresh morning air! The roar of the small train as it tore through dark, tangled patches of wood and delightful open fields of grain! Ed and I, with our baskets and buckets, were placed in the centre of a "gondola" (an empty coal car calculated to hold about a dozen tons, I fancy). On both sides were splendid reaches of darksome wood, broken here and there by rolling farmland, all yellow with July wheat or red with clover. Occasionally little white cottages were to be seen. Orchards, meadows, small towns: what a fairyland! And we were rushing through at what seemed endless miles an hour! Despite orders against wandering to and fro in the car or hanging over its sides, we did so wander and hang over and were in heaven. Ahead of us was Westfall, in blue overalls and jumper, a thin, greasy, black cap on his head, an oilcan in his hip pocket, sitting with one hand on the throttle, his head out of the window, and occasionally turning to see what we were up to. On the floor of the car were piled two clothes-baskets, a wash-boiler, and four buckets and a bag, all the receptacles we could muster. Every now and then—out of sheer gaiety of heart, I presume— he would blow a long blast on the thin peanut whistle with which this toy engine was equipped, or would ring its dinky bell, whereat our joy was complete. What a wonder world! Here, for me, were all of the things the human heart might desire: change, speed, colour, variety, life.

Arriving at the spot designated, we were put down in a splendid orchard, the trees of which were fairly loaded with fruit. Told by Westfall to help ourselves, we did so. I never ate so much fruit in my life. Mother had given us our lunch, but we had no need for it. In four or five hours, according to his promise, Westfall returned and picked us up and with the help of other men put our fruit on board. Presently as a reward for our energy, Ed and I were taken up in the engine with him. But, oh, his rage when on arriving at Sullivan, he discovered that some labourers he was bringing back had purloined some of our choicest fruit! The curses! I can still hear him as red-faced and angry he yelled and gazed about him.

"I've a good notion to come back there and throw every God-damn one of you off the train!" Yet he did not. A powerful man physically, he was really a mild and genial one, and that evening as he was washing his face in the tin pail which stood on a post near our back porch, he was heard to recount volubly to mother, who was inside preparing our supper, how scandalously "those damned Italians" had acted.

My mother had an absolute gift for accepting kindnesses graciously. Very distinctly I recall her rubbing her soft, velvety hands over this as over other windfalls of Providence and exclaiming as to the beauty of the fruit and her gratitude. Westfall's face fairly glowed as he insisted that "It's all right, mother. Just nothing at all, Mrs. Dreiser." And all about us was the rich fragrance of a farmland evening filling the air with delight. For once in these memories of Sullivan I have a sense of plenty, geniality and comfort in something well done. I do not recall that Westfall ever did anything that was not helpful or pleasant. I have been told that he was eager to marry my sister Amy, but like others before him, he was eventually allowed to go his way, not good enough or interesting enough, I presume.

CHAPTER XIX

O F the other characters who passed in and out of the scheme of things as here arranged was one who always looms up as dark, even sinister, and yet pathetic, a kind of American Dick Silver or Jack Cade. He was a big Jovian fellow, with short black beard and curly black hair which hung over his forehead in ringlets. His great hands were hard and knotted, and his feet immense. The coal mine of which he was a slave was perhaps a mile away. From it had already come our share of applicants for room and board. Why I do not know. Perhaps because our home was clean and the food good and possibly more reasonable than it might have been elsewhere. Trust my mother to be a poor bargainer!

But this big Jack—Wildfellow, let us call him—had applied to mother for board as the friend of another miner who was with us, a small, peaceful, retiring man who sat before the fire of an evening reading his paper or occasionally, principally of a Saturday evening, went downtown. But Jack, it developed in no very great space of time, had no desire to go downtown or anywhere much. Considering his boisterous and at times even sinister temperament, this might have struck some as strange. But perhaps not my mother. At any rate there he was quite every evening during his stay, on occasion a drunken, frowning demon, swearing, talking of his love affairs with women, and of his gambling. At other times though and when not drinking he would sit silently about of an evening before the fire in a darksome frame of mind, betimes urging mother to let Ed or myself go for a pitcher of beer. It was soon made plain to him that he was not even to suggest this and might better leave, which silenced him. When not drinking and so always in a more pleasant frame of mind, he was fond of showing us card tricks, also singing in a guttural voice about the joys of a roving life. In his capacious pockets he always carried "squibs," as they were locally called by the miners. These were thin pipes or threads of paper filled with powder and used to fire the small charges of powder which were placed at the bank head to dislodge a "throw" of coal. It appeared to amuse him to light these in order that we might see them sputter or fizzle. Sometimes though, he would throw them under our feet in order to see us jump. And I remember also that once, being slightly in his cups, he threatened to put me in the fire head first, seizing me and holding me so near that I screamed, whereupon my mother interfered. Also he would on occasion take out an enormous horn-handled knife and threaten to cut someone—a most sinister proceeding. At other times he liked to gather us children about him and tell about mine explosions in which he had been and how he had dug his way out through banks of coal and earth.

His career had obviously been a rough one, for it was whispered to mother by one or another of the miners, and so to us, that he was hiding from the police, and as if in proof of this, instead of going into the heart of town at week-ends as the others did, he preferred to lurk here or go with a miner friend to some out-of-the-way place. At that, it was not more than five weeks after he came with us that one night as he was sitting in front of the fire, two men appeared and walked in without a "by your leave." Detectives in plain clothes they proved to be. As they confronted him, he jumped up and instinctively seized the chair on which he had been sitting, backing the while toward the bedroom door. However, both men being armed, he appeared to realise that his position was critical and merely stood still.

"Hello, Jack! So you're here? We've been looking for you for some time. It's no use going out that way. There's two more of us out there." As this last was said, I saw two eyes peering under the curtain of one of the windows.

One of the men showed his badge while the other produced a pair of glistening steel cuffs. At that, Jack's frame seemed to tower savagely, but after a moment's reflection he went peaceably enough, one of his hands linked by steel to that of his detective captor. It came out later that he was wanted for a murder in Brazil, Indiana, where he was said to have killed a man in a saloon brawl. How guilty he was, if at all, we never learned. Anyhow, here he had been, working day after day for a few dollars, leading at least a partially sober life, and now he was off for trial and punishment. Great was the impression made by all this upon me, and I can see him now as he went out the door, his great, shaggy head and broad back slumping. My mother's face was white and tense. She was ever so distressed by the results of error and the panoply of the law, and called our attention to the dire consequences of evil in any form. A rough bundle was later made of Jack's belongings and sent to Brazil. And so he passed. But for years my mother often spoke of this Big Jack and his strange, animal disposition. She did not dislike him and always said that perhaps he was as much sinned against as sinning. Her slight share in this pathetic section of his life seemed to grieve her. She was sorry that men had to suffer so in this mortal scheme.

A third person who drifted across our path in this way was a certain Professor Solax, a small, trig, dandified man, in a cut-away coat and high silk hat, with shoebrush whiskers and Jovian curls. He came to the door selling "Hill's Manual of Etiquette and Social and Commercial Forms." Here was your born book agent, if there ever was one, and the peddler of the first book that was to influence me. A to me fascinating and, as I shall now testify, highly illuminating volume! To this hour I hark back to it in fancy at times, not to any particular item of its contents but to the wonderful sense of strangeness and mystery and beauty and delight which the most inane things in it evoked in me. There is fire and there is tow, but without tow, however humble, no fire, and without this book, its delicious, suggestive commonplaces . . .

I would sit and read in it by the hour whenever I could get it away from Trina, who seized upon it as soon as she discovered that it contained material and rules for checking up the ways and manners of others. (Lord, what a pest that girl could be, and how in time I came to dislike her! Always picking and always criticising or reporting our errors or neglects or bad doings to mother, who would scold accordingly.) But the book! "How to write a business letter." "How to write a letter of condolence." "How to write a letter of appreciation." "How to write a love-letter." And pictures, actual pen and ink illustrations, showing the right and wrong way to enter a room, the right and wrong way to make a bow and doff the hat on meeting an acquaintance or your best girl, or on being introduced to anyone, especially a lady. Pictures of how and how not to rise from or sit down to a table; how and how not to hold the knife and fork at meals; and how and how not to eat soup from a spoon. (Darksome mysteries all to me at the time, and since.) Pictures of the seven wonders of the world; the principal rivers, mountains, lakes of America and elsewhere; pictures of cities and great buildings and of men who began as nothing in this great sad world but rose by honesty and industry and thrift and kind thoughts and deeds to be great: such men as George Washington and Thomas Jefferson and Benjamin Franklin and Thomas Paine and Christopher Columbus! Heigh ho!

There were also stories and poems and songs about anything and everything: "Just a Song at Twilight," "The Old Oaken Bucket," and "Over the Hills to the Poorhouse" (a poem that always reminded me of my brother Paul's attitude toward his mother), and Longfellow's "I Stood on the Bridge at Midnight," and that one about Paul Revere, and the one that begins: "I see the lights of the village gleam through the rain and the mist." Ah, how poetry and romance, ambition and achievement, burst upon me as realities and possibilities from the pages of that book! It was large and red and heavy and lumpish, with thick leaves and lead-lined borders, but I devoured it page by page, holding it on my knees or spread out on the grass in the shade at the side or back or front of the house, my mind mounting upon the wings of fancy, my body upon the magic carpet of Sulieman. Ah, to have been with Washington at Valley Forge, with Whittington tramping the long, weary road back to London town! If I could but see New York, Paris, Rome, St. Petersburg!

Among all these other things I now recall that it also contained several pages of elaborate and decorative penmanship, the different "styles," I presume, of celebrated penmen of the time. These I studied with the greatest awe. How was it one came by such grand flourishes and curlicues, especially when by screwing oneself into the most complicated of positions and protruding one's tongue as far as possible and lowering one's nose and eyes to within a sixteenth of an inch of the paper, one could barely achieve the distinction of setting down in an almost undecipherable hand such a gem as "The cat is watching the rat," or "Will the cat catch the rat?" or "Yes, the cat will catch the rat." It was a mystery to me.

Yet know, oh, reader, sometimes a trivial thing, a bit of coloured glass, will take on all the lustre of a precious stone to a child. So it was with me and this book. My mother, astonished at my avidity for this sort of thing, was pleased, of course, for no doubt she had had dinned into her ears the precept that children should be studious and that to succeed in life one must apply oneself to good books. And was not this a good book? Did not Professor Solax say so? I can see him now entering our front gate, "Hill's Manual" done up in a handsome leather portfolio under his arm and in less than three minutes bewildering my mother by such a coruscating flow of language as would befuddle and undo any honest housewife anywhere. This volume as he painted it was the be-all and end-all of social and commercial education. Every family needed one. The book was a complete education in itself. Study it diligently, and you would need no further equipment for your contest with life. So he raved, and so my good mother was induced to buy it (its price was $3.50) or at least to agree to exchange board for it.

I cannot say exactly what it was that brought about the final dénouement in connection with Professor Solax—his coming to board with us while he was in Sullivan—but I think it was one of my pretty sisters. We had no other boarders at the time, and so he decided to stay with us. He would return at night after his labours, rubbing his carefully manicured hands together and disposing of his sample and his silk hat and frock-coat, make himself as much at home as if he were the head of the house. After that and after dinner he would sit before the fire—the pretty daughter at hand, of course—and recite "'Ostler Joe" and "Over the Hills to the Poorhouse," which last succeeded in moving us all to tears. Or he would sing sentimental songs with great feeling.

The particular daughter that the "Professor" fixed upon as most charming was my sister Amy, who with her usual proclivity for flirting was most agreeable to being courted by him. Only this disturbed my mother so much that she was after her early and late with instructions in regard to "keeping her place." But this, for Amy, was a difficult thing to do. As she afterwards confessed to me, she and the Professor often met outside, and finally he begged her to run away with him.   And while his curly hair and amazing whiskers were entrancing enough, she feared that he had a wife somewhere (by this time this had come to mean an obstacle to her) and she did not go.

But for my part I have never forgotten that he left me "Hill's Manual," and from that I absorbed a world of fascinating lore.

CHAPTER XX

BOARDERS or no boarders, this effort of my mother's to keep this humble home and this fragment of a family together must have spelled complete defeat had it not been for an arrival and a source of aid which I shall now recount.

But before I do this, I wish to say that it was at this very impressionable period, and because of the various events I have narrated, that I became mentally coloured or tinged with a sense of poverty and defeat and social ill-being in connection with our family that took me years and years, and then only in part, to overcome, and traces of which I still find darkly ensconced in certain corners of that subconscious which is a part of the deeper and more mysterious self of me. For years, even so late as my thirty-fifth or fortieth year, the approach of winter invariably filled me with an indefinable and highly oppressive dread, and that at periods when I needed not to be in dread of anything that winter and poverty, or the two of them together, could do to me. Similarly, any form of social distress—a wretched, down-at-heels neighbourhood, a poor farm, an asylum, a jail, or an individual or group of individuals anywhere that seemed to be lacking in the means of subsistence or to be devoid of the normal comforts of life—was sufficient to set up in me thoughts and emotions which had a close kinship to actual and severe physical pain. At such times I felt not only an actual physical heart pain but a heavy, sinking sensation at the pit of my stomach, which all but unfitted me for any serious work I might have in hand. In sum, so immeasurably depressed was I by encounters with poverty or misery in any form anywhere that I was always feeling called upon to relieve it, to do something about it, the while my better judgment often told me there was little beyond the bare necessities—food, shelter, clothing—that one could offer to anyone without, in part at least, altering their very mental and physical texture.

I also early realised, in this connection, that where health and mentality go together, there is a positive joy in working, the while I also realised that nature handicaps people most damnably and then tosses them into the vortex of life to sink or swim. And this caused me to pity all such and to be inclined toward the belief that poverty and rags, while not always the symbols of social injustice, were nevertheless connected, in part, with economic maladjustment somewhere as well as social ignorance, though how anybody less than God himself was to arrange for the proper social equipment of every individual was beyond me. The creative forces that bring life to the surface spectacle which we behold are certainly to blame. Be that as it may, I still feel that I can clearly retrace to Sullivan and the last winter we spent there, the genesis of my awesome fear of winter and cold and want of good clothes and good food, which, spectre-wise, marched at my heels for years.

For it was during that last winter that my mother appeared to lose faith in this earnest and very decent adventure of hers and to sink back and down into a kind of dumb despair. The necessity of once more taking in washing—the local coal mine having shut down—and of running credit accounts at the stores, also of seeing her children carry coal and wood, and hearing them and herself denounced as "trash" by such ne'er-do-wells as the Thompsons and others, was sufficient, I take it, to depress anyone. Add to it the final problem of boarders who did not always stay and did not always pay, and you have a composite burden which must have been more than difficult for her to bear.

And yet I know now how valueless and, worse yet, ironic, at this time are mere compliments and filial pity, to say nothing of social and family respect, when extended to her, and especially in connection with the social and spiritual debt due her, by myself and the other members of her family at least. The courage, the charity, the affection, the complete subjection to the so-called "social contract" which must have been involved in her incentive! Add to all this the fact that for the first twenty years of their lives, all of her children appeared to be lacking in any trace of what might be called a social or constructive sense, that they mooned and dreamed and fiddled away their time, and you have a spectacle that must have frightened and made sad a woman of greater constructive force than was hers.

For, as I have indicated, she was never one who might have been called mentally incisive, nor had she ever had any of the advantages open at this day, educationally speaking, to the children of the very poorest. And already she had suffered enough blows and defeats and disasters to dissipate the fighting strength of even a stronger and more capable woman. And yet here she was, hidden away in this rag of a town, seeking to make a living for herself and her three younger children, to say nothing of some of the older ones as they appeared from time to time.

That final winter in Sullivan, though! The boarding and rooming venture finally failed—too large food portions, very likely, for the amount charged—and very soon she was refused credit (and that quite justly, I assume) at every grocery store. There was a period also at this time during which my father was out of work, though he stayed on in Terre Haute looking for something to do. And all of the older children were literally compelled to depart and seek work elsewhere, because there was nothing for them here. I recall a Christmas that passed with scarcely a toy worth mentioning (some little things sent by a sister from Chicago) and no candy or candles or any of the things which make the feast of the Christ-child worth while. I recall being sent to the distant mill to buy fifteen cents' worth of cornmeal, because it was cheaper there and one got more of it. I recall cornmeal mush eaten without milk because we had none. I recall clothes so old and so made over and patched that they were a joke. Even the rent was long overdue, though we were allowed to stay on because she did the washing of the landlord's family and hoped to pay eventually in that way, I presume.

And then, behold, a miracle! That eldest brother Paul, who after having been forbidden the shelter of the family roof in Terre Haute had disappeared and attempted to carve out a career for himself, returned, and that in the nick of time in so far as the affairs of his mother were concerned. His story is much too long to relate here; it belongs in a novel, which I shall never find the time to write. After leaving a local Catholic school for boys, in which, by the aid of a priest, he had been placed at the time of the blow-up in my father's affairs—so that he might study for the priesthood and so place himself in life —he had led a most chequered career. He had decamped from said school six or seven months after entering, and made his way on foot to that same Switz City in Indiana which was the terminal of the narrow-gauge railroad on which Jim Westfall worked, in search of a farmer friend (possibly a distant relative of mother's) in the hope that he would give him work. He found the farmer, but the work proved to be toil of the most back-breaking sort, and without reward save in food and shelter. He had to sleep in a haymow, and there was never a cent for clothes or entertainment in any form. (I am quoting from notes which he gave me a few weeks before his death.) The food was poor and he had to get up before daylight in order to do many chores before the real work of the day began. By night, he said, he was so weary that he could think of nothing save his hayloft, so that he might get sufficient rest to permit him to rise early and go through another such day.

So one night, when he was possessed of little more than rags and absolutely no money, he left, this time to walk to Indianapolis, sixty or seventy miles away, in the hope of enlisting aid from a Catholic priest who once had ministered in Terre Haute, and whom he knew. And this man proved to be a real Samaritan. He not only bought him a suit of clothes but gave him a room and meals in his parish house and some money wherewith to make a new attempt. But before that, what a sad journey for one so temperamental and inexperienced and emotional as was he at the time! Applying to one farmer for a meal on his way, a dog was set upon him. Applying to another at dusk for a night's lodging, he was ordered off at the point of a pitchfork, his wretched clothes giving him the appearance of a tramp, no doubt. For the most part he went hungry and slept in the open or under the shelter of some hay or straw stack. In Indianapolis he was picked up by the police as a vagrant, and only saved from a term on the rockpile by the appearance of the priest whose name he gave. (And this the future author of "On the Banks of the Wabash.")

In Indianapolis, fortunately enough, once his appearance and mental attitude were thus repaired, he was able to connect himself with an itinerant cure-all company, a troupe or wagon caravan which travelled gipsy fashion from city to city or rather from small town to small town, and sold "Hamlin's Wizard Oil" to the yokels. By this time he had discovered that he could sing and play in a rather amusing fashion; that is, he could accompany himself on an organ or piano; and it was this skill that brought him the opportunity to join this troupe.

And so he journeyed with this aggregation over Ohio, Indiana and Illinois, gradually winning for himself a better position. For he soon found that he could also write the type of comic song that the yokels loved to hear. Also that with the aid of a burnt cork make-up, he could positively convulse his auditors. This earned him some fame as a minstrel, so much, indeed, that the manager raised his salary and bound him by contract for three years. At the end of that time, though, he accepted a flattering offer from one of the best minstrel companies of that day, starting in Cincinnati as a blackface monologist, interlocutor and "end man." And now, after several years of this—and with a definite measure of popularity attending him—he appeared in Sullivan, and at the very time when his mother's affairs were at the lowest ebb.

But why, I once asked him? His reply was that for four years before this he had been dogged by a desire to see her; he had been haunted by the feeling that all was not well with her. So at last, finding himself within reasonable distance of Terre Haute, he had gone there, only to find that she had removed to Sullivan, for which place he boarded the first train he could get.

CHAPTER XXI

WHEN I think of my brother Paul, I often think of Gray's thought in regard to unknown Miltons and Cæsars walking obscure ways in obscure places. For here was one of those great Falstaffian souls who, for lack of a little iron or sodium or carbon dioxide in his chemical compost, was not able to bestride the world like a Colossus. (And how narrowly many others miss infinitely better fates than are actually theirs!) I can think of him now, with his large range of sympathies and interests, as easily condensed or elaborated into a Henry VIII, say, or an Omar (of the Caliphate) or a shrewd Saladin or. a Leo X. A little more selfishness, a little more iron or lithium, maybe; as it was, with these missing, he could only sing, jest and grow fat.

Even at this time, this strolling minstrel—who already at twenty-four had acquired a rotundity or girth that was good to look upon—had achieved the distinction of having had issued "The Paul Dresser Songster," a slim, gaudy pamphlet containing comic songs supposed to have been original with him and which he sold on royalty to such members of his audience as cared to buy. (Note the change of the name "Dreiser" to "Dresser." He thought this more pronounceable and suitable to his stage life.)

And now, cap-a-pie as to clothes—fur coat and silk hat— he arrived in our depleted home. I shall never forget the excitement his visit created. As I have said, our fortunes were at their lowest ebb, my mother at her wits' end. Al, Janet and Eleanor had gone to Chicago to seek work; Ruth and Amy had returned to Terre Haute to seek employment. This left my mother and us three youngest alone and waiting aimlessly for something to turn up. It was a cold, snowy day in February. Late in the afternoon there was a knock at the door, and there, to mother's amazement, stood her lost and presumably erring son. As she said afterwards, she scarcely recognised him; he had grown so much stouter and no doubt the fur coat and silk hat confused her. But the uncertainty was not for long, and then came embraces and tears, the while we children stood about and listened to tales of his success in the great world without, and then within the hour witnessed a most palatable change for all of us. For at once, of course, he relieved mother of her most pressing wants with ready cash, and thereafter, so long as he was able, sent her money every week. In fact, for a period of ten years thereafter or until her death in 1890, he never failed in this.

Only to me, the arrival of this brother was the same as the arrival of a total stranger—or nearly so—and yet, fascinatingly enough, a stranger who was more like a fairy godfather or the well-known occidental Santa Claus. As I have said before, he was like the sun, or a warm, cheering fire. He beamed upon us all, and when he left (as he did, after only a few hours, but promising faithfully to return soon), he gave Ed and me copies of "The Paul Dresser Songster," with his picture on the cover just above the price (ten cents)! It contained all sorts of comic and sentimental jingles and underneath each was printed: "Copyright Willis, Woodward & Company, New York, N.Y." (And so he was connected with that big city, too!) And he spoke of a lot of his old but still good clothes which mother might make into suits for Ed and myself. And a week after he left, a box arrived, containing these clothes as well as a dress and slippers for mother and many groceries— a development or phase of prosperity which left me fairly agape. Later came new shoes and hats for each of us and a complete outfit for Trina, who was to "make her first communion" at the small Catholic Church. The labour of washing and ironing and taking care of boarders and roomers which had so harassed my mother for these several years was given over, never again to be resumed by her in this world, thanks be, and I trust in no other. Her heavy gloom was replaced by a normal optimism and sunny geniality, for, given the least aid, she emanated rays of humour and hope.

Perhaps the conception of a fate or fortune in the affairs of men—an interfering hand that beyond our understanding or willing makes or mars our inconceivably petty lives—was at this time born in me. At any rate, this change from a gnawing, driving misery to the ease and relief that comes with a little money, was sufficient to burn itself for ever in my memory, and there it remains to-day. My mother's tears of relief! Her son's loving, helpful arms! Truly, I think it is better to give than to receive!

And truly, I think there is nothing in life more wonderful than the tang of new experiences in childhood. The world is all so strange, so mysterious and full of promise. Our soul, or essence, whatever its previous state or lack of one, appears to come fresh from an entirely different realm, intensely avid and curious as to this one. And the impressionable slate or wax it brings is so clean, so unmarred. On it may be written anything, and so forcefully and enduringly. And youth does not crave the truth, only its dreams and illusions—which is well enough. For what a dreary world it would be if it did! Youth prefers and seeks mostly the vague, expansive, uncertain imaginings which crowd its mind, always so much more wonderful than reality itself.

And now, following Paul's departure, a new element or personality was injected into our lives, a woman whose relationship to Paul was probably one of the motivating causes for our removal to Evansville the following spring or summer. This Annie Brace (alias Sallie Walker) was, if I must confess it, the keeper or owner of a very successful, even imposing, "house of ill repute" in Evansville—a "madam," no less—but still young and very beautiful, as I came to see for myself. Somewhere she had encountered Paul and, becoming enamoured of him, was seeking at this time to join her life with his, and did, as it later appeared, for a time. Having heard from Paul, no doubt, as to his mother and her whereabouts and condition, she now hastened to make social and affectional capital with both him and his mother by coming to see her. As I recall her now (for I was always about and watching), she was a handsome woman of perhaps twenty-seven or eight—which seemed very old to me at the time—very dark as to hair and eyes and rounded and graceful as to figure, and with, as it seemed to me at the time, an exotic taste for black. The assumption, on my part at least, was that she was in mourning. But those clear, incisive, black eyes, and the exaggerated whiteness of her face and hands! I recall her sitting in our front room and beaming warmly on my mother, the mother of her lover. It was a brief visit between trains. Say that at best she spent an hour with us, but thereafter came boxes of groceries and baskets of fruit and packages of cloth, together with a number of cast-off and rather remarkable garments, the source and exact use of which were not discovered by my mother for some time, if ever.

And then, the following spring or summer, the actual removal of our family, or very fragmentary portion of a family, to Evansville, traceable, no doubt, to the kindly, if self-interested, desire of this Annie Brace to win or maintain an affectional control over Paul while he was so keen to do something for his mother. Whether he saw through this, or seeing felt it to be satisfactory, I do not know. Certain it is that he fell in with the proposal, first made by her to mother and later to him, and which in the course of a few months she engineered to a successful conclusion. First there was an extended visit —four or five days—on the part of Paul to our home in Sullivan, and then, in late May or early June, we left for Evansville.

In connection with this particular removal, though, are some facts which relate to the hodge-podge which life makes of what we are pleased to term morality and immorality, and of this I now prefer to speak. For although this particular change was effected as much as abetted by perhaps the reigning courtesan of her region, working through the always vulnerable emotions of my very good brother, still, at the time the change was brought about, my mother knew no more of Annie Brace than she knew of anything else in connection with her eldest son's immediate past. And whether or not she knew, it is my conviction that it would have made no least difference in her opinion of his right to his particular interests or affairs. For and although concerned always with the necessity and duty of keeping step with the social and economic standards of whatsoever community she was a part—herself working most and hardest to maintain them—still, where her grown children were concerned, she was never one to pry into their affairs. In their youth it was that she had had her say, but never to the extent of demanding interest in or respect for the hard and fast conventions of narrow-minded or socially biased persons. Human beings, as she often indicated in many ways, had trouble enough in maintaining themselves without being harried further by finicky and non-understanding social opinion or social notions. Knowing much, and this by direct experience, of the driving passions and weaknesses that affect us all, she was far too generous and innately understanding to criticise much. Rather, if her own or the children of others erred, it was because, as she usually insisted, of many things, most of which they could not help or forfend against, and it was her emotional fate as well as spiritual duty to continue to love them. She might quarrel and sigh, and even cry, but in the end they were her children and she bowed to the instinct that drew her to them.

But how intense was my own elation at the thought of change and seeing more of the world! Sullivan had been satisfactory enough at one time and another, though we had seen some grim hours there, but oh, to be up and away! I remember the packing, the seeing about boxes and a drayman to transport our few belongings to the freight office. And then at last the great day! I recall looking at the tall, scarred, eagle tree in the field and thinking that I should miss it. Also there was the problem of the future of our two dogs, Hound and Rover, which troubled me not a little, for it was finally decided that they were to be abandoned to a roving fate, because, forsooth, we lacked leather straps and collars wherewith to control them en route or the money to have them expressed. (These were trifling matters, I presume, which could not be brought to the attention of our successful brother.) At best, they were used to poverty and want and probably fared just as well without us. I hope so.

I recall the long, slow junketing of a five o'clock local train from Sullivan to Evansville, and of passing ten or twelve small villages, most of them less important even than Sullivan. One, Princeton, a resort of sorts, impressed me as being exceedingly alive and flourishing, with carriages to meet people at the trains and bright store windows seen through the trees. And with Vincennes came memories of Sue Bellette and the firehouse and Tinby. And at one other station, Paxton, came the vision of a certain family there whom we chanced to know. A wonderful ride!

But transcending all this by far was the novelty of entering a city of so considerable a size as Evansville. So slow was this train that it was nearly ten o'clock before we finally reached our destination, and by then I had grown too sleepy to realise much of what was going on about me. But at sight and sound of numerous engines and engine bells and the clattering of cars —all part of a big yard we were entering—as well as the sight of gas lamps flaring in the night, I sat up and took a renewed interest in life. Came a Union Station, capacious and lively, the terminal point of several roads, and here, with a crowd of others, we were ordered to get off. And then the wonder of a city night scene! Those poor scum back in Sullivan, I thought! What could they know of a place like this? A city! And such a city! And they had dared to look down on us! If only they could see us now, gloriously entering this city, a city such as they might never have the privilege of entering!

We were not allowed to wander about, though, or meditate too much in this fashion, for there at the train was this amazing brother and son, who now led us through a glowing waiting-room to the street (East Main Street), where were, as it seemed to me at the time, great crowds and countless lights and vehicles and street cars and brightly-lighted shops. True, the street cars were small, drawn by one lone mule and in charge of one man as conductor and driver, but what would you? They had bright-coloured bits of glass at the top near the roof and bright brass handles. Even now I can see myself hanging on to the hand or skirt of my distrait and pestered mother (who was, no doubt, as wide-eyed and wondering as ourselves), as led by Paul we boarded one of the cars labelled "Salt Wells" and rode off to unravel the mysteries of our new home.

Neither my mother nor any of us had been given the slightest inkling as to what our new home was to be like. Imagine, then, our surprise and delight when after some piloting along a dark street we came upon a small one-and-a-half story brick cottage, set in a neatly-fenced big yard, with a barn and chicken run at the back! And flowers in the foreground! About the house and yard also a wide, grass-covered common which stretched unobstructed to a distant wood on one side and a far-off railroad yard on another, for we were at the edge of the city. South and westward was the city, the sky glowing with its lights. And entering, we beheld a completely-furnished home. No shabby makeshifts and leavings here, as at Sullivan. Instead, in the dining-room a shining new table with a complete set of chairs, and in the parlour, not only parlour furniture but a piano! Carpets on the floors, new carpets, and in the kitchen a shining cookstove, with dishes and an ample array of cooking utensils!

Quite like one who has seen a fairy wave her wand and work a miracle, stood my mother, looking at it all from one doorway and then another. And behind her, patting her shoulder, because she was crying, my brother Paul. Blessed are the merciful, for, verily, they have their reward! Paul, the good son, the loving brother: write his name high among those who have wrought for affection's sake. Jail-bird, writer of pointless ballads, singer of trivial songs—even so, write his name large as one who loved his fellow-men!

In the midst of these wonders—almost a surfeit of them—we went to bed, and next morning arose to new glories. I shall never forget the intense delight I felt in stepping out on to the lawn of our backyard and over the low fence to view the city, the great common, the new life. And bright and early came Paul again, to suggest and direct. To Ed and myself he brought a ball and bat; to Trina some gewgaw of some kind. To the piano also he went and played some of his latest compositions, folderol comic songs, but how wonderful to us! So the new hours began to slip by and Sullivan to sink into the dim and misty past, never to rise or obtrude itself again.

CHAPTER XXII

THOSE first days in Evansville! Looking back on it now, it seems a kind of dream city—made so, of course, by my very fervid and youthful imagination. A marvellous river, a sylvan creek, trees, birds, flowers, open common, spires, towers, sunlight and moonlight; indeed, a perfect swirl of youth and life in which everything moves as in a dream, sentient and delightful.

It was a splendid thing, in a city of this size, to live in the last house, or almost the last house, of a region not inconvenient to the city heart and yet blessed with all of the idyllic charm of the country. It was so remote and quiet and rural and yet so convenient to everything. Inside its brown picket fence in the centre of the great common of grass, it possessed congruity and charm. (Returning years later, I found the common all built in and this little house crowded tenementwise without yard or tree into a close row of commonplace cottages.) A good brick walk with which East Franklin Street was paved led out to it. Gas-lamps and water-plugs were near at hand. The mail-carrier, the milkman, the newspaper boy, and now and then a peripatetic policeman, were to be seen, the latter only accidentally and peradventure. Why should a policeman waste his time wandering about pleasant, grass-grown suburbs when he could idle much more comfortably in a saloon?

About half or three-quarters of a mile to the south of us were the tracks and switching yards of a railroad that ran from Evansville to Louisville, and on which later my brother Al worked for a little while as "butcher" or train-boy, selling candies and magazines. Between our house and that road was level grass, starred with white clover and a few fine, broad-branched trees. And to the east also was grass, with a house or two farther out. And beyond it all at one point an immense red brick pottery, with a number of kraal-like kilns of great size showing over a low wall of brick. And to the north was open common, with a pond here and there. And beyond, nothing but grass and well-favoured trees, until one came to the muddy Pigeon Creek, a tributary of the Ohio, where were the Devil's Elbow and the Yellow Banks—swimming holes— and pockets on either side of dam and falls where bass and perch and other fish were to be had in great quantities. To the west was the city proper, a straggling, sprawling affair, with the east end of Main Street trailing to within two or three blocks of our door, and Blount's Plough Works, with giant hammers beating steel bars into ploughshares and belching flame and smoke, often by night as well as day.

And then, to the extreme west of the city, and bounding it, was the wide-surfaced, yellow-bodied Ohio River, rolling its enormous flood from the Alleghenies and the States of Ohio and Kentucky and Indiana into the Mississippi at Cairo. Never shall I forget the first day I beheld it, from the end of Main Street, which debouched upon an enormous sloping levee, paved with great grey cobblestones and stocked with enormous piles of cotton in bales, groceries and hardware in boxes, and watermelons and other fruits and vegetables in piles or crated, boxed, bagged or barrelled. Among these were little artificial streets or lanes, along which travelled constantly scores of small mule-drawn drays driven by Negroes in sleeve- less cotton undershirts and belted trousers gripped tightly about the hips. At the foot of the levee, where it met the water, were long, brown wharves or floating docks, anchored lengthwise of the shore, and lashed to those again, a number of the old-time, stern wheel river steamers, with their black double stacks, double and treble decks, gilt and red or blue or green decorations, and piles of freight being taken on or unloaded. It was the first active river scene I had ever beheld, except for pictures in our school geography.

And so, the glory of that first summer! The sense of new- ness, strangeness, mysteries to be explored, together with freedom and content with life! White clouds in the sky, trees, grass, a river and creek, journeys to far, mysterious parts of the city! Life went around in a circle of delicious and yet vain imaginings. And what a splendid company of playfellows we found here! At last Ed was in his glory, relieved, I am sure, and for the first time in his life, of my dreamy and all too meditative temperament and now able to pick and choose his own companions.

I have not described this brother, but I will do so now. He was the soul of physical activity. I see him now, in short trousers, a blousy kind of shirtwaist buttoned to his trousers, a round brown hat or cap pulled well down to his ears, solid buttoned shoes, brown or black stockings. A most formidable youth and one fast developing more courage and hail-fellow-well-met air than I could ever boast. From the very beginning he proved himself an adept at all sports: baseball, football, shinny, skating, swimming, marbles, tops, anything you please. Indeed for a time he became a marble and top champion, backing his field victories with the ability to fight, and piling up cans of marbles and tops until in one of our understairs closets was a kind of treasure trove composed of the fruits of his victories. In so far as I was concerned, he was ever the most generous of playmates, sharing with me half of all that he won, because, forsooth, I never won anything at all. I was more for books and pictures, the visible scene about me, and all the wonders of life and work.

I have often wondered in these later years why Ed found me so desirable a companion, or, for that matter, I him. In any scheme he undertook, he invariably included me, and only after persistent refusals on my part did he take up with others. And together we soon managed to make a number of friends and be hail-fellow-well-met with all types and conditions. For one reason, our home condition was now respectable, even seemingly prosperous; for another, we wore good clothes, at least as good as the average, and were not deprived of most of the necessities—though I cannot say luxuries—which go to make youth delightful. Paul being interested in baseball (already the reigning sport of America) and liking to knock a few "flies" himself so long as he had someone to fag for him, was quick to add to Ed's collection a $1.50 National League baseball and not one but several bats. Persuaded by our pleas, he also bought us baseball caps and shoes and once (Paul having furnished the money) mother made us baseball suits out of some amazing material of our own selection, across the breast of which was lettered in white tape: "Evansville Reds." The suits—I rise to remark as an afterthought—were a dark, rich maroon, to be worn only with white stockings and brown shoes—an artistic evocation of our own bursting brains.

The boys hereabouts were numerous and of genial character.

128

I remember, for instance, big Bill Snyder, who though only fourteen or fifteen was as tall as a beanpole and as slender, a veritable vine of a boy. He had an unconsciously comic face, long and thin and wide of mouth and long of nose and more or less vacant of eye, and wore, as a rule, a small round peaked hat which gave him the look of a clown. More, he was very near-sighted and wore thick glasses, which magnified his eye-balls into starry orbs. Whenever Bill lost his glasses, he had to get down on his hands and knees and feel about, his nose not more than an inch from the ground. His legs were so long that they bowed like the blade of a jackknife as he walked, and his arms, as he ran bases, had the appearance of flails or loose boards attached to his body. But what a genial idler! He loved to loaf in the sun or in the shade of our barn and play mumbly-peg or talk of what he intended to do in the future or read *The Family Story Paper* or *Brave and Bold*.

There was another lad, "Stub" Peters, who was the foremost figure in another gang of a much less polite character than ours which flourished in a section of the city we rarely visited: the region beyond those tracks which could be seen from our house. He loved to visit our gang, perhaps because he thought we were of a superior world and that his talents entitled him to our companionship. I can see him now, undersized, stocky and well built, in coat and trousers of ancient vintage and great size, evidently once his father's, since the trousers had been cut off at the bottom to make them fit. His shirt was of rough blue gingham, well-worn and faded and dirty, and his legs and body were always innocent of underwear, shoes or stockings. He was, in the main, a blowsy little scut, brown and unwashed, a hard swearer and fighter, but friendly enough when he wished to be, yet always with a suggestion of something subtle and traitorous about him. He was at once too oily and too agreeable, unless irritated, whereupon, and all too suddenly, he could become vicious and cruel. A peculiarity about him was that when it came to the more serious discussions of things, pleasant round-robin arguments with all of us lying on the grass, he would get up and leave. He obviously preferred a more active form of existence. None of us ever looked into his neighbourhood or his family connections and knew nothing about him except that like some stray pigeon he came to our part of the town to play.

There was still another, one out of perhaps twenty all told, who had a genuine fascination for me, even though in my heart I secretly condemned him. He was a curious compound, half good and half bad, that at that time I was in nowise capable of understanding. His father was a combination or mixture of horse-doctor, horse-trader and horse-thief, half gipsy and half Negro or Indian, using as his card of introduction: "Truckee's Celebrated Poison Ivy Liniment, Good for Man and Beast," with which and an old tumbledown vehicle attached to a most astonishing and uncertain animal which he assured all and sundry was a horse, he travelled about the countryside, buying and selling and trading; and while he was about this business, seeking to steal anything he could—a horse, a dog, a cat, a bird, a chair, even fruit and vegetables and meat. I say this after due thought, for not only were strange or stray animals tethered about his place but it was commonly known in the neighbourhood that the Truckees rarely bought anything from any store.

I wish you might have seen "Old Man Truckee," as we always called him. He was so small and wiry and birdlike and withal so misshapen and ill-clothed and dirty that you would have said he was a suitable companion for the poorest and boniest of his steeds. His eyes were like those of a ferret, beady, darting and suspicious, and his hands were veritable claws, with long, bony fingers and long, dirty nails. He was by no means opposed to companionship with or inquiry from anyone; instead, he seemed to like to talk in the most friendly way, letting us boys gather round him while he worked at currying or doctoring his execrable horses. One of his sources of income was the selling of the carcasses of dead animals to a soap factory. Another was the pickling and selling of the hides to a tannery. I think he also did away with dogs and cats and other small animals for their pelts, for ever and anon we would see the skins of animals hanging on a line in his yard.

The Truckee household itself was a nondescript affair, such as an Indian or Negro or gipsy half-breed might sling together. It lay a little to the east of us, a house not unakin in quality to the bony, limping, spavined, blind-eyed horses which its master kept about him. A lean-to of poorly-planed boards had been added to an original single living room or kitchen, and back of that was a workroom patched together out of scraps of wood and rusty strips of tin or flattened cans. There was a shed or stable at the back, made out of the same materials, in which he maintained his tatterdemalion laboratory for the concoction of his famous liniment, and in the tin-can barn or tethered out on the common to eat the grass were his spavined horses. Harry, the son, in a burst of confidence, once informed me that his father had a method of making a horse, any old horse, "look as good as new" for a little while—by the use of a drug of some kind, I assume. But drugs or no drugs, dirt or no dirt, these Truckees appeared to want for nothing essential to their happiness. They fished in the Ohio, returning with great baskets of fish which they sold; and they had an organ on which Mrs. Truckee (a creature not unlike her husband) played, and they laughed and talked and jested betimes with whomsoever would have to do with them.

There are still others who linger in my mind. Arthur Eisenfelt, a Jew, and Sydney Grant, the son of a drunken Civil War veteran who was a lather and plasterer by trade. Eisenfelt was a smug, round, pleasant and yet reticent fellow who lived a block or two west of us and who liked to play ball and other games well enough to come out and join the common crowd. Sydney Grant, by contrast, was pale and lethargic, a youth of not much spirit, always suggesting a wax candle to me. His father, a drunkard and ne'er-do-well, always treated his son wretchedly, beating him on occasion when things did not go to suit him. When work was plentiful, he used Sydney as an assistant and I recall seeing this boy making off in the early morning to some distant part of the city, a pair of small mortar boards, trowels, hammers and the like in a white canvas bag thrown over his shoulder. Old Grant and his son cooked their own meals and did their own housekeeping, in two rooms of a miserable tenement near by, the wife and mother having died years before. A shabby place it was they lived in; a bare, carpetless, furniture-less affair. I remember seeing Sydney one day in a snivelling state of despair because his father was drunk and he feared he would be beaten. He was thinking of running away, he said, but he was a poor, spiritless fellow, and instead of running away he rubbed his eyes with his coat-sleeves and worked on.

When I think of him and so many others like him that I have known in the past, I wish it were true, as the religionists would have us believe, that there was someone to whom man in his misery might turn for succour or at least a kindly word; some definite universal heart of whom the declaration "Come unto me, all ye that are weary and heavy-laden, and I will give you rest," were true. If only there were some God whose sanctuary were in a church, or many churches! Yet only in the vagrom heart of man is this dream realised for himself by groundless faith apparently. If we as individuals do not wish it to be true, do not make it true by our thoughts and deeds, then it is not true. If you wish a loving God to exist and have mercy, *be* Him! There is no other way.

But these new boys were, in the main, so good-natured and agreeable, a fun-loving and essentially democratic crew. They were always about with a proposal for a game of some kind. The matter of girls was as yet—in quite all of us, I think—a dormant instinct, or at least a sealed mystery. Certainly girls, to me at least, were no more at that time than boys, if as much, just another type of creature but not suitable for athletic games. At about this time, too, I was beginning to read, in an idle, indiscriminate way, an odd mixture of books which I found in the loft of our new house. These comprised such works as Gray's Elegy, "The Deserted Village," "The Traveller," "Wanda," by Ouida, and Lytton's "Ernest Maltravers." And how I did enjoy them! It may seem strange, but it was as if I had met up with things I had long known and loved and understood. I did not know all of the words and did not trouble to look them up, yet I am sure that I gathered the import of most of that which I read. I can neither understand nor explain it, seeing that I was but between ten and eleven years of age. Yet so it was.

And at the very same time, if you will believe it, I began to read with interest *The Family Story Paper, The Fireside Companion* and *The New York Weekly*, all romantic periodicals which flourished at that time and sample copies of which were thrown over our fence almost weekly. Finding one lying on our front lawn one day, I picked it up and began reading one of those dramatic introductions by which the reader is lured to "continue in our next." Forthwith I was lost. I just had to see what became of the poor but beautiful working-girl who was seized by thugs on her way to work and driven, gagged and blindfolded, to a wretched shanty far out on the Hackensack meadows, where she was confronted by her lustful and immoral pursuer. Having from either my mother or Paul extracted the required nickels, I proceeded every Friday or Saturday to the nearest news-stand to purchase, as might a drug addict, this latest delight.

But along with these also I was introduced, by some of the youths who gathered in the shade of our barn, to "Diamond Dick," "Brave and Bold," "Pluck and Luck," "Work and Win," and those other predecessors of the later "Nick Carters," "Frank Merriwells," etc. . . . It was a colourful world which they presented, impossible from a practical point of view and yet suggesting that freedom of action which we so often experience in dreams. How often at that time I trotted over the plains of Africa or Australia or Asia with these famous boy heroes whose names I have long since forgotten, but who possessed some practical device or other—iron horse or buggy or man, and bullet or arrow-proof jacket and suits even—in which one could travel in safety, if not peace, and, at the same time, defy and destroy all manner of savages and wild animals, and so with impunity invade the wildest, the most dangerous and therefore the most fascinating regions! At times, in short, I became so excited over the wonder of the life pictured that I would become intensely dissatisfied with the life I was living and was all for running away and finding a device of my own— a horse, a covered wagon, a bicycle, anything—and so seeing the world. But always practical considerations arose and interfered—money for one thing; parting from mother, Ed and others of the family. So instead I went along tamely enough, to school and church, and contented myself with baseball or fishing or reading of the deeds and adventures of newer and even grander heroes.

CHAPTER XXIII

AT first we were alone—my mother, Trina, Ed and myself —but soon (and at my mother's behest, I am sure), Trina wrote to the others and they began to flock to us. Although my mother always protested that she did not care to be followed by all of her children wherever she went, still I noticed that they were made welcome enough and for the most part remained, for a time anyhow.

Al was the first to appear, coming from Chicago, getting work in a chair factory and remaining with us. And after him came Ruth and Amy, together with my father, from Terre Haute to visit for the entire summer and longer. Also from heaven knows where (Mexico, I think) came Rome. And after him, Janet and Eleanor from Chicago. After the first three months, the house was always peopled by at least one and sometimes three or four of these elders who had not been included in the original pilgrimage. What my brother Paul and his lady sponsor thought of it all I am not able to say. But to me they brought a refreshing aroma of adventure and they made a comfortable home scene. And certainly, in so far as I sensed things at that time, there was little that was not pleasant and even delightful about our home life.

Would that I could say as much for our compulsory church and school life, here once more entered upon! For my father, the moment he appeared on the scene, and with his usual zeal for the welfare of our souls, sought out the nearest German Catholic Church and forthwith enrolled the entire family as communicants. Think of a man who had already made a botch of his life, a man whose theories of prevailing justice and reward had been gainsaid and battered by every form of accident and circumstance, being so deeply concerned over the immortality of not only his own soul but the souls of others! The business of adjusting us to the church must certainly have followed some explanation on the part of someone—either my

134

mother or Paul—as to how we were managing to subsist here. That should not have been very difficult, however, since obviously Paul was enjoying comparative affluence. (Because of Annie Brace he had deserted the minstrel troupe and accepted the position of star comedian at the Apollo Theatre in Evansville, a vaudeville or burlesque house which maintained a small stock company, supplemented at times by such comedians as Paul and the minor troupe which he trained and controlled.) And this evidence of prosperity must have had a soothing influence on my father, for weary he must have been of his own lacks and labours, and Paul, no doubt, was now seen in a different light from that of the jail-bird who had been forbidden our wretched home in Terre Haute. Since he had chosen to return and help his mother in this lavish way, what could one say? Christianity, apparently, dictated that he be forgiven under such circumstances, and so there you are, he was forgiven! We were all smiled upon as being part of a better state, whether actually, in a moral sense, we were or not.

That my mother, even at this time, knew that my brother's inamorata was the mistress of a house of prostitution I do not believe. I do know that she knew she was Paul's mistress or at least related to him in some intimate way, for when she visited us in Sullivan she had confessed her passion for him. Many years later, Paul himself, in a panegyric relative to Annie Brace and her virtues, told me that it was she who had rented and furnished the cottage, though it was he who maintained it. It was her idea that his mother need not know of her profession, since she would be dwelling in a different and remote part of the city and would keep aloof.

At any rate, here was my father concerned with the moral welfare of his family, and in the fall Trina, Ed and myself placed in the German parochial school connected with Holy Trinity, or "Heilige Dreifaltigkeit Kirche," a church whose spire could be seen from our house. Often I have heard the Angelus tolled by its bells coming to me across the level grass where I played, from the distant city beyond. Evansville, as we soon discovered, was, in the main, a German city, and there were at least three very large and prosperous German Catholic churches with their attendant parochial schools, every one of which was crowded with German-American Catholic children. In these one heard only German sermons and only German was taught

135

in the schools. My father, being heartily Teutonic in his notions and ideals, approved of this, and my mother was still sufficiently under his mental direction to be unable to withstand his will in the matter, though I am fairly well satisfied that she was even more than ever then dubious of the value of this faith in "educational" system.

The church was well enough in its way, as Catholic churches go. Of red brick, with stone trimmings, its pointed spire rose high above the surrounding buildings. Three priests—one rector and two assistants—administered its parochial needs. In spite of a certain gaudy artificiality as to decorations and a hacklike reproduction of various ancient altar-pieces, ceilings and the like, it was still impressive because of the height of its ceiling, the depth of its recesses, and the heavily-fluted character of its tall columns. A showy and yet impressive (because large) altar filled the apse, and there was a large and sonorous pipe organ which filled the west gallery or organ-loft.

I recall now, with considerable satisfaction, being permitted, once I was a member of the school, to pump this organ (there were no electrical attachments in those days) on Sundays or weekdays, for behind the organ one was not visible to either priest or teacher or nun and one could whisper and laugh and play about and at the same time escape the routine of mass responses, genuflections, prayers and the like. Wonderful! For by then I was so weary of these things that the mere thought of them was torturing. Yet at the elevation of the Host, so cowed was I by dogma that I invariably knelt, even behind the organ, not because I felt it to be so sacred or spiritual a moment but because of the fear that if I did not I might die in the act of committing a mortal sin and so be consigned to eternal fire. Fear, not spiritual understanding or reverence, compelled me.

If the church was dignified, interesting or impressive, the school was as poor a shift for an institution of that kind as I have ever seen. Why should deficient, non-standardised private schools be permitted, anyhow, I would like to know? Hasn't the world had enough of unsubstantiated dogma by now? Why permit an unwitting child to be dosed with all of the impossible vagaries of religious and social folderol when there are masses of exact data at hand?

This school adjoined the church and was a sizeable affair of eight rooms, one-half of them devoted to boys and the other to girls. It was presided over, as to the boys, by the very *hoch-würdig* Professor Ludwig von Valkenburg, one of the most amazing and individual educators it has been my privilege to know. I cannot, unfortunately, speak of him as an advantage, but as a bit of colour he was wonderful. Imagine a young man, whiskered like Michaelangelo's Moses, and a Vulcan for size and energy, functioning here as principal of this school and devoting all of his time to those pupils who were too old, too unruly or too advanced in their studies (the latter very rarely) to be taught by the nuns. A most formidable man, Brobdingnagian, archaic, Norse. I never knew one with a more dreadful frown or a more seemingly difficult smile. But his position must have been very trying, for he was at once schoolmaster, principal, organist (at which last he was considered exceptional) and general factotum where most of the church functions were concerned—communion, confirmation, graduating exercises, picnics and the like—and this under the direction of a most irritable and domineering pastor, the Reverend Anton Dudenhausen by name. Stout, pompous, aggressive, this priest had the presence and solidity of a ferocious bull. The mere sight of him terrified me, so much so that when he was anywhere near, in the schoolroom, on the street, on the playground, I lost all self-possession and stood agape, wondering what terror, punishment or deprivation might not be in preparation.

Picture a room, possibly twenty by thirty feet, crowded with boys of from ten to fourteen years of age (sons of workingmen or small shopkeepers for the most part), whose one aim in life seemed to be to get through their days and classes in the most shiftless or shifty manner and so get out at four o'clock to play, fight, loaf, or do anything that their very idle fancies might suggest. No curriculum worthy of the name. A mixed gibberish of minor arithmetic, beginner's grammar, reading, Bible history, spelling, catechism, and then at about twelve years of age most of these spiritually afflicted underlings turned out to begin the work of making a living and planning their careers! Think of it! And that goes on to this day!

This school taught nothing of the history of the United States, nothing concerning geography, algebra, geometry, zoology, botany, nor indeed any of the sciences or arts, the rudiments of which are frequently of so much interest to children. The main thing was to get them through the three Rs and out into some humdrum workshop full-fledged and solidly-believing Catholics. To this end the school was opened and closed with prayers. Even now I can hear the anticipatory clatter of books and feet as we prepared to recite our prayers in double-quick time and so escape to the open air and play. We were always supposed to go to early mass before entering school, and twice failing so to do resulted in a visit on the part of the Herr Professor or the priest to the father or mother of the delinquent. And after that, if the boy was at fault and the parents consented, or did not consent, a good, sound beating. Beginning in January or February of each year, regardless of anything save age (ignorance, dullness, antipathy not considered), all those from any grade who were nearing the twelfth year were assembled every morning at eleven to receive, under the personal direction of the Very Reverend Anton Dudenhausen, instructions in the history, ritual and spiritual foundation of the Catholic Church, in order that they might be properly confessed and absolved and admitted to their first holy communion with the Holy Roman Catholic Church on a certain day in May.

Above all things, I desire not to be unfair to an organisation that may have a reasonable, or even an unreasonable, foundation in the inalienable emotions of unthinking men, but making every allowance, I can think of nothing more stupid than the system which prevailed here and which must have affected quite definitely the lives of at least several thousand who passed in and out of this school in the course of a score of years.

CHAPTER XXIV

I SHALL never forget the prolonged and desperate struggle my brother Ed made to be excluded from the grip of this school's disturbing curriculum. On the first Monday in September, when with heavy heart and desperate forebodings of evil, I set forth on this very sad adventure, Ed firmly refused to budge. Having played free and loose all summer and for several years before, he now refused to be thus tamely bridled and led like a broken horse to dreary labour. And because my father had returned to Terre Haute and my mother was too lax to exercise his stern force, such scenes as now followed were possible. Also Ed had much more than what might be called a will of his own; he could be as stubborn and unreasoning as a mule.

For the first few days, therefore, my mother coaxed and thereafter frowned, threatened, offered interesting rewards of money or future pleasures, but all to no avail. Then Trina and myself were induced, for the sake of Ed's future intellectual career, to bring home glowing reports of how nice it was in school. And in spite of a severe depression of spirit which had fallen on me at sight of all I have described, I lied manfully. (May Heaven forgive me!) But Ed merely eyed me as one who had turned traitor and gone over to the enemy. Then there was talk of sending for the priest or the teacher or both. But even this did not frighten him. He merely stuck out a contentious underlip and remained obdurate. In despair, Amy, of whom he was very fond, volunteered to go to school with him and even sit with him. No, he would not go. Finally, one of the parish priests—a Father Liverman, a mild, gentle, little man who seemed to be called upon to settle odd jobs of this kind—came to the house and talked to him, and in such a soothing way that he even intrigued me a little. This softened Ed somewhat, but he would not agree to go. Then one morning, finding himself quite alone in the neighbourhood with no one to play with, he was induced to go as far as the school building and look at it, Amy, Trina, Al and myself accompanying him and all working en route to make him see how essential and agreeable and interesting it was. But I know he looked upon us as traitors or at least as Greeks bearing evil gifts.

Once in sight of the school, however, he was seized with renewed qualms of horror and refused to budge. But having brought him thus far with great difficulty, it was now our turn. We refused to permit him to retire. A struggle ensued, a physical one, and this on one of the main highways of the city. There were yells, kicks, moans; strangers were moved to pause and see the "fight." But the four of us finally managed to get him as far as the school gate, whereupon he yelled so loudly that the Herr Professor von Valkenburg, no less, hearing him and wondering what new human catastrophe was upon the region, came out and seizing him about the waist, attempted to carry him in. But Ed, by some caution of the imagination having laid hold of several fence pickets, was not to be torn loose without all but tearing the fence away, all the while screaming so loudly that Amy feared he was being injured by von Valkenburg and suddenly decided that it might be as well to rescue him from this dire monster. In consequence she now began to push and strike the Herr Professor, demanding that he let her brother go, and he, not recognising her as anyone connected with the school and probably overawed by her expression, decided to desist, but not without many scathing remarks as to the nonsense of the whole procedure. Then several nuns and others who had come upon the scene— among them the worthy Father Liverman—undertook to pour sweet words upon us. Thus there was much talk of how nice this Catholic school life really was, how good the nuns would be to him if only he would enter. And finally, by dint of persuasion on the part of Father Liverman, he was induced to enter, but only on condition that Amy be allowed to sit with him.

Once inside, he appeared to subside and let things go as they would. The nun in charge had sufficient sense to leave him very much to himself for a day or two. Finding himself uninjured in any way and also that the playground at noon recess and other times offered some means of recreation, he soon accustomed himself to the situation, only now the difficulty lay in making him study or come home afterwards at a reasonable hour. For practically all of the two years we were in this school, we were always hunting Ed before or after school. When we did find him, it was necessary to use force to compel him to leave off playing marbles, top, ball, pitch-penny, or to get him off the snow or ice in the winter.

So much for Ed. In regard to myself I now rise to state that I am convinced that I gained from this school no least atom of anything helpful to me in any way. My father, of course, imagined that I would be strengthened in Catholicism and that my soul would be saved, but you know how it is as to this last. I am in truth, dogmatically speaking, a total loss. In fact, it was the seeds here sown that definitely alienated me from the Church. My mother, of course, was still suffering from the delusion that something of what was here taught would be helpful in the business of making a living later or might at least aid one in deciding on how to survive economic-ally. But this was the sheerest moonshine; nothing of any practical value whatsoever was either acquired or even offered. For my part, I merely mooned and blundered among things which were said to be important and which meant little or nothing to me. Spelling was easy enough, and reading delight-ful. But what reading! Fortunately, there was an Eclectic Fourth or Fifth Reader used here which contained some gems —passages out of "Undine," Heine, Schiller and other German classics. Then there was a Bible History which, however biased it was in favour of Catholicism, contained not a few lovely interpretations of religiously classic scenes: the Sermon on the Mount, the wedding at Cana, the Garden of Eden, the Flood, the death of Christ, the Resurrection. These impressed me not so much as religious dogma; they seemed to me simple, human stories. More than once I was struck over the knuckles with a ruler by the noble Herr Ludwig for reading in my reader or Bible history when I should have been mastering grammar or arithmetic.

More, the boys I found here were in no way suited to my mental or emotional taste or mood. With but few exceptions they struck me as coarse, rough, vulgar, ignorant, contentious. Always among them a fight was brewing, largely as tests of strength. Your best friend of to-day would suddenly turn on you for the least look or disagreement and decide that he wanted to fight you, and the honour of yourself and the school demanded that you fight back at once or accept a challenge to settle it after school. This procedure being agreed upon, there came then a great crowd to see the result. Adherents naturally fell to your or the other fellow's share, just why you could not say. Books would be thrown down, coats taken off, and the milling would begin. More than once I was forced into rows of this kind, entirely against my will. The fact is, I was a great coward, mortally afraid of being hurt. Yet on at least two occasions, being forced into combat, and though frozen with fear, I managed to fight and did not come off so badly. And once an upward self-defensive blow, wholly unconscious and involuntary on my part, caught a boy on the jaw and knocked him flat. He thought it was calculated and that I was a powerful fighter, whereupon he refused to rise and sat holding his jaw. At once I was acclaimed a hero when I knew I was an arrant coward. But before these others I did not object to being thought a hero.

But life—my individual reactions to the natural beauties about me—was ever with me as a counsellor and friend, setting at naught these things that were otherwise so unsatisfactory. Always, I may say, I was looking at the clouds, watching the birds, noting the swaying of a tree in the wind, speculating upon the doings and thoughts of others, their homes, pleasures, means, travels. A passing train or boat, even an ambling street car, was ever a delight. On my walks to and from school, I invariably paused to linger before shop or factory windows. I recall an old potter who had a very small shop or factory on one of the streets along which I daily travelled—Vine Street, I think it was. A small, spare, reflective and worn man, he sat before an open window, winter and summer, his wheel or whirling platform before him, shaping clay into pitchers, cups, saucers, bowls and the like. It was my first introduction to the mystery of form and I marvelled and at the same time rejoiced that he could so easily make out of this yielding substance these things of varying hue and often beauty.

Elsewhere on my route was a foundry, through the open doorway of which I could see an inner yard filled with great stacks of pig-iron and vast quantities of broken stoves, wheels, pots and pans, endless parts of machinery, all red with rust and waiting to be smelted into a new, clean mass. Beyond all this was a great furnace towering upward and seething with flame, the while men emptied into it masses of iron or drew off cauldrons of sputtering, glowing metal. In beds of sand near by were traced delicate designs of stove panels, legs, doors, tops, lids, into which this molten fluid was poured. Men were constantly carrying about pots of metal and pouring the same into these forms, or lifting out the rough results and brushing them with steel brushes to make them smooth. Their faces were black, their eyelids red, their eyeballs showing white, strange, grimy figures, and yet they laughed and sang and whistled as they worked. And as they did so, my soul whistled and sang with them.

There was still another delight—that of the growing city itself. Everywhere new houses or factories were springing up. In the centre of a great common near the heart of the city, a public library was being erected, the bequest of a deceased resident. It was of a beautiful, creamy sandstone and of not unpleasing design, and from time to time I watched with interest the placing of these blocks into one harmonious whole. Its arched doors and fluted columns and cornices remain with me to this day. In another section was being erected a giant chair works which promised employment to hundreds for years to come. And here was a new church, its double spires rising sharply in the air. And there a row of workingmen's cottages, very small and plain, all, all alike. And skyward were being reared, even at that date (1882), tall skeleton towers of iron, spidery triangles of thin posts or tubes that at a height of one hundred feet or more were to carry six arc lights each. Electricity had just arrived, and arc lights were beginning to be used in one and another of the stores. (The incandescent lamp had not yet appeared.) And here now was a street being paved. People were laying out new lawns and adorning them with metal figures of Cupids or stags or dogs. A five-mile car line jingled all day long, with cars trundling from the water front to a place known as Salt Wells. Whistles screeched at morning, noon and night. A half-dozen Catholic churches tolled the Angelus. Boys and girls idled to and from school with their books under their arms.

At such moments of contemplation I did not know a care. All was well with me. Overhead might be clouds or sun; within myself was life with its hungers and I was being satisfied.

143

From blacksmith, baker, tinsmith, grocer, I was learning the intricate lesson of the social organisation of life. Barter, sale, the perfect, the imperfect, wealth, poverty, the idler, the industrious—all were paraded before me. What need to teach me of the useless mercy of God or His rage? Here was my Maker: the creative life force all about me; and it was showing me how it worked, almost why. I did not need to look for the reason in books. "I am because I wish to be, and this is my way," it might have said to me. Did I wish to fit in with the scheme of things, then I must learn some of these things and join in its constructive tasks. No more and no less. All ethics were being taught me by life itself. Of what service to me the wretched school? Better the open forge and the potter's window. From these I gathered enduring lessons of both beauty and truth.

CHAPTER XXV

IT was after I had been in this school for two years and was by then twelve years old that the Very Reverend Dudenhausen appeared one morning, his eyes commanding and yet not unfriendly, and announced that from now on until the end of school all those who were twelve years of age were to report to him in an adjoining room between eleven and twelve every morning and there receive such instruction as would fit them for their first communion and subsequent confirmation.

You may well guess with what a mixture of surprise, fear and doubt this announcement was received by these poor scrubs of boys who had no more conception of what it meant to be instructed in the tenets of the Catholic Church than they had of what it would mean to be called upon to sail to the moon. Literally, outside of *hearing* what was said and then going to the altar and going through certain motions and genuflections, they knew nothing of what was meant. Catechism? What was that? "And the Word was made flesh and dwelt among men."—how might the import of that be imparted to a child, and a dull one at that? What could the elevation of the Host or the body and blood of Jesus Christ mean to them? Yet it was the business of these heavy religionists, regardless of the mental equipment of these silly lads, to "instruct" or rather demand acceptance (and all unexplained), of all of the obscurities of dogmatic theology, or failing that, catch them by threatened ills and the hopes of the possible remission of the same providing they agreed or came to look upon the Holy Catholic Church as insuperable and so absolutely necessary to their future spiritual salvation. In other words, assure a man that he has a soul and then frighten him with old wives' tales as to what is to become of it afterwards, and you have a hooked fish, a mental slave! And so once more I ask, why permit this dogged insistence on religious theory which cannot be proven but must be accepted on faith—especially in the case of children? Why not confine it to the grown mind? There are libraries enough for all, and we can all theorise for ourselves when the time comes.

I wish you might have been with me, though, to see the Reverend Anton Dudenhausen as he was at that time. Fat, domineering, albeit honestly (possibly) and blindly convinced. And before him, in that big, bare classroom, these fumbling, duncy boys being instructed for an hour each day in the mysteries and subtleties of the Catholic faith. Their mental inefficiency, their lack of interest, and yet their fear of being punished for any noted inattention! And the Reverend Anton so broad and solemn and stern, towering above them, himself so bigoted and deficient. Yet there was at the same time something so bland, so smug, so oilily affectionate about him. In short, I actually believe of this porker that he was of the very stuff of zealotry. He believed in so far as he could understand, and what he did not understand he accepted on hearsay and faith, and demanded, most violently at times, that these others do likewise. For instance, how he dwelt on the horrors of hell and the punishment awaiting all who failed to conform to what the Church had ordained as necessary to salvation! But no plausible explanations and none there capable of understanding had any been made. No honest presentation of the history of the Church as such; mere rules and regulations and then denunciations of all Protestantism and infidelity and of all those who dared to think otherwise than did Rome!

At this time lived the redoubtable Ingersoll, travelling, lecturing, writing, making a hash of the dogmatic as well as spiritual pretensions of quite all of the sectarian religions of his day, and him the Reverend Anton excoriated with fiery zeal. This demon! This actual devil in men's clothing, dragging these foolish and mistaken souls down into hell with him! And for what? Well, he, the very Reverend Anton, would tell you for what! And here and now! For the crime, no less, of listening to this demon sent here by the devil and then daring to believe him, when here at hand, free to the wish and will of everybody, was Holy Church, with its Christ-given authority and its holy laws and sacraments ordained by God himself and confirmed by Peter, the first Pope; by no less a person than Jesus himself, the Almighty Ruler of the Universe! Only to think of this scoundrel in a high hat attempting to persuade inattentive souls to the notion that the divine teachings of the Holy Church were not true!! But wait! Wait until he died! Wait until at his very bedside in death the Devil himself appeared and seized him! For God still ruled. And what He ordained the Devil had to obey. And for his sins against the Church, he and all of his victims here on earth would be properly punished! Just wait. . . .

I leave you to disentangle this fine bundle of logic and dogma as well as its probable effect on these immature and gaping and altogether fearful minds, the while I conclude the picture of the noble Anton and his labours. For while he talked, there was something iron in his eye, something dictatorial and final about his fat paunch. In cassock and lace and chasuble— for effect, I presume—he strolled among these children and either glared or laid a soft, white, priestly hand on a tousled head here and there, and talked, and talked, and talked.

I have often thought it a pity that this man, with all of his native force and enthusiasm for his work, was without mental understanding or equipment of any kind. He was probably not a bad man, just a fool, a narrow bigot like my father, his one idea being to make good Catholics of these children and nothing more. Years later he was found dead in his bedroom—kneeling at his bedside, so I was told, his head upon his hands which clasped (or had) a cross. He had died praying! In short, he was a good Catholic. But why such a lunatic firebrand in charge of the minds of children? Why?

CHAPTER XXVI

DURING all of this time the most interesting figure in our family, to me and the others, was Paul. He was our bright and progressively growing and glowing luminary.

I have told of one of the reasons why he came to Evansville and then chose to remain there. Yet all of the time we were there I saw this Annie Brace (or Sallie Walker, as she was locally known) but twice, and then only for moments; once sitting in front of our door in a carriage and another time when I was sent to deliver a basket of preserves, the gift of my mother. And from this one fact alone, I have long since deduced that my mother could not have known of the nature of the business conducted by Annie Brace, for in every thought and direction connected with her younger children, she was always concerned lest our contacts be other than such as would tend to improve our social standing, to strengthen rather than weaken our interest and faith in the value of such social customs and rules as she understood and held to be valuable.

Still, on this one occasion I was thrust into the very centre of this so-called "den of iniquity," although I think my mother's intention was that I was to deliver my basket at the door and come away without parley of any kind. (There was a note in the basket which was supposed to explain everything.) I found the place with some difficulty, wandering up a long street which paralleled the Ohio River and provided some striking views. I rang the bell and before I could explain was ushered into an entryway by a Negro servant and told to wait. Nothing loath, and curious as to the character of the place (I only knew of such things by hearsay), I stared about until the Negro returned and told me to follow her, that my brother wanted to see me. I was then led upstairs and along a passage to a suite of charmingly furnished rooms which commanded a splendid view of the river. It was hot and bright in this semi-southern world, and there was Paul, in the trousers of a light, summery suit and a silk shirt, making his morning toilet. With him was his Annie, in a pink and white, heavily beflounced dressing gown, and surveying me with an amused if not very much interested eye. The rooms—living room, bedroom and bath—were not yet made up for the day, but to my uninformed eyes they were beautiful, everything in them rich and wonderful, a marvellous place. Striped awnings were at the window to shut out the hot morning sun, and the living room was furnished with comfortable-looking wicker furniture, covered with tan linen. There were potted plants and a piano, strewn with music. Silver-backed toilet articles graced a dresser in the near by bedroom, and beyond this was a bathroom such as I had never seen before, large and bright and equipped with toilet accessories in great profusion. It seemed a kind of fairyland.

But to reach this suite there had been that passage through the house, during which I had peered into several open doors and seen things so strange and to me exotically moving that I felt I must not acknowledge them even to myself. Segments of beds, for instance; dressers and odd bits of furniture; and in one case a yellow-haired siren half naked before her mirror. I can see her now, in chemisette, her arms and breast exposed, "making-up" her cheeks and eyes. The bedding in every case, as I noted, was tumbled, the garments of the occupant strewn about in an indifferent and (to me even then) blood-tingling way. In a flash, and without being told, a full appreciation of the utility of the male as such came to me. I wished that I might stay and see more, even that one of these women would take a fancy to me. Yet I also knew quite well that such things were still in the dim, distant future for me, if at all. But these pink-meated sirens, however vulgar they might have been in their physical as well as mental texture, were wonderful to me as forms, that spirometric formula that appears not only to control but compel desire in the male.

And while we are on this subject, let me here and now pay my respects to the prostitute as such. I have often attempted to unravel for myself, from a philosophic point of view, this mystery of the orgiastic life and why it has fallen to so low a state in the modern world. It was not always so, as Greece and Rome and Japan will testify. And yet there has grown up about sex licence a painted terror which for asininity of mind rivals, if it does not outrival, all the silly folderol of the Middle Ages in regard to heaven and hell. For instance, it is regularly charged that (1) it is an unproductive profession; (2) that for some individuals (not all) it is a debilitating and depleting profession; (3) that nature itself has stigmatised its liberties by frustrating or pursuing them with all forms of disease. But, to take the last point first, what organic function or liberty has not nature severely stigmatised by disease or difficulty? The lungs (breathing): pneumonia, consumption, coughs, colds. The heart (pulsation): angina pectoris, cardiac fever, fatty degeneration, lesion. The brain: lesion, degeneration of the tissue or its psychic functions. Indeed, every function and organ of the body preyed upon in the same zymotic and disgusting manner.

Science has already proved, of course, that the supposed heaven-inflicted diseases which are presumed to trail sex liberty are no more elusive of unravelling and cure than any of the others that afflict the human frame and spirit. Syphilis and gonorrhœa have yielded to treatment, whereas cancer, consumption and Bright's disease still claim their countless victims.

If one examines the charges of unproductiveness and depletion in connection with prostitution, they also fall into the limbo of the improbable, for while some women and some men are depleted and diseased, others are sustained through a period when poverty and possibly physical and mental bashfulness or unattractiveness make them the victims of a horrible loneliness or sense of unfitness or sex defeat, which would do as much to make them mentally and physically debilitated and unfit as anything else, the so-called sex evil included. I speak from personal knowledge, which I shall not stop to elucidate here.

More, the persistent presence and popularity of houses of prostitution and of the harlot in the face of an age-old war upon them (religious, ethical, social, moral), would indicate that they satisfy an urgent and defiant need, a need as definite as that supplied by the theatre and the drug store, if not the grocery. Literature, art, science and trade must subscribe to the intellectual as well as the physical stimulus supplied by those whose lesser gifts in the matter of blandishment, magnetism, beauty and the like, drive them to this purely mercenary outlet for their impulses and desires. Nature knows better than man what it needs. Its flare of self-expression indicates a keener logic than all man's petty and spindling fumbling with ethics and morals. Neither Ashtoreth nor Venus is dead. Their shrines are lit by eternal fires.

The thing that I wish to make plain, however, in connection with Annie Brace is that once the secret of her profession was known to me, I guarded it as a great mystery, saying nothing of all I had seen to my mother or anyone else. During my visit to her house I was treated very genially by my brother, who gave me some money to spend on my way home. Pagan that he was, never economically or socially adjusted anywhere, he seemed to think nothing of my being there or of what I had seen.

In the course of time, however, it appeared to have become known, at least in our immediate neighbourhood, that this handsome, well-positioned brother of ours was in some way connected with this institution; and along toward the end of our second summer, I received a shock in connection with Paul and his affairs which brought the matter of public opinion very much to the fore. I was passing the home of that Harry Truckee previously mentioned as he was whitewashing his front fence. "Hey, Thee!" he called, "what's the name of that woman your brother lives with downtown?" He was a sly and shifty-eyed youth, and on this occasion there was something about the way he spoke which warned me that he was about some ferrety business. Surprised and taken aback by this direct assault, I hardly knew what to say. Since no one, even in the family, had ever ventured to refer to the matter, if they knew, I had come to believe that it might still be a dark secret to others. I know I flushed and made some jumbled reply that I knew nothing about it, whereupon he followed up his first inquiry with a bold, irritating: "Aw, get out!" and then added: "Sure about that?"

"Certainly, I am sure about it," I retorted, for I was never in the least overawed by Truckee.

"Well, other people seem to know about it," he went on. "Ever heard of Sallie Walker?" There was a malicious look in his eye which simply defied contradiction. Still I denied knowing her, though I had seen that name over Annie Brace's door and guessed then that it must be she.

"You're a funny fella," he continued. "Never heard of Sallie Walker! Why, everybody knows her. She keeps a fast house down on the waterfront. You ask your brother some time, he'll tell yuh. They say she's stuck on him and he lives there."

He smiled pleasantly and yet defiantly as if to say: "Put that in your pipe and smoke it!" and went on whitewashing. I turned away, a little sick, and went on about my errand with a keen sense of having been placed in a very embarrassing position. My thoughts were about as follows: Yes, Paul lives with Sallie Walker, and I know it. And Harry Truckee knows it. And he knows that I know it. But who is Harry Truckee? Trash! And his family? Trash! Paul has a big name. His pictures are all over town on the theatre billboards. He writes songs and lives at the St. George when he wants to and supports us and gives us things. And Sallie Walker is a beautiful woman. I wish I were as fine and prosperous as Paul and that some beautiful woman would fall in love with me. But it's too bad to be found out. But what difference does it make? He's not hurting anybody, and neither is she, and they're both good to us.

But there was never a word from any other source in Evansville. Every day or two Paul would appear at our home and stay for lunch or dinner, sometimes even all night. He loved to sit near mother or follow her about as she worked, telling her funny stories or asking her advice in some problem or plan. Often during the summer he would play ball with Ed and myself. Always he brought something: a watermelon, ice cream, candy, books, papers. At Christmas and Fourth of July it was he who made the day for us, bringing great bundles of toys or huge packages or firecrackers—rockets, pinwheels and the like. And often he would give us all tickets to see this or that show at the Apollo, which, of course, included himself. (It was seeing him on the stage and going behind the scenes that later prompted Ed, Al, Trina and myself to give a minstrel show in our barn, incidentally infecting all of the children in the audience with chicken lice!)

For by the end of the first summer, Paul was already a part of a stock vaudeville or minstrel organisation which held the boards winter and summer at the Apollo—later the Evansville Opera House. In this connection he served not only as "end man" but betimes interlocutor, monologist, song and dance man, and I know not what else. The fences and billboards everywhere attested to his popularity. Large red and yellow and black single-sheets bore his picture and the legend: "Paul Dresser, Comedian—Evansville Opera House—Week of . . ." And nightly, before the show, or of an afternoon, he was to be found, along with friends of the stage, the sporting and newspaper worlds, about the lobby or bar of the old St. George Hotel, at that time Evansville's principal hostelry. I often sought him out there, with a note from my mother or to get tickets he was holding for us, or to perform some small errand for him, and I always carried away an impression of a man perfectly dressed, his suits and linen fresh and well-fitting, his ties and socks and shoes of the latest mode. Also, before the end of the first winter, he connected himself with a local semi-comic weekly—*The Evansville Argus*—as a paragrapher. His weekly column was copied into other papers east and west; he used to bring them out to the house for us to see.

You may well guess what all this meant to me. For was this not my own brother, strong and rich, a veritable bulwark, as it seemed to me, against further misfortune? He loved us and would see that we did not have to suffer. What other thing could make any brother anywhere half so important?

CHAPTER XXVII

THOSE of my brothers and sisters who came to visit us were so struck by the charm of the city that they at once attempted to get work and remain.

Al, for instance, my small and different sort of brother! Always when I think of him, I think of a natural intelligence thwarted by untoward conditions. There is a type of mind or intelligence that seems to leap into the world full-armed and as though equipped by previous experience elsewhere to move without error or faltering here. On the other hand, there is a lesser order of force, equally intuitive and possibly even more sensitive, which, like some of the hardy though none the less gorgeous flowers, requires special nurture in order to bring it to its proper stature and value. The hardy weed that fights and in the face of obstacles and opposition comes to such beauty as is in it, we can admire for its courage as well as forgive its defects. But of the sensitive soul that requires both shelter and aid in order to be all that it might be, and yet fails of the same, what shall we say?

Despite his cultural lacks—due to having been kept in a Catholic school until he was twelve and then sent to a farm to work and learn as best he could—his was a genial, sincere and industrious spirit. He liked to work and tried so hard to get along, though lack of education continued to prove a heavy handicap. He realised this and often spoke of it. He urged me to study, so that I might amount to something. His soul, as I saw it, was fixed on the colour and beauty of life. He liked to read; a fine poem or a good book or play meant much to him. He had a keen sense of humour, and, like Paul, was always imitating people, their language, facial expressions, gestures. One of his dreams was to become a blackface comedian or a green-whiskered Irish farceur. Later he had a keen desire to become a writer, but always he seemed to be frustrated by the thought that he was not sufficiently prepared and needed a little capital whereon to lean while essaying these fields. Too little force, say you? Too poor a grip on his dreams? Very likely. Yet his dreams cut and burned, making of his early life a yearning search and of his later years a series of bitter disappointments. We crave so much and we win so little, the majority of us.

On leaving Sullivan he had found work as a varnisher in a coffin factory in Chicago (a fact which I have not narrated), and now in Evansville, he secured, first, a place in a barber shop; then as a "butcher" on a local passenger train; and finally as varnisher with Neinaber & Fitton, a large chair factory. Here he worked until we left Evansville. And many were the Saturday afternoons that I went to the shop and helped him to varnish or gold-leaf a design upon the very commonplace kitchen chairs which were the sole product of this factory. His foreman was a lean, blue-eyed, large-moustached man who had no quarrel with an employee turning an honest penny in this way. If his employees did not work, they did not get paid, so why should he care? And to me the work was so easy and delightful! There was a stencil which one placed against the chair and against which was pressed the gold-leaf with a brush. As for the varnishing, there were large buckets of clear varnish and good brushes. Incidentally, Al seemed to like to have me with him. We talked and talked, about everything under the sun. Working about as he did, he had acquired the habit of swearing, and occasionally he drank too much, thereby terrorising my mother and the rest of us with the fear that he might follow in the footsteps of Rome. Yet he never did.

My sisters Amy and Janet, whom for reasons of temperament I class together, also secured work here—one in a candy factory and the other in a five-and-ten cent store. The candy factory, as I chanced to discover by going there one noonday with something for my sister, was a grand place, full of great buckets and boxes of candy, an absolute paradise. And on several Saturday nights Ed and myself were introduced as helpers or errand-boys in the five-and-ten cent store. For this we were paid thirty-five cents each, to say nothing of being able to purloin all of the dates and figs and candy we could eat or stuff into our pockets. And more, a girl at the soda fountain gave us each a glass of soda and a dish of ice cream before we went home at eleven. Oh, Aladdin! Oh, Ali Baba! What fortune!

But why these two girls should have preferred to remain here with their mother, who was constantly preaching sobriety in thought and action, when they might have remained away and led the lives they chose, is beyond me. But here they preferred to be, and if it was a cheap life they led, it was still an eager and enthusiastic one. Both were ever on the go—picnics, boat rides, dances, buggy rides. Here were a pair of idlewilds, driven helplessly and persistently by their own internal fires and emotions and illusions and not to be regulated by the solemn advice of any well-meaning parent, however yearningly or tenderly given. They were not so much calculating as vain and unthinking.

Thus, Amy, speaking in later years of experiences in Evansville, told me that once her employer at the candy factory had attempted to seduce her. When it came to the crucial moment and after she had accompanied him to a room in a hotel (and knowing he was married), she was stricken with remorse and cried so loud and long that he let her go.

Janet, on the contrary, was already so experienced in matters of sex that at crucial moments she would desert her sister and go her own way. Her whole life, outside of labour, was devoted, apparently, to the selection of men she considered as having sufficient charm of face and manner to enjoy a share of her favours. Incidentally, the proprietor of the five-and-ten cent store where she worked (a man who subsequently became very wealthy and opened stores in many cities) appeared on the scene as a friend of the family, Janet being the attraction. But he was not handsome enough or she did not like him enough. The worthiness or import of a man as a husband, or lover rather, in these instances was not measured by his character or capacity as a merchant, craftsman or thinker, but by his clothes, moustache, airs, looks, his qualifications as a beau, and by these only.

My father, coming home occasionally for week-ends, was so infuriated at the goings-on of these two girls that he would have driven them out had it not been for my mother. As for myself, being still so young and knowing so little of the driving force of sex and what, if anything, was going on, I felt that there was a great deal of to-do over something that did not amount to very much. But now I know how futile are all earthly doctrines as to morals and virtues and how incapable the most well-meaning and puritanic of virtue-seekers of establishing the thing of which they dream. Who filled these girls with this eager fire which made them seek relief at any cost? Who caused their eyes to blazon their hunger for love? Who made their eager feet to run, their hearts to pant with desire? There is in this world much too little grasp of the nature-made chemisms and impulses that evoke and condition our deeds.

Again, there was Eleanor, about from time to time with reports of the son of a wealthy dry-goods merchant in the east whom she had met in Chicago. She had gone to Chicago to seek work and her encounter with this man—Harahan, I shall call him—interestingly enough, came about in a boarding house in which she was employed and where he came to gamble—a clubroom of sorts being conducted there. This affair, as time was to prove, was destined to end only in death, for I personally lived to see this lover of my sister's grow old and full of years, a stubborn and yet undefeated Solon of sorts, still wise but broken, and yet attended by love, as after his fashion he gave love, or at least loyalty and faithfulness.

And then Ruth. A beautiful girl, if there ever was one. I never saw a more sylphlike figure. And now, at eighteen or twenty, she also was in love. This I gathered from hearing her talk to mother about some rich manufacturer in Chicago. And then at last, his appearance one day, meticulously dressed and light-treading, a springy sort of optimist of perhaps forty or more years of age. And shrewd and reserved and courteous— a quiet, pleasant and decidedly observant man. What fascinated me most in connection with him was that he came all the way from Chicago to visit Ruth and her parents and was apparently very much interested and impressed by my mother as well as Ruth, and so us.

In this connection my mother must have led a rich emotional as well as mental life, with all of the affairs of her many children so completely in her hands. I can see her now, moving about her latest kingdom, interested in the flowers, the scenery, the sky, the chickens, and always the doings of her children. One of her tricks, in so far as we younger children were concerned and whenever we became too obstreperous, was to threaten to leave us. If no contrition on our part was visible, she would produce her shawl and Mennonite bonnet, and, packing a small basket, would hang it on her arm and start to go. This invariably evoked a storm of wails and tears, until she was moved to relent. The mere thought of her possible departure was sufficient to produce in me as well as Ed, and even Trina at times, an intense depression and the most dissolving of emotions. In fact, long after I had passed my thirtieth birthday, and when she had already been dead for some years, I still used to dream of her as being alive but threatening to go off and leave me, and would awake to find myself in tears. Even to this day, dreams of her invariably evoke in me a great sadness and longing, the result, I presume, of the psychic impact of those terrors of long ago.

CHAPTER XXVIII

THE more serious phases of our life here—which eventually brought our stay to a close—occurred toward the end of our second year and caused us all, but more especially my mother, no end of distress and worry.

For one thing, along about that time my brother Rome, who had been wandering in all sorts of places—Mexico, Honduras, California—came to pay us another visit. He arrived, as usual, with nothing more than a small handbag. But this brother's method of travelling was always most informal. He never made any formal farewells; might even announce that he was going out for a little while and then we would neither see nor hear more of him for say one, two, three, and in one instance four years. Sometimes, after six months, and when mother had finally worried all her worries out, a postal card would arrive from some far-off place, on which would be scrawled: "En route to Cheyenne (or Dallas) (or Matamoras). All right with me. Don't worry. See you Christmas," or something like that. As years passed and he became more and more of a drinker and waster, the family began to dread these periodic visits. They spelled little more than drunkenness, imposition, clashes with the local police and fines to be paid by some member of the family, followed by tearful repentances and promises to lead a better life and find work—at the end of which period he was to "wear diamonds" and do something for us all—and then another sudden departure, more postal cards, more returns, and so on. To me he seemed to be possessed of an incurable lust for wandering as well as a desire to unravel the mysteries of a phase of life considered unmentionable. Saloons, gambling houses, low dives, constituted the centres of his interest. For always his pockets whenever he arrived home were crammed with letter-heads and cards of saloonkeepers and politicians. In short, he seemed to have a genuine genius for getting about and seeing things of sorts, but with plainly no desire for work of any kind—at least no work that spelled permanence in any one place or field. Not he!

On this occasion, after an absence of two years or more, he suddenly appeared, having been directed by someone in Sullivan or Terre Haute. As usual, he was without a dime and in the elapsed time had gone from bad to worse. Finding his mother glad to see him again, he laid his head in her lap and cried bitterly, and she, as usual, cried with him.

His stay in Evansville, however, resulted in one thing: a sharp disagreement between himself and Paul, which boded no good for him in the future. For he was divorcing himself from the most successful and helpful member of the family. This family of ours, living, in part, at least, on what Paul provided, was more or less responsible to him for its moral conduct—an easy matter, requiring little more than a cheerful acceptance of his kindness—and yet Rome was an irritation and a grief to him. They could never agree; they had too little in common. Rome was both ironic and sardonic, with considerable opposition to the methods and necessities of organised society (although he partook of as many of its benefits as possible), while Paul was generous, sympathetic, easy and quick to laugh, and although without any too deep understanding always constructive or creative.

Soon after his arrival, Rome proceeded to the downtown section, where, finding that Paul was so popular and well-placed, he immediately proceeded to advertise himself as his brother, borrowing money, drinking, gambling, passing worthless cheques, and presently landing in jail. Of course, you can imagine Paul's chagrin. It was not long, therefore, before there were words as well as the hardest kind of feelings, since Paul had to use his influence to get him out of jail in addition to making good the worthless cheques. Then one afternoon, soon after being released from jail, this Rome, in company with another wastrel, climbed into a buggy which stood hitched to a post and drove off, visiting saloon after saloon and finally leaving the buggy in some outlying livery stable. Alas, for both himself and his companion they had miscalculated as to the memory of saloonkeepers and strangers, and were finally apprehended and taken up, Rome in our home at two in the morning. Of course, he was again taken to the county jail and held on a charge of grand larceny, and it took considerable manœuvring on the part of Paul to get him free. I think my song-writing brother even went so far as to make the pardon granted by the judge dependent upon Rome's immediately leaving the city. At any rate, he left, after another of those trying scenes between him and mother. And this time he was gone for three years or more, during which there was constant worry on her part. Where was he? What was he doing? Perhaps sick or in jail. Or dead. To her dying hour, and in spite of everything he did, she felt sorry for him.

And then toward the end of this same second year of our stay in Evansville, an affectional difference between Paul and his lady arose, due, I believe, to his decidedly promiscuous and variable disposition. I have never known a man more interested in women from the sex point of view (unless perchance it might be myself), nor one to whom women were more attracted. Amazingly attractive, the women of the world in which he moved as well as others of different levels were constantly on his trail with proffers of diversion and support. He began early and, like Jack Falstaff, died unregenerate. He was a genial and lovable Lothario or Don Juan, devoting his time, thought, energy and money to his unquenchable desire.

And yet, for the virtues of sweetness, liberality and charity, I commend him to your memory. He had little or no knowledge of social organisation or government, and little understanding of the social virtues. It was useless to talk to him of the welfare of the state. Not that he was not imbued with that enthusiasm for America and things American known as patriotism, but he knew little apart from the theories or pretences of those whom he encountered. An unregenerate sex enthusiast, he was still a good Catholic. A wanton invader, he was still desirous that the integrity of his own family be respected. His sisters, for instance, should be virtuous, his brothers also. Yet in so far as all other sisters were concerned, they were just girls to be sought and overcome if possible.

Need I point out that such a disposition might naturally give rise to difficulties where the affections were concerned? His lady was his elder by four or five years at least, and being human, she was humanly jealous, all the more so perhaps because she was her lover's senior. And eventually differences arose between them over his affairs with others. One of the girls in the house of Annie Brace, as he afterwards told me, managed to lure him away for a week and was thereafter summarily dismissed (though he was not) after all but a riot. Also another woman, of financial if not social position in Evansville, became interested in him, whereupon followed quarrels and separations covering days and even weeks. At the same time, whether he said so or not, he was probably finding his family a burden, even though by now it was already partially self-sustaining.

At any rate, and for some reason not by any means clear to me at the time, it began to look as though it would be better if he took to the road again and the family move somewhere else. And this was actually what happened toward the opening of our third spring in Evansville. A family conference was held, and because of the widely heralded growth of Chicago and the fact that Eleanor, Ruth and Amy were working there, the wind of favour was set to blowing in that direction. I have no knowledge or recollection of how the finances were eventually adjusted, but I do know that Paul agreed to contribute regularly and the others were to work and make up the difference. One of the girls—Ruth, I believe—always the most eager to do something for her mother—secured a rear six-room apartment in West Madison Street in Chicago, and finally we left. Al remained behind, since there was a girl in Evansville who interested him, and Paul allied himself with Rice & West's Minstrels as end man. Within the next year or two he established himself as blackface monologist at Tony Pastor's and The London Varieties in New York, and we did not see him again for several years.

CHAPTER XXIX

THE city of which I am now about to write never was on land or sea; or if it appears to have the outlines of reality, they are but shadow to the glory that was in my own mind. Compassed by a shell or skull, there was a mirror inside me which coloured all it reflected. There was some mulch of chemistry that transmuted walls of yellow brick and streets of cedar block and horses and men into amethyst and gold and silver and pegasi and archangels of flaming light. There was a lute or harp which sang as the wind sings. The city of which I sing was not of land or sea or any time or place. Look for it in vain! I can scarcely find it in my own soul now.

Hail, Chicago! First of the daughters of the new world! Strange illusion of hope and happiness that resounded as a pæan by your lake of blue! Here came the children of the new world and the old, avid for life and love, seeking a patrimony. How glorious was your substance in the hearts of those who wrought you! Of what dreams and songs were your walls and ways compounded!

What a privilege to come as a child and see a modern city in the making! I have described my feelings on entering Evansville, but this was so much more wonderful and beautiful. I had heard so much of Chicago. Rome had come and reported the magic of its temperament. Then Al had gone, not once but several times, and had returned to sing of Halstead Street and State and Madison and the lake and the great factories and the river. Then had gone Eleanor and Ruth and Janet and Amy, to return with more tales of its wonders. And now we were all to be there. In northern Indiana, not so very far from Chicago, had been my mother's home after her marriage—in Fort Wayne, no less—and here, at this time in a village called Benton she still owned a small tract of land (five acres) willed to her by her father, which she was anxious either to sell, farm or occupy. In the intricate and curious planning and counter-planning that was constantly going on in our family, the occupation or sale of this land had become inexplicably involved with its proximity to Chicago and the wisdom of locating at this latter place in order to manipulate it. I cannot quite straighten it all out in my own mind, but I think the general idea was that we would first try Chicago and if that did not prove as practicable as she now hoped, mother would take her three youngest to Benton, where she could live cheaply and send us to school, while the others would work in Chicago until such time as conditions warranted a change.

Never was there such a dreamer or mental web-spinner as my mother! Her eye was always on the future, where lay wonder and delight, if not fame and power. Like the thick smoke that rises from the glow of a few small coals, so rose her fancy, glorifying the very air. For such enthusiastic individualists as her children were proving to be, there must certainly be a glorious future. I think a part of the love of her children for her was due to her faith in and enthusiasm for them. Something in her eye, her words, her half-spoken dreams, built up in each one of us a longing to go forth and do. I cannot recall a single one of my youthful plans for the future in which, somehow, my mother was not included.

Our apartment (secured by Ruth) was one in a row of cream-coloured flats, two blocks in extent, on West Madison Street at Throop. It was a semi-bright, semi-gloomy affair of six rooms on the third floor. Its windows lighted a kitchen and general living room and looked over a great central space or inner court which was flanked on both sides by great yellow blocks like our own. The "yards," about twenty-five by forty feet each, at the rear of these houses or flats were divided by high, solid wooden fences. An alley system shaped like an H served on all four sides.

Across the street in front, and covering the entire block, was the old—but now disappeared—Waverly Theatre and, in summer, open-air beer garden, where nightly was to be heard music and the applause of a pleasurably entertained public. For here, too, was dancing—in the mornings roller-skating for the young—and along its roof's edge, on all three sides, bright-coloured flags—of all nations, I presume. It was perhaps this gay place, with its crowds night and morning, that gave to Ruth her zest for this vicinity.

At any rate, there we were. And as for myself, I was not long in discovering various interesting things. There were hucksters, calling out all manner of wares, from kindling to vegetables, and collectors of rags, iron, bones and gum-shoes. They drove rickety wagons attached to equally rickety horses and lifted their voices in an appealing singsong way. And there were so many strange types to be seen from our rear windows: Russian Jews, with long beards and long coats; Poles, Irish, Germans, Swedes, and ordinary Americans, all buying or calling out something.

And then the rats! At this time Chicago was the City of Rats. (I think the word "rats" as a disbelieving or contemptuous term originated there.) Immense ones, the product of an amazingly deficient sewer and garbage system, were constantly scampering to and fro in the alleys and occasionally in the streets. They even uncovered garbage pails, rooting out scraps and hurrying away. Some of them were almost as large as small cats, ferocious and defiant, holding at bay not only cats but dogs. Along with other boys of the neighbourhood a little later, Ed and I fished for rats with corn or bread on a hook lowered into sewers or rat-holes or through windows that gave on to dank basements. When caught they were killed, of course. Another of our tricks was to place bread or fruit outside a given hole and when a rat appeared, stone it. However destructive our intentions, almost always we failed, so swift the rats and so scattering our showers of rocks.

In addition, there were cats and dogs, droves of them, probably attracted by the rats. Also maids in white aprons and caps, who hung out clothes—for this was a residence neighbourhood of a better sort at that time. In Monroe Street, paralleling Madison to the south was a charming little park—Waverly, I think it was called—where people sat of an evening and viewed a small lake, upon which were bright-coloured boats for hire. Before our very windows also was a constant and varying panorama: girls or women who made endless toilets near open windows; clerks who came bustling in at five-thirty or six to dress, lounge in a hammock in a yard, or rush forth to evening engagements. Also there were those who attempted small gardens or window-boxes, or who sat and read or walked to and fro enjoying their 25 × 40 evening worlds. Betimes, by day or evening, great fleecy or black thunderheads which preceded thunder-showers showed over the tops of the houses. Pigeons and sparrows flew here and there, the only visible birds other than canaries in cages. Window shades or curtains flapped or stirred idly in the breeze. Pianos sounded, voices sang, occasionally a zither or mandolin was heard. Lights glowed in the shadows at night. This was the Chicago of our block.

It is not necessary for me to say that all this made a deep impression on me. I was for watching it for ever, the theatre over the way, the park in the next street, or, hanging out of one of our windows, the rear panorama. It was all so different from anything I had ever seen or known. In Evansville was no such congestion, no such moving tide of people, no such enthusiasm for living. I was lost in a vapour of something so rich that it was like food to the hungry, odorous and meaningful like flowers to those who love. Life was glorious and sensate, avid and gay, shimmering and tingling. I recall that at four o'clock of our first afternoon there, leaning out of one of these back windows surveying this new world, I fell asleep from sheer weariness of wonder—the tinkling of street-car bells, the noises of distant wagons and engine-whistles and bells sounding gratefully in my drowsy ears.

How shall one hymn, let alone suggest, a city as great as this in spirit? Possibly it had six or seven hundred thousand population at this time. To it, and at the rate of perhaps fifty thousand or more a year, were hurrying all of the life-hungry natives of a hundred thousand farming areas, of small cities and towns, in America and elsewhere. The American of this time, native, for the most part, of endless backwoods communities, was a naïve creature, coming with all the notions which political charlatans of the most uninformed character had poured into his ears. He was gauche, green, ignorant. But how ambitious and courageous! (Think of our family!) Such bumptiousness! Such assurance! Such a mixture of illusions concerning God, the characteristics of the human animal, and himself! He was distinctly one thing the while he was ever imagining himself another.

Would that I might sense it all again! Would that I were able to suggest in prose the throb and urge and sting of my first days in Chicago! A veritable miracle of pleasing sensations and astounding and fascinating scenes. The spirit of Chicago flowed into me and made me ecstatic. Its personality was different from anything I had ever known; it was a compound of hope and joy in existence, intense hope and intense joy. Cities, like individuals, can flare up with a great flare of hope. They have that miracle, personality, which as in the case of the individual is always so fascinating and so arresting.

A free agent, for the summer at least, I wandered alone or with Ed over the nearer portions of the city, watching the paving of the streets, the manufacturing processes of factories as seen through windows, the stores, the crowds. Once, for a few days, I secured a place as cash-boy in a west side dry-goods store on Madison Street (Tuohy & Company, I think it was), but something intervened to take me out of it very soon. I think my mother decided I was too young to work, or I may have complained. I have a faint recollection of an afternoon or two spent on a wooden bench in a great store, with a signal box opposite showing the number of the counter calling, and to which I was to run and carry a bundle. But my thoughts were so nebulous and cloudy, so immaterial and unorganised, that I could scarcely gain a working conception of what it was all about—where the counter, what the errand—simple as it was. The people tramping about the store, the counters of material, the hurrying clerks, were all so strange and confusing. I became frightened, abashed, ashamed, and even mentally confused, or like one slightly out of his senses. More, I wanted to cry. (And I was twelve years old!) My mother, sensing something of all this, decided that I need not return.

But there was one thing that did appeal to me, and that was selling newspapers—a thing with but few aspects of solid commerciality or industry as here conducted, but which every idle youth of the vicinity under ten years of age seemed to enjoy attempting. In those days there were scarcely any newsstands, in the modern sense. This deficiency—if so it might be called—was more than supplied by a host of impromptu newsboys who visited the nearest distributing centres for papers, buying them at half price and selling them for the full value stamped on the face of the paper. *The Evening News*, *The Evening Mail* and perhaps one or two others were in existence, but the one that sold most, and at one cent, was *The News*.

I think it was due to Ed that we came to be newsboys. He was always so quick to associate himself with one type of urchin and another, and from one of the boys in our block he had learned how and where this evening sale of papers was conducted. Anyway, it was not long before each of us was investing as much as ten and fifteen cents a day in papers. If luck favoured us, we were through with our sales by six-thirty or seven and so ready to invest our profits in candy or some athletic article we very much wanted. A student of character would have known that we were not destined to be merchants by the thriftless manner in which we spent our gains. One of the things that dawned on my fancy on our arrival here was cream caramels. Underneath our apartment was a manufacturing confectioner whose windows were always full of these tempting delicacies and whose place was as deliciously odorous as heaven itself. Long before I had finished selling my papers I would be thinking of the fine time I would have eating caramels or ice cream. And once or twice, the confectioner, seeing me looking longingly into his window, commissioned me to carry pans of caramels to a certain State Street store, for which he gave me car-fare and some caramels besides. In consequence, I was beside myself with joy and a sense of prosperity. For was there not this ride, the caramels, the sights of the city, all combining to form a symphony of entertainment and delight? The memory of it thrills me to this hour. Life-hunger was the spirit of me.

In regard to our newspaper vending, though, quite invariably we confined our merchandising to our own block. Neither Ed nor myself was much for pioneering as yet; even our defensive courage was not too great, barely enough to keep us in fair countenance with ourselves. And so these narrow confines. But in regard to another matter, how different! For although it was against the local ordinance, even then, for boys to jump on and off the ambling horse-cars which crowded this street, and conductors were most persistent in their enforcement of this rule, still, since the majority of sales were to be made to those homeward bound on these open-air cars, it was a delight as well as a profitable adventure to jump on and off them and make these quick exchanges on their running boards. In my case the opportunity for riding outweighed even the hope of profit, and the rage of the busily employed conductors troubled me no more than it did the others. But once, and once only, I jumped on a car to sell a paper and the man gave me a nickel to change. Thinking it a penny, I jumped off. There were cries after me but I did not understand until the car had gone on a full half block. Instantly the matter of ethics was injected into the situation. I became conscious of the matter of equation or something for something which is at the bottom of all commercial transactions. This man should have had his four cents back. Yet I hesitated. The man could not get off and catch me if I didn't want to be caught, nor could I very well catch the car, and so I stood there. Had the nickel tempted me? Yes! Only and just the same I was not so glad afterward; rather I was sorry and secretly ashamed. Nevertheless, I spent the nickel, trusting that if the man ever saw me again and demanded the return of his money, I would have the cash, and at the same time wishing I were not so evil as to want to take money in this way.

CHAPTER XXX

IT was not long after we arrived in Chicago that my father paid us a visit, and with him I gained an even clearer conception of the size and character of the city. For the few weeks of his visit I was for some reason invited to accompany him on all of his rambles. I am satisfied that he had never seen the city before, and besides being impressed by its already great size, he was more than astonished by the hourly visible growth that was everywhere in evidence. I have seen New York and Los Angeles grow—furiously, as it were—adding homes and stores for as many as fifty to one hundred thousand people in a single year. But the impression of rapid growth gained in Chicago at that time has never since been equalled for me by any other city.

At that time the city was protected from the lake by a retaining wall of piles and earth, since the land lay below the lake level. In consequence, all streets and sidewalks had to be built up from four to six feet above the land level. This was accomplished by laying parallel walls as far apart as the proposed width of the street and then filling in between them with ashes, tin cans, rock or earth. On top of this, once it had been rolled by a steam roller, was laid two-inch planking eight or ten inches wide, and on top of this again, round cedar blocks six inches in length (or height). Over this was poured sand as fill, then gravel and tar, making a clean and delightfully odorous roadway which was most satisfactory as long as it bore up against the traffic. But as the "fill" packed down and heavy trucks wore down the edges of the blocks, it became a wavy and even jagged mess in places, and sometimes the cedar blocks were torn out by the residents in the tenement sections and used as firewood.

But at the time of which I am writing, the streets were mostly new and sightly. In addition they were being lined by red and yellow and grey and cream-coloured brick apartment or flat houses, in anticipation of waves of people that would presently flow in. There was the Chicago River, too, a stream so dirty, narrow and traffic-laden that it was ever a source of wonder and delight. I had never seen a tug before, nor any masted vessel, large or small. And this river was full of them, to say nothing of steamships far superior to the steamboats on the Ohio River. Swinging bridges spanned the river at various streets, and through their draws passed a procession of ships all day long. The city tinkled and whistled and clattered of life and trade. Along the lake front " downtown," was a narrow strip of land, faced on the land side by small stores and livery stables and on the lake side by a wooden wall, to which small yachts and passenger boats pinioned themselves in expectation of trade, and from which scores of fishermen were constantly fishing. And caught many fish, principally perch. Eastward over the lake, the skyline was broken by a "crib" or protecting breakwater of wood and stone. On a sunny day it was wonderful to see this seemingly shoreless body of blue water dotted with white sails, great woolly argosies of clouds floating above.

Those days in Chicago marked my first really intimate contact with my father, for since leaving Terre Haute four or five years before we had seen little of him. Now he was here for about a month (the mill with which he was connected having shut down), and during that time we walked and talked, he having conceived an actual fancy for me—or perhaps I would better call it an affectional admiration—which lasted until he died. And now, and for the first time, I began to sense a little of his personality, which apart from religion, if only one could have disentangled it, was mild and observant enough. He liked nature and character, and where religion was not involved, could make amusing and sometimes quite clarifying comments about people—their abilities, lacks, eccentricities and the like. And while I had always resented —and still did—his driving, dictatorial and even harsh author- ity, now I began to feel the least bit sorry for him. Already he was so clear an illustration of the beaten or at best psychically depressed man, and was ready to admit even to me that he could not very well bring himself to enter upon any other contest with the world, however generous or inviting the opportunity. (At that time he was but sixty-one or two and, as time proved, still had twenty years of life before him.) At the same time, he was not in the position of one who lacked a trade or profession. He had a very good one, or two or three. He could qualify as manager of a woollen mill or a buyer or tester of wool, and lastly, if least, as a master machinist in so far as wool-weaving machines were concerned, since he could set up and operate quite every machine used. And why it was he lacked the courage of his own value, I to this day fail to understand. For all of thirty years he had been an expert in everything relating to wool and its various manufacturing processes. In fact, the Wabash Mill, of Terre Haute, also the Vigo Mill, rarely operated without seeking his services as superintendent or general factotum in charge of every process. Only they were so often shut down in those days and he did not trouble to look elsewhere.

One of the Ellis Brothers, who in that day controlled the well-known Wabash Mill, once told me (years later) that there never was a better buyer of wool than my father; nor one that knew more about wool and its manufacture. "All that your father lacked to become one of the most successful woollen manufacturers was the courage to go ahead and organise another plant of his own," he said. "But after that fire and accident in Sullivan he seemed to lack initiative and to be afraid that he wouldn't come out all right. And then toward the last, he seemed to be so wrapped up in religion that he couldn't think of anything else."

And I know this to be a true statement, for so late as 1900, at which time he was eighty-one years old, the American Woollen Company of Massachusetts sent a representative to him offering him a salary of twenty thousand dollars a year as expert adviser in connection with their buying forces. But by then, of course, his strength was gone.

But at this time in Chicago, he was still a man of strength and energy. A little success in his own field would have made a most presentable and satisfactory figure of him, and he could have forced that success. Here was a great new city, fairly thrilling and shouting with opportunity. In Water Street were scores of merchants who dealt in wool, and in northern Illinois and Indiana were several woollen mills with which, with his experience and reputation, he might easily have identified himself. Far from being an ignoramus, he was a man of considerable experience if not culture. He had travelled no little in France and Germany and America; had lived in Paris for several years, from which place, with several German and French adventurers, he had set sail for America. In Dayton, Fort Wayne and Terre Haute he had been either foreman or superintendent in the different mills, and in Sullivan he had operated his own mill. (If you were to look at St. Joseph's Roman Catholic Church there, you would behold land given by him to that organisation, and inside you would find a stained glass window bearing his name as donor.) Yet at the time of which I speak he was a man already lost in religious zealotry and absolutely bankrupt of courage and initiative. Life was a dark, religious mystery presided over by a jealous and vengeful God.

Nothing in Chicago, therefore, concerned him quite as much at this time as the whereabouts of a Roman Catholic Church and school. Troubled by the labour of getting settled, my mother had not looked up any church, but now he found one and we were all made to go. This irritated and at the same time interested me, for much as I might dislike the routine of the Catholic Church, it was ever of interest to me as a spectacle, and I was never weary of comparing a new church and its priests with those of some other, Holy Trinity, for instance, in Evansville. But it soon developed that this church was not as pretentious as the last one of which we were a part, and the small, drab, wooden school attached, with various rosary-clicking, wide-bonneted nuns fluttering about, filled me with my usual disgust. Yet since this was very early summer, the horror of another Catholic school was a few months away, and so not as oppressive as otherwise it might have been.

CHAPTER XXXI

ANOTHER matter, and of more interest, was that here and for the first time in my life I felt the tang and pang of love. It came about in this way. Among the idling boys and girls of this vicinity was one girl dwelling in this very block—across our alley—and in one of the better private homes facing on Throop Street, who on sight struck me dumb with delight and desire. Only to touch her hand, say, or look into her eyes and have them respond, or, her mood favouring me, to kiss her red, full lips! Ah! For she was a gay, shapely, buxom, young hoyden of perhaps ten or twelve, and for days after my first glimpse of her, I could scarcely sleep. Her face, her eyes, her hair, her smile, her gestures!

For the second, third and fourth decades of my life—or from fifteen to thirty-five—there appeared to be a toxic something in form itself—that of the female of the species where beautiful—that could effect veritable paroxysms of emotion and desire in me, and that over distances of time and space. The mystery! The subtleties of physics and chemistry behind it! The suggestion of possible intention in it all—or an eternal system! We call it love. A word! Any other label that implies that a chemical formula such as a human temperament, embodied as flesh and displayed as a design, can evoke, in another such form, emotion and so release and exchange tides of desire and sensual relationship, would do as well. The form of a woman is the best expression of that design or geometric formula, and the word "aphrodisiac" (Aphrodite) the best expression of the power of that form or formula upon its companion formula, the male.

Let us say that my blood has been either ill or well compounded, as you will. But because of this pre-arranged system —about the perfection of which certain forces in nature appear to be so busy and which the self-constituted religionists and moralists appear to be incapable of either examining or explaining—I have thrilled again and again from head to toe, the sight of this particular formula (female) resulting in the invasion of homes, the destruction of happy arrangements among others, lies, persuasions, this, that. In short, thus moved, I have adored until satiated, so satiated, indeed, as to turn betimes in weariness, even disgust, and so fleeing. Whether this, in the last analysis and from any test arising out of or evoked by the needs of organised society or the rights or pleasures of the individual, is ill or not, I cannot say. I commend it at once to the biologists, economists, and philosophers for examination. Certain it is that the religionists and moralists have already been heard from sufficiently, and in vain. It is time for science to speak.

But to return to this girl, this charming child. Was she as beautiful as I thought she was? She may have been. She was wonderful to me then. Hundreds of such girls have come and gone since I saw her, yet the joy and tensity and agony holds from generation to generation, age after age. Moralists come and go; religionists fulminate and declare the pronouncements of God as to this; but Aphrodite still reigns. Embowered in the festal depths of spring, set above her altars of porphyry, chalcedony, ivory and gold, see her smile the smile that is at once the texture and essence of delight, the glory and despair of the world! Dream on, oh Buddha, asleep on your lotus leaf, of an undisturbed Nirvana! Sweat, oh Jesus, your last agonising drops over an unregenerate world! In the forests of Pan still ring the cries of the worshippers of Aphrodite! From her altars the incense of adoration ever rises! And see, the new red grapes dripping where votive hands new-press them!

But there was a flaw in all this, as I soon discovered, and a most inimical one. For there was a boy whom she favoured far beyond me, if ever she gave me so much as a considered glance, and he, as I soon discovered, was one of those self-impressed as well as highly courageous youthful dandies of the neighbourhood who presumably lorded it over a small but faithful group of boys that attended him wherever he went. And perhaps it was this very girl, upon whom I persisted in gazing in such an awe- as well as love-stricken way, who called me to his attention. At any rate, and presently, I became very definitely aware of him, for not only did I see him once chase and kiss her in the alley directly below our apartment, but later, seeing me standing in the street doorway of our building, he stopped and looked at me, most contemptuously, as I thought. But there was no word or action of any kind at the time.

Yet even so, my admiration persisted. I could not desist from looking at her admiringly. And whether this news, favourable or unfavourable, was carried to the youth I have just mentioned, I do not know, but certainly, and in the course of a very few days, a very definite thing happened. I was standing in the doorway as before, or just outside of it, when, either accidentally or intentionally, this youth, with his attendant satellites, appeared and approached. I was conscious now of a cool, handsome, sophisticated and well-dressed "lady killer." On the little finger of his left hand (as I have good reason to recall), he wore a turquoise ring, and in his scarf a gold stick-pin. His clothes were arrestingly superior to mine as well as those of all of the other boys who attended him: a fact which seemed to me at the time to set him apart as a creature of a much better world than mine, someone with whom it would be a delight to associate on equal terms. But, and for all my *parvenu* ideas, this was not to be. Instead, on seeing me—and as if to demonstrate to me how brash and foolish I was so much as to venture to look at the girl in whom he was interested—he now came forward, and surveying me coldly, asked of one of his attendants: "Isn't this the fellow?" "Yes," returned this Achates. Without more ado, he walked over to me, and without a word the hand with the ring shot out! It caught and cut my lip. At once I was aware of the import of it all—his recognition of my effrontery and his desire to show me my place—yet thinking myself the weaker, and in consequence horribly ashamed and dismayed, I stood there, making no move other than the one intended to protect myself from a second blow. With a lordly air of strength and contempt, he surveyed me the while I nursed my cut mouth. Then lifting the ring finger of his left hand, he said, with an easy air: "That ring always cuts my finger. I ought to take it off," and so walked away.

A day or two later I saw him talking to the paragon of maidenly beauty who was not for me, and for want of sufficient fighting courage at the time, I was compelled instead to think keenly on my lack of strength, or rather, courage, and the ills to which it was now subjecting me. Also the indifference with which this paragon of beauty would think on me—if at all— once she knew. Surely, the battle was to the swift, the race to the strong. And yet at last I swelled with a great rage against myself, which in time bore fruit enough.

CHAPTER XXXII

THE arrangement for the support of the family in Chicago was based in part, I am sure, on the supposition that the majority of all present would obtain employment and contribute each a fixed amount, any delinquency to be made up by a cash contribution from my brother Paul, he being by now presumably prosperous and hence, and justly, the proper prey of his dependent relatives. Secondly, there was my father, who although slipping along in years and most unremuneratively and irregularly employed, was still assumed to be able to assist in carrying at least a part of this burden—(out of what deeps of nature came this law?)—although his chief mental concern was the liquidation of family debts incurred years before. This labour, according to him, involved his spiritual salvation—his entry into heaven, as it were—and so debarred him from any important contributions and, more, of any normal enjoyment of his stay here on earth.

But there were other hitches. Work for all (and this in spite of the brisk energy of the city), was not always obtainable or continuous. Besides, my brother Paul (due to personal difficulties of his own, I assume) was not always heard from. As I learned afterwards, his stage or, as one might otherwise see it, his industrial life, had been affected by his disastrous love life. Certainly he was all but felled temporarily by the desertion of his Annie and for a number of months, as he told me later, could barely endure this fleeting thing we call life. Actually, a few years later—as many as five or six—he embodied his bitterness in a most melodramatic and yet somewhat arresting song which he titled "The Curse." As I recall the words, he cursed his once fascinating sweetheart from one depth of hell or misery to another, until, assuming each curse to have been consecutively and not concurrently applied, she would be—or shall I say, will be?—roasting and boiling, et cetera, until our honourable universe should be or shall have been no more! How's that for a curse? And yet still later, as late as 1897 or '98, he re-embodied his mood in regard to her in a far more appealing ballad and one that is still sung at this date and bids fair to grow in fame and life for many years to come. The name of it—and many may now know it—is "My Gal Sal."

But as bad if not worse were the heart romances of each of the several daughters to be taken into account. For my own confused part, between selling newspapers and running errands for the caramel man downstairs, I was nevertheless dimly aware of a certain emotional activity in connection with my sisters and their suitors; the manufacturer who admired my sister Ruth appearing to take her out driving of an afternoon or evening; the aristocratic Harahan stopping at one of the principal hotels and inviting Eleanor, Ruth and a friend of theirs to dinner; Janet and Amy and even Trina, as young as she was, finding youths or men who, attracted by their looks, were anxious to occupy their time. I might attempt to disentangle what was unquestionably a knot or network of emotions and interests, all relating to the particular love life of each, but I would fail for lack of any real knowledge of the underlying subtleties and beauties—as, of course, beauties and subtleties there were.

I have described, for instance, how Eleanor came to Chicago and met Harahan, but not, I think, how he in turn introduced her and Ruth to the wealthy manufacturer who came to Evansville to visit Ruth. From all appearances, his courtship of Ruth, or at least his friendship for her, was sanctioned by my mother. Whether this was wise or unwise, I cannot say. He was much older albeit a widower and wealthy. My one idea of it is that as usual my mother was at once strangely nebulous and optimistic. She had no ability to advise shrewdly in a situation of this kind, had she thought it important to advise. Being dubious of life and its various manifestations, I think she thought it as well to let her daughters face their own problems—a viewpoint with which I find myself in agreement. Life is to be learned from life, and in no other way. That Ruth was obviously intrigued by this man I came to know when I chanced to enter the apartment one day when all of the others were out and discovered her in his arms. By what arrangement, if any, he chanced to be there, I do not know. No doubt, she had calculated on the house being empty. At any rate, she requested me afterward to say nothing about it, and while I was shocked or moved in a strange way, I did as she wished. It seemed to me that my sister, being so much older, should be able to regulate her own life.

Similarly, Janet, who had been chided for her conduct this long while, had on coming to Chicago taken up with an able and well-to-do, though somewhat aged, architect, and was now living with him in a hotel on South Halstead Street. I recall her giving Ed and myself a meal ticket issued by a semi-public restaurant attached to this hotel and afterwards being invited to her rooms in the absence of the liege lord. I was filled with wonder at her clothes, furniture and the like, which seemed to contrast more than favourably with our own. Her boudoir dressing-table, for instance, was piled with bright silver toilet articles and a closet into which I peered was plentifully supplied with clothes. Janet herself looked prosperous and cheerful. I remember going back through the grey, foggy streets of Chicago, looking at the huge sign-boards of the shows then playing: "Humpty Dumpty," "Eight Bells"—and thinking how fine it all was.

Moral problems such as the lives of my several sisters presented to me had no great weight. And have not now—any more than do those of other men's sisters or daughters. It is the way of life, however much socially it may be denied, concealed, or disguised. At times, assuming I heard someone else discussing them moralistically—my father, say—I was inclined to experience a depression or reduction in pride which was purely osmatic—a process of emotional absorption—no more. Had I not heard someone else criticising, I would not have been so moved. And yet, at times, and because of this, I had the notion that they were not doing right; that men (this must have been gathered from my father's many preachments) were using them as mere playthings; but most of the time I had a feeling that they were their own masters, or might be if they would. Also that perhaps they enjoyed being playthings. Why not? And through it all ran the feeling that good, bad, or indifferent as individuals or things might be, life was a splendid surge, a rich sensation, and that it was fine to be alive. And in so far as my sister Janet was concerned, my final feeling was that she was prosperous and individual and perhaps as well off as some others, if not more so.

But to return to my sister Eleanor. Being in love and waiting to be taken over completely by Harahan, she was leading a trying, and yet to her, I assume, invaluable life. In later years I heard all about the love woes of this period: the eagerness for letters, the despair at not receiving them, the agony of suspecting other flirtations, and so on and so forth. Until at last she had found herself desperately in love with this man, as she once told me, she had been moderately entertained by the admirations and attentions of first one man and then another. But mere flirtations these—not complete sex relations. She had not been sufficiently interested. The thought that comes to me now, though, is that by reason of criticism on the part of others—taboos and the like—and however generally evaded or ignored—we do not prefer to contemplate these youthful sex variations, either in real life or in literature. And yet, how common! You may measure the thinness of literature and of moral dogma and religious control by your own observations and experiences. Look back over your own life and see!

CHAPTER XXXIII

OTHER phases of this Chicago life were more amusing than anything else. Thus, there was a musician and his wife living on the floor above us—I remember them well —who disagreed so constantly as to the various details of their life as to constitute a nuisance. The husband in this instance was a short, stocky, almost beefy individual, whose musical ability consisted in a certain mediocre mastery of the bass horn but who seemed to make up for any artistic weakness in that direction by his greater ability to drink and gamble. His wife was young, tow-headed, talkative and irascible. And not infrequently they fell afoul of each other. And to such an extent as to make the night in this particular flat building hideous. Liar! Dog! Brute! Bitch! Who the hell were you when I married you? What do I care? Suppose I am drunk! I'll kick the blank-blank furniture out the window! A large airshaft carried the sounds perfectly and in our bed-rooms beneath we were entertained by all this and in addition the slamming of doors and squeals and screeches of opposition or protest on the part of the wife as occasionally she was choked or beaten or chased to the street—or all three. In due time, of course, aroused neighbours would get up and threaten to complain to the police, but as a rule, the midnight, or later, storm ran its course without outside interference.

One night, though, our family was brought into the matter by an exceptional row, which began in a storm of curses and blows and ended with knives, spoons and crockery being hurled into the airshaft and falling with a resounding crash into the basement. My father, who was visiting us at the time, was highly indignant.

"What is this, then?" he asked, in German, putting his head out of the shaft window and looking upward. "Hey, you! Stop this now! This is enough! Some of your stuff is falling in our window."

"What's that, you German stiff? Who the hell are you? I'll throw something at you if you get fresh!"

"Yah," replied my father. "Just you do that once! I show you yet!" Scandalised beyond belief at this sudden burst of life, he surveyed the rest of us who had gathered. "That scoundrel!" he added, deeply incensed. "He has done enough now! He should be arrested!"

Some additional screams and a shower of plates convincing him that a policeman should be called, he set forth and in a very little while returned with one—a large Irishman—who rapped vigorously at the musician's door.

"What do you want?" came a liquorish, contentious voice from within.

"Open the door, will yez! It's an officer. Be openin' it now!"

Whereupon silence, and then the door, after the policeman had shaken it vigorously, opened. And within standing, in shirt and trousers, the cause of all the row, this irate and contentious musician, his hair awry, his face flushed, and in his cups.

"What's the trouble here?" demanded the policeman. "Whad'ye mean, throwin' things down the airshaft and kapin' people up all hours of the night?"

"Who's keepin' who up?" inquired the musician, belligerently and yet evasively. "I don't know of any trouble outside my own rooms."

"Yes!" declared my father. "He says that now because you are here. A while ago he was going to hit me with something. He's been throwing things down the airshaft. Yust look! This isn't the first time either!"

"Who are you?" demanded the furioso, truculently. "Can't I have an argument in my own home if I want?"

"Yes, and throw dishes down the airshaft, and beat your wife!" declared my father, who was choking with excitement.

"Come now," continued the policeman, "none of that now!" Then to my father: "You say he's been throwin' things down the airshaft? Do you want to make a charge against him?"

"Will you be good?" inquired my father, mellowing slightly and feeling perhaps that it was rather hard on this man after all that he should be thus summarily yanked off to jail when behind him were his wife and a three-year-old child.

But instead of seizing upon this kindly-proffered opportunity of escaping, he replied, and as truculently as ever: "Why should I talk to you? Who are you? I don't want to talk to you at all!"

"Come now, what do you want to do? Say the word and I'll take him off. Do you want to make a charge?" (This from the officer to my father.)

Always soft-hearted, my father hesitated until someone in the crowd behind him (a woman) exclaimed: "He ought to be arrested. This is getting to be an every-night affair. He's just a nasty, wife-beating brute!"

"Well, then take him along," said my father. "I'll make a charge."

A small company, including myself, followed them interestedly to the street, where the policeman rang for a patrol wagon. And the next morning my father, as a reward for his civic service, had to be up and dressed by seven in order to appear at some downtown police court at nine. And more, had the severe satisfaction of seeing the musician fined twenty-five dollars and remanded to jail, since he was unable to pay it. And so sorrow on my father's part. For by now he was regretful. Did not the man have a wife and child and job? And what about them now? In a reduced Teutonic mood he commented on all this afterwards. It was certainly too bad—a strong and in other respects well-conducted man getting himself in such trouble through drink! Ach!

But the usual unsatisfactory sequel to all this, you may be sure. For the next morning, Mrs. Musician, no longer drunk and by now sorrowful and repentant, was at the police court to plead for her rampant husband. And my father being the soul of truthfulness, compelled by his own conscience to repeat all he had seen, heard and suffered. And so, the husband in jail, the lachrymose wife descending on us to explain how hard this would be on him and her. For where would she find twenty-five dollars? And there was his work (at some theatre). And this and that. "Oh, weary I—that ever I was born to set this world aright!"

At any rate, my father and mother and sisters in a long, sad conversation with this woman in regard to her past woes and present ills. For to be sure, he was a bad husband and abused her shamefully, but after all, was not he the only husband she had? And worked nearly regularly. The fact that she would have to pawn all her trinkets, etc., in order to pay his fine was brought out. And now, my mother and several sisters, being soft-hearted and sociable—the latter inclined to make friends where too often it was best they should not—were moved and interested to such an extent as to seek to devise ways of raising the necessary twenty-five! And thereafter not infrequently calling in order to console her. Only the husband, outraged by his irritating arrest, returning after a few days, not only to beat but also to attempt to chloroform his good wife—or so it was said. The purpose of this latter act was truly not quite clear. His wife's belief, later related to all, was that he had attempted to kill her and then depart for ever—a deed which the method employed did not make plausible. For he did no more than fill the room one night with fumes from a sponge dipped in chloroform and laid near her nose as she slept. But the purpose of that, as some argued, was for no other reason than to secure his various belongings without either detection or opposition, and so to depart in peace. (I trust so.) But awakening the following morning to find this strange-smelling sponge close to her nose, the air in the room stifling and herself suffering from an intense nausea, she proclaimed attempted murder. Whether any legal action was ever taken by her or others I have no knowledge.

CHAPTER XXXIV

IT was just at this time that the problem of our making out in Chicago appeared to culminate. For one thing, there was my father, coming here because of a temporary shut-down in Terre Haute and unable to find work, and so a burden. Next, there was the matter of the elder children, who, because of long suffering at his critical hands and because of the practical contributions they were making from time to time toward the support of the home, were no longer prepared to listen, much less accept, his diatribes on conduct. They had seen too much of life and unquestionably had suffered too much because of the want of a practical education, the result of enforced attendance at Catholic schools. And since their freedom of conduct was continually criticised by him, it was soon a question of whether he would desist or go away or whether they would leave—at least some of them—and so destroy this home.

From hearsay—words dropped by my mother or sisters—I gathered that all was not as easy here as in Evansville. For one thing, there was the matter of rent—"only thirty-five dollars," as one would say of it now, but exceedingly high after none at all in Evansville and only seven or eight in Sullivan. Next, there was the monthly—or perhaps it was weekly—payment on six hundred dollars' worth of furniture bought on the easy payment plan from a large West Side furniture house—some twenty-five dollars per month—and which had to be paid regularly or after the lapse of two payments the furniture would be removed and the money paid in lost. As something like seventy-five dollars had been paid down originally and several payments since made, this was a real burden as well as a fear. Then the idleness and expense of us three youngest—assumed to be too young to work—as well as the maintenance of my mother—the total constituting a considerable and not easily met budget.

So presently, a council between my mother and her elder

daughters as to the advisability of removing to some smaller place—preferably near Chicago, for all, or nearly so, were now here—where food and rent would be cheaper and we three youngest could go to school. For by now my mother had awakened to the folly of having sent her children to the parochial schools, since all of the older ones were complaining of the results in their cases. More, in connection with this matter of moving, there was the interesting fact that not far from Chicago—to be exact, 109 miles south-east on the Pennsylvania as well as Nickel Plate Railroad, in northern Indiana—was the very region in which my mother and father had lived shortly after they were married. For, if you will recall, it was in Fort Wayne, Indiana, that my father had had charge of a woollen mill. And it was to Silver Lake and Bourbon, Indiana, that my mother's parents, together with a number of relatives and friends—a kind of Mennonite migration of that day—had gone to settle on farms. At this very time, there was here, or quite near here, a brother who was an elder (the equivalent of a bishop) in the Mennonite or, as it was then known there, United Brethren Church. Also a sister—Susan Arnold by name—married to a farmer near Silver Lake. Again, there was a half-sister of my mother's—that one who was the wife of the prosperous farmer near Manchester, Indiana. But still more important in these trying days was the fact that near Bourbon was that five-acre plot of ground which had been willed my mother by the father who never more in his lifetime would receive her and which might now be reclaimed and either farmed or sold—a reality which in connection with the straitened circumstances of the moment was not to be sneezed at!

And so it was now that after several trips to this region on the part of my mother and her chief confidante, Ruth, and after due consideration of the various pros and cons in the matter, the truly beautiful little city or town of Warsaw, Indiana—some ten or twelve miles east of Bourbon and itself the county seat of this region—was selected: a town to which I owe some of my most helpful as well as most pleasing hours—hours of schooling, of play, of romance, of dreams under the shade of great trees or in swimming holes, lakes, the Tippecanoe River, on ice ponds and snow-covered farms and woodlands that made this region a kind of paradise.

But before this, as you may well guess in connection with

such an impractical group, one of the characteristic incidents which seemed ever and ever to punctuate our family life. I have explained how our furniture was secured. Only I must now add that in connection with this proposed change, this furniture, regardless of the amount still due on it, was—at least as Ruth and Eleanor, who had signed the contract for it, desired and described—to be transferred to Warsaw and thereafter arranged for—well, I scarcely know how—by such payments as could be exacted by a none-too-near and perhaps not even informed creditor. Only under the laws of Illinois, furniture bought on the instalment plan and not yet fully paid for could not be removed from the State without permission of the seller. Since only something like $150 or $175 on a total bill of $600 had been paid and the plan was to remove the furniture first and argue about the legality of it afterwards, there was certainly a question of right and wrong here. Just the same, I am by no means sure that my sister Ruth, who was engineering this matter, was boldly and coldly contemplating fraud. Hers was a decidedly nebulous as well as romantic rather than a directly intellectual temperament, and I seriously believe that her chief thought and sole desire was to make her mother comfortable, the while she schemed out some method of payment less drastic and regular than that agreed upon in the contract. Perhaps not. At any rate, as was later shown, the furniture was to be removed and paid for afterward.

The modus operandi of all this was as follows: my mother was to go to Warsaw with Ed, Trina, and, for the moment, Eleanor, leaving Ruth with myself as companion to follow the next day. On the evening of the day preceding our proposed departure, though, a van was sent for and the furniture (actually still belonging to the furniture company) transferred to the freight house for shipment to Warsaw. Receipts were taken and all was considered well and arranged for—no further troubles of any kind. And we were actually about to start when, lo, and behold, a knock, and since the door of the apartment was not opened immediately, more and fiercer knocks and calls. Then, and in spite of some original plan to the contrary, I believe, the door opened by my pale, golden-haired, dreamy sister, most nervous and disturbed, as you may well guess. And before her a brisk and slender and almost immaculately-arrayed gentleman (cutaway coat, black fedora hat, black shoes, black and proliferous and highly-barbered hair and whiskers) but very angry and threatening—a veritable Jove with his lightnings, no less. And the same the owner of the easy payment furniture house! (Some watchful neighbour —paid to do so, perhaps—had reported.) At any rate, in he strolled, strong, electrifying, determined. And looking around and seeing no furniture, exclaiming: "So! You have removed the furniture, have you? Well, where have you taken it?"

My sister—never one to battle the world as it likes to battle and be battled—was so taken aback by the cold, incisive presence of this man as well as the fact that she had been taken red-handed in her plot, as it were, facing him quite colourless and limp. For a few moments it appeared to me as if she might faint. But recovering herself, she managed to reply: "We're moving."

"Yes, I see that well enough, but where to? Where have you taken the furniture?"

"To the country."

"Some town outside of Chicago?"

"Yes, sir."

"In this State?"

"No, sir; we're moving to Indiana."

"What part of Indiana?"

"I won't tell you. We intend to pay for the furniture. We've paid a hundred and seventy-five dollars as it is."

"Come, now, my fine young lady, none of that! Don't you try to come any game over me. The law in this State doesn't permit you to take any furniture out of the State without the written consent of the owner. You can't even move from one block to another without my permission. It's in the contract. This is plain robbery, and unless you tell me right now where you've sent it, I can and will have you locked up. Now you either tell me the name of the place you're moving to and the depot to which you took the furniture and the name of the moving man that moved you, or I'll call a policeman and clap you in a cell! Now what are you going to do? Go to jail or tell me where the furniture is? I'll have a policeman here in three minutes unless you answer me promptly and truthfully."

Is this the exact conversation? No: the substance as near as I can remember. This grim individual, Mephistophelian in build, stood before us cool and iron. A more sophisticated and worse-intentioned soul might have found some way out of this situation, but not so my sister Ruth. She was too vague and dreamy. Indeed, she seemed quite undone, and meditated only a moment before she said: "Warsaw, Indiana. I sent the furniture to the Pennsylvania freight depot."

"Well, now, that's better. I'm glad to see you acting sensibly. This is a very serious business, my dear young lady. I don't suppose you know that, but it is. I could put you in jail for even attempting to take this furniture away. You must have received a freight receipt for it. Where is it?"

Without a word my sister went to her purse and took out the freight receipt and surrendered it. "But all of this is not yours," she said. "Some of it belongs to us. The barrels and drawers are filled with our things."

The vigorous easy-payment man examined the freight list most carefully. "We only want what belongs to us. You come down to the depot now and I'll permit you to sort out your own things."

There was then and there a humiliating journey in company with this man, which resulted in the separation of our property from his. Everything which we had thus far paid on was by this process lost. The rest—some dishes, clothes, this, that —retained, but not much. And my sister bewildered and in tears. Yet, as she afterwards told me, on the way to the freight depot and later, once the furniture was found and withdrawn from shipment, this frowning Cerberus, cheering up and even troubling to explain the difficulties of his trade. There were so many such losses to endure. The company, because of it, scarcely making anything and so compelled to act thus rudely. More, her personal charms being what they were, himself moved by them. He realised, he said, how trying this must be for a young girl like herself. Was she herself going to Warsaw or was she going to remain in Chicago? She explained that she was going to stay in Chicago, but with relatives, whereupon he added that if the family were to remain in Chicago and ample security could be found, the furniture might be returned (cartage charges, etc., added) and the remainder of the bill permitted to be paid in instalments as before. As ample security could not be furnished, this offer was of small use.

But as someone later pointed out, it was entirely possible that had an open and frank policy been pursued in the first place—the company notified and pleaded with—we might have been permitted to take the furniture to Warsaw. As it was, we lost both furniture and money.

Two years later, my sister Ruth, chancing to visit one of the fashionable churches in Chicago of a Sunday morning, was startled and interested. For who should pass the plate with a most reverent air but this same furniture dealer! (I am not introducing this as a bit of irony on my part; I mention it solely for the purpose of elucidating my sister's view in regard to it—which is more important.)

"There he stood, the sanctimonious old sharp!" was how she expressed herself to me. "Holding out the plate and never even looking at me! You never saw such an air of 'holier than thou'! I don't suppose he would have recognised me. But at the time he found his furniture safe, he wanted to be so nice to me. What a pity such wretches should be permitted to impose upon people, rob the poor all week and go to church on Sunday!"

To which I can only reply: Of such stuff are morals, public opinion, the common understanding of "mine and thine" and so forth, ad infinitum. I leave the subtleties of this for the cogitation of those who can qualify as logicians and expert expounders of ethics and morals and other such passing social arrangements.

CHAPTER XXXV

MOST of the cities and towns of America, to say nothing of the Middle West, have always seemed to me to be deficient in both individuality and charm. Nearly all of them, as one may see in passing, are spotted on the flat prairies, where no water is to be found, and all too often too few trees. And as for architecture! But Warsaw, the town to which my mother and we three youngest now repaired, remains in my memory as one of the most agreeable minor residence towns it has ever been my pleasure to know. At that time it lay in the very centre of three small but beautiful lakes, two of them so close that they formed an integral part of the town, its streets and houses following their nearer shore lines. The third—Eagle (at present Winona)—was only two miles distant from the public square, in the centre of which was the court-house, a pleasing although none too graceful white sandstone building, possibly seventy-five by one hundred feet, with a dome or clock tower possibly a hundred feet high, the four faces of which were to be seen and the great bell within it heard for miles. (I was always charmed by that public square, its court-house and clock.)

Center Lake, the nearest and most accessible of the three, was a quite impressive body all of a mile wide and perhaps half as much again long. On its nearer or town shore—at the foot of Buffalo Street, I believe—stood a handsome boat-house offering all manner of small boats for hire. On the other two —Pike and Eagle—were summer parks or playgrounds, and excellent fishing and boating in all three. On Center and Pike Lakes were not a few small sail craft of the sharpy type and because of the various sandy beaches and wooded spots, attractive settings for picnics and roving expeditions, especially in summertime. Another of the charms of these waters, as I soon came to know, was that they induced a spirit of romance. Many times, from my thirteenth to my sixteenth year, I stood on the shore of one or another of these lakes at evening listening to the music of zither, mandolin or guitar, wind-wafted from some craft off-shore. And in winter as well as summer—and especially after midnight—the lights and fires of fishermen who were fishing with other than hook and lines—a matter locally prohibited by law—might be seen. Indeed Warsaw's lakes and river, its kempt groves and winding lanes, its handsome schools and bright square, are now identified with the most poetic and thrilling of all my youthful moods. How better than by flaming desires, mirage-like moods and anguishing, unfulfilled desires, can the loveliness of any given region be made to endure in the memory of man!

By some misfortune of chance, though, the small brick cottage which my mother first hit upon, though pleasingly and comfortably situated on the outskirts of the northern part of the town, was, as we were to learn, part of a region occupied by several women of questionable repute. One of them, in fact, occupied the house adjoining ours. Of a Samaritan turn of temperament possibly, and on the very first day of my mother's presence here—and especially in the absence of furniture which was never to arrive—she proceeded to offer conveniences and to make herself otherwise as sociable and agreeable as possible. Since ladies of loose virtue do not always wear a scarlet "A" on the forehead nor advertise their trade by their manner, my mother was certainly none the wiser. And had she been, I doubt if under the circumstances she would have summoned a pharisaism not common to her. Certainly the several sisters who for the single purpose of helping my mother and getting her settled had come on, found this woman not only congenial but helpful. New furniture, of course, had to be secured, and it was in her company that two of my sisters appeared on the street visiting this and that store. And in consequence, a few days later, in passing a local wagon manufacturer's on my way home from the post office, I was hailed by the proprietor. He was a slim, blond, bony young man, of a peculiarly severe expression, as I thought, but not at all unfriendly—quite the contrary, in fact. But now stepping before me and saying: "Aren't you the people who have just moved into the little brick house at the end of Berry Street?"

"Yes, sir," I replied.

"Well, will you tell your mother not to let your sisters go with that woman next door to you—Mrs. Gilchrist? She hasn't a very good name around here, and I know you're strangers and don't know. So I'm telling you. If they go with her, other people won't go with them, you see."

I thanked him for his kindness and immediately went home and told my mother, who appeared more distressed than shocked. "Oh, dear! Oh, dear!" she exclaimed. "He said that, did he? Now isn't that terrible?" And forthwith proceeded to consult with her daughters. After Sullivan, Evansville and Chicago, you may be sure she was determined to make a success of this latest effort to set the remainder of the family on the straight and narrow path. And in consequence—and really immediately—and to escape the attentions of this woman, another and really much more attractive house in an entirely different neighbourhood was sought out —one adjoining one of the two ward schools. And into that we immediately moved.

This house, as it proved, was much larger and far more comfortable—and interesting, even—than the first one, since, accompanying it at the rear was an extensive garden, bordered by many healthy and varied fruit trees, and the body of which the following spring we were able to plant to capacity with many valuable vegetables. The rent was a little more—eight dollars instead of six, I think. It faced a blind street, unpaved, which gave, by courtesy of a stile, into the adjoining school yard, and so into another blind street on the other side. Over the way directly to the south was a large, old-fashioned brick house set in a grove of pine trees at least two acres in extent, which in earlier days had, no doubt, been part of a very comfortable estate at the edge of the town but now stood vacant and so constituted an extra playground. (Some two years later we removed to this house.) To the rear of our very large garden, divided from the lawn by a very handsome hedge, was a great grove of ash trees, from which we were permitted to cut such wood as we desired. Beyond that again were fields and marshes filled with tall brown cat-tails—the environs of the town in that direction that sloped down to the Tippecanoe River. And so many were the hours, swayed by a romancing mood, that I spent in one or another of the topmost branches of one or another of these trees, surveying the silvery windings of this little river and thinking. Of what? The great world beyond and where I should be and what doing, came the mysterious years that were then still confronting me.

It is always a comforting thing to me to know that here— for once—our family life began in the simple, conservative, well-mannered way that my mother most desired. At last, as she thought, I am sure, she really had a taste of that satisfaction of knowing that she had surrounded at least the three youngest of her children with conditions which she considered most favourable to their mental and spiritual development. As I think of my mother, she reminds me of a pale, spindling flower left to vegetate in a dark room, yet earnestly struggling to reach the light. Yet her efforts were so groping, and for the most part so futile; not sufficiently retroactive, alas, and yet in the main so like nature's own. To her very last hour, indeed, and in spite of a marked physical if not mental degeneration, she sought to retain her enthusiasm for life, an enthusiasm lovely because altogether childlike in quality. It was not that she personally wished to appear so well before the world as that she so strongly desired to have her children succeed in a definite way, since, alas, and as she now knew, neither the understanding nor the direction of herself or their father had been sufficient to aid them to any great extent. (Ah, the pang of that, I fear!) If there is a continuance of life after death, no doubt my mother took up her further development with a gay heart.

And I . . . I, too, was possessed of a sense of peace as well as beauty here—such sylvan and idyllic beauty as rarely elsewhere I have met—at least in the same mood as then possessed me. For after Chicago and those last few days in Evansville, this place suggested not only security but evoked a feeling of beauty and adventure. For not so very far away, straight east along the street which passed our front door, was Center Lake, and over the way was that large, old, deserted house, centred in a grove of pines, where for me at least it was so satisfying to loiter and dream. And below that again, as I soon learned, was a pond or tarn which furnished water for the boilers of a small saw mill and furniture factory adjoining its shore line, and at the same time provided skating in winter and log-jumping in spring, summer and fall. For always about it were stacked large, thick logs of oak, the future furniture of the factory, any one of which could be rolled into the water and propelled here and there or from one to another of which, with the aid of a strong pole, one could leap.

Besides, through the efforts of Paul and the older girls and Al (still in Chicago), the finances of the family were at least in such shape that by such care and thrift as my mother was always capable of exercising, there was no immediate sense of worry or strain. In short, in so far as I could see, she appeared as contented here as during those first days in Evansville. And more, there was every facility here for a modest feeling of prosperity. For in the orchard at the back—and although the season was late—there were still any number of apples to be gathered. And in a left-over kitchen garden, cabbages, turnips, beets and onions. I recall now the practical enthusiasm with which my mother ordered or urged these to be harvested. And, of course, there was work to do : grass to be cut, flower-beds and walks to be weeded; a somewhat decayed fence to be repaired; and the entire house cleaned and refurbished. But all of these things being finally disposed of—the hardest kind of personal labour on my mother's part aiding most, you may be sure—a period of really joyful peace ensued—a period in which we three youngest were at last entered in the public schools, and where I first sensed clearly—and with what relief!—what it had been all along that had most oppressed and delayed me in every way—the dogmatic and always threatening dominance of the Catholic Church and school.

CHAPTER XXXVI

WHENEVER I think of the American school system as it was then—the genial shepherding of millions of children after the fashion of loving parents, and with more love and much more intelligence and care than most of the poorer parents have to offer—I still hold to some slight faith in, if not democracy, at least some form of social organisation which would permit of the child being as advantageously and intensively cultivated as any other living and cultivable thing. That this is probable I am not here to say, for certainly the present drift of our American form of democracy is by no means promising. Yet also, the mental road of man is a long one, and obviously, the path of any and all forms of government is beset with the seemingly inalienable and unchanging stupidities, greeds and venal ambitions of man. It is also true, perhaps, that vain, ignorant, prejudiced, yearningly and selfishly ambitious and sex-hungry young women have too often taught the young—to-day more so than ever, I hear—but, as frequently, they teach them very well. In so far as I could see at that time, they inspired as well as suggested ways and means for the future that were of great value and import, and that is all that any educational system can do, is it not?

My teachers, from the beginning to the end of my opportunities in this direction, were by no means intellectual giants, but they were kindly, helpful and sympathetic individuals, one and all, and in line with the current American characteristics of hope and desire for knowledge, and as such, fit teachers, in my humble judgment, for American children of that day. They may or may not have held to stubborn and ignorant religious beliefs. I know that in the main they had the conventional American moralistic notions which made it a crime for a man or woman to know anything about life sexually unless safeguarded by the profoundest Protestant religious and moral convictions. Also they looked on all tendencies toward sex interest as evil

197

and, in a sense, devastating. But even so . . . they had no objection to a sane conception of history, botany, sociology, zoology, a hundred fields and avenues of information—which was much more than could be said for the Catholics. It was, all in all, a rather free intellectual world in which they lived. The sanctity of the home and of women had already become somewhat of a binding bugaboo, but even so, it was a freer intellectual atmosphere than any with which I previously had been in contact.

More, the atmosphere of the school here was radically different from that which had terrorised me at Evansville and elsewhere. Gone were the black-garbed nuns, with their ultra-solemn countenances and their dull, dogma-repressed minds. And the Reverend Anton Dudenhauser and the very Honourable Professor, their equals and likes. Terrified by my previous experiences, I was at first most loath to enter. It seemed to me that of all the devilish inventions of man intended to plague childhood, schools of any kind were the worst. And Ed, as I smile to recall, refused to enter, and as at Evansville, had once more to be wheedled, coaxed, and finally bought. When, however, he, Trina and myself were finally induced to go next door to the principal of B Ward School, as it was then known, and found instead of a frowning Cerberus of a nun or principal, a bland, smiling, pink-cheeked girl of twenty-two or three, who asked what our previous training had been and said she would try me in Grade seven and Ed in Grade four until she found out whether we were suited to the work there, I could hardly believe my senses. And when I entered Grade seven and found, instead of a gloomy nun ordering us indifferently about, a chestnut-haired girl of not more than twenty-one, whose incorrigible ringlets made a halo about her head and whose laughing brown eyes spoke only of good nature and love of life, I felt exceedingly different about it all.

Besides, the attitude of the pupils was so radically different. Here were boys and girls freely intermingling in the same room, babbling concerning the new arrangements, what had become of whom, who had gone where, the charms and defects of the new teacher, and so on. Imagine this after the Reverend Anton at Evansville! Truly, I think my young American soul gave one bound and thereby attained to the meaning of freedom! I could almost hear the timbers of an antiquated and repressive educational system creaking and crashing about me. This girl, who was to be my teacher and who did really teach me in the best sense of the word, spelled opportunity instead of repression. With shy eyes I followed her movements, taking the desk she indicated. Betimes I was given a list of books to secure: Harvey's Grammar, Swinton's Geography, somebody's Arithmetic, and so on. By noon, Trina, Ed and myself had been to the village book store and secured all. By noon I was telling my mother that I thought it was going to be very nice.

Only Ed, incorrigible Ed, had been relegated to the primary grade, where he had to begin all over again. Apparently his two years of slavery in the Catholic school at Evansville had done him no good whatsoever.

"It serves him just right!" pecked my sister Trina, her black, birdlike eyes snapping. "He never would study! Now see what he gets for wanting to play all the time! Ha, ha!" (The intonation alone was the very substance of irony and ridicule.)

And I myself was in no great feather intellectually, for although I made the same grade as my much smarter sister, I was doubtful of my ability to remain there. Arithmetic? It seemed the substance of mystery and difficulty. Grammar? I could gain no least inkling of what it was all about. Why nouns and verbs and participles, anyhow? What was the good of them? When it came to the Fifth Reader, geography, spelling, I felt more or less at home. These interested me, especially geography.

But, ah, the charm of that seventh grade room! Its warm, bright space; clean, varnished desks; wide and bright windows, framing what lovely views! And May Calvert, the teacher, with her sunny smile, seated on the platform at the front. Her soft, kind eyes. And her friendly voice. At once, and for some reason, she seemed to take an interest in me. Did I like Warsaw? Did I think I would like this school? I was so moved by this consideration that I was silent, and yet really tremulous with pleasure.

And after that, the pleasant routine of the school itself. Under the questioning and subsequent sympathetic direction of this particular teacher, I felt more at ease here than anywhere else I had ever been, I think. Her eyes, always bent on me so quietly and even appealingly, as it seemed to me. Would I read the third paragraph on page 70 of so and so's Reader?

Would I tell her what were the leading industries of the State of Maine? What was the meaning of the word "pique," and how did one spell it? Parse the following: —— Whereupon, and ignominiously, I confessed that I did not know how.

But was that the end of me in that grade? Not at all! Instead, after school that evening, a cooing and even affectionate investigation into my lacks and defects as a grammarian. And so then and there the whole truth—that I knew nothing whatsoever about it; had never known. But then to cure that, a talk with my sister—who did. More, private noontime or after-school half hours in which various difficulties in regard to grammar were gone over and over and over, until at last some few feeble glimmerings as to its import seemed, X-ray fashion, to pierce the thickness of my skull. But along with that, amazement, plus compliments, in regard to the English I could write and speak. "But, Theodore dear, you write good English. Your longest sentences and paragraphs are correct and orderly. I don't understand." Neither did I, although I flushed with some mystical vicarious pride. I myself wondered—and very much so—how it was that I did it, for I could not say how.

And somehow, with all this, a growing something that was very close or akin to affection—love, even. Her eyes, her pretty mouth, her hair, her pink cheeks! Her face at all close to mine, I trembled and felt what . . . actually that *she* would put her arm around me and hold me, rather than that I might put my arm around her and hold her. Had words come, they would have been "Love me; love me, love me, please!" And so often her soft eyes looked as though that were true.

So then, graceful, easy, charming hours! The tang of them comes back, as does that of the sea to the sailor. For about me now were such new and agreeable types of boys and girls. For before, behind, to either side of me, in this bench-filled schoolroom, were girls whose cheeks and hair and eyes in their wondrous combinations, were a constant provocation and delight. And in other rooms of this same school, scores more of them, and at noon, night, recess, tripping out so gaily and arm-in-arm going where . . . ah!

Whether it was due to family banter or the repression of any tendency to take an interest in girls, or a natural shyness which caused me to underestimate my own merits—it might have been one or all three, or something else—I now began to develop a poignant consciousness of being unattractive to the other sex and not very popular with my own. What could have produced it? Growth? That defeat in Chicago? Being thrown with girls? Opposition or comment? I cannot say. Primarily it may have sprung from a lack of courage or a too lively sense of the virtues and merits of others. But when I studied the grace or material equipment of other boys and girls I saw here—girls, in particular, whose least smile I would have welcomed with a fainting enthusiasm—my immediate conclusion was that I was terribly homely and without courage or charm of speech or manner.

And yet, out of perhaps thirty or forty who here met my eyes, many of them in the same room with me, and whom I came to know and in other cases to admire at a distance, four or five immediately stood out as of definite import for me. Augusta Phillipson, a Jewess, black-haired, brown-cheeked, friendly, daring, hoyden; Myrtle Trego, whose face and eyes—violet-blue eyes and of a pale complexion—sent a thrill of mingled delight and misery through me every time I looked at her; "Cad" Tuttle, tawny of hair as a Norse, whose full brown eyes and rounded chin and heavy, shapely neck, were richly sensuous; her sister Maud, soft and plump and blonde, the type sure to be fat at forty; Berta Boone, dark as jet her hair and eyes, and with a slim, waspish figure. And then my teacher, May Calvert, plump, rosy, fair-haired, a type of robust beauty, and as intelligent as the Middle West of this period (no more), and as lovely as the cornflowers that grew in such profusion here in the spring.

In regard to this teacher, I have a story to tell which may as well be told here. Before three months had passed she had fallen into the habit of pinching my ear as she passed or putting her hand on my hair and smoothing it. One day, after I had finished reading two paragraphs from "The Legend of Sleepy Hollow," she said: "Theodore, you read beautifully. There is something so like outdoors in your voice. You read as you are. It is perfect." I sat down abashed and flustered, the blood burning in my cheeks and ears. I thought for the moment that she was making light of me, so little vanity had I, but finally it came to me and I was very proud. I felt a warm, yearning kinship with her for all the while I was in her room thereafter. I wanted to get close to her and hold her. She was so warm and of such a generous mould.

Toward the end of the year, finding I was still backward in grammar, she asked me to stay after school one day. Leaning over her desk following the details of her advice, I felt her hair brush my cheek. Finally I felt her hand on my shoulder. I snuggled up to her, because I was magnetically drawn and because I thought she was lovely. I could scarcely think of what she was telling me. I wanted to put my arms about her, but I did not dare. I went home that night elated and yet disappointed. I felt that I was entitled to cling close and love her, and yet I had not the courage. This relationship between us existed without interruption until the end of the year. But as to grammar, I failed dismally.

"You have done well in everything else, Theodore," she said to me one afternoon, "but you don't know anything about grammar. Yet because I know you don't need to, I'm going to pass you just the same. You're too bright to be held back for that. You're going to be in Miss Reid's room next year, and I'll speak to her. She'll understand and help you through. Grammar isn't everything."

She paused and looked at me. Outside I could see the school lawn and beyond it the pattern of the branches of the trees on the ground made by the sunlight. But I had nothing to say.

"Shy boy," she added, and then she reached over and took my hand. "I hope you'll have a happy future," she said, and kissed me.

I was so overcome with surprise and delight that I could not speak. Bashful to the extent of being ridiculous, I had no courage for an opportunity such as this. Instead I flushed to the roots of my hair, thanked her, and left. As I went out the door, she called after me: "Good-bye." I turned and saw her smiling and looking affectionately after me. I wanted to run back, but I did not dare.

When next I saw May Calvert, she was married and the mother of two children. It was a great shock. But, oh, the dreamy import of that last scene with her! Though men and women change and fade and are cut down like the grass, yet some scenes and some words and some thoughts and emotions have a deathless quality of their own.

CHAPTER XXXVII

THE charm of Warsaw as a town and, perhaps better, as a mental and emotional experience, was enhanced by other things. This was my mother's home country, the region in which she had seen the three spirit lights of her children, and a lovely country it was. Not twelve miles away, at Silver Lake, lived Aunt Sue, my mother's sister, and her family. Not more than fifteen miles away, at Bourbon, lived Uncle Henry, her brother, a bishop in the United Brethren Church and a man of consequence. At Manchester, not more than forty miles away, lived her half-sister and her husband, the one who had taken Al and tried to make a farmer out of him. All about us were the evidences that mother had enjoyed comfortable prosperity and some successful relationships, and that was something to elevate our spirits.

I recall sitting at my desk in school one day and reading an item in my geography to the effect that Warsaw was considered to be the most beautiful town in the State and one blessed with many lovely features of both land and water. I sat up with pride, for *we* were living in Warsaw! More, this was my mother's home region, if you please!

In spring, summer and fall here—quite as much so in winter, really—the lakes, the Tippecanoe River, and the woods, were delightful. Though one might not own a rowboat, one could fish and swim from the banks or the public and private piers, the owners of which did not object to their use. Also boats were to be hired for very little—twenty-five cents for an afternoon or evening. Or there were neighbour boys or schoolmates who had rowboats and were willing enough to share or lend them. When winter set in, there was ice skating on all of the lakes, their surfaces frequently frozen to the thickness of a foot or more. The town was prosperous, its boys and girls, for the most part, well-dressed and playful.

Yet by now I was beginning to wonder about our family, its

relationship to this new community, which somehow seemed better and perhaps more class-conscious than any I had ever known. I saw boys and girls whose parents possessed homes much more luxurious than ours. In school I was shoulder to shoulder with those who were better-dressed and generally better equipped materially than we were. Skates, sleighs, furs in winter, and an ample wardrobe in summer, plus tennis sets, canoes and the like, were the portion of many of those whom I knew, at least by sight. One of the disturbing observations which presently I made was that we could not afford a handsome canoe, where handsome canoes were common, nor yet a sleigh when in season sleighs were numerous, nor yet the clothes and amusements of so many who were of the wealthier fraction of the town. In short, my budding personal attitude was that of an ambitious but pleasure-loving *parvenu*. Instead of taking to heart the emphasis in our home and elsewhere on the need of energy, study of a practical character, ambition, self-denial and some other things in order that one might properly prepare oneself for the battle of life, I was for mooning about and dreaming of how delightful it would be to do this and that, have this and that—without effort—by luck or birth, as it were. The attitude of a maundering ne'er-do-well, I grant you, but trying or painful enough just the same—the unconquerable and incurable vagaries of the ignorant and inexperienced mind.

But fortunately, at about this time my interest in literature flowed higher and found better pasturage. Previous to this I had been reading but odds and ends of things, and without much, if any, discrimination or direction—*Puck, Judge, The Family Story Paper, The New York Weekly, The Fireside Companion*—the substance of these papers being either the cheap partisan politics of the nation, as in the case of the first two, or the mystery of the disappearance of some shop girl, beloved of a scion of wealth, whose parents sought to hold her in abeyance until his love should cool or he or she was forced into a relationship which would end the objectionable infatuation.

Just why at this time I was so much interested in all this I did not understand. That sex desire was developing with great strides was a biological fact far beyond my ken. Or that, as ever, it was associated with ease, luxury and beauty, was all beyond me. What I did sense, and so clearly, in connection with these impossible romances was that my sympathies were all with the maiden forlorn. The drawn, distrait faces of these story-paper heroines, the appealingly outstretched arms, the wind-blown hair, moved me as has little else since.

It was May Calvert who first suggested to me the privilege, which was mine for the asking, of drawing books from the local public library in the basement of the High School. I remember securing and taking my privilege card for her signature as guarantor, and then returning with it to the attendant at the library. And then, shelves upon shelves of books; and all open to me for the asking! True enough, from a public library point of view, they were few—perhaps twelve hundred volumes all told—but for me at my age, an amazing number. At first I selected only such books as had been recommended to me. Later, though, I began to choose for myself, because of suggestions made in prefaces or because the subject matter enticed me. Hawthorne's "House of the Seven Gables," for instance, and "The Scarlet Letter"; Irving's "Alhambra," "The Sketch Book," and "The Conquest of Granada"; Kingsley's "Water Babies"; and Goldsmith's "Deserted Village." I think of all that passed before me at this time, the two books that impressed me most were "Water Babies" and "The House of the Seven Gables." I was not then—consciously, at least—a realist, and the mystery of the water world as portrayed in "Water Babies," the metaphysical and mystic impulses which project life and which were suggested therein, appealed to me strongly. It somehow brought back those days at Sullivan, when and where I sat beside pools and waterholes watching for crawfish and salamanders.

And there were other books. I recall reading "Evangeline" and thinking it wonderful. Also many of the other poems of Longfellow, as well as Bryant, Whittier (much recommended in the schools of those days) and, much better, Poe's "Raven," "Annabel Lee," and "The Bells." From some source came a volume or two of Fenimore Cooper—recommended by a schoolmate, I think—"The Pathfinder," "Deerslayer," and others of his. Only presently I turned again to romance, seeking in Ouida, Mrs. Harrison and even Laura Jean Libby some phase of impossible sentimentalism which my nature appeared to crave. In short, I have since thought that for all my modest repute as a realist, I seem, to my self-analysing eyes, somewhat more of a romanticist than a realist. The wonder of something that I cannot analyse! The mystic something of beauty that perennially transfigures the world! The freshness of dawns and evenings! The endless changes of state and condition in individuals! How these things grip and mystify! Life itself so unstable, water-slippery, shifty, cruel, insatiate, and yet so generous, merciful, forgiving. How like all or nothing it seems, according to one's compound and experiences! Yet never would I say of any picture of it, realistic or otherwise, that so much as fragmentarily suggests its variety or force, that it is dull. The individual himself—the writer, I mean—might well be a fool, and therefore all that he attempts to convey would taste of his foolishness or lack of wisdom or drama, but life, true life, by whomsoever set forth or discussed, cannot want utterly of romance or drama, and realism in its most artistic and forceful form is the very substance of both. It is only the ignorant or insensitive who fail to perceive it.

But to continue. These books which now commanded my attention lifted me into an entirely different state, gave me a new outlook on life, and in a way aided me better to formulate myself to myself. Hitherto I had been quite nebulous as to what I might do or could hope to do. But now, by these readings, or because of them, while I cannot say that I consciously arrived at the thought that I was to be a writer, I might say that I had found something which I felt I should like to imitate. Among other things I read Samuel Smiles's "Self Help," commended by May Calvert, and however trivial that may appear to some, I felt a self-helping force developing in me. It made me see that there were many things to do and many, many ways of finding how to do them. Some people drifted into things, and most successfully; others thought them out. Perhaps when the time came, I should think my way out.

More, I was no longer the same boy I was in Evansville or Chicago. It mattered not how uncertain my future seemed to me, I was soothed by the consciousness that I had come in contact with an immense reservoir of ideas, scenes, materials which could and would enlarge my vision. And then, too, the authors of these books were men whose interests appeared in many instances to be identical with my own. In many presentations of human difficulties, pleasures and actions, I recognised my own moods and emotions. The world is not like the

Catholic Church says it is, was one of the first things that occurred to me. My father is a narrow, hide-bound religionist, was another. My mother, not strange to relate, grew in stature and import in the light of these revelations. I looked upon her now as an open-minded personality; she had not, like my father, stopped growing.

Books! Books! Books! How wonderful, fascinating, revealing! Whenever I found it possible, I would steal away and ascend to a front bedroom on the second floor of our house, and there bury myself in the pages of first one volume and then another. Outside, overhead, might be a blue or grey sky, sunshine or rain or snow; it made little difference. For I was reading and awakening to a consciousness of many things, the mere knowledge of which appeared to coincide with power. The skies in my books were blue. One could do things with sufficient power.

CHAPTER XXXVIII

THERE were many boys here whom after a very little while I came to know reasonably well. In thinking of them in this way, I feel as though I were about to attempt to describe the personal and social characteristics of a regiment. Among them were several who took up with me not because I was really suited to them in mood, but because I was Ed's brother and because they thought that in spite of all the evidence I might prove to be all right.

In that connection let me say that never anywhere, I think, was there a more avid playboy or sport-lover than Ed. He was tireless in his pursuit of pleasure after this fashion. Although never willing to get up early in the morning, he invariably made up for this by his unwillingness to retire at night as long as there was the least possibility of his getting or staying outside and playing at a game. Yet a greater dullard at books never lived. I can safely say that up to the age of fourteen, to say nothing of a much later period, and outside of such general knowledge as he gained at his play or work, he knew nothing at all. Whether the earth was flat or round was one and the same thing to him. Was there a good skating pond somewhere? Would the weather be fair enough to play ball on the morrow? Would vacation last from May fifteenth to September fifteenth as it had the year before? Whom could he get to fill a certain position on a ball team which he was attempting to organise: the Warsaw Blues, say? All these were leading and engrossing questions with him. Never once, up to the age of twenty at least, did I see him pick up a book and attempt to read it, not even the five-cent or dime boy libraries that were then so popular. Girls interested him not much more than books. He appeared to like them well enough, but in so simple or animal a way as to contrast sharply with the blood and brain fury which they set up in me. In short, he was generally deemed a healthy, normal boy, whereas I was already looked upon by some as of a brooding, mooning turn, by others (my immediate family and some of the school-teachers and students) as a potential student, one who might later choose to shut himself away from the cares of the world to dwell in books. You know the tendency of the average family to deify the numbskull student, should he chance to make his appearance in its midst. Only in my case, there was a greater leaven of laughing understanding, cynicism and worldly experience than might have been found in some others.

For one thing—to digress somewhat further—our family was by now convinced that I had distinct intellectual tendencies. My father, coming home from Terre Haute on one occasion, for instance, and finding me reading so much, actually approved of the purchase of a set of Washington Irving's works (bound in most unwieldy fashion, as I recall) offered by a mendicant agent on the ground that these books were a liberal education. In due course of time, sets of Dickens, Thackeray and Scott were added in the same way, though that my father, had he known, would have allowed "Vanity Fair" or indeed many parts of Irving, to enter his home, I cannot believe. The truth was, the superior phases of the world's literature were beyond his ken. And so these, as much talked-of volumes, probably seemed worthy and so reasonably safe, but that was all.

Just the same, though, having succumbed to our entrance into the public school (under a brisk fire of argument as well as opposition from my mother, no doubt), he continued to fight briskly, and with the most amazing array of dogmatic assertions, every untoward reference to the Catholic Church, or indeed any fact which we encountered and chose to report—out of pure cussedness on our part, I suppose—and which chanced to run counter to the asinine teachings of his Church. Thus it might be that I reported that the reason why the Reformation came about was because some Catholic monks in Germany dared openly to sell indulgences to all and sundry—which because of the price paid permitted escape from purgatory, or that Martin Luther was a good man, or that the Church had punished Galileo for saying that the earth was round—statements so infuriating to my father that he fairly foamed with rage.

"Scoundrels!" (I can still hear him.) "Liars! That such things should be allowed to be taught in these public schools, and when the facts are written down where everybody can read them! That scoundrel Luther, with his lies! That whore-master! That seducer and marrier of nuns! That false swearer! And now they dare to teach that he was a good man! It is all his fault, the scoundrel, the drunkard, the reprobate, that the Reformation was ever started! The Church! The Church! They dare to deny the Church! St. Peter was given the keys to heaven, and this scoundrel comes along and tries to deny it and cause trouble here on earth! Very good! But he is burning in hell for what he did! God is fixing him! But here on earth things are in a bad way yet because of him, and apparently they are getting no better!"

"These schools, look at them!" he went on to me once, his face a study of impotent rage, bitterness and grief. "No Bible in them, or if there is one, a Protestant Bible, gotten up by that scoundrel and full of lies! No separation of the boys and girls as there should be in any well-regulated state of society! The shamelessness of these American children! Boys and girls together! Terrible! No vow-bound, God-fearing nuns or priests to curb them, but silly girls, their heads full of beaux, to teach these innocent children! God will visit His wrath on such a country! Wait and see! Wait and see!"

Occasionally, if mother was present, he would turn to her and declare: "It is you, with the way you think and the excuses you make for them, that are the cause of all our troubles with our children!"—which, of course, would start a new argument. And then would come crimination and recrimination for possibly hours at a time.

Needless to say, most of his boisterous and intemperate language fell upon indifferent or sealed ears. My sister Trina, who in her shrewd way had discovered that Catholic schools were poor places in which to learn anything, was now daily pouring into my mother's ears a live stream of censorious facts destructive to the claims of the Catholic Church as well as a host of complimentary ones designed to paint the merits of the public schools in high colours. In this respect, or once she was convinced of anything, she was a relentless fighter. If she did not like a thing, that ended it, and her batteries never flagged. Finding the public schools pleasing to her, she was now deter-mined to stay in them, as was I, and anything my father dared venture against was fought by the two of us. In short, my mother's suspicions as to the worthlessness of the Catholic schools as educational institutions became a certainty under our persistent fire.

If I may be permitted a still further digression, I should like to say that I cannot recall that there was the least tendency in any of the public schools I ever attended to say anything derogatory to the Catholic Church, either publicly or privately, even so much as by innuendo or juxtaposition of unfavourable facts, to cast doubt upon its dogmatic teachings. The educational direction of the State did not permit it. And although, as I happen to know, there was a strong local anti-Catholic feeling abroad (and in my humble judgment, rightly so), it was constantly curbed and held in restraint in order that the very minor Catholic element in the schools might not be offended. Yet the opposition of my father to our presence in the public schools and his estimate of their baneful, anti-religious influence was little short of fanatic and provoked statements from me which I did not hear in the public school but rather encountered in my general reading.

But to return to the gang of boys that we had gathered around us or of which we had become a part. It consisted of at least twenty—never all present at once—some more respectable than others, some less so, but no one of whom was particularly vicious. Of all of these, though, I recall at least three or four who seemed to me exceptionally clever or venturesome, or both, and of whom personally I grew quite fond. Chief among these was one Gavin McNutt, the cleverest, most reckless, most spirited, and certainly the most courageous of any. The daring of him! And the something of animal violence that at times animated him! He was neither very respectable nor very vulgar, but decidedly not vicious at heart.

To begin with, this same Gavin was a great sport. He could do and outdo all of the things we could do. For one thing, he could sustain himself by his teeth from a rope or tree limb, provided the latter could bear his weight. He was a graceful skater, a good fighter, a long-distance runner, a trick diver, and a pole vaulter. In one of his limpid, blue-grey eyes was a cast, and in moments of excitement this gave him a semi-demoniac expression not always pleasant to contemplate. On the other hand, when not too excited, he was the soul of gay humour, banter and general good nature—sometimes even of helpfulness when someone came by an injury or was in danger of drowning or losing a fight or being tormented by an enemy.

And one of his greatest stunts, as I recall it, was log-jumping in and around that saw-mill log pond on the other side of the old Thrall's house south of us and which I have described. Here, after school or on Saturdays or holidays, he would frequently collect and lead a log-leaping party, himself executing great flights through the air by means of a long pole and landing like a bird on some eminence too difficult for the rest of us to attain. Some of his other pleasures were to dare any or all of us to wade through a piece of dangerously deep water or walk a high and treacherous rail or invade private property. However, outside of a heavy contempt for unathletic classmen or indeed for all who could not take life as he did, he was truly a lovable fellow, generous, frolicsome and humorous.

"Hey, Ed!" (I can see his tousled, blond head over our side fence.) "Get your bat and ball and come on out!"

"My mother won't let me."

"Aw, yes, she will. Tell 'er you're just goin' to play ball. She won't mind."

"But I gotta do some work first."

"Aw, let it wait. I'll help you afterwards. Tell 'er that, will ye?" And so baseball.

Or: "Hey, Ed! Come on, we're goin' swimmin',"—and in confirmation of this he would hold up two cryptic fingers, the swimming sign. Or: "Ooo-eee, log-jumpin'!" whereupon, perchance, my father or mother, hearing his voice and seeing Ed trying to sneak out a side door, would call: "Ed! Ed! Don't you go out! You come back here now! Don't you pay any attention to him! Just you go and get your lessons done. You can play afterwards."

My father, however, really liked Gavin, I think, for on at least one occasion I heard him say, staring in the direction where McNutt's head had appeared and disappeared: "There he is again, the idlest good-for-nothing in the neighbourhood! When does he study, I'd like to know? What sort of parents has he? All he thinks of is play. A right scamp, this one! I don't think Ed ought to be seen with him. He can do you boys no good!" But just the same, he never forbade him the premises.

And McNutt, unabashed· by this obviously unfavourable opinion of him reported by Ed or myself or seen in my father's face, had no hesitancy in pursuing the even tenor of his way My father and mother might frown, but what of it? If he encountered either of them publicly, he would take off his hat and greet them most cordially, but he had no intention of reforming or letting Ed alone. Frequently my father declared that he was on the point of going to McNutt's father and pointing out his son's defects, but he never went. Instead mother and Mrs. McNutt came eventually to exchange civilities, largely on account of us children, I presume.

For my part, from the very beginning I took a strong fancy to Gavin. He did not dominate me intellectually as he seemed to do in the case of Ed and others, though he led me athletically and in other ways, as in his adventuring here and there. But the reason for that was that he was so frank, pagan, gay. Boys talk of so many things their parents never dream they talk of, and Gavin's mind was stored with details as to the methods by which life is generated. Also what girls were being pursued by what boys in Warsaw, and vice versa. In addition, he had a seemingly inexhaustible fund of semi-lecherous yet always humorous stories which he retailed in privacy and with much gusto. "Free bus to the Astor House" was one of his I recall. And the story of the preacher who was a solace to the entire family. But I am sure that I never listened to a more pictur-esque or original story-teller nor one who took more joy in retailing them, and they illuminated life as much as any school could, and, in one field, more. I should add, though, and in defence of Gavin, that his oaths and stories were coupled with bounding forthright energy and animal interest in play.

We think of healthy human animal energy as being divorced from a mucky interest in sex and brutal language and so-called pornographic thoughts. But I did not find it so in my own case nor among any of those I knew. On the contrary, those who gave freest vent to their knowledge of and interest in things morally and ethically frowned upon in a community of this kind were apt to be the most vigorous physically and even mentally.

Since probably I shall not deal with Gavin again, I should like to add that at nineteen he died of lockjaw from a rusty nail driven into his foot while running; and that shortly there-after there developed a grave local scandal. A girl by the name of Flora Woods, with whom he had been "running," as the locale had it, was found to be with child by him. All the scandal-loving tongues of the town—*à la* the "Tom Jones" world of Henry Fielding—were at once set wagging, and finally the girl's family, in a state of deep disgrace, left town. And so the community reaffirmed its public morals.

CHAPTER XXXIX

ALTHOUGH, as I have said, I took this sensible liking for McNutt, there were others I did not like: youths of lecherous, saturnine and frequently brutal disposition, whose thoughts and moods I could not abide. One—Chick Peters—a lean, slathery, ambling type, for subtlety, silence and instability compared not unfavourably with Dock Johnson and Al Thompson and Harry Truckee. How he came to get in with our group I do not know, save that in summertime the bounds of friendship were enlarged. He was always proposing some mischief I did not like: the invading of someone's property; stealing something to make an occasion or a meal —a boat, a chicken, fruit, vegetables—or running away to some other town in a box car.

Then there was "Ash" Thurston and Willie Kettle, boys of better family whose parents I never met but with whom I frequently wandered and talked, on heaven only knows what topics: school, work, teachers, books. And finally, George and John Shoup, distantly related cousins of ours on my mother's side, whose father was part owner of the principal flour mill here. Both George and John were alternately friends or enemies, as the time or mood suggested—friendly during one week and enemies the next. I really did not like either of them any too much, because in the course of time I found that they were not a little snobbish, their father's flour mill causing them to look down on the flour-mill-less and up to those who had more than their flour mill represented. In short, what we attained was only a partial relationship, never anything that extended to the homes of either of us.

But there was one other boy who for at least two of these opening years here was almost my inseparable companion. His name was Harry Croxton, and his father traded in sewing machines. He was an innocently wild, irresponsible youth, full of the maddest dreams of adventure for the future: China,

India, Mexico, South America. (He finally died in Mexico a mining engineer and expert representing a company there.) But better yet, he was of an insatiable intellectual turn, and because of him as spur and impetus I was compelled to discuss some of the more serious and driving thoughts concerning sex which were already beginning to haunt him as well as myself.

Indeed, when we were out in the woods, or swimming, or in our secret or unobserved places, nearly always all of these boys would fall to talking of girls. Some of their talk was positively vile. A woman at a window, a child in a yard, a boy and girl or man and woman walking were certain to provoke the most pornographic comments. "Come on over here in the woods!" or "Say, I wouldn't do a thing to her if I had her here." Quite entirely, of course, all of this was the product of a bounding animality, almost wholly restrained in the policed and so orderly world around them, and accordingly its intenseness transmuted itself to thought and comment, only partially satisfying, you may be sure. Legs, breasts, thighs, underwear, wild stories of encounters, of seeing things through windows or keyholes, of boys and girls seen lying together in the depths of the woods, were dwelt on as the most exciting of all things.

On the other hand—and by reason of the temperament of this particular youth—another, and for me much more illuminating type of sex discussion was introduced. For whether by reason of the mental direction of either his father or mother—both New Englanders and intellectuals of the country or small-town type—he appeared thus early well aware of the physical anatomy of sex—the actual (as then known) physiology as well as, in a modest way, emotional psychology of the organs and their reactions, and also, as then taught, the attendant dangers of masturbation, lack of sanitation, and the various diseases and contagions to which that lack gives rise. And liked to talk about all these things. Only finding, in our gang at least, few if any hearers other than myself, he devoted much of his time and quite all of his discoveries as well as speculations in this field to me. And hearing of a lecture for men only which was soon to come, was determined that I should hear that. But the admission charge—fifty cents—as well as the shame that I felt at that time of explaining to my mother exactly what the fifty cents was for, caused me to give over the idea.

But Croxton, determined on learning all in this field, and having himself attended, returned with news of all he had heard —not much more than previously he had known except this: that he had seen large coloured maps of each particular organ, with the mechanics of the same clearly set forth—some of which he roughly sketched and so made very clear to me much more of my own mechanism as well as that of the opposite sex than I had ever guessed—but all with his now repeated warnings of the dangers that accompanied licence—a series of facts in regard to contagions and their devastating effects which impressed me not a little.

I was as determined by then to avoid loose or evil women— as my father described them—as I would the devil himself!

None the less, sex, sex, sex! How the hot fire nature had lighted in my body was driving me to almost frantic efforts at self-satiation! And how, for the next two or three years (to say nothing of the next twenty-five) it harried me from hell to hell! Although my mother and father and the pleasant father confessor of our church were constantly counselling me to keep pure in thought and feeling, yet my proper nature was gratifying itself with insistent thoughts and emotions that concerned girls and this sex function. And while I did not even then quite realise fully the immense force and power of male and female contact, still in a vague way, I did, too. I cannot explain the something of vagueness that lingered about all this, only that it must have been evoked by inexperience. Men and women revelled with one another in some way . . . but how? It seemed—and even after young Croxton, if you will believe it—that it must relate more to hugging and kissing than anything else, although I now knew definitely of that *else*. For the lines of a woman's form were beginning to be of blazing import to me, and just that—the pleasure of viewing and caressing it—seemed almost enough—indeed in some of my sex-worshipping fancies, all but too much. Could I endure? Would I have the vitality, the self-repression even, so that I should not faint? For often at the mere sight of an unheralded Venus displayed in a book or some picture that chanced to fall into my hands, my blood ran hot and cold. I was transfixed, fearsome, and invariably looked cautiously about for fear someone might be looking with or at me. Yet assuring myself of being alone, I would make bold to feast my eyes upon the potent lines. Then a veritable feeling of fear or weakness, an actual wave of bashful terror and almost insupportable breathlessness, as I paused to think on what I should do if I were suddenly confronted by such a reality—what—in love—I should be called upon to do! Ah, how devastating as well as rewarding! How fire-sweet and yet fire-injurious, too!

Sing the dark flower of passion that glorifies and terrifies the world! Once—in my youth, at least—we lied so about it. As one might skirt the quaking cauldron of a crater, red and glinting with the molten slag below, so humanity throughout the Christian era has gone about it on tiptoe, fearing to examine what it most greatly desired to possess. But since then, what a change! The stage—books—Freud—life!

At that time, though, I found myself on the *qui vive* for every form of life; all was no more than a minor accompaniment to the molten, sputtering main theme pulsating and winding like a great river within the depths of my inner self. Shall I call it passion? It had no least relationship to the actuality which a passion for some one definite individuality evokes. The feverish unrest to see a given face or hear a certain voice! That was wanting. Instead, though, there was a wild, flaming enthusiasm for the colour of life itself: all the colour which contributes to the settings of sex. The flowers, trees, grass, sky, beautiful homes, bright shops, music, the artistry of clothing—all combined to produce a thrilling harmony which sang of but one thing: love.

And by love I do not mean that poetic abstraction celebrated by the religionists—devoid of sex—nor yet the guttural sensuality understood of the materialist. My dreams were a blend of each: the diaphanous radiance of the morning, plus a suggestion of the dark, harsh sensuality of the lecher and the libertine—a suggestion merely, none the less a potent one which gave to all beauty and all reality a meaning. This, this, this contact joy between two was its meaning! And this was its reward! This and no other! Architecture, trade, commerce, law, the political and social rules and activities of life: servants, servants merely, the underpinning and surface-decorating of the great world altar on which the creative love or sex impulse made its bed!

CHAPTER XL

THE first girl to take my attention seriously and cause me to experience that unutterable, inexpressible something we call love, was a dark-haired, pale-faced child whose father was one of the two or three druggists whose stores, because of ice cream and soda principally (but not ice cream soda as we know it to-day) constituted the centre of a gay traffic.

I should like to interpolate in passing that all of the wonder paraphernalia of the modern soda fountain was then practically unknown. The ice cream soda, with its endless variety of flavours and colours, and the glories of marbled and mirrored counters, had not yet arrived, although in the second year of our stay in Warsaw, the "milk shake" (a drink which from 1885 to 1889 ran a brilliant course of popularity) was introduced. I also recall that forthwith I was one of the earliest and most enthusiastic addicts of this product, expending all of my begged or earned dimes for it, but later when ice cream soda put in an appearance, along with everyone else I became an apostate from milk shake, a convert to ice cream soda. But at the precise time of which I write, only ice cream and soda water variously flavoured, as well as pop, sarsaparilla, ginger ale and the like were displayed and dispensed.

But to return to my thrilling, if not primal, sex contagion, which like some sweet disease gave me weeks and months of mingled anguish and delight. Myrtle Trego studied in the same room with me, under May Calvert, during our first year here. A shy little maid, as I recall her, her beauty suggesting the pictures of Quaker and Puritan maids of history and school literature rather than the girls of our own day. A simple, unpretentious creature, not as blazingly impressive as many another, I am sure, yet for some reason most painfully appealing to me. Her soft eyes! Her shy smile! A sinuous and yet evasive walk, demure and with a sweet innocence that grew on me daily until the grace of her became a kind of fire of delight. And her eyes, of a chestnut brown, and holding a look always retiring and even bashful. And her cheeks so pale, with only the most delicate suggestion of a flush in them at times.

Nature, I am prone to believe, rather indifferently achieves the miracle of flower-like passion or illusion in youth and spring. Yet unquestionably it suggests an urgent desire for rebuilding, over and over, the machinery of physical and mental life and love, and love is its prime mover; love that is at once its method and its purpose. But in so far as the individual is concerned, it certainly values the particular machinery and usefulness of him at almost nothing, or for so brief a time, so few years, as to mean the same. Yet it builds anew and anew, as though quantity, not quality, were the point. The slums! The bagnios! The amazing wastes of war and disease! And yet, think of the sun's rays, splattering almost for ever upon this earth and producing over and over, seasonably and unseasonably, the mystery and complexity of this thing we know as life: human beings, animals, trees; plants of five leaves, four leaves, three leaves; the amazingly sensitive tendrils and blossoms; and through all these again, life's rude and bloody vigour! And the moon—a frozen stone—evoking, endlessly almost, destroying dreams and emotions! And under them, such minute things as myself and the beings who move me! And desire that can destroy! And hate!

I have waited for years to make some reference to this engrossing affair, intending to paint it with the dawn-like delicacy which it always seemed to me to deserve. But now that the time has come, words fail me. I might rhapsodise—I am even moved to. The shell-like colouring of it all! The sky-ey, dawny delicacy of the mood that possessed me—remote, intangible, elusive and yet consuming—it calls me even now to the effort. But how? For here was a sacrosanct realm, its confines fragile and delicate, of amethystine clarity, as of the dawn and spring, and redolent of flowers and faint spices. So wondrous, lovely and delicate indeed that I could only wonder at it and her from afar. No adoring devotee, laying with faltering hands a votive offering on the altar of a high and powerful god, could have had more of the quality of adoration in his eyes than lay in mine whenever I beheld this Myrtle.

But to what end! For months I waited without once speaking to this first true love. Yet eventually, and to my quaking amazement, heaven itself opened and received me for a moment into its deepest heart. It was at a schoolboy and girl party, the first one I ever attended. The party was to be given at Myrtle's house. And the list, to my amazement as well as that of Trina, my sister, included my name. Why me? And marvels—wonders—mysteries!—Trina had all the prospective details from a girl friend—there were to be games of all sorts. And at once I was alive with wonder as to what their character would be. But as if in answer to my curiosity or need, it was Harry Croxton who strolling home with me of an evening troubled to enlighten me by predicting "post office." "Gee, I hope they play that!" he added. "If they do, and I'm called, I'm going to call Sadie Morris." (Another pretty girl of our room.) He was so excited that he executed a number of handsprings in our yard to relieve his feelings. But as for myself, at the mere thought of possibly facing Myrtle alone, I alternately shivered and flushed. For now—or then on that occasion—I could ... But would I? Would I dare? Would I? For days beforehand, really, whenever a lull in other thoughts permitted, there was Myrtle Trego—eyes, walk, shyness. And whenever she appeared, I shook as with a chill almost. That coming hour! That approaching fatal moment! At times I sat in the swing under an apple tree in our yard, and swaying to and fro, meditated on the possibilities of such an encounter. The joy! The weakness! What if I won the opportunity of kissing her! Then what!

I call the attention of all moralists and ethical experts to the fact that in the face of this innocent and quite reverential ecstasy in connection with Myrtle, I was even then and there suffering perturbations of a somewhat different nature. In the schoolroom with me at that time were many other girls who affected me in various ways. There was "Cad" Tuttle, a warm, vital beauty who moved me to such rash, sensual thoughts in connection with herself as to cause my confessor to caution me in regard to mortal sins of the flesh that dragged one to hell. And her sister Maud, shorter and heavier, but scarcely less beautiful. And Nata Weyler, whose full pink lips and swimming eyes suggested what fleshly languors! And Gusta Phillipson, a curly-haired Jewess, who once chased me around a lilac bush to kiss me. There were so many. I think I dreamed constantly of their hidden physical lines. Yet with Myrtle it was as I have said. Sensuality in connection with her appeared to be held at bay. It was as when one contemplates a sunrise at sea or a cool, crisp, dewy morning in the woods. There was no sensuality. Only adoration and yearning. But for what? No more than to kiss or touch her, to have her look into my eyes and indicate that she cared —desired to touch or at least tolerate the touch that I would bestow upon her—no more and no less.

But in considering and interpreting (if possible) these two emotions in one person, what shall one say? Was one of them evil, the other good? Then in me were both evil and good, evoked by forces which I did not even know of, much less understand.

Those who like to separate and pare the emotions and thoughts of man into material and super-mental or so-called spiritual entities and then to insist that he should think one kind of thought of one group of things, or of life itself, and avoid or suppress all others, may chew on my dilemma. For I insist that I could no more have avoided the one kind any more than I could have shut out the other. There may be those who are capable of such feats—but I do not think so—and where they assert yes, I think they lie. I conclude that it may be well enough as an ethical or moral exercise, suited to develop or strengthen certain tendencies or impulses already existent, to attempt to think against one's emotions, but I do not believe in its success. It is only the emotions or fevers themselves that can weaken or fail and so cease to annoy or control. But as for altering the fundamental compounds which produce emotions of all kinds in all of us, or altering nature which breeds man—whether in its own image or not—that is neither here nor there, since it breeds him subtle, treacherous, lustful and other things, and I, for one, refuse to believe that life is other than as it manifests itself. We are its product and therefore its representatives. Morals do not hold save where the temperamental balance is in favour of them. Men are "good" (I use the word as representing those ethical tendencies so much admired by the moralists), because their impulses (primal, chemic and ineradicable) are so; they are "bad" (same exceptions as above) for the same reasons.

CHAPTER XLI

MYRTLE TREGO'S home was curiously like her. Small, neat, white, embowered. She lived with her mother and father and brother Charlie, in a white-sheathed, green-shuttered little house, in front of which a low white picket fence enclosed a green lawn, set with roses and small bushes. Once of a chill November evening, hanging about to see if I might catch a glimpse of her, I spied her through a window, reading a book, her head bowed, her smooth young cheek heightened by the shadow of the background against which she was outlined. Bitter sweet were my sensations, fire and ice, coloured and tinted as are the dawns and evenings of spring in the eyes of youth.

But now, the fateful evening. I do not recall, but I must have dressed myself with extraordinary care. By some process, new suits for myself and Ed had been produced that winter. I wore mine, a dark, woolly blue. Perchance I wore a red tie—I hope so—the flag of my urgent disposition. But I recall that I suffered an intense nervous depression, springing from the feeling that I would prove unsuited to an occasion of this kind. My sister Trina was always insisting that I was awkward and ungainly, lacking this and that: looks, presence, courage, flair.

At any rate, my thoughts of myself shrivelled me. Would I prove attractive to anyone, let alone *the* one? Would I not instead sit there, neglected, a hobbledehoy, destroyed by my own lacks? For think of it, I did not even have a girl to take! All the other boys were taking girls, even the erratic and not too handsome Croxton. But as for myself, and despite various glances and smiles in the past, I was still so restrained by my own conviction of want of skill as a gallant that I had never even approached one, never talked or laughed with any, had merely looked and looked. And so now I was compelled to escort my sister! And she angry with me for it, for she could have gone with a boy. Yet off we marched finally, and because of inexperience on the part of both, too early, a mere sprinkling of guests there when we arrived.

At first I sat frozen or freezing, my tongue leather, my hands unplaceable, trying to think of something to say, some intelligent, if not pleasing, way to look, some least move to make that would make it plain that I was not paralysed. But no: only stiffness, an amazing conviction of mental as well as physical collapse. In vain it was that Mrs. Trego—an efficient, sensible little woman, as I recall her—and presently Myrtle, bustled here and there, speaking to each in turn and bidding us make ourselves at home. I stared as might a stone image. How did one feel at home? What did one do, say, under such circumstances?

And then, just as I was nearing coma, the entry appeared to be crowded with arriving guests. There were voices, laughter, the removing of wraps. Yet this merely complicated matters. From having no one to speak to, there were some twenty-five to whom one should make overtures, appear human! Someone —I believe it was Augusta Phillipson—came and sitting down beside me, said, quite warmly: "Hello, Theo!" but so terrorised me by so doing as to leave me tongue-tied. I could only twitch and fidget in speechless agony, until finding me hopeless, I presume, she arose and left me.

It was even worse with Cad Tuttle and her sister Maud, Nata Weyler, Lovie Morris, and indeed all of the others. However friendly and helpful they attempted to be, I was too much for them. Cad Tuttle—who had long taken note of my glances, as I had reason to believe—said: "Isn't it fun, Theo? Aren't you glad to be here?" But this from her red mouth and smiling eyes reduced me to sheer idiocy. If I said anything, it was stuttered, I am sure, for in such crises as this stammering usually descended upon me. Then Harry Croxton came over after a while and said: "Gee, what's the matter with you, anyhow? What do you want to sit here for? Why don't you come over and talk?" Terrorised by the suggestion, I actually shrank and asked him, and not too kindly, to let me alone. Whereupon, since we had been the best of friends up to this moment, he stared at me and said: "What's got into you?" I could not have told him myself.

Fortunately, and at last, a number of simple and all-inclusive games were begun, and I was part of the party. Apple-bobbing (it was Hallowe'en); word-making for forfeits, someone beginning with a single letter, the next adding a letter before or after until a word was completed, the last person adding the completing letter being the winner and receiving a prize. Another game was sentence-building or "histories." One wrote the name of a given person, male or female, at the head of a slip of paper, turning it under. Then each person added a sentence describing what the person said or did, also turning the paper under. The result, as may be guessed, was frequently ridiculous. "Demosthenes going to the hardware store told her mother to chew gum!"

The situation heightened considerably for me with the beginning of these games. I was a part of the life and recovered myself sufficiently to be able to interpolate an exclamation of gaiety now and then. But never for a moment unconscious of Myrtle. In a simple, demure little dress, she was here and there, and once in a game stood before me asking me the answer to something. Out of my rapturous, tongue-tied state I managed to speak, to answer. Perhaps it was because I saw that she, too, was as pale and nervous as myself.

Finally, about ten o'clock, when the trepidation of the majority—if it had ever existed—had almost completely worn off, the game of "post office" was proposed: a game which was nothing more nor less than a temporary licence to kiss and embrace. Someone, a boy or girl, would go into a dark room and call for a favourite of the opposite sex to come and get his or her mail. This meant being kissed, and then remaining in the room as postmaster to call someone else. The only rules which seemed to govern the situation were these: no two persons could call each other back and forth, thus monopolising the situation, nor could anyone remain more than a moment without creating a ripple of excitement outside, where others, no doubt, were anxious for their turn, the bolder spirits, anyhow. As the game was played here, a call to come and receive stamps, a post card or a letter (any number of one variety or all three at once, according to the wish of the acting postmaster) meant, in the case of a stamp, a stamp on the toe, and a post card or letter a kiss or a "hair-pull," according to the mood of the postmaster. Occasionally (very), some wag would send out for another boy to come and get "stamps," though in the main kisses and hugs were exchanged in the recesses of the darkened chamber.

I can only suggest the perturbation of spirit which seized upon me as this game began. I have been in many, many trying situations in my life; my spirit has been perturbed by anticipations of delight or pain that have not always materialised; but the clarity and vividness of this particular evening remain unmodified. I do not recall how long it was before I was called, but I do know that I watched the rout of gaiety with a hungry and yet frightened yearning. For the time being, no one seemed to want me, and I was becoming terrified lest I be passed over entirely, when presently Gusta Phillipson becoming postmistress, I was immediately sent for to receive a letter. I did not yearn for her as I did for some of the others, yet when she called, I went gaily, though nervously, enough, glad that anyone had called me, yet ashamed at having sat uncalled for so long. When I entered I saw her outlined against the shadow, and the next moment with a "Poor Theo!" she put her arms around my neck and kissed me twice. It was so soothing to be sympathised with in this way that I was ready to cry; it was almost as though she were mothering me, and perhaps she was.

But when she left, as she did immediately, my own troubles began, for now the crier or messenger appeared to ask who was wanted. With a fainting heart I thought of Myrtle Trego, but I did not have the courage to send for her. The mere thought made me reel. I was really afraid she would not come. I compromised, therefore, on Cad Tuttle. Yet the moment I had done so, I was not only fearsome of the result but in addition sick with grief over my compromise. For had I not wanted Myrtle? And what might not she think of me, if she thought at all? But before I could speculate much, in fact, even as I thought, here was Cad before me, debonair, quick and warm, and saying, as she kissed me: "You're not so shy after all, are you?" I almost fainted with delight because of my success with her, for she embraced me warmly. I recall her thick hair, her warm, clinging lips, redolent of faint perfume. And yet, frozen by my own effrontery in calling her, I could not reply. Instead I thrilled from head to toe, for a word of commendation from her meant much; she liked me then a little. Yet as I came out, there was Myrtle, and in the midst

226

of all this honeyed delight I paused to think on her. What a coward I had been not to call her! And I was regretting this deeply at quite the same time that I was experiencing a sense of triumph at having at last kissed o rbeen kissed by two really pretty girls. Then I was not so hopeless after all!

But Cad Tuttle came out, having, to my chagrin, called another boy, one of the beaux of the school (whom Harry Croxton immediately told me she was "stuck on"). And he in turn called Nata Weyler, who called Charlie Trego, who in turn called Maud Tuttle, who called me. This second call precipitated a new crisis. For vaguely I sensed that Maud was fond of me, though such a fool was I that I could never bring myself to take advantage of the inviting smiles and knowing glances she occasionally turned in my direction. Now, though, I put my arms around her, trembling with excitement, and kissed her warm mouth. She yielded in so willing a way that I knew I was at liberty to take more than one, yet such was my shyness that even here my courage failed and I turned to go, when suddenly I recalled that it was my duty to stay and call another. And now, if I would, I might call Myrtle Trego. But would she come? Did she like me enough? Knowing there was no time to lose, I blurted out to the girl postmistress who looked in: "Myrtle Trego, a letter." And then my knees all but gave way. Myrtle! How I managed to remain standing I did not know, for in a moment she might be here, a moment which seemed to me an age. At the same time there was the thought of where to obtain sufficient courage to kiss her, touch her even, so remote from me and all that I was did she seem.

Yet as I pondered—a brief moment or two, I am sure—the door opened, and there she stood. A veritable shy mouse of a girl, gliding toward me, her head down, about her an atmosphere of shrinking unfamiliarity with life. I stood before her limp and choking, throat dry and body numb. I trembled so violently that I think she must have noticed. I tried to say something, but no sound came. She drew close to me, but I could do no more than lay my hands on her arms. As I bent to kiss her, her head slipped shyly into her arm and only her cheek was exposed. Even so, it seemed like the surface of the Cooba, that gate to paradise. I hurried out, weak and voiceless. When it came her turn to call someone, she called Etta Reed, a school chum of hers. Then more than ever I felt that I had shamelessly intruded on her, and at the same time felt glorified that she had not called a boy. She was not a boy's girl, that was plain. She had not wanted any boy to kiss her. And no other boy sent for her. After a while the game was dropped for taffy-pulling and refreshments, but I continued to seethe with the wonder of it.

Only when it came time to leave, I was thrown into an additional panic by the fact that I had no girl other than my sister to take home. I waited about nervously until the crowd thinned, when finding Trina, I slipped out and hurried away. But the shame of it! The loneliness and defeat!

But afterwards when it was over and I thought back on how I had kissed Myrtle and Maud and Cad and Gusta, my spirits rose and I did not feel so bad. I went over the details again and again: the call, each step, my trembling, all! In memory I kissed Myrtle a million times. Actually my lips quivered at the thought. I sat in our swing, studying the blue sky and the fleecy clouds, and the world seemed to me extremely beautiful. I swung and dreamed of the feel of Cad Tuttle's arms, the fragrance of Maud's personality. Gusta Phillipson's "Poor Theo!" haunted me as a commentary on my social inefficiency, but always when I was nearing the danger point as to that, Myrtle's shy, delicate presence confronted me and all else was blotted out. I re-experienced the tingle of that paradisiacal moment. Once more I choked with delight. Would she speak to me now when we met? Would I ever be able to walk and talk with her? The thought haunted and frightened me. I know I should never be able to build up the courage, nor she, even if she cared. But the splendour, the wonder of the dream!

CHAPTER XLII

NOT long after this—in late May or early June—the even tenor of our family life, so pleasantly inaugurated and maintained by my mother, was disturbed by the reappearance not only of my brother Rome, last seen in Evansville, as you will recall, but of my sisters Amy and Janet, who ever since our departure from Chicago had been making common lot there in an economic and household way. A vivid, harum-scarum pair this, but as life was to prove, marching tamely and conventionally enough throughout their maturer years.

But let me deal with my brother Rome first. Upon his arrival, he proceeded, as usual, to give a demonstration of his unchanging tastes and proclivities. In a day, perhaps, he sought out one or two downtown saloons, coming home at least partially intoxicated and making such an exhibition of himself as was sufficient to darken our character in the eyes of those who knew us. For here, as in other places of the same size or slightly larger, everybody's business was everybody's business, and the joy taken in drawing one's Christian or social skirts about one was only equalled by the fear that a bit of news, however derogatory or painful to another, might escape. The better families, of all grades of comfort, were most mindful of their outward and presumably inward state and well-being. There was much church-going and careful socialising among the elect. The records of all newcomers were carefully looked into, in so far as possible, and few, if any, were taken up by that elder, central group which dominated the town. Among the lesser families, some children's parties such as I have just described were countenanced, but even here the list was carefully viséd. It was a mark of high distinction for us to have been invited to that first school party of this first fall of our residence here, and I most distinctly recall that my mother viewed it in that light.

But with Rome's arrival our state began to darken. We had

a drunken brother. My mother was plainly grieved. Not that she did not love him as much as ever, but she was so determined that we three should have a better chance than the others had had. I recall her turning on him with a kind of pleading fury one day: "Why do you come down here now, Rome, and spoil everything? Here I have planned for years to get to a place where the family could at least appear respectable, and now you come again and do this! You know I would love to have you stay here if you would get work and lead a sober life. But to come here this way and when the children are just starting into school and doing so nicely—it is too much. Why do you . . .?"

This argument, made in the kitchen while she was working over the stove and he was sitting, in a semi-defiant, semi-drunken stupor, on a wooden chair near the window, affected me greatly. By now I had come to look on him—because of various things said and seen—as the family Nemesis. Nearly every time I saw him he was at least partially intoxicated, and that was disgusting to me. When thirsting for liquor, he would even go so far as to rob a toy bank. Now on his first visit to Warsaw, he even attempted to persuade mother to get him some money—a request which suggests his temperament when drinking. But in some two or three weeks, he left, but not before he had fished in the lakes in the fine summer weather and not without cursing the town as a "rube town," its citizens "dubs."

"The damn' scum!" I once heard him say, as he sat in a small boat of a Saturday afternoon on Center Lake, where catfish were supposed to be numerous. "Who in the hell are they? Mother is always worrying about them. A lot of cattle and jays!"

As before, though, he related experiences in the copper and lumber camps of northern Michigan, upon the railroad lines of western Kansas and southern Canada, and in Vancouver. Life only knows how he lived and spent his time or where he got the money to travel. I suspect that he rode in box cars at times, slept in lumber yards and jails. At other times, resplendent in good clothing, a cane, a watch and some jewellery, he paraded the more showy spots of the world.

And after he was gone came Amy, who, having hung about Janet and the others in Chicago until she had worn out her welcome, now returned here, to be looked after by mother, of course. Being too nebulous-minded to carve out a career for herself, she could think of no place else to go, nothing else to do but return home and dream her days away. At this time, she was pagan, sensuous, decidedly attractive physically, and fairly spoiling for sex contacts, but with no mental skill or reasoning faculty in so far as I could see. I recall her as nearly always before her mirror, rouging her cheeks and lips, darkening her eyebrows and lashes (which were effective enough without any exterior aids), or fastening bows of ribbon on her dresses, or trying on hats, or feeling her waist and hips to see if they were trim enough to suit her. A perfect fool of a girl, as I thought at the time, and one concerning whom there would be talk unless rigidly guarded. In fact, I doubt whether in all her youth she ever indulged in an unconscious laugh, smile, look or action.

But let that be as it will. Following her arrival came Janet, on a summer visit—in July or August, I forget which. At any rate, it was for the sole purpose of playing about a bit. And about the same time—worse or better luck, as you will— my father, who upon our leaving Chicago had returned to Terre Haute and there had remained during the winter. But now it was spring again, the local mill there closed, and here he was, our religious and moral mentor always. Yet Janet and Amy, companions of old, now made plans to enjoy themselves here socially, although apart from the minor school contacts made by Trina and myself, no particular social relationship or standing had been achieved. Any male companionship they desired would have to be arrived at flirtatiously and in passing —a method or process which, as anyone might have known, would never be countenanced in so good and pure a town. Were there not the churches, the schools, and the parlours of those who were properly introduced?

I should also explain here, though, that at this very time this town abounded in a certain type of gay youth—eighteen, nineteen, twenty, twenty-one and so on—who kept the scandal-mongers busy, particularly in regard to the type of girl who associated with him. Let us give them any names: Fred and Harry Ticket, sons of the leading hardware merchant of the place; Frank Dall, son of the County Treasurer; Bert Savage, another heir to a small-town future. At any rate, they contributed a coterie of small-town roués and Beau Brummells whose reputation was really, at most, unsavoury. Fred Ticket, in particular, was a shining example of both small-town vivacity and animality. He drank, gambled, and disported himself in such fashion as eventually to become a town scandal. Indeed, the seduction of half a dozen poverty-stricken girls was openly attributed to him. His father, a churchly man, was reputed to have bought off one girl after another, before finally he disowned him, driving him forth, a local Ishmael, to make his own living and his future as best he might. But what a future! I may as well relate it here, because I know the end of him was that at forty he returned to Warsaw and his old haunts, a broken, old-young man, a shabby spectre of his former force and enthusiasm. So low had he fallen in life that by then he was a cleaner-out of bar-rooms and on occasion —when he could get such work and was sober and strong enough to do it—a layer of brick and gravel walks, but as assistant only. And when he did get work, and so a little money, his one object was to keep moderately drunk, in order that he might not remember, perhaps. No more quips or bright jests; no more cynical gaiety at the expense of others less fortunate than himself. A wreck, and, after his fashion, pitiful. And yet my sole wonder then and now was and is that one of so much youthful energy and lust, and regardless of his vices, could come to so poor an end physically. Financially, of course, one's descent may well be sharp.

The Tickets, however, were a mere item in the local cosmos. There were many others. Next to mind come Harry and Frank Vigus, two charming-mannered youths, sons of a local banker. They, too, ran a gay, if not so desperate, course. The younger, Frank, was a kind of minute Beau Brummell, a mouse-like Chesterfield, who was always to be seen around the smartest part of the public square. For some reason he rarely worked, although he always wore the showiest of clothing, drove a spanking team hitched to a shining buggy, and owned a small sailboat in which he voyaged the belles of the village. His brother Harry was of a somewhat more sober turn, larger, better built, and with a seraphic smile. Almost every attractive girl—and some who were not so much so—tagged after him for a smile. My sister Trina, although only in her fifteenth year, was actually sadly smitten with him the year following our arrival there. Oh, his eyes were so lovely, his nose so straight, he had such a sweet smile, he was so courtly, kind, generous! The truth was that Harry, like his brother, was a beau, and, if anything, even more dangerous. For during our stay in Warsaw, a number of girls were rumoured to have fallen victims to his charms, although, unlike most youths, he apparently possessed some serpentine knowledge of how to save them from calamity. In fact, I fancy that was his chief crime. Be that as it may, he eventually left Warsaw at nineteen or thereabouts and joined the forces of a western railroad, with which he eventually shone as general advertising manager.

Again, there was Bob Baker, son of the principal grocer, and a clever type of clerk himself; Harry Woods, son of the President of the First National Bank; Walter Saulis, son of the Vice-President of the Warsaw State Bank; and so on, a large company, really. Clever people all, in a small-town way—who, among themselves, at the homes of one and another and around the town generally managed to establish a veritable social circle and to move and live in a whirl of parties, dances, balls, lawn fêtes, water festivals and the like. The local papers chronicled their comings and goings and doings. "George and Harry Ticket ran up to Chicago for the week-end." "Harry Woods and Bob Baker are planning an ice carnival, with the Baker boat house as a central gathering point, the evening of Thursday, January 18th." "The Misses Bertha and Etta Saulis have planned a lawn fête for their friends, to be held on the Saulis grounds the evening of Friday, August 10th, weather permitting. The dancing will be in the Saulis parlours and the west veranda, which will be made as gay and summery as flowers and Chinese lanterns will permit."

Being a youth highly susceptible to such joys as are here indicated, I was heartbroken to think that my youth, my looks and lack of means, prevented me from entering upon or even anticipating any of the heavenly privileges here indicated. This one I envied for his looks, another for his clothes, another for his courage, and so on through a long catalogue of earthly and very youthful woes. The beauty of the girls, which in this town, and as it seemed to me then, had a stinging richness, ravished me of my very wits. As I saw them at this floodtime of youth, when the whole world was gilded by a substance which may have a deeper origin than blazing suns or circling planets, they were little short of magic and moon madness. Who has planned these gorgeous individualities that like the odour and witchery of flowers, they should addle the wits of youth in springtime? Who set the diamond firmament to glow in its black-blue arc and put the subtle hands of man to weaving textures that bring the colours of the rainbow and softness of flowers to the service of the flesh? Those springtime years in that small town! How they vibrated with that ancient energy that has made the world young through timeless floods of time! Before man was, it was, and after him, through forgotten days and nations, will come again; spring: of the body, the heart, the soul, no less than of the year!

CHAPTER XLIII

BUT, as I have said, here were Amy and Janet now on the scene, and bent on entertainment. And no sooner had they arrived than they set forth to "parade the streets," as my father described it, to see what "loafers" or "mashers" they could involve in their toils. And, of course, it was not difficult for them to do this. The principal street corners at almost any hour of the day were certain to be occupied by at least one or two gallants whose principal occupation was that of seeing who and what was to be seen.

My sisters must have shone as a pair of choice morsels, for they were soon sought after and attended. We heard of it from one source and another, you may be sure. A lack of training and social discretion, perhaps, led them to certain exaggerated effects of costume and coiffure which might reasonably be described as gauche, if not bold. The ignorant mind loves to exaggerate, or perhaps one would better say, only the exaggerated in everything appeals to the ignorant mind. Yet time has not proved that these girls were dull in any general sense, merely that they were unsophisticated and errant in regard to certain small-town conventions or aspirations. An indiscriminate love of colour and life was binding them. At any rate, no sooner had they taken up with one or another of the youths in question than by night or day they were to be found planning or executing boat rides on the lakes, buggy rides into the country, trips to dances in neighbouring towns, and the like. But my father, soon aware of the social licence into which their gay amiability led them, was watching, and presently a storm.

"Such a bold, shameless way to dress!" he declared one evening when Janet shortly after her arrival here appeared at the family table with "spit curls" pasted down the sides of her cheeks and her lips and cheeks rouged. "Those shoes! That hat!"

Dressed for the street, she was always cap-a-pie, in patent leather shoes with white tops and a broad-brimmed hat which flared with an immense ostrich plume. Amy also, assisted out of Janet's wardrobe, was flashing in borrowed finery: dress, shoes, rings, pins, furbelows; and also painted and powdered, as you may well guess.

"And you!" went on my father, addressing her. "You have gotten yourself up more ridiculous than ever!" He turned and addressed my mother. "Is that the way they are going to carry on while they are here? I thought once that Janet was going to turn out to be a good girl, she liked to work so, but now look at her!"

Mother herself was obviously nonplussed. She agreed to talk to them, begging him not to make a scene until she had used her influence to make them see the necessity of a more circumspect presence here. But all that she could do or say was of little force against their burning impetuosity and desire to live. In consequence, a number of succeeding storms; arguments and tirades.

But these two were now determined to dress and do as they chose: a determination which was fortified in so far as this house was concerned by the fact that my father was contributing so little to its upkeep. His days as a material producer were practically over. He might have been called a moral adviser at this crisis, but little more. Yet a fanatic Catholicism led him to feel that it was his duty to protest and to interpose physical force if necessary. My mother, while no longer blazing with the passion she obviously had had for him in her youth and beginning to see that he had wrecked not only his own life but hers by his blind devotion to religion and public morals, was yet not satisfied to set aside his authority entirely. A man was needed in this home as well as every other, if no more than a pantalooned figure of one. While no doubt she wished his authority modified or done away with in some matters, she was not willing to have it set aside in all, or to assume the rôle of moral censor and master where his will did not operate. In consequence, there was a modified form of social if not moral rebellion in our home, an absence of respectable authority.

For instance, my sisters believed (as did we all on occasion) that if they had only mother to deal with, they could do much as they chose. On the other hand, my mother appeared to wish to hold my father in reserve as a weapon to be brandished or even used in critical moments. Realising her attitude and that of the children, I think he would gladly have washed his hands of the whole matter, save that his moral and religious bias would not permit him so to do. I think that at times, in moments of anger, he actually hated my mother, looking on her as the cause of the moral wreck of the family. At other times, I am sure he regarded her as one whose intentions were good but whose judgment was weak; he felt she agreed with him, only she disliked the radical measures which he felt impelled to apply, and yet was not shrewd enough to devise better ones. Many of these arguments impressed me as much as at times they depressed me. For one thing, they kept me speculating constantly on what was right and wrong in connection with human wishes and human conduct: a type of meditation that has never since deserted me.

The immediate result, of course, was conduct which though partially repressed was not sufficiently so to save us from some local criticism. For one thing, these two girls made friends with the Tickets and Harry Woods and Bob Baker, individuals whose very companionship, unless limited to their own set, was sure to evoke social suspicion and even ill repute. There were boat rides of an afternoon or evening. A small pleasure park on Pike Lake, newly opened, received their attention, and there were evening disappearances of which no satisfactory account was made.

"This thing is not going to go on any longer!" declared my father one night to my mother when the twain having slipped out unseen remained out until after twelve. "Here I sit if I have to wait up all night! They shall not ride down my opposition if they do yours! I will show them! If they do not get home before one o'clock, they do not get in! Let them go where they spent the first part of the night! Such shameless creatures, coming here when you are trying to make a new start, and conducting themselves so that already the whole town talks about them!" (He did not know this really; it probably was not so; but he made the assertion for what it was worth.) "Who knows where they are? Who knows what they do?"

My mother admitted feebly that much of this was true, yet afraid of his harshness and brutality, she still hesitated to side with him. He would probably lock them out or attempt to strike them when they came in, which prospect terrified her as much as it did me who overheard it. Worse, it raised in my immature mind such exaggerated thoughts as to the shame and scandal their conduct was likely to inflict on the rest of us as to reduce me socially not a little. To have to be a part of such a life! To have to suffer because of it! All of us! I personally began to be nervous, depressed—very.

Realising that her services would be needed as an equaliser, and so afraid to go to bed, my mother sat there along with father until two in the morning, when the miscreants at last returned. But then! My father stormed so loud that we three youngest children, who had gone to bed and were fast asleep, were aroused and came down. But to witness what? First, an argument as to whether they were to be permitted to enter—the two of them standing outside in the night— and then, after much rage on my father's part and the reducing statement on the part of my mother that after all she had found this place and made this new home, not he, and that willy-nilly they were to be permitted to enter, the climax of their entrance. But then again, the shouted demands of my father as to where they had been and what doing, and their semi-defiant, dubious, and yet possibly truthful, reply that they had been rowing on the lake.

"The lake! The lake! Yes, the lake at two o'clock in the morning! And with the trashy loafers of the town! Shameless scoundrels no better than yourselves!" But in addition, a long tirade, too long to be added here, at the end of which, Amy, staring defiantly, and certainly not guilty of any immorality up to that time, exclaiming: "Why, my goodness, can't we even go for a row on the lake without all this row? Other people's children aren't threatened and abused when they go anywhere. You'd think we were a lot of dogs and slaves!" She could always employ a cynical, condescending, resentful and semi-defiant air when and where her whims were crossed or her father involved. On this occasion her face was white and tense and her eyes blazed an irreducible opposition.

"You strumpet!" shouted my father, advancing upon her savagely. "You vile hussy! I know what you want! I know what you would do! Before I will stand by and see such goings-on, the family name trailed in the mud again here, I will twist your neck! I'll choke you to death and throw you out in the street where you belong, you vile-hearted, good-for-nothing, evil-minded little demon!" (I have not given the exact words, of course, but in substance this is correct.) In addition he actually laid tense hands on her and attempted to choke and subdue her.

But by this time, Amy, finding herself assaulted and realising that her best weapon lay in simulating terror and pain, began to scream at the top of her voice, long, shrill, terrifying shrieks, which in a tenement would have brought hundreds to her side. As it was, this house was reasonably isolated, and so in so far as the neighbourhood was concerned, insulated. In addition, however, Janet joined in with a few terrified cries of her own, and the total accumulation was one of moans, imprecations, charges and countercharges on all sides.

"Stop! Stop now!" called my mother, coming forward and attempting to thrust herself between them. "This is enough! You mustn't choke her! You don't know how to handle children. I know they are in the wrong in staying out so late, but there are other ways of correcting them besides shouting and waking up the whole neighbourhood. You are too rough. You always were."

A scene that Henry Fielding, or Goldsmith, or even Irving, would have rejoiced in; yet to me it was so dreadful that it fairly burned itself into my brain. What sort of people were we, anyway? Yelling and screaming when the world outside demanded order, peace, self-respect! I remember standing and staring wide-eyed, frightened, hurt. Oh . . . oh . . . oh!

And worse, next day a certain Alfred Sisson, who lived in the first house west from ours, separated by perhaps two or three hundred feet of ground, wanted to know if anyone had been ill at our house the night before. His mother had said she heard someone crying.

"No," I replied, denying everything, but a flush of shame mantling my cheeks and probably noted by him.

But the reducing impact of all this on me! I was so shaken that for days I could not get it out of my mind. In school, on the streets, wherever I was, I thought of it. For, willy-nilly and reason as I might (and my reasoning powers were not so good at the time), I was impressed by this town, the new and better social order of which now we bade plainly to be a part.

Those pretty girls in the schoolroom! The small, clean, and seemingly orderly (mentally and in every other way) homes by which we were surrounded. The boys of good homes and good manners who now approached Ed and myself with proffers of friendship! It made me not a little sad. I tried to think that maybe it would make no real difference, but also there was the haunting thought that it would or might. My mother's constantly reiterated hope that the family would be able to do better here was actually sinking into my blood.

Nevertheless, this storm ended by Janet being urged to go back to Chicago, where she had work of some kind and where she would be out of the range of her father's wrath: a proposition she seemed glad enough to accept. As for Amy, being still very young, she was permitted to stay, on the ground that separated from Janet she was not entirely intractable, though my father had no regard for her and would have been glad to see her go also, I think.

Just the same, and as I feared from the beginning, there was an unpleasant aftermath to all this, and soon. For apparently at least some of the youths, if not the families of the town, were apprised of the fact that John Ticket and Harry Woods had been associating, at times at least, with both Amy and Janet: a fact or charge the significance of which was not clear to me at first. For while I could understand, clearly enough as I thought, the evil of late hours—the talk that the same might invoke, I mean, with, say, kissing and hugging as concomitants —still, anything more than that in connection with these, my sisters, at least, I did not grasp. It was only when one day, perhaps as much as a month or two later, a boy whom I did not even know very well (and whom I found knocking butternuts from two trees at the extreme rear of our leasehold, and whom, with the aid of Ed and a stick and much bluffing, I succeeded in driving off) called back as he went: "Ah, why don't you get your two Ticket sisters to help you?"

"Our two Ticket sisters!" What did he mean? Already I knew of Ticket's large hardware store. We bought things there. Also in a dim way I knew of two or three sons and a daughter. They lived in one of the best houses in town. But even so! And yet presently it came to me. It must mean, yes, it must mean that he—whichever Ticket it was—was considered loose and immoral and was or had been associating

240

with my sisters, or they with him. And that in consequence they were looked upon as no better than he. Then, after all, perhaps my father was right! Perhaps he should be just as severe as he was, and more so. And so, dark thoughts as to the effect of all this on our social station here. That a boy like that, a stranger to me, really, should call that to me!

For weeks and months after that I pondered over this, wondering what people might be thinking of us; also envying those families, who because of wealth or cleverness or the circumspect conduct of their children, were respected and looked up to; wishing, in fact, that we might be like them; although at relatively the same time I was also wishing that I might have all of the privileges I chose with some of the lovely girls I was seeing here. A bit of social unbalance which may be meditated upon for what it is worth. Some will assume that it spelled definite moral unbalance as well as mental degradation; others that it fits in with the arrant hypocrisy of life itself. My belief is that it was and is in line with a curious and inherent unbalance of nature itself; an unbalance pre-supposing, as it must, balance, yet due to an innate tendency toward variety, plus a tendency toward unity and harmony, plus a necessity for equation between the two, resulting in what we know as life, that shimmering, pleasing vibration or movement which we know to be trivial and reasonless but which, in its passing, is so vital to our desires.

But then, that very winter, following close on these social discrepancies, came news of my sister Janet's marriage in Chicago. I recall being very much impressed, for after all of the almost riotous condemnation of her I had heard from my father, if not my mother, here was (as my parents seemed to see it) this much desired thing, marriage, and that to a man who if "no great shakes" socially in our world was nevertheless of some little position elsewhere, in New York City, no less; a New York politician, as I heard him called, a deputy or second deputy somebody in the New York Street Cleaning Department, who also, as time was to prove, was of some small political influence, and hence means. That is, he was connected with Tammany Hall—one of its ward or district lieutenants—and as such up to his arm-pits, as I, if no other, learned later, in the shameful political conniving and legerdemain that was a part of all politics and jobholding in New York City in the 1890's.

But what appeared to be conveyed at this time was that he was still comparatively young—forty or so—and had means, for subsequently there were rumours of a charming apartment in 15th Street in New York, also jewels, furs, an exciting trip to Saratoga and other places, and finally the birth of a boy, and later a girl, both well-favoured physically as time was to prove, and in their subsequent years as successful and conventional as the average person, no more and no less so.

But in regard to all this, I recall meditating not a little at the time. For after all, the tirades I have spoken of were of so recent a day. And I had been so reduced by them, emotionally and physically. And more, considering all that had been said, I had been strongly of the opinion that no respectable man anywhere would have either Janet or Amy. And yet here was Janet already taken over by one, and that one, presumably at least, respectable. For was he not an officeholder in the great city of New York, and more, as a letter in regard to all this stated, a Catholic? This latter fact appeared to relieve if not impress my mother, and as I well knew would pass as pure gold with my father. For what more than that could be desired in a man? Honesty was excellent enough, but even the lack of that forgiven if one remained a true Catholic! I saw the fact sticking out of all my father's arguments. Weakness of character? A commonplace mind? Trudging dumbness? Were not nearly all Catholics like that? But faith in the Church! Ah, how excellent! What more could be desired?

And true enough, when my father heard of this very sudden and all too dimly outlined marriage, complete silence as to Janet's past. So she was married at last! High time! And to a Catholic! Well, she was lucky! So harum-scarum a girl scarcely deserved so much. Had anyone witnessed the marriage? Was there any proof? There appeared to be, since both Ruth and Eleanor vouched for it. They had witnessed the marriage in some outlandish Saint Something-or-other Church in Chicago. Very good, let bygones be bygones! And in so far as Janet and her father were concerned, they were. In short, the typical happy ending. Or, as we say in these days: "Swell!"

CHAPTER XLIV

ANOTHER thing that cast a not wholly satisfactory light on at least one member of my mother's family in this region was the social condition of one of her sisters, Susan Wybold by name, whose husband and family—to whom we were introduced during our first winter in Warsaw—were socially not so much, to say the least. To me, at the time, and with all my sensitivity as to how we should make out here, this group, once I came in contact with it, appeared most unsatisfactory. Aunt Susan and her husband Amos and their children lived in, or rather near, a little town called Silver Lake, some twelve miles from Warsaw. It had but one north and south road (railway) which ran from Indianapolis to Michigan City and cut it off from the main line of growth and improvement, which seemed in those days to concern only the towns and cities that were pierced by the great trunk lines running from east to west.

Neither this aunt nor my uncle, the bishop, was notified of our presence in Warsaw until some little time after our arrival. When Susan did learn, though, she came quickly enough to visit us—since in the first place my mother was very dear to her, and next, because her idle, shiftless, good-for-nothing husband found in this situation an opportunity of visiting without much expense. In short, he was only too willing to drive her the twelve miles because of the prospect of staying and sightseeing here in Warsaw, the county seat, to his heart's content.

Pardon me if I digress too far in portraying this very peculiar group. A stranger, queerer family I never really encountered —so truly rural, down-at-heels and, in so far as the father was concerned, shiftless, as to constitute a valuable study in what in America is known as "poor white." My Uncle Amos was a little man, whiskered after the manner of a Scotch terrier, with about as much intelligent, serious interest in life as a fly.

He only pretended to be a farmer, really, for he had no farm of his own, only a small leasehold of seven acres which he worked on shares. (I smile when I think of what an intelligent French or Italian or German farmer could do with even that!) Grey-blue of eye; a foolish, talkative mind concerned with every folderol, prank, error, failure, crime and scandal for miles around, and with these only; grey jeans suit, shabby, wrinkled, patched, mud-bespattered, the trouser-legs tucked into wrinkled high-top boots, and an old brown felt hat with a hole in it; these were the superficial and sub-surface details of a temperament which struck me on sight as strangely vapid and uncouth.

In addition, there were two boys and a girl, both brought along to greet their unknown relatives: the elder of the boys, Wilbur by name, a tall, gangling farmhand type, strong and intelligent and valuable enough, as time was to prove, but then a mere gawky, untrained country boy; the younger, James or Jimmie, a hunchback and dwarf for size, all of twelve years old but no larger than a boy of seven or eight, with thin, clawlike hands, a face like a parched nut; eyes black, piercing and impish, and a restless, inquisitive temperament, bustling here and there but understanding or accomplishing little, and as soiled and badly dressed as his farmer father. The girl, Jess, was in many respects a fair example of a degenerate stock. Like her younger brother, she was dark, very, with the same piercing, savage, catlike black eyes and the same brown, claw-like hands. She had no beauty, unless it was that of a savage Indian girl. Her dress was almost nondescript, blue and green gingham, with a cotton or linen collar of some inharmonious colour, and bits of red sewed on here and there. Instead of a hat she wore a gingham farm bonnet, and her feet were shod with shoes of an impossible size and weight. And at no time had she anything to say beyond the mere yea-yeas and nay-nays of the farm world. I learned later that she also swore on occasion and was about as conscious of her virtue as a cat. Concerning a youth who married her the following year, and because their child was born three months after their marriage, Jimmie, the dwarf, once told me, and with impish glee, that the new husband being taxed by his father-in-law with the crime of premature cohabitation, had exclaimed: "Well, I never buy a boot without first trying it on!" Whereat old Amos, hearing this told again, laughed heartily.

Susan, my aunt, was a woman of a different sort again, one of those relatively superior and sensitive spirits, but with no more than a farm education—and that of those days—and hopelessly stricken and shamed by the course her life had taken. Unlike my mother, she was dark and sombre of skin, with a look at times like that of a hooded fate. Naturally of a genial temperament and once very beautiful, as I understood, she had degenerated into a slattern, possibly because of brooding over an unimpedible tide of misfortune. For like my mother again, she had married against her parents' wishes, though as I saw it she had done much worse than my mother. For whatever might be said against my father, aside from his astounding religious prejudices and emotional impressionability, he was not a bad citizen nor one who had always been unsuccessful. Amos Wybold never had a commercial or other idea of import in his life. Indeed, even my father was amazed at his cotton-brained imponderability.

"What a man!" he declared once, astonished at the evidence of instability, low breeding and utter shiftlessness. "Hat on one side of his head, teeth dirty with tobacco, boots muddy, and never a thought of whether he has a dollar or not! And there sits his boy with patches on his pants and his wife without a dress to her name, and he whistles and sings, yet a man all of fifty-eight years of age! This crazy American world! No religion! No taste! He spits on the floor and puts his feet on the table and calls me by my first name! And that girl! There she sits, without a word to say, her hands folded! Such ignorance! Such dullness! Such shiftlessness! I never saw the beat!"

I laughed at my father's characterisation, which he carefully refrained from repeating to my mother because he did not care to stir up a countercharge. (She had not seen any of his relatives.) But what he said was relatively true. At the same time, in spite of their defects, I came after a little while to have a liking for them, and because of a hearty invitation extended to all to come and take pot-luck with them for as long as we liked, I, companioned by Ed, once journeyed of a summer day to their place and was received with a geniality and cheer which was captivating. Their house and barn were ramshackle, adjoining the small acreage which was farmed on shares. In the barn were two horses, a cow, a wagon, some farming implements, several pigs and three or four lean dogs and cats. There was also a tame ferret used to catch and kill rats and woodchucks. I recall also a huge straw-stack near the house, down which Ed and I, along with the young hunchback Jimmie, set to tumbling soon after our arrival. I also recall that at intervals on the way here I had stopped to listen to the whir of reapers and the calls to the horses to be heard on every hand. It was the time for taking in the grain: hot, clear July or August weather. I could not help contrasting the lovely fields about, the fresh winds and sun, with these relatives of mine, who mentally seemed so totally unresponsive to all this. For, as anyone could see in connection with all save Aunt Sue, either the beauty of all this was an old and wearisome story or there had never been sensitivity to any phase of it to begin with: mere indoor or front stoop chatter about idle things—dances, fiddle parties, prospective trips to town, who was courting whom. Positively, in the face of the immense dignity and awe-compelling beauty of the fields and hills which enfolded this grey and weather-beaten hut or cabin, their home, I was astonished by the vagrom and brainless moods of those who occupied it.

None the less and notwithstanding, my Aunt Sue appealed to me greatly. She was in some ways so like my mother, soft-spoken, dreamy, wistful, resigned. And her soft, weary, appealing, defeated eyes! And like my mother, she, too, wore the simple black dress with turned-down collar affected by the Mennonites, a costume so simple and unassuming that it suggested that of a man, a Shaker or a Quaker.

Aside from cleanness or uncleanness, I doubt whether I have ever had strong preferences among humanity at large. The rich have not appealed to me any more than the poor, if as much. Individuality or oddity of character I would put first among my personal preferences, although along with that I would accept, although by no means demand, cleanliness, unless it was that I was to be compelled to associate with such individuals at close range. But so compelled, the remaining idiosyncrasies of humanity do not trouble me so much. But one thing that happily I can say for my Aunt Sue is that she was reasonably clean. Against overwhelming odds and practically nothing to do with, she obviously struggled for a kind of order and spruceness. Her costume, as plain as it was, and at best a thing of rags and patches, was clean, and the furniture of her small home, clumsy farm-made furniture, of what vintage I cannot say, was not unattractive to me. For one thing, I recall an old four-poster bed with rope slats, which to-day might be of some value. The remaining pieces, if my memory does not fail me, were tumbledown, paintless, and without charm of design. One or two old rag rugs, worn thin and tramped muddy, as a rule, were laid upon bare plank floors, the planks themselves wide, worn and loose. But without, just the same, clean winds blew; trees and wild flowers flourished; the sun, the moon, the stars peeped in; the earth rotated and night followed day, and day night. Undisturbed by my aunt, I wandered about, musing idly over all I saw and storing impressions such as these which here come to life after so many years.

But to return. The day after Ed and I arrived came visiting the daughter previously described, with her husband, as well as a niece of my uncle's and her husband, and a neighbourhood farmhand or farmer. All, as I noted, sat about and joked in a crude, coarse way. There was some argument, not only on the night of our arrival but this next day also, between my uncle and aunt as to where to procure fresh meat for so many, since there was none in the larder, but finally and after much discussion, and in the face of so much poverty, two good-sized chickens were brought forward, from somewhere and there and then killed near the doorstep, and fried.

It is strange how impressions of this kind always linger. I recall even now the bare table, with the tin lamp, at evening; Uncle Amos and Wilbur coming in from the fields at sundown, raw yokels both as they seemed to me at the time, and washing their hands at a tin basin on a post outside. I recall also the mournful steel-blue and red of the sky, the chirp of crickets and the hum of insects, and the welcome sound of the crackling wood fire in the kitchen. Also that unlike Ed and myself (who after a hot day were invariably compelled to bathe) these sweating farmers, bedtime having arrived, did not bathe; also that the beds in the loft, under a sloping roof beaten upon all day by the sun, were hot and dry and stuffy, and that although cool evening winds blew outside, no windows were opened. There were beds in each angle or corner of the room, one occupied by Wilbur and Frank, another by Ed and myself, a third by my aunt and a fourth by Uncle Amos. Also that there was almost no attempt at privacy, possibly because of the heat—I do not know—although in front of her bed, I noticed my aunt had hung some sort of cloth, for the occasion, possibly. The next night, though, the daughter Jess and her husband occupied one of these upper beds and the niece and her husband another directly adjoining the one in which Ed and I slept. And in the dim moonlight which pervaded the room later I saw both of these wives undress, the niece, as I noted, being large and graceful and rather attractive. And the next morning I saw them dress and, to my astonishment and perturbation, the yokel husband play with the breasts of his wife in a joking, unashamed, animal way. "Whad'ya call these, Jess?" he asked, pulling at them, while she protested: "Oh, let me alone, Jim!" Finally they dressed and went downstairs.

If I have indicated in any way that I was unutterably shocked by this atmosphere, I do not mean to do so. On the contrary, and once I found my Aunt Sue so appealing, this shabby, viney, leafy, animal-like world appealed to me. It was, after a fashion, like being housed with certain curious and not too offensive animals, my dear aunt excluded, of course. As usual also, my uncle was as gay as he was inconsequential.

"'Spect I'll get all o' sixty bushels to the acre outta that thar wheat, don't you, Will?" (He was speaking to Wilbur the night before as they came in.) And then: "Ey-gad, I'm tired! I hope I don't have to work that hard soon again. The sun mighty near baked me to-day. Eh, old gal," to his wife, "you'd oughter be glad you don't have to work like that, what?"

"Oh, yes, work!" I can still hear my aunt's soft, resigned voice. "I don't work either, I suppose." But she was not morose at that moment, rather cheerful, because of these several presences, probably.

After a time also, as I recall, Wilbur got out a French mouth harp and played most lugubriously. Also as usual (I presume) Jimmie refused to wash his feet before going to bed, and when I asked him why not, said: "Because I don't wanta! I'm not goin' to wash my feet."

"Don't your mother ever make you?" I asked.

"I'd like to see 'er," he half snarled, and yet somewhat ironically. "Ey-gad, I'd cuss her out, and the old man, too, if he tried to make *me!*" He was, in the main, a viperish, impish child, but with some genial and playful moments at that.

The daughter, as I also observed this second day (it was probably Sunday), sat around and trifled with her husband, or rather he with her, making overtures which could have but one meaning. Near by, however, was Silver Lake, a bluish-green gem set in high green pines, which save for the occasional presence of a lone fisherman or two, was silent and deserted. And about the cabin, as I have said, were great stretches of field and wood, grain so yellow it was like gold, and woods so deeply green that by contrast with sky and wheat they were black, also so silent that the song of birds and the chirp of insects was loud. Wide-branched trees spread their arms about this weather-beaten hut, and from the back porch, which faced to the south and west, was a view of green meadow. Here, as quickly as I found one, I placed a rocking chair and watched the fading light, listened to the birds, the bells of distant cattle, the whir of reapers, and the trudging steps of my aunt. And finally night fell, the stars came out, and I went to bed, happy in the strangeness and newness of all things about me.

It was this same aunt, though, who the next afternoon gave me a forecast of my life which haunted me for a long time and which has since largely been realised. We were sitting on the porch at the time, eating what the more sophisticated would call lunch but which here was known as dinner. All of the others had left us and my aunt casually took up my empty coffee cup and looked at the grounds left therein.

"Did you ever have your fortune told?" she asked.

"Oh, please tell it, auntie!" I exclaimed.

She smiled in an enigmatic way, and giving me the cup told me to turn it bottom-side up and then around three times, whereupon she took it from me and after examining the brown grains—with what mystic intuition I know not—said: "I see where you are going to travel, travel, travel. I see cities and towns and crowds, great cities and great crowds. And here," she added, holding the cup toward me for me to look, "are books, I think, and girls. There are girls behind you over there." She pointed to two great hills of dark coffee-grounds. I looked, but my veiled eyes could not see.

'You will never be rich," she added, "and not very happy,

249

but people are going to follow you. I see great crowds and great cities."

That was all she told me, but it made a deep impression on me. It seemed, as I sat there, as if suddenly a window had been opened and I had looked out on a world which concerned years and years to come. And at once I felt a great inward surging of the blood or mind, as if then and there I must be up and away. Those mystic cities! Already they were calling me. I would not be rich, nor very happy, but there would be travel, girls, crowds! At that moment, I presume, I wanted to be neither rich nor happy, but to arise and traverse the new, strange, mysterious world that was beyond and calling to me, the world that was to be known as only mysteries are known.

Oh, world so wide! Oh, world so strange! What, after all, have all my eager seekings brought me?

CHAPTER XLV

DURING this same summer and fall, I passed or was promoted from May Calvert's room in B Ward School to the eighth grade Central High, where a Miss Luella Reid, a stern, dark, sallow woman, with black-brown eyes, who looked and acted more like an Indian brave than a spinster of thirty-odd then functioned, took me in charge and furthered my education. She was reputed to be a most capable teacher of boys and girls from thirteen to fifteen years of age, and distributed her praises and censure impartially. Though she terrified me at first, I came by degrees to like her, and at the end of the year parted from her with regret.

Incidentally, it was during my progress through this last year of the common school that I came in contact with various boys and girls who affected my local viewpoint profoundly and who by the same token helped form a very definite outlook on life which endured for years. They were of the older and more central portion of the town and attended the combination Central and High School to which I now, along with Trina, was removed. Among them were the younger members of the Ticket, Vigus, Baker, Oldfather, Moon and other families too numerous to mention, who, comparatively wealthy and therefore socially prominent, composed a form of local aristocracy to which mere passing strangers such as ourselves were not admitted.

Nevertheless, in one or two senses, and for the time being, we were admitted into friendly relations with these younger members, although just why I may not say. We certainly had no means wherewith to do as they did. One member of my class, for instance, John Ticket, a brother of that Harry Ticket of previous pages, soon after my encounter with him decided to make friends with me, as did most of these others. In many ways he reminded me of that elegant young beau in Chicago who had struck me in the mouth: the same airs and this and that, only now friendly instead of the reverse. Incidentally also, there was Will Vigus, the younger brother of that Frank of whom I have spoken, whom I came to know and like very well and with whom I went about some, skating and the like, only so much engaged was he with some of the pretty girls of the school and town that he had not much time for me or any other boy. And it was just in connection with girls that I envied him most, not only his looks but his clothes, freedom, courage, and money, with which last he seemed always so plentifully provided. In short, at most times, seeing him hurrying here and there so smartly dressed and talking on such friendly terms with most of these girls whom I so greatly admired, I was made more sad than happy by his liking for me.

Again, there was Arthur Moon, cold, disdainful, well-dressed, recessive, who even invited me to his home, but with the air of one who was condescending rather than equalising, an attitude which finally reduced the friendship to nothing. And after him, Walter Flood, Odin Oldfather, John Reid, Judson Morris, all sons of successful and hence fairly prominent men. I can truly say that during all of the time I knew them and for years afterward when I thought of them, I foolishly envied them the financial and social start which life appeared to have given them—but which, as time teaches us, it so readily revokes. Indeed, in my youth, as I see myself now, at least, I must have been very much of a climber.

Among the girls, also, there were a number who, because of beauty, prosperity, innate hauteur and the like—but principally because of beauty—stirred in me an ever-present if sometimes recessive and fearsome desire to possess or at least to move and so control them in my favour, so much so that at times it swelled to an animal yearning. Mary Ticket, for instance, the sister of Harry and John. I see her now, a buxom maid of fifteen, whose face and figure suggested so enticingly and gaily the animal delight with which she took life and which later, as I heard, resulted in a full experience. During that year she sat in front of me in school and seemed at times actually to challenge the desire and daring which at the same time she scorned. Those green, catlike eyes of hers! That supercilious smile! She was so direct, vigorous, forthright; looking at you with hard, bold eyes that flashed messages of admiration or scorn in no uncertain way. Like her brothers, she was a hoyden—their female counterpart—and demanded a degree of smartness and gaiety in her admirers to which I could not, as I so well then knew, aspire.

Again, there was Stella Davenant, blonde, lithe, active, graceful. She was so genial, playful and what not else that had I had the least courage, I might have shared the delight of her smiles, companionship and conversation, which apparently with seeming impartiality she bestowed on so many. She even smiled on me at times, in school and out, her big blue eyes as clear as sapphires, seeming to say: "Come, now, don't be bashful; I won't hurt you!" But the mere sight of her looking at me caused my heart to beat so fast that I would almost choke, my eyes unable to meet the frank implication of her own; I had no courage.

Again, there was that Nata Weyler whom I have described. In the seventh grade she had paid no least attention to me, but here in the eighth grew more friendly, hailing me at times and doing her best to draw me into a flirtation of sorts, which, none the less, for want of clothes, this and that, I thought myself unworthy of. At the same time, my natural bashfulness was so constantly frustrating me that I was in torment daily, hourly. How unchangingly I longed, and how persistently I failed! The truth was, as I have said before, that I was a mortal coward when it came to girls, having no way of either cleverly expressing or concealing the awe, delight and wonder with which their varying beauty filled me. Hypnotised, tongue-tied, spellbound, I could only gaze, feeling myself to be hopelessly deficient and having no power to interest them. Yet had I only known it or could I have mustered a little faith in myself, this was by no means true.

For during that winter came numerous parties, straw rides, sleigh rides, gay gatherings on the ice Saturday afternoons and evenings, which tended to make clear to me that in spite of my lacks—looks, clothes, bashfulness, what you will—I was destined to have friends, and not a few of them. Among the boys above mentioned I appeared slowly but surely to grow in favour, on what grounds I could never quite make out, until at last, and especially in connection with those after-school palavers in Morris's drug store, the senior Moon's grocery, and where not else—I was quite regularly a part of one small group or another that was bent on doing what? Skating, getting up a Hallowe'en party, playing chess or cards in the County Clerk's office or the back of Morris's drug store, or calling on some girls somewhere. Although in so far as cards or girls were concerned, I invariably found some way of avoiding any final participation, lack of means and daring warning me against unhappy dénouements of any kind.

None the less, there were the parties, sleigh rides and ice gatherings, all properly chaperoned, to which Trina and I were invited, and throughout these I fared more successfully than I had ever hoped. For with several of these girls with whom I did not dare familiarise myself singly or alone in school or on the street, here I found myself much more directly faced and compelled to talk, and under such circumstances at least proved more at ease than ever I could elsewhere. Thus, on a sleigh ride one night—an immense box sleigh made of the bed of an enormous wagon, filled with straw and placed on runners—I found myself seated by that same Nata Weyler, whose dark, curly hair and black eyes and olive skin so enticed me, and who now finding me in this immediate contact, exclaimed: "Oh, it's Theo! Now you can't get away, can you?" And after I had mumbled that I didn't want to, but did no more than that, she turned to talk to one or two others before finally turning again to me to say, with a warm, cheerful laugh: "Oh, I'm sure I'm going to be cold without something warm around me!" Whereupon, my protective dullness having been penetrated, I actually ventured to supply the necessary something! But did anything ever come of this? Believe it or not, not a single additional thing worth recording! I could not talk. I had no small aggressive patter, because I had no courage. Perhaps I did kiss her, or she kissed me, but if so, with freezing tremor on my part. (If only the myself of that day were here present, in order that I might hand him a strong, illuminating kick!)

And as for Stella Davenant, I was kissed by her at a party. And by a certain Dollie Stead, a plump, rosy girl whom I did not take to because she seemed too assertive and even aggressive or possessive: a show of temperament which, since she was not as attractive as some of these others, alienated me completely.

But one thing more surprising than any other in my life up to that time, and which effected in me a certain phase of practical understanding in regard to girls, their ultimate desires, daring (if any), and my own intimate relationship to the same. It happened in this way. On my way from school, going out our street regularly morning and evening, I passed a combined bakery and restaurant which was the property of a mid-European and his wife, but of exactly what nationality—German, Dutch, Swiss, Hungarian or Czech—I cannot now say. It was a none-too-clean place, as I used to think, since occasionally I stopped there for bread, but clean or not, and especially since it stood on the best commercial side of the public square opposite the county court-house, did a thriving business. Many people ate there at noon and evening: country visitors, excursionists to our lakes, and some of the schoolboys who had money to spend in that way.

Working for this couple from time to time—principally after school, as I noticed—was their fourteen or fifteen-year-old daughter, a stocky, smiling, healthy, vigorous and playful girl to whom the boys of the town made easy, suggestive, though rarely coarse, remarks, to which, in the absence of her parents, she did not reply in kind by any means but took it all somewhat too good-naturedly, as it seemed to me: an attitude which caused her to appear the least bit common, not of the same caste exactly as these others whom I so greatly admired. And yet, going for bread or stopping in with these others, there she was, and when not too busy with others occasionally giving me a smile which I thought merely friendly. But at other times, as I also thought, something which I could not pass over as just a friendly smile: an urgent, contemplative something. Her eyelids, as I recall, and her eye sockets— the pink, puffy flesh just beneath the eyes—evoked a sudden, unanticipated heat in me. She had a sensual, meaty attractiveness, there was no doubt of that. Just the same, I was no beau and could not respond or make gay or idle, let alone explorative and progressive, conversation. I never knew how to begin.

But one early April evening, passing her father's bakery just at the close of the supper hour rush (if there was one) and when it was quite dusk, there she was outside the door. And at that hour, whatever might be doing within the restaurant, there were few if any pedestrians about the square. Nearly all were at home eating their dinners. And as important as this contact then proved to be, I cannot now recall whether I spoke to her first or she to me, or whether seeing me and knowing how bashful I was, she made some playful remark which caused me to pause, although knowing my *then* self as I do now, it must have been something like that. At any rate, before I knew it, she had pushed me with her hand or shoulder and in her smiling, enticing way had said: "I'll bet you can't catch me," and started running along the alley which lay to one side of the bakery, separating it from the adjoining stores to the south and, turning into quite a large open space, partially enclosed by a high board fence, and within which were stacked or scattered any number of large and small packing cases, some of them large enough to house a piano or a veritable mass of dry goods or hardware, large enough, at least, to house several children at play. And once we reached this aisled maze, where not a few of these great cases lay sidewise and open on the ground, dashing into one, and since I dizzily followed, pretending to be trapped.

And since so it was, and myself being seized by that sudden, hot desire which she so easily evoked, seizing her, and since she buried her face, mock-helplessly, in a corner, seeking to kiss her. Whereupon ensued a brief if mock-defensive wrestling match, all the more exciting and enticing because of the obvious yielding and yet seemingly contesting desire on her part to be in such close contact with me, so much so that we twisted here and there and then presently stumbled or fell, or at least she did, and so dragged me down with her, but in such a way that once prone on the floor of the box, she was beneath me, her face close to mine. But more, and without any effort on my part—rather an enormous and almost tremulous confusion—I found her as suddenly and swiftly assisting me to a relationship which, while I had contemplated the same in many ways with so many others in my imagination in the past, I had never so much as dreamed of in connection with her. And yet achieving the same with her, or having it achieved for me, and so completely and thrillingly and at the same time confusingly that I scarcely knew what to think. Good girl? Bad girl? The more or the less attractive for what had just happened? Shameless and so evil, as my mother would have said, and perhaps the more so to me since she was by no means the one whom I voluntarily would have sought or pursued. And yet, and quite in spite of myself at the time, really tricked into this intimate relationship with her. And now what . . .?

256

For obviously, she was not a good girl, and therefore a bad one. And since I had never considered her so very attractive —not nearly as graceful or mentally or artfully temperamental as all of these others—common. Worse, and plainly, and in this way, she must be going with those other boys who winked and made sly remarks to her. Besides, both of her parents were common—restaurant-keepers, bakers, foreigners. And so . . . well . . . what was it I had already heard of boys who went with girls indiscriminately, or of girls who went with boys in the same way? "The clap!" I remember that word as something menacing, something signifying a disease which one caught if one did not know with whom one was playing in this way. Harry Croxton had used it. (And yet to this hour I still do not know what it really means.) Not only that, but while I was considering this and that in connection with this new adventure, its pleasure, its danger, its vileness, I was also, and fully and wholly, congratulating myself on the fact that now I knew the exact nature of this relationship, for I had experienced it. And more, and however little I thought of this girl for her bold, shameless assault on me, still there welled up in me the sudden conviction that however bashful or retiring or this or that I might be in connection with other girls, here was one who had seen through my shyness and conquered it. More, that if she, after such few and somewhat retiring contacts as I had had with her, could feel so definitely about me as to desire and then achieve this to me most amazing dénouement, and against any intention or provocation on the part of my very innocent self, well . . . then . . .

Only as I was stumbling to my feet in some (surely) grotesque and ridiculous way and seeking to regain my mental poise, she—her mother's querulous voice sounding from the back door—was up and out, saying as she shook her skirts and fumbled at her hair: "Oh, I have to run! Good-bye!" And was gone.

And then myself in this wilderness of packing cases and in the early dark now also slipping off toward the other end of the alley which gave on to the street, and puzzling and pondering as I went. Yet so shaken and thrilled and puzzled and frightened, and also heightened in my own esteem, was I that while I continued to think, and most intensely and incessantly, concerning it all, yet never was it with any desire or intention of returning to her, since she was not only bad and common but not nearly as attractive as these other girls whom I so very much admired and desired. And so finding myself no more furthered than before in either my courage or my intentions in regard to these others who were so much better, so much more recessive, sophisticated, superior, and heaven only knows what else, and who as before, and because of my lacks in money, daring, this and that, would never permit even so much as a trace of such familiarities as this girl not only demanded but had achieved.

But oh, should they ever! And now, this new knowledge of mine! Oh. . . .

What is wisdom? What learning? And who planned it so, and why? That to each generation it must come fresh and strange and fearful and dumb to what is so old and so common that the constructive forces of life as we know them —those nearest us in our creative process—must have known and used them functionally æon upon æon, time without end?

CHAPTER XLVI

BECAUSE of some slight advantage in the matter of rent and a more convenient arrangement of ground and orchard, we moved during the following fall across the street into what was known as the old Thrall's house—a brick house of fourteen or fifteen rooms, with ample basement and subcellar. It stood in the centre of a piece of ground fully three acres in extent, large and gloomy and almost concealed in a thick grove of pines that sighed and whispered with every breath of air. Because of this, my mother liked it all the more. She was romantic. There was no bath or toilet, only an exterior and distant water-closet covered by vines and led to by a tumbledown grape arbour. To the east and north was a combination of fruit trees: apple, cherry, peach, plum; and space for a garden. To the south the ground sloped precipitously to that large pond or tarn which lay directly outside the fence. It was not so small as to lack charm, despite the fact that it was surrounded on two sides by the log and lumber yard of the saw mill and furniture factory previously described. To the east was the large school yard and the wide grass-grown street leading up to it, with the houses of the McNutts and Bakers as its eastern ornaments. To the south spread a handsome panorama of Warsaw itself: the tarn, the pretty wide-lawned homes and the tall white sandstone court-house, with its great oval dome and clock face.

Sitting in my room of a morning or evening and studying or reading, or in the general living room on the first floor, I could command a full view of all this the while I meditated and dreamed what dreams! For of all places in which we ever lived, this was the most charming. Those great fir trees! And a long cobblestone walk which led between orderly rows of them, straight as an arrow, to a far gate opening on to a main north and south thoroughfare. And all about grass and wild flowers in the open spaces between. And in the summertime, a legion of blackbirds that roosted and nested here by night, the while by day they fed in the adjoining wild rice fields that embosomed the lakes and the meandering curves of the Tippecanoe River. I was never weary of observing them setting forth of a morning or returning at night, the screech of their voices and the flutter of their myriad wings evoking a homelike rather than an alien mood.

And life here, as it seemed to me then, was so lush, full and sweet, a veritable youth-dream of lotus land. For here, between swimming, fishing, boating and loafing about in the holiday season, I read Dickens and Thackeray, Carlyle, Bunyan, Fielding, Dryden, Pope—a long and notable company. And here I became aware of some American authors of no less import: Thoreau, Emerson, Twain, and that author of one interesting book—Lew Wallace and his "Ben Hur." For then the current magazines, distributed as were books by the school library, were full of the lesser rushlights and peculiar or vari-coloured flames of literature.

More, here, and for the first time in my life, I was beginning to look back with a touch of regret on Sullivan, Evansville, Terre Haute and Chicago. Those childhood perfections, and wonders, as I now saw them, were gone. Never would I be so young again! Fifteen or sixteen looking back with regret on seven, eight, nine, ten! Besides, the morning of sex was full upon me: those dreams of happiness we speak of as love. And in school, when it convened, I was studying history, geography, physics, zoology, English and American literature. On every hand life was pouring in, and oh, how sweet! I can only think of this time as concerning clouds that banked themselves in noble, snowy piles; of trees that sighed and swayed, budding, flowering, blowing; of broad lakes of smooth ice in winter; of warm, comfortable schoolrooms into which to retreat, together with pleasant instructors and, in the main, interesting or enviable personalities or companions on every hand.

My only outstanding ills, as I saw them then, were that I had no pocket money—there was never any of that for me— and the fact that while our local reputation was by no means tainted as yet, still, as compared with these others here—and with whom I by now so much desired to associate—we were as nothing, mere outsiders who could never expect to be much of anything here, try as we younger ones might.

And yet at one point, and after we had moved into this larger and altogether more pleasing home, there was quite a rise in our social state as I looked upon it. For it was at just this time that we were visited by two cousins who impressed me not a little: Oliver and Mark Snepp (a corruption of "Schanab," my mother's family name, just as my brother used "Dresser" as a concession to the American middle west of that day, which thought little of all foreign names other than English). They were sons of that previously mentioned elder or bishop of the United Brethren Church of this region, my mother's brother, living at Bourbon, Indiana, and frequently visiting Warsaw on his travels. And by reason of their airs, carefully selected raiment, sophisticated witticisms and thoughts of their position in life, they created no little commotion in our midst. In fact and in contradistinction to the unsatisfactory impact which the condition of the Wybolds had had on me, that of the Snepps, or Schanabs, was considerably more encouraging, or so I chose to think. For at that time in my life and mind, they represented about the same elevated state of intelligence and social position as the Tickets, the Viguses and other notables of Warsaw. Financially also, they were reasonably well-placed for this region, and by my mother, I think (which naturally would have influenced me) their favour and friendship were very much desired. At any rate, they were welcomed by our family with no little consciousness of what they represented in this part of the world.

The youngest, Mark, at the time he called was the newly appointed assistant ticket agent and telegraph operator in Warsaw, and quite anxious that we should know as much. The position, as he soon told us, paid him sixty dollars a month —a considerable sum for this area—and caused him to be looked upon as a coming man. His brother, Oliver, trained as a journeyman printer and compositor, had been connected with the management of one or more small country newspapers as editor, assistant manager and the like, and was now working for the Warsaw *Republican*. Approximately twenty-seven or eight years of age, he was possessed of considerable knowledge and aplomb, or so I fancied; better still, was of a dry and kindly humour. Also, he was handsome—very—and courteous, and his generally friendly and tolerant attitude toward all commended him almost instantly to our goodwill. On the other hand, Mark, although considerably more of the dandy and social favourite locally, was more pinchbeck and conventional in his views. At times he appeared to be positively obsessed by a desire to remain on calling or at least speaking terms with the "best people."

Neither of these youths, as we soon learned, had the least trace of religion, even though their father was a bishop. As I understood afterward, some feeling on this score had made it more pleasing for them to live and work away from home. My mother, when they first put in an appearance, seemed—to me at least—fearful lest we should not be able to make the proper social showing in their presence and so win their good-will. Later, when after a first call they still appeared inclined to be friendly, her fear appeared to be that Amy, the trouble-some Juliet of the family, and later Ruth (who arrived on the scene for a few weeks' visit the same spring) might not conduct herself in such a circumspect way as would raise all in the estimation of the Snepps—the bishop, his wife, and these sons of his. Just the same, Mark seemed to find Ruth attractive and very soon there were boat rides on Center Lake, buggy rides, and train trips to his parents' home in Bourbon.

But as usual Amy chose the more attractive of the two—Oliver—for her attentions. And since he responded in kind, soon there were not only walks and talks but public demonstrations of affection which seemed to all of us not only premature but overly bold and hence disgusting. Also, as we soon learned, there were protests and pleas on the part of my mother and thoughtless, stubborn persistence on Amy's part. Worse, as all of us saw it (her dear relatives, you see?), she proceeded to dress more like an odalisque than a contemporary Warsaw maiden, a fact which scandalised my mother beyond measure. What would Oliver think? Or the prim Mark? Or the bishop or his wife, should they see or hear? Oh, what could they think? Once also, as one of my sisters told me, my mother herself chose to appeal to Oliver, telling him something of Amy's disposition as well as his own duty in this matter, and he proving, outwardly at least, amenable to reason, there was a modification of some of the most trouble-some outcroppings effected by this contact. And then some eight or ten months later—fortunately or unfortunately, as some might see it—he was taken with lung trouble and left for his home. Later he went to Arizona, only to return some two years afterward to die. But before he took ill, and also afterwards, he desired that Amy be permitted to visit him at his home. My mother, afraid of complications with her brother's wife (a chill and religionistic woman), did her best to prevent this. But after innumerable storms and tears (it looked up to the day of his seizure as if this might end in a runaway marriage), Amy was finally permitted to go to Bourbon to visit him. His parents, seeking to aid in his cure by gratifying every whim, consented to this. Later, as I say, he departed for Arizona and died. (I have often wondered whether my mother looked on this as the direct intervention of heaven.)

The friendship of Mark was of a different character, but was soon alienated by another condition which followed swiftly on the heels of Amy's affair with his brother. For in the absence of my father and after Oliver's removal to Arizona, Amy, who had during this time managed to get much more of her own way, took up with one Don Ashley, a member of that group of village ne'er-do-wells previously described. Ashley, as I recall, was twenty-five or six, lean in body and carefully tailored, with a long, thin, wolfish and yet handsome face, shiny, hard eyes, and long, graceful hands. Locally he was known as a sport, a philanderer and gambler, much admired by women. His younger sister, Willette, whom later I encountered in the Central High School and liked very much, was a much more reserved, thoughtful and kindly person, who did her best during the time I knew her to be agreeable to me. His father was an ex-Colonel of the Civil War, quite well-to-do, and they lived in a fairly pretentious home, somewhat nearer the heart of town than ours. Colonel Ashley, so report had it, had been, if he was not then, of the same tendencies as his son. He was tall, grey, thin, severe, soldierly, courteous and slow-spoken, and looked up to here as a social leader. I recall often seeing him walking with three or four handsome greyhounds in leash. The wife and mother of this family was a tall, cold, incisive woman, who used to overawe me when I passed by the chill force of her occasional glance as she worked among her flowers. Willette, as I have said, was different. I knew all of her life later and came to know that she was as sensitive and seeking and fair-minded as any, and one who finally, by suicide, escaped from the harshness of a world she could not endure.

Just when and where Don Ashley and my sister met I never knew, but I am satisfied that he was just the man my sister would assume was perfect. She was that kind of a dunce. Indeed, my first suspicion that there was anyone other than our cousin Oliver came one evening when at nine o'clock, and the rest of us making for bed, she asked me if I would not step out with her, since she wished me to accompany her to a certain corner or near it, because if a certain man was not there she wished to return with me; if he was, as she added, he would bring her home. It was then I began to wonder who the young man could be, but did not learn until some time later, when because of conferences between Amy and my mother, this new beau was permitted to call. Incidentally, on seeing Ashley, and as young as I was, I could have told my mother that no particular good would come of the contact. He was entirely too distant and condescending in his manner: the grand young person of means deigning to meet the family of the girl whose hand in marriage he was presumably seeking. He was too utterly cool and obviously so contemptuous of all that he saw. In short, the best I can say for my mother's psychology at this time is that it remains a most curious enigma to me, for she seemed to think that he was agreeable enough. At any rate, on a few spare occasions when he came to take Amy out —never to stay for any length of time—she seemed to think that there was no particular harm in him, although once or twice when the walk or whatever it was endured until after midnight, she protested and perhaps an earlier return was enforced. I do not recall.

At any rate, this continued for a month or more, after which the visits of young Ashley ceased, and there followed a drooping, spiritless attitude on the part of Amy, which arrested even my attention. She was now and of a sudden so utterly lackadaisical, and more, hypochondriacal. The primping, fussing restlessness, combined as it always had been with a vain and almost critical condescension toward us all—myself less than most, since I was always considerate of and frequently useful to her—was replaced by a sad, drooping mood which showed in her closeting herself in her room or wandering out unaccompanied of an evening, only to return and retire to her room, where she would stay until the next day regardless of any suggestion as to parlour contact or games with the rest of us.

Next, venturing into her room one day when she was out, I noted for the first time—and with what curious foreboding I can now scarcely indicate—certain bottles of medicine, one a bright red, concealed in one of her bureau drawers. My rummaging there was due, in part, to an insatiate curiosity which possessed me in those days. I was hungry for any bauble or curio I might find. I never stole anything of great value, but I remember once taking a round, smooth, gold locket from the room of one of my sisters, merely intending to carry it around. After a time, when the hue and cry as to its loss and my own conscience-ache had partially subsided, I grew tired of the thing as a means of enjoyment and returned it, much to the delight of my sister, who fancied she had overlooked it in her previous numerous searches. But these bottles of medicine seemed to me odd, since in all ways Amy was always so almost ridiculously healthy. One was labelled "poison" and "to be taken as directed." Another: "one spoonful every three hours." I wondered what she was doing with them, and a day or two later, seeing one of them lying on the top of her dresser—accidentally overlooked, I presume—I asked: "What are you taking that for, Amy?"

"Oh, I'm not feeling well," she replied.

But the way she said it, together with the fact, as I had noticed, that her new flame did not call any more, and that instead she went out to meet him, caused me to think. Was she really sick, or was she grieving, or both? Then one lowery September night, when the clouds hung so low and heavy that they looked ready to pour buckets of water upon the earth, she asked me if I would not walk with her as far as a certain street corner; she wanted to see if Don was there. I went cheerfully enough, and we stood under some heavy-leaved, damp and dripping maples, waiting and watching. But he did not come, and after a half-hour we went home, she more gloomy than ever. In short, she had little to say, and when we reached home, went into her room and closed the door and I went into my own, but thinking of her and her low mental state and the fact that this young beau whom I had never liked had so obviously failed her. Was there anything really wrong between them, I wondered?

Not long after this, one late October night, as I was coming home from the post office by a downtown detour such as I usually made to see what and whom I could see, I met her slipping out of the house and down the leafstrewn lane which led to the principal street adjoining. It was nearly dark. She had a small bundle under her arm.

"Where are you going?" I asked.

"Ssh!" she replied. "Don't say anything to mother. I may be going away for a little while, and I may not. If I do, I'll write. Will you miss me if I don't come back soon?" She seemed in a depressed, emotional mood.

"Sure, I'll miss you," I said. "But what makes you talk like that? You're not going away for good, are you?"

"Oh, no, I may come back. But you mustn't say anything. Only kiss me in case I don't, will you?"

She put her arms around me and kissed my cheek, and then went on. For the first time I sensed in her a desire for love and sympathy, or both, almost a pervading loneliness, which was quite moving. I felt so sad after she had gone. Also in connection with this was the feeling of some love difficulty. This Don Ashley! Where was he? Why had he not called? I wondered as to both of them and what my mother would think once she learned of her departure.

But this departure, as I also learned, was not for long. For the next morning, there she was, in her room as usual, and I wondered as to that. On seeing me she again cautioned me not to say anything, that she might leave a little later, and as to this I obeyed her. But her face was a study in severe depression. She looked so wholly reduced. Nothing developed for fully a week, during which time she grew more and more depressed, moped in her room and cried a great deal. One blue Monday, when my mother was preparing to do the week's washing as was her custom (and after a Sunday in which Amy had secluded herself in her room and, as mother declared, spent the day in crying), she went upstairs to find out why Amy did not come down to breakfast and found her still crying. There was a period of sympathetic, yet persistent and mandatory inquiry, at the end of which my mother finally extracted the reason for her depression. She was *enceinte*, and Don Ashley was the acknowledged cause. He had promised to marry her and take her away, but when she had gone to the appointed place to meet him, he had not appeared. She had written him, even called at his home, only to be told he had left Warsaw.

266

An unsigned letter, in a disguised hand, beginning "Dearest Amy," arrived some weeks later, urging her not to grieve, that his flight was compulsory, owing to debt, etc., and that money would be sent her later. But no money ever came, nor any other word.

Following this, she sat about moping and crying and composing love verses to her "darling Don," expressive of her misguided faith, plight and despair—a development which I uncovered by wandering into her room at various times and talking to her as well as picking up anything which might be lying about. (The curiosity age!) Also I discovered these literary efforts to be poorly-rhymed, mushy affairs, which attempted to deal with the great loneliness and defeat that had descended upon her. Not that I scorn the misery and will that prompted them—decidedly not!—only that beyond the comfort and diversion they may have furnished her, they had no great value.

But my mother! That discovery! Her helplessness in the face of her broken local dreams! Ah! For there was her brother, the bishop, also her nephews, and her plans for us, her three youngest. And now, see! At first she cried bitterly, standing in the corner of the downstairs living room and holding the end of an apron to her eyes. Ah, that much disappointed and life-betrayed woman! Next, there were depressed ravings against the headstrong folly of this girl, her vanity and ridiculous sentimentality, together with urgings in regard to bestirring herself and preparing for the troublesome future immediately before her by working at suitable garments. Also there were letters to be written to Eleanor and Ruth in Chicago in order to obtain of both advice and possibly aid. And more tears, and even prayers, I believe.

As for Amy herself, she merely gave way to additional floods of tears and dreamy, secluded broodings, which, as her subsequent history proved, were without reformative significance. To be sure, she was anxious to find some way out, since she considered herself most cruelly betrayed, but as for any helpful worldly wisdom, none. The problem as to what was to be done for her was my poor mother's, not hers, you may be sure.

CHAPTER XLVII

THE attitude of the Ashley family in this crisis, as I learned a number of years later—not then—was interesting. It appears that Don Ashley had kept the matter a secret. Amy was really little more than a street girl to him, a mere temporary diversion. (I cannot say that I can quarrel with his lack of interest; outside of this one bent, Amy, as I see it now, could scarcely, at that time at least, have inspired any man to real love.) As she afterwards explained, he first attempted to assure her that nothing probably really ailed her, then that he would treat her himself, and then, as a last resort, that he would elope with her on a given date. Silly dolt that she was, she swallowed it all. She actually believed that he loved her and that she had made a great capture. Only his unheralded departure aroused her from her dream, and then, of course, it was too late.

The Ashleys, very naturally, deemed it as much of an unfortunate mix-up as any group in their position would. Mrs. Ashley, cold, forthright, and possibly unsentimental, made short work of Amy when once, shortly after her lover's flight, she ventured, as she subsequently related—unknown to mother —to call on her and ask where Don was. (What Laura Jean Libby type of romantic thought prompted this I do not know!) Mrs. Ashley met her at the door, and on being told her reason for coming, said: "Why do you come to see me? My son is not here. I do not know where he is." Amy said she began to attempt to explain that Don had seduced her under a promise of marriage and that she wanted his address in order to obtain aid, when Mrs. Ashley interrupted her with: "This looks like blackmail to me. You mustn't trouble me with this matter. My son couldn't marry you if he wanted to. He has other obligations. Besides, how do I know you weren't bad long before you met him?"

Amy flared at this, but the older woman dismissed her with

icy courtesy. "You must go now," she said. "I cannot give you any more of my time. If you want to find my son, you must hunt him in other places. I do not know where he is."

Amy left, soaked, no doubt, in the best type of melodramatic misery. If she had only gained a clearer working conception of the realities, it would have been worth the cost. As it was, merely endless tangled steps, ending in confusion. After conferences and I know not what reflections, a suit for at least sufficient money to maintain the prospective child was contemplated and carried as far as consulting a lawyer. There was at this time in Warsaw a somewhat famous criminal lawyer and Republican politician—a State representative at one time —and solely because my mother had heard his name a number of times, she decided to go to him.

Orrin Barnes (that was the lawyer's name) was a tall, ungainly, genial, ambling type. I had often seen him about the public square, in a long black frock coat, fawn-coloured waistcoat, and soft black, broad-brimmed felt hat. I should say now that he was the type of sophisticated small-town lawyer who would take an incident of this kind as more or less of a joke, pulling a serious face and extracting as large a cash reward as possible for himself. The matter was communicated to Eleanor and Ruth in Chicago, the former coming home to help out. When she and Amy approached Barnes in his office over the corner bookstore, he pulled a very solemn face and said: "You don't say! Don Ashley! Why, I can scarcely believe it! Well, I shall have to take the matter under advisement and let you know."

It developed later, so I heard, that the elder Ashley was one of his chief political supporters and that he could not well have moved against him. However, some scheme of reconciliation or self-aggrandisement must have been in his mind, for he advised Amy to visit a certain well-known Dr. Woolley, one of the town's old family practitioners, and to tell him, if he insisted, the name of the culprit. It turned out afterwards that Dr. Woolley had been for years the family physician of the Ashleys, but it is not possible to say that his intentions were not of the best, even under these compromising circumstances. The reason Barnes gave for sending her there was that he wanted irrefutable medical testimony as to her condition.

The old doctor, grey, shock-headed, full-whiskered and all of sixty-five years of age, listened to her, shook his head gravely, and exclaimed: "The young scamp! Now you see what comes of wilful conduct! There are many young girls like you, trusting these young scamps and disobeying their parents. Do your parents know?" Amy admitted that she had confessed to her mother. "Yes, yes," he went on, "poor woman! I am just as sorry, though, for Mr. and Mrs. Ashley. They don't want a scamp of a boy any more than your mother wants a thoughtless girl." He made sure that her condition was serious, and then added: "Well, there's just one thing to do, and that is to have your baby. I can't do anything for you except to tell you how to take care of yourself. You mustn't think of trying to prevent it. That would be a much greater crime than anything else that has been done."

He lectured on about duty and virtue, as Amy herself related, but said nothing about young Ashley's duty except to call him a scamp. Subsequently he called on mother and offered to go to Ashley senior and see what could be done. When he learned that a suit was contemplated, he withdrew, saying Barnes could handle it quite as well. I saw him at various times afterward, a crusty, domineering, patriarchal old soul, who would growl like a bear whenever he was compelled to get up in the night to visit anyone but who invariably came when he considered the request sufficiently serious. Once I fell out of a second-story window at three o'clock in the morning, walking in my sleep, and he arrived, my father bringing him, very much concerned. Another time he treated Ruth for a serious tumour, and my father for an attack of gallstones which bade fair to result in death. On this occasion he sent me far out into the country to procure fresh peach twigs, from which my mother made tea. I see him now, a grave and reverend senior, riding about the countryside in an old, dusty, rickety buggy, or walking the streets, always in a musty, baggy, grey suit, his slouch hat over his eyes, always saying "How do you do? How is your mother? How is your father?" and always looking as though he really recognised you and knew all about you—which I doubt. He was famous for his knowledge of medicine and his goodness of heart, and my mother testified that his bills were exceedingly low in our case.

But autumn deepened into winter, and winter into spring, and no good came of the appeal to Barnes and no medical aid from the examination by Woolley. If any money settlement was made—as there may well have been—the lawyer appropriated it as his fee. Because of danger of local exposure and the inability of mother to handle the situation in the face of my father's probable return (he was in Terre Haute at the time), it was finally deemed best that Amy go away, preferably to New York, since her sister Janet was well-placed there and could look after her. Just exactly how all this was arranged I knew not at all then. Later I learned that there had been correspondence between Eleanor and Janet, which resulted in a helpful arrangement and money for Amy's fare and other necessities.

I seem to have a semi-clear recollection of the hubbub, or perhaps I would better say repressed excitement, which attended her departure on a midnight express for New York. Someone went with her, probably Eleanor. At any rate, gone she was, and for the time being at least, there was surcease of this impending misery for my mother and all of us.

CHAPTER XLVIII

BUT this matter of my sister and Don Ashley had a semi-stabilising effect on me because it drove home quite definitely not only the physical results of sex contact but more interesting still, the chill resentment, or at least evasive dread, which failure to conform to socially accepted arrangements invariably evokes in those who, willingly or not, bow to the conventions which inwardly they may contemn. The sudden whispers, evasions, desires to avoid those who have failed to conform to the customs and taboos of any given region! In this case, I saw, and yet at first I didn't. For although hitherto there had been, as I have said, some inclination to receive us —we three younger children at least—into the best school society of the town, all this was now quickly ended by the rumours in regard to Amy. We were a scandal.

At the same time, I have often tried to calculate my own feelings and moods in regard to all this. Sex was the most important thing in life, apparently. Why was it wrong? I did not have wit enough to discover that it was marriage that was being safeguarded, and that life, if any such social scheme as the present one is to be accepted or held to, must, of necessity, guard against such violent extremes, even though they may be certain to occur for ever and ever. The strange polarity of life, the tendency to variation in every direction, the counter-tendency to and necessity for equation, were matters for later discovery. Just now, the Catholic Church, my father, the social belief in the necessity for marriage as life around us was constituted, were all in apparent conflict in me, and yet I was in favour of sex contact and eager for it. My thoughts were coming to be constantly on girls, as my sisters' were on men, and since I still deemed them wrong, I frequently confessed them to the Catholic priest. The latter, under the seal of the confessional, gravely warned me against them. If I should die with such thoughts unconfessed, I would descend at once into hell. At the same time, as I have stated, I had this long time been finding decidedly heterodox references and counter-beliefs in almost all that I read. In such a mental state, and physically surrounded as I was, I was literally blazing physically.

And yet now—and just at this time, of course—a sudden lull in or conclusion to this local school and town relationship that had seemed so promising. Sly or curious looks, if not inquiries on the part of such youths as had been most friendly and in some instances intimate with me; and worse, in so far as the smarter ones were concerned, a tendency not so much to avoid me directly as to fail to make the former friendly contacts with me. And as for the girls, there were the customary nods and sometimes smiles, but in so far as those school affairs, parties and outings to which Trina and myself had been regularly invited were concerned, there were no more invitations. I felt that deeply, because I was always dreaming of some particular relationship that was to prove so wonderful here, but now that this had occurred, I was certain that this was not to be.

And so, the restoration for the time being of that old mood in regard to us—our several and combined prospects—together with a revivification of my poetic if (just now) somewhat melancholy delight in nature, which, set over against my thwarted dreams of romance, always took an intense if not exaggerated lustre. I have never been able to feel that.

I spent hours upon hours walking alone and brooding, contemplating the flight of blackbirds and crows which gathered in this section by thousands to feed in the wild rice fields not many miles distant. Warsaw, barring a break of five miles, was the beginning of a chain of small lakes which extended north-east for thirty miles or more, and here were large swampy areas overrun with cat-tails or wild rice. In late July and August, when this ungarnered grain was ready for the reaping, the ethereal highways were traversed by long lines of blackbirds and crows, great black armies generated by what instinct? The grove surrounding our house was at times populated by hundreds of these birds resting for the night. As I watched them, and just then in particular, my own spirit took wing and travelled with them over measureless spaces. I was irked by the limitation of our life here as well as that of the human body, and quarrelled with it. Why had not man been born with wings as well as feet?

And now more than ever broodings as to my personal (material) as well as physical lacks, since one of my constant thoughts was that had I looks sufficient and money, what great difference, where attractive girls were concerned, would poverty or disgrace make? They would like me anyhow. But to lack looks and means, and to suffer from social lowness into the bargain! Actually such thoughts as these burned in my brain as retarding facts. I was so hungry for life and love! And what lovely and enticing girl, such as so many of these were, would endure a boy with big ears or large teeth or a mouth not cut like that of a soldier or a beau? Obviously then, I was now doomed to sex loneliness, and at the very time when I was most desirous of it. Whereas others were walking under the trees or rowing on the lakes, holding hands or kissing or whispering sweet nothings, here I was, destined to brood alone. And in connection with this at this time, the least recessive or uncertain look on the part of any girl, a thoughtless or nervous giggle, a pout or frown—those make-believe antagonisms and assumed oppositions which are a part of all sex life, animal or human—were to me, in my wrought-up state, a sign of contempt or worse. Sometimes, after such an encounter, I walked for days, frozen by my belief in probably purely imagined rebuke. At the same time, in the presence of some girls at least, I pretended a gaiety and indifference. I tried to think that I could get along without them, or that other boys and girls were not having as good a time as I thought, but life always gave the lie to my imaginings. Girls were too plentiful, their boy admirers too clever and too open in their attentions and frolics.

In short, and at this very time, alas, the town was rife, in boyland at least, with stories of who was in love with whom, of who was going with whom, and those darker, more fiery tales of secret trysts and doings in unlighted parlours and groves. I recall that once one of the local papers published an editorial to the effect that certain shameless boys and girls, the names of whom were known to it but withheld, had been guilty of bathing together nude in a certain part of the Tippecanoe not far from Warsaw, and that if the performance was repeated, these names would be published. Imagine the implied repression, envy, desire! To me, closed as all this now seemed to be, it was the same as a fiery revelation ou of paradise.

Then such things were! And here and now! In youth, in sunlight, in summer warmth! And unpunished! Ah, to be a part of that—to share it all! For weeks, even years, thereafter, I was haunted by a vision of nude nymphs and satyrs sporting in the clear water and frolicking in the dark green woods! Who were they? Which of all the beauties that I had known had been so courageous? Ah! The orgiastic sting of such union amid such sylvan scenes! Pan with his reeds! Could I not hear his call? The mere thought of it was heaven!

CHAPTER XLIX

ABOUT this time it was that, because of my growing sex interest as well as my contact with the baker's daughter and at the same time my inability to front the elusive subtlety of the more attractive girls of the town, I fell into the ridiculous and unsatisfactory practice of masturbation, which finally became a habit that endured—broken, of course, by occasional normal sex relations with passing women and girls—until I married.

One hot summer day, alone in my room after a bath, I sat down on the side of my bed thinking of what I would do if Gusta Phillipson, or Stella Davenant or Nata Weyler, as opposed to my baker girl, were in my arms. To me at least they were such torrid flames of beauty! And, in this state of emotion, I suddenly and quite unexpectedly brought on a sensation which, as in the case of my contact with the baker's daughter, thrilled and yet quite terrified me. For I had not intended any such result and had not even assumed that in this case it would occur. When it did, I jumped up fearful lest I had injured myself. I dressed quickly, resolved not to trifle with myself in this fashion again nor to think the thoughts which our local parish priest was always telling me were evil.

Following this came several days of strenuous effort to remain pure in mind and body. But this decision lasted only some three or four days. The physical beauty of girls as well as the delight and relief of the process I had discovered—the only substitute for the sex contact I so much craved—came back to me with overwhelming force. I forgot my good resolutions. No harm had come to me, apparently from either this or my preceding single relationship with a woman. Subsequently I longed, of course, and with flaming eagerness, to find some girl other than the one mentioned with whom I could continue, but in lieu of that, this other, this something that stung and thrilled, must serve. I ran to my room and indulged in the act again. A heavy reaction of mood again followed, but a few days served to efface the memory of anything save the intense delight. For weeks and months, every two or three days at the utmost, I now indulged myself in a kind of fury of passion. I would run to my room or any secret place I had appointed, and there in a kind of excess of passion and delight, give myself over to this form of self-abuse. At the same time, I would combine it with passional thoughts of one of the girls whom I most admired: Carrie Tuttle, Stella Davenant, or Nata Weyler. It has always been a matter of curiosity to me that the personality of Myrtle Trego was never visualised in this connection. It never occurred to me that I could satisfy myself with her in this fashion.

The natural result of this was, first, a radical change in point of view, and, second, and to a lesser extent, a change in my physical condition. For one thing, temporarily my face became blotched and marred by pimples, which caused Harry Croxton to exclaim one day: "What are you doing to yourself, Ted? Your face is all covered with pimples!" Abashed at the thought that my face was advertising my secret, I resolved to quit. But I could not. The pleasure and relief to my desires were too great. Besides, now that Croxton had indicated this facial condition as a sure sign, I noted other boys and girls to be in the same state. Better, though, I came to talk more freely of all this (sex) with Croxton, McNutt and others and to learn of seemingly endless variations of it. Judson Morris, the hunchback son of the bookstore man, had secured a number of immoral, fly-by-night pamphlets, which in those days were allowed to pass through the mails undetected and which for the price of ten cents retailed all the delights of the wedding night. John and George Shoup, Gavin McNutt, Beachey Reid and others—quite a circle of the youths of the school—used to gather to read them at Jud's father's corner bookstore. A Rabelaisian, immoral business, but so it was. Not a morbid crowd either, if I except myself, but rather of a laughing, jesting jovial turn. And incidentally, and coeval with this—very likely because of it—I came to know of books that dealt with sex in a revelatory if more or less classic way: "Tom Jones," "Joseph Andrews," "Moll Flanders"; also passages from Dryden, Pope, Shakespeare's Sonnets. For several years after that my main concern with old or famous books was to find the portions which dealt with sex, though the merit of a conservative work was by no means beyond me.

But after a time—due to my morbidity in connection with it all—a nervous depression. I was sitting one night at the dinner table some three or four months after I had begun this practice, when all of a sudden I was taken with a whirring in my head and ringing in my ears, which frightened me nearly out of my wits. For a few moments I thought I was going to die. Nature's way, apparently, when an internal physical adjustment is to be made, is not to give warning beforehand but to keep up an appearance of normal health until it can no longer possibly be maintained. In this case I cannot even suggest, I fear, the ominous portents of physical change or readjustment that seemed suddenly to play about my mental horizon. If you can imagine a black landscape with a yellow storm in the offing, or a fever victim pursued by spying, lurking devils, or an inferno glimpsed in half light and quaking with strange and hitherto unimagined sights and sounds, you may arrive at some idea of what I endured. If I had not been sitting, I would have fallen. As it was, I put down my knife and fork, placed my hands on the table to steady myself, and closed my eyes. In my brain was spinning a whirligig of spectral lights: yellow, red, green, blue, grey, white. In place of my normal heart-beat was a feeble fluttering, which alternated with a heavy thumping which seemed to spell instantaneous collapse. I tried to get up, but could not. Then after, say, thirty seconds —by which time I was nearly exhausted—the uproar in my ears ceased, my heart beat less feebly, the grinding and clanking in my brain subsided, and I arose and went upstairs saying I had forgotten something.

In my room, though, I sat and meditated on all this. Sickness! Brain trouble! Total physical collapse, no doubt! The truth was, I was really thinking of those innumerable advertisements addressed to "Weak Men" or "Victims of Self-Abuse," as the advertisements of those days ran, which Croxton and others by their talks had called to my attention and concerning which we used to jest. But now no more. The emaciated, sunken-eyed victims of youthful excess always illustrated by them haunted me. For now was I not one of these? If not as yet, then obviously I was to become one, emaciated, with hair and teeth falling out, eyes sunken, and no hope of any future of any kind save in the particular pills or nostrums advertised or such periods of treatment as could be procured from "Old Dr. Grindle" of Buffalo, New York, or "Old Dr. Grey," of Scranton, Pennsylvania. The particular "swamp root" or tannic acid pills or electric belt or "Neurophag" prescribed by these was all that was left. I shook in terror, for I had no money. My mother would not be able to afford sufficient money to permit me to undergo any one of these saving treatments, even though I had sufficient courage to tell her what had befallen me. And then what?

And worse, the whirrings and interior disturbances returned and at seemingly regular intervals for at least a month or two. Also I had the most terrifying dreams, in which ghosts or skeletons walked and threatened imminent destruction. At two in the morning—the zero hour at which the earth seems to suffer a change or period of inhalation or exhalation—I was wont to awake, feeling as though I were about to expire. A peculiar whistling in my ears would begin and might continue for several hours. I had, or imagined I had, all the symptoms of prolonged insomnia, only with this difference: that when I became exhausted, I would fall into a heavy sleep. After much thought, I hit upon the idea of copying out a prescription which I found in somebody's "Family Medical Guide" and asking the most friendly of the two local druggists—the one who was not Myrtle Trego's father—to fill it and charge it for a month. He did so, but with true rural sagacity, mailed the bill to my mother: a bill for $4.25. Now I know, as I half suspected then, that the medicine (like ninety per cent. of all medicine) was worthless. It brought me merely a few day's hope, then greater despair, because the night sweats, etc., continued, and there was the necessity of explaining, or attempting to explain, the matter of the bill to my mother. Curiously enough, that strangely sympathetic woman did not press the mystery of the purchase too far. When she saw I was confused and distressed, she let the matter rest.

"If you think something is the matter with you that you don't want to tell me about, why don't you go and see Dr. Woolley?" she said. Her voice was as soft and pleasing as that of a sweetheart.

But one service the author of "The Family Guide" rendered me was to point out the efficacy of cold baths, exercise, sleeping with the windows open, on a hard bed, etc. All this, coupled with the gradual realisation that I was not to die at once, gradually led to a modified view of my condition. Perhaps I was only to be crippled sexually for life, as the advertisements I had been reading by the ton invariably asserted. That was bad enough, of course, but after all it was not insanity or death.

Poor, ignorant humanity! I wish that all of the religious and moral piffle and nonsense from which I suffered in connection with this matter could be undone completely for the rest of the world by merely writing about it. What tons of rot have been written and published concerning the spiritual and moral degradation of this practice! Old wives' tales, for the most part. Quacks and thieves printing lying advertisements to sell nostrums to the ignorant, and so terrifying poor fools who stand in no more real physical or mental danger than a man with a taste for green plums! Doctors, more religionistic than medical, writing endless silly books on hearsay or because of early asinine terrors of their own! I have often wished that the pagan or Hebraic view of things had prevailed in my own family and that at this age I had been taken in hand and introduced to a bagnio, or that I had possessed sufficient courage to persuade a girl to have physical relations with me. I was of the temperament that required it. As it was, for four or five years I was thrown into the most, at times, gloomy mental state, that is, whenever I thought of my assumed condition, and yet there was no more the matter with me than there is with any healthy, normal boy who takes to this exotic practice.

CHAPTER L

I DON'T know but what our family fortunes appeared to me to be at their lowest ebb at this time, although there were one or two faintly redeeming features. Thus, my brother Paul had gradually bettered himself and was now a comedian of some repute and the author of two or three popular songs, one of which—"The Letter that Never Came" —was being played and sung everywhere in the United States. It had even travelled to Warsaw, although when we claimed kinship with the author we were scarcely believed, largely because he had changed his name to "Dresser." Eventually, though, we came into our own in this matter. An actual visit on his part, and in state, tended to verify all this, and among other things it appeared that the manager of the local "opera house" knew of him.

Again, my sister Eleanor had finally married that Harahan I have previously mentioned. But considering himself above her intellectually, socially and in every other way, he could not make up his mind to remove her east, where most of his social connections were, but preferred to maintain a more or less temporary residence on the north side in Chicago, where they dwelt for many years.

But there were many drawbacks to our situation. Amy's baby, a boy, arrived at our home late in this fall, already four or five months old but requiring endless care. I remember the constant wailing we had to endure and the time each one of us had to give to "minding" it. I resented my labour in this capacity intensely.

In the next place, Ruth's affair with the Chicago manufacturer had terminated as such affairs most frequently terminate. She was deserted and almost broken in health. For a time we thought she would die. Dr. Woolley took her in hand and by degrees restored her to health, so that the following spring she was up and around and returned to Chicago.

Again, my father returned from Terre Haute about the time Amy's child arrived, and there was a most darksome period of explanation, crimination and recrimination. In fact, he cherished a bitter feeling toward Amy to his dying day. (I do not know how he reconciled this with his religious injunction to mercy, etc., etc.) Then on top of all this, he himself was taken seriously ill with bladder trouble, and for a long time we thought he would die. From a weight of about one hundred and eighty-five, he wasted to one hundred and thirty-five or thereabouts. His body was as lean as that of the arrow-pierced Saint Sebastian. He prayed much, took his medicine regularly, groaned, and occasionally shrieked with pain.

But in the midst of all this, there was for me a most interesting inspirational school life. There were two women teachers in this High School at the time who came to exercise a most hopeful and helpful influence over me, to make for somewhat more of optimism in connection with myself than hitherto had been. One of these was a tall old maid from Malden, Massachusetts, a certain Mildred Fielding, who at thirty-three or thereabouts was for the first time in her life finding herself moderately attractive, and thinking, no doubt, therefore, that the world was not so bad. As I afterwards learned from her, she had had a very hard life. In her youth she had been poor, socially nobody, cursed with an ungainly form, protruding teeth, in short, every physical disadvantage which could afflict a young and otherwise healthy girl. At last she had fought her way up to being a teacher and in addition had had her teeth straightened, her hair properly dressed, had learned to wear appropriate clothes and only now was beginning to reap the fruits of her long struggle. In spite of all her difficulties, she had retained a sweet, gentle and lovable disposition. Her attitude now was one of broad tolerance and generosity. At thirty-five, her light brown hair, grey-blue eyes, and pink complexion made her seem younger than she was. It was this woman who was destined to come to my aid in a very curious way some two years later. Just then, as director of the High School recitation room, she was in touch with me, my studies in connection with algebra, physical geography, general history, botany, and so on, being recited to and corrected or directed by her.

The other teacher—Alvira Skarr, I think her name was— who controlled the study room, was a very different type. Small, red-haired, finicky, and showy in a material and yet conservative way, she was at the same time lively, friendly and attractive. She wore gold-bridge glasses and a showy gold watch fastened at her breast by a jewelled pin. A taste for appearing in new dresses of rich material and talking of her family in Erie, Pennsylvania, indicated either a plentiful supply of money or a good salary. I think it was the former, for her salary could not have been more than twelve hundred dollars a year.

Both of these women, soon after my entrance into first year High, evinced a genial personal interest in me and my views and aspirations, which flattered me not a little, and by degrees seriously affected my personal estimate of myself. It must be remembered that I was then at the age when one is most easily influenced. Miss Fielding, to my surprise and embarrassed pleasure, frequently assisted me after school with my algebra, with which I had some difficulty. More, and at the same time, she appeared to be aware of our local history, and while this troubled me not a little, at the same time it was coupled with, in her case, a tender and quite obvious solicitude as well as desire to fortify me against any depressing effect our home troubles might be having on me.

Thus, one afternoon, and quite out of a clear sky, in the midst of an explanation in connection with an algebra problem, she paused and said: "Theodore, I want to say something to you. It is not prompted by anything but a real interest in you and your welfare." I instantly shivered with the thought that she was going to tell me I was not sufficiently trained as yet for the work I was undertaking and would need to return to the previous grade. But instead she went on: "I can see that you are not like the other boys and girls here. You are different, Theodore. Very sensitive. Your mind is very different. You understand well enough where you are interested. It is only where you aren't that you do so poorly. But you mustn't let that worry you. You must study and go on, for your mind will find its way. I know it!" And then looking directly into my eyes, her own lit with a warm, tender, even affectionate, glow, she concluded: "But there is something else. You mustn't mind my saying this, Theodore, because

283

I am fond of you and want you to succeed in life. And you will, if you wish. Please don't mind anything that is said or done in a small town like this, and don't let it hurt you. I was brought up in one, and I know how small people can be and how they talk. But please don't let it affect you. You will soon grow up and go away and then all that has happened here will seem as nothing to you. It is only you that can hurt yourself, not the actions or words or opinions of anyone else. You understand me, Theodore, don't you?"

I was moved almost to tears, and so grateful that though I wished to speak, I could not. Instead I merely looked. But she must have gathered what I felt, for she laid a gentle, caressing hand on my arm and added, smilingly: "Now shall we see if we can solve this?" I tried to follow her, but seeing that I could not, she said: "Well, we'll put it over until to-morrow. You might look it over to-night. It will come to you." And—reluctantly, as it seemed to me—she walked away, and I gathered up my books and hurried out.

But the thrill of it! The bracing, encouraging thrill! Instantly and because of this strong, affectionate support, I felt so much better about everything. Pooh! Warsaw and its people! What of them? Who were they? Had I not just been told that I had a different and good mind and that once I was out in the world I could get along? Supposing our family was talked about—evidently it was, since she chose to refer to it—was that certain to affect me? She seemed to think not, had practically assured me that it could not. I felt so much braver, stronger, walked with an air, a trifle of vanity swelling in me.

And better—if such things really are better—this was added to, if in a lesser degree, by Miss Skarr. My interest in English and world literature seemed to appeal to her. As busy as she was—and she was in charge of a very large roomful of scholars—she too (possibly at Miss Fielding's behest) managed to find time to talk to me and to point out books in which I might be interested, some lectures that were occasionally given on literature at the home of Professor Saunders, our school superintendent, and lastly, after learning I was half German, urged me to take a German course which she was conducting and which would open the door to Schiller, Goethe, Heine and others. I could read a little German, and here was all this superior wisdom at my hand. At once, my estimate of my father's native land (hitherto, because of his religious dogmatising, exceedingly low) rose. I joined the course, and during the remainder of that year, along with ten others (one of them Nata Weyler, if you please) scanned—cursorily, as one may guess—a history of German literature.

Unquestionably, I think, I progressed as fast intellectually during this one year as I ever did at any other time. I picked up bits of information relating to the meaning as well as scope of geology, physics, chemistry, all studies coming under Miss Fielding's direction. I began to think of things below the mere surface of life and to wonder in regard to them. What was energy or the life force? Where did it come from? Had it always existed? Why electricity and its laws? What was it? Why strange, powerful chemicals and their regulated combinations? I knew after less than one month of blundering in this realm that there were immense fields of energy obviously of great import to humanity which as yet no one could explain. And so I began to think about them. Electric lighting and water systems had been recently introduced into Warsaw, and these I found were related primarily to physics and afterwards to electrical and the older steam engineering. The connection of botany with chemistry, of chemistry and physiology with medicine, and of arithmetic and algebra with nearly all of them, as well as astronomy, was plainly indicated. I began to speculate for myself in regard to these things—the stars, people, animals, life—the mystery of their origin and continuance.

I had, if I may say it, a passion for understanding, without the willingness at that time, however, to delve into the intricacies and subtleties of things. Rather I liked to meditate than to pause and inquire closely. Besides, I was horribly pestered by thoughts of love and beauty. A chemical bias of this kind does not make for serious, detailed or involute technical knowledge. Instead, if anything, it tends to philosophy, poetry and the arts, and although I had no least inkling of it at the time, I was for the arts. Life did not appeal to me so much on its technical or purely structural and trade aspects as it did on its general forms and surface appearances. The rains, clouds, fogs, blue and grey days, sunlight, moonlight, trees, grass, flowers, birds. I was never made, as I learned in after years, to be a specialist in any or many fields, but rather a general if close observer of the form and motion of things, their effect upon and import to the individual as well as society at large. That I was to become a writer I never so much as dreamed until years later. To myself I seemed little more than a mooning, dreaming youth who was so largely speculative that he could never hope to master details.

Just the same, I was never weary of physiology, botany, astronomy, zoology. The world as revealed by these branches of science was so astounding. The sea, the stars, the earth, the blood—how they fascinated me! At the same time I never grew tired of reading history. In my school General History, which I took up in first year High, Cæsar and Napoleon took a strong grip on my fancy, as also did our own Washington and Lincoln. Novels, plays, poems, of course, were always interesting, rich in their suggestion of our varied and far-flung world. My mother might be worrying from day to day as to where to get means to feed and clothe us, but I was thinking of the splendid fields and opportunities of life. One day I might acquire technical knowledge of some kind that would astonish the world! Why not? One day I might even go to college— the boys and girls of the better families here were going to De Pauw, Rose Polytechnic at Terre Haute, the State University at Bloomington, the University of Michigan at Ann Arbor. My idea of college was, I think, that if you could only once get there, you would come out—by what process I did not really know—fit to hold a well-paying position and worthy of being looked up to by everyone. I used to sit and dream of these things: changes, peoples, adventures. How life might make me a general, a ruler, a judge, a doctor, a lawyer, anything you please. Even on occasion some vague notion of writing something, like Dickens or Thackeray, floated across my consciousness—in about the same way as I dreamed of being a general or a judge—but with no more definiteness or validity. (Just at the moment I was immersed in Dickens—one or another of his many novels—and Thackeray, with his clearer, cleaner logic, seemed second-rate. Later he was moved into first place, until Balzac appeared.)

At about this time, too, the rumour appeared to gain ground that I was a youth of exceptional mental ability. A small paper I wrote in our literature class—a description of a local scene—brought me direct encomiums which caused the blood to mount to my cheeks. One day the superintendent of schools, a lean, pedagogic, temperamental and enthusiastic man, walked home with me to tell me how much he thought of my work, what a great thing it was to have a good mind, etc., etc. He spoke of novels, histories and plays which I would do well to read, as well as philosophies which I might eventually inquire into. Also, and more definitely, he recommended a study of the rise of the German Empire (which was then under William I, Von Moltke and Bismarck), and a careful reading of Shakespeare, two worlds to which I had never given so much as a thought. He was all on fire for youth, development, future deeds of force, and he made me feel it. Indeed, by his talk he put me in a kind of nervous frenzy from which I did not recover for days. Even now I can see the street, the overhanging trees, the lawns of the houses we passed as we walked, and this man's lean, sallow, tense face and burning black eyes. I have often wondered since whether he was really a capable educator and whether he subsequently succeeded in the work which he seemed to like so much. One thing is sure: by his praise and advice he lifted me out of the slough of despond into which I had been sinking. "No accident of birth or condition can harm or delay a determined individual," he said to me at one place, and added: "I want you to write that down and think about it."

I suspected at the time that he probably knew some of our family troubles and was trying to hearten me. Be that as it may, I went home and thought and thought. Out of the library I secured somebody's "Rise of the German Empire," Carlyle's "French Revolution"—a book I scarcely understood—Shakespeare's "Macbeth," "Julius Cæsar," "Antony and Cleopatra," "Hamlet," "Merchant of Venice;" and "Wilhelm Meister." I wish he had introduced me to Balzac. As it was, I felt myself to be a coming somebody. What, in view of all I was learning concerning the world at large, could our petty local difficulties matter? The race was surely to the swift, the battle to the strong. So in a swing, a hammock, a rocking-chair, under the trees or within the house, I thought, reading and dreaming, to carve out something for myself in the future regardless of what my family might do or say. But with no zest for any immediate action.

CHAPTER LI

AND then, one spring evening, after attending the graduation exercises at the local opera house, with boys and girls in their best clothes, addresses, flowers, the awarding of diplomas, I was moved to think seriously on the ending of youth and schooldays. I still had three years to go if I completed the High School course, but what was I going to do at the end of that time? Where was I going, if anywhere? I really did not know. One thing that brought on a sense of loneliness, and so perhaps thoughts of change, was the fact that shortly after the close of school my two teachers, Miss Skarr and Miss Fielding, left, Miss Skarr for ever out of my life (although I did not know that at the time) and Miss Fielding not to be encountered for several years. I felt lonely and disconsolate. There was, as I now saw, so little opportunity for boys in Warsaw, unless perchance their parents controlled industries or shops which might accommodate them, as not a few did. The Ticket Boys, for instance, occasionally clerked for their father; the Viguses assisted their father in his bank whenever he needed assistance; Charlie Trego, Myrtle's brother, clerked in his father's drug store at nights and in summer. But what had my parents for me?

In the next place, my brother Paul, home this June from the east and more successful than ever, was causing me to wonder whether there was not some place for me in the wider world. Then my sister Eleanor and her husband coming to pay us a visit on their way to Saratoga brought with them a sense of a wider and more prosperous world—travel and resorts—a life beyond us and our means, but still full of suggestions toward adventure. Why should not I move in some way, bring some form of action to and so adventure and development into my life? Why not? It was plain to me in her case that after a stormy youth her life was broadening into something better, and so held a hint for me. Had she not adventured? Sought? And now, see!

Eleanor's husband, strong, reserved, aggressive, with an air of wealth and experience, was soi-disant and not particularly eager to stay in our home. Rather he appeared to be submitting to a queer, showy devotion on the part of Eleanor to her mother—a devotion that, if anything, meant more work for mother—yet also he indicated his affection for and so submission to Eleanor by so doing. An amazing and powerful thing this matter of love, as I then and there saw, since through a poorly educated and decidedly emotional and exotic temperament such as Eleanor's, it could hold and, after a fashion, direct so strong and prosperous and interesting a man as this. Incidentally, my brother Al, who had been in Chicago all this time working at one thing and another, now came home for a stay of several months, and was planning to launch a small-town minstrel show. His great desire then, apparently, was to be a black-face or Irish comedian (or both), lines or professions for which he seemed sufficiently talented, being witty and with a knack for devising outlandish costumes as well as popular or comic songs and "lines" or "gags" (his words) which seemed amusing enough to me. For some reason, though, he found it difficult to connect with success, even if, as I saw, he finally did succeed in organising a local minstrel show and took it to four or five surrounding towns. But the financial return was not sufficient and he was compelled to return to Chicago— a great blow to him.

In connection with all this—the arrival of Paul, Eleanor with her husband, Al, and, as I recall, our sister Ruth for a short stay—our social state was actually no better than it had been before. We mustered no more than a living. Besides, Trina, after a promising opening friendship, if not intimacy, with a number of the more securely-placed girls and young men of the town, had slowly been reduced to three or four who though agreeable enough were not of the group to which she originally aspired. As for myself, as I have shown, while excluded by the group which not long after our arrival had accepted Trina and myself, I now found myself in touch with only separate individuals here and there, and these mainly girls, as I also noted. For during my first year in High, I had encountered Anita Brand. She lived opposite us. Beautiful? She was as beautiful as one roseate apple is more exquisite than another. As I saw her, she seemed serious—fairly studious in school—and not at all flirtatious. And yet after school, and when I was heading (only not too briskly) for Ezra Morris's bookstore with Jud, his son, and one or two others, I was always reasonably sure to encounter her. And as often, the enticing glow of her cheeks and eyes caught my fancy, only girl-shy as usual, I avoided her. But one day, walking homeward past the post office, there she was. And though I did not choose to pause, in step with me she fell.

"You live near us, don't you?"

"Yes."

"I've seen you walking out our way."

Silence, nervous and intense.

"You have some nice chestnut trees in your yard. Would you mind my coming over some time after school and gathering some?"

"No! Oh, no! I wish you would!"

"Well, I will, then."

Silence.

"To-morrow evening, maybe."

"Yes, do."

"Will you be there?"

"Oh, yes."

"You must come over and see me some time, too."

"Yes, I will, thank you."

And so, with a throat quite tight and an almost unendurable heartbeat, coming to her block, her house, or at least opposite to it on our side, and yet not even crossing over, just saying weakly: "Good evening!" and leaving her to cross over alone. Yet wishing to go with her. How much! And she thinking what? Numbskull? Dunce? None the less, she came to pick chestnuts with me, and secured a basketful, yet never so much as a kiss or a squeeze. Not one! And so leaving me alone and miserable. Horribly so!

Similarly one day of this same summer I was sitting in a hammock in the shade of a pine tree in front of our house, when Stella Davenant, Bertha Reilly and Dolly Reed came by. Stella called: "Hello, Theo!"—a daring overture in so far as I was concerned, not presumed since the sudden exclusion of the year before. Yet now thrilling me—how much! And causing me to call back "Hello!" yet with half-hope, half-fear that they would go on. But instead: "Why don't you let us come in and swing in your hammock?" from Dolly Reed, whom I did not like, although, leaning on our front gate, she made a charming picture. Her plump beauty, enhanced by a white dress with a blue sash and wide straw hat, was considerable. I jumped up, nervous and flustered. It seemed as though our old social favour might be coming back. "Why, of course," I managed to say, "do come in." Giggling comfortably and audaciously, they came in, and stayed all of three quarters of an hour, laughing, jesting, swinging, and unquestionably seeking, as even I could guess at the time, to efface through this present proffer of friendship not only the previous coldness but my present and unchanging bashfulness, which in the past as now caused me to feel so futile. And yet grateful too, for now they were so friendly. And had I had any real skill, how easy it would have been to effect new contacts and friendships. But, as ever before, beaten by girl-shyness, my curse until nearly twenty. And so I was beside myself with nervousness and unable to stammer more than platitudes. And so making out most poorly. They stayed and played but without any love-making or follow-up agreements of any kind.

Similarly, there was another girl: Myrtle Taylor, a pale, dark-haired Myrtle-Trego-ish creature, the daughter of a travelling salesman, whom I had adored through all of the preceding winter without a word of any kind. Her little mouth, her dark violet eyes with their lavender lids, her soft black hair: all was so ravishing to me. But she went her way. Four years later I learned with a pang that she had married Walter Keller, the local jeweller's son.

And then, one day that summer, Nata Weyler—she of the blue-black hair and olive skin—seeing me roving in the north-west corner of our front yard where mushrooms grew, came over to say: "Oh, hello! What are you doing?"

"I'm looking for mushrooms," I said, staring at a face and figure Medusa-like in their paralysing charm for me.

"Oh, do mushrooms grow here? May I see them? Oh, aren't they nice? You have such a large place here, haven't you? Isn't that a swing over there? It's a wonder you wouldn't invite somebody once in a while. It's so nice and cool in here."

"Oh, do come in; I wish you would!" I said, but without

making any move to open the gate, which was some distance away.

"Well, come open the gate for me!" she prompted.

Whereupon I nervously awoke to the duties of a host if not of a gallant, and hurried to let her in. But what a half-hour! The agonising vacillation between the desire there and then to put my arms around her and so shatter the binding sex fear, and the queer conviction that if I did so (and this in the face of her all too obvious intention to allure me to just this), she would turn on me with belittling comment which would set at naught my hungry presumption. And yet there was nothing for it but that I should swing her, her trim ankles and calves showing beneath the long skirts of the day, blown back by the wind. And her squeals and pretended fear and this and that intended to move me to the part I should have played! But in spite of that, no more than my hands about her waist in swinging her. Not a kiss for her laughing and enticing lips. And yet, saying to me as she left: "You and your sister know where we live, don't you? Why don't you come out some time?" And this after our really sharp exclusion of the previous year!

But in my mind was not so much that—the fact that during the winter just past there had been group festivities in which she and others had participated and from which Trina and I had been excluded—but rather that the residence region as well as the house in which she lived was so much better than ours, and that to and with her went the smarter and richer boys of the town who still ignored me. Actually, and at last, there was swelling in me a resentful pride. Had it not been said of me that I had a good mind and a good future? And was it not best that I should turn to that? But how? How? And yet because of this, no immediate resumption of these relations. Rather new, if vague, dreams of how and what to do. I really could not stay here any longer. I must find some way of doing something, not continue on here to loaf and grieve and dream.

CHAPTER LII

AND then one July day, and because of all this, I decided that I ought to work. But how, and at what? After thinking it all over very seriously, I talked the matter over with Ed, and he, amenable to my thoughts as to this, was decidedly interested. I pointed out to him, sitting in a hammock under the trees, that as things stood, we were mere loafers sponging on our mother. Other boys worked, if only for their fathers. Besides, had I not heard Judson Morris say, and this for weeks past, that this was the time of year when farmers were looking for people to work in their truck patches or fields? In consequence, Ed and I started out one morning about nine o'clock (a good farm-labour-seeking hour, as you will notice) and fired with the notion, if you will believe it, that farmers paid fifteen to eighteen dollars a month and board for inexperienced farm-hands, and such farm-hands as we were! Under the arm of one of us was our midday lunch prepared by mother, and in our hearts mingled hopes and fears. In my own heart also, as I recall, was a sense of loneliness or *heimweh* at the thought of parting with the sense of peace and possession which filled the old brick house among the pines. For as I could feel, it was really slipping from us. Our years were multiplying. And while we might not be going away for ever, still was this not the beginning of the end of our youth? You may imagine the depression!

However, as you may well guess, my emotion was premature and unfounded. We walked and walked. The long roads, overhung with trees; the simple farm-houses snuggling close to the soil; the wide, silent fields of growing corn or wheat, impressed me as a lovely but lonely opportunity. How silent it would all be at night! And only work. And our dear and comfortable mother so far away. Only, fortunately or not fortunately, the farmers to whom we applied did not want our help. Instead, and to my disgust and depression, either harsh or ribald and haw-haw comments on our fitness for the work applied for.

Thus: "Where do you boys come from?" asked one grey-thatched, sun-tanned old farmer as we approached and made inquiry as to whether he needed any farm help. I can see his wry, critical face even now.

"Warsaw."

"Ever work at anything before?"

"No, sir."

"Well, boys, I tell you," he said, with a quizzical smile. "Neither of ye have got heft enough across here and here," and he indicated our sterns and shoulders. "Ye ain't big enough. Yer hands are too little," and he examined one of mine.

"I thought we might pick weeds or plough, maybe," I suggested. "Plough, hey?" He smiled. "Well, that's good. A farm day lasts from sunup to sundown. It's hay pitchin' and corn and potato ploughin' just now. Some days the sun gits mighty hot. How much did ye expect anybody would pay ye?"

"Oh, our board and whatever is fair a month," I replied.

"You can't do it, boys," he said, genially. "Ye ain't been brought up to it, I can see that. Better go back home and get some city job, in a store or somethin'. You're too light in the poop deck, both on ye," and he smiled genially. We returned disconsolately across the field to the road.

At another point, around the noon hour, we met three husky farmer boys coming out of a field, following several large horses.

"Where ye goin', boys?" asked one of them, a buff-brown Samson of eighteen or twenty, in jeans and a homespun shirt.

"We're looking for work," I replied.

"On a farm?" he asked, spreading out his legs and running a hand through his damp, loose hair.

"Sure!" I said, a little defiantly, irritated by his manner.

"Ho, ho, ho!" he laughed, and the other two joined him. Then of a sudden he pulled a serious face. "Come to think of it, I know a man down here that wants two boys." He waited to see the brightening effect of his remark. "He wants 'em to pound sand in a lot o' rat holes." He ho-hoed again and the others joined him, while Ed and I, crestfallen, trudged on. Under a tree we sat down to eat our sandwiches and some berries we had gathered in the lanes.

What a long day that was! We walked and walked. Under green trees, tired and disheartened after a time, we rested and debated as to whether we should apply at a certain distant farm door and which one should do it. Frequently Ed rebelled at my trying to make him the spokesman. By nightfall we were footsore and weary and still six miles from home. No one wanted us. To be sure, motherly old ladies here and there had commended us for our courage. We were nice boys and shouldn't get too disheartened. Younger ones, busy with the cares of the day, had turned us sharply away, usually with jests. Old men, as we discovered, were easiest to talk to, but these only gave us kindly advice. We were too spare and young.

At nine o'clock that night we arrived at our own door, so tired and footsore and hungry that we could scarcely walk. As I saw it, we had had a miserable and laborious day just walking. But supposing there had been real farm labour to do? As for myself, I was already sure that there was not much hope for me. Ed was always more courageous. But there was mother outside the door, waiting and wondering about us.

"Well?" she asked, sweetly, as we came trudging up the path, much too reduced to speak. "Did you get anything to do?"

"No," we replied, drearily.

"And I suppose you're starved, too," she added. "Well, go take off your shoes and wash your feet and I'll get you something." She even took one of my hands and smoothed it as I passed her, then went slowly into the kitchen.

My next venture was more and yet less successful. After taking a few days to recover from this discomfiting adventure, I talked to Jud Morris about the matter of work. Clerking in his father's store, he seemed to me to be likely to be in touch with everything that was going on. "Why don't you go and see old man Gears at the hardware store?" he suggested. "He has a farm four or five miles out of town and I hear he wants boys to weed out his truck patches. He has thirty acres of onions alone."

I jumped at the chance. "How much does it pay?" I asked.

"Only fifty cents a day, but then you get your board and

room and you can come home Sundays. That's twelve or thirteen dollars a month, and the work'll certainly last that long. You can get a good suit of clothes out of that." I decided to act at once, for I needed the clothes as well as other things.

Old man Gears, in his still, cool, dark hardware store, with its buzzing blue-bottle flies in the window, and its advertisements of reapers and binders and tools, looked me over quizzically.

"Ever worked on a farm?"

"No, sir!"

"Do you think you could earn fifty cents a day if I give you the chance? It's hard work and my superintendent out there won't stand for no loafers!" He stared at me over the counter as though I were a curious insect.

"I wish you'd let me try," I said. "I'll do the very best I can."

"Very well, go on out! Tell Mr. Palmer I told you to come."

He gave me no directions, but I learned them from Morris, and that very afternoon I set forth, walking the entire distance and arriving there at about three o'clock. The superintendent, a crude, sandy-haired man, in rough overalls and a ragged straw hat, received me. He was sharpening a tool in the barn.

"Well, what do you want?" he growled. His manner was most uncomplimentary, even pugnacious.

"Mr. Gears sent me out here. He said you would put me to work if I told you he sent me."

"Jesus Christ!" he commented, and turned away. After allowing me to stand for a while unnoticed and seeing that I did not leave, he added: "Another of his damn' town-boy farm-hands! I wonder how he expects me to run this place out here." He held a scythe blade against a grindstone and sparks flew. Presently he turned to me and asked: "How much did he say you were to have a day?"

"Fifty cents," I replied.

"And your board and room?"

"Yes, sir."

"Well, I suppose I'll have to try you if he says so," he added, wearily. "Wait a minute."

I stood there while he completed his task. Then, with a

rolling, defiant swing of the shoulders and a heavy tread, he led the way toward a great field of young onions about a quarter of a mile distant, where in a still blazing sun he set me to work with a small steel fork loosening the earth and picking the weeds from around a row of onions that must have been all of a thousand feet long. There were scores of such rows. In other rows were several other farm-hands, two of them women.

Briskly enough I began. The man's manner had impressed as much as it had depressed me. After quickly illustrating what he wanted done and watching over me and two or three other groups as I hurried to do as he directed, he departed, shaking his head. Because of his obvious doubt of my ability, I worked as hard and fast as my strength would permit. Under the shade of an old straw hat which I had brought with me, I hunched along on my knees, pulling weeds as fast as I could. At first it seemed easy enough, and I began to think I might satisfy him. Later, as my unused back muscles began to ache and my fingers to tire, I was not sure. Still, I thought I must get used to it. I worked and worked until I began to think it must be at least six or seven. The sun did not set until long after seven o'clock. Finally, from the distant house —a long way off, as it seemed to me then—a farm bell sounded and since I saw the other labourers rise from their knees, I wondered whether I had better not do so. Not being sure, though, of my own privileges, I worked on until my master's voice sounded from the distant fence. He was making for the house. "Come on an' git your supper!" he called.

I don't believe I ever ate a more unsatisfactory meal, tired and hungry as I was. The day had been very warm, and the flies in the dining-room or kitchen—whichever you prefer— were legion. It was a still, close evening and the food was served steaming hot. There were ears of corn, stewed chicken, mashed potatoes, and biscuit: the American farm formula. But tired as I was, I could scarcely eat. The joints of my knees, shoulders and back ached and were sore from sunburn, and my hands too, as well as being tired. To add to my discomfort, there were seven or eight farm-hands, the veriest yokels, whose loud comments, laughter and noisy and smacky manner of eating struck me as boorish. At one end of the table sat Mr. Palmer, my employer, and called for an ample supply of food from the two bustling women, one of whom was probably his wife. Curiously, the whole situation was more confusing than anything else. It was so different from anything I had ever known. I was miserable.

After this meal, which lasted say fifteen or twenty minutes, pipes were lit and there was a brief period of idling in the small, barren, littered farmyard. Then suddenly a restless: "Come on, Jake, we have that hay to put in yet!" from Mr. Palmer, and to my astonishment and dismay, I learned that more work was expected. "We work until the light gives out!" explained the foreman to me in passing.

I bustled back to my row, resentful of such unremitting toil. This man directing me seemed to me a clown and a boor, not really worth considering. He reminded me of a strong but fractious and little-reasoning horse. And so eager to work. And for what? This hot, hard, poorly paid life here? Of what value were such people? I asked myself. Or did life demand this heavy struggle from the many? Would it demand it of me? If not, for what else was I fitted? Actually, when it came to my first hand-to-hand contest with the struggle for existence, I was by no means sure but that the lowest of menial labour within my strength was all I was fitted for. For otherwise, what had I to offer? Had I been trained for anything else? Could I so train myself? By no means, as I saw myself here in this first contact with work, did I conceive of myself as a personage or one called to the arts, professions, or even higher trades? I seemed to myself just then as thoughtless, footless, without aim or direction.

Finally night fell—for it had been no more than six when we were called to dinner, and two hours had since elapsed—and while I was still in the field with these others, a number of stars were already twinkling in the sky. Besides, the west had become a pale violet, the woods darkling black masses, cool and mysterious. Finally called with the others to quit, I trudged wearily back to the house, doubting whether I could endure another hour, let alone another day of this strenuous regimen, and even though a night's rest were now to intervene. It was all so hard on my back, knees and hands. Dourly enough, I washed my hands in a tin pan on a post outside the door, wondering at the same time where I was to sleep providing I was not already discharged, for I felt so unwelcome here, merely tolerated. Most of the other farm-hands, as I now noticed, though, had betaken themselves elsewhere, certainly not to sleep as I could see, for they were not as I was, spindling and weak, a mere string of a boy or man. Inside in one of the rooms, as I could also see, a tin lamp was glowing hotly, and overhead now the sky was thick with stars. I was not so done but that I was conscious of their beauty, although I was wondering where, if anywhere, was my bed. I hung about hopelessly and quite afraid to speak to anyone, until at last my employer appeared to say that I could have one of the four cots in the attic.

There being no way of sponging off, as at home in our improvised bathroom with its large tin tub, I crawled, unwashed, on to a narrow, saggy couch under the low slope of the roof, a tin lamp on a small stand near me, mosquitoes singing about, even visible through the screens of the two small windows when the light was out. It was hot, stuffy, dull, but just the same here I rested, unconscious of the arrival of some three others some time later. And then at what seemed to me could be little more than past midnight, I heard the clang of the farm bell outside and saw the occupants of these other cots straightening up. It was dawn. In the east was already noticeable a faint dilution of the dark.

"Come on, Sam, if you want any breakfast!" one called to the other, and down the stairs they clattered, having seemingly tumbled into their clothes. I heard the sound of dishes and smelled boiling coffee, and I knew that my second day's work was at hand.

I doubt whether I ever spent a more strenuous day or one that pleased me less. Not that this farm world was not lovely. It was. The smooth fields, sown to corn, wheat, potatoes, onions, tomatoes, were truly beautiful, especially in this early light. There was even a slight dew on the onion stalks, and the distant sentinel groves of trees was now so pleasingly green and so shot with silver patches of light as to be Corot-like in the morning mist. Birds were calling, and there was that spicy odour of endless plant and insect life so fragrant and pleasing in summer. But as the morning wore on, a climbing sun drove down stronger and more blistering rays. Light! Light! What is it? And that blazing ball, the sun, creating and driving us! I worked and worked, moving along on my hands and knees, wondering how long it would be before noon, or before I could not endure it any longer. Yet not noon but only nine o'clock came, at which time a second meal was served—cold meat, jam, bread and butter milk. And then at nine-thirty we returned to the fields and worked until one, when owing to aches and pains and a curious dizziness in my head, I lost all track of time and thought it must be evening. Yet it was only one, and the meal proffered nothing to me, for I really could not eat. But at one-thirty again I returned to the field, only to ask myself how was I to stand this. I knew I could not. Yet a kind of pride—the need of making a start in the world—caused me to go on. Every few minutes I would change my position in order to rest my back or knees and to wipe my face, and so made wretched progress. And finally, at three or four, my grim master was once more there, and exclaiming: "My God, this will never do! You can't do this work! You won't do a row a day at this rate!" I think I had just finished the row I started the evening before. "I wish to Christ Gears would stop sending me city boys!" he added, and walked off.

I realised now that I was of no value to him and would unquestionably be discharged at nightfall, but still I kept on, how or why I don't know. Pride should have made me quit or do better. The marvel to me is that I was not felled by sunstroke. But I stuck it out, though drooping like a fagged horse, pulling feebly at weeds. Finally at nightfall, I walked heavily and doggedly to the house and sat down at the noisy table, but unable to eat. After dinner, as I stepped out into the yard, my employer came over and said: "Here you are, sonny, fifty cents. You can't work for me. You're not strong enough. Better go back to town."

And so I realised that my job was done, also that I had to walk back to Warsaw this same evening. But I started just the same, grateful that it was all over. I was so tired that occasionally I lay down by the roadside. And once I sat down at the edge of Eagle Lake and put my feet in the water, thinking how plain it was that I was not meant to be a farmer. Yet if not that, what? I thought of the cities and towns my Aunt Sue had predicted and of Paul and Al and my sister Eleanor's husband, their distant wanderings, experiences, pleasures, successes. Would ever I become part of so great a world, travel so far, do so well? Between ten and eleven at night I arrived at our home and found my mother sitting on the steps outside the door.

"Well, Theo?" she asked, sweetly. "You couldn't stand it, could you?"

"The sun was too hot," I replied. "It made my head hurt."

"Of course it did!" she said. "It's too hard work for a boy like you. I knew it would be. You're very tired, aren't you? You'll want something to eat, won't you?"

She put out milk, bread, cold meat and jam. And here at home I felt much better and ate, sunburned and aching as I was, for her sympathy was as a bath and a balm. Already Mr. Palmer, his farm, the hot sun, and all my ills, were no more than distant memories. They would not return. I remember, though, that before eating I fished into my pocket and produced the half-dollar, which I laid down before my mother as evidence of the fact that I had really worked.

"A half-dollar!" she exclaimed. "You really earned all that! Well, now, isn't that nice? It's the first money you've ever earned. Well, I'm sure some day you'll earn a lot more," and she smiled approvingly. I was half inclined to feel that I had rendered a distinguished service not only to her but to humanity at large.

CHAPTER LIII

WARSAW was becoming famed at this time for its scenic beauty. Excursions, planned by the railroads, came from Fort Wayne, Indianapolis, South Bend, and even points farther off. A great new pleasure park was opened on Eagle Lake, and the stores and shops generally began to look more prosperous. The variety and beauty of the craft on the several lakes increased at a great rate. A canal was cut between Pike and Center Lakes, so as to provide a longer water trip for visitors. I was beginning to be caught by the American spirit of material advancement. Here was no land or day to be satisfied with well enough. Anyone could legitimately aspire to be anything in America, and nearly all aspired. Not to want to be rich or to be willing and able to work for riches was to write yourself down as a nobody. Material possessions were already the goal as well as the sum of most American life, and so one could not help feeling the state of isolation and indifference which accompanied a lack of means.

At the same time, I was beginning to be caught by news of the tremendous activity of Chicago, to which so many were repairing. Since we had left there three years before, it had been growing at the rate of at least fifty thousand a year. The daily papers which we took recounted vast activities: the building of new depots and street car lines, the extension of social and financial activities in every direction. I remember being fascinated by descriptions published in the Chicago daily papers of odd bits of city life: Goose Island in the Chicago River with boats and scows made into houses, ducks and geese waddling about and lines of wash fluttering in the smoky wind; West Madison Street, where we had lived, teeming with life and lights; Halstead Street, north and south, then a clattering, stirring thoroughfare, with its eighteen miles of stores and houses; and the lake and river, with its steamers and large and small sailing-vessels! If we could only return to Chicago again, I thought! There our neighbours would not care what we were. The fact that some of us had not done quite as was socially expected of us or that we had not fitted in as I at least desired would not be held against us or me there. I could get work, all of us could. In Chicago were crowds, opportunities, theatres, libraries, museums, a great world!

What trivial or minor things will occasionally move an individual to action! I think it was a Sunday newspaper account of Halstead Street's life and activities that finally caused me to act. Besides, many boys I knew were leaving for other places. Arthur Moon and Harry Bitner had gone to Chicago. Harry Croxton's father had decided to remove to Medicine Lodge, Kansas. By now I was sixteen years old, old enough to make my own way, I thought. My brothers Paul and Al had already made theirs. My father, recovered, was once more in Terre Haute, and here we were, we four: mother, Trina, Ed and myself. Entering the house I found my mother in the living room.

"Ma, I am going to Chicago!"

"Why, what do you mean? When?" she asked, astonished.

"To-day!"

"What for?"

"I want to get work, if I can. I'm tired of Warsaw. If you'll give me my fare and three dollars, I'll go to-day. I can get something. I know I can. I see lots of places advertised in the papers." I was very sure of what I was saying.

I think, as I look back on it, that my mother must have been temperamentally biased in favour of change. Or was her justifiable dissatisfaction with the *now* reason enough for her constant eager contemplation of the future? Possibly she saw in my state of mind a precursor of better things for me, and so for herself. Who knows? Or maybe she felt that she dare not take upon herself the thwarting of ambition in any form? At any rate, she looked at me solemnly and said: "You really want to go, do you?"

"Yes, I know I can get something. I don't want to sit around this place any longer. We can't get anywhere here. People only talk about us."

I remember her curious, distantly contemplative look as she sat and stared at me. "Well, maybe you're right," she replied. "But I wouldn't go just yet. Why don't you wait a few days and think it over? You're very young. I wanted you and Trina and Ed to go to school and get an education and be somebody."

"I'll get an education," I replied—and at the moment I knew I would—how I could not say. "I know how now, and anyhow I'd like to work. I learn a great deal reading."

She hesitated, musing. "But you can't get along on your fare and three dollars."

"Yes, I can, too! Anyhow, let me try. It's only three hours away. If I get work, maybe I can do something for you."

I could see her still youthful, hopeful eyes brighten. What storms had she not endured, what hopes seen fade, and yet she still hoped!

"Maybe you might," she said, simply, after a time. "Anyhow, it's only three hours away and the others are there." (She meant Eleanor and Ruth.) "You can look them up. I'll give you six dollars, and if you need more you can write me. Maybe I can help you, or you can come back." (The fare was $1.75.)

"I won't come back," I said—I don't know why, for I had no certainty that I would get anything to do.

"Well, then," she said, "I suppose I ought to say go. I don't want to hold you back, if you think you can do anything for yourself."

I hurried to pack a bag. And then, after kissing her good-bye, to the train which left at three. I did not trouble to tell Ed or Trina; I could not be sure how long I would be away.

That ride to Chicago was one of the most intense and wonderful of my life. For to me it was of the very substance of adventure. I remember, for instance, the quality of the day: it was so fair and cool, not arrestingly bright. And when I kissed my mother good-bye, I did not do so with any great regret; I did not feel for some reason that we were to be parted for long. The train rushed on through woods, fields, and towns, which, although I had come this way three years before, seemed wholly new. Besides, never before had I made a railroad journey alone, and here now I was, bag in hand, going to Chicago and wondering what I should do and where I should stay once I was there and for how long. And strange as it may seem, although I knew where both were, as well as Al, as I thought, I had no desire to visit either of my sisters at once. Rather, and most determinedly, I wanted to reconnoitre this fairyland alone, to wander about and get work. I was not afraid; rather, I was pleased and assured. Had I not been there before, and did I not really love it?

As we progressed and neared Chicago, the sky changed and threatened a thunderstorm. In the west, over green, smooth fields, brushed here and there with soft, foggy groves as at Valparaiso, hung a great thunder-head, and I had not bothered to carry an umbrella. In my bag were but a single change of underwear and socks, an extra shirt or two, some handkerchiefs: no more than a bare equipment. When we reached South Chicago, with its sudden smudge of factory life against great green plains, a crowd of Italians, Huns, Poles, Czechs, all chattering in their own tongue, boarded the train, their pipes smelling vilely. A little farther on, lumpy roads appeared, strung with telephone and telegraph poles and dotted with wagons. Then came railway lines paralleling the one on which I was riding, immense car yards packed with thousands of cars, and street crossings outside the gates of which waited shabby cars and a congestion of traffic. Farther in came the Desplaines and later Chicago River, which I recognised at once and with pleasure, and then the long, low sheds of the then Pennsylvania Depot paralleling Canal Street, with its hurlyburly of trunks and porters and bags, lines of cabs and buses outside.

Stepping out of the train, it was as though I were ready to conquer the world. Neither fear nor loneliness possessed me; rather, if anything, there was something determined and even aggressive in my attitude, why I cannot say. Also I knew then and there that I loved Chicago. It was so strong, so rough, so shabby, and yet so vital and determined. It seemed more like a young giant afraid of nothing, and that it was that appealed to me. It was dusk and the lamps in the stores were just being lighted. Because we had once lived in Madison Street, I tramped out that way, eager to walk, anxious to find a room for $1.50 or $2.00 per week. But after I had walked far past our former abode and was becoming thoughtful as to where I should find a room, I finally encountered a section which seemed to call to me. It was simple, clean, neighbourly.

Outside a livery stable door, tipped back in a chair, was a fat, red-faced man who seemed also simple and genial.

"Do you know where I could find a small room around here?" I asked.

He looked me over critically. "See that window over there with the flower pot in it? Number 732?"

"Yes," I replied, noting a two-story frame building, a store below, an apartment above.

"There's a Mrs. Pilcher lives there. A very nice old lady. She has a room, I think. Go and ask her."

I crossed over and rang the downstairs bell. Presently I heard a step, and then the door was opened by a sweet-faced, slender, grey lady, who beamed on me with such intelligence, geniality and sweetness as to cause me to feel, and at once, at home, or shall I say on old and friendly terms with her. She looked at me directly and estimatingly, and with some slight favour, as I could see and feel. "You want to see me?" she asked.

"The gentleman across the street in the livery stable said I might get a room here," I replied. "I want a room to-night if I can find one." As I talked, it began to rain.

"Are you a stranger in the city?" she asked.

"Yes, ma'am, I just came in to-night."

"Like every other person in Chicago, you're trying to make a start in the world, I suppose," she said. "We're trying to start too, here, my husband and I, only we're not as young as you are. Just come up and I'll show you what I have." She allowed me to precede her up the steps, closed the door, and then added, leading the way: "Now you can have either this little front or back bedroom for a dollar and a half. I did intend to ask two dollars. But since you're just a boy and I know you need your money, I'll let you have it for that. I have a boy starting out in life in Kansas City."

I felt so pleased and touched that I scarcely knew how to answer her. She was so gentle and cordial and frank, and the place was so clean and neat. One look at the front bedroom, with its small white bed and window looking down on the street where the cars passed, decided me. "I'll take this one," I said.

"Now I know you want to wash your hands and face and tidy up, so I'll just bring you water and towels."

She bustled out and returned with these, leaving me to my-self. I washed my face and brushed my clothes, then knelt down by the window—because I could hang farther out by doing so—and looked out. East and west, for miles, as it seemed to me, was a double row of gas lamps already flaring in the dusk, and behind them the lighted faces of shops, and, as they seemed to me, very brightly lighted, glowing in fact. And again, there were those Madison Street horse-cars, yellow in colour, jingling to and fro, their horses' feet plop-plopping as they came and went, and just as they had when I sold papers here four years before. And the scores and scores of pedes-trians walking in the rain, some with umbrellas, some not, some hurrying, some not. New land, new life, was what my heart was singing! Inside the street cars, like toy men and women, were the acclimated Chicagoans, those who had been here long before I came, no doubt. Beautiful! Like a scene in a play: an Aladdin view in the Arabian nights. Cars, people, lights, shops! The odour and flavour of the city, the vastness of its reaches, seemed to speak or sing or tinkle like a living, breathing thing. It came to me again with inexpressible variety and richness, as if to say: "I am the soul of a million people! I am their joys, their prides, their loves, their appe-tites, their hungers, their sorrows! I am their good clothes and their poor ones, their light, their food, their lusts, their industries, their enthusiasms, their dreams! In me are all the pulses and wonders and tastes and loves of life itself! I am life! This is paradise! This is that mirage of the heart and brain and blood of which people dream. I am the pulsing urge of the universe! You are a part of me, I of you! All that life or hope is or can be or do, this I am, and it is here be-fore you! Take of it! Live, live, satisfy your heart! Strive to be what you wish to be now while you are young and of it! Reflect its fire, its tang, its colour, its greatness! Be, be, wonderful or strong or great, if you will but be!"

CHAPTER LIV

THE next morning I proceeded to reinvestigate this vast plasm of hope. The freshness, strangeness, wonder! Had I one gift to offer the world, it would be the delight of sensing the world as I then sensed it! This city was to me a land of promise, a fabled realm of milk and honey, but only approximately true, of course; poverty's only paradise, a new door to the illy-equipped, the dreamer's mirage of something better! For all things were so new, and so many new things springing up. One could see it as well as feel it as one walked here and there. Here, as nowhere else, youth might make its way; even old age retrieve its broken fortunes. Almost all save the dying might hope. What more?

On leaving Warsaw my mother had put in a shoe-box a whole cold chicken, part of a pie, some bread and apples. This lasted me for three days. In the meantime, I walked the streets, miles and miles, seeking work before looking up either of my sisters. Ours was no family for leaning heavily on blood relationship. I liked my brothers and sisters fairly well according to their merits as individuals, but never more so. Hence, although close to them here, I still felt myself to be alone, one who must act and think for himself. I remember entering immense factories and stores, seeking anything in the way of work. But what task it was I should be able to perform I scarcely troubled to think about. Maybe I could wait behind a counter or clean a store or wash windows or drive a wagon. I could not be sure, but obviously I must find something, and quickly. The idea of a small salary, six or seven dollars a week, inspired me. With it, as I figured, after paying $1.50 for a room and perhaps two or three dollars for board, I should have two or three dollars a week left. And what might not be done with that? Ha!

Needless to say, my dream was periodically interrupted by sudden sinkings of heart, disconcerting flashes of failure, as venturing into one place after another—concerns that appeared to employ thousands—I was received with an indifferent: "Nothing to-day!" or, more frequently, a sign posted conspicuously in the centre of the door: "No help wanted." And yet the thousands of young men and women, as one could see through the windows, bustling here and there, neat, energetic, and possessed of just some such place as I desired! Oh, how did one rise to so comfortable a state in so great a city? Then the very first day, after many of these discouraging experiences, at two o'clock I consulted the "help wanted" columns in the afternoon edition of *The Daily News*, the great want advertisement paper of the city at that time. "Boy wanted" seemed somehow to suggest me to myself. But I discovered, and with considerable uncertainty and even fear, that it was not so much cheap inexperience that was required as experience: that of a druggist, butcher, bricklayer, carpenter, baker, printer, salesman, painter, driver, tailor, waiter, or his assistant. That word "experienced"—it was everywhere. And the list of beginners exceedingly brief, almost terrifyingly so. More, such opportunities as there were for beginners concerned trades or conditions which I did not like or in which I was by no means sure that I could prove successful.

Nevertheless, I ran here and there: to a hotel that wanted a boy to work in its laundry; to a store where they wanted a boy to run errands; to a drug store that wanted a boy to clean up and help at a soda fountain; to a machine company that wanted a boy to learn to be a machinist by beginning as a machinist's helper. Those advertisements worded "*Strong* boy wanted" reduced me not a little, for I did not consider myself a strong boy. Yet I went just the same. As a rule, though, I found that I could not make more than two or three calls in an afternoon. All too often the distances were considerable, and in some cases car-fare was required, and when I did arrive I usually found five or ten or even twenty boys ahead of me, and all as eager and anxious as myself, so much so as to appear quite unfriendly at times. More, they had been, in many instances, swifter to reach the place, and in many instances appeared better fitted for the work, stronger, more inured to this sort of thing. Sometimes a druggist or laundry manager announced that the advertisement had been run the day before and the position had already been filled.

In more cases, they merely decided that I was not satisfactory: too large, too weak, too nebulous, too dull. Anyhow, I got no work.

On the third evening, though, a brother-in-law of the woman with whom I was lodging, arrived with his fifteen-year-old son to pay a call. They were Kansans. By now I was on such good terms with my landlady and her husband, who was a house-painter, that they seemed not only interested to include me in their family circle but to help me find something to do. My frugal eating, my early hours, and my daily search for work had impressed them mightily. On the strength of this, they introduced me to these visiting relatives, who also seemed to be interested. The father, a lean, wiry, close-mouthed, industrious type, asked me not a few questions about myself and said he was sure I would find something, that everybody did who tried. His son, on the other hand—a loutish youth of sorts, who had had only a fraction of a common school education—appeared to like me and suggested a walk along Madison Street. As we walked, he talked, contrasting Kansas and the small-town life which he and his father had only recently left, all too favourably, as I thought, with what was here in Chicago. At the same time he told me that they had found work not long since far out on the South Side—57th Street, I believe—where a great railway stable and refrigerator car company had its yards. Both were employed as cleaners, he said, he and his father working together.

"Why don't you come out to our place and see if you can't get work there?" he suggested, finally. "It's pretty good. They often put on new people. All you have to do is ask the foreman." He was munching a peach at the time, one thing he was willing to admit was better than he could get in Kansas for the money, fruit being scarce there.

Although I was not really drawn to either him or his father at the time, I was so desirous of furthering myself in some way that I simulated a warmth of interest that was as unreal as it was effective. Sure! Fine! How kind he was! I certainly would go! And then presently we returned to the house, where his father, though by no means as enthusiastic as the son, extended to me a not wholly uncordial invitation to come out the next morning along with them. Accordingly, at five, or before, the next morning I arose, in order to catch a five-thirty train, and at six-fifteen or thereabouts we arrived at these great yards, which because of their intricacy and far-flung arrangement of sheds, tracks and cars, confused me not a little. I think that at times the vastness of the city was almost too much for my by now almost rural brain. How staggering these industries—this one and so many others—the stock yards, the steel works, the great can and nail companies, the lumber yards, breweries, grain elevators, soap factories! Truly, so many of them, and all in one city, had a reducing effect on me, so much so that I was not sure of myself in any way. To work here—here and now—seemed to me more like contending with some vast mystery, the details of which could never be mastered, by me or anyone. Also I believe that what I was really thinking of was the whole city, not any particular part or task, which could not have been so confusing. At any rate, errors—those of clumsiness, if nothing more, for I was given a try-out by the foreman of this father and son.

But I must have done poorly—decidedly so—for as it turned out, the foreman did not want me, only he phrased it differently —he didn't need any more men just then. Later, he might. And after a half or three-quarters of a day spent at this, and no pay, a long trip back to the business heart. But before returning, and just the same, an intensive study of this region and this work—these great yards and cars—and the conclusion that I was too poorly equipped for it, not as strong and energetic as I should be. For as I saw it, the industry of this father and son was quite wonderful. They worked briskly and hard, rubbing down zinc ceilings and walls with soapy water and rubber mops in no time at all, then pouring floods of fresh water through certain holes and over the interiors of these cars, and after that polishing locks and ice pockets with such speed as discouraged me. No, I was not swift enough for this.

And so the next day spent in a desultory search which did no more than reduce my spirits still further. For I had so little money, and in spite of the greatest caution had consumed all that was in my shoe-box and eighty-five cents' worth of food besides. This left me exactly one dollar and ninety cents wherewith to face the future. Fortunately I had paid for my room in advance. In addition, I had written to my mother to say where I was and what I was doing. That evening brought me a letter containing not only encouraging thoughts but two dollars, all my mother could spare. She also voiced the thought that if I succeeded in obtaining work and if Ruth and Eleanor should choose to live with us later and help a little, she herself might be willing to come to Chicago and establish a home—a statement that made me feel as good as if I had found a job, and inspired me to search all the harder.

And whether because of that or not, I did find a job—a small and most unsatisfactory one, to be sure, but a job. It was nothing more than a combination dish-washer and bus boy to a Greek who ran a dirty but apparently prosperous restaurant in Halstead Street near Van Buren, a neighbourhood teeming with life but all a mixture of apparently degraded and semi-degraded individuals who interested me more by their strange looks, gestures, methods of living and meeting the difficulties of life than by any outstanding charm or merit.

And that restaurant! Heavens! It was a dirty, low-ceilinged, fly-specked affair or room—a long, thin store—lit by two single-branched gasoliers, ornamented for their entire length and breadth by fly-specked, dirty, red and white fringed paper. Also there were as many as eighteen tables, three rows of six each. On the floor was dirty, worn oilcloth, once brown-and-white squared but now all a dirty brown. And on the tables, dirty and torn tablecloths of thin linen and marked by coffee and what other stains I may not say. I think these were changed once a week.

And the kitchen! John Paradiso's kitchen! For such was my employer's name. However appealing his personality (I used it in after years), he was a smudgy, pudgy Greek, such as might be found in any of the long roster of dirty Greek restaurants in the America of that day. His fat, pale, oily body! And round and, as they seemed to me, almost meaningless eyes, dark and oily, not radiant or vivid. And his black hair and eyebrows and moustache! In the short period in which I learned of Greeks and their restaurants from him, I was unchangingly amazed that anyone could be so consistently and oilily and odorously dirty and still maintain so cheerful and even intriguing a presence or mien. For with all this, he was kindly and agreeable, a really genial and likeable man. If only one might have cleaned and brightened him up a bit, mentally and physically!

My first sight of him was in his own fly-specked and smudgy window, setting on end a dirty, fly-specked placard which read: "Dish-washer wanted." The sign was obviously old and had seen much service, and I could soon see why. Not even Greeks or down-and-outs or the veriest vagrants accustomed to the most unsanitary conditions could have been induced to work for long for Mr. Paradiso, more particularly in his kitchen. For it was not only hot and crowded with food and dishes (washed and unwashed) and slops, but smeary and slippery and odorous besides. A large-surfaced and serviceable old range, black and shiny because of many gravies and oils spilled upon it, stood in one corner, and supported innumerable pots and pans. Above it were shelves and hooks with more pots and pans. A once no doubt bright tin coffee boiler, holding not less than three or four gallons, had become, when I viewed it, an arresting combination of blacks and browns. What, wash the coffee pot? "Iss better dissaway!" So it got no washing during the seemingly endless period of my stay, although often I wished to have a go at it, so truly old and coffee-caked was it. Also during this time, what from dirt, work and an almost chronically irritated stomach due to the smells about me, I thought I should die, but I think mostly from dirt. My hours were from six-thirty to ten; eleven-thirty to two-thirty, the noon rush, by which time I was supposed to have washed and stacked the dishes; and again from five-thirty to eight-thirty or nine, by which time—and meanwhile having eaten the three meals provided me—I was free. Long but not arduous hours for one with experience. Yet probably it was only my inexperience and physical and practical sparseness which made it as trying as it certainly seemed.

Mr. Paradiso, on the other hand, was not a hard master by any means. On the contrary, he was, when things were not too pressing, genial and talkative, and in addition appeared to like the profession or art selected by him. On occasion, and even in the midst of the noonday rush—and this was July, the hottest month in the year in Chicago—he managed to whistle some notes or bars of a then current popular song, but whether sorrowful or gay I could not make out, and occasionally to curl up his moustachios and push back his hair, as if to say: "There now, I must look somewhat better!" And betimes he would tell of places and countries in which he had been—Mexico, San Francisco, New Orleans, New York. But Chicago was very good, he said. He had been here now fifteen years. Garbed in a pair of dirty black trousers, a once perhaps cream-coloured but now grey undershirt, brown slippers on his bare feet, an apron that for filth might have captured blue ribbons, he trudged here and there, now talking, now whistling, and betimes paring and potting the various vegetables or dressing and carving the invariably aged and none too fresh-smelling meats which went into his various concoctions. In fact, they were nearly always bad, as I came hopelessly to note, so bad that I could never eat them. It was only the eggs and vegetables and milk on which I could make out. Also betimes, in slack hours, he would repair to a room or apartment upstairs, where he roomed or lived with a girl—different girls at different times, as I noted—although there was one particular one who was nearly always around—at which times I had the place to myself and could steal and cook such little food as I desired. My poor stomach! And after my mother's cooking, too! The one girl whom I noted most and whom I suspected, because of her appearance, of being something more than a passing figure in his life, was young, plump, pink, tow-headed and frowsy. Too often she wandered about half-dressed, a cigarette between her fingers. Once as he came down from upstairs at four in the afternoon, I heard him mumble: "By jingo, she think I wait on her all time! I no wait on her all time!" Yet when I left, she was still present.

But now as to my duties. They consisted of washing dishes as the sign said, placing them in the drying rack near the stove, where they would dry themselves; scraping the leavings of the plates into large, wrought-iron slop-cans, which smelled to heaven and which when filled I had to trundle or rather roll (on one edge) out through the small yard into an alley beyond. This back yard itself was no dream of flowers and grass but a rattletrap collection of boxes, cans, paper, pieces of wood, and some coal in a shed, which latter had to be carried in buckets by me and fed into the yawning series of glowing pot-holes. "Little bucket coal, Theodore! Quick! Some wood, too! Muss make quick fire, now!" And out I would dash to get the coal or wood. But overhead was often a blue sky, a flying bird, a cloud, and I looked aloft at these out of my grimy yard.

One of the worst features of my job, though, was not to peel potatoes or onions or turnips or carrots or to cut up bits of beef, pork, veal, chickens (all stale and lying in barrels and tins, God knows how long!) and to all of which as labour I did not object, but to watch Paradiso do it! For he was almost unbelievably filthy in that respect. Rarely, if ever, did he wash his large fat hands or face, much less his body, I am sure. The best that at any time he would do was to seize a towel, usually as filthy as his apron, and wipe his hands or face quickly and indifferently on that. And that greasy, perspiring face! More, without turning a hair he would remove the smelly entrails of a stale chicken and then pick up new, clean pieces of pared and sliced potatoes or onions or this or that and drop them into whatever pot or pan was arranged for them. Also, and how often, he would pick up a piece of pie or cake with his unwashed fingers and put it on a dish to be shoved through the aperture which was the avenue for food passing into the dining-room or for dirty dishes on their way back to the kitchen.

As I have said, all of his chickens and meats were aged and blue and smelling of infection or decay, bought, no doubt, wretchedly cheap in order to make a profit on the low prices with which he baited his bill of fare. Lamb stew, 25 cents. Beef stew, 25 cents. Potted chicken, 35 cents. Roast chicken, 40 cents. Roast beef, 40 cents—and so on. And all with vegetables, coffee, bread, butter, pie even—or maybe not. I can't recall now. And believe it or not, I actually heard him haggling one day with the butcher or poulterer who was wheeling in a fair-sized box of these chickens and meats, not as to their freshness but as to their *relative* freshness! As he talked, he picked up one and another and smelled them, finally saying, quite solemnly and all in the way of business: "No, no! Too strong! Better you take 'em back! I get from some other fella!" What other words there were I have forgotten, but the dealer in turn, a dusky marketeer of what nationality I cannot recall (probably Greek, too, or Jewish), pretended an enormous astonishment. "Whatsa matta those chickens? Just the same chickens what you always get! Just so good, I betcha!" "No, no, no!" returned Paradiso. "I pay for good chickens, so I get 'em! Bettern you take 'em back, and we no deal no more." Whereupon the poulterer, aghast, rushed back to his wagon and produced an equal-sized bucket, full of chickens that to me looked practically the same. They were just as water-logged and flaccid. Yet seizing one from the lot, he held it aloft. "Smell 'im! Smell 'im. Maybe you like 'im better. What? You no like 'im better? Fresh as any chicken you can get anywhere for the money, I betcha!" Whereupon Paradiso, taking an additional whiff or two, declared, "'S'allright! These not so bad. No can fool me! Bettern you not try!"

And so, the chickens piled on a dirty table and the noonday lunch proceeding apace. For Paradiso had a way of doctoring them up with what salts and onions and oils! Had it been to-day, they would have been listed on the bill of fare as "Fresh Philadelphia milk-fed chickens." You may be sure of it! It is the custom of the country.

CHAPTER LV

AS anyone may guess, this was work which one of my temperament could not long endure, let alone respect. It was not only too wholly miserable for words, but worse, humdrum. Peeling potatoes, peeling onions, washing carrots and lettuce, enduring the smell of stale meat and chickens and rancid garbage cans, and the sight and odour of Mr. Paradiso, greasy, if genial! And no cessation of work, no real break, for the hours of the morning and afternoon in which I did not have to work left me no real time for anything. Did I choose to go to my room, it seemed as though I had scarcely arrived and lain down to rest—as I did at first—when it was time to be up and off again. And worse, paying $1.50 for my room and all of seventy cents a week and sometimes more for car-fare, there was but little left for any of those other things for which I was mentally and emotionally clamouring: clothes, entertainment, the companionship of someone, either boy or girl. For did I say, or did I not, that my financial reward was five dollars a week plus my meals, such as they were?

So throughout, and as before, I was always wondering as to what was to become of me, what I could do to better myself, for I had so little time, working as I did here, to seek elsewhere. More, from my experience in seeking, I was not so sure that jobs were easy to get, not good ones, that is—not for me. And yet I was determined, after a time, not to stay here if I could help it. One of my ideas of how I was to do was to save a dollar or two a week until, if I could only continue here long enough, I should have enough to stop and look elsewhere, to live for three or four weeks, say, without work while I looked around. Another thing which held some promise was that now having this job, I might look up my sisters with better grace and without saying definitely what it was at which I was working, give them the impression of a youth who was at least succeeding at something, and so perhaps get them to advise and maybe even help me. I could not say how or why, but so it was.

And so, one morning, after working at least two or three more weeks in this fashion and feeling that I was not getting anywhere at all, I finally decided that I would call on my sister Ruth, not to say that I was working as a dish-washer but just working, and so if possible learn of her, Al, and my married sister Eleanor, and their plans and what if any chance I had of profiting by the same. Neither my pride nor my courage were as high as they were at first. My mother had written me the address on West Madison Street where Ruth was living, and to that I repaired, wondering how I should find her. She had always seemed the most interesting of all my sisters to me, more quiet, thoughtful, intelligent, and so on. And true enough, I found her working, assisting a West Madison Street dentist who had an office near by. But just at this time he had departed, it seemed, on a short vacation and had allowed her to take hers at the same time. She was rooming with another girl and they were still in bed when I knocked. But when she came to the door, she exclaimed in friendly astonishment: "Why, Theo! Wherever did you come from?" and offered me cordial if not enthusiastic lips. Since she had not yet had breakfast, we went after a time to a near-by restaurant.

Her first questions were what was I doing in Chicago and how was mother. And since I was in a position to say that I had work and that mother was well, she appeared to brighten. Also since I was by no means anxious to report myself as a dish-washer and in such a restaurant, I immediately assured her that I had a small clerkship which paid me about seven dollars a week. This she appeared to think was very good and said so, also that she hadn't thought I would leave Warsaw so soon, but since I had, it was nice that I had been able to place myself so well so soon—a pleasant acceptance of my present circumstance which caused my own prospects to darken. For I had been expecting something more than this—a somewhat more cheerful greeting and better news about something, I scarcely knew what. But no—instead presently she proceeded to inform me that Eleanor and her husband had gone away for the summer, and that Al was not in the city either—a bit of news that reduced me greatly—but at last, she added, and this quite casually, that since she was here alone now, and with her vacation at hand, she had been thinking of paying a visit to Warsaw. But now that I was here and working and mother, as I now told her, had hinted that it might be best if we left Warsaw, she seemed to brighten rather than take it dourly, as I thought she might, and even to suggest that if mother felt that way, it might be best. Her first thought had been that I had merely left in the face of the fact that the others were to stay on, which was, in part, true. But as I talked and it appeared that mother was willing to change—or so she had said to me—well, that was different. Wouldn't it be really a very good thing if mother and we three youngest and Al and herself could be reassembled here? She would like that so much. And I knew that she would, since she adored mother. If only Al could be found and induced to return and join us, she said. Besides, Trina and Ed were old enough to find work of some kind. So why should we not get along? In short, we were to do so! Of course, what was in the back of her mind was the joy of being part of any home arrangement of which mother would be the head. It was quite always so with all of us.

And so, and immediately, much talk as to how to do. We had all been so happy in Evansville, and even Sullivan, and why couldn't we again be so here? She began to talk of some new apartments she had seen going up in Ogden Avenue near Robey Street. They were nice and new and not so very expensive, she was sure. If mother were to freight the furniture, it would be enough to furnish such a place, and more. Besides, she had some things in use in her room, and some in charge of Eleanor, whose apartment was on the North Side. She could get them, and with an apartment furnished and only a small rent to pay, and all of us working as we would be, and Paul contributing as usual, how could we fail? She would write mother immediately, and she would spend the rest of that very day trying to find an apartment. If she did, I could go with her this same evening in order to see how I felt about it, for it must be convenient for me as well as herself. My wretched job, I thought! How long would I be able to endure it? Still, my desire to be a part of our home, any phase of it that might possibly be recaptured, was so great that I became enthusiastic and decided that I would stay at my job as long as my smudgy Greek was willing that I should.

And so, back to work until eight-thirty that night. And then the next day a trip to several apartments with Ruth. And the two of us finally deciding—and this without thought on the part of either of us as to what the others might think —that one in Ogden Avenue near Robey Street was *the one*. It was only thirty or thirty-five dollars a month, and with room enough for all: a front view and a back porch overlooking one of those typical Chicago back courts such as I had enjoyed in Madison Street on our first visit here. And a day or two after that, word from my mother, who was always the soul of optimism—and especially where any change was concerned— that she would be glad to come if we thought that we and she could make out. Her optimistic soul! And after that, and in consequence, a letter to Al, working in Milwaukee somewhere, with presently word from him that he would be glad to come and rejoin us if this intended home were certain. Also a letter from Paul. And finally word from Trina, who was also intrigued, that a freight car (and for as little as eight dollars in those days!) was being chartered for the furniture. Also that on the day the furniture left the house, mother would appear.

CHAPTER LVI

BUT in the meantime, and in what little spare time I had, what a running of errands—for soap, brushes, a broom, a mop, and what not else! And my sister and I cleaning—windows, woodwork, floors!

I was able during this time to gather a clearer and better impression of my sister Ruth than ever before, for previously I had not been sufficiently mature and certainly not nearly as much interested. Her large, still, contemplative blue eyes. Her heavy light hair and delicate face. Her spare and yet reasonably strong body, which with her delicate hands and feet seemed to match the softness and evenness of her voice. In all the days that I knew her I cannot recall her speaking harshly or cruelly to anyone. There was, as I have shown, a form of reserve and meditative self-balance, but little, if any, irony in any of her expressions or gestures. More than any of the girls I feel she resembled my mother, being, where she was interested, affectionate, peaceful, romantic and beauty-loving. Of all the girls she was the one who, as I had observed, carried her mother's necessities and interests most closely at heart. She really understood and sympathised with her needs, even though she had not always been with her. Away from home, as she had been during most of the years in which we were moving from town to town, she was in constant correspondence with her, sending her either cash or gifts whenever her means permitted. Here in Chicago now she complained to me regarding Amy, Eleanor and Janet. They had, as she declared, caused mother too much trouble: a thought which squared rationally with her own helpful attitude. And she was also intelligent. In Warsaw, during her visit home to recover from that serious illness, I had found her on occasion reading some of the most valuable books of which I then knew.

At last all was ready. Then there came a letter or wire saying when my mother would arrive. As for myself, it seemed impossible for me to get off to meet her—the dish-washing work piling up so—but when I explained to Mr. Paradiso one day, but with considerable hesitancy, that my mother was coming the next, he was more interested and helpful than I had hoped. "Your modder? You want meet 'er? All right! You meet her! Will be all right!" My gratitude swelled within me.

And so to the old, shabby Pennsylvania depot, with its long, dirty train sheds. And my mother being assisted off the train —with Trina and Amy's baby and a dozen bags—by two friendly trainmen who en route and because of the irresistible human appeal of her, had become interested. And she smiling her customary unaffected, winsome and therefore beguiling smile. I can hear her voice even now: "Well, well, Ruth! And you, Dorse! It's very noisy here, isn't it? Dear, dear, we have so many things." And Ruth tightening her arms about her in a tearful embrace. And myself getting as close as possible, squeezing her waist and arm and saying—I don't know what—that I had a job and that, gee, it was fine to have her here—but feeling that life would be nothing without her, so close had I always been held by the strong cord, the silver tether of her affection, understanding, sweetness, sacrifice.

But Trina eyeing me as ironically as ever, my many deficiencies appearing to provoke only humour in her, and offering me dry, pecky lips to be touched. Ed had not come with them; he had been left behind to see that the car carrying the furniture was properly locked, tagged and sealed. It was on a somewhat later train that he was expected. At once, though, my mother, Trina, and Amy's baby removed for the night, or until the furniture should arrive, to a room which Ruth had secured next to her own. As for myself, I was left at the depot to await the arrival of Ed and take him with me to my room for the night.

But here again was another troublesome mix-up. He did not arrive on the train scheduled. Instead, something interfering, he had been compelled to take a later one. But no wire to say so. And myself fearing he had made a mistake and gotten off at some suburban station, hurrying out to the Ogden Avenue apartment to see if by any chance he was there. But in my absence he arrived, and not finding anyone

322

there to meet him, travelled out to the Ogden Avenue address. Meanwhile I was trundling back to the station, more and more excited as the hour grew later. After waiting an hour, hoping that he might return to the station if he had gone to Ogden Avenue, I once more hurried back there. But again, while I was riding out to Ogden Avenue, he was riding back to the depot. God! On reaching Ogden Avenue the last time and not finding him, I had the good sense to tell my troubles to a policeman, who told me not to worry, that he would keep watch and if he saw Ed would ask him to wait. Then once more I dashed back to the station, while he returned to Ogden Avenue!

Finally, some time after midnight, I captured him. He was standing outside the Ogden Avenue address, in the yellow gaslight, not so much disconsolate as disgruntled. Unlike myself, he was not of the worrying, fretful sort.

"You people are fine ones!" he grumbled when I came puffing along, almost ready to weep for joy.

"Oh, Ed!" I exclaimed. "I thought you were lost!"

"Lost! It's a wonder I wasn't! Why didn't you come to the station to meet me?"

"Why didn't you come on the train you said you would?"

"They didn't tell me any train!" he declared. "I had to wait till the furniture was in the car, didn't I?"

Delight? I desired to hug him! But he was of no emotionally demonstrative turn. Solid facts interested him. Where were mother and Trina? Where could he get something to eat? He was hungry and tired and cross, and after searching for a cheap restaurant and not finding one open, we gave it up as a hopeless job and went to my room. I believe we did find a fruitstand, from which he made a grumbling, and by no means compensating selection.

The next afternoon, though, the furniture arrived and was delivered at about dusk. And at midnight we were ready to retire in the newly set-up beds amidst the usual moving disorder and so begin a new phase of our lives. And by degrees, order was brought out of chaos and we began to live the ordinary life of a Chicago flat. Ruth and myself, having work, attended it; Ed and Trina were about the matter of seeking something. But that was a thing that was serious enough in their cases. After the schools of Warsaw, to study the newspapers and run here and there after this and that! We heard plenty as to the difficulties of it.

In a short time Al too arrived, having resigned whatever he was doing to come here. But that meant a third to search. He had given up his stage ambitions, apparently, and sought only to obtain a reasonable wage and incidentally master some craft on which he could rely. Eventually it was electrical work that put him to rights, but meanwhile there was little before him save the usual crude economic struggle which because of his naturally studious and reflective turn grated on him. He was so anxious to escape the low weekly wage class, to find the door or path to a better life. That he ever did I do not know.

And again, a little later Eleanor and her husband from the east settled on the North Side, but with Eleanor, like all of the others, anxious to be about mother as much as possible, in her husband's absence spending most of her time with us.

As for myself during this transitory period, I was so much troubled by the work I was doing and how I was to pass from it into something more respectable that I scarcely knew how to think or do. For the fact of my securing a place so soon after my arrival here and so much better, according to my telling, than it really was (I had pictured myself as a clerk in a Halstead Street store), had obviously impressed my mother and the others so much that I was fearsome of weakening or modifying this impression in any way. It was so flattering, had raised so much hope in the breasts of these others. My mother's comment soon after her arrival was: "Well, Dorse, I thought maybe you'd have to come back, but you didn't, did you?" And this implying, as it did, energy, determination and apparent success on my part, was too heartening to be readily clouded, although I knew, and only too well, on what a slim, shaky foundation it rested. Always I stood in a form of terror lest Al or Ed in their wanderings should come upon me, discover in some way where I was working (since they were about the business of looking for work themselves), and not only expose me for what I was—a liar—but have their own courage or enthusiasm sapped by what they saw me doing. It was an exaggerated emotional notion on my part, but that was the sort of youth I was. As for Al and Ed, they had more energy and flair for this sort of thing than ever I could boast, as small as theirs might be.

Also just at this time, as luck would have it, Al was intensely interested to know what and how I was doing, how I had succeeded in finding such a place, since I claimed I was working in a haberdashery in Halstead Street which kept open Sundays as well as weekdays, also why might there not be something in the same place for him? This was most trying, since I had given him a fictitious store address and name. And now I was in constant dread lest he should look me up, which was what would have happened had I not presently forestalled this by telling him all and explaining how anxious I was to find something else.

But what really moved me to confess to him, after he had been with us not much more than a week, was, first, his own frank description of his own reduced and trying state; how sorry he was that he had not been able to make the stage and now must run here and there, and at his age (he was nearly twenty), and wishing that he could learn something, study something. At the same time, now and then in his despair he would take to drinking—a thing which terrified me beyond measure, for was not that what had ruined my brother Rome? I felt intensely sorry for him, and did my best to hearten him at the same time that I begged him not to drink, certainly not as an escape from failure. I sensed what that meant. And then one day there was his saying (we had begun meeting for walks during my hours off) that it was a shame a young fellow like me, with my mind and education (?), could not get something better to do; a position which would mean something to me in later years, not leave me floating around like Rome and himself then were—a comment so ridiculous in so far as what I was doing was concerned that I wanted to burst out in protest. My own dark thoughts as to what I was doing! And so I said, and almost without stopping to think: "Well, but what I'm doing isn't even as good as you think it is!" And then followed with a complete clarification of my duties, my earlier search, and why I felt so badly about it all. Whereupon he suggested that I give it up and try for something better. I could say I was discharged or laid off and could go about with him and Ed, and certainly within two or three weeks we would find something. For at the present, the family could look to Paul and Eleanor and Ruth, could it not? We were certain to find something. He even suggested that he would try and secure the place I was vacating (which seemed to me the very limit of brotherly affection and helpfulness), so that we would have that to live on, only he felt sure both of us could do better. Fall was coming on and things were better in the fall. He talked as one who had sought and found many jobs and was ordinarily not afraid of seeking.

And so, a bald statement one day to Mr. Paradiso that I was determined to quit. I·had to help my family and get something better. And to my astonishment, and as poorly as I thought I had done, he seemed loath to part with me. True, I had broken dishes, had by no means always kept up with the downpour of work in rush hours, and quite frequently had to be reminded of things I had overlooked, but his was an easy and by no means too exacting nature. Whereupon, to soften the blow, or rather to seem less ungrateful, I told him that our family was going to move far out on the South Side and that it would be impossible for me—distance, car-fare, and what not—to keep the hours he required.

"So, so, you moves now?" he observed, genially enough. "Sout' Side, heh? When you go? Saturday, heh? You no like this work? No good, heh? Well, maybe you right; bess I think you go. This no place fer a young feller like you. Too rough. You get better job somewhere. I get stronger man, not so fine like you, but better for this, see? I put him sign in the window. Some feller he come along I take him, right away, see? Then you no need bother." But seeing, possibly, a troubled look in my eye, he added: "I pay you juss same, Theodore. You makes good man some day, maybe. You works, no drinks, no too much womens. No good, drinks, women—too much." I smiled at this, as did he, only we did not smile for the same reason, I think.

The very same day a new man arrived, a rough young hobo, as hardy as a sailor or a tramp, and I was given my five until the end of the week. And so, heartened by this, announcing quite boldly to my mother and the others that I was laid off —an announcement that was not too cheering but which I glossed over by rosy assurances as to the quick and successful search I was to make for something else—an assurance which

326

for the moment I believed in myself. But just the same, by my mother's face and eyes I could see that such announcements were old and not decidedly encouraging things to her. She had seen too much of life. Its ills and the brevity of her own possible future made a not too encouraging picture, you may be sure. And yet she said to me: "Yes, well, that's all right. Don't you feel too bad about it. You'll get something else, I know"—a typical reply that was out of the depths of a simulated and all too tired courage, but which somehow for all her disappointments and defeats never failed her or her children.

CHAPTER LVII

BUT then the dreary weeks that followed (nearly four in all) before any one of us found a place. In fact, it was not until late September or early October, and not before the family as now constituted was considerably disturbed by its latest adventure. Living in Chicago, where food prices were relatively high and rents comparatively exorbitant, was different from living in Warsaw, where home-grown chickens, a fair-sized truck garden, and fruit trees helped to lighten the burden. I know that I, for one, was greatly depressed by my share in the affair and had about concluded that I was of no value whatsoever. I was so anxious that we should all be happy here (my mother's desires had in some way become my own, I think), and it was so discouraging to be met with the sign: "No help wanted!" and too often the added words: "Keep Out!"

However, walking into a large retail hardware place in our vicinity one afternoon, I encountered a man whose eye did not exactly spell indifference. He was a little man, as I recall him now, with a big head and a big mouth, shrewd, practical, commercial.

"Do you need any help?" I presume I asked. And for answer he asked if I had ever worked in a hardware store. When I told him I had not, he said: "Well, I think I can use you anyhow for a while," and asked if I had any objection to cleaning stoves. His establishment dealt principally in stoves, storing, cleaning and repairing them.

Although I had pictured myself as a smiling clerk behind a counter, I replied in the negative, whereupon he led the way up three flights of steps to a great rambling, dusty, smelly loft, crowded with old and rusty or smudgy stoves of every description, and among which I saw two men at work, or rather a man and a half; and saying as we went and entered that he would pay me five dollars a week for the labour of helping these others here.

But the two heavy-countenanced, somewhat saturnine

328

men, one large and one small and both of the tradeless, shiftless, drinking type, who were engaged in cleaning and polishing here, did no little to darken my thought as to what was in store for me. A stove polisher! A rust and dust brusher! Excellent! And after all of my thoughts as to something better! But now was no time to argue or retreat. It was work that I needed, and badly, and so I went forward, the larger of the two men, a veritable "Bill Sikes" for size and savageness, and looking to have about as much intelligence as a lumbering ox, eyeing me about as cheerfully as might a tiger or lion. "Here's another man to work with you," was all my employer said. My heart sank because of "Mr. Sikes." His clothes were dirty, oily, shapeless. His hands, like his face and feet, were large and rough. His fellow, the smaller one, was evidently his satellite and not a little afraid of him, as anyone could see—a squirmy slave, really. His trousers and coat sleeves were frayed, and he worked in a frittering, indeterminate way, which indicated that he intended to do no more than he had to, the while he hoped to get enough done to retain his place—an attitude which at once irritated and amused me, it was so futile. In the presence of the boss, as I noticed, they seemed respectful and courteous enough, apparently willing to be courteous and even civil to me. But once he had gone, their manner changed, the larger one's in particular, and both stared indifferently or were cross and silent. "There's a hell of a lot of work to be done around here," was the first or opening comment of Mr. Sikes, who added: "You'd better be getting to it. Brush and polish these here stove-legs!"—an order he accompanied by indicating a pile of rusty stove-legs all numbered, a brush and a box of polish; also a bench on which I was to sit if I wished. And at once I felt I had entered on a rough and unpromising world, more arduous if not so smelly as that of Mr. Paradiso.

I have indicated quite clearly, I think, that I was a dreamy, moony youth. And now in this room, with its stoves and rags and brushes and its cloud of rust and stove polish everywhere, I was not so much impressed by the work before me, hard or not as it might be, as by the curious and almost unimportant action it represented. No real thought at all. And I was for thought. At the same time, there was the mystery of the social worlds from which these stoves came.

In what homes had they previously been? What girls, boys, old people, had sat around them? Some were large and handsome, with many little isinglass windows; others were small, round, tin-bodied, some the meanest of little garret stoves. But all to be cleaned. And as I worked, my fancy ranged from extreme poverty to great wealth. I was romantically afloat in stove-land.

More, outside the window before which I sat on a wooden bench polishing stove-legs and lids, spread another fragment of this same Chicago world of which I was enamoured. Below me, for instance, was such a court as I have previously described as existing in West Madison Street. There were clothes-lines, trash boxes, ash cans, and again, yards still partially green, grass if not flowers, some windows open to the sun, a sky of sapphire, and everywhere diamond rays of pure light. Hucksters were calling their age-old songs of "rags," "old iron"; "tomatoes, potatoes, sweet corn"; along the streets wagons were clattering, and for miles northward stretched the new, brisk city. Do you wonder that I sat and dreamed?

But these two men, or at least the larger one, decided—and that after a very little while—that I was a fool or a shirker or both, and no doubt from a practical point of view I was. My labour with the unexacting Mr. Paradiso had certainly not trained me any too well. At any rate, I was startled the very first hour, I think, by a "Give a hand here, will you!" from Sikes, standing by a big rusty stove which obviously he proposed I should help him to move. Now it had been assumed by me when I was brought in here that I was to do the lighter work of polishing while these two men did the heavier. There certainly was not a little difference between our builds and ages, as the proprietor must have noted on interviewing me. In consequence, I hesitated. "You mean me?" I asked. "Yes, you!" growled my fellow-servant. I arose and went over to him, but when I seized the stove I realised that it was not anything I could lift either alone or with him. It was large, round-bellied, heavy. A two-wheeled hand-truck could and should have been employed, and although one was present, Mr. Sikes was bent on my lifting it with him the while the third man did something else. My spirit at once sank and rose or rebelled, and I announced, with as much outward calm as I could muster: "I can't lift this."

"The hell you can't!" announced Mr. Sikes, glaring at me. "You're paid to do just the same work as we are, freshie! You give a hand here!"

"But I can't lift it!" I said, determinedly.

He brooked no further conversation from one so spindling; instead came toward me with a swift, sudden stride and gave me a resounding kick with his heavy boot. It both hurt and frightened me, but I think more than anything else it shamed and disgraced me, so much so that although I was ready to cry, I was also ready to fight and kill had I only known how. Anyhow, more used to life and its ways by this time than I had been, I quite instinctively seized a stove-leg that lay near and drew back.

"Drop that!" growled Mr. Sikes, approaching. "Drop that, you bean-pole, and lay hold here!"

Again I drew further away, saying: "You let me alone, you damn' smart-aleck! I'm not paid to work for you."

"The hell you ain't! I'll show you whether you ain't or not!" And he began following me, vicious and determined.

"Aw, call it off, Bill," pleaded his partner, not a little frightened, I think. He may have suffered at this man's hand himself. "Don't hit him again. If you don't like him, send him downstairs."

Yet I have no doubt that he would have kicked me again had I not been moving, and toward the door, at the same time that I held the stove-leg threateningly aloft, and besides, by then I was near enough to the door to escape. "Chase yourself, then, you string!" he called after me. "Get the hell outta here, and don't come back!"

I put down the stove-leg just outside the door, and in a kind of frenzy of anger and depression, went below, where I found my new (and so recent) employer. "That big brute up there kicked me just now," I blurted out. "He wants me to lift those big stoves up there, and he knows that I can't, the damn' dog!" I added.

My employer looked at me quizzically, but not very sympathetically or with much interest, I fear. "They're pretty rough men. It's not light work, and I was afraid you wouldn't be able to get along with them," he added, "but I thought I'd try you. I guess you're not strong enough. Here you are," he said, and laid a dollar on the counter, anxious perhaps to allay any resentment I might feel against his establishment while at the same time desiring to retain men who got work done, whether by force or not.

So, not only kicked but discharged, as I saw, I went forth again into the bright September afternoon, bitter and swelling with semi-impotent rage against life and its hardships and creatures. At the same time I was half consoling myself, or trying to, with the thought that life was like this. Lack of strength or means or education made of a man a mongrel to be kicked at! Yet that lout! That swine! Had I only been able to kick him as he had kicked me, and more! And asking myself when, if ever, would I be strong enough to do unto others as they did unto me. An eye for an eye, as it were. Or maybe two or three eyes for one, and an ear into the bargain.

It was not long after this, though, that Al secured a place, also in a retail hardware store, but less arduous than mine, as he appeared to think. It was a very little store, near our home, shabby and dusty. There he earned ten dollars a week, as he proclaimed, and retained his place for three or four weeks when, according to his story, his employer, anxious to get rid of him because of the natural end of the early fall trade—the selling and cleaning season, as they called it—caused him to quit by charging that some little money—three or four dollars all told—had disappeared from the cash drawer. I could not believe that Al had stolen it, since he himself proclaimed the charge, only I half wished he had not told why. Like that kick I endured, it seemed to be bound up with something degrading, and I wished it were not so. I had rather he had said he was discharged.

But now Trina, who had been looking for work in the downtown district, finally secured a place with a crayon enlargement company—the North American Art Company, or some such name—a swindling concern which, as she testified, daily robbed the ignorant by offering to enlarge a photo for say fifty cents and then introducing some ferret-holed agreement whereby in the end it appeared that the person so favoured had agreed to pay from seven to fourteen dollars for some wretched daub in a plaster-gilt frame. Misinformed in the first instance as to the nature of this business, Trina had undertaken a minor bookkeeping phase of it, but now in explanation and perhaps self-justification to us of why she did not resign (needing the

332

money being the principal reason, of course), she had to tack on the words that her work did not really require her to countenance directly this swindling she knew was going on, and since she had nothing to do with it, merely kept the books, why should she not work there? The explanation seemed weak to me, although at the same time I was glad she was not throwing up the job on moral grounds—we needed the money too badly.

The logicians of Christian morals will certainly argue her as wrong, as she herself did. What else can they do? But as to necessity, compulsion, how little will you hear of that from them! But since she was compelled to spend sixty cents of her earnings in car-fare and we needed the money, I will take it upon myself to salve her conscience for her. In short, here and now and publicly, I deign to forgive her. Let the Creator of Life see me as to this.

Then to our wonder, little Ed secured a place in a small though prosperous grocery store near our flat, at the noble salary of three dollars a week and grocery wagon rides free—a job which necessitated his driving one of the grocer's two wagons when the senior clerk was busy. This senior clerk, as I recall him now, was a rare example of how nature, out of straw and waste, can make an imitation or papier-mâché man. A mere grimacing, brainless, smiling, bustling Jack-in-the-box, with large ears, a pointed head, yellow hair, whose one or none thought was to appear like somebody else, some man who came or went—no thought, mere sensory reflection of and reaction to whatever might be. The bond of union between him and Ed, which was strong from the very first, seemed to consist of a mutual interest in the great American game of base-ball, and little more. On Sundays and holidays, whenever they possessed the cash, these two were off to a game, either as spectators or players.

But how it was that Ed first came to make this connection I do not know, most likely by his usual practice of hanging about. He was the greatest boy to hang about and beg and wheedle and mourn and moan until he got what he wanted. I haven't the slightest doubt that a harassed grocery clerk—even this one—laid siege to in this fashion, finally let him help to get rid of him. I cannot see how else it could have been. At any rate, one Saturday afternoon Al coming home from work reported that he thought he had seen Ed driving around in a grocery wagon, and driving at a furious gallop at that!

"Now what do you think of that?" exclaimed my mother. "I expect he's gotten in with some grocer's boy and is riding around with him. Dorse"—that was my family name—"you go downstairs and see if you can find him anywhere."

Engaged by this development I went, but no Ed anywhere. I did not even know what store wagon he was connected with, and so after sneaking up on various grocery wagons and stores and peering into them, I was restlessly and irritably standing in front of one—one Jacob Miller's—and looking seekingly about when what should come clattering up but Mr. Miller's own wagon, and on the front seat Ed, no less, as brave and bold as any Trojan. And at once jumping down, an iron stay weight in his hand ready to fasten the horse, and with an eye on some empty boxes and baskets in the wagon itself.

"Ed!" I called. "What are you doing, anyhow? Don't you know it's after six o'clock? Ma wants you to come home right away!"

"Who, me?" he inquired innocently and indifferently enough. "I can't. Can't you see I got a job? I gotta deliver all these groceries. Want to come along and help me?"

Curiously, and as sober as I was, this sudden and restless and adventurous development laid as strong hold on me as seemingly it had on him. Saturday night. Lights. A crowd. Bright stores. People buying things and having them delivered. At once I gave in to the idea as one would to a game. He wanted to work. Well, so did I. And here he had a job. And I did not. And so: "Sure!" I replied, delighted at this upward turn of our affairs. "Will the grocer let me?"

"Sure! I'll ask him. Come on!"

He bustled in and conferred with the clerk whom I have just described. The grocer himself, a solemn German, had gone home to dinner.

"But sure, sure," said the smiling clerk after Ed had introduced me. "Go right ahead, only if I were you I wouldn't let the boss see him. Let him get on the wagon after you get around the corner. Then he won't know."

So on the wagon I got and clattered about these Saturday night streets with Ed, joyfully carrying baskets into homes—as joyfully as if they were coming to us—and feeling myself—

I cannot tell you how or why—an indescribable factor in all the comfort and colour I was seeing, or imagining I was seeing, on every hand. What fine homes! What nice, edible groceries! And everyone seemingly so cheerful on this late Saturday evening, the week's work done. And all of these nice groceries being delivered. And so . . .

"Say," said Ed once to me in the midst of this gloating and rejoicing. "If you just find work now, we'll be fixed, won't we? We can live on what we make, can't we, and get some clothes?"

At nine or ten o'clock Al also appeared, final emissary in search of the two of us. He had been sent to unravel the astounding mystery of the progressive disappearance of the Dreiser family. But after a few moments of description and mutual congratulation, he also was induced to join and help deliver a few final things. After about a half-hour of this, however, he departed to inform the family, and at eleven I was willing enough to go, but I stayed on for Ed's sake. He was to get a job out of this, as he said. And then at twelve or thereabouts, after unharnessing a tired horse in a tumbledown barn, we entered our own home, wholly triumphant, Ed to lay down a shining half-dollar as the proceeds of his first afternoon's and evening's work, I to say that I had helped and that it had been fun. I can see my mother's face, as round as an apple and smiling. A long delayed supper of fried veal and potatoes with gravy was now served. And Ed looking every inch the hero, as you may well guess. His healthy, genial, stubborn face glowed with satisfaction. Work was his forte, any kind of work that required exercise, and here it was.

"Look at him!" remarked Trina, as he ate his food. "You'd think he was Alexander the Great come home from the wars! Ha, ha!"

"Aw, shut up!" was his only comment, as he went on eating.

CHAPTER LVIII

AT this time there lived next door in our row of flats, and sharing a back porch divided only by a low wooden fence, a literary-minded painter of photographic backgrounds. With my sister Ruth in the course of a little while he struck up an acquaintance which presently ripened into friendship, and eventually marriage, after which they lived together for years in what appeared, to me at least, to be a true harmony of spirit. Maybe not. For, incidentally, they were watched over by his very jealous mother, who having lived alone with her son since her husband's death many years before, resented the intrusion of either sweetheart or wife. For, of course, it first threatened and then did destroy her domination—a conclusion which resulted in great bitterness of heart and not a little unhappiness for Ruth some six or seven years later. In 1897 this sister of mine was killed by a train, and only shortly after her husband's mother died, a circumstance which Eleanor invariably maintained was brought about by the spirit of this woman. After Ruth's death, it appears that Eleanor had a dream in which the mother-in-law appeared and told her that if *she* did not let her son alone, sever all social relations, as it were (though just why I cannot see), she would bring about an accidental death for her also—a dream threat which I offer for what it is worth.

But to return to this opening friendship. This man, whose name was Davis, calling on my sister to take her to the theatre and elsewhere, had noted Ed, Al and myself and our temporary idleness. Finding me interested in books, he endeavoured to persuade me to read Walt Whitman and Christopher Marlowe, two poets the value of whose work, although I did read it at the time, I did not appreciate until years later. And then, because of my seeming bent toward learning, or because of Ruth's intercession, or both, he offered me work as an assistant in his studio at seven dollars a week. That I accepted with

336

alacrity may be guessed. In fact, I at once concluded that I had found a world eminently suited to my tastes: a large, barn-like studio set with innumerable white canvases, which first had to be covered with a yellowish-white "sizing" or sticky paste which prepared each canvas for a second coat of light grey water colour, on which later would be outlined and painted such scenes as this trade artist deemed suitable for his customers, among whom were many photographers and theatres. Since my work required no more skill than accompanies whitewashing a fence, I deemed myself a success, going briskly from canvas to canvas or job to job, but talking to my employer the while—a line of immature philosophic comment which I felt would entertain him greatly and *pari passu* raise me in his estimation, whereas, after a week or two, and whatever he thought of my labours, he decided, however diplomatically and gently, to dispense with my services. Reason: I talked too much. My gab, if not my work, was unendurable: a discovery which shocked me so much that it produced a silence which endured throughout my next and several other jobs.

For winter was coming on, and to lose so good a place—so artistically promising, I thought—and all for want of wit enough to keep my mouth shut . . . oh! Afterwards he told my sister, and she told me, that I needed to grow and cultivate reticence—an observation which still holds true. A greater blow than that even was that after I was gone he chose my brother Ed who, anxious to secure something better than the grocery job, had also been importuning my sister for the same work. And he, not at all afflicted by such literary or artistic soufflé as stuffed and hence emanated from me, was taught the rudiments of photographic painting and retained for some three or four years.

It is an actual fact, which I very much wish to emphasise here, that in spite of Warsaw and my weeks of work with Paradiso, my hardware man and Davis, my conception of things, earthly or material, was still extremely vague; no least inkling of the organic necessities of life in any field seeming sufficiently to impress me and bring me down to earth. Always the sky, the clouds, the outlines of building, streets, colours, sounds, movements, voices, gestures of people, held me more than the actual structure, necessities and economics of the same. In short, the specific current and pressing necessities, or the lack of them, of most people were out. I did not know how life was run, how driving most of its needs. And while I know that many children are like this, it is also obvious that many others are early practical and so able to see more clearly to their advantage. Besides, it has never been quite clear to me just why a boy of my age should have been so dreadfully moonshiny and dreamy.

To illustrate—and just at this time—there was a street car strike on in Chicago, which tied up quite all the West Side lines and brought into use as passenger conveyances trucks and drays filled with chairs or improvised benches. And while this was obviously one of those tense labour-capitalistic wars which bear so hard on the poor and the public and eventually bring on social revolution, I was in nowise interested in the economic facts which produced it. For me it was little more than an odd spectacle of persons, ordinarily accustomed to ride in street cars, now seated on chairs in wagons and hauled to and fro. In short, placed before a given series of facts which, had I been in the least economically or society or individually-minded, must have given rise to at least some modest social speculation, I saw only the surface scene, and other than artistically my mind was a blank. I had no gift for organic sociology. Trade and all that related to it was interesting as a strange, at times even lovely, spectacle, but as a problem or compulsion, at once, under certain conditions, desperate and terrifying, I was not able to register it. Rather, my one gift, and one only, appeared to be to stare about and admire this world so wide, though, as Kipling has gaily phrased it, "it never did no good to me" then, or very little. As a writer and thinker, it profited me, for this picture stuck, and in time I was able to identify its true economic and social significance, and so my own personal relationship thereto. But not then. Rather, it was only the exterior of America, its surface forms, not its internal nature, that registered.

But now, with my serviceability as an artist-labourer ended, I had once more to take to the streets. And what streets! Grey, windy, rainy, cold! To complicate matters from the home point of view, Al, as I have said, had lost his small hardware position and now walked with me. That keen appreciation of the storms and stress of life that later may have

338

manifested itself in my writings was then being forced on me. For so often I was touched by the figures of other seekers like myself and Al—their eyes, worn faces, bodies, clothes, the weariness of them in line at so many doors! As a matter of fact, this was but the beginning of a long observation of the struggles and fortunes of man. The whole cruel as well as kind, rough as well as smooth, working schemes of life set over against my enforced spectatorship and idleness stood fairly close, and in what sharp lines! Nevertheless, desiring so much, I wanted to work and be a part of things and to share, if possible, the sweets of this loving cup. I was cheered by the possibility that I might, and that made my seeking somewhat less hard. Yet daily, and for how long, as it seemed to me, I was pushed aside while and where so many were at table!

A brief experience which I had about this time demonstrated to me my seeming incapacity. It came about through my brother Rome, who one late October day appeared on the scene. By now, all of us, being used to his eccentricities of character, were none too glad to see him, unless perhaps my mother, since always she sympathised with him and was anxious to move him to better ways. But as usual we soon discovered that he had not changed. At once he began to drink and borrow money, and my mother was desperate. But one thing he did do, and that was to attempt to secure me a place with one of the great railroads entering Chicago; just why I cannot say—he had never interested himself in me before—a position as tracing clerk in one of the giant railroad freight yards which lay in the extreme south-west section of Chicago. In connection with this, one morning he took me to see a friend of his —the General Western Freight Agent, no less, of the C. B. & Q.—in the hope that my personality would so impress this man that he would give me a position. How he came to know him or indeed a number of others who were of considerable importance in Chicago and to whom he introduced me at different times—lawyers, politicians, railroad men—I do not know, and I have often wondered about it.

Just the same, I recall this trip and the stocky, corpulent man of forty-five or fifty who received us and looked me over Able men have, as a rule, able faces, and this man's was broad, high of forehead, deep of eye, a heavy but not ungenial countenance.

"Well, Mark," he said to my brother—Rome's first name was Marcus—"so this is the boy you were telling me about?"

"Yes, this is my brother," Rome replied. "I want to know if you can't give him a small place of some kind. He's just beginning and we think he's all right. He's a good boy, I believe."

I recall that I resented his patronising air. Previous to our coming here he had drilled me in my manners, urging me to look brisk and not to talk any more than was required.

My prospective employer eyed me solemnly. "The truth is, Mark," he finally brought out, "we have very little here that he could do; no inside clerkship at all. There is one place, though, out at our Hegewisch yards, where we might use him. They need a car tracer out there. It's a long way, all of ten miles, and he'd have to take a train at six-thirty."

"That wouldn't bother me any," I interrupted blithely.

"Ssh, don't interrupt!" complained my brother, irritably. "Certainly he can do it. He'll be glad to."

"The salary isn't very much either," went on this master of labour. "Only forty-five dollars a month, but he could work up to something better in the course of time if he holds on. It all depends on whether he shows any aptitude for rail-roading."

Forty-five dollars, I thought! For God's sake, that's almost eleven dollars a week! And here I have been hoping to get only as much as six or seven! I'll be rich! Visions of fine clothes and a happy affluence generally swept before my gaze.

"Well, do you think you would like to try it?" demanded my brother, turning to me.

"Nothing would suit me better," I replied, beaming.

"Very well, then," observed this lesser god of the railroad machine. "Have him report to Mr. Kroll at Hegewisch any time in the morning and I'll see that he puts him to work."

After a few exchanges of compliments between my brother and this man, we went out, I so excited inwardly that I could scarcely contain myself. Forty-five dollars a month! Gee whiz, what could I not do with that? My most colourful dreams seemed once more on the verge of realisation.

CHAPTER LIX

EARLY the next morning, accompanied by Rome, I set out for Hegewisch. My brother insisted on stopping to have a drink or two on the way: a fact which troubled me much, because I always dreaded the change that drink made in him. On the train, and devoid of any organic or constructive impulse in himself which might have justified his criticism of life in general, he commented sardonically on the fantastic nature of life; how some men here, the Armours, Swifts, Morrises, Pullmans, etc., were piling up astounding fortunes, while other men toiled at the bottom for their "sissy sons and daughters." Simultaneously with these remarks, and as we rode, he took out a small penknife and jabbed the blade over and over into the red plush of the seat.

"Rome!" I said, irritated and sickened by such vandalism. "Why do you do that? Good velvet like that!"

"Oh, the company's rich!" he sneered. "It can afford it," and went on jabbing until he wearied and the plush had been badly damaged. I so often thought of that afterwards as characteristic of not only him but so many.

Around nine or ten o'clock (we were delayed by his drinking), we arrived at the yards, a great plexus of tracks, perhaps forty or fifty, side by side, with an intricate arrangement of switches, y's and cross-overs. Through all this we made our way to a little brown shanty that stood in the centre and asked for Mr. Kroll. A tall, lank, malarial person, with a short growth of black beard and a bored air, appeared and took me in charge.

"I'm a railroad man myself," volunteered my brother archly. "He's new at this game, just starting in, and he doesn't know this neighbourhood out here. I work for the road beyond Burlington."

This was not true; said for effect, no doubt. The yard-master merely looked at me non-committally. "All right,

I'll look after him," he said, and after some advisory words to me he left.

I have never forgotten my first afternoon in this place. It was so novel, uncertain, and therefore fascinating. Never before had I memorised for myself the names of so many railroads; these cars here were gathered, apparently, from all of the lines in the country. The air-brake for freight cars had not yet been invented; even the modern, highly-equipped stock and refrigerator cars were still somewhat of a novelty. No semaphores on tall steel poles here but rather the old-time switches displaying their warning lights. Engines puffed here and there in a desultory way, great plumes of smoke hanging above them. Now and then a long line of cars would crash and begin to move, suddenly, jerkily or with an even, slow and almost silent movement.

My duty, as I soon discovered, was to trace cars: a task simple enough for any beginner, and yet so dull was I in all practical matters that for several days it was almost a complete enigma. In the first place, the man under whom I was directly employed gave me no least inkling of the method or system I was supposed to follow. In fact, I had not been there four minutes before he handed me a dozen yellow slips, on which were printed a number of inquiries. Thus: Line .... Contents. .... Weight .... Destination .... Consignee .... Consignor .... and other data which I have forgotten. As a rule, a track or section of the yard was indicated.

"See if you can find these!" was his first command, and when I hesitated, he added "Out there! Out there!" and waved toward the large plexus of tracks.

I took my slips and began feverishly to bustle up and down between long lines of cars, some of them moving, wondering nervously how I was to find the tags or labels which corresponded to the numbers and questions on these slips. Where was Track 9? And where Track 32? All of the information my slip contained was the name of the line, the number of the car, the track on to which it had been shunted—for instance : C. W. & M. 8863, track 16 East. But by no means was it always there, as I found. Whole lines of cars were frequently in motion, or gone, perhaps to be restored later, but not easily to be found then. I hunted and hunted, crawling under or over cars, dodging about the ends, climbing up sides to examine roughly or vaguely pencilled names and addresses. A friendly brakeman told me how the tracks were numbered and where certain types of freight were to be found. But it seemed to me that I was making an awful botch of what I was doing.

And then, that very first day, as I came back toward the shanty at dusk, I saw a small crowd gathered about a crumpled object over which a faded brown overcoat had been thrown. I had been nervous all afternoon—the sudden or slow starts of the cars, their dark rows—and now this dead body proved the substantiality of my fears. I put down the completed reports with which I had returned and picked up ten or twelve more which had been dropped in a small box outside the depot door, and went to work again, but seeing as I did so a caboose, hauled by a yard engine, back in near the station in order to take the body away. You may imagine how I felt after that, in the growing dusk, slipping about with a lantern and thinking of the dead man and my own life, trying in the thickening shadows to decipher the handwritten information on the small tags tacked on the car doors. But even now, as I must pause to emphasise, the beauty rather than the utility of this scene moved me: the shadows; the red, white, blue, green and yellow switch lights winking and glowing like flowers, the suggestion of distant cities, and the chemic shift and play of things in general.

When the day ended at six o'clock I learned that there was no passenger train to the city, but that a work train travelling on another line which crossed this one at right angles some half or three-quarters of a mile west would carry me to Ogden Avenue and West Fortieth Street, about two or three miles south-west of our apartment. This same train stopped at this station or crossing at six-thirty every morning, arriving at Hegewisch at seven. That meant I had to leave the house at five-forty-five in the morning and would reach home at seven, or thereabouts.

I wish sincerely that those who live in comfort in this world could look for one day or thereabouts into the working strain of many, many lives. Not that I wish them any such unsatisfactory fate, but that I feel that it would add to the interest of their lives. Contrast makes all that we know of life. Differences present life's edge and give it its zest. We enjoy or disdain what we have because of contrast with what we do or do not have, what we do or do not endure.

The work train was made up of box cars lined with wooden seats about the four sides and fitted in the centre with a round-bellied coal stove. There were no side steps, instead a short iron ladder reaching to within two feet of the ground. The interior woodwork, as I saw on entering, was rank with decayed tobacco juice and smoke. Mostly the men were foreigners—Swedes, Poles, Huns, Czechs, all largely a product of Central or Slavic Europe. They looked heavy, or fierce, or old, or thick, as the case might be. And whether they were or not, they seemed inured to lean and meagre lives, such lives as, contrasted with ours (and we thought ourselves poor enough), depressed me greatly. If I had only been sure that my temperament would never permit me to become a part of all this, I would not have felt so bad. But something— the fact that my father was a working-man, and that by chance or fate almost anyone could fall to a low or defeated state which might compel anything—evoked the more or less unthinking notion that I might be compelled to endure a like fate, and with it a morbidity that was all but devastating.

And again, here is something that I would like to propound. What is that something in youth that sets it at war with age and dirt and shame and weariness, but for the period of youth only? Youth will not believe that the end of life is death. Life must go on. Beauty must reign eternal. Hope must be justified. It must be so. So cries youth, and well it may, for the unending vibration of life is its justification. It is that vibration. It is the sun's newest heat made over into the shape of man. "And the sun's rays were made into flesh and they stood up as men"—so might one say of the light and heat of the sun, and so physics and chemistry prove.

Just the same, I did not give up this first day, and had no intention of so doing. My one thought was that I must go on, and how fine my forty-five dollars would be once I got it into my hands. At seven-thirty that night in our flat I ate my evening meal, and at nine, after a bath, went to bed in order to get up at four and be off. When my mother heard of the nature of my work and the distance I had to travel, she was considerably disturbed and sympathetic, an attitude not too helpful for those who should work and make their own way.

344

Just the same, the forty-five dollars lured her as it did me, and I had to go on.

The next day was a fine day, a red sky in the east, and I thought I was doing very well, until about noon it began to rain, a fine, cold drizzle which continued all afternoon. I had only an old, light overcoat, and I wore this until it seemed to weigh a dozen pounds or more. My suit and underclothes became damp, and with much running and climbing I became exceedingly tired. The next day I developed a severe cold; by afternoon my head was fairly ringing and that night as I rode home, even my bones ached. The next morning I was really ill, or imagined I was, and unable to get up.

But all this might not have ended so badly had I had the good sense to have someone write or call and explain to my employer the reason for my absence. But alas, my brother Rome had disappeared for the time being, and as for the other members of the family, they were busy, or so it seemed to me, and so the whole day went without any word being sent. On the second day, and due to my urging, someone bethought himself of the importance of this, and a note was sent, but whether it was of any avail or not I never had the courage to investigate. I was ill for a number of days, and when I got up again my mother had concluded that the work was too hard for me. Naturally ease-loving and inclined to indolence at times—and especially when I was not feeling any too well—I was willing enough, though the thought of that forty-five dollars pained me.

CHAPTER LX

AND so now, once more, the streets, from seven, eight or nine in the morning until four-thirty or five in the evening. And my thoughts, speculations! For once more outside of every store of any size, the great wholesale houses in particular, I stood viewing a land of promise. In one of these, surely, was my future. Did I but attain to another place, then henceforth would I work and study and become some kind of a manager. I saw myself, a great roll-top desk before me, a large enclosed office around me, myself dictating to whom? And about what? Great matters and affairs, of course. At other times, weary and jobless, I saw myself as one for whom there was no future at all. For what could I really hope, untrained, inexpert, a failure at everything save dish-washing under a genial, dirty Greek?

But at last a job, if a small one. It loomed up one day after hours of weary tramping through cold and smoky greyness. It was with an immense wholesale hardware company at Wabash and Lake Streets: Messrs. Hibbard, Spencer, Bartlett & Company. An arresting feature of this establishment was a series of bright, mahogany-furnished offices, following both street lines on Wabash and Lake, separated from the street and the cold outside by huge, clear, plate-glass windows, and at the hour at which I applied, flooded with electric lights. At the back of these, in the interior of the store, as it were, at tall-legged desks on high stools sat an army of clerks, their bent eyes protected by green shades. About the great structure, which stretched for a half-dozen doors along one street and as many along another, were a score or more of giant trucks drawn by well-groomed teams or even spans of three and four horses. Men with box-hooks and clad in gingham shirts, non-descript trousers and coffee-sack aprons were piling boxes into or unloading them from these vans. It was plain that an enormous and profitable business was going on here. But on the plate glass of the front door was the usual sign: "No help wanted!"

346

"I believe I'll try in here," I said to Al, who was accompanying me. I did not explain that the old, white-haired man seated at a small desk just inside the door looked more genial than some others I had seen.

"Well, young man?" he asked, quite sternly, as I entered.

"Do you need any help?"

"Let me see; I believe they are taking on one or two more," he said. "Wait here a few minutes and I'll find out. Did you ever work in a hardware place?"

"No, sir," I replied, fearing to refer to my previous experience. "I only left school last spring."

"School, eh? Well, wait a minute, I'll see."

A few moments later he motioned me into the presence of another old man. "Mr. Hibbard, here is a young man who wants work," he observed, rather pompously.

I started, for Hibbard was one of the names I saw lettered on the windows. Could this be *the* Mr. Hibbard?

"Mr. Jayne tells me," said this Mr. Hibbard, looking me over from head to toe, "that you have never worked anywhere before."

"No, sir."

"Well, we like to start with young men who have never worked anywhere before. We like to have them learn the business and work up. We never pay much to begin with, only five dollars, but we raise our young men just as fast as they show themselves to be capable. But I don't want you to come in here if you don't want to learn the hardware business. We'd rather not waste our time and yours training you in something you're not fitted for and that you aren't going to like and won't do well at. Now if you think you'd like to learn this business, go on home and come back here Monday morning and tell me so. Then I'll put you to work."

I think I said that I was very eager to learn the hardware business, but he waved me indifferently out. "Come back Monday; come back Monday!" was all he said.

I hurried out rejoicing. Five dollars! Small, to be sure, but immensely better than nothing. Al had gotten tired waiting for me and left. That night, though, there was general rejoicing over my success, and the next Monday I presented myself, vainly assuming that I might again be seen by

Mr. Hibbard. But that gentleman had not as yet stirred from his Prairie Avenue residence.

"You needn't bother about him," observed Mr. Jayne when I stated that Mr. Hibbard had told me to come back Monday. "He's forgotten all about that by now. Just you wait here and I'll find Mr. Purdon. He's the man you want."

In a little while he returned, accompanied by Mr. Purdon, an angular, store-clothesy, squeaky-shoed Irishman, whom I despised at sight, so obviously suspicious, contemptuous, domineering was he. After catechising me as to my history and connections and almost angrily demanding if I really did want to learn the hardware business, he took me to the third floor, a bewildering region of shelves crowded with a thousand items of hardware, where I was placed in charge of Mr. Arbuthnot, manager, and informed as to my duties as box-rustler and stock-piler. This second individual was, as I immediately sensed, more pleasing: a solemn, pink-cheeked, pop-eyed man of about thirty-two, of Scotch ancestry, I believe, who, as I learned afterwards, was so greatly concerned as to his position that he had no thoughts on any other subject, at least for public expression. It was his duty to see that newly-arrived cases were promptly and carefully opened, checked and their contents piled away, also to check up the contents of small trunks or bins on wheels rolled before him by the order clerks. There was a constant procession of these order clerks, passing from room to room and floor to floor, pushing before them large four-wheeled crates or boxes into which they deposited the articles called for by orders from below stairs. I discovered later that this order clerk work was considered a preliminary to a travelling salesmanship, a position which paid as high as thirty-five dollars a week and expenses, and was much sought after by all of the various clerks.

And now as to Mr. Thomas Purdon, whom I have described. Mentally he was certainly beneath and yet officially above all those on whom it was his duty to spy. He had a sort of roving commission as detective and spy, reporting to the President, Vice-President and Secretary of the company, individually and collectively, concerning all that he saw and heard. Were the several managers keeping their floors clean and their staffs well employed? Were the bins clean or dirty, full or empty? Were the fire buckets properly filled every night? Were all of the order clerks industrious? Did anyone steal or loiter? Were incoming invoices allowed to clutter the floors without being promptly unpacked and put away? Could anyone be profitably or savingly discharged, a better man put in some- one's place, etc., etc.? It was Mr. Purdon's place to know and suggest. And his eyes looked his duties to the full. Also his reports were very seriously consulted when it came to the matter of promotions, raises in salary, or discharges. In short, it was rumoured that young men whom he favoured almost invariably rose rapidly, whereas those whom he disliked did not succeed very well and occasionally disappeared.

I had to smile at the newy-newy clothes that he always wore—commonplace browns and greys that fairly smelled of the shelf, and always too big and creased. And his spick and span, and yet much too small, hat, that made him look ridiculous. And his solid and usually squeaky shoes, for sometimes (in order to convey the impression, I think, that he was incapable of spying on anyone), he would wear shoes which could be heard some distance off. At other times, though, he wore what might be called "quiet shoes," thus managing on occasion to entrap a momentary idler and per- haps even to overhear scraps of conversation most uncompli- mentary to himself and other officials. If he did, though, the career of the critic was short. For in him was no least sympathy for weakness, folderol or horseplay, in or out of working hours. He conversed with no one except his supe- riors, on whom he openly fawned, and his manner to an under- ling was the acme of contempt. Early he fixed on me, as I have good reason to know, as a shambling, scatterbrained, meaningless and mooning incompetent, and at that I think that his opinion was entirely justified.

But aside from my duties, this firm and this floor on which I worked were of immense interest to me. This great insti- tution, one of the largest of its kind in America at the time, was truly a school of economics and, in its way, sociology. For here crossed currents of invention and effort of as wide a range of character and economic and sociologic significance as one could possibly hope to find anywhere. For here, if nowhere else, it was so easy to discover that somewhere in the east was an enormous factory pouring forth a veritable Niagara of so-called "agate ware," of which almost daily we were receiving car-loads. Also a thousand other things which ordinarily the human mind is not called upon to contemplate, either in the aggregate or the particular—ironware, tinware, rivets, nails, brooms, mops, can-openers, glass jars, razors, shaving mugs and brushes, spoons, ladles, coal scuttles, fire sets, fire buckets, kitchenware (I could go on for pages), but which here astonished and even fascinated me by their number and variety. In fact, the number of things I was awakened to and that in some way suggested themselves to me as things that I might use or even need, was legion—a fair commentary on the unescapable growth of materialism. "You need me! You need me! You need me!" so they talked, or should have.

And worse, it did seem to me at the time to suggest and even offer a most undetectable opportunity for thieving. For how easy—and yet not that I desired to take very much, or ever did—to pick up and conceal a shaving brush and mug, worth, I believe, fifty or sixty cents, or a razor or pocket knife or a small lamp or some candles or a candleholder, and then suffer, as no doubt many did, the mental distress pursuant on the same for how long a time afterward! For whatever system of logic or earnest reasoning I might achieve, I had not then proved to myself that ethics are purely minor group arrangements having no relationship to the larger movements and positive and dominating forces of the universe but rather to the contrasting things that grow out of them, and in such an elastic way at times as to prove the ethics of savages and religionists and moralists in certain parts of the world to be ridiculous, and worse, destructive.

Be that as it may, this firm had adopted rules for protecting itself. I soon learned that packages were not permitted to be taken out of the building without examination. The old doorman to whom I had first applied was authorised to open any packages on suspicion. Also, incoming packages had to be opened and their contents registered. Occasionally a suspect was searched and arrested. But aside from this, the firm exercised a quite liberal policy in dealing with its employees. Articles could be bought at wholesale prices, which meant at about one-third less than the retail. Also in the event of sickness—for reasonable periods at least—wages were not deducted; and at Christmas every employee who had been working there for a year or more received a turkey.

CHAPTER LXI

BUT at this time I was going through what might be looked upon as one intellectual storm after another, and this, if you will believe it, on the score of work and wages, wealth and poverty, ignorance and intelligence, and the accepted differences in social station which gave boys of birth and station precedence primarily over youths of greater physical and mental capacity. For I was working with men who were getting twice my salary and who had been hired principally because of their physical strength, and yet so working I was spared no whit in the matter of severe tasks. For example, there was Axel Lindstrom, a short, thick, dull Danish peasant, say thirty-five years of age, as strong as a small horse, with whom often I unpacked and binned iron pots and kettles —immense truckloads of them pouring in hour after hour throughout an entire day. Also Ed Raff, a great blond German clown, of nineteen or thereabouts, who was joined with us in this and related work. And yet as I knew, originally they had been hired to do this floor trucking and heavy piling exclusively, and they received nine and ten dollars respectively as opposed to my five.

Again, there were Arthur Newy and Thayer Gates, relatives or friends of the owners, who came in from the east somewhere —New York or Boston—to study western hardware methods and needs before returning east again and to their parents' establishments—scions of wealth, in short. And wearing gloves to protect their hands and silk shirts under their blue denim jumpers. But with what an air of condescension as well as remoteness—since to all of us had been made plain that they were there solely for this purpose and for a time, and not to be confused with ordinary labourers, only to acquire as quickly and sketchily as possible such knowledge as would permit of their being transferred to the division of order clerks, and then home. Yet even here they got ten as opposed

351

to my five, and were quickly elevated, returning after a week or two or three to patronise me and tell me how soon they were to be salesmen on the road and at what wages. And always they were so well manicured as to nails and politely barbered as to hair, and each keeping a dress suit in a locker in the basement in order, once their day's work was done, so as not to be delayed in reaching some local dinner or dance or what you will. Constantly, and most emphatically, I was impressed by the luck of being born rich, but without as yet any working knowledge of the chance or ill luck that can befall anyone, rich or poor. Newy, who seemed to have a conversational liking for me, was a graduate of Amherst; Gates was also an eastern college man, but in every way both seemed to illustrate most clearly to me the insufferable difference between wealth and poverty.

And the other gods of this little world! Mr. Hibbard was said to have an immense residence in Prairie Avenue, with a great stone-pillared iron gate guarding a wide drive (I subsequently went to view this for myself); Mr. Spencer, a corpulent, jovial, red-faced person in a loud check suit, was said to be equally splendidly housed in Michigan Avenue, and to have two beautiful, socially popular daughters and a smart, society-loving son. Mr. Bartlett, a tall, gentlemanly figure, reported to be the shrewdest member of the firm because he had entered last and risen to his present height from the lowly position of office boy, had a country seat at Oconomowac as well as a residence on Lake Shore Drive, and betimes amused himself with civic and charitable affairs, for which he received frequent honourable mention in the newspapers. To me he seemed an attractive man, searching of eye, silent and refined of manner; the best example, as I saw it then, of your cool, discerning American business man.

There was another man here—a part of the company, apparently—also very much respected; a little, stocky, incisive person of a decidedly Jewish cast of countenance, though his name (I forget it now) sounded Irish. One Christian Aaberg, working on the same floor with me and with whom I became extremely friendly, insisted it had been stolen or assumed. "He is a Jew, make no mistake about it!" he insisted. "He is a Romanian or Hungarian Jew, but he will neffer admit it!"

This Christian Aaberg! What an influence he immediately

began to exercise on me! That degenerate, nerve-racked body, and that mind! He was a Dane, unquestionably stemming from a well-placed family. A little rickety, out-at-elbows, shambling man, with a wrinkled, emaciated, obviously emotion-scarred face, who at forty or forty-five and after God knows what storms and rages of physical and mental dissipation, still had about him that indescribable something which for want of a better word I must speak of as breeding, not English or French or Teutonic but Scandinavian. His hair, not too closely cropped and parted in a careless and yet somehow arresting way, was limp and thin; his forehead high and protruding, almost massive; and in his eyes an arrestingly bright and almost psychopathic lustre. His hands were thin and delicate, and his feet small, almost ladylike. His face, like so many of his countrymen, suggested Andersen, Ibsen, Strindberg, Grieg. (I am thinking of the type only.)

As I learned soon enough, he was here on sufferance—by courtesy, as it were, not of Hibbard, Spencer, Bartlett & Company but of that Mr. Bartlett alone of whom I have just spoken. And as I recall Mr. Bartlett now, he seemed just the type of man who for intellectual or other reasons might befriend a wastrel like Aaberg. He had sufficient brains and temperament to apprehend the varied and storm- or emotion-rocked nature of the mind within. At any rate, and decidedly, Aaberg was of little or no value to the firm, for he could do no hard work and the powers that were could not trust him with the more complicated, though less strenuous, task of filling orders. As he himself admitted, he drank and dissipated here as in the past and often wondered aloud why it was that either Mr. Bartlett or the firm stood for him. " I am no good. I am no good," he even asserted to me. "I drink and run around with women. I say I am sick, but Mr. Bartlett knows better. He lets me stay because he feels sorry for me." And truly, drink and women had affected his health, and now he was shabby and sickly to look upon. Yet, as I have said, there was that strong, seeking, vital light in his eye at times; at other times a look of ineffable weariness and contempt. It said as plainly as could any words how wretchedly unimportant and dreary all this was to him. How I came to get in with him I cannot say—piling goods together, I presume. At any rate, within two or three weeks we were fast friends intellectually, and there followed a series of conversations on life and character, the import of which has endured to this day.

"My Gott, how I have lived!" was one of his expressions. Occasionally he would arrive on Monday morning exclaiming: "My Gott! My Gott, how drunk I was yesterday!" or: "Oh, these women! These devils of women!" When I ventured to admonish him or inquire too closely into his affairs, he would look out at me from under shaggy, protruding eyebrows and smile sardonically or shake his head in contempt. "You kit, you! Don't talk such silly stuff to me! Wait until you are forty-five and broken like me. Wait until you have lived a little and know something about life. Here you are at sixteen, just beginning, and you talk to me! Ha, ha! Well, the gods must know what they are about, but I don't!" And he would subside into a moody silence.

He had read—God knows what!—everything! And he it was who talked to me of Ibsen, Strindberg, Grieg, Goethe, Wagner, Schopenhauer. He would talk to me by the hour, as we piled pots and pans or buckets or bolts or rivets, of the French Revolution and the great figures in it, of Napoleon, Wellington, Tsar Alexander. Also of Peter the Great and Catherine of Russia, Frederick the Great and Voltaire, whom he admired enormously. But not the silly, glossed, emasculated data of the school histories with which I had been made familiar, but the harsh, jagged realities and savageries of the too real world in which all of them moved. And again, of Greece, of the age of the philosophers, logicians, playwrights, sculptors, architects, statesmen, warriors. He revealed as much as any history could—why it was that Aristotle was the first of the organic and realistic thinkers; why Heraclitus would always be remembered. He also told me why Socrates had been compelled to drink the hemlock; that the cross was originally a phallic symbol; elucidated for me the mysteries of the Egyptian temples, the religious festivals of the Parsees, Chaldeans, Assyrians, Persians. He talked of Danish court life in a guarded and yet suggestive way. Somewhere he had lived, and lived well. When I told him that our family was Catholic and that I still went to church, he smiled. "You will come out of that," he said. "You are already out and don't know it."

Although he was very poor, and living, as I gathered, on a

West Side street in a Danish community on the ten dollars a week he earned, he was in nowise interested in the economic and social problems which were then—and afterwards—disturbing this country. Nor was he for any cause which looked to the bettering of the condition of the so-called "poor working-man." As a matter of fact, he was an aristocrat of the most definite type, and the condition of the poor and lowly interested him not at all. More, I think he condemned them as beasts of muddy brain, having some regard for their simple virtues or abilities, but none for their thoughts. Rather, his eyes were turned to philosophy and history. Novels were weak, he said, mostly pictures of unreality. Also he was insistent in his assertion that America—aside from Poe—had no literature worthy of the name and laughed at the attempts at social life in Chicago. At the same time, he had a profound respect for American commercial ability. Of Bartlett he observed: "We have few such men as that abroad. He is a common type over here."

Always infuriated by the ignorant, the dull or the inefficient, particularly when they gave themselves airs, he was inclined to belittle those around him, even too much so, and to their faces betimes, making unconscious clowns of such individuals as Raff, Lindstrom, and even Newy. And for my benefit. His method was simple. He would ask amazingly ridiculous questions with an air of the greatest gravity, pretending an interest entirely out of keeping with the subject matter, but which completely deceived those with whom he dealt. Then when they took him seriously, he would smile and wink. The youth Newy he would lead on as to matters of history, art, science, politics, literature, until he had him far beyond his depth and making statements which were plainly not true. Then he would nod and smile, not even troubling to contradict him, so obvious were the errors into which he had led him. For the rest, he laughed at life, the types of human insects and numbskulls it produced, and as for the American pretension to liberty, equality, fraternity, "Who has liberty?" he demanded. "He who can get it, no other! Liberty is in here!" and he would tap his forehead significantly. "As for the rest, priests and the strong drive people like horses. The dumb pay tribute to everyone who can think faster than they can. Liberty! Pah!"

The great fact which contact with Aaberg brought home to me was that mind, and mind alone, makes the essential difference between the masses and the classes, and thus caused me to understand that mind, and mind alone, would make or break me. Either I had it or I did not have it. If I had it, I might do much; if not nothing. At the same time, he was quick to point out that while we had no princes or lords—individuals whom in my American fashion I deemed to be ridiculous—still here in America, and after the fashion of the feudal barons, were already men who by means of money and special privilege were seeking to establish themselves as just such and to leave immense fortunes to their children in order that they might establish caste, a money aristocracy, no less. And with that he had no quarrel either, any more than he had with our efforts to obviate the same. It was all of the very essence of life, love of change, and in his estimation strong men would always rule.

The trouble with his conclusion in regard to mind, once I came to accept it, was that I confused it with the ability to acquire what is known as polite learning and did not identify it as the directing essence of great and not necessarily scrupulous energy or force in any field. In short, I was still making the mistake of valuing polite learning and emotional joy in life as against or over special aptitudes and special bents fortified by study, and backed by generic mind, as first among the things of the earth. And so, while I saw in him a man who was learned in the various phases which I admired, he still seemed to me a failure, because he had nothing at all materially. Even such coarse animals as Ed Rapp contemned him because, forsooth, he lacked physical vitality. And our mincing friends, Newy and Gates, looked down on him because he had a "foreign" look. To them he had not come credentialed, as should a foreign gentleman. Our narrow-measuring floor manager could not see anything in him either, first because he was a drunkard, a parasite and physically ill, and next because he did not appear to appreciate the great dignity attaching to the position of floor manager. No doubt, he too wondered why Mr. Bartlett retained him.

Burning with desire as I was to use in an aggressive way the brain which Aaberg said I had, so that I might share in the material splendours which everywhere, as I saw, men were struggling for, I thought more and more of learning, and as my meagre free hours permitted, read—principally history and biography. And doing so, continued to think more and more of myself, regardless of my low material state. One could rise! One could rise! Actually, in a nebulous, almost unconscious way, I forecast to myself some sort of life which was not to be anything like this—some luck or energy, or both, which was to come to me and guide me. Sometimes it was a life like Napoleon's that I desired to imitate; again, one like that of Bismarck or Pitt, of whom I was reading. Between times it was Macaulay or Carlyle or Dickens or Fielding whom I was ready to emulate, not as a writer exactly but as figures to whom writing had brought attention. And yet even here I was not thinking of myself as a writer, merely as one who ought to be able to distinguish himself in a particular field.

But the squeaky shoes of Purdon in the distance, or the face of Mr. Blaikie, the foreman, contemplating me from near by, would by day recall me from my high dreams, and shamefacedly I would hustle through what I had been idling over and hasten to a new task.

CHAPTER LXII

ACTUALLY this period stands out with a colourful electric lustre for me, so feverish was my mental effort. I was burning with desire, yearning for everything and anything which my eyes or my mind contemplated. And about me, as luck would have it, was this new city, as feverish in its quest as myself, for even then was beginning talk of the World's Fair, which came to pass in 1892; the revising and rebuilding of the Chicago University by John D. Rockefeller; the extension and cabling of the West and North Side street railways by Charles T. Yerkes; and the enormous extensions in the plants of the great packers and trades generally. In addition, there were in full swing the exciting wheat pit, the arrival and rapid construction of the skyscraper, the for that time broad extension of the city's park system—all things moving steadily and swiftly toward the metropolis that Chicago was to become.

To join with this just at this time was the fact that beginning with Ed's and Trina's positions, things in our cubbyhole of an apartment or flat were taking a turn for the better. For Eleanor returned late this first fall and took up her abode with us, urging my mother to take a larger place in order that she might occupy a portion of it with her husband when he was in the city, and for that reason contributing something, I forget how much. Again, Al had finally secured employment with a small but rapidly growing patent cure-all company —Dr. Fahrney's "Kuriko," Fahrney's Pills, Fahrney's Wild Carrot Ointment—which provided him with some mental ease and, I believe, twelve dollars a week. In passing, I may report that soon all of us were being properly dosed with all these nostrums (tonic to salve), since Al brought all of them home along with recommendations which, for the time being at least, seemed convincing. (Who does not like to try new medicines?) And lastly, Ed, growing in favour with Davis, our prospective brother-in-law, had been "raised" from seven to eight dollars a week. (As I have said, unlike myself he had the gift of holding his tongue.) And Trina, after finally giving up her position with the swindling picture company, had secured one as profitable with The Fair, a local department store, where she was a clerk in the stationery department. Antithetical to all this was the return of my father from Terre Haute, the mill there having shut down again, and he now began to look for work in his own line here, but without finding anything, after which he again returned to Terre Haute. Providentially, by this time my brother Rome had departed again, but only after having caused as much family distress as was humanly possible—drunkenness, arrests, quarrels. How he managed to live when away always puzzled me; he travelled so constantly and in the main dressed so well.

In short, the state of our family as a collective unit at this time was perhaps as good as it ever was, before or after. As against the injuries and disappointments of the past, it was now comparatively sound, marriages and work having, temporarily at least, disposed of a number of ills. To be sure, we four youngest did not contribute very much. Al six or seven dollars, because he was earning twelve; Ed four or five because he was earning eight; Trina three dollars because she was earning six, and I three because I was earning five; a total of somewhere near seventy dollars a month as against a rent of thirty-five dollars and food amounting to perhaps considerably more. The difference between this income and outgo must have been supplied by Eleanor, Ruth and Paul, and possibly something now and then from my sister Janet, who was financially well-placed in New York.

But now because of speaking of my father as above, I wish to offer a few words in explanation. I am not now and was not then really bitter toward him. The truth was that he was never either sufficiently liberal or engaging to evoke or deserve that affection which my mother earned. Worse, so mentally cribbed and cabined was he by his religious obsessions that he could not but prove a reducing and irritating element in any family. For in spite of his more natural and really, for the most part, human elements, he could not possibly encounter any of us without at once beginning with disturbing and even irritating inquiries as to our moral and religious conduct, which never, of course, achieved anything. True, we will admit that he had much provocation and that all were under suspicion. And when he suspected that we were becoming indifferent to the Catholic Church or that we—the girls particularly—were in danger of countenancing practices or relations which could only end in the destruction of our, to him, immortal souls, his misery was too great for words. At such times, of course—which meant nearly always—he took refuge in silent prayer. I can see him now, in his worn-out clothes, a derby or soft hat pulled low over his eyes, his shoes oiled (not shined) in order to make them wear longer, and in rainy weather a large cotton umbrella in his hand, trudging off at seven or eight every morning, rain or shine, to hear his beloved mass. If some persons take to drink and others to drugs, a far greater number become addicted to religious formulæ, and with equally fatal results. Their brains simply ossify, since independent inquiry is no longer needed, and their natural emotions, being vainly rejected as sinful, transform themselves into a single aspect or expression, and they are for ever on their knees before an immense and inscrutable something which cares no more for their adoration or supplications than it does for those of an expiring beetle. In short, all of the impulses to live and strive (life's first command) are completely dissipated in appeals for mercy and spiritual salvation. Horrible! And to this are dedicated the endless religious edifices of the world!

But to return to my position with Hibbard, Spencer, Bartlett & Company. Need I rise to report that the same was not a flourishing one? Also, alas, that owing to my almost incurable tendency to converse or intellectualise or moon as I worked, I must have struck all and sundry as a poor investment, for so organised and systematised was this large and practical commercial house that no mooner or dreamer could long escape. True enough, I tried to work briskly, and in the main maybe I did—I cannot now say truly—but one's attitude is worth almost more than one's work in most places, and mine certainly was not in line with the best interests of a wholesale hardware house. What, me a bin-cleaner and case-opener, and for five dollars a week where others doing the same work were receiving seven, eight or nine! Outrageous, I thought! And this, mind you, after so recently walking the streets and eager and willing, as I thought at the time, to accept almost anything!

Only in palliation of all this, I may add that carrying home my wretched five every week, I was regularly so depressed by my really anomalous and hence quite ridiculous position in life, that I did not know what to do, which way to turn in order to better myself. For certainly I was in need of decent clothing; next, a little entertainment. And then, girls, girls, girls! Were they not always in my mind? And how was I to interest any girl in a person who was so economically impossible as to have less than two dollars a week for spending money? Who could believe it? Why, I could not even afford a theatre ticket for myself, let alone another. And worse, as I saw it, I was not actually interested in the hardware business. For did I want to be a travelling salesman for a wholesale hardware firm? I knew I did not, even though at times I tried to believe that I did. To go from town to town and try to persuade people to buy things—how could one do that? I knew I could not. Besides, almost constantly at my ear, there was that same Aaberg, with his notions of what he as a prince among men, socially and otherwise, and I as a promising young intellectual, deserved. I would grow and be somebody, but not in this field, as he insisted.

And so, looking out of one or another of the windows of the firm, and always at such times as I was supposed to be working, and noting the rumbling traffic of the city and its converging and separating streams of pedestrians, I was merely wistful, dreamful, and, because of my limited state, unhappy. Ha, the wealth and power of others, those to whom for some inscrutable reason I chose to believe that I belonged! The mansions that should belong to me! The footmen, even slaves, who should bow and genuflect before me! The beauties who should note and receive me, eagerly and with passionate admiration and love! The throngs that should huzzah and at the same time part and bow before me! But for what reason, exactly? I would not have ventured to whisper it to another at the time, but if you must know, it was because I was I, no more and no less!

Make sense of that who can!

But taking it all in all, perhaps the worst phase of my state at this time was that I was not in good physical condition. My appendix, as was surgically proved years later, must have been in a bad condition even at this time, since at thirty it carried seven protective layers or coats of skin due to as many youthful attacks of "inflammation of the stomach"—the usual medical interpretation of any fevers or disturbances in that region at that time. In consequence, my stomach and bowels were almost constantly out of order. My appetite (perhaps Mr. Paradiso had something to do with this) was bad, and I was compelled at the time of which I am writing to confine myself for not a little while to lemons, eaten undiluted—a food which gave me some relief but no great strength. Additionally, my belief that I had ruined myself sexually was as acute as ever, and the fact that I had no money to invest in the many nostrums I saw advertised seemed one of the horrors of my unfortunate state. Worse, the dust which I found it impossible to escape in cleaning bins or opening packing-cases stuffed with chaff, decayed straw or excelsior, finally acted on my lungs in a very unsatisfactory manner. I began to cough a great deal and my throat and nose were in a constantly irritated state. The total result of all this was that I felt languid, without strength, and found it almost impossible to get up in the morning at the hour demanded: five-forty-five. In short, some twenty years later, as the X-ray then proved, I had at this time suffered a severe lesion of the upper left lung, which subsequently, and due to various outdoor and so fresh air tasks, as you will see, healed and finally left me as strong, apparently, as I would have been had I never suffered any lung lesion whatsoever.

But the peculiar semi-morbid and semi-poetic state of that day! The at last resigned and melancholy eye with which I viewed all beauty! It might be raining. And from one of the windows of this store I could see the immense crowds of the city, bobbing along, and so rhythmically, under umbrellas, so that at last I was more conscious of the material rhythm than I was of the crowds or the units that composed them. There was rhythm, rhythm, rhythm—and somehow men and crowds and wagons and every moving thing fell into it, although they were unconscious of it. And in the rain and under umbrellas or raincoats or covered wagon-tops, all life seemed to flow so softly and smoothly. But to where? And for what? To their homes—to their work; to their homes—to their work—went my mind, rhyming the more. And as for the horses and wagons and cars, they too—to their homes, the barns, or to the city's heart and back again—systole—diastole—and as for the rain itself, it came in gusts and lulls, like the wind, on the back of which it rode. And now here were clouds, and then bright weather, clouds and bright weather, or rain and no rain, or a job and then no job, or hunger and then not hunger, or sleeping and then waking, and then sleeping and then waking.

Yet behind me might be a box which I should be opening instead of rhyming so, and Mr. Purdon (who knows?) watching me from afar, for I could never be sure.

But then again there would be pigeons, flying over some portion of the downtown section which I could see from where I worked, and these I would follow, now high, now low, now into the very streets and gutters where they sought food. And at once I would be off and away—how high, how far, how free! And dreaming to fly with them—up into the heart of a blazing noon, or an evening setting sun, but never, never to cease flying or seeing or dreaming.

Oh, never!

But from all·this, how well you can gather and understand that it was but a short time before Mr. Purdon, squeaky shoes or no squeaky shoes, began to observe and to make clear that he thought me a useless person. And so from then on I suffered from the added conviction that shortly, if not just then, I was to be discharged. His suspicious eyes! His dark, disconcerting frown and occasional inquiries! Why had I not found time to do this or that? Why? And I so much wanted to be fixed somewhere and earning money! Naturally I became very despondent, since about me were endless evidences of the rewards which follow on patient industry of sorts. Our floor manager, for **instance** and as I had soon learned, had been with the house fifteen years and was now earning the, to me, amazing sum of forty-five dollars a week! Mr. Purdon, my shoe-squeaking Nemesis, had begun as an errand-boy and was now superintendent, and at fifty dollars a week. The road salesmen were all once order clerks but now earning thirty-five dollars and expenses. Bookkeepers, bill clerks, checkers, had risen to be managers, stock invoicers and the like. A great world! But as for me . . . I thought of quitting, yet hadn't I failed at everything else so far?

Finally Christmas came, and with it general excitement

about the place, for this was the time when discharges as well as promotions, raises in salary and the like were put into effect. And really, from the first of December on—but now especially during the last four or five days before Christmas—quite everyone was openly speculating as to whether his salary would be raised—even myself, if you will believe it. For did I really believe that I was as hopeless as Mr. Purdon made out or that he could be—well, you know—cruel enough, etc.? I really did not—not wholly. Besides, it was the custom of the firm to raise all faithful employees at least one dollar a year. And, better or worse, one week before Christmas an annual gift of turkeys was posted: signs on each floor to the effect that in a great cold room in the basement were hung the birds to which all employees properly entitled to the same were free. But were all entitled? Only those who had worked for the company a year or more. No others. Therefore, all I could do at this time was to look in and see how enticing they were, and wish. For how happy I would have been to carry one home to my mother! The pride! The glow! Yet the turkeys came and went—all gone before Christmas even—and so that sorrow over.

But next, on Christmas Eve itself, came the pay envelopes and promotions and discharges and the like, for it was a custom of this firm to deliver the pay for that week regardless of the fact that it might be two or three days early, and to place in the envelope whatever raise or promotion had been fixed upon. Also—a most cruel custom this one—a blue slip in the envelopes of those who were to be discharged, and which stated as much: "After December 31st next your services will no longer be required." And it was Mr. Thomas Purdon, no less, who was delivering all these. And with what a cheerful air, a smile even, not alone to those who were to receive more pay but to those who were to be discharged. I recall his smile as he handed me mine. Yet when he arrived on our floor on this day and gathered, as was his custom, all of the employees of that floor about him, I was actually tremulous with both hope and fear—not fear alone, really. And though he bent on me his cynical and even contemptuous eye and smirk as he handed me my envelope, I thought, well, he may not be so bad after all. He certainly looks and acts very cheerful. (To this moment I can see the sizable crowd of human flotsam, myself among them, all so eagerly watchful of what he held in his hand and what he was likely to say.) "Theodore Dreiser!" he called, the small envelope held in his hand, and then that smirk: "Here you are!"

I stepped aside and opened my envelope. And there it was! No increase! Instead a blue slip, with the words stated. And along with that, my final week's five! Ah! I can see the little scene as plainly as if it had happened yesterday. And the morrow might have been so wonderful had this envelope been favourable. But now as it was, my dream of a merry Christmas was over. Instead I was not only shaken but frightened as I thought of another long search for work. The grey, the cold, the admission to my mother and all that I was discharged! I was ready to cry, and did later. Only at the moment I went and got my hat and coat preparatory to slipping out as unobtrusively as possible. I did not intend to return the day after Christmas; I was too ashamed.

But as I was putting on my coat, the thought came to me that if I could see Mr. Bartlett, the tall, cool, military gentleman who was so active in the firm's affairs and who had always appeared to me so intelligent, sensitive and somehow kindly-minded, I might explain to him how hard it was on me to discharge me just now; that I was ashamed to have my family know, and that if he would let me go on for a little while longer I would try and do better. Uncertain of my courage and yet still thinking of doing this, I hurried downstairs, but when I saw him standing near his own office, which faced the aisle to the door, and greeting the various employees as they went out, I first paused, thinking—impossible—then next my mother and home coming to mind, managed to approach and exclaim: "Mr. Bartlett!" Wondering, no doubt, what of all his employees I could want of him, he turned and surveyed me keenly through his glasses. I doubt whether he had ever noticed me before.

"Yes?" he said.

"I work on the fourth floor under Mr. Blaikie," I began, quickly. "I have been here since October. I thought I was going to get a raise to-night, but I have been discharged. I didn't want to be discharged now, because the family . . . '
Here my voice gave out and I began to cry.

"Yes, yes," he said, "don't cry. I suppose you were discharged because you were not useful enough or the floor didn't require you. You don't want your family to know, is that it?"

"Yes, sir," I managed to choke out. "If I could just stay a little while longer, I . . ."

"Never mind, now," he said, consolingly, "you got a blue slip, didn't you? Where is your envelope? What is your name?"

He took my torn envelope and checked my name and salary.

"Very good, now," he said, "I should not really do this; we have many such appeals. But perhaps you will do better next year. Anyhow, you are not discharged, and I wish you a merry Christmas."

He laid one hand on my shoulder, and the touch of sympathy quite upset me. I turned my head toward his office door to avoid detection on the part of the many in the great room. Then I hurried away to try to enjoy one of the most depressing Christmas Eves and Christmas days I have ever endured.

CHAPTER LXIII

LIKE all such compromises with inefficiency, this retention of my services was of little, if any, value to myself, and none at all, I am sure, to the firm. Unfortunately, Mr. Bartlett's better judgment was overcome by my emotion, but Mr. Purdon, when he saw me retained, was not so moved. Meeting me in one of the aisles on the second or third of January, he observed, rather dourly: "You got off by crying this time, but you won't get off another year." Since then I have always been ashamed that my spirit was so poor that it would endure an insult of this kind and still hang on, but so it was. Why I was so lacking in courage I do not know—throughout all of these subsequent years I have sought to make amends. The only excuse I can think of is that all told, and as I have said, my physical condition was low and I was probably lacking in vitality. At any rate, my lungs really were in a serious condition, and I stood in great need of getting out in the air again rather than staying on at such a dusty task as that. Yet stay on I did. And for begging! And to my greater physical injury, as I will show. Yet with Aaberg as a sort of professor of philosophy, history, religion, and even science, I drifted on physically and intellectually for six or seven months more, and was at least improved by that, although at no time did I think of a way out or of even quitting. Fear, and nothing more.

Meanwhile, in my own home I was garnering lessons in economics, sociology, or inefficiency versus efficiency, plus order, force and the like. For our home at this time, as always, was a kind of chaffering camp in which every theory of living and sustaining oneself was either advocated or discussed. Along with a kind of blood affection or rapprochement, there was in all of us a growing sense of individuality which effected eventually decidedly sharp differences in tastes and aims. Indeed, every single member of our family, in so far as I could

367

see, from then on was first and foremost an individualist, guarding his individuality with an almost savage vitality, and yet not attempting to interfere very much with the individuality of the others. Only one of us, my sister Eleanor, seemed to have any real penchant for interfering and imposing ways and theories upon us, and that sprang not only from a restless and, as I sometimes thought, scatterbrained desire to improve herself but her very recent success in capturing a strong, vital, successful man. It had given her notions far beyond her real insight and set her to lecturing, criticising and dictating where as yet was no real equipment for the same. At the same time, while really re-mouthing such scraps as she gathered from her liege lord, she was giving herself airs which tended to anger if not wholly alienate every other member of the family. By no means as liberal or as gropingly speculative as was Ruth, and without the basic educational training which Trina had thus far obtained, she set herself to asserting that she was the one to tell all of us, including my mother, how to do.

Thus, first of all, and no sooner had she returned, than she was convinced and determined that we should move to a larger apartment, or rather house—a good one in a better neighbourhood. For her husband would never countenance such a shabby flat as that in which we were then living. More: "Jim, you know," she was constantly saying, "comes from such a fine family. His parents are very well-to-do, one of the best families in Rochester. They have such a beautiful home there. My goodness, you should just see his sisters and brothers! They move in the very best society!"

As a matter of fact, the Harahans, while wealthy and of good standing in their own community, were little more than a new-rich Irish Catholic family, with the usual Irish Catholic pretensions to social superiority. But beyond that, nothing —not a novel intellectual or artistic idea among the lot of them. Instead, a huge commonplace house set in a great lawn, carriages, the standardised furniture and doings of their day and neighbourhood. In short, silks and velvets and red and yellow plush. The only time I ever saw this house —which was years later—it was stuffed with the usual atrocities of furniture and art conceived in Grand Rapids, La Crosse and Keokuk, the neo-American idea of the artistic and the beautiful.

But unaccustomed to anything so pretentious and having no artistic standards whatsoever to fall back upon, Eleanor was, of course, impressed by all this. She appeared to feel that she had been lifted into and made a part of something which, while it transcended her present understanding and training, was not beyond the limits of her comprehension. How weak her understanding of it all really was may be gathered from the fact that she desired to be worthy of it, and being worthy of it meant that she must give herself airs, dress to the extreme limit of her purse, and do her best to inculcate her new conceptions of taste and culture into the remaining members of her family.

The only trouble was that in her insistence on manners and culture *à la* the Harahans, she became almost as obnoxious as my father with his religious views or my brother Rome with his drinking. As I have said before, we must not do thus and so; we must not say this or that. Our furniture was, of course, out of date and taste and must be replaced by such atrocities or their copies as now filled the house of Harahan. This last had one disadvantage—much of the furniture having been paid for by money collected from most of the rest of us, we were not prepared to see it thrown out unless it should be replaced at her expense—a conclusion which kept most of the furniture just where it was.

"Why don't she go and live with the Harahans if they're so very superior, instead of coming here and living with us, contribution or no contribution?" was the comment of Trina, I believe. But we did not take into consideration, I fear, her love for her mother, which was as great as that of any of us. In short, as I have said, and in order to be close to her mother, she brought Harahan to the house—a suite of rooms having been arranged for them—and together they went carriage-riding of a Sunday, visited the theatres, dined at the principal restaurants, and gave themselves many airs. At the same time, if I recall some quarrels and charges correctly, she failed to contribute very much more than her pro-rata share toward the family expenses.

Perhaps it was knowledge of this fact that by degrees came to irritate the rest of us—Ruth, Al, Trina and myself—who, as we saw it, were constantly being told what and how we should do, without in any material or definite way being helped to do it. I, for one, as I saw it, had scarcely any decent clothes to wear. And this was nearly as true of the others, Ruth excepted—a state which brought about frequent discussions as to whether this second Chicago venture was any better than the first. For all such talk and goings-on, there was too little money, too little order; "an awful botch," as Al used to phrase it. And yet we hung on together, Trina, Ed, Al, and myself, feeling that we really constituted a unit within the family and so ought to hang together, read such books as we could agree on, go to such cheap shows as we could afford, or attend such lectures or free public affairs as the city was constantly providing for the poor. Yet among us four again were divisions, for Trina and myself, as well as Trina and Al, did not always get along together. Trina, as I was seeing her at that time, was too critical, stingy, and strait-laced. As for Ed, he was frequently too youthful in his tastes or mood to suit our older whims. Thus it came about that a strong mental as well as social alliance between Al and myself, as opposed to a simpler and less mental bond between Ed and myself, sprang up. I it was who induced Al to read Dickens, Scott, Hawthorne, Irving, Stevenson, Crockett, Barrie, and Jerome K. Jerome. Deeming him, by reason of his enforced attendance at a Catholic school and his early childish apprenticeship to labour, to have been robbed of his rightful claim to an education, I found myself trying to make up to him for his lost opportunity. Ethically enthused in his behalf, I repeated to him the arguments of Aaberg as they came to me, and together we practically agreed that there was little or nothing to Catholicism. Yet believe it or not, we went to church. Again, because he was original, witty, and a clever mimic, I endeavoured to restore his enthusiasm for the stage, and urged him not to sink back into the humdrum of day labour. He agreed, but the struggle for time as well as means, working as he did, was too severe.

Personally, and in spite of all these things of which I have complained, I continued constantly to read, and in that way to broaden my understanding and so to get some line on my future. But I could not. For nothing in the trade world seemed to interest me. I could think of other jobs, such as thus far I had had, but beyond those, nothing. Reason, as I saw it then: no technical training. And worse, no capacity for the same. Then *how* in God's name, as I sometimes asked myself? What was I to do? How make anything of myself? And should I not be able, and soon, to solve that, where was I to end? I confess that at times my depression was enormous. At other times, minor diversions aiding me, I lost myself in dreams, experienced sudden and unexplained elations, only to swing back toward enormous morbidities. Yet when with others, and dreaming of girls, life, money, somewhere, some-how, I found myself proclaiming the doctrine of opportunity and hope, and so convinced myself of the tremendous import of life. The hope, for instance, of fighting my way to the heart of a beautiful girl was a constant stimulus. Of succeeding in some distinguished way (yet how?) was another. Joy, as I was determined, was to be fished out of the sea of life; sorrow to be evaded, maybe. Only sorrow's presence, the slowness of joy's coming, the uncertainty of everything, were the great drawbacks. I might dream and dream, and proclaim and proclaim, yet alone I returned to sorrow.

CHAPTER LXIV

O NE of my great reliefs, and even delights, at this time was the theatre, a form of diversion which palled upon me in later years but at this particular period seemed the epitome of all transcendent earthly blisses. In Evansville, years before, I had seen my first show, given by a minstrel troupe of which Paul made one—the interlocutor—Ed, Al and myself, occupying seats in the gallery. Later, in Warsaw, both Ed and I constantly pestered our mother for as much as fifteen cents per week in order that we might see the strolling repertoire shows which occasionally visited that town. What dramas and comedies have I not seen given by the most inadequate and limited of companies: East Lynne, Uncle Tom's Cabin, The Bells of Corneville, The Octoroon, The Mikado (with a chorus of two girls only!), The Silver King, The Danites —a long list!

The Opera House, or combined store and theatre building, in Warsaw boasted an orchestra of seven or eight pieces, conducted by a local carpenter who was also the leader of the town band, and this orchestra—part band and part orchestra —was almost as much of a delight to me as the show itself. For interpreted by it—and badly, as you may well guess—I first heard "La Paloma" (fitting in with my current delight in Irving's "Alhambra"), selections from "The Beggar Student," "Carmen," "Poet and Peasant," and "William Tell," operas the import of which I could not even guess, though their names I much admired—they smacked of romance. Not only that, but the variety of the instruments, including, as they did, two violins, a trombone, a cornet, a bass viol, a 'cello, a flute and several drums of different sizes and all beaten by the same man, permitted of wonderment, if nothing more. For in this orchestra was one man who played not only the cornet but the flute, changing from one to the other very swiftly at times, trilling a few notes on one and then giving a short, quick blast on the other, an operation most amazing if not always tuneful. However, knowing nothing of music, technically or otherwise, these little difficulties could not really disturb me much, lost as I was in the contemplation of perfections which had no relation—or small, at least—to the shabby world of fact before me.

For the youthful imagination of almost any race or community always glides over, I think, the homely defects or simplicities with which it has to deal. Your small-town audience—of that day, at least—and even the members of its barnstorming casts, were not dealing with the paste and papier-mâché of their humble art, but rather with what life always seeks to create and that which for the most part it succeeds in achieving—a delightful illusion. Thus, these commonplace members of this Warsaw orchestra, who by day were barbers, clerks, grocers and the like, were by no means commonplace individuals to me. They had become, and that by virtue not only of their instruments—which were important enough and capable of effecting a great illusion in regard to them—but by reason of their being now and at night a part of that glistening paradise which belongs to no country and no time—the stage itself—not only different but strange and even wonderful. All of them wore dress suits, of course; all had their hair and moustaches carefully dressed. All seemed most earnestly concerned with the hieroglyphics of their music pages before them, and so by dint of thought and arrangement they passed over into a realm so perfect that they seemed more related to paradise than to life.

And in the matter of music, the transmutation of reality into paradisiacal fancy was even more astonishing. It did not occur to me, for instance, that the Overture to William Tell or The Beggar Student was being either well or badly interpreted. I was in no position to judge as to that. But under the spell of some simple passage, feelingly conceived in the first instance and here translated as well as the sensitivity of our local workmen-musicians would permit, and under such conditions as I have set forth, my fancy expanded and responded in such a way as to make veritable and present realms on which no merely mortal eye has ever looked. Imperial stallions thundering over immensities of space; cloud castles lying bathed in the sapphire of unknown moons; giants and dwarfs conferring in Cymric shadows; gorgons and salamanders of fire fighting in the sun; hosts of angels in ordered and rushing flight winnowing the immensities of time and eternity.

And yet, with all this, claptrap scenery and most wretched mimes, I am sure. But glorified by the imagination and illusions of youth. A paper rock backed by painted if torn canvas, and presto, a mountain view of unparalleled grandeur! A wooden bench, a tin basin, and a wooden door near at hand —behold, you were before a woodland cottage of great beauty and most gloriously placed! Three bearded and black-garbed men huddled about a small red glass and gas-jet stage fire, and behold the entire and almost illimitable bandit-infested West of 1849! In short, a thunder-storm upon the stage was almost more real than about our own door. And besides, and just then (why?), there was no beauty equal to that of a stage beauty. More, when I first saw a girl in tights, I was so shocked that I trembled. And so on, through many "representations" of life.

This even extended to our local stage curtain. Surrounded by advertisements of butcher and baker, tailor and grocer, druggist and banker, was painted a small turret balcony, overhanging, presumably, a Swiss or Scandinavian lake scene. And in the foreground a few swans drifted, their necks romantically arched, their bodies regally and lightly floating on the water; in the distance a mere dab of a sail suggesting occupants and—morning or evening—a dreamy hour of contemplation. But was I the swan upon the lake, the idle dreamer in the tower, the idle dreamer under the sail? I was! And where the water rippled, I was the water and the ripple; the trees, the wind, the silence, the light. And beyond it again, among the sublime peaks, there was I, my heart and soul enlarged as under the spell of a magic opiate! Already upon entering the Opera House, the commonplace local world about me had vanished, and in its place had appeared this super-cosmic realm wherein my wand-commanded fancy had forgotten all commonplace things. I was in that land of illusion which seemingly has no relation to reality and yet ever has its roots therein, like those water plants that reaching down through muck and ooze still find something that is neither muck nor ooze.

374

But to return to Chicago. The plays I had seen in Warsaw had whetted my appetite for the stage to such an extent that by now I was enamoured of every play-form or scheme of entertainment of which I was conscious. The heavy tragedian, the ruthless villain, the dishevelled maiden tortured by love or deprivation in any form, the frittering clown or comedian, were all bedded in my fancy as among the most fascinating of earthly delights. Similarly, those ragamuffin farceurs of the vaudeville stage—the Irish comedian, with red hair and green whiskers; the fat Germans with immense paunches, wooden shoes, and pancake hats; the blackface comedians, with thick, red lips, woolly hair and white eyes; and the baggy-trousered, full-whiskered Jews, their hats spreading their ears sidewise, tickled my fancy to the verge of convulsions. Armed with a bag of peanuts and the handbill of the play, I was wont, when means permitted—sometimes with Al and Ed, sometimes alone—to betake myself to the topmost gallery, there to look down on all the delightful sea of life below. And what a sea —the heads, so orderly that they resembled cherries in a box; the air itself so hot and stuffy and tobacco-laden as to threaten suffocation! But still perfect to me. And therein, what hours! What anticipations! And afterward, were Al or Ed or both along, we would go home pretending ourselves to be comedians and repeating all of the bon mots and delicacies of accent and gesture which we could recall.

·I would not dwell on all this in this fashion save for the fact that the playhouse as I tasted it at that time was responsible for the endurance in me of many illusions far beyond their normal length of life. As unbelievable as it may be—my reading, experiences and other things considered—I still took stage drama, or rather stage melodrama, for practically what it represented itself to be. Love, as I saw it here, was not as it was in life—I did not then know how it was in real life, but only as I *thought* it was or should be—sensual and enticing— but here I found it exalted, enduring, reforming, refining, a long list; in other words, as the melodramatist appeared to believe it was, and as I there and then accepted it—on the stage. And so for me, and in spite of Aaberg and others, the doctrine of a moral order, with evil garbed as evil and easily detectable, and good arrayed as good, was still obviously true, in the theatre. Bad men and women were obviously to be known by their clothes. At the same time, many notions which my father valiantly retained and defended were here shown to be of no binding force to others, for gay girls romped with men in a most unseemly manner, and tights and low-cut dresses were flaunted in a most unChristian fashion.

Not only that, but amazing to me were the various phases of luxury which I saw most adequately portrayed and which contrasted so sharply with the life I was leading: banquet scenes, men in evening dress, balls and garden parties, and such Aladdin-like spectacles as "The Crystal Slipper," "Ali Baba and the Forty Thieves," "The Isle of Champagne," "The Queen's Mate," and "Sinbad, The Sailor." All were given for the most part in the old Chicago Opera House, a building which was subsequently widely heralded as the first sky-scraper of the western world. It was ten stories high. Here I viewed those, to me, amazing miracles of the ballet master's art: hundreds of girls in fleshings, capes and costumes of all the colours of the rainbow, turning and parading in evolutions which were as mystically sweet as motions can be, the while comedians of subsequently national reputation entertained all by their antics. Thus I recall Eddie Foy, De Wolf Hopper, William Seabrooke, Frank Bush. Also I saw property flowers unfold only to reveal a naïve semi-nude maiden at each heart. And before stage waterfalls, in glistening caves and chasms in the mountains and under the sea, I beheld those diverting creations of the scene-painter and the electrician here for the first time employed on any stage, I do believe—the electrical effects, I mean—and needless to say, I clothed these illusions in even richer colours than the pantomimist dreamed of attempting.

Ah, the long history of the world! Its written word! The endless exposures and explanations of life that have been made! And to think that millions are hourly born into the world to whom even the misleading written "knowledge" of the world is and will remain a sealed book! Planets and their inhabitants coming and going. Continents on this one rising from and sinking into the sea again; a moon splitting off and swinging about this one (its mother), as a satellite, a cow and her calf. Now submerged and now visible continents such as here and now have arisen and faded, as plants, as fields of strange grains, races and nations. The North and South

American continents above or under the sea how often? And the memory of their various flora and fauna, where? Is it not plain that man is not intended for wisdom?

And yet here was I nibbling at wisdom, my petty self capable of gathering but little of all that had gone before, seeking to know. But what? The futilities of the economics and sociology of this world? Its emotions, hopes and despairs—or its reflection, the stage? The *comédie humaine*! And yet, born without cognisance of it, and without even sufficient time to discover a tithe of all that had been and had always been made plain on this planet alone.

CHAPTER LXV

BY such a mixture of the pleasant and the unpleasant, I finally reached the summer of 1888, by which time I was seventeen. My body was about as emaciated as it might well be. And yet, in spite of this, I was still fairly vital and mentally alert. At that, though, the dusty task of bin-cleaning was really telling on my lungs; for a time my sputum was faintly tinged with blood. Also I was feeling more and more weary of all that I was doing and would stand at one of the windows of this wholesale hardware house, reasonably concealed by boxes, and sigh for the freedom of the world which I saw outside. I have described the pigeons, the crowds, the Lake. At work or idling, I was always dreaming.

At the same time, I do not wish the reader to understand, in spite of all I have said, that I was really so completely sick or broken physically as to be more than hypochondriacal and mentally discordant. After all, weak or oppressed lungs, a disordered stomach, and an imaginary sex weakness do not necessarily spell much more than varying hours of hypochondria. And underlying my ills was an intense nervous or mental health which needed little more than a change of air and some assurance as to the future to lift me physically also. Even as it was, as I have said, I was not without hours of intense and vivid pleasure in the scenes about me. Nature, my shoulder companion, on Sundays, holidays, nights and mornings, was ever before and with me. Despite all my ills, imagined or real, I fairly revelled in the quiet and unobtrusive as well as the spectacular phases of life—its unfailing and so moving artistry. Working Chicago! Working Chicago! Its smoke palls, fogs, rains, snows, blizzards—with people bending their bodies low against shrieking winds! The crowds of commonplace boys and girls, men and women, who journeyed to and from work morning and evening, crowded so grotesquely in the vari-coloured, small horse-cars. The factories and shops!

Their screaming whistles! the sublimity of crowds in half lights —those of the night or the early hours before dawn! Actually I think the mystery, charm and poetry of life were as high and clear in me then as ever before or since. But as for expression, I lacked even the thought of it—no suitable form or words, though paintings and writings were always a part of my intellectual as well as emotional life. I think I even preferred galleries of paintings to libraries of books. Certainly I cared for them as much.

As for the other members of my family—more particularly my father and mother and those brothers and sisters closest to me in years—I have often wondered since how that particular winter impressed them. For reactions such as mine are more or less common to all; most certainly they were to my mother, who often paused to remark on them, and so feelingly. My father, too. And Al, if not the others. And one of the definite and moving impressions of my mother that I took at just this time was of a lovely, poetic and yet cabined and quite enslaved spirit, who because of poverty and a lack of practical training, as well as the absence of any marked strain of selfishness or unrest in herself, was content to remain and act as servant to as well as cement between the various and restless and changing spirits of her children.

And in that connection let me say, and with feeling, that I cannot imagine what this home, any more than any of the others earlier, would have been without her. For that curiously binding spirit which she exercised and which bound us all was here as powerful as elsewhere, and to me so moving and even dramatic in a strong, compelling way. For already at forty-eight or thereabouts, she had come such a long way in poverty, and yet was still labouring through its aftermath. And at five-thirty each weekday morning was up and preparing the lunches of those of us who were going early to work. Indeed, I see her now, a fleshy if not large woman, from whom most of the delicacy of youth had departed and yet whose soul was as sweet as any girl's, moving here and there about her almost servant-like labours. And with no good dresses to speak of any more, mostly that modified Moravian habit of black, with the nun-like collar, which I must say became her truly sacrificial spirit. Yet her dreams of a superior home of any kind by now surely dissipated. And little thought of anything other than that we youngest ones were to succeed and be happy. It was so evident, from all that she did. Yes, even then, and not for her own sake but theirs.

For who shall sing the song of the true mothers of the world?
Or dare curse life when patient, unrequited hands take up so
    heavy a load?
Or assert that cruelty in this life realm is not balanced by
    tenderness?
Or that self-immolation does not even the scale against
    selfishness?

      *   *   *   *   *   *

For over against grasping greed I place the endless patient
    risings at dawn of mothers;
And opposite vanity and selfish indifference I set down the
    white, strained faces of watching mothers;
And against the fevers and cruelties of desire
I put over the self-immolations of the mothers of the off-
    spring of that desire—
And I defy you to say that the scales that weigh inequity
    are not even!

I may add that these lines spring from my boyish impressions of my experiences with my mother; the sympathy and delicacy that on all occasions—the most trying—could refrain from inquiry or prying criticism; the mercy so wide that there was no ill or infirmity that could not be sheltered beneath it, no weakness of temper that her sweetness of mood could not dilute. I have seen fears in her eyes which never found vocal expression, and defeated hopes which never crossed the portals of her mouth. So often she knew, while refraining from the censure of seemingly knowing; she understood, and yet her understanding was all too often veiled in her eyes.

In those days I was up and doing as early as five-forty-five. By six I would have a cold bath, and from then on for perhaps twenty or twenty-five minutes I might be dressing and eating (the little that I could eat). I had learned by experience to calculate the running time of the cars to such a nicety that I could almost foretell the possible delays of any morning and so arrive exactly at seven. Usually between breakfast and the time of leaving I had six or seven minutes of leisure, and these I would spend in a rocking-chair on the back porch which overlooked our court and the stretch of houses beyond, or, in very cold weather, I would sit by a window, singing and thinking of the mystery of life and of my future. Like the rest of the flora and fauna of the world, I was growing toward fruition or bloom without knowledge of the processes involved. The art of the jumbled streets, the rancid alleys, the little cars jingling along all day for profit, the little stores, the dirty river, with its dark, inscrutable waters: all moving, soothing, beautiful, rewarding. It was like listening to an enticing symphony. Most of all, the art of the accidental experiences of individuals appealed to me: the bits of death, wealth, fame, failure, with which the newspapers were crowded. Life was a living, dancing picture; it was a realm in which on every hand plays and operas were being enacted. People whispered to each other of their unutterable tragedies or believed their salving hopes; they sat on commonplace chairs and told of doings which were related in texture to the great novels as I knew them. I was beginning to suspect already that life was better than any book. Who could transfer to me by writing the life that I was seeing and feeling? No, the thing was inviolate, perfect in itself; it encompassed all in its perfection, was all perfection. Why, right in my own home, as I saw it even then, was the best time ever, only it was slipping away. My mother, my father, my brothers and sisters, my life and all that had hitherto been a part of it! All! That was the thing I was beginning to feel and see as an undertone. This perfection was not static, although for ever young, for ever dramatic, for ever tense. Only I and all others who were now moving along and out of it, were not permanently of it, in this form, anyhow. We, too, all of us, were fading and eventually ending. Ah!

But just as I was beginning to think that the material aspects of my necessities were about as bad as they could be, there arrived on the scene, and at the office of Hibbard, Spencer, Bartlett & Company, that tall New England spinster of my Warsaw school days—Miss Fielding, if you please—from whom I had parted without a word and had heard nothing of since leaving except that she had accepted a position in Worcester, Massachusetts, the year after I left school. Nevertheless, here she was, called to become principal of an outlying Chicago High School—Irvington, I think—and her proposal after explaining that she had just been over to see my mother and secured my address, was that I resign the work that I was now shirking and spend the next year, or two, at best, at the State University of Indiana. And at her expense, if you please! And in order to discover whether or not I had a peculiar bent or aptitude which I could develop and then follow to success. For she was insistent of her conviction that such was the case. More, that under the circumstances it was my duty to go, since having taught me one year in Warsaw she had not been able to get me out of her mind. And since now she had more money and a good position and was feeling so keenly about this, well . . . therefore.

But imagine my astonishment, as well as my doubts, plus, if you will believe it, not a little shame in regard to my work here—not my idling and discharge, but the commonplaceness of it all, if you please, and especially after all that had been said to me in Warsaw in regard to my possibilities. Ah! In consequence, instead of acquiescing with alacrity, as might have been expected, I retreated, pretending to be interested not in the work so much as the prospects of this place, and so, and as usual, made a gauche spectacle of myself, as you may well guess.

But Miss Fielding! Her eyes! Her sympathetic, helpful smile! How clearly I see her looking at me as of yore in Warsaw!

"Now, Theodore," she explained quickly when she saw my puzzled and uncertain look, "I have come here especially to do this, and you must help me. I have the money. I do not need it myself, and it is something I want to do for you and for myself, and you must let me do it. I have thought of you ever since you left Warsaw. I know so much more than you think; I understand you, Theodore, so much better than you think I do. And I need to do this for myself. It is a shame you shouldn't have been permitted to finish your high school work there." (She did not know that I had personally deserted it.) "You are too young, really, to know the importance of finding yourself. A year or two at college, if it doesn't do anything else, will make you think."

She hurried on over many points relative to education and

my life which I have forgotten. The principal thing was her intense enthusiasm for me, her determination to make me leave this work, the joy she insisted would be hers in assisting me in this way.

That I speculated much on the fortuitousness and fortune of this is natural. It was such an unexpected and almost spectacular way out of my difficulties. I forgot to say that my father in the interim of the spring months had again returned to Terre Haute and that my mother alone was left to judge of the import of this proposition. As usual, I shifted the responsibility as lightly as I could to her, whereupon Miss Fielding said she would at once return and place the matter before her.

As anyone might have known, it was not difficult to convince my mother. When did she ever balk at any scheme which would give happiness or advancement to her children? As I recall it, she was greatly impressed and even astonished at this windfall in my direction. That a woman so well-placed (for she was by now, as I have said, a principal in one of the outlying high schools of Chicago) should look me up in this fashion was, to say the least, a great tribute to me in her eyes. I think my standing in the family rose at once, and to a very high point. Also I remember pluming myself on my individuality and feeling that there must be something to me after all. Why not? Was not Miss Fielding actually inviting me to her rooms in order to give me some advice, instructing me in the general nature of the work at the State University and the character and personality of one David Starr Jordan, who was then President of this college. More, as she made clear to me at this time, she had resented the, as she put it, unjust disrepute into which our family had fallen in Warsaw. It was all petty and unfair and dangerous to my personal moral and budding talent, if any.

"You need not feel so badly about it, Theodore," she said, although by this time I was not feeling badly about it at all. Quite other things were filling my mind, as you have seen. "I tell you, the world is full of half-concealed shames and tragedies. But they are not really important here, there, or anywhere. What I want you to do is to study and develop your mind. Read philosophy and history. You will see how life works and how mistaken or untrue most beliefs are. Read

Spencer. Read a life of Socrates. Read Marcus Aurelius and Emerson. You have the capacity for rising high in the world, and I want you to do it. Don't let any little beliefs as to family scandals or disgraces lower your personal pride. Your life is yours, and people will take you as an individual, and only so. They will not trouble about your family if you are all that you ought to be."

I felt, for the time being at least, that I was one of the most important youths that ever was.

CHAPTER LXVI

THE ensuing weeks after this proposal and decision were spent, in part at least, in visiting about with Miss Fielding and reading at home and in the city library with a view to finding something of what college life was likely to be, even if from no better source than works of fiction: "Tom Brown at Rugby," "Four Years at Harvard," "A Collegiate's Remembrances of Princeton," together with such college curricula as I could find. But with little result, since they did not bear directly on what I wished to know or what I might expect at the State school for which I was destined. Again, the time was short—it was somewhere around August first when Miss Fielding first called to talk to me, and about September first when she came to say I must quit what I was doing and prepare to leave. I had been afraid to tell anyone at the hardware house about my good fortune, for fear I should be discharged before I was ready to go, so I kept mum until four or five days before I was ready to go and then began telling those immediately about me. The effect was electric, as change always is.

I have always rejoiced in the eagerness of so-called living things for change, that strange something in nature that wants to be on the go. We talk of stable things, but nothing is stable. If you let things alone, they change almost as swiftly as if you attack them personally. Buildings, cities, nations, ideas, gods, and even ethical conceptions, go by the board. The rains, the winds, the frosts, the tides, the moods, angers and delights of men, are eating at all visible and invisible things. The vast creative impulses of life, or in the phrase of the world, God Himself, are on the move, and the fixed envies the unstable and the unstable the fixed. Only a love of beauty endures: that strange taste for joy and delight in mental and material harmonies, although even there change is conceivable —a variation from what is here known as beauty. Is beauty the same to the savage as to the poet, to the animal as to man?

Among these men whom I had come to know—Aaberg, Rapp, Kiber, Newy and others—I had noted this tendency to envy every suggestion of beneficial change or promotion for others. No one was really made sorry by another's downfall, though a certain amount of wordy sympathy was always expressed, but when anyone rose higher, then came the look of envy, distress, self-commiseration, a certain something which suggested that if thought could prevent it, you would really not get what you felt you had. I think Aaberg was as sincere as anyone, and his congratulations were more genuine than most of the others.

"Ha!" he exclaimed when I told him. "So you are leaving! I am glad for you, but that leaves me here with no one to talk to but these swine! God damn! Why should you have to go to college? Still, your life is not mine, and you are young. I know you will get along. You have no vices, and you think. But I am sorry. My own life is a hell of a thing. What a botch I have made of it! But so it is!" He waved his thin, almost emaciated hands. He seemed to see before him long, darkening years for which he could find no remedy.

To young Ed Rapp, our horse-like floor-worker, I spoke of my coming change, but more by way of jest than earnest, to see what effect it would have on him.

"College, eh?" he exclaimed, lustily, with a blinking attempt at solemnity. "Well, I went to school up here in Lakeview four or five years ago, but Jees, I couldn't learn nothin'. They used to try to make me study arithmetic, but I told 'em to go to hell. The old man wanted me to go, but I wouldn't. I threatened to lick the teacher once, and they put me out. 'Tain't nothin' that I care anything about."

In him apparently was no faintest notion of what it was all about.

Theodore Kiber, a youth whom I may or may not have mentioned but a beginner like myself and deeply interested in prohibition as a cure for nearly all social ills, was curious as to my future.

"Why don't you look up the drink question when you get down there, and get interested in prohibition?" he suggested. "It's the coming political issue. The party that advocates it will be *the* party! You could get somewhere that way. You may laugh at me now, but you won't laugh at me ten or fifteen years from now. I'm going to stick to it and get somewhere politically."

If he is alive and has witnessed how, without the support of any party but solely by the machinations of moralists and reformers, prohibition was foisted upon Americans, and that quite without consent of the governed, he probably does not think so highly of his political judgment or his imagined dominant party.

But if no one was especially stricken at my going, one was especially pleased, and that was Mr. Thomas Purdon. I did not personally tell him but reported to Mr. Hibbard, who had originally hired me. A rather pursy and vain old gentleman, he eyed me philosophically. "Now you see how it is," he commented. "We take young men like you in here to teach them the business and keep them here a year or more and then they resign. Where are you going?"

I told him.

"College! Very good! You'll probably do better there than with us. The only pity is that you couldn't have known before working here so long what you were interested in. Anyhow, good luck." He waved me out with a fat smile and a fat hand.

But Thomas Purdon, Esquire, was angry because he had not had the pleasure of discharging me. "I hear you're goin' Saturday," he said to me on the afternoon of the same day as he approached where I was working. "Well, that's good. You wouldn't have lasted another year. I told Mr. Bartlett as much last Christmas. Well, that's what they get for listenin' to whiners."

If I had had more courage, I would probably have given him a beating, but not being of the fighting kind at the time, the thought of the swiftly approaching change consoled me and I did not so much care.

The State University now beginning to dawn on me as a reality worried me not a little, for I was most puzzled as to what I was to do once I got there. In a rough way possibly I might be said to have had a notion, yet I did not know. Life—as to its built-up technicalities, at least—was seen by me through a glass, darkly. One thing I saw clearly enough, and

387

that was the interest and value of knowledge in general, but as for special knowledge, the enormous advantage to the individual of technical equipment in a given field, how different! I heard Miss Fielding and others repeat and repeat how important it was to fix on some particular technique and acquire it, since in America specialisation was already in such great demand, but the import of that failed to lay hold of my mind in any thoroughgoing way. Technique! Technique! I could scarcely grasp the meaning of the word. And as for specialisation, in what field should I specialise? Law, medicine, engineering, education, what? With the aid of Miss Fielding I had secured a catalogue of the curriculum of the University, but, if anything, was more puzzled than ever. Languages, the sciences, sociology, biology, history, law, a long list! Positively I could scarcely grasp what was meant by any or the lot of them. True, there was the dictionary and the encyclopædia, but in the main it was almost useless for me to consult either. The foundation or study whereby one comes to understand the terminology of a given branch of science, trade, or art had never been laid or made by me.

In answer to my various inquiries, though, which indicated a very dubious and no doubt confused state of mind, Miss Fielding said a very intelligent thing. Roughly it went something like this: "You have never had any direction in your mental life, Theodore. No one appears to have had sufficient knowledge to understand or guide you. Nevertheless, you are mental. Your reading and your interests show that. Go down there and pick out such things as interest you and study those. The catalogue speaks of various examinations, but I can have those waived for the present. What you will do will be to learn what is being done by some people, and why. That will help to clear up your own thoughts. You will find out what other young men are intending to do and why. In the course of time that will tend to make clear to you what you would like to do, and why. So don't worry. Go! Pick out from this catalogue anything you think really interests you, and study that. I will write to Dr. Jordan and I am sure he will let you do this. I will give you a letter to him."

And so, heartened as well as soothed by this advice, I looked over the catalogue and found that I liked history, literature, old English, English literature, and such generalities. It was stated in the catalogue that either algebra or geometry or trigonometry as well as Latin were compulsory unless I had already taken these. Regardless of whether I should succeed or fail in these, I decided on geometry and Latin; since such things as chemistry and physics were closed to me the first year unless I had done some high school work in preliminary studies, which I had not, I decided not to bother about these. Even so, how I ever came to get into the University without preliminary examinations—which would have quickly debarred me—I cannot say. Apparently the correspondence between Miss Fielding and Dr. Jordan resulted in my being admitted without examination, and so the coast was clear. With some little money I had saved—very little—and some the family provided, I secured a very cheap new suit and overcoat. My linen and underwear were put in good condition, and my belongings packed in an old trunk. Miss Fielding, on my leaving, handed me fifty dollars, wished me good luck, and told me that I should hear from her regularly. My mother kissed me good-bye and cried. Al suggested archly that I should not get a "swelled head" and Trina remarked that there would probably be no living with me when I returned. En route, as I also recall, the train ride seemed an exciting adventure. How remarkable that so suddenly I had been lifted out of that hardware house and into this so very different form of existence! I was to be a student, become . . . what? Alas, I could not say what, could not even think what!

CHAPTER LXVII

WHENEVER I think of my one year at the State University, I have to smile, for aside from the differing mental and scenic aspects of the life there as contrasted with what I had left, its technical educational value to me was zero, or nearly so. For in my thinking I was so nebulous, so general and undifferentiating as opposed to special and particular. Possibly, as I have since thought, large masses of facts of a general character about life were being stored, but as to the particulars of any specific field of education—while I cannot say that I was not curious as to what they concerned and their possible value to me or anyone—most certainly I was not practically interested. In the main, I argued, I think, that if in any way I was troubled, I might single out some one line or field of technical information, and by inquiry learn something of which later I could speak.

For here, as I saw on entering, were chemical and physical laboratories, departments of sociology, economics, history, mathematics, law, to say nothing of geology, astronomy, and what not else. And while the necessary preliminaries for these had not anywhere been laid by me, still might I not seize on one or two, those nearest my own taste, and follow as best I might? As for achieving anything definite in connection with them, that was another story.

In the main, what I really did do, as I saw later—and as Miss Fielding had indicated—was to contact and observe other youths of my own years coming here with distinct fields of study and achievement in mind, and through them, their gay and in the main purely social exchanges with me, hear as to what they were studying, and why and how. Yet that many of those contacts and exchanges helped me, I cannot say. I was already or still too much interested in my own thoughts and observations of life, and while I listened to these various youths—boys and girls, but principally boys, since I was still intensely girl-shy—I was not always impressed let alone moved by their ambitions. For here was one who was going to be a lawyer, because it should earn him so much a year; and here another who was determined to be an educator, but in so humdrum and practical a way as positively to bore me with his programme; and yet a third was studying history in order to teach it, and that one economics and politics in order to enter the State legislature. Another—a most interesting youth—was bent on philosophy, in order to teach philosophy. But as for life, inquiry, and the mystery and flare of it all—apart from a commonplace, humdrum reputation and a salary—I could not see that there was anything much in the minds of any of them. And yet here was this great, flashing, extended, mysterious world, as I saw it, and it was these commonplaces of living and salary and some little reputation that interested almost all.

Thus all of these fields left me cold. True, I wanted to read and know a little about all of them—not too much—and yet just why I could not have said at the time either. As for following any one of them as a life course, God, how narrow, dull, even futile! I recall thinking of Latin (and because I had heard that if you were going to study anything: law, medicine, the sciences, this, that, you would need Latin; having been a mother tongue it had passed into all of the educational compilations of the world; was, in short, an open door to the knowledge of many lands) and asking myself after my first few days' study of it, was I going to enter upon anything so technical that it would require this open sesame? Was I? I questioned it very much, but decided, since it was required, that I would do the best I could. As for history and literature, I was from the beginning intensely interested and pursued these with avidity.

But what interested me more than anything else was this school or university as a whole—its buildings, professors, students, the life and character of the town of which it was all a part—and a very good school of its kind, as I learned later, and one then housing as teachers a number of men subsequently to become widely known: Jordan, the president; Jeremiah Jenks, economist and sociologist; Von Holst, historian; Green and Crocker, mathematicians, and their like. And as I subsequently learned, it was just then in the heyday or at least opening of a new era. The year before, for instance, the attendance for the first time in its history had crossed the six hundred mark, and the State legislature, under some burst of educational interest, had devoted the interesting sum of one hundred and fifty thousand dollars to the building of a new limestone library building. There were, in addition, six or seven other buildings, of brick or wood, scattered rather casually over a large and physically varied campus, which to me as I first saw it, and especially after my confined Chicago days, seemed very beautiful. A wide brick walk led from the principal street of the town up a hill, at the crest of which and to the sides as one approached stood these several buildings. Below, westward and to the south and north, lay a charming panorama of the town, with a small, quaint old court-house in the centre. And to the east, north-east and south-east, were hills and seemingly heavy growths of trees leading interminably hence. In so far as the whole State was concerned, this was considered to be a very backward county, commercially, and in every other way, and the adjoining county east—Brown— had no railroad and no town of any size, a most primitive region. It also contained—so our geographies said—the highest hill in the state—one Weedpatch by name—there being no mountains.

And in Bloomington I found a charming old town to look at, and surcease from all my recent woes in so far as dust, early hours, work and the like were concerned. For here all, by comparison, was so leisurely and restful. Besides, before me were at least eight months of comparative peace and security. Board and room, as I learned, could be had for not more than five dollars per week, and almost instantly I found a room in the home of an aged widow, not so far from the heart of the town and still a most pleasant walk from the university. Its yard was large and attractive with trees, flowers, a grape arbour in full fruitage, and a smooth lawn all about that was a delight to look upon. And the homes surrounding it, with their kempt lawns and trees, constituted an equally pleasing prospect. A lovely rural land, as it seemed to me, with pre-ternaturally warm September and October days, so warm, in fact, that I could leave all my windows open, and, ensconced in a ground floor room, the doors and windows of which gave out upon grass and flowers and pleasing vistas of other lawns and trees and ambling pedestrians, dream what dreams! After the vitality and urge of Chicago, it was like coming into a still chamber and preparing to rest and sleep.

On the first morning after my arrival, though, I visited the office of the Registrar of the University, and was shown how to register for classes, and from the catalogue picked out the men under whom I was to study. The Reverend Amzi Atwater, a tall, bewhiskered, funereal person, one of the pillars of the University and an ardent Presbyterian, as I immediately discovered, was to teach me Latin; John Cooper Davidson, a heavily-whiskered yokel about thirty years of age, was to teach me geometry; Willard Pelton Green, a dreamy mathematician, was to teach me advanced algebra; Arthur Peddoe Gates, a weird, bony specimen and a pedant of the first order, was to teach me English literature and Anglo-Saxon at one and the same time; Donald Moranville Strunk, Litt.D., Ph.D., was to teach me history, and so it went. I do not know whether these were all who were to lend me the light of their counsel, but no other comes definitely to mind.

But if ever, physically, at least, a year proved an oasis in a life, this one did. For much to my astonishment, the lessons, outside of Latin, were not so very difficult, though as for algebra and geometry, I could not quite see the import of these, to me if to life. They seemed, I having no turn for mathematics or the technique of the sciences to which they so aptly apply, such a useless waste of calculation. Yet history, English literature and the study of words fascinated me, since thusward was the bent of my temperament, but far and above these again in import to me was the life of the town, the character of its people, the professors and the students, and the mechanism, politics and social interests of the University body proper.

For, as I soon found, nearly all, professors and students, were as busy about these things as any other. There were so many hivelike conversations in so many rooms: professors surrounded by eager and anxious students asking questions, and the group walks and palavers among the students themselves; the solemn and concerned mouthings relative to this and that duty only now in the immediate offing. I was puzzled, troubled, and in part even amused. For I was not so dull or so inexperienced but that even here I sensed a certain amount of unnecessary solemnity and over-emphasis of this and that, together with merely vain parade and show. So many of these students were so ultra-solemnly impressed with their own importance. Where I was not made envious or sad, I was compelled to smile at the variety-like show it made.

Yet the food at the various boarding clubs where one gathered with as many as twenty or thirty others was good, and the intelligence and spirit of at least some of the students so high and their characters so diverting, that it was not long before I was friend to many, actually hail-fellow-well-met with not a few. And by degrees this led to games, a freshman society to be organised, Greek letter societies to be considered, debating, exploring. Eager for life, I began at once to speculate as to what fortune and friends would bring me in the way of entertainment and possibly love, for what youth does not think of love? For now here was the college girl or co-ed to contemplate. And what airs and self-imagined station she introduced into this world! The affected way of dressing, the affected walk or swagger, the implications of her eyes as she examined one for such marks of social station as she valued or knew in her own home town! And by reason of the same, a sudden, sharp realisation of the humble place I most likely occupied in the eyes of these girls. My clothes, as contrasted with those of the swagger students; my limited purse, with so many of the others here with all and more money than they required—pampered pets, in short, of pampered parents —the usual college lah-de-da or social loafer. And was it not obvious that it would be they who would triumph in this field in which I was so much interested? For me it was.

In short, by now the beauty of girls had become a kind of fetich with me. Deprivation of even genial familiarity with most of them had built them up in my mind as absolute paragons. Round that ever-moving line of beauty which is their body, supplemented by that perfection of romance which is sex, I wandered, thrilled by a seeming subtlety which was not unlike that which veils the chalice to a Greek or Roman believer. Never was Aphrodite more glitteringly or inviolably enshrined than by me, and yet I was wildly longing to tear the chalice from its shrine and place it on my dresser.

CHAPTER LXVIII

NEXT door to me, as I settled down in this delightful world, was a girl whose memory endures to this day. Her family was commonplace, a small-town working-class family. If I were to see her to-day as she was then, I would probably consider her trivial. Yet for some four or five weeks of these opening college days, she tortured me.

She was a small, vivacious hoyden—blonde, pink-cheeked, blue-eyed. I spied her not long after I adopted a certain east window as my favourite study spot, drawn by the grass, sunlight and flowers outside. It was blissful, as I now found, just to sit there and pretend to concentrate on the subjects I had selected. But more blissful still was the discovery soon made that the charming view of the garden led to a fence which enclosed the house mentioned and showed not only a long window peeping through the branches of a tree but this girl, presumably studying and—after a day or two—precisely at those hours in the early morning and mid and late afternoon which I had chosen for my work. More, as I soon noticed, she had a habit of loosing her hair, which was plentiful, and letting it fall over her books, a trick which tended to halo her face in a most pleasing way. Occasionally also I caught her slyly studying me, and more, allowing a shadow of a smile to play about her lips—evoking such a nervous disturbance in me as was scarcely endurable, so disturbing, in short, that I could not concentrate but had to lay down my book and look, and even sometimes give up any further attempt to study. Yet having no courage in these matters and no least scrap of self-assurance or appreciation, I made no attempt to flirt with her. And this I cannot possibly understand, since at the very same time I was positively convinced that it was a flirtation with me she desired and was seeking.

This went on day after day for the better part of a week, when one afternoon at about three my landlady, who was a feeble old crone, soft-hearted and genial, came in and with a nervous and gentle "Tee hee" stated that the young lady next door wanted to know if I would help her with her grammar. There was a problem in connection with grammar then confronting her which required immediate solution, and she did not know to whom else to turn. But grammar! And me! But worse, imagine my assuming that any grammatical problem had anything to do with this, and worrying about that! My genial old crone, with her bent back and grey hair and shawl, stood holding the door and inviting me to come back into her musty living room, where this artful Circe was already waiting. I rose to follow with alacrity, and yet fear, cold chills already chasing themselves up and down my spine. Grammar! This pretty girl! A real flirtation! But now how, how in God's name?

None the less, proceeding as to a grave or a death pit, I was given the briefest and I must say somewhat shamefaced introduction and then left by my crone to survive or perish as best I might. She had gone back into her kitchen and closed the door. So here I was at last in the presence of this audacious appleblossom, and with no skill whatsoever to turn so advantageous a situation to my profit. Yet with her smiling up at me and opening her book, and then pointing to a sentence which she said she did not know how to parse. Which was the subject, which the predicate? What did something modify? God! Without any trace of grammar in my system, I stood trembling before another Waterloo. As usual, my tongue began to swell—swole, swill—which is it? Looking into her warm, welcoming eyes, I might easily have been convicted of semi-paralysis, I am sure. My hands and knees trembled. I stared the while she appeared not to notice, determined, no doubt that having gone so far, she must prosecute this adventure to a happy conclusion. In proof of which she now threw herself into a chair, motioned to me to bring another close to hers, and when I looked over the book put her head confidingly close to mine. Euthenasia! Ecstasomania! Delirium! Dream! Another youth, of even minimum audacity, would have made short work of this occasion. He would at least have taken her hand and proceeded to a kiss, arranged for a future contact, and at once. As for me, I made no such use of my great opportunity.

Rather, stuttering, fumbling, uttering God only knows what sounds, the occasion slipped through my fingers. To be somewhat more exact, I stammered and blushed and pretended, if you can believe it, to take the matter seriously.

Well, anyhow, and for a few moments pretending to take me seriously, the while a chill of realisation on her part invaded the air, she exclaimed: "Oh, I see now. It's much clearer than it was before. Thank you ever so much." And then jumping up and smiling herself out of the door, skipped gaily across the lawn into her own home the while I stood there macerated and self-contemptuous among the ruins of my perfect opportunity. Ah! And worse, feeling that because of this lunatic inhibition housed within myself, she never would be mine now, however much I might desire her. Some damned sprite of the anachronistic, some imp of the perverse as Poe understood him, was ever walking or even parading before me, bringing to nothing my keenest aspirations, my dearest dreams. And so in my own heart, misery. What lurking wraiths of the might have been!

And after this, though, and just the same, for a week or two, if not longer, she gave me ample opportunity to be friendly with her, nodding and smiling to me whenever she saw me, the while I, dying to be bold, still remained without the courage to approach her, so cursed with paralysis or a halting, clumsy tongue that I could not speak or even call hello. Literally, as when on one occasion and another, I screwed up my courage and was about to approach and attempt some pleasantry, carefully worded in my mind beforehand, I got the shakes, ran cold, and retreated to a safe distance, from which I finally decided never to emerge again.

But the sequel to all this was, if anything, even more painful than my original failure. For after a very few days subsequent to my realisation that I was hopeless, there arrived on the scene—from Greenfield, Indiana, I believe—one William Levitt, law student, no less, who, entering a little late and finding rooms scarce, although his own purse was not light, and after some conversation with my landlady—who desired to make as much as possible out of her rooms, of course—appeared with her to inquire if I would not share my room with him, the assumed inconvenience to me being compensated for by a dollar reduction in rent to me—a tempting bait to one who needed every possible dime. More, on sight I took a fancy to him. He was young, athletic, with a mass of heavy black hair, well-brushed and oiled, and since he smiled cheerfully, talked briskly and jovially and announced that he was sure we would get along gloriously together, I agreed at once. For whereas I was all for meditation or quiet and always speculative and observative, he represented that active athletic phase of college life—football—which interested me much. More, in a very few days after he had joined up with me in this rooming arrangement, he was swept into the fall football team and finally ended as one of its half-backs, kicking long goals, running and fighting and eventually becoming one of the stars of the year—a year of victory for the local team, by the way.

Better, though, he was so interesting to me as a type that I have never forgotten him. He was clever as well as practical in the social sense of the word, also liberal and good-natured, a fighter for the love of fighting and the glory of it. In sum, his was a light-hearted swashbuckling nature of that western day and world, fair at his studies, and genial as a companion. More, he was possessed of many popular or college charms —looks, strength, grace, means, which made him a hero and an idol before the year was out. Yet he never took any undue advantage of me or made any base, let alone rasping, comment on my inferior skill in these various matters. Rather, after a little while, as I saw, he tried, in a semi-affectionate way, to bring me out of my shell and if possible build up my physical strength—a task which I am sure he must have considered all but hopeless.

Be that as it may, imagine this youth then, with his handsome face and figure, his rippling, intriguing smile and interpretive and understanding eyes, noting on almost the very first day this girl at her window, and after a glance or two, taking his place at the very window which I had been accustomed to occupy and exclaiming: "Ah, who's that little cutie over there? Little golden locks, eh! We'll have to see what we can do about her." And at once smiling broadly, as I saw, and receiving in return just such a smile as had been originally visited and wasted on me. And my sensing forthwith the allurement as well as the accursed fickleness of women, the ease with which, where beauty was their portion, they passed, with one and the same beckoning smile, from one to another. And no real fixation or special or exclusive interest intended. On the contrary, as I was seeing here and now. For had it not been but yesterday that Circe was smiling on me? And now this Levitt, handsome and daring, and behold, where am I? Stuck as with a knife, the same permanent in my very back!

Actually I stood agape, thinking could it be possible that she had cared so little for me that under my very eyes she could do this, myself there and then present, as she could all too plainly see? And yet, why not? Was I not a fool, an oaf, really, and he a dashing, daring, handsome cavalier? Had not the dish been offered to me, and had I partaken of it? Until from somewhere I could muster daring, aplomb, looks, means, had I any just right to complain?

I considered and considered, since instinctively I knew this to be one of the great problems of life, if not the sure and intended problem, far more important than Latin or Old English, for instance, or any technique or science. Also as to whom or what I should blame—Life—for my want of this or that—daring, et cetera—or my possibly too indifferent contemplation of possible forces and powers within myself. Yet with a knife like this in my ribs I could not think very clearly. More definitely, if anything I was moved by a reducing mixture of self as well as life pity—the state of man as well as myself—his as well as my own personal lacks, his as well as my own personal advantages, if any—our duties, our rights to despair or optimism. But to no avail, as I was to learn, since this was a field in which he who was called was to prosper maddeningly, whereas he who like myself was wanting in charm or skill, was to be cast aside.

And Levitt was so handsome that, whenever I saw him—on the street, in our room, on the football field, or where you will—I was full of admiration. He seemed so complete, magnetic, and so effective in the matter of achieving friendships, repute, and what not else. From the bottom of my heart I envied him, and constantly after his arrival I used to look at him and then at myself in the mirror after he was gone and ask myself what chance had I? For had he not come with two trunks and a bag in which were clothes such as I had never been able to boast of? More, in a short time, our room was a meeting-place for not only private football councils and the genial overtures of various fraternities who were frantically interested in him, but the councils of other friends on other matters: points of law, week-end trips to one town or another with or to see girls, and so on. So popular he seemed with a certain clever type of law student as well as these athletes and others that academically I took it as a good sign and one which made up for other and less valuable, as I saw it then, phases of his popularity.

But imagine, then, my chances with the young girl next door! He was so popular and had had so much experience with girls of all types that to engage the attention of any of them was scarcely a moment's work. One day, when I returned from the college library, there he was leaning over the fence, talking to her. And in a halfhour or so, and after I had sat in a part of the room where I might not be seen, he came back to report.

"Say, she's a cute little bitch, that!" (He was a profane youth, in a gay, almost meaningless way.) "She thinks she's going to string me along, I think, but she'll have to get up early enough in the morning to do that. Say, I'll just get a pinch of salt and put it on her little behind, and the next thing you know, I'll have her right in my hand, tight, just like that! She's a pippin, though, I'll admit that. Cute ain't the word, but she can't kid me. Although I don't think she does anything as yet," he added, meditatively, scratching his chin and surveying himself in the mirror preparatory to shaving, "still, I think she can be induced to," and he began to pull his shirt over his head.

Oh, woe!

"Why didn't you tell me you knew her?" he went on, reflectively, after he had begun shaving. "She said she had been trying to make up with you for a week but that you wouldn't have anything to do with her. Don't you like her? Or are you bashful?"

For the life of me, I could not help flushing, and he noticed it. "Well, I'm damned," he commented, "you're a funny. And for a little . . ." and then he stopped, a sudden, threatening anger in my eyes reducing the thought to nothing. After a period of apologetic silence, in which he completed his toilet, he ventured to add: "Well, she won't string me. She's very cute and sweet all right, but she's got to do business or quit. If I don't get away with her, I'll let you know."

And thereafter, I would see him lounging over the fence engaged in earnest conversation with her or chasing her in scurrying encounters, in one of which she lost her slipper, which he refused to give back for a day while it ornamented our bureau. A kiss was nothing when he managed to catch her, and then she would pout and disappear, seemingly angry, only to show by her smiles the next day that all was well. As this went on, I naturally grew distant and reserved, pretending that I did not see or care, and as he grew more successful he had less and less to say of his progress.

Did he, or did he not, are you thinking? I do not know for sure, but from one or more tell-tale signs I think he did. But I think from what I heard afterward from another source that it was no new thing with her, that for some little time before either he or I appeared on the scene, she had and did. But the prize was never mine.

CHAPTER LXIX

IN spite of this, there followed halcyon days crowded with college interests and novelties, which had I been more of a student and freer of the bite of beauty and the desire of the flesh, would have brought me as near to peace as one may come in this world. Being far from either student or philosopher or free of the lusts of living, or, indeed, of anything other than an immense and intense yearning which gave me little mental peace, I did not fare as well as I might. For there were so many things here, which in spite of my translation from a most unsatisfactory and from many points of view almost destructive state in Chicago, immediately set up new wants and new ambitions which served—and this in spite of such grateful thoughts as I could muster to oppose them— to contrast my condition even more sharply with themselves than had the great prosperities of Chicago with its great poverties. For, after all, in a world metropolis, such as even then Chicago was, one could find contrasts to wealth into which one could not too painfully sink and which served to assuage, for the time being at least, the pangs of deprivation and envy. But in this small world, sharp with imported levels and castes and God knows what prides and prejudices, there were no such sloughs to sink into, no vast neighbourhoods of which one might say: "Well, those here are no worse off than I am." Rather from this level of general, though very simple, comfort, new and biting contrasts arose, all the more sharp for their unfamiliarity.

Thus, I had never even heard of the college fraternities which now I found here; in short, almost nothing of college life, my reading of the same to the contrary notwithstanding. For it is not what one reads but what one lives that truly marks the mind. And here, as I found, the social segregations which owing to the varied amounts of money with which many students came, and on which they prided themselves, were inescapable and took on varied and at times brilliant forms. Thus, the Greek letter society entertainments and dances: the arbitrary and yet very real differentiation between freshmen, sophomores, juniors and seniors; the airs and distances of the latter, to say nothing of the airs and distances created by means or the lack of the same—and these in our young and gentle and so-called democratic or social republic! But so it was—as in Chicago and Warsaw—only sharper, I am sure. And they touched me to the quick, for I was, of course, in no least measure any part of them, though I will admit that with more audacity I might have been, in part anyhow. But I did not realise that at the time either.

Thus, I had not been there more than two or three weeks, or a month at the outside, when I began to realise, in a dim and uncertain way at first, that there were definite, and even secret, forces at work among all the newcomers which tended to sort them: first, and generally speaking, into the socially acceptable or unacceptable, and next into fitness for membership in various organisations which thereafter removed many from the current of ordinary sociability and groomed and aided them in social and educational ways in which the ordinary or non-fraternity element, which in itself was quite large, did not share. Also, I soon learned that if you joined a fraternity, you were thereafter generally spoken of as a fraternity man or "frat" and wore a pin, whereas if you did not, you were a plebeian or "pleb" and had no pin and no real standing in any social sense. You were just a student, nondescript and so of no real import to any of the above. Worse, or so I was led to believe by these whispering and seeking students, many professors belonged to one or another of these superior Greek letter societies and prided themselves on the fact. More, that the influence of these same societies, with their chapter houses, extended throughout all of the colleges and even the social and commercial life of the world outside, and therefore (mere youth palaver this) would aid one in later years. Indeed, these really piddling and meaningless organisations were then and there painted to me by those in favour of them and those who knew about them from the inside as ideal bonds of brotherhood which ended only with death! Imagine! And all who were "tapped" for membership here seemed to labour under the belief that they were thenceforth to derive inestimable benefits from these same brothers, because in the first place their being selected at all indicated or would bring to them a certain social fitness and adaptability of temperament which later on here and elsewhere would make them acceptable to their brother or prospective brother fraternity men the world over.

Need I say that no fraternity selected me? There was some rumour—I learned that later—that I had been or was still being seriously considered by the Delta Tau Deltas, assumedly a rather studious group here, but that I never was personally consulted I know. On the other hand, Levitt as well as a number of others with whom presently I was at least on nodding terms were immediately seized upon and presently began to show by their companionship, their exclusions and inclusions, where and how they stood. One felt it in nearly all personal contacts nearly everywhere. The reserve! The snobbery! Indeed, and as these first days showed, there was not only here but had been before ever college was reached, a perfect scramble for the more eligible youths—and among the women's Greek letter organisations, maidens—which, as I came to look at it afterwards, was not only petty but barren of any really valuable result, and so ridiculous.

Just the same, though, the social life of the college, and therefore, by reflex action, the social life of the town (the more exclusive social life, of course), was largely determined by the selections which the Greek letter societies made. For once the chapters were full, the élite of them set the pace in the social world. Their hops, dances, musicales, suppers and junkets of one kind and another were the all-to-be-desired centres of social activity. It is all very trivial, of course, when viewed in the large and from a philosophic standpoint, but viewed in little and as a part of the everyday life to which we were all subjected and by which most were judged and guided, it was not so pleasant. For one, I, when I once learned how these discriminations and adjustments were made—how one was selected for his looks or clothes or social connections and adaptability, another for his athletic prowess, a third for his money, a fourth for his educational superiority —was reduced as well as irritated and nonplussed. For being left out in this way argued so plainly—if not in one's own eyes, then in the eyes of others—that for lack of a little money, savoir faire, social experience and the like, one was not eligible for the supreme, or at least more select, of all college affairs. And this made one palpably conscious of the fact that here one was considered undesirable, good for some forms of contact perhaps, but not these. And hence and soon I found myself thinking that I was of no real importance here to anyone, destined to be taboo to these elements at work here or wherever else their influence might extend.

And say what one will, however trivial these matters may come to look in the course of any career in the stern, grim world outside, where force and swiftness of mind alone can make anybody, here in this cabined and clearly defined world, and where youth had the power to impinge upon youth in a trying and at times even brutal fashion, the result was not inconsiderable. It erected in one's mind the disturbing and reducing thought of caste as well as of favourable as well as unfavourable physical qualities, also of fair and unfair play in the working of nature itself. For here was I, lacking this and that, and hence and for no willed reasons of my own or greatly distinguishable errors on my part, out of it for good. For after a month or so, it was very plain. And yet, in the course of time, as I also saw and learned, various youths of various fraternities, and many non-fraternity men began by degrees to seek me out and to make friends with me on one personal ground and another. In part, this may have been due to the fact that this room now shared by Levitt and myself had become a meeting-place for his friends—many —and some of those who came to see him came to be friends of mine, and vice versa. And since these in no way rested on any local social base but were personal and final, they were good—but at that left me where I was before—in the main excluded.

To offset this, though, and by degrees, I fell in with a number of youths who, while they were interesting, were little if any better positioned than myself. They had no money, no entrée anywhere, and therefore did not count much locally, although to me all of them proved most interesting as individuals and at times companions. One of these whom I liked quite well, although he was not much mentally, was an earnest, undersized and meticulous law student by the name of Howard Hall, blond, light weight, and spare built, who shortly after my arrival took a very small hall bedroom on the floor above me and at once asserted —for reasons of private mental comfort, I am sure—that he could study so much better in a small, cool space than in a large, warm room. Such poverty-philosophies are amusing or pathetic, as the case may be. Like the Jews in history, the poor make a virtue of their necessities. But what of it? They really deceive no one, least of all themselves. As for myself, I was always for looking life in the eye as directly as possible, and in this case this subterfuge irritated me. At once, and as usual, I charged life then, as I do now, with loading the dice and playing favouritism, and with unbelievable cunning and cruelty. For just when was the least fillip of joy removed from Dives at the sight of Lazarus? I doubt if ever. Rather, as life is organised, Lazarus appears to be necessary to complete the picture. He is seemingly the only measure wherewith Dives may gauge his success, the true assurance of his prosperity.

In addition to his poverty, though, Hall had an impediment in his speech that promised to prevent his pleading before any jury. This suggested to me that necessarily he would be compelled to confine himself to gathering data and preparing cases, a line remunerative enough, no doubt, where one has sufficient subtlety or vision to seek out those loopholes by which pleaders before our so-called courts of justice can circumvent or bedevil the intended meaning of the law. Only Hall had no such intellect, as I could see. He was too snarled in social and moral scruples to begin with. One idea he had I rather admired. It was that, like Demosthenes, he could overcome the impediment in his speech by talking slowly and with a pebble in his mouth. And in consonance with this, he confessed to visiting remote and unfrequented open places, where alone and pebble in mouth he orated aloud. "And it's helping me, too," he once insisted. And later, and when we were much more intimate, he invited me to hear him, and although I was by no means impressed with his progress, I did not tell him so. I did not want to hurt his feelings.

Also, as I presently noted, he practised regularly with dumb-bells in order to develop his small chest, and together, at his urging, we set up a horizontal bar to keep ourselves in trim, for he easily converted me to this idea of exercise, since I needed it so much. The one thing that oppressed me not a little in connection with all this, though, was that he was so fearful of consumption, a plague that had killed others in his family. And by thinking and talking of it, he not only oppressed me at times, but I really believe strengthened his own fear that he could scarcely escape it. In sum, a frail youth, restricted as to cash, and who, if he succeeded in finishing his two years' course here, intended, as he said, to return to Michigan from whence he hailed and practise law in his home town.

But he never did practise law. At the age of twenty-four, and after he had studied some four or five years in law offices as well as college trying to prepare himself for life's sharp contests, he died, the victim of a constitution not sufficiently robust to endure the raw forces of life. But his struggles and hopes at the time! That small oil stove, bedroom, his lean purse, voice impediment, weak lungs! How indifferently, as I thought at the time, does man fare on this planet! How little, if at all, nature cares! How completely unimportant our presence or absence! As Carlyle once said of Nature: "We hae nay pairt or lot wie her or she wie us." And Goethe (accepting one of the remarks of Faust as his own) appeared to think the same.

There was another youth who arrived on the scene shortly after Levitt and I were fixed here: Russell Sutcliffe by name; a poet, philosopher, vegetarian, democrat, and student of modern nationalism, who, because of his high courage, ready and willing acceptance of the inequalities as well as the difficulties of life as things to be met and struggled with, if not conquered, interested me enormously and at once, and presently came to exercise a serene and broadening influence on me. So much so that I came to look on him as of more mental and ideally instructive as well as creative value to me than all other phases and persons of the university combined. In short, so appealing was he to me that to this day he stands out in my memory as fresh and pleasing as when I first saw him: the most intellectually sincere and valuable of all the students I met at college.

And how was it that we met? He came to solicit of me my

laundry, he being, as he said, the agent for an Indianapolis concern which through him, as agent and delivery wagon, as he laughingly explained, took and delivered all work promptly. Under his arm, sometimes on his head or back, was a large wicker basket in which he collected the bundles of his customers. But that warm, gay, smiling face! Those large, round, blue and friendly eyes! I took to him at once, as he to me, and in as little as five minutes, I think, we were as true and fast friends as ever we were to be. Physically, or exteriorly at least, he appeared to be of a spongy, soft-jointed, Bakstian type, of about the roundness and meatiness of a youthful Ingersoll, and with a head almost as round as a sphere. But mentally, how different, how stern, uncompromising and clean! But with good-natured and smiling eyes and mouth and a chin that would indicate defiance. By some industry or cleverness or politics the year before, he had managed to secure, as he now told me, the agency of the above-mentioned laundry, and by the aid of this, as well as a share in a vegetarian dining club which also he had helped to organise, he provided himself with the necessaries, if not exactly the comforts, of a college career. A sophomore, he was specialising in economics, sociology and philosophy. Whether he had any money from any other source I cannot recall, but I think not. Having won me over, I decided to introduce him to Hall and Levitt, both of whom proceeded to patronise him.

"That's a queer cuss, that fellow Sutcliffe," Levitt once observed to me. "Think of paying your way by collecting laundry! Not that I don't think it's a fine thing to do," he went on as I began to bristle, "I'd do it myself if I had to. But he's a sort of a bug on philosophy, isn't he? And reform. I heard him talking to you about vegetarianism the other day."

"Sure!" I replied. "He's a vegetarian, and he's part owner of the vegetarian dining club, but he's not exactly bugs about it. He laughs at some things in it just as you do. But he believes that people can live without meat and that it's wrong to kill any more animals than necessary. There may be something in it. I don't know."

"Oh, these nuts! There's no end to them!" was Levitt's material reply. And I had to smile, for I liked him, too. Innately generous and gladly giving Sutcliffe his laundry, still he could not help talking thus. And as for Hall, while not exactly approving of Sutcliffe's other-worldliness, still he did not wholly disapprove of him either.

"He's a queer fellow, isn't he?" he said to me one day. "Studying philosophy, isn't he? Well, he looks like a philosopher. Does he make anything out of the laundry business?"

"His living," I replied, "or nearly so."

"George, I wish I could get hold of something like that! I'd do it if I thought I could pay my way."

But he had neither the industry nor the social charm, and hence persuasiveness, to put through so practical an enterprise. He was not popular with students, whereas Sutcliffe was. And besides, I could not see Hall as a charming figure in the capacity of working to support himself, whereas Sutcliffe seemed to me nothing less than an ornament in the medley of pleasing and at times unpleasing features of college life.

Sutcliffe was particularly interested in philosophy and the necessary social as well as physical and other scientific data on which it rests. He was tireless in his efforts at ferreting out the social anachronisms and idiosyncrasies of life and its arrangements: chemical, physical, biological. An omnivorous reader, he was already stuffed with data of a wide variety which he was trying to classify in his own mind and from the same deduce some conclusions of his own. Just then, as he said, he was immensely interested in not only the naturalism of Spencer, Huxley, Darwin, Alfred Russel Wallace, Lecky, Draper and others, but had just found and was considering the religio-social panaceas of Tolstoi. "What To Do" as well as some other pamphlets were already in the small and booky room which he occupied in a barracks-like college rooming house. And here, after perhaps a week or two of more or less casual contacts, we began to meet and talk and read together, because, forsooth, I saw in him a most worthy preceptor of the Greek academy type and myself as a neophyte or disciple.

CHAPTER LXX

WHENEVER I think of Sutcliffe, I think of him as one does of a rare and good book or a fine picture or a beautiful poem. His was a delicate, finely attuned, high-motived, and yet solidly self-controlled personality. As a passionist or hedonist, he was as nothing at all—a failure. I doubt whether the feminine element moved him more than a minute fraction in all his moods which led to actions. But as a student and an idealist in the best sense of the words—a fine, studious, Spinoza-like personality, to whom the riddle of life, and particularly the riddle and muddle of social organisation or disorganisation (want, vice, poverty, crime) seems something which might be deciphered in the light and by the aid of altruism—he was illuminating and most stimulating. Generous youth! I have often wondered what became of him and his dreams. I never had but one letter from him after he left college, and that years after, when I was an editor and he wrote to tell me that he had seen my name and approved of my work. Also, he told me that then he was secretary of something or other under the government—some Indian agency or other, with various scientific extensions and privileges, but even so, he expressed himself as dubious of the import, other than in a very temporary sense, of either science or philosophy. As I recall the letter now, it carried a phrase: "the deeps to which the plumb-lines of philosophy or science will never sink; the heights to which their eager arrows will never fly." Prophet or failure? Which?

At any rate, in these opening days, Sutcliffe was really a comfort to me philosophically and helped me to bear somewhat more gracefully than I ordinarily would have the envies, despairs, unrests and self-disapprobations with which I was afflicted. He was tender and loving toward the errors and ills of life, and from the very beginning endeavoured to turn my ability and taste, such as it was, into the line of altruistic inquiry and, if need be subsequently, work. Reading "What To Do" aloud, we discussed together all of Tolstoi's theories and questioned somewhat whether they were applicable or workable, human nature being what it was and Darwin's "Survival of the Fittest" having sunk deep. Nevertheless and notwithstanding, he was also keen to discover whether or not the ills of society could be healed, since, as he insisted, there had been some progress, and might there not be more? Also he was inclined to believe—as what kindly disposed philosopher is not?—that what is needed is less lust, less hate, less vanity, and less of the other sins of appetite and aspiration with which we find nature endowed, but what he could not clear up for himself was how they were to be done away with. Tolstoi, in his small volume, preached a return to simple, normal labour to the end of self-sustenance merely and also of refusing to strike back when imposed upon: the ancient doctrine of non-resistance. Sutcliffe saw (or appeared to), though, that many—yea, most—persons are avid, selfish, hungry, envious. How was one to get them to accept the Tolstoian point of view, to desire naturally that which they did not naturally desire: a very fine point in chemistry and biology, as you may well guess, and which neither he nor I could solve.

An interesting phase of this relationship, as expressed by these weekly contacts or evening reading, was that opposite the wooden barracks in which he lived—from the rear and looking out of one of his windows—were a number of the better town homes and college fraternity clubs, wherein regularly on the nights we met together were social doings of a more or less elaborate character, music and dancing of those more socially favoured, if no more inclined, than ourselves. And though for myself I was always serious enough about the intellectual work in hand at the moment, nevertheless the sound of this music as well as the sight of these dancers, visible through open windows on pleasant fall and spring evenings, was sufficient to flagellate my other eager and studious impulses. Ah, to forget for the moment the solemn and often quite depressing considerations of the ills and compulsions of man! To turn freely and indifferently to pleasure! To ignore for the time being the weak, the tangled, the perhaps unsolvable, and consider, or rather sensate without consideration, those who were ideally and joyfully functioning as toys infused by nature with the power of action and the sensations of pleasure! And noting this one evening, seeing me lounging wistfully near a window where I could both see and hear these revelries the while I listened to him read or concentrated, or tried to, on some of his social propositions, he paused long enough to comment: "It is hard, isn't it?" Although instantly I understood, I was neither simple nor honest enough to reply "Yes," but said rather: "What is hard?" "That," he replied, motioning in the direction of the music. "I myself feel it. You probably more so. But I still feel that there is some justification for standing out against the calls of pleasure. It cannot be an end in itself, not in the world as it is to-day, and if that is the case, why not look on these evenings as one of our necessary sacrifices?" I looked at him, flushing and ashamed, for I respected him deeply. And on me he bent a helpful and consoling smile. Yet in me was not wholly stilled the yearning which these gaieties evoked.

While sometimes I feel as though I ought to apologise for my attitude at this time, at other times I do not, for I was not one for waiting. No idea of a far-off supremacy, however much it might occupy my mind as a probability or necessity, had anything to do with my love of and eagerness for life at the moment. I wanted to live now as I saw others living, and the fact that I could not was a gnawing irritation. I do not believe any human being ever watched the pleasures of others with a hungrier eye, or by reason of a vivid imagination, more grievously exaggerated their import. I say "exaggerated," and yet I do not know that I mean that exactly. Exaggerated, perhaps, to those to whom social show places and social show mean nothing. But suppose, for some inexplicable reason—a flaw in your temperament, if you please —the beauty of women, the exotic artistries of the drawing-room, and all the paraphernalia which relates to sex in its struggles to fascinate and conquer, completely fill your eye? Suppose at a certain period, life takes its meaning—what little it has—from the hope of conquest in connection with women, and that all the machinery and artistry connected therewith are practically beyond your reach and therefore beyond your experience, and you see it as a shimmering mirage passing alluringly in the distance? And suppose that you feel yourself to be temperamentally defective and that the best of life is scurrying by, a gay rout of Pierrot and Columbine? Then what?

Never in my life have I been more heart hungry—or sex-hungry, if you will—than I was then, and never, as I soon began to discover when the college activities fell into their stride, was I so completely out of almost everything. This small town, as it then seemed to me, was so full of gay pictures of youths and maidens interested in each other. I do not mean to say that the thought of sex was predominant in every case nor any special group, but there was a great deal of it. A kind of fever for dancing, supping late, serenading and junketing at week-ends, was in the air. Dressing for evening parties and functions of all kinds was almost the order of the day in some houses. A kind of fever to lead in the matter of sex triumphs dominated some of these youths, Levitt, for one. Therefore, the world that I beheld seemed all a-tingle with sex love in my eyes, and the thing that pained me most was that there was no least indication that I would ever have the least taste of all that I most craved and envied.

And practically I did not, nothing at all during the time that I was there. For although by a little cleverness or subterfuge, or both perhaps, I might have secured the price of a dress suit and other clothes, either from my mother or Miss Fielding, I did not consider it fair so to do, even though I was so resentful. Also, while it was true that by reason of a little more courage I might have satisfied myself with the sympathy and even affection of one or another of the less ambitious and pretentious types of girls about this college town—the girl next door, for instance, who still occasionally manifested an interest in me—still that was not anything which I could develop since I simply did not have it. And in consequence, while there were others craving a richer state, I was really craving most the affection and companionship of a truly beautiful girl, and that, as I was here, I could not acquire. Naturally, I laid it to the want of clothes and of formal introductions, whereas more audacity would have eased my distress quite swiftly. And as if to convince me that the first was true, I was compelled before the year was over to make use of reconstructed clothes: an overcoat, for instance, made over from one of my brother Paul's, and collars, ties and

413

socks which Paul and Eleanor's husband had discarded and sent home.

But the misery of this type of youthful brooding! The marvels of beauty and joys of tender intimacy that in connection with every photograph of a pretty girl standing upon some student's table or hanging upon his wall—sister, cousin, or sweetheart—I conjured up! The sense of permanently defeated dreams and aspirations that pervaded me! For was not there and then the proper love-time, if not playtime, and was I, I, making any use of the same? Was I not being defeated? Defrauded? Worse, Levitt was the worst type of room-mate for me, for he was constantly pluming himself on his intimacies, his varietistic conquests, the cleverness and beauty of those who succumbed to him. In his own home town (of his standing in which he was always boasting), and neighbouring cities as well, he had been (to hear him tell about it) and still was a kind of devil among the girls, a small-town Don Juan. And no doubt there was a great deal of truth in what he said. More, and always, he talked of girls in that easy, intimate way used only by those youths who successfully prosecute affairs of this type. (And had I not seen him with one whom I craved?) This one was "a little sport"; that one a "peach"; a third "a regular little devil"; a fourth "a bitch." Letters came for him superscribed in the most affectionate way and he left them carelessly lying about. Every Saturday and Sunday, unless football or other duties claimed him, he devoted to a trip, either alone or with other worthies of his ilk, to his home town or to Indianapolis or Louisville, girls, girls, girls his companions. According to him, also, all of these girls yielded to him joyfully. His, as he indicated, was always the enticing and conquering personality. Not with any would he trifle unless they yielded.

For one like myself who was sex-hungry, it was inexpressibly painful, and kept so as is a wound by irritation. I listened to him greedily, enviously, and wished myself as handsome, bold, magnetic, devil-may-care. In fact, I used to walk about, thinking of all I was missing, looking at lamp-lighted windows and wondering what pleasures might be concealed behind drawn curtains. And often after he was gone to an interesting evening affair and I was left to my books, as it were, I would stand by my window and look out on the moonlit yards or rain-washed streets and ask myself what I was to do, how proceed. For this period, my one escape was through books, my college and other studies, and to these I turned in a defeated if not, as I saw it afterwards, unprofitable way. Since I could not play, I read and learned.

CHAPTER LXXI

BE that as it may, these two youths, Hall and Sutcliffe, with
Levitt as a counter-irritant, as it were, exercised a
considerable influence over me and caused me to seek for the
wellsprings of life and human actions more carefully than I
ever had before. Hall, as I have said, was such a spindling
little soul, with an eagerness for life which matched my own
at points; at others we diverged widely. Sutcliffe, serene and
introspective, like a Hindoo seer or a cat outside a mouse-hole,
waiting for the secret or meaning of life to pop out, and on
which he could seize, was of the utmost in the way of mental
fascination and development for me. He was so tutor-like in
some of his approaches, seeing me for what I was, I suppose,
and what I needed, uninformed and seeking for knowledge in
others. He it was, even more than Miss Fielding, who tried
to make clear to me that this college world was little more
than a realm in which one might find oneself intellectually—
if one had an intellect—a table spread with good things of
which one could partake if one had an appetite. The curriculum—a mere bill of fare. The professors and instructors—
waiters who served what was provided but who could neither
eat nor digest for you. So, by degrees, I came to think of
him as the only true instructor I had, the one from whom I
could and did gain most.

My relationship with Hall, on the other hand, took the
form of long walks and talks and certain courting and sex
expeditions which were, in the main, futile. One of these,
as I would like to pause here to report, the outcropping of
a sex hunger by no means appeased, led us once far into the
country to a certain spelling bee of which Hall had heard
and where we secretly hoped—both of us, I am sure—to impress the country maidens present by reason of our superiority
to the country youths who could not, so we reasoned, hope to
compete with our city-bred ways. An ignoble mission!

As a matter of fact, though, our surmise was correct, and before the evening was over, we managed to make friends with two country maids to whom we talked constantly and who on the way home invited us to call again. There our ways parted, and I on my part being somewhat taken by the ways and airs of the one I had met—a country belle of laughing and flirtatious ways—pursued her during several weeks, walking out once or twice weekly until she (sensing, I am sure, that all I desired was an easy and quick sex victory whereas she was more normally interested in a true and gallant admirer who would presently declare his love and propose marriage) told me at the end of the third or fourth visit that I would better not call again—a rebuke which served me right but did not, the circumstances being what they were, reduce me as much as it otherwise might have. The walk was long and my interest not really vital. As I learned afterward from Hall himself, who was a quite honest and self-criticising sort, he had suffered the same fate and for much the same reason.

In regard to this region itself, having no social connections of any importance to occupy our time, we did endless exploring, and that for the very good reason that it was a decidedly remarkable country to explore. One or two counties, as we soon learned, were practically underlain with caves, fantastic and tortuous aisles, pits and caverns through which, in one instance at least, ran an underground river and in which eyeless fish were said to live. (What endless reaches of time must have been required to do away with their eyes!) On more than one occasion, in walking across a field about Bloomington, I either accidentally or deliberately put my foot through a small opening in the grass, and kicking and digging at it to see what it amounted to, finally succeeded in either falling or sinking to my knee or waist before I could extricate myself. Subsequent investigation invariably showed a runway leading into what was probably one of the branching arms of one or another of the various caves hereabouts, whether previously explored or not I never knew. And once Hall and I had the disturbing experience of being lost in a cave, and in which he came very near dying of heart failure and from which I took a haunting dream which caused me to wake at night for a long period thereafter.

Every fall and spring, expeditions were organised by the

geological department of the university for the purpose of visiting these caves with a view to studying the rock formations, which were of peculiar and often magnificent and even astounding proportions and character. Giant stalagmites and stalactites of lime rose from the floor or fell from the ceiling, as the case might be, forming not infrequently yellow columns of lime which looked not unlike sulphur. Tall, pointed, arched caverns frequently led away for so great a distance as eight hundred or a thousand feet, giving the impression of correct if not exactly tremendous cathedral aisles. The pits, broad chambers, corkscrew declivities and the like were so frequent as to be confusing, and in one place one could pause with a candle while others went ahead only to detect each other later, perhaps a hundred or so feet apart in a perpendicular line, the voices of those below and above sounding hollowly as they hailed each other through great cracks of stone. Several chambers through which the river flowed impressed me tremendously by their height, breadth and blackness and the sound of the darksome water gurgling hollowly under the vaulted roofs.

On the advice of Sutcliffe, Hall and I joined one of these expeditions, the equipment being an old suit, a half-dozen or more candles of good length—there were no treacherous draughts in these caves—and lunch. The leaders carried torches with short handles. I think as many as twenty or twenty-five joined on this first expedition, and we had a glorious time listening to the instructive remarks of the geologist, feeling our way about narrow ledges and through bodytight openings which almost invariably gave into spacious chambers or passageways. Once we all sat on a large natural bench or chair, and another time dropped blazing horns of oiled paper down a pit, into which they fell and fell without interruption until they became minute specks of light and disappeared. The geologist explained that the state of the air might quickly reduce the flame to a mere pin-point as it fell.

Not satisfied with following the crowd, though, Hall and I decided on another occasion to explore the cave alone. We had seen much, but as the geologist had explained, there were several routes for which there was not time. It was one of these turning to the right perhaps a thousand feet from the main entrance that interested us. We calculated beforehand that it might be true that there was danger of getting lost and that twenty were better able to care for themselves than two, yet we decided we could manage it. Explorers, no less! Our plan was to take half a dozen candles and a dozen or more balls of stout twine which, once we had passed the great opening cavern, a long, broad hall, we would fasten to something and play out, taking it up again as we decided to investigate this or that side route or passage along our main course. And this would have been well enough if we had had the sense to stick to our plan. Once we had entered the cave, though, and the novelty of stillness and darkness having worn off, we began to grow bolder. By long passages and spiral ways and amazingly complicated turns, we used up our twine and tied the ends of the balls together as we went on. Finally, after we had gone as far as twelve or fifteen balls would permit, we came to a long, narrow, unbroken passage which was, for all the world, like the side aisle of a cathedral and which, since it was so direct, we decided to explore, string or no string, since we could always come back to the end of it and find our twine.

This, unfortunately, was where we made our mistake, for at the end of it was a flat wall, with, however, sufficient bits of projecting stone on its face to form a ladder of sorts. This we decided to ascend in order to see if there was an opening at the top. It was Hall who took the initiative in this matter, and, candle fastened to the front of his hat, climbed up and for a moment or two disappeared. Then, with an enthusiastic "Oh, say!" he suddenly put his head back to announce that just above was an immense chamber hidden by the ledge over which he had disappeared and that in it a plain of smooth rock and sand led down to the shores of an underground river, and that the roof was smooth and black. "Come on up!" he yelled. "You never saw anything like it! This is the best yet!"

I needed no urging but climbed up and through, setting my candle down on the other side but picking it up again as I stood up to survey the sepulchral immensity, which lit by the thin gold flames of our candles seemed to recede and close in as the eye moved from space to space. I have seen many impressive things in my time, but none more impressive than this long, dark underground chamber, through which, as Hall had said, was audibly flowing an underground river, spread out lake fashion and suggesting the silent reaches of the river Styx. It was all so dark, the flames of our candles making ghostly light spots. The beach approaching it was gently sloping and sandy, and from somewhere came a sipping and gurgling, mysterious and remote. We had not, as we recalled, been here before. Lighting one of the last of our remaining candles and putting it down where I stood, to mark the place of our entry, we went to the river brink. There we separated, Hall following the bank downstream and I up, and both marvelling at the ages of time during which this river must have flowed here in silence, unseen perhaps by human eyes, and at the splendour of this cavernous chamber which might have been the throne room of an underworld king. All sorts of weird and fantastic fancies fluttered through my brain, and I finally sat down on the shore, watching Hall's light in the distance, the better to consume the wonder of it all.

After a while, though, he called for me to come and see where the river obviously debouched into a rock and disappeared, for a sheer wall seemed to end its further progress in that direction, though a bit of paper cast on the water showed that it went farther, for it disappeared. And so, fascinated, we talked of holding a great festival in here and of fishing one day for eyeless fishes. Finally we decided it was about time to return, though so loath were we to leave that we took laggard steps toward our sign candle. Reaching it, we concluded that there was no mystery as to our whereabouts, for there was the hole through which we had entered, close to the candle, and into this Hall began to descend. But as he did so, he suddenly exclaimed: "Say, this doesn't look like the place we came out of. That big aisle isn't there, and this goes off into another big room."

I stopped, a chill of fear passing over me, for by now we were reduced to three candles all told, and our lunch had been consumed some time before. But I tried to maintain an even tone as I said: "But it must be! That's the hole we came out of."

"But it isn't, I tell you!" he said, climbing back, his own voice shaking a little. "That's a stony passage that divides in three or four directions, and there's a big room just beyond. That other was a straight aisle."

"Let me see!" I exclaimed, a cold sweat exuding from my brow, and I climbed down only to find it so. The place was jagged, diffuse, and went off in unknown directions.

Never in my life have I been seized with a colder chill. I climbed out quickly, knowing well that we must be near the spot, and yet where was it? Had I moved after setting down my candle? If so, in which direction had I moved? To my intense relief, I saw another hole considerably to the right of the one out of which I had just emerged and which appeared likely to be the one. Ah, yes, that was it! There were two holes and we had mistaken the second for the first. So I held my candle in that to see if it bore any resemblance to the flat wall we had scaled. There was a wall of sorts, but different, not so sheer, more flat and sliding, as I discovered on descending cautiously, and going down and down, into what depths? But no least sign of a Gothic aisle!

Once more, that sickening sense of impending disaster, the terror of darkness, loneliness, possibly starvation, who might say? For why should anyone find us, and when? We had not told anyone. And more, even had we been seen coming here, how would they track us to this hall, and when people did not come here to explore every day, or every ten days for that matter? At best it was a trying business, unless one had a taste for it, and in the meantime here we might sit in loneliness and darkness, our food and candles gone, not knowing night from day, and waiting. Never before in my life, as you may guess, had I entered upon such a soul-searching moment. Death, which in youth is so important as the threatened interruption of an appointed cycle of experience which may hold the most intense delights and glories, stared me out of countenance in its heavy, relentless way. The fortuitousness of life, its accidental and indifferent character, loomed tense and immense.

"What shall we do?" asked Hall, in a thin, tremulous falsetto, as announcing my discovery and coming out again I stood beside him, tremulous and dismayed. As for him, he had already lost his head, and frail and nervous, was wringing his hands in the dim light, the immense blackness and the dark river behind him. "What shall we do? We're lost! My God!"

"Oh, no, we're not lost," I replied, with an assumption of

courage and superiority which I did not feel. "We came in through a hole somewhere along here, and it must be here. It must!" My own voice was shaky. "I put the candle down right there!" I added.

I bent over and pointed to the spot, then with the candle followed the wall some distance away until I came to another hole, quite large, which was plainly not the one we were seeking. I could see that after ten steps. Hall also had gone trembling along the wall in the other direction and returned to say that he could find no way out there. Suddenly he sat down in front of me, quite exhausted from fright, and said: "What shall we do? What *shall* we do?"

I have no desire to boast—I was wet with sweat myself—but I went along the wall again and down into the first hole. It was not the one. I came back and tried to think, and in doing so I sat down, as much from weakness as anything else. I was painting to myself all of the terrors which being lost in here involved. As I did so, it occurred to me to look again at the wall in the dim light furnished by our two candles, and as I did so I noticed a low projecting shelf or tongue of dark stone, very low and projecting enough to indicate that there was a shelf, not ordinarily noticeable when you were standing up. I jumped up and went over to it, dropping to my knees and then on to my stomach to look under it. True enough, there was a hole under that stone, but was it *the* one or another deception? I worked my way under and noticed a sheer wall much like the one we had climbed.

"Here it is!" I shouted. "It's under here!" and backing out, turned around to push myself in feet first.

"Oh, do be careful!" called Hall, coming over. "Do be sure where you're going!"

I went cautiously enough while he held a candle above me, fixing my feet firmly as I went for fear of slipping into an abyss below, but once at the bottom noted the long, narrow, high-pointed aisle. I shouted and almost danced for joy. And after me he scrambled, pale as a ghost, the two of us trembling like frightened rabbits. I recall also that I tried to pretend that I was not really frightened, but had anyone seen me scuttling along the long aisle, breathing heavily and stumbling here and there, he would have known that had it been possible to run out of that cave, I would have. But between us lay all of a mile of twistings and turnings, ascents and descents, and places where one crawled through small holes on one's belly or squeezed through narrow slits which a stout man could not have negotiated. And worse, at one point a new and final terror confronted me. For a long passage, which as we had entered had seemed straight enough, now on returning showed that we had not noticed two others which joined with it at this point and now appeared as three separate routes which might lead out. But which one? For to complicate matters just then, the string we had so carefully laid and were now following back ended. Apparently it had been broken and pulled along. But had it? Might not a passing animal have dragged and broken it? A German might have imagined a *Poltergeist* at work—a demon of mischief. Half German myself, I began to think of evil spirits, Jinns, those German imps of the perverse, for who could have broken and taken that string? Had we unconsciously, we asked ourselves, pulled it too hard? Our plan had been to lay it loosely. Or had someone come in and stumbled over it and taken it up? We dropped to our knees and began feeling the floor with our hands, now up this aisle, now up that.

"If ever I get out of here," I said, feelingly, "I'll never go in another cave as long as I live!" (A broken promise.)

"What damned fools we were to come in here, anyhow, without telling anyone!" grumbled Hall. "God, what awful fools!"

Up each passageway we crawled, seeking feelingly, in the true sense of the word. At last, in the extreme right passage, about one hundred feet from where it ended, we found the other end of twine. Only, and just then, the horrible thought —was this truly our string? For the passage ahead was so long, dark, difficult. So instead of skeining it up as we had up to this point, we let it lie, since we might need to return. At the end of some eight hundred yards, though—and oh, so weak!—a dim light, a very feeble ray, like one of the new concealed arc lights of the time. Gaily, madly, stumbling over stones and falling here and there, we scuttled toward it, eventually emerging through the small hole which had admitted us and which gave out upon a level field of green, late grass, on one corner of which the evening sun was still shining. That sun! Its light! The feeling of immense relief, almost prayerful gratitude! For now we were out—a red sun in the west. We threw ourselves on the grass and shouted for joy. Gone the fear of death, of possible hunger or loneliness, like a dream that had never been. Here, in this delightful sun, with the grass still green and evening cottage fires detectable by their smokes in the distance, we sat and sighed and laughed and congratulated ourselves. Behind and below us was this great cave, which some said extended for all of sixty or seventy miles in various directions—no one really knew. Somewhere in there was the dark river, with its eyeless fishes, and the great chambers, many of them, no doubt, more magnificent than those we had seen. But we did not want to go back, ever. We said it over and over, only adding: "Gee, what an experience!"

And for years thereafter—until Hall's death—we talked or wrote of this in letters, and proudly. It had become by then a great adventure, *our* great adventure. But with no particular emphasis on our terror, rather mere embellishments of the terrors we had so bravely met and overcome. It is of such stuff that at least one hero is made—myself, no less.

CHAPTER LXXII

ONE of the amusing things in connection with this college spectacle—and I trust the reader will not assume that I am trying to be ribald, for I am not—was the collection of professors, their wives, their ambitions, and their work. Since I was in at least six or seven classes, and since, lamb-like enough, I went to the various professorial functions to which I, in common with all other under-classmen, was invited —and, according to custom, was expected to attend—I saw much of this life, and while admiring it from the point of view of its seeming comfort and leisurely ease, I could not help smiling at the stagy seriousness of most of it. It was so ultra-cultural, so to speak, and so cautious. This whole business of living was taken, not with a grain of salt but with a protective armour of propriety. What will people say? might have been run up as a fire sign over the entire college world. One could feel the heavy pressure of those moral and religious standards which then dominated the Middle West and which exacted the last jot and tithe in the matter of exterior conformity and mental preciseness. All were here, presumably, to think original thoughts, or at least to make the attempt, yet if anyone had really dared . . .! And concerning this particular fact, I was feeling that ethically and morally, in the matter of thoughts as well as deeds, I was, in the true sense of the word, an intransigent, and worse, one who was slyly concealing his true thoughts and intentions, whereas these various people were honest and perhaps more valuable to life in general because so deeply convinced of the truth and import of various moral things, and so earnestly and happily living. I was to learn differently in the course of time, but this did not alter the feeling of scoundrelism on the part of myself as I contemplated them and considered myself and what I thought.

Of the professors, one, though, who was most amusing to me—and whose classes I attended—was Arthur Peddoe Gates,

Litt.D., Ph.D., an osseous, skeleton-like creature, who taught English Literature, Anglo-Saxon, and the Study of Words. An eccentric and tense scholar if ever there was one—Don Scotus no less. As my father to religion, so this man to bookish knowledge. A library to him was the same as a cathedral to a devotee. I can see him now, always carrying one or more large volumes which seemed too heavy for him, so frail, gaunt and emaciated was he—a slave of the midnight lamp. I truly believe this man toiled by night as well as by day, trying to extract wisdom and understanding from his tomes, when the least gift of imagination, the tiniest spark, would have saved him years of toil. In a small, kempt cottage it was that he lived, very carefully furnished according to college standards, with books and Copley prints and plaster statuary freely distributed, and supervised by a pale and housewifely wife who looked after him and two children. He gave "literary evenings," at which he read Shakespeare and even acted him, abominably, I thought. But his belief in himself and his love of literature was high, and I am only sorry he had no more imagination. Actually, I think he had toiled so hard in his youth under really poverty-stricken conditions to get where he was that his constitution had been more or less undermined. Possibly, too, a better mind. At any rate, only by what process I cannot guess—the desire to do something for a complete ignoramus—he conceived of a certain friendship for me and after his last morning class, of which I was one, seemed to like to walk home with me and talk as he went. And indeed I listened and asked question after question, until at times, I am sure, he would have been glad to get rid of me. Learning by question was my great forte.

But such love of what might be called the mere technique of scholarship was most pathetic. I remember that at the time the first edition of the ten-volume Century Dictionary was coming out. Nothing could excel this man's interest in and even excitement over the long and careful explanations of derivations and meanings of various words therein. Thrilled was no name! He grew tremulous, in classroom and out, as he contemplated or thought of these various volumes, which arrived one by one over a period of time at his classroom, and which he fairly hung over with outspread, worshipful palms and popping eyes. He had one word—"copious"—which he

426

used over and over. This was so "copious"; that so "copious."
I remember seeing him bend over an open page of this dictionary, his hollow-set and yet popping eyes gleaming with an
ascetic fire as he rubbed his hands as might a freezing man
over a fire or a hungry one over a feast, and exclaimed: "It is
so copious in its presentation of the various shades of meaning,
so copious! Positively it is a delight to search out the history
of words here! One feels so amply repaid!" (Good heavens,
I thought, this man is mad on the subject of dictionaries!)
And in the matter of encyclopædias and thesauri, he was
even worse. I remember greeting him one windy November
evening just outside one of the two bookstores of the city,
where the lights were gleaming and students hustling by,
and where seeing me he paused to say a word. He was just
emerging from the store, under his arm a bundle of books,
new purchases. He smiled, for although I was not one who
valued dictionaries too greatly, still I was civil and attentive
and interested. More, I think he had come to feel in me a
sympathy for if not pleasure in his weakness. And so . . .
"I have just made two such interesting purchases," he paused
to say. "These two dictionaries. Most useful! This one
has such a copious glossary." He rearranged his packages,
the books not being wrapped, and revealed "The Geography
of the Ancient World" and "A Larger Classical Dictionary,
with Maps and Illustrations," the latter a most imposing affair
printed on very thin paper and bound in red leather. His
eyes had the glint of a hungry gourmet as he thumbed the
pages. He seemed like a half-starved wastrel viewing a
feast through a window. Fraternally, even, he told me who
the editors were and what the price was. I think he must
have imagined that I was intensely interested in these matters,
when as a matter of fact the mere thought of them gave me a
kind of brain-ache.

But if he was queer in one way, spindling along with his
endless tomes, his associate—under whom, by the way, I took
no work—was even more so. I gained my knowledge of him
only by outside observation, going once or twice to his house
to hear him read, hearing him lecture once, and listening
to the astounding compliments paid by others to his scholarship
and his genius. But scholarship, after all, can be a rum and
dry thing. Like machinery, it seems to be related to quantity

in mental productiveness or invention, not quality, and yet in the main it is little more than an aimless garnering stored eventually in the dry, dusty bins of libraries which no one has the heart to examine and which eventually rots under the dust of new days and new technicalities. Or perhaps it is like the savings of a man who lays up much money in order to leave it to his spendthrift children who do not understand its value at all.

Be that as it may, here was a youth who at the age of twenty-two had read—or so I believed—all the literary treasures of not only the English but all other languages. His scholarship was so profound that all we numbskull freshmen stood in awe of him as much as if he had conquered Europe or penetrated to the Oxus. He was tall, frail, graceful, a willowy, candle-waxy man, or boy really, with a head that hung like a great, heavy flower on a thin stem. His brow was sentiently protuberant, a veritable dome or belly of thought, thatched with pale, greenish-brown hair that floated and curled and fell in graceful wisps. Also, his hands were so pale, so long, so graceful, and his nose, chin and cheek-bones so waxy-white, that they resembled old ivory. Packed and jammed with culture, he even appeared to exude it. Bustling collegeward, his long legs giving slightly at the knees, his head bent, his soft black hat only partially concealing his curly hair, one arm akimbo under splendid books, his frock coat-tails swaying in a dignified way, the total effect of him was to make one feel that culture was the be-all and end-all and that mere money —its possession—was a degradation and even a crime. Personally, I sensed him as a youth who had been reared under the most refined, and even artistically exotic, conditions; as though his parents must have loved culture and made him read important books at say the age of five or earlier—although exactly why I thought this I cannot say. But another thought that haunted me in connection with him was this: Exactly when, if not where, had he begun to gather this vast store of knowledge? And—thinking of myself, of course—how could an ordinary mortal like myself ever hope to cope with a brain that took to books as a musical genius takes to music, at say the age of two or three. "Johnny Boston-Beans" could have nothing on him! He was an intellectual giant, a high-flying condor of literature, soaring always at the topmast altitude of thought. His eyes, as I saw them, burned with a sacred lustre, his presence suggested not only a sacerdotal devotion to supreme thought but an equal remoteness from ordinary, humdrum reality. In short, and to me at least, he breathed of academic shades and cloistered windows, and I am not exaggerating this description one jot.

Well, Walter Deming Willikus, Ph.D., Litt.D., etc. (we will call him) was a graduate of this university, but like some of its professors, had done post-graduate work at Princeton and Harvard. He taught English Literature first year and had classes amazing for size, the largest of any at college. Also he lived in a small pea-green house near the campus with a thin, intellectual girl—he had just married her—who was so frail that she appeared to be a mere rumour of a woman, an artistic abstraction. Yet a month or so before I arrived, she had had a baby. Like many of the others—the more successful professors—this same Willikus held literary or artistic or musical evenings, and by the ever kindly Sutcliffe I was piloted there once or twice, as also elsewhere, to have my mind as well as my knowledge of the social colour of this college broadened. He thought it would be good for me. At the same time, he giggled most cheerfully as he insisted on this. Just the same, I was never more depressed intellectually by anyone in all my life. Not that I condemned intellectuality or scholarship, but I was so reduced by it. Ah, if only I had been born with a taste for heavy books! Ah, if only my mind had been such that I could plunge into anything and everything and understand it! Damn! I actually grieved as I thought of my dopy inefficiencies, my inability to grasp mathematical, economical and scientific abstrusities, to say nothing of such a commonplace as grammar. What the devil was the matter with me, anyhow?

The upshot of all this, though, was that one of the most disturbing memories I took from college and retained for years was that there were living and walking around such stupendous compendiums of knowledge as this and compared to which such brains as mine were mere feathers. I asked myself over and over: Why work in stores and factories when, could I but concentrate and think as did Willikus, I might (maybe) be like him, surrounded by all of the refinements of intellectual and college life? The delight of living in such a refined and nobly intellectual world! Ah, why was I born to be a dub? Later I heard that he had gone to Ann Arbor, then to Princeton. Still more years later, I read of him as a lecturer on art and life, speaking to large audiences and writing for *The Ladies' Home Journal* and *The Atlantic Monthly*. And by those things I was more impressed. Yet once again I saw him. It was in the Lenox Library in New York. He was still poring over books, and again I was awed, only not quite so much. For by that time a number of things had happened. I had studied, travelled and read. Five years later, I finally ventured to read one of his effusions. It was, as I sensed it then, scholastic, intellectual, and from the point of view of traditional learning profound, but not otherwise. For of newness, strangeness, power, revelation, how little! In short, his work was plainly like he was: exotic, insubstantial, full of the mere repetition of great thoughts. Then and there he vanished—not with an arresting detonation but as mist vanishes before heat and light, the light and heat of the strong, ordinary, creeping, grinding life that I had come to know. And I smiled, but not at him, only at myself. And with reason.

CHAPTER LXXIII

ANOTHER individual, who, while not so exciting was more amusing in an odd way, was the Reverend Amzi Atwater, LL.D., Ph.D., etc., sometime professor of Greek literature and the Latin tongue. He was a tall, angular, sanctimonious individual, one of the most prayerful-looking men I have ever seen. And so suited to the region and the day of which he was then a part. For one thing, he had a long, heavy-boned face, with deep, solemn eyes and a long upper lip, very, and clean-shaven. Below, on the underside of an aggressive chin, a heavy growth of black beard, which stood out goat-fashion whenever he turned his face heavenward, as he frequently did, but when lowered suggested an Irish patriarch or a forty-niner. He wore always a wide-brimmed, soft hat and a long, flowing frock-coat. In classroom he sat or stood with a kind of archiepiscopal dignity behind a high table and slowly folded and unfolded his hands. As he talked he wore an expression of unbroken gravity, amazing because of its solemnity. Profound? Not at all. He was too pre-ternaturally solemn, without a suggestion of humour in so far as I could see, and because of this he probably impressed many, as he did me at the time. But as for ideas, not a trace —the mere echo of older ways and methods. His was the kind of impressiveness that attaches to a country deacon, and he had the country deacon's idea of duty, virtue, morality and the like. I have always thought that in the last analysis he must have been exceedingly dull.

How he came to be a student of the Roman language, and presumably its literature, is more than I can understand. I once asked Sutcliffe about this, and he replied: "He carries his Latin in one half of his brain and his religion in the other. They never meet." In addition to holding the chair of Latin, he was also vice-president of the college, moderator of some national or international religious body, and was frequently spoken of as one who was good at raising money. He often prayed or preached in the college chapel or a local church, preached in the old-fashioned, high-flown, religious way, and seemed to believe in the Bible as the country deacon believes in it. I recall that one of the students once inquired, apropos of a wager concerning Atwater's attitude toward the story of Jonah and the whale and the gourd vine, whether the Bible as translated could be accepted literally.

"Literally!" he is said to have replied. "Every portion has a direct or a mystic meaning which faith and prayer will make clear."

Faith and prayer! What questioning could go beyond that?

Levitt's opinion of him—and I always liked Levitt's opinions because they were so ribald, middle-class and American—was that he was "a damned old fool." Levitt had an amazing contempt for this type of antiquated religionist and never failed to express it where he thought it would be appreciated. In class or chapel he would sit and contemplate Atwater, exclaiming, *sotto voce*: "Get on to old Amzi this morning, will you? He's brushed and oiled his hair and beard. How is that for Perkins Corners?" Or it might be his tie or his collar or some other phase of his apparel that he was referring to. "Isn't that a swell twist to Amzi's tie? I do believe he spends a few moments before the mirror every now and then, the old buck! I wouldn't put it past the old cock to chase a young girl if he thought no one was looking." Sometimes he would even slap me on the back in order to emphasise his delight, a liberty I would return by a poke in the ribs.

And again, John Caspar Davidson, the associate of Willard Pelton Green, the chief mathematician of the college, was another who was almost as amazing to me, though not quite. Green, I am compelled to explain first, was a limp, mousy little man, wearing, as a rule, a pea-green suit and brown fedora hat. He was considered to be—there, I mean—one of the most remarkable mathematicians the college had ever seen, or so it was said. Also in class, as I often heard, he astonished the most capable of his students by applying theorems and logarithms with such rapidity in the process of his calculations as to leave them open-mouthed and lost in puzzled thought. On the street he wandered along, himself lost in thought, his round, pale blue eyes as fresh and starry as a child's, appearing to contemplate no thing, no person. Davidson, his assistant, on the other hand, was one of your big, ox-like, bush-whiskered youths of say twenty-seven or eight, whose whiskers and hair always struck me as an affectation, wholly unnatural for his years. And among other things, I think he tried not only to imitate Green's walk, which was limp and lackadaisical, but his apparently profound abstraction.

The reason for this was that Green was acknowledged to be a great mathematician, and Davidson was not. Davidson had been educated by Green, and his awe was that of the satellite for the primary. He was jealous of him, too, no doubt, for now he was a professor and trying to rise in the world. Speaking of both, Sutcliffe once told me that for a long time Davidson affected an outstanding mannerism of Green's: that of holding his chin in his hand for four or five minutes at a stretch; but later, finding it uncomfortable, gave it up.

I knew little of Green personally, but once heard him remark to Sutcliffe that mathematics constituted a serene and unchangeable essence, the forms of which were without substance, pure thought, the possible absolute as opposed to the material and visible: a series of remarks which so impressed me that I wrote them down in the hope of puzzling them out later. I did so puzzle, but the import did not reach me for a long time afterward, and then only vaguely.

Davidson, like Walter Deming Willikus, had married a frail, pale, high-browed girl whom occasionally I used to see washing the windows or sweeping the porch of their small home and who looked as if transcendentalism was much more important than breakfast. They, too, had a baby, also presumably intellectual. The house, the one time I called there of an evening, looked tasteless and rather poorly taken care of.

But the intellectual palaver that went on in connection with all these! The bubbling, youthful enthusiasm for this, that and the other ism, theory, personality, and the

433

like! One group, as I recall, was fond of asserting that the president of the college was a most marvellous man, able to read old French at sight and translate as he went, teaching mathematics, physiology, geology, palæontology or botany, as the mood happened to strike him. Also that he had several distinguished lectures which he gave here, there and everywhere throughout the United States, but only on request here, the student body acting as a whole to this end. Whether this was true or not, I do not know. But that he was really popular with the students was obvious, so much so that on occasion nearly all would vote to suppress anything which they felt might offend or trouble him.

Lastly, so far as this roster goes, there was Donald Maranville Strunk, A.B., Ph.D., Professor of History, who had one of the homeliest women to wife I ever saw. She was so homely that she was painfully arresting in this respect, and to this all students of that year loudly subscribed. "My God!" shouted my incorrigible Levitt on his first glimpse of her as with Strunk, A.B., she passed our door one sunny November day. "Look at that! Imagine walking abroad with that, or waking up in the night and seeing that! Do you mean to tell me he can love that?"

"She may have her virtues," I suggested.

"Well, she may," he said, "but if she belonged to me, I'd make her keep her head in a bag."

But the cruelty of this bald sex decision was by no means lost on me. It was a thing of which I as well as most youths of my years was thoughtlessly guilty. If a woman was not good-looking, what else mattered? And yet, wisdom and achievement were assumed to carry and bear weight. But with youth? And in the instance of a woman?

Along toward the end of the first semester—approximately Christmas time—I began to feel myself reasonably established as a student and a freshman. I had actually taken and passed several examinations, had joined in several class festivities, fights and the like, had, in addition to Levitt, Hall and Sutcliffe, established a number of contacts with students of all classes, freshmen to seniors, and was finally told by two members of Delta Tau Delta that while owing to lobbying, my newness, strangeness, this and that, I had escaped being invited to make one with them this year, when I came back (and assuming that they were there, as they intended to be), there would be a different story to tell. Only . . . but that can wait.

What really pleased me as much as anything was the growing and finally enthusiastic and almost too possessive friendship of Levitt, for he seemed bent, after a time and for some emotional reason of his own, on elevating and strengthening me in every way. I was to practise with a football, no less, kicking and chasing with him of a morning, noontime or evening. This to build me up. And he supplied the football. Also, I was to take certain setting-up exercises which he suggested, and out on the open lawn in the cold, because my chest was not broad enough. Whereto and wherefore he would wake me up with a yell at times, saying: "Come on, now, Bones! Move and get strong!" And since he was so insistent, I went. And at other times, as I protested, and not too well as you may guess, he might add: "Good God, man, a fellow of your height ought to have at least a four-inch chest expansion! You're terrible! Awful! And you can be strong! Look at me!" And to illustrate, and while adding that he was no taller than I was, he would stretch a strong and sinewy pair of naked arms before my gaze. Ah, to be like that, I thought! Like him! And handsome! And while I exercised accordingly, bending and jumping and lifting, still I was also conscious, and even convinced, of the fact that exercise would not make me so. And so, why sweat so much? I would still be homely, wouldn't I? And more, and while for reasons of want of wardrobe as well as my obviously retiring disposition, he did not seem to think it best to attempt to include me in his philanderings, still I felt that if I were only really handsome, I would not need fine clothes and I might be ignoring him instead of him me. At that, though, and at one time and another, he did suggest taking me on an outing or two. Once in particular, as I recall, he urged me to come to his home town with him over Saturday and Sunday; he would introduce me to some girls there, one of whom, as he insisted, would fall for me—she'd have to!—a crude presentation of his power and charity which killed the idea completely for me. Yet whether in his genial, warm-hearted, asinine way, he guessed that, I doubt. Anyhow, the mere suggestion of it so frightened me —the probability of my making a tongue-tied fool of myself

435

—that I declined: a declination he fought to the utmost, yet with no success.

And another time, if you will believe it—and in some ribald, condescending spirit which nearly, if not quite, severed our friendship—he wanted to "fix it up" between me and the girl next door—and after his own success, as I judged—a yokelly piece of tenderness which so infuriated me that I was ready to fight. And yet too I could understand the honest liking that lay behind it. Lastly, he wanted to adopt me as his football mascot, saying he could not play a decent game unless I was there, and to please him I did go once or twice, although with no thought of my import as a mascot. Yet the team won, not once but twice, and I was given a free ride to the next college city where the opposing team went down to defeat. But I tolerated no mention of me as any mascot. It may have been whispered, but not in my presence. In the main, I gave him no chance of patronising me in any way, as affectionate as was his mood, for outside his physical strength, skill with women, and his looks, I deemed him inestimably below myself in real grip and understanding. Gaily and daily, in short, I jested with him about one and another phase of his peculiarities, making him wince at times, as I could see, although apart from a slight dourness on such occasions and some contentiousness, he would still continue to boast of his feats of strength, his popularity and his conquests. At such times I would merely smile in a supercilious way and suggest how necessary it was for some to be good fighters and a triumph with the ladies, since they brightened life a little for some, whereupon he would take his books and go to some other student's room, or rave about my "damned smart-aleck tongue." But he liked me just the same and often brought his football team and other friends to see me—a diversion which did not thrill me any too greatly. I was thinking of other needs. And once he persuaded me (it was a witty experiment formulated by him and two or three others) to go with him to his washer-woman's (I forgot to say that Sutcliffe's laundry only handled collars, cuffs and shirts) in order, as he and they hoped, that I might be induced to go with an adopted daughter, a large, commonplace, mushy type of girl, who, like her mother, washed clothes, and like her mother (after her day in this field, though, I believe) accom-

436

modated sexually those students who gave her their washing to do.

When we reached the place, the girl, a big, simple, ox-like creature, was working at something under a lamp. And Levitt, after pretending to make some inquiry as to a missing shirt, observed to me, in her presence: "Well, do you want to do anything before you go?"

"Do what?" I inquired, simply, for I did not grasp what was meant. "What do you mean?"

At this I saw the girl smile in an amused, genial way, but without, however, looking up from her work.

"Why, you know. What are girls for? There's Ella over there." He grinned broadly and then whispered the one cryptic word which all understand. I flushed, and probably stammered. I had never been with but one girl in my life —the baker's daughter—and to put it thus boldly, and in the presence of the lady herself, was too much. Besides, I had no idea what the charge would be, and was I not trying to be as saving as possible with my meagre means? Yet rather than make a fool of myself by getting angry, I passed it off with a wry smile and exclaimed: "No, thank you, not this time."

We went outside, and the three youths hee-hawed and yoo-hooed as we went along, laughing over what seemed to them a good joke. Yet I also recall the fine, crisp November night, the actinic sparkle of the stars, the rustle of brown leaves still on the trees, and the low, glow-wormlike windows of cottages, of which the one we had come from was the most humble. More, I speculated on this woman and her daughter, and the combination of toil and sex-bartering by which they eked out their living, and added to myself—since I knew I could not talk to these others of such things (they would not understand)—that here was one case where immorality was not buying the silks and satins denounced of the moralist— merely a meagre living, as anyone could see. That cheap, frame cottage at the outskirts of a small town, weakly warmed and poorly lighted! The daughter, as I thought her over, not unattractive but working, with her mother, at washing —and yet in addition and in order to eke out a rueful livelihood, taking the risk of disease and the name of a prostitute! I had heard so much as to that. But the principal thing that was running through my mind, and which made me hesitate in my secret shame of returning some day or night and satisfying myself sexually with her, if I could spare the money, was that I was afraid when the crucial moment came I would find myself impotent—since, and if you will believe it, I was still harbouring the fool notion that I might have made myself impotent, or nearly so.

CHAPTER LXXIV

I HAVE some reason to believe that any craving or desire based on some necessity of the individual essence, and which lurks as a wish or thought in the mind long enough, will eventually make its further appearance in a form reasonably suitable to and characteristic of the individual of which it is a part. Thus, and by degrees, possessions as well as material forms and states of being will appear as actual material or emotional realisations of that which was longed for and so brooded upon in the mind as thought. Indeed, so much do I believe in this that I think I may affirm the old Biblical phrase: "The evil that I greatly feared has come upon me." Only I would change it to: "The thing which I have most thought upon and craved has at last appeared." For I have come to believe that entirely apart from death or persistence, thoughts are things, and like seeds dropped in this mulch of flesh which we call man—generated in what psychic abysses of eternal energy we know not—(I am thinking of another Biblical phrase: "And the Word was made flesh")—grow and eventually present themselves, their full development depending in part upon the substance or quality of the earthly body in which they are sown. I have had such thoughts and I have seen them take material form and confront me—not always opportunely.

More, as anyone can see, we are only spring-mouths through which subterranean fluids arise and bubble. We are gardens or envelopes in which grow strange things which give rise to man. And when the soil is accidentally favourable, astonishing things result—chemic bursts which actually wreck the individuality that has given them nourishment. Indeed, our uttermost dreams of love or possession or power are transmuted —by what magic I know not—into lands, power, works of art, achievements in science or thought, houses, position, affection, public applause; in short, achievement in any field.

As we think, not only so we are, but so we become, time and chance favouring or breaking.

It is Nietzsche who says that every man is the victim or favourite of his typical experience, and this is also true. The two propositions are really related. Persistences in the form of dreams or desires eventually produce our typical experiences. It is certainly true in my case. For here was I, at that time yearning definitely for not only the courage, the skill, the ability to interest women, but to have them approach me —skill or no skill—and then of a sudden and at my door several who were most eager to aid me, really made my path as easy as it could have been made without actually depositing the necessary force within me. And in connection with this, there has been a thought which has sometimes haunted me. Supposing, say, that these wishes of mine had been other than they were—virtuous, in the Christian or moralistic sense—then the Christians would say that God had answered my prayer. Since they were evil (so called), I suppose they would say I had drawn the devil to me, or that he was setting gins to destroy me. But fulfilled they were, as I will now proceed to show.

For just at this time, a new individual appeared on the scene, one who was not only more pagan than Levitt but also more diplomatic, cunning, insistent and emphatic in regard to quite everything that he desired, and so more able to fulfil, and at once, for me some of the things I most desired. To begin with, he was the quite well-to-do son of a judge of one of the northern circuits of Indiana, a law student and possessed of much more money and *savoir faire* than Levitt ever dreamed of—a minor country beau of the legal and Richelieu type. And I liked him for that—his spidery temperament as well as his good clothes, good looks, free and easy means and ways. For at once, and without my encouraging him any more than did I any other, he actually proceeded to devote himself to me. I was, as he insisted, a valuable and fascinating addition to his life—just the man he wanted to meet and one with whom, and as time showed, he was prepared to make common lot—a proposition or proceeding which astonished Hall, Sutcliffe and Levitt, who noting his sudden arrival and continued more or less possessive presence, began to comment on his personality and his ways, and betimes to warn me against him. For he was sly, and though outwardly pleasant and agreeable, vain—one of those coming "trick lawyers" was the way Levitt characterised him. Worse, he was, as Sutcliffe pointed out, a Phi Beta Kappa, the one really "smart" Greek letter society in the university, and so anathema to Sutcliffe as well as Levitt, who were not of it. And his clothes! "A college dude!" was Hall's comment. The suavest and sweetest remark was one made by Sutcliffe, who once said to me after he saw me becoming friends with him: "Some time after you know him better, I wish you would tell me what you find in him. I can see that you like him."

Our encounter came about in this way. Rather early in the fall, some time in October, I think, there was a folderol contest between the "freshies," of whom I was one, and the sophomores, over a certain gate and a certain street leading out of the campus. It appeared that several years before a rule had been promulgated by the sophomores that no freshie should take a certain route home—the main gate of the college —on a certain day. Naturally, the timid, the cautious, and the severely intellectual preferred to abide by this rule and go their way around, while a sporting element in others led them to break it. A very definite mistrust of my own prowess, which amounted to actual fear at times, led me to wish to avoid this contest, but pride would not permit it. I fancied Levitt would be there, and Hall, who however spindling and ill was spirited enough, and anyhow, I was anxious enough to see and be if only I could but hold my own.

It was at this contest that O'Connor appeared. For in the rush for opponents by both sides, he, being a sophomore, singled me out, or I singled him, I cannot recall which. At any rate, as he grabbed me by the arms, or I him, I noted a Machiavellian gleam in his eye. It was too wise, winsome and diplomatic to be either ignored or disliked. And he was so well dressed.

"See here!" he began. "What's your name?"

"Dreiser," I replied.

"Well, my name's O'Connor. I'm in the law department. Now you and I don't want to roll around in the dirt here, do we, Dreiser? Why not let's just let these kids here fight it out while we go through the motions?" His eye twinkled, he spat out the stub of a cigar he was chewing and swayed to and fro in an amused kind of dance the while he added: "We're paired. That's enough. What good would I be as a lawyer if I couldn't fix up a little thing like this?"

I laughed and aided in the pretence as best I could. And a lucky turn of fortune for me, for I might have encountered some football husky of the Levitt type who would have thrown me over his shoulder. (In one of the contests indeed—this one was at night—my friend Hall was shot in the leg and laid up for several weeks, his work neglected and a doctor's bill he could ill afford piled up into the bargain.) As it was, though, we kept up this farce for three or four minutes, perhaps longer, when the first force of the storm having blown over, a number of private friendships began to manifest themselves and the crowd began to skip, jest, and tell jokes. As a basis of compromise—to turn the contest in some other direction— I suggested that I had learned this day that a non-student who occupied a room in our house had just gotten married and was to bring his bride home this night for a stay of a few days, until a small house could be found. (It was Hall who gathered this information from the landlady.) My proposition to O'Connor was, I think, that we induce as many as we could to come around after midnight and help celebrate the bride's home-coming. A great uproar or charivari just outside the married couple's window after they had retired. And when I suggested this a whoop went up, for it introduced what all most craved, apparently, the ever enfevering sex element, and someone called: "What shall we bring? Drums, tin cans, cowbells?" to which I replied, excitedly: "Never mind bringing anything. Bring your voices. They'll be plenty." Where- upon my new friend O'Connor began to laugh ecstatically. I think he had been drinking a little beforehand. "Did you hear that?" he began to call to one and another. "He says 'bring your voices.' Do you hear that? Ha, ha! Do you hear that? He says you're just to bring your voices. Ha, ha!" Then he came over to me and hung on my arm. "Let's you and I go somewhere first and get something to eat, will you?" he cooed. "You and I ought to be better friends, dontcha know? I like you. You're just the sort of a fellow I do like."

He went on to explain that somewhere downtown was an excellent restaurant, where oysters, fish, steaks, chops and broiled chicken were always on the bill of fare, and where, because of the drinks that could be ordered, it was, as I learned afterwards, smart to eat. Wouldn't I come there with him? There were to be seen many frat youths who, gaily apparelled, stopped in on their way to some evening adventure, dined, smoked cigarettes, jested and departed with an air. On this occasion I accepted the offer rather doubtfully, because of the obligation, present if not implied, to return such a favour, but I went just the same. I said nothing just then as to my financial state, hoping to avoid further obligations of this kind, but such was not the case. He came to the charivari, which turned out to be almost a town scandal, with red fire, cannon-crackers and the like. The poor bride must have been frightened out of her wits! But long before it was over (and he had been home to study between whiles), he came over to me and taking my arm in the most familiar and affectionate way, said: "Come on, Dreiser, let's you and I cut this. Let's go downtown to Bohmer's"—the restaurant we had just left. An inspiration to frankness seized me. I saw that I had him really interested and could afford to be frank.

"See here, O'Connor," I replied, "I can't go your pace, and there's no use my trying it. You have money, or enough to do this anyway. I haven't. I have to be content with a simple boarding house."

"That's all right, old man! That's all right!" he exclaimed, without any change of manner or interest in his voice. "I know how it is with you, if you want me to know. Come down, anyhow."

I protested.

"Come on," he went on. "It's a nice night, and I don't want to go home yet. You needn't buy a thing. We'll just have a little beer or whiskey and then we can go home if you want."

He tugged at my arm and wheedled and coaxed until at last I went, a thing which both Levitt and Hall, since I had gotten them in on this, resented. There had been a crazy programme arranged between us—songs, the blocking of doors, the explosion of crackers, and I do not recall what else.

"You're a hell of a fellow!" was Hall's comment the next

morning. "To sneak away just when we had everything going fine! Where the devil did you go to?"

I told him.

"Well, you're a snide, to run away and leave a thing after you start it! Who the hell is this fellow O'Connor anyhow? What do you want to run off with him for?"

"Oh, he wouldn't let me alone," I explained, apologetically.

"Well, the next time I go in with you on anything, you'll know it," he grumbled. "Start a thing and then run off!"

It suddenly occurred to me that in this instance at least, and in this small way, I had proved a leader of sorts. (A most surprising discovery for me.) Also that both Hall and Levitt were interested in me enough to have noted my absence— a flattering thing in itself as things were going here. But after that came other incidents of the same kind: more visits by O'Connor, return visits on my part to his room, a dinner at his fraternity house, with friendly introductions to others—a procedure, in short, which indicated that unless I resolved to be rid of him, he would persist in his friendly overtures, and this complicated by the fact that I really liked him.

In passing I may say that one of my typical experiences has been this same unconscious drawing to me of individuals— forceful, artistic, interesting—who while not always interesting me intensely have been sufficiently agreeable not to make them unacceptable—a type of approach and friendship which has somewhat puzzled me even while I have in part enjoyed it. For on occasion they have been so intense in their interest, literally thrusting themselves upon me, injecting, where possible, their moods and desires into my life and, as it were and often with the best intentions, seeking to motivate me, woman-wise, for their own pleasure as well as mine. Only and all too often, I have proved a mulish and intractable pet. They have worked hard, but rather fruitlessly. I can only explain this on the ground that during the first half of my life, at least, I must have been a very deceptive person, seemingly mild, aimless, indifferent, dreamy—particularly in regard to trivial things and matters—whereas in reality, in regard to my own deepest currents and interests, at least, I could be adamant.

444

For one thing—and quite consciously so—by now I was determined never to be sculled to and fro by any other's whims or notions or interests, however well intended, unless truly they bore some reasonable relation to my own. More, I was beginning to understand quite a few things in connection with my own temperament, my limitations as well as my possibilities, and to accept the former, and so avoid personal pain, or to think on ways of escaping them. Only in regard to what I really thought, I rarely said anything. It was my policy to smile and smile, even though I disagreed vitally. At some crucial moment, if I was dissatisfied with any plan or relation, I could swiftly enough end it by saying no, only it was rare in my case that the moment seemed sufficiently crucial. I craved friends and friendship. In many, many instances, I neither cared nor bothered as to what was said or done —it was less bother to yield than to fight—whereupon some deficient observer, dull or clever, was apt to assume that he or she could take charge of me, that all I needed was sympathetic direction, and that whoever chose to furnish that direction would rule. In consequence, these sudden descents and manipulations would occur and go on pleasantly enough as long as they were interesting or amusing. But of a sudden, some fine morning, I would find myself bored or would conclude that I was wasting my time or being made a dunce of, whereupon presto, unless greatly moved by sympathy, I would call a halt. If sympathy interfered, I might gracefully and gradually extricate myself (as I often did) as gracefully and gradually as one may without being too much bored.

But to return to this youth, David Ben O'Connor. (And by the way, that name has come back to me now for the first time in twenty years.) He was a most precocious youth or man of twenty, lean, somewhat swagger after the small-town standards of the Middle West, of good standing here and at home. He was possessed of that amplitude of means (furnished by his parents, of course) which permitted him to dress smartly, travel here and there as freely as he wished, and amuse himself in such fashion as would have completely exhausted my meagre year's allowance in a month or week, even. My mother had very justifiably decided that she had no money for this educational adventure and that if Miss Fielding was determined that I should go, she must pay my way. So all I had was the sum of fifty dollars or thereabouts monthly, with something extra for tuition fees, out of which various things besides board and room had to come: laundry, entertainment (almost enforced lecture courses, I mean), clothes and the like. Naturally, I was troubled and cautious as to my expenditures and viewed any proposition to entertain or be publicly sportive with a nervous eye.

Nevertheless, this did not render me immune to O'Connor or others of his type who later, and through him, I met. Rather, having means and finding me to his liking, as I say, he was seemingly determined to shower entertainment upon me, had I not persistently stood out against it. For one thing, and at once, he was wanting me to go to Indianapolis or Terre Haute or Louisville or this or that other place each week-end. And willing and anxious to pay all expenses, which I determinedly declined. The thought of anything so parasitic was a little too much for me. Failing that, and most speedily, I was introduced to this and that Phi Beta Kappa brother, as well as several girls with whom socially he had become intimate, and this in spite of all my lacks and fears. For occasionally on the street or in his room, when we chanced to be together, would be a girl, and before I could think yes or no or decide, there I would be, introduced. Thus, there was Eva Casper, for one, whom we met on the street one day, and to whom as well as her girl companion he instantly introduced me with strong encomiums of myself which embarrassed me not a little (my clothes were always in my mind) and so caused a silence which I assumed would prove fatal. As it was, he was back the next day with a suggestion that I meet with him and her and another girl that night for dinner in his rooms—an invitation I declined. I had no dinner clothes and he had. This explanation he waved aside with the assertion that dress clothes were not necessary; he was going to wear what he had on—an intended mitigation which had no least value for me, since, as anyone could see, he was better dressed than most of the students. But where I should have laughed and accepted, refusing to feel degraded by lacks which had no real authority, I did not. Lacking the courage of my innate conviction about myself, I refused and spent an unhappy evening alone.

Just the same, O'Connor was of that mental urgency which

is not to be gainsaid. He was as tireless as he was diplomatic and in my case affectionate. In his very comfortable apartment, not so very far from where I lived, were all those effects which a student of means can afford: clothes, books, pictures, knick-knacks—a pleasing student array. Besides, as I found, there were these girl friends of his occasionally dropping in, that same Eva Casper among them, and proceeding, although not under his direct instructions, I am sure, but through the agency of the girl with whom he was most intimate at the time—and who was taking her cue from him—then and there to make such obvious approaches that in spite of myself I could not really escape. For if I could not talk, whoever was present at the time could. More, Eva Casper, who came first in this matter, sat close beside me on a couch (more particularly after O'Connor and his girl had chosen to retire to an adjoining bedroom, of which there were two), and smiling and smiling, until excited and tormented by what was so obviously in mind, it became absolutely impossible not to understand and accede. And yet with the horrible thought in my mind that here and now I was at last, and in spite of myself, to be exposed as impotent. And this in spite of a virility that would have done credit to a young bull. My hands and knees were really shaking, the more so since directed by her, and seemingly unconsciously, first her knee was touching mine and next, about her waist and over one breast was one of my arms and its hand. She had been willing it, and so it came to pass. Devil! Beast! Also her face was so close to mine, one girlish cheek pressed against my own, that kisses were unescapable. From that it was but a step to the other room. (I was even thinking of the baker's daughter and her methods at the time.) But instead of heartening me as that might have (since I came off well enough at that time), I was now reduced by that lunatic word or thought: *impotence,* which I had read in so many of those driving ads relating to "lost manhood." And all because of some night emissions, the only reasonable explanation of which should have been potence of the first order. Can you imagine! And I was insisting on the direct contrary!

And yet in one sense that was true. For so nervous and excited and fearsome was I that although she was attractive and yielded most graciously to my every gesture of approach

447

—and more, like my baker's girl, even aided me—nevertheless once the contact was made, I was instantly finished; a conclusion which left me impotent enough for the moment and herself unsatisfied—a dénouement which possibly she herself lacked sufficient experience to understand.

At any rate, so it was. And myself in consequence reduced to the most miserable state of mind. I cannot tell you! And feeling . . . God! how ashamed . . . and so, really impotent for that night—my one thought how to extricate myself without appearing lunatic as well as impotent. For in my mind was literally roaring—what can she be thinking? And what would she be telling O'Connor's girl, and after that, she him? And so henceforward, how useless to any woman here or elsewhere—even public knowledge of my weakness! The horror! The desolation! So sensitively shaken was I by all this that I scarcely knew what to say, least of all what to do. I recall some weak comment, relative, probably, to her loveliness, and that because of it I could not long withstand the charm of her. But just the same, I noted that after a few moments she escaped by saying: "I think we'd better be going out. They'll be coming back in a few minutes." A statement which was true, but which was her easiest way out of an embarrassing situation.

Worse, though, a miserable half-hour for me ensued before either O'Connor or his girl did appear, smiling and inquiring —an immense relief from an almost wordless state on my part —and after that still another three-quarters of an hour before Eva explained that she must be going: an explanation which projected the problem of who was to accompany her and so completed my defeat. For at once I foresaw an almost speechless and perspiring walk. But, and thanks be, after some whispered conversation between Eva and her girl friend, it was decided that since both were going the same way, they would just go on together, their places being in the opposite direction from mine. (Bloomington girls both.) And to this, and in spite of the innate gallantry that was always his, O'Connor consenting, an obviously suspicious circumstance in itself. For as I knew, he would not, except for my predicament, let his girl go off by herself. As for myself, I was dying to be gone. But off they went presently, he insisting that I stay to have a drink with him, after which he inquired, casually enough, how I liked the little girl. And my saying honestly enough that she was lovely. But thinking what of myself? Had I only had the courage to explain to him or someone! The upshot of it was that I finally took my leave, and after an almost sleepless and most miserable night, decided that I would not keep company with him any more, would not, if possible, even see him.

*

CHAPTER LXXV

BUT that, as I soon learned, and in spite of my deepest determination, was by no means to be. O'Connor's friendship, thus curiously begun, was by no means so easily to be broken off. For apparently it was not affected by my ability or inability to deal diplomatically or potently with girls, but hinged on my personal appeal to him alone. So that the very next day, or the day after, meeting me on the street, he hailed me as cordially and understandingly as ever. Why not come around to the room about six and have dinner with him? Or why not go downtown and have something together, and then I could go back to my room and study if I had to, or bring my books and study in his? But these requests, though I deeply appreciated them, I almost rudely rejected, being hurt and in consequence defiant. Yet as to what he thought of that, or what, if anything, he sensed or knew, I subsequently wondered, for he said so cordially: "Oh, all right, old man. But we'll have some other meals together some time soon, won't we?" And smiled his most cordial smile. Too damned cunning and sly, was what I then and there decided, at the same time almost loving him for his tact. Yet, as before, deciding that I would have nothing more to do with him.

Just the same, and as I have said, it was not to be. For soon—one afternoon late—there he was at my room again, and with a good-looking horse attached to a two-seated sulky in which he wanted me to ride. He was thinking of buying the horse, he said. He looked so genial and inviting and so superior, waiting for me outside that worn house where all could see. With both Levitt and Hall as well as that little white mouse next door looking on, I decided to go, if for no more than the effect—a crude, selfish, vain thought, as you can see. But after that, a dinner at that same restaurant. And then a walk to his room, where once more he began to talk about girls and trips. For regardless of my fiasco with Eva Casper, he still seemed determined that I should share in his world, such as it was, and because of my liking for him, so I did for a time.

For I actually came to see and feel that he looked on me as a genius of sorts, even frankly said so, although just why I could not see. I certainly felt at loose ends mentally. And because of praises and compliments thickly strewn before, as I also noted, he always managed to interest one or another of his girls to the extent of awaking in her a desire at least to see me. Yet so conscious was I always of the fact that he was overrating me and my powers and that I could never prove as gallant or clever in the presence of women as was he, I remained painfully shy and evasive whenever he even so much as suggested one of these meetings. Yet always he was ready with the word that it was just for the evening, and no more—he had to be back to his books by twelve—I need not do anything more than talk a little—a method which quite always led me into the trap, seeing that from the point of view of the girls to whom he introduced me, I seemingly appeared acceptable. Yet his idea of a delightful evening, as I well knew, was to call on a girl—two if I went with him —and after some light conversation, a stroll, and possibly ice cream or oysters somewhere, return to his home or that of the charmer, there to sit on her porch or within a darkened chamber, and hold her hand or do whatever else was permitted.

To begin with—in connection with this new arrangement —there was one girl, a certain Lila Woody, a rather biggish, blue-eyed doll of Bloomington, living with her mother and studying music and something else—I forget what—a most loosely-governed piece, who seemed to do very much as she pleased. We called, but she and I found nothing in common, as I thought. It appeared that I was what I was: dull, I suppose; and that was the end of that. Then next came a short, plump maiden, with an oval, pale face, and a wealth of sleepy yellow hair, whom, long before I was introduced to her by O'Connor, I had noticed sitting on the vine-covered steps of one of the more exclusive boarding houses of the town (there were no dormitories here) and whom often I had wished that I might know. A certain fullness of the neck, the beauty of which she heightened by low-necked, collarless dresses, took my eye at once. She was specialising in English literature and chemistry, as some other students told me, and was a fraternity girl as well as a member of an excellent family— a bit of information which O'Connor later imparted with gusto, since that was a phase of life which he, assuming himself to be a part of it, most admired. But nothing came of that either. She was far more interested in O'Connor than she was in me; a fact so obvious from the first that it cut and burned. I went no more.

There was a third girl, a certain Kathie Millership, very plump, very sensual, very pretty, and very eager, I am sure, to enter on an affair with almost anyone whom O'Connor and any one of his favourites could agree upon, and accordingly to her I was introduced one evening, and then and there a trip to Louisville proposed. Just why I do not recall—a fair or something. But in this connection and before the, I am sure, previously arranged trip was suggested, this same girl —no doubt at the behest of O'Connor's latest girl friend— seeking to draw near me, and with as much of an air of camaraderie and liking as with his previous ballyhoo she was able to achieve. Yet just how under these circumstances she could have liked me, I cannot think. (These advertised friends, you know!) Worse, in my mind all the time and just the same was my memory of Eva Casper and what happened there. I had no faith. Disaster, and only disaster, could follow on all this.

Just the same, as I was noting, here was yet another instance of an answer to that intense wish of mine which seemed to be dragging girls for me from out of the very air. For not only had Levitt sought to aid me, but now O'Connor! And more, against this barrier within myself, and which I did not seem to be able to overcome, although it was being fairly assailed by charmers of this type. Had I thought clearly of it at the time, I most certainly would have been psychically astounded. For now, and on O'Connor's say-so alone, and like all the others, this girl was as ready to receive me, apparently, as though I personally had sought her out. Not only that, but for the sake of the quartette O'Connor desired, ready to like me or at least make the best of me until such time as she could discover whether or not she could endure me. For now she smiled gaily, said she had heard so much about me, and then waited for me to indulge in some light badinage. That I failed miserably was due, of course, to my failure with Eva Casper and my highly exaggerated notion that I was being called upon to say the most sparkling things and make a vivid and lasting impression, whereas all that was demanded of me was a courageous manifestation of the fact that I was interested in her, certainly not afraid of her. As it was, I spent a most painful evening, emerging limp under the heavy thought of failure and that I had made a fool of myself, had not dared a single intimacy, either of look or word, where that was so obviously expected of me. As on the previous occasion, I had been left alone with her while O'Connor courted his Miss Somebody (I forget the name) in another room. And I had dared come no nearer than the width of the room! Think of it!

Just the same, this was not the end. For about this time, due to nervousness and undue concentration on my books, lighted by a much too feeble oil lamp, my eyes, or rather the one eye I was ever able to use, were out of commission. I could not read—the type blurring. Hence a visit to a local doctor, one of whose side-lines was eyeglasses and their prescription. He at once suggested that I visit either Louisville or Indianapolis and consult a specialist. I was thinking of Indianapolis, the nearer place, when suddenly in walked O'Connor. Now hearing of my predicament and of Louisville and Indianapolis in connection with the same, he quickly joined up his proposed trip with my eye trouble. Why not two birds with one stone? It was just about Thanksgiving time—a day or two before. Why not take Miss Wright and Miss Millership to Louisville over Thanksgiving? "It would be just fine," he added. "She likes you, you know, and we could all have a fine time." A thought which evoked little more than panic in me. To be thus pursued when I wanted so much to be pursued in just this way, and yet to have this fear! And more, to lack the means wherewith to pursue just this type of gaiety for which I yearned! I was actually thrown into a kind of fever by the thought of it, yet at the same time pretended an easy efficiency which was only spoiled by my lack of money—an excuse which O'Connor, as I knew, would never accept. For at once, and as I expected, he interpolated:

"If it's money, old chap, you know I have enough for everybody. I'll fix everything up." And when I demurred as to that, modified it by saying: "Well, you have to go somewhere, Indianapolis or Louisville. Why not make it Louisville, pay your own way there and back if you wish, and let me do the rest?"

Fool that I was, and in the face of my certainty as to the result—the Eva Casper debacle all over—still, so desperately was I clutched by the thought, the opportunity, I consented to go, and then spent several days worrying over why I had accepted and why I did not retreat while there was yet time. Supposing, supposing I should try, and succeed? Supposing? I *might* talk. I *might* summon the courage. Who knows? But then also, and supposing (dark thought that!) that love and kisses achieved and we two alone, what then? God!

However, when the time came, and because of the fear of a scandal, it was deemed best by O'Connor that we should board the train separately, all of us, and wait until we had ridden past a station or two before we pretended to find each other. When we went to the station Thanksgiving morning, it was without the knowledge which the morning papers would have brought had we received them in time (they never arrived before three in the afternoon) that a great cyclone had struck Louisville the night before and that amazing and pathetic damage had been done. Hundreds upon hundreds of buildings had been blown down. The car yards of this very road on which we were riding had been strewn with wreckage. Great engines of imposing tonnage had been lifted up and piled one on top of the other. All of this we were to see as we drew near, and it might have deterred us.

However, uninformed, and most unconcernedly as far as O'Connor and these girls were concerned, we boarded the train. I saw Miss Millership and Miss Wright, the former smartly dressed in a light blue walking suit, with a tasselled cap, after the fashion of that fall, pulled down over her hair. Her cheeks were rosy—a girl bursting with health—and she walked with a kind of defiant stride which fascinated and yet frightened me. When I realised that shortly I should have to entertain her, and that when we reached Louisville I should have to play the gallant and win her to the scheme O'Connor had proposed, I ran hot and cold. I was terrorised.

Fortunately as we rode together after the third station, O'Connor became most diverting, devoting himself to the four of us rather than to his girl alone. We sat in facing seats, did card tricks and gambled for pennies. But noting an exceedingly stormy sky as we proceeded south, we began to wonder at it, even to worry a little. And then soon someone brought information as to the storm itself, the great damage, and so diverted attention from our real purpose or mission. I think we were all distressed for fear the storm might compel our return or itself return to Louisville while we were there and do more damage—a thought which caused me to feel that my fears need not be as great as they were. I might have no real problem. To make a long story short, I found it possible under these favourable circumstances to talk to my girl and even hold her arm or nibble feebly at her fingers with mine, though my over-timidity unquestionably reacted unfavourably on her and she scarcely knew how to look or what to say, so lamely did I receive her least genial glance or word.

Arriving in Louisville, though, and because it was early and because much damage was visible on every hand from the train as we entered—great hogsheads of tobacco broken and spilled about the streets, endless bales of cotton rolled here and there by the wind, corners of buildings clipped off, as well as hundreds of buildings destroyed and vehicles of all kinds upturned and broken—we stayed to survey the ruin. O'Connor's plan, as he had confided to me, was this: that the two girls were to take a room together and we one each, and then if any hitch or separation occurred or his plan failed to go through, all would be well, for we could return to our respective rooms and in the morning meet for breakfast. But just the same, and from this period on until they, O'Connor and the two girls, returned to Bloomington the next afternoon and I remained over to await the return of my oculist and have my eyes treated the next day, I spent as wretched a twenty-four hours as I ever spent in my life.

In the first place, now that we were on the ground and I was supposed to take charge of this girl, my courage, as usual, completely blew out. True, with O'Connor and Miss Wright as companions, we at first wandered about, staring at the immense ruin wrought. But what of that? As terrible and moving as it might be to some, how little it meant to us four young persons who had come on so different an errand. And how thoroughly it proved the utter selfishness of sensual desire as opposed to all else. For regardless of the dead and the ruins, here were we four, the other three at least, thinking of a hotel room and what might there be achieved between us. And even I, after my all-too-pathetic failure with Eva Casper, wondering whether it was not possible, and even in the face of that, so to control myself, or at least to overcome my deadly fear of subsequent exposure and shame, as to attempt a successful relationship. Was it really true that I was so completely done for? And so early in life? A light, cold sweat was upon me. My hands were cold. For despite my poor showing on the train and elsewhere, here she was, as young and attractive as one would want, and hanging on my arm, anticipating, no doubt, at least some light suggestion of the gallant in me. Yet thoughts or no thoughts, not one forward or appealing word on my part. And after an hour or less, I was fully aware that she was becoming bored. For long stretches at a time, even under these interesting circumstances, I had nothing to say, for I could think of nothing to say. Not that I did not know what was expected of me. I could feel most clearly that in unfrequented places I was expected to slip my arm about her and urge her with gentle badinage to return to the hotel with me. Yet I did not. Instead made the most of noting that always ahead of us somewhere, for a time at least, were O'Connor and Miss Wright in full view, lost in pleasant confidences, for they had reached an understanding, apparently, long before. Only presently, even he returned to say that he and Miss Wright were going back and that Miss Millership and I could arrange things between ourselves.

So at last my hour! The gallows! And as before with Eva Casper, it was do or die! But with me it was die, as I now began to feel. For I really could not contemplate another fiasco and began to think what a fool I had been to permit O'Connor to wheedle me into this predicament. And yet not saying as much to my girl, as we now returned to the hotel—she was too enticing and vital—the all-to-be-desired, really—or that O'Connor having previously arranged for a room for me as well as one for the two girls, she might come

456

with me to mine if she would. Never! And yet it was now my duty really—my death duty almost, as I felt it to be—so to persuade her. For unlike Eva Casper, although willing, she was not forward. It was I who would have to say and do the leading.

Inadequacy, consciousness of defeat, failure, shame. Yet marching into the hotel with her as might an automaton or robot, and thinking, or better, not thinking, merely miserably sensating. And so, because of my silence, we two taking seats in one of the parlours on the second floor. And there, alone together, O'Connor and his girl having gone to his room, as I assumed—they were not seen again for several hours— I attempted to put my arm around her, but in such an awkward, fearful way that nothing came of it. I did not go far enough, nor did I say what so obviously it was my duty to say. In fact, I did not show that I had any intention of doing anything more at all, after which and after a time, and after giving me ample opportunity to go farther, she excused herself and left me. Thereafter I saw nothing of her until O'Connor and his girl having reappeared, she rejoined us. She had been in her room. And that night, after dinner somewhere for the four of us, she presumably slept with Miss Wright.

And although the next day all were genial enough, O'Connor suggesting that after I had seen my oculist, we take a carriage and see the city, still, since it developed that I should have to wait over another day, these three finally compelled to return together, myself left alone to have my eyes, instead of my mind, examined and to meditate on what a total and ridiculous failure I was—a meditation which resulted in my resolving never, never, never to accept another girl invitation from anyone, since obviously it only led to such torturesome and self-belittling things as had but now occurred. And that resolution for once was kept, and so my peace of mind gradually restored. For O'Connor, having at last discovered what a hopeless failure I really was, gave over this particular phase of his desires for me. He called, it is true, occasionally, and was most friendly, but as for adventures such as this . . . Selah.

CHAPTER LXXVI

A S the Christmas holidays drew near, I found that quite everyone except myself was going home. My first intention, seeing that the family was by no means as well placed as it might have been and that things here were interesting enough for me, was to stay, but seeing everyone else leaving —O'Connor, Hall, Levitt, Sutcliffe—and they asking me was I not going, I finally decided, for form's sake, that I must. (Beaten by convention, as it were.)

More, about this time, O'Connor, having recovered apparently from his despair over my inefficiency at Louisville, began to show up and be as interested and cheerful as ever. He was coming to Chicago, after a day or two spent at his home, he said, and wanted me to meet him and idle about during the holidays. Being convinced, because of his personal grandeur, etc., that he would not find my family sufficiently interesting or suited to his notions, I decided not to let them meet. As for going out with him myself, that was a different matter and concerned none but ourselves.

We made the trip northward together, and since he was getting off at 3 a.m., we decided to sit up in the smoker. (This made my inability to afford a berth less demeaning.) Approaching Chicago and my own home, I experienced, for the first time in my life, I think, a sense of change in myself —something more toward individuality—the intense centripetal integrality of the same—as opposed to what hitherto might have been looked upon as a merged or group feeling —integrality with the other members of my family and home —my mother, of course, the central centripetal star of the same and one not to be affected, let alone reduced or modified in any way. And nothing since has ever altered her peculiar emotional and vital relationship to me, however numerous the years.

But as to the others! Although only three months had

passed, I had grown so much. These different and strange contacts, how seriously they had affected me! The university, with its faculty and student body; the various fields of mind and effort of which, in so short a time, I had become apprised; the earnestness or folly or weakness of so many of the students who were there supposedly seeking the technique of the larger world realms without and yet, like myself and for reason of this lack or that weakness or incapacity, fumbling or fooling—myself as I saw myself one of the most pathetic illustrations of this, yet without the will or power to fight these same impulses which, as I saw them then, were deflecting me from the so necessary concentration and effort, from which (and from which only, as I also saw it then) true achievement could arise. Of course, long since I have changed my mind as to the import of much upon which I might then have concentrated. And education has dimmed into little more than a polishing process for innate ability and a sense of direction. To-day, in so far as education is concerned, my first concern would be not as to how much concentration was achieved, but rather what type of mind or character, or both, was doing the studying and concentrating. For from that, and that alone, can spring results. The rest? Mere page-turning and thought-marking. No more.

But to return to Chicago and our home. While I found things about as I had left them—the same jobs for all, the same nebulous wonder on the part of my mother as to this and that in connection with life, the same intense religiosity on the part of my father, Eleanor and her husband away somewhere, Ruth and Davis about to be married; the problem of the family budget as irritating, or nearly so, as ever, each one desiring to contribute no more than was necessary—still the same curious family accord, or affection shot through with disaffection, union fighting with the slow but sure growth of disunion. One could feel it even then—myself wandering forth for a time as much as any other, possibly the least bit more.

Finding my father out of work once more, I contemplated him about as might any student of psychology or biology, interested in the life history or processes of any given species. (I had not joined up with Sutcliffe and some others in vain.) On the other hand, and for the first time, I was cognisant of a sense of mental loneliness, even here in the very heart of my own home, where never before had I been lonely in that sense. As I could see, and regardless of whether I had studied or not, I had absorbed so much, mentally osmosed in connection with this and that. The various students with whom and in what various fields I had met and argued or listened and of whom I had asked questions! And the result? After three short months, a sense of class as opposed to mass, the intellectual as opposed to the non-intellectual; the trained as opposed to the untrained; the socially favoured or lucky as opposed to the socially unfavoured and unlucky. But by no means robbed of that consciousness of the state or weariness of the many who are not so favoured or trained or lucky, and for that very reason—my own father, mother, younger brother and sister among them—treading ways which as contrasted with those asinine bourgeois comforts and equipment so much insisted upon by the O'Connors and others might seem hopelessly inferior. They might not be among the strong, wise, this or that, but they were of my own blood. And that mysterious and psychic something which is blood or functions through it, dictating sympathy and tenderness which would not down. They were of me; I of them, in this strange sense, and come what might, I knew that psychically at least, I would never be able to desert them. (And never have.) I knew that at the very time that in some contrary phase of my mind, I was setting some little store by O'Connor and his friendship for me.

For how little it mattered to me then that I, by luck alone, had been lifted out of a most objectionable form of employment and given a chance to find myself, if possible! For while a mere look into a few petty phases of what then seemed so superior was sufficient to set me on tenterhooks in regard to my own noble social future—not that of these others who had sacrificed so much to help me thus far—still my true sympathies were here at home. And yet I wanted—or thought I did—a profession and money and a *good* family such as other people could boast of, and a girl like Kathie Millership or any of those others whom through O'Connor I had so easily and pleasantly contacted. Not only that, but for the time being I wanted to swagger about the world like Levitt or O'Connor, to show off (me!), have good clothes, smart friends, and this and that. I can only smile indulgently concerning myself as I was then, think not too drastically of that boy whose heir and, in part, creation I am. For, in part at least, is he not still here and thinking on his own follies?

And so O'Connor came to Chicago, and with that lusty determination of the college youth to show off and have a good time, beset me at once. Telephones were rare in those days—one in some corner drug store was considered a great commercial and even social convenience and equipment. And so, without my consent, after a day or two he came out to the house to look me up. He had taken a room at the Palmer House, as he now told me, and after visiting certain friends by day and calling on certain girls who could be taken with only the most serious and conservative formality, as he also explained, his deepest desire was to reconnoitre the great red light district, which then centred in and about South Clark, Pacific and other streets in that vicinity as far south as Harrison. And in order to be free—a matter I could have arranged easily enough but which left me dubious as to difficulties and annoyances that might arise because of him—I was to stay with him at the hotel. He could be so insistent! (And this after Louisville, if you would believe it!) But now, we need not go with any of these girls, unless we found just the right ones. As for expense, well, as usual, it was to cost me nothing.

Concerning all this I cannot say why I went or why he was so desirous of having me accompany him. Personally I was really only interested in some girl whom I could know and admire—a special contact—whereas he, for all his special contacts, could still be interested in those public and quite common inmates. I could not see why. Did he not have enough already? As for myself, I was really going to please him, and nothing else. Left to myself, I would not have bothered. But one thing that helped was that I had more courage for this type of adventure than for any of the others thus far proposed, since it did not involve any final intimacies for me, and, in addition, gave me a look into a field about which I was curious, my protective delusion in regard to impotency making it certain that I would not want to bother with anyone. My one fear, if any (and that is too laughable) was that finding myself in such a place, and being left by

O'Connor, I might by some strange chance or fatality or force even (who could tell?) be inveigled into some expensive and yet, and as usual, ineffective contact, whereupon my enraged and vigorous houri might rise and after demanding more money than I had, denounce me in ringing terms, say, for my physical impotence! "How dare you attempt relations with me when you are not capable of performing the sex function?" Or perhaps I was afraid she would merely laugh and leave me. In spite of these fears, I went—was even anxious to go.

Those brazen females of the bagnio! Their showy shamelessness! In connection with them I often think of the picture given in Proverbs 7: 6: "I looked through my casement and beheld among the simple ones . . . a young man void of understanding passing through the street near her corner; and he went the way to her house, in the twilight, in the evening, in the black and dark night. And, behold, there met him a woman with the attire of an harlot, and subtil of heart. (She is loud and stubborn; her feet abide not in her house: Now is she without, now in the streets, and lieth in wait at every corner.) So she caught him, and kissed him, and with an impudent face said unto him: 'I have peace offerings with me: this day have I paid my vows. Therefore came I forth to meet thee, diligently to seek thy face, and I have found thee. I have decked my bed with coverings of tapestry, with carved works, with fine linen of Egypt. I have perfumed my bed with myrrh, aloes, and cinnamon. Come, let us take our fill of love until the morning: let us solace ourselves with loves.' "

And think how little the world has changed since then! Over two thousand years in which Christianity and other forms of belief have struggled to reduce the sex import of man to woman and woman to man, and one can still look through his casement and see youths "void of understanding" and women "with the attire of an harlot" meeting in the ways! I often ask myself why do not the argued morals of the world prevail if they are so important, or if the immorality of the world is so destructive and plague-like, why has it not destroyed the world? Why the everlasting contest between them, the everlasting palaver as to their sinfulness? Is it not obvious that both are essential and that equation which we know as Life is thus struck between them? I think so. Also that beyond them, in either direction, lie depths or heights as yet unplumbed or undreamed of by man.

These Chicago red light streets as we ventured into them after dark—as has always been the custom—were as typical of the raw, brawling force of sex, and particularly of this hardy city, as anything could be. For cheek by jowl with immense manufacturing buildings which were then springing up on every hand—tall fourteen- and sixteen-story buildings which were then already the marvel of America, and unknown to New York among other things—were the low brick residences formerly the homes of conservative citizens who had long since moved before the encroaching manufacturing and sales life of the city. In one way, too, these were quiet, dark streets, with here and there only patches of shabby frame dwellings devoted to saloons, pool-rooms, stores, rooming houses and the like, whereas for the rest, they were prowled over and through by hungry and seeking or, as we now say, sex-starved men, from all parts of America, really. But so minutely as seen before these taller, newer buildings, great skyscrapers dark and silent and now towering shadow-like above these rows of houses with their red or pink fanlights over the door and occasionally a name emblazoned: invariably that of a woman. (Might it not as well have been *Aphrodite?*) Policemen too, here and there to be seen,—grafters and henchmen, belike—and, on occasion, robbers—and along with all this a line of cabs in one or another section, the scene resembling an etching. And throughout all, a muffled sound of activity; the feet of men coming out of or going into houses or swinging along the street in groups or pairs, and talking in low tones, and occasionally a woman crossing from one section to another.

It was an old picture, but to me, then, exciting. We set out after a dinner at Rector's, a basement restaurant then gaining considerable fame, and wandered into this region, looking for the signal lights over the doors. Although insisting he had never been here before, still O'Connor seemed familiar enough with the process of discovery and entry, for saying: "Let's look in here!" he knocked at a door and was at once admitted by a Negro maid, who remarked cheerfully: "Come right in, boys!" I recall well the flaring red plush curtains that divided the front room from another in the rear, the tall gilt mirrors, the bright gilt chairs, and the upright piano, at which, no sooner were we seated, a blasé youth, entering from the rear room, seated himself and began to play, but without paying any attention to us whatever. And as actresses entering upon a stage, and from a rear room set off by heavy plush curtains—from which had been issuing sounds of laughter and conversation—presently came several girls, detached portions apparently, of a larger group of men and women already congregated there.

"Hello, boys!" Even yet I can hear the voice of the meaty German girl who approached me. She was clad in a pink silk chemise, with stockings to match, her yellow hair piled in a high spiral at the back of her head, her fat, gross face apparently glowing with health. "How you like this costume?" she asked, stepping forward, moving her lips suggestively, and leaning over and pressing against me the better to impress—or should I say infect—me with her charm. A slimmer, more graceful girl, in evening dress, had already approached O'Connor and in his lap was being fondled by him.

I confess that as coarse and gross as all this was, there was still a vigorous, healthy reality about it which quite interested me. It smacked so of vigour and lust and hunger and a kind of brainless mad reward for the brainless mad ills of this world from which no healthy male or female is really ever wholly free. To my hungry sex sense then, how reviving and at the same time torturing, this consciousness of the value of potency as well as youth and means! Ah, to have all! Not be as I was —impoverished and impotent! At the very same time and in spite of this, I was luxuriated as might one who is cold, say, and permitted to enjoy a fire. Really, I think I was so enraptured by this particular and generic phase of life, or this particular showy setting of it, that its various and often crude details did not trouble me at all. For here a woman was a woman, provided she was plump and rosy. Her mental characteristics or tendencies were of no particular import. It was her form, that mystic geometric formula which something has invented and which when contemplated by the eye of man inflames his passions. I say "invented," for I think man really is an invention, a schemed-out machine, useful to a larger something which desires to function through him

464

as a machine, be that air, fire, water, electricity, cosmic rays, or what you will. At any rate, and most assuredly, man is no self-propelling body by any means; air and water and heat and other things most certainly make him go. As a flying machine may to-day be operated by invisible rays, so man. A part of the motivating power, perhaps, enters through the eye, another part through the mouth, the nose; touch is responsible for some reactions, and so it goes. But certainly one of the geometric formulæ which causes man to act, to energise or procreate in the very necessary process which the continuation of human life on earth compels, is the form of a woman, and its energising force is communicated through the eye. What humorous master decided on this double mechanism which a man and a woman constitute, and why?

Be that as it may, and just at that time, a woman was a woman to me, a pretty girl a charming implement for effecting sex delight. I fondled this offering of the fates, regardless of the fact that she was as dull and coarse as any girl might well be, and was thrilled by the discovery that she had nothing on save this pink chemise, that I was in contact with her rounded solid flesh. Ecstasised sensorially, yet also made to remember that I had no money and no potency wherewith to entertain her, I accepted the snuggling and its effect about as a man eats a meal, knowing he cannot pay for it. And this was all the more emphasised by an early inquiry on the part of the girl as to whether I did not want to go upstairs, and since I did not, by the additional inquiry of a coloured maid who came to ask what we wished to drink—cigars, beer, wine, or what? Cigars at fifty cents each, beer at a dollar the bottle, alleged champagne at five dollars but of American make and very bad, presumably cultivated cider.

Since I could not pay the price that was demanded by this girl—five dollars for a single relationship—I was about to extricate myself by pretending to be dissatisfied, when O'Connor coming over to me, signalled: "Come on!" and then, *sotto voce*: "You don't want that!" To smooth matters, we each took a cigar off the tray, which he paid for, and affecting a serenity and indifference which I did not feel, we set forth again.

"There's nothing worth while in there," was his comment as we went down the steps, myself wondering why after all the girls he knew and played with in Bloomington, he should choose to come here. "They're just tough, vulgar bitches," he went on. But just the same, my mind was full of the wonder of being able to join issues with such a plump piece of pastry as I had just released, of being able to spend hours in such meaty, perfumed embraces.

There were thereafter other houses, and into several of these we entered, O'Connor paying as we did so. (I still wonder why.) And before we were through, I had become almost expert in sampling these beauties (exteriorly, at least) the while maintaining a seemingly judicial and undetermined state of mind. For I found, and that quickly, that it would not do to seem appreciative or inclined to any one girl, lest one failed of an excuse to depart. At the same time, what a beggar I felt! How cheap! With each additional entrance and exit I grew more and more disgusted with myself than with anything I saw, and wanted much to get away. As for O'Connor, with his money and aplomb and determined and critical selective sense, he was by no means abashed. For, as he said, when he found what he wanted, he would stay, and not before. Hence, while remote and non-committal, as I could see, he, like myself, was looking these several candidates over and sensualising at his ease. Yet presently, and as I saw, he did find one who seemed to attract him, and so stayed. And although he urged me to do the same, offering me bills wherewith to continue my search, I refused. The whole process for me had been ruined for the want of independent means.

And though looked at askance and even frowned upon by maid and "professor"—as the musician was called—at last I made my way out. Yet not without some expense. For although O'Connor had paid for most, I presently had spent three dollars for three bottles of beer—my financial limit, and more. In consequence, depressed by this experience, I decided to go no more—would not see O'Connor any more on this trip, and managed so.

Afterwards, I thought—some years afterwards, though —what spindling beginners we must have seemed to those women, accustomed as they were to politicians, priests, and that heavy type of business man who comes with a roll of money and a solid, matter-of-fact conception of these mundane

466

pleasures! How trivial! But then again, the thought of these women receiving all and sundry staggered me. For although one could not really see the man ahead of one or the man behind, still there he was. And you shared only function-ally in what could be no more than a machine process. More, the same girls approached me as every other with a pretence of special interest—an affectation of a fresh delight with you, me. And so—not only a little pathetic, but worse, a farce, really.

But how ridiculous! Astounding!

Surely somewhere must be forces of intelligence that look on and laugh, as we do at comic toys. But where, oh, where is the toy-maker who makes us? And can it be that he is ashamed to show us his face?

CHAPTER LXXVII

AFTER Bloomington and its easy college life, it will be obvious that the home life from which I had been so suddenly extracted should seem less attractive—most suggestive of the economic and social struggle that would await me once my college year was over. And at the same time, and because of the idling I had done and was doing, and the feeling that apart from mere colour—the functioning of this particular university as an institution or social organism—it had meant and probably never could mean much to me, I was troubled by the thought that honestly I could not accept another year from Miss Fielding or anyone—that it was really unfair to go on from this point and that I should tell her so.

At the same time, it was the Christmas period, always seemingly dull in the commercial world to which I should have to turn. And how hard to say to Miss Fielding, as well as to my mother and others, that here as in other fields I did not appear to fit in, was once more a failure! And then start out in the cold to look for a job! Whereas if I said nothing and returned, I should at least be as comfortable as I was before. And when the college year ended, it would be spring and I could so much more comfortably seek work then. Whereas now . . .

To my discredit let it be said that I chose the easiest way, and with obviously no such qualms of conscience as should have deterred me, "elsen" (as we used to say as children) I would not have returned. One thing I did do was to talk to Miss Fielding, who seemed, whatever I said—and I know that I did not boast of my progress—to feel that I should continue for the rest of the year anyhow. And her argument was quite the same—or nearly so—as it was in the first instance. That I need not expect that I could fit myself for any definite thing in a year. I could not. And that was not the idea. What was really desired was that in some modest way mentally

468

I should begin to find myself. Wonderful! I thought. But supposing she should guess how I was "finding" myself—what it really was that was troubling my chief sensory faculties, or at least responses.

Just the same and thus heartened I returned, but with somewhat of a more serious view than before. Obviously, as I saw it now, I could not enter upon any technical course which would get me anywhere in any reasonable course of time; so why bother? As for the general and quite conventional and more or less literary courses I was pursuing, well, as I argued, it was, with my wholly deficient equipment, the best that I could do. One thing that I could do, though—or at least I thought I could—was to take my mind off girls and sex and put it on my selected studies and their related reading. And to that end, I decided that it might be best if I moved. For before Christmas, not only Sutcliffe but Hall and others had remarked that I seemed to be bothering with a lot of social as well as athletic nonsense which could in no way benefit me—which was true. For Levitt and O'Connor—the one interested in football and athletics in every form, the other in girls, college society and his superior social connections—and the two of them finding relatively common denominators in not only law but me—had come to a sort of gentlemen's agreement not to quarrel but rather to be sociable. And so it had been that some time before Christmas, the large one-time living room, which was now equipped with a bed and our books, had become a rendezvous for all sorts and conditions of students, from those who liked society and law and girls to those who liked to play cards and talk athletics or college politics—a development which appeared to me and Hall and Sutcliffe to spell the end of all serious thought, and brought about the conclusion on my part that as much as I liked O'Connor and Levitt, it would be best for me if I separated from them and went, as in the beginning, my way alone.

And so it was that not more than two weeks after my return, and after duly looking here and there for some quiet place in which I was not likely to be disturbed, I found one at the extreme east end of the town, near the college, where because of a boarding club which was a part of the same, were assembled —at meal time only, not otherwise—some of the abler though poorer, and incidentally more studious, students of the college, who having no time for such nonsense as O'Connor, Levitt and myself had been permitting ourselves, spurned all thought of it. It came out in various conversations at table, as I soon found.

On finding this place, though, I immediately returned to my room-mate and announced my intention of moving, whereupon Levitt, who was probably a little conscience-stricken himself, agreed with me. He, too, he said, had been wasting time, devoting too much attention to athletics. Since he only had two years in which to complete his law studies here, it was high time he settled down and did something. And besides, since I was moving, he would prefer to be in another part of the town in a house where apparently were gathered a number of his fraternity brothers. Result—an immediate notice to our mild old housekeeper of our intention to depart. And within the week our joint removal, though not without protests on the part of Hall and O'Connor. Why, if I had to move, did I choose such an outlandish spot—so far removed from everything—whereas here, close at hand . . .? In as politic a way as I could, I explained why, and went. And for the time at least appeared to have lost almost everybody, save Sutcliffe and Hall. And even they at first did not appear to be anxious to walk the long distance it required to get there.

But the difference between this atmosphere and the old —the comparative silence and peace! For here, and much to my satisfaction, I had a room to myself. And better, after the hectic and for me mental as well as emotional tortures in which I had been steeped ever since my contact with Levitt and O'Connor—their girls and their means—I found a phase of peace and quiet such as previously I had not experienced here.

The charm of this house was that it stood on a hill or quite considerable rise of ground, giving a broad and almost unobstructed view not only of Bloomington, which lay in a hollow below, and the university, which lay to the north, but the wooded hills, interspaced with level fields which lay to the south and east. And how pleasant, as I found the following spring, to sit on the long front veranda which faced to the south and watch not only the early ploughmen of those fields but the gathering birds and the delicate pepperings of green

470

which finally tinted and then mantled in a rich green cloak the bare and leafless arms of the trees that stood out so stark and crow-haunted in the January days in which I arrived.

Next, Mr. and Mrs. Santee, who conducted this place, and their son Frank were three of the most earnest, honest, quiet and industrious people that I have ever known. Santee, Senior, before he and his wife and son removed to Bloomington, had been a fire insurance agent in some very small town in southern Indiana, where in addition he farmed, or sought to, a very small farm or truck garden. But both his and his wife's pride as well as life was centred in and around their very handsome and strong young son, Frank, who only the year before had been graduated from the university with a degree. The only reason they ever came to Bloomington, as Mrs. Santee told me, was to be with this son, whom they adored and who in return seemed wholly devoted to them. He was as yet unmarried, and held a position as superintendent of a large, local spoke factory. In a family sense, I think I never saw a happier or more contented family. And this happiness blew like a sweet breath of air upon all those about them, myself as well as the several members—some fourteen or sixteen in all—of the East Hill Boarding Club, which at the beginning of each college year appeared to wish to renew its contact with Mrs. Santee for not only the supplies but her supervision, which to them appeared necessary to its proper conduct. For Mrs. Santee, in addition to being a charming wife and mother, was not only an orderly and tasteful house-keeper but an excellent cook, or at least the manager of a good cook whose labours she supplemented and directed.

Within a week—certainly a fortnight—it seemed to me as though I had encountered an entirely new and to me quite fascinating world. The introductions and new contacts which this club provided! Wilkins Byworth, for instance, a tall, bony, worn man, of forty-eight, who after years of farming, river-boating, logging, in the north, and what not else, had managed finally (he was a bachelor still) to put by sufficient money to take a course in philosophy. But he was so worn and weary-looking, and not bright, as I discovered through various conversations, but so delighted, so ecstatic really, at being able at last to enter upon the fulfilment of his great dream.

And after him again, one Harry Bullen, a young, clean, vigorous, argumentative sophomore, of no particular means but with such upstanding and penny-jingling independence as evoked, after a very short time, a veritable flood of admiration out of the deeps of me. He was from the Ohio River line, half Southern, half mountain type, but interested in economics, sociology, politics, taxation, government and the like, and determined, as he said, to invade the State and later the National legislature in order to make effective certain ideas which were already haunting him—improvements in education, the machinery of government, taxation and the like. He liked to talk, and very soon to me as I found, and presently of a late afternoon would appear with the suggestion that we walk and talk, he bringing a small twenty-two calibre rifle with which he used to aim at bottles, rocks, leaves and the like, and get me to do the same. And occasionally he shot rabbits and pheasants, of which he promptly made Mrs. Santee a present. And while she always deplored his cruelty, I noticed that in due course they appeared on our club table. At which he laughed, or defended himself, and well, even in the face of the fact that this was mostly a vegetarian club— some eight eating vegetables only and constantly defending themselves—the others meat, and as stoutly defending themselves. And so, much banter and persiflage, as you may well guess. "Pale, anæmic vegetarians" and "bloody, bullying meat eaters!"

Among others who came near me in this new quarter was a certain young German-American by the name of Albrecht, first or second assistant in geology—I forget which—a bachelor, athlete and great walker, who liked to conduct small groups on long tramps in search of this or that geological stratum or specimen or to demonstrate something in connection with Indiana formations, and who, although I was no part of his department, still after a general table conversation or two in which I did not join but to which I listened intently, invited me to come along, once to so far as Brown County, where, among rough hills and woodlands, I was shown where the sea had once been and left what traces of fish and shell life in what ancient rocks—a demonstration which was broadening as well as refreshing.

And after him again, a big intellectual bully by the name of

Trodgers—a huge, lank specimen of a student, majoring in history, philosophy, logic, and what not else—who liked to start an argument on any and every subject in order to drive into their holes all and sundry who ventured to oppose him. In some ways he was a most ponderous and threatening-looking fellow, built, in part, like a great baboon, and in some ways looking and acting not unlike one. Often in the silence of my newness and strangeness, I contemplated him, fearing for a long time to contest any point he chose to defend, for was he not a senior working for a master's degree and rather more pleased than not to thunder out his conclusions in a great rough voice which nearly always quieted all? For nearly all of the students who surrounded him here, as I found, were quite certain that as soon as his course was done he would be called to some important chair somewhere, or possibly enter politics in his own state, which was Michigan, for among his other accomplishments was oratory.

On one occasion, though—it was toward the close of dinner one evening—at which time strong arguments quite often developed—the question arose as to whether a man propagandising for any ism or theory or trying to persuade the world intellectually to any cause or thought was better equipped to attract attention and win if he were supported by an organisation—a chair in a university, say, or a pulpit—or whether being merely a free lance and using such methods as he might (the same not always permitted by a church or school), he would not be more effective. For some reason—possibly because the majority hoped to hold chairs or positions of one kind or another—the stoutest argument maintained that organisations were more of a help than a hindrance—they gave a man standing, prestige, etc.—to which I privately demurred, as publicly did Trodgers. My personal reason for so demurring was that a real free lance of great mental capacity neither would nor could endure the tag of a school or church. But since Trodgers—and with that argument —was slowly but surely beating every other into silence, I finally interjected a question. It was whether material means (money, church pulpit, college chair, or what you will) could possibly, if unhampered by conditions of any kind, really hinder a man.

Since I had never ventured to join issues with him before,

or indeed say anything at all in his presence, he looked at me with frowning contempt, then began to scrape around for reasons to prove that any argument other than his was ridiculous. There was, in the first place, the uselessness or dead weight of a tag of any kind, pulpit or chair; also, having such or money or all, there was the danger of sloth and love of ease.

"But we are postulating a man who is on fire with an idea, one who, however situated, is seeking the nearest and best way to address the world. Now an idea that would not necessarily be popular with the mass on the street corner might well get its start in a church or college, or through the use of money." (You see, I was arguing just to be arguing.) "Hence, why assume that if given means or an unhampered chair of philosophy or a pulpit, he would be idle or slothful?"

"But it is human nature," he declared.

"But we are postulating the extra-human, the man who is somewhat above current weaknesses."

"Still, he would have the haunting sense of privilege, of taking an unfair advantage of his fellows in order to further his ideas, wouldn't he?"

"But would he? Haven't we just said that he is trying to serve his fellow-men by his ideas, and all means that fall to his aid would then be good means or could be made so. Why not?"

"Why not? Because a man in a pulpit or a chair has only an audience of five hundred or a thousand; the other man has the whole world to address."

"So has my man," I replied, "the whole world, plus the immediate five hundred or one thousand he is privileged to address, and unhampered."

There was a silence. It had been a brief but new phase of the argument, and just before my last reply he had risen to go, as though all was over. But now he paused and looked at me, intending, I am sure, to hurl some last crushing remark in my direction and then walk out leaving me windless and musing. As I sat there, though, I saw the light dying out of his eye, for, as I could see, he had no instant reply and I could not see where he was to get one. But then, with a contemptuous laugh, he concluded: "Well, maybe. Anyhow, I haven't any more time to discuss it now," and started to go.

"No answer," I called as he hustled past me, and then I sat there wondering whether I had been beaten or not.

"Good for you!" exclaimed a stout and not too mentally strong student sitting next to me. "That's the first time I've seen anybody take a draw with him at this table. It'll do him good."

"Darned if you didn't lick him, Dreiser!" exclaimed Frank Santee, my landlady's son, who ate at this same table. Others gathered around to continue the discussion, but flushed by my success, I arose also and walked off, feeling very much like the gladiator Trodgers certainly was, for plainly I had won in a heated and popular contest, and for the first time, and was being told so. Then why shouldn't I get along in the world, I now asked myself, if I could argue like that with a philosophy senior?

But the victory was not for very long. For in a later argument I was beaten or tied by lack of facts.

CHAPTER LXXVIII

AS the spring drew near, though, I began to realise that outside of general impressions and a somewhat less vague understanding of colleges and the character of the men who thought them valuable, I was no whit farther than when I came. No technical, as opposed to general and non-technical, education; no way, once I was out, of doing anything different from what I had previously done. Heavens! And now bemoaning, and most unreasoningly, the fact that I had not chosen a special as opposed to a general course of reading. Yet how in a year, as I afterward said to myself, was I to grasp anything practical, anyhow? That must come later, apparently, through contact with some business or profession. But how? I dreaded business as well as any practical profession, since I could not see myself as having any capacity for either, any intuitional skill or enthusiasm for the same. And as for clerking or serving in any unprofitable way, how wretched and destroying, even painful, to contemplate!

Nevertheless, seeing that no practical course was open to me here, I read and read, everything that I could lay my hands on—history, philosophy, art—but with the thought, for the most part, that I was drifting, and that straight toward the rocks of poverty and failure. If I only knew bookkeeping, I now said to myself, or even commercial mathematics, or some trade like carpentering, bricklaying, plastering! But I did not. And by now, silly as it may seem to many, I was imagining that I had wasted most of my best years and opportunities and that it was already too late to learn a trade, and that I should never have sufficient means to acquire a profession. For by this next summer I would be eighteen. What was I to do—which way to turn?

Finally I decided, and quite determinedly, that once I returned to Chicago, I would try to get in some line of work which would provide a course of commercial training in itself

—such as manufacture or railroading. It was not a very cheering prospect, since all I really cared for was the beauty of life, its spectacles and pleasures. By fits and starts, therefore, I was restless, gay, sombre, or wholly defeated and despondent. Hypochondriacal by nature, I could rise to the greatest heights and fevers of expectation and delight, the next moment sink to the lowest pits of certain failure. One thing that grew upon me was the conviction that neither O'Connor nor Levitt was likely to be of any service to me, their minds being mainly concerned with entertainment. And both together had been becoming not only too importunate but had been filling my mind with things with which I should not have been bothering. The devil! And only to be defeated as I had been!

Nevertheless, and in spite of excellent resolutions, more love or sex interruptions, and in this lovely, quiet home where I expected (apart from meal hours) no least emotional disturbance of any kind. It was this way.

One of them was a little Quaker co-ed who roomed in this same house—a pale, shapely, retiring girl, who seemed amazingly simple and shy at first, though I have since doubted whether she was either as simple or as retiring as she seemed. For as I went on living here, she came to talk to me much, usually contriving to be playing the piano when I was sitting outside viewing the scenery. Also at times, I having confessed to difficulties in Latin and algebra, she offered to help me with these studies. At other times we talked history and literature. But with what smiling glances in my direction, and how often, inclining her head to mine, her hair touching my cheek, in order to be near me in those moments when the problems involved appeared to require two pairs of eyes to contemplate the same page. And yet, in spite of this proximity, nothing came of it, I swear. After O'Connor and Chicago and what not, I was still too fearful of a reproach or rebuke. And although she did nothing but frankly smile and encourage me in such ways as she could, as amazingly as in the past, I retired, confused and distressed, not with her but with myself.

In connection with all this, though, a thought has since come to me, and that is that perhaps at this period it was better rather than worse that I was so self-inhibited in my desire to achieve all of these various intimacies which my intense desire appeared to attract. For assuredly, not only for lack of time but for lack of strength—which would have followed upon such satiations—I would have been diverted from the major portions of not only my studies and introspections but such contacts with serious and informed personalities as, through Sutcliffe and others, were constantly swimming into my ken. In other words, it so chanced that I was not to waste myself on contacts which certainly would have undermined my none too good health and diverted my mind from such serious thinking and reading as I was then capable of.

A second girl was the fifteen- or sixteen-year-old daughter of one of the best physicians of the city—a grave medical gentleman as tall, silent and impressive as any physician might wish to be—who lived not far from where I now resided and whose home was a perfect bird-box of rustic beauty. It was farther in toward the heart of the town than my own place, and whenever I went to the city for mail or any other purpose, I had to pass it. And so, as the winter wore on and spring came, I could not but observe the dulcet home life that was led here. In so far as I could make out, there were but two daughters—no other children—one, the elder, an amateur violinist, who played with either her father or mother as accompanist—the open French windows in the spring revealing this quite plainly—the other, this young girl, whom I frequently saw, usually, in the raw spring weather, in a blue cape with a red hood, her books under her arm—a slender, white-faced, sylph-like girl, making her way daily to and from the local High School.

And now once more, and as in Warsaw with Myrtle Trego, love at first sight—a physiological epoch, as valid as the explosion which follows the union of certain chemical elements in the laboratory. And however valueless my testimony may appear, I cannot refrain from stating my belief that this was another example of the only true union, however disastrous it may seem in current affairs, and that around this type of union or attraction cluster all great tragedies as well as all true blisses. For I am not one to deny that for some (many), one such union, recognition, physiological epoch, might prove permanently binding. On the other hand, I am not prepared to deny that many such astounding recognitions, explosions, true unions, are possible in one life and to one person, where previous recognitions by accident or circumstance are not permitted to come to their normal fruitage. As many as five times in my life has this happened to me to date, and in three of them the natural fruition of the contact was interrupted, so that I cannot say what the ultimate result would have been. But in each instance, the transition from a normal to an agonised state was almost instantaneous. And in each case the pain endured for months, and in two instances, years. Not that other attractions did not manifest themselves after, or that minor emotions did not ride on the swell of the greater one, as little waves do on big, but the former was valid, instantaneous, and in all three cases the women had very much in common. I am thinking of Myrtle and after her, the daughter of this doctor, whose name I do not recall, but whose import to me at the time is by no means invalidated thereby. The others will be described elsewhere. In all other cases, I have merely tolerated, not loved, though under other conditions—if, for instance, union had not resulted first—love might have been evoked.

In each of the cases above mentioned, a certain nebulousness of mood, a certain fearsomeness as to love, a certain white-faced serenity which seemed to bode terrible storms of mood and feeling, gripped me with an intensity which defies description and which no one of all of the other women I have known has been able to convey. You may see a suggestion of what I mean in Dante's Beatrice, in Rosa Bonheur's Joan of Arc, in Faust's Marguerite. It remains an enigma. I only know that whenever and wherever I have encountered it, I have been laid hold of as by an iron force, I have succumbed and become wild, although in three of the five cases—this being one of them —I never exchanged more than a few troubled words with the soul that so aroused me.

And the thought that sometimes haunts me is (though from the fourth experience I have to assume it is not valid) that possibly the thing that I saw or imagined—that something so seraphic that I cannot even describe it—was not there at all. Or perhaps it was no more than a projection of my own mood. Life's greatest lures are a compound of illusion —phantasms, mirages, *ignes fatui*, I fear—I do not know— but like the mystery which binds people to religious beliefs, so was I bound. I have also sometimes wondered whether the power of nature to delude us is ever broken, even in the days when we are but the thin and decayed fibre of former physical strength. If imagination endures, unquestionably the power of nature to charm and betray is there.

But even so. In regard to this girl, I was, after a few views of her, simply beside myself. I cannot tell you what it was that held me—a weaving airiness of motion, a softness and shyness of eye, a wisp of windblown chestnut hair curling out from under her hood, a slimness and curve of chin or cheek, which was like music. In spite of all these other matters that here claimed me, I began spending so much time at the window of my room, which commanded a view of her home, and looking for some sign of her, that I was not only almost wholly idle but as wholly miserable. For what was life without such a dream? What could it be? Oh, those aching moods, that almost unendurable longing for her, just her face, her eyes, her steps, her total loveliness! And worse, I was not so far removed but that I could see her and she me if she looked, yet not so near but that my feeble attempts at flirtation—the waving of a hand or a handkerchief—took on a kind of uncertainty, and therefore safety or innocence. Yet after a very little while, and in spite of this distance, she appeared to become aware, and as I looked, she looked, and when I was nearer, morning or evening as she went to or came from school, what shyness! And how disconcerted, passing me with head bowed and sometimes face averted! Yet after a time, since I often managed to pass her on the street as she came or went, managing to glance, once perhaps, but how shyly, and then pass on, not to look again, maybe, until she was entering her own door or turning a corner, when suddenly she might pause to fling me a white rose-leaf glance over her shoulder, and then as swiftly entering and closing the door of that paradise, her home, to which I was not admitted but outside of which I stood, lorn and adoring.

Once—on one of those warm, premonitory and almost enervating nights that come in late February or early March—I saw her sitting at her piano, while across the way among the trees I stood adream. Already visible in the sky was the "big dipper" and some minor stars, parts of those strange galaxies that people the deeps of space. Spring fires of raked leaves had been burning, and the air was redolent of their smoke. She wore a light dress; by the light of the lamp near her I could see her face and form as she bent over her music. Perhaps it was the artistry of life itself that enthralled and bit so savagely. Yet to me it was desire—aching, knifing—and for her. And in my mind as she played were songs of and to her—poems, dreams. Ligeia.

Another time—another spring evening—there was a dance at her home. I do not think that she danced—it was for grown-ups—but I imagined she was there. In a clump of trees across the way, in the shadow, I stood and looked for her, waiting, waiting, and wishing that I were dancing with her.

Youthful romance is such a delicate and enthralling thing. In my own case, in desperation as to some method of overcoming this barrier of distance and non-relationship, I composed all sorts of notes to her, suggesting that she meet me somewhere, that she permit me to call, that she attend a college lecture with me, and the like. Each one was based on the idea that I was to interrupt her somewhere and hand her the note, though why, if I could do that, I could not address her directly, I do not know. Just the same, I tore up these notes one after the other, but not before carrying them in my pocket for days, and as certainly not being able to bring myself to present any of them. Finally, in desperation, I waited outside her school, then outside her church on a Wednesday evening. Each time someone or something interfered or in some way frustrated my hope or thinly built-up daring. For now it would be that someone was looking, or again that she was with another girl or girls, though I believed she saw me. At last I did approach her one day as she was strolling down a side street near her home, as shy and meditative as ever, and drew my note from my pocket and swiftly handed it to her. In a sort of wide-eyed and yet by no means antagonistic amazement, quite pale and tremulous, she looked at me, then took it and hurried away. And I was as thrilled as though she had spoken. For she had taken it—and her eyes—how inexpressibly weak and frightened and yet kind they were!

What did the note say? I have no clear recollection except that I believe I asked her to meet me somewhere not far from her home. What did she do? Nothing! I don't think I really expected her to do anything, so nervous was I about the whole affair. Yet because I had not the courage to speak to her when I had this very good opportunity, I gave the matter up in despair, knowing that nothing would ever come of it in so far as my direct efforts were concerned. Just the same, I think I even implored chance—the sightless substances of nature—to grant me the boon of knowing her, of being able to touch her hand. And as in all of the truly serious cases of affection where I have been thus smitten, my passion was in no way involved with any thought of the flesh. That, if at all, was far too remote to permit of any thought of anything save possibly a kiss or kisses, of being able to sit by her in some dreamland of beauty, of walking with her by lovely waters or under the pointed stars, and listening to the night winds and the murmuring of waters and dreaming and dreaming of all beautiful things.

But no more. My love in such cases did not come to any such happy fruition.

CHAPTER LXXIX

AND so, with such things, and my few books and lectures and occasional examinations, and my talks and arguments with one person and another, on to the end of the year. Curiously, and in spite of my feeling that practically (so far as concerned my making a place for myself in this world) I was no further advanced than when I came, and recurrent and sombre depressions in connection with that, I did *feel* advanced. For apart from the imposing and to me oppressive curriculum of the university, its ramified fields of endeavour—almost every one of which required an intense form of specialisation which left me not so much cold as suffering from a feeling of inadequacy before so many extremes of mental adventure—there had been these various contacts, that with Sutcliffe the most impressive. And the walks and talks, and betimes arguments most hotly and not infrequently successfully conducted, which had made clear to me that however mute I might stand before the curriculum as a whole, its professors and their required courses of reading and experiment (present and past), still, when it came to the individual anywhere, and past reading or no past reading, I appeared instinctively to apprehend many things and to be able to demonstrate my apprehensions sometimes quite satisfactorily, to myself at least. More, I enjoyed listening and inquiring so much that at times I could actually weary if not exactly exhaust anyone who was so foolish as to suggest knowledge in a given field. For I could go on and on, asking one and then another question until at last the unhappy victim would extricate himself in any possible way he could. And once Sutcliffe, in friendly weariness, exclaimed: "Well, if asking will get you knowledge, you certainly will get it!"

But just that remark, together with my unschemed ability to draw to and about me a quite impressive group of students, shaped up somewhat a sense of individuality, though still far from well, let alone egotistically, formed in my mind. Within the classrooms, as I well knew, I had done nothing much—capturing here an idea, there a memorable statement —nothing very logical or sequential or valuable to me as part of a course—but outside, as I have shown, I was really being privately tutored, and by many who were successfully prosecuting their studies within the walls of the college—a system or procedure not unrelated to the Greek peripatetic school with its mentors. And while I could not say to myself or even see then in exactly what particulars I was being prepared for the life outside, in reality I was so being and taking on at least some of the directness and surety of those who, with less skill for argument and questioning than I possessed, were nevertheless satisfied that they were reasonably well fitted for the world they were about to face. To be sure, many of them had parents with means or were the natural heirs to position or controls in this or that built-up industry or property, whereas I . . . Only, after associating with Sutcliffe so long, I could not help but feel that if he could face life so bravely and cheerfully on just nothing at all—what he actually earned by the meanest kind of labour—so could I, and with honour, so long as my mental ideals were not betrayed thereby.

How much I owe to that one sturdy, inquiring, generous, thinking soul! How much!

But now these closing days, a warm, sunshiny spring glorifying the beauty of this university campus and town, and all of these students dreamy and speculative or practical and unpoetic, going here and there, to and fro, their examinations and their hoped-for degrees bringing on a mental tensity and even energy not previously noticeable in the college air—the all-penetrating wave-lengths of their escaping thoughts and moods. But although all sorts of things were going on—class conferences of juniors and seniors, functions in connection with the Greek letter societies, students bent over their finals—I myself felt more or less apart or alone. Try as I might, I could not think of myself as a suitable, let alone essential, part of anything that was here going forward or to what subsequently it might lead. To be sure, I took some examinations and did well enough in history, literature, and such phases of mathematics and economics as I had taken. But what of it, I asked myself? Of what service, since I was not to return here or follow them up in any definite way?

And yet, and in spite of this, I had grown mentally to love this patchwork college or university, which was as yet a mere spindling suggestion of its future, and was dreading to leave it. For after it, Chicago, the world, my future, and then what? Ah, that mystical, strange, exciting and fearsome future! After what fashion, in what state—sorrowful or courageous, wearied or encouraged, helpful or helpless—should I fare? Besides, the spirit of this school, as I now perceived, was admirable enough—its principal message the love of correct information on the part of all of its students as to all things reasonably verified or helpful, the rejection of all others. To be sure, it had no tradition, no least trace of the mellow patina of time; but what of that?—it did have a kind of youthful ambition and optimism which said to all, "Try!" And although already various phases of snobbery were manifest, still as yet these same were but spindling things and with years might die. Who should say? I felt so sure that in spite of this or that idiosyncrasy, this or that petty notion of life or society, so many of these boys and girls were blundering on to real individuality and material or spiritual success, for they were so earnest. (Sutcliffe, for instance.) As for the rest, they were going back to be small-town citizen lawyers, doctors, chemists, physicists, members of faculties in minor schools, or mere ornaments to the small property someone might leave them. At that, I envied most of them, since for them was no great problem of how to do—their aims were too commonplace and practical—they knew exactly what they were to do and what they wanted to be, whereas I did not know what I was to do or be.

But finally my last examination concluded, and knowing that all was over, I sat in my room one afternoon wondering whether I should start at once or linger on a day or two on any pretext in order to enjoy for so much more time the spring and these last sweet days. As no reports were furnished as to whether one had failed or passed (they were to be mailed later), I did not have that to worry over. I knew that in class I had never really registered. But Sutcliffe called to say that he was coming to Chicago to seek any sort of work, even that of waiter or car driver, until he could find out what he wanted to do or where he fitted in, and that set up in me the thought that I should depart at once. He had an idea that it was his duty to serve humanity in some way; how, he could not say. Hall also called to say that he was going back to Michigan to study law in a law office, and at once; Levitt also, but to find out whether I was coming back next year. Hall, as he said, was eager for me to visit him in Michigan, for we were still the best of friends, but (a gloomy Hamlet) I told him that I could not be sure, that he should look me up in Chicago. O'Connor was also there, and many others, individuals whom I have not mentioned but with whom I was friendly enough. The gloom that was on my soul, though, was so thick you might have cut it with a knife, yet I pretended to be gay, even was gay, for so often we are two things at once.

And then at last my departure—and in shabby state, as I saw it—no spring suit such as most of the students were displaying—an old trunk that I hated because it was not as good as most of the trunks on the depot platform. The night before I left, there was the burning of books on the campus— a borrowed custom, I assume, common to all college freshmen classes everywhere—but I did not attend because I did not feel myself a part of these, to me, silly revelries. In fact, now that I looked back on my college year, I was irritated by the deprivations I had endured, the things in which I had not been included, the joys which many had had and which I had not.

"They can all go to hell!" I said of these youths, girls and elements which had ignored me. And for the first time, I think, I set my teeth in hard defiance of life and fate. "I will get along and be somebody in spite of them! Beautiful girls will yet be interested in me, and society, too!" But as to how I was to accomplish all this, I had no notion. None. Unquestionably, the greatest pain in me now related to the lovely daughter of the physician, who for the time being represented all that I desired of romance and beauty. For her I saved my last brooding thoughts, and on the evening before I left, returning late at night from visits to Sutcliffe and Hall, stood opposite her home and under the moonlight studied its humble protective form. For inside was she, asleep, adream, perhaps, or looking out of the window at this same moon. That face. Those small white hands. That waver-

ing, shy, recessive tread. Darling . . . darling . . . I thought
. . . and hurt to the heart, fled. But with me went the
bushes and trees of the yard, the vines that clambered up the
walls and shaded the windows; her smooth, pale, oval face,
delicate hands, and thin, petal-like eyelids. And ever since
have stayed just as they were, identified with the moonlight
and odours and stars of a long-ago spring.

When I returned to Chicago the second morning after that,
riding all night to get there, it was with such thoughts of
deprivation, inefficiency, and impending difficulties of all
kinds, crowding hard upon me. My year of pleasure was
over. And although I should now have to report to Miss
Fielding that I was grateful and ready to face the world, I
really was not—must pretend (though I felt that I should not)
that I had been vastly benefited and that I was going forth
to do many things. As a matter of fact, I had been benefited,
in the ways stated, but as to this I was still not sufficiently
clear. I did not understand myself well enough, either then
or much later. Only in spite of all my idling and dreaming,
I was by no means the same youth who had left Chicago the
fall before. I was more courageous, more ambitious, and at
moments had an opinion of my possible future achievement
in some field which would have shocked all those immediately
about me if they had known.

Only now, more days in Chicago throughout which I
took up my seeking—for work as well as the key to my own
disposition and life. For in me were bubbling the most
ethereal and yet colourful dreams and possibilities. As for
Chicago, it seemed stronger, brisker, more colourful even than
before, although and at the same time it was so coarse and
crude, in spots vicious as well as tatterdemalion. I liked
it much, for here one sensed vigorous, definite projects under
way, great dreams and great achievements, and behind them
strong, definite-minded, if not so terrifically visionful, men at
work. It was more money, money, money, and the fame
of the same, the great fortune idea. But still, was not the
fame of this city to ring about the world? One could feel it.
Even our neighbourhood, now that I saw it anew in June,
seemed more interesting, with new houses going up everywhere. I remember thinking, as I made my way home, that
everything was before everybody in Chicago, if they but

thought so, and that in spite of all my doubts, I would find work and joy somewhere here. So many people were making money. So many new enterprises under way. Even the dullest could see that and would be certain to be moved by the hope of prosperity.

I know that I started out with a better feeling than ever I had experienced for any undertaking before. For one thing, the state of the family seemed to be much better than it had been at Christmas. All were still working as before. The medicine company, Al reported, had raised his wages. They were planning to build a large plant on the west side, and Dr. Fahrney, the proprietor, was building himself a pretentious residence in the most exclusive section of Washington Boulevard, near Garfield Park. Ed was with his dear Davis; they had come to be fast friends. In fact, his salary had been increased from five to seven dollars. It is true my father was downcast as to further effort in his field, but on the other hand Trina had prospered in her work at The Fair and was getting six or seven dollars and indulging herself in some additions to her wardrobe. Ruth was still being courted by Davis, and in view of their approaching marriage was receiving aid from him quite as might a wife, although because of this and her approaching displacement in his home, his mother hated her and would have nothing to do with her. As for Eleanor and her husband, their life was as before—travel joined with stays at this home. As I have said before, because of her obvious prosperity, there was some feeling between her and Trina and Ruth, but not of a disrupting character—the magnetism of my mother being too great to permit of any final break. Ruth, as I recall it, was a little jealous of Eleanor's prosperity, since she now gave herself airs in all matters respecting taste and social experience. And Trina, as I recall it, thought of both Ruth and Eleanor as not only vain and somewhat parasitic but by no means sufficiently considerate of those who, like her, had to work hard.

Perhaps the most important thing, psychologically as well as practically, that had happened since I had left was the increasing success, and even national repute of sorts, of my brother Paul, who since my leaving the preceding Christmas had suddenly come to nation-wide notice again with another sentimental and hence very popular song, entitled: "I Believe

It For My Mother Told Me So"—one of those charming and babyish expressions of his inmost self as well as his unchanging adoration of his mother—an expression of affection which, since it was not only dedicated to her but expressed in very primary and yet effective language his profound love of her and so her emotional control of him, must have comforted her no little. In fact, I was told afterwards that when the song first arrived and she saw the title and dedication, and later when Paul himself played it for her, she was moved to that always restrained expression of her deepest feeling— slightly moist eyes and a twitching of the lips—which when witnessed by me immediately effected companionate tears. I could not look at her when she was like that and not cry. (And we are told that the giant chemisms and mechanisms of space are without tenderness or emotion; that suns being hot and moons being cold cannot cry; that rocks and stones and trees are insensate! Yes? Well, maybe. And maybe not.)

But my very good brother was not only successful with this song but was at that very time about to arrive in Chicago (already billed so to do) as one of the leading comedians in "The Tin Soldier," and later so did arrive, fortunately, as we all saw it, this time to be made comfortable in the much more pretentious and comfortable dwelling—two stories and basement—into which since my departure in the fall the family had moved.

If there was one rift in all this, it was the attitude of Trina, who could be so critical and angry at times. According to her, Eleanor was too pretentious and indifferent or stingy, demanding all for her husband and giving little in return, and expecting to be waited on in the bargain. And Ruth, by the same token, was a parasite, living in and on the prospects of marriage to that Davis. As for myself—who was I? I had had one year in college at the expense of Miss Fielding, who could not very well afford it, and now thought myself smart, qualified to show off and criticise! Ha, ha! A line of comment that burned and infuriated as much as fire can burn and infuriate. It made for rows, recriminations as well as dark thoughts as to what I was to do, and how, in order to efface this evidence of parasitism on my part, to make her as well as others know that my year at college had not been wasted on

489

me. And so, an intense desire to get something to do. And at once.

But through it all the dominating sympathy and magnetism and "live and let live" mood and attitude of my mother, which—and which alone—made possible this combination of disparaging temperaments with these steadily diverging ways—all ages, sizes, weights, forces or the lack of the same. And all, for reason of her comforting and so soothing maternal wings, here and remaining here, and for that and no other reason whatsoever.

CHAPTER LXXX

IN a little while—some three weeks at the outside—I obtained a place in a real estate office newly opened in Ogden Avenue, near our home, but on conditions which made it scarcely worth the having. I was to get an assured three dollars a week, with an additional nine dollars out of any earnings which exceeded the monthly cost of rent, gas, stationery, office expenditures and a salary of at least twenty-five dollars a week to my employer. In other words, after he had received twenty-five dollars a week and all his expenses, I was to get as much as twelve dollars.

That would have been well enough if my employer had been a business man of any capacity. But he was not. As a very little time was to show, I was dealing with a really defeated and worn-out religious fuzzy-wuzzy, whose intentions and aspirations were probably of the best but whose ideas of the commercial practicalities and necessities of life were of the vaguest. It may interest some to know that he was the living prototype of Asa Griffiths in "An American Tragedy." His name was Asa Conklin, and his office, a most imposing affair on the ground floor of a new and rather handsome triangular building at the corner of Ogden Avenue and Van Buren Street, was just then being opened by him. In those days, it was a very promising corner. Ogden Avenue, one of the principal thoroughfares of the West Side, ran south-westward from Madison to Douglas Park, and so on across the grass plain which is Illinois to a suburban residence town known as Cypress Grove—there being no cypresses whatsoever in that region.

Conklin's ambition to sell property, rent and care for houses on commission, execute mortgages and the like, was called to my attention by a large gold-leaf sign which one morning I saw a young man lettering on two immense plate-glass windows which constituted the Ogden Avenue front of this building. It read: "A. Conklin, Real Estate, Rentals, Insurance, Loans." Where and how he came by the idea that he could do all of these things I never was able to fathom. Perhaps he saw them on other real estate windows. At any rate he had no money to loan—although, as he once said to me, that could be arranged on commission through some bank, providing the security offered was sufficient. As for the real estate and rentals, these were still to come from somewhere, and on commission also. Next, the insurance offered meant, in the main, soliciting—and he was no solicitor. In short, as I gradually learned for myself, he had no commercial ability of any kind.

Just the same, when I saw the sign I paused and asked the man where A. Conklin was to be found. For might he not be in need of a clerk? Real estate offices were very numerous in Chicago at that time, and since nearly all seemed quite prosperous, I thought I might become a clerk in such an office. For had I not seen many young men, all obviously working for some such concern, running here and there with "For Rent" or "For Sale" signs or cards tucked under their arms and on occasion tacking them on doors, walls or fences, or pasting them on the window-panes of empty flats, houses, stores, which their employers had secured for this purpose, and on a commission basis, of course? More, in open vacant lots, had I not seen them driving stakes, on to which they nailed boards which read: "For Sale or Lease"? I had gained the notion that this sign-placing business must be a full day's or week's or month's work for any clerk, and at a good salary. At any rate, there was the young man painting the sign on Conklin's prospective office, and here was I. And well . . .

Under ordinary circumstances, if I had secured the right kind of a position I think I would have been successful, for I was brisk enough now that nine months of college life had toned me up. But now . . . And Conklin! And the ridiculous part of it was that I really suspected the worst on sight, for I sought and found him at his home, which was part of a religious mission in West Indiana Street not so many blocks away. And he was such a little man, perhaps five feet three or four, stout and yet flabby-looking, and with a grizzled beard and a shock of silver-white hair such as you might see on some tanned and blustery down-east Yankee sea captain, only without the usual sea-captain force or fierceness. He had none of that. On the contrary, a man most weak and variable, easy to persuade to this or that, even by me. An impractical dreamer, who knew nothing of the intricate and psychologic and necessarily diplomatic field on which he had now ventured.

When I think of him, really I have to smile. For actually he was little more than one of those ex-Civil War veterans or G.A.R. men, as we called them—a common soldier of no great skill as such, I venture to say—who was even then and there drawing a pension for some alleged war injury. And worst of all, addicted to a baggy blue Army suit, with brass buttons; for some reason he had eschewed the wide-brimmed and gold-tasselled Army veteran's hat which was almost a byword in my youthful school days (an old soldier hat), and wore instead a wide-brimmed, low-crowned derby, pulled firmly over his ears—in summer a straw hat—from under which his long, curly, white hair protruded most patriarchally and, may I add, foolishly. Add to this, if you will, a penchant for snuff (because his religious wife objected to his smoking), and a snuffy smell, and you have him. In addition, though, was a gold wedding ring on one of his fat fingers, a general look of incompetence in his blue eyes and, oh yes, a habit of twiddling his thumbs when in repose, and when pained or irritated or defeated, of clicking or clucking with his tongue.

The reason for this real estate adventure on his part was this. Someone had recently willed him or his wife, or both, the sum of five hundred dollars, and he was determined to make a success in real estate. He had been reading the endless stories of sudden rises in property values and the great incomes made by renting agents. Without knowing anything about the district, except that it seemed to be growing, and without knowing anything about the renting or selling of properties, he proceeded to lease this large and really attractive office and put in some furniture—a high accountant's desk, for one thing; a roll-top desk for himself; a railing across the front to keep out the inquisitive and make others believe that real business was being done beyond it. At the back, left by some toilet or perfume company which had previously dwelt here, was a partition shutting off a small wash-room, toilet, clothes closet and the like. As clerk and general factotum, as I presently found myself to be, I was to occupy or stand before

493

the accountant's desk and keep the books, as well as wait on customers, while he bustled about on the outside and secured business. As it turned out, just the reverse of this was true. But how was I to know that? To begin with, though, it troubled me not a little that I did not know anything about bookkeeping—since I had concealed the fact from him—but since he did not either, as I soon discovered, it made very little difference to the two of us. I might add that I might have learned in a very few evenings if I had troubled so to do, for later I found it simple enough. But I did not. Instead I worried and invented a crude system of my own, which seemed to satisfy him and me. It consisted of a day book, a cash book, and a ledger, which I posted, heaven knows how! For one thing, we had so few transactions that it made little difference whether or not I entered them.

The mainstay of both Conklin and his wife was religion. They set great and honest store by it. At first, the fact that Mrs. Conklin, as I soon learned, turned religion to good account at such times and in such a way as served to tide them over periods when he was out of employment, militated most decidedly against her in my judgment. Later, though, it did not matter so much. For as I came to know her better, she took on some very arresting and quite admirable qualities. She was, in my eyes at least, so earnest and truly believing. Tall, worn, pale and spiritual-looking she was, the kind of a woman, or mentality rather, that smacks, in part, of a social as well as personal misery which finally finds escape in religion or faith of some kind. I have said of religion that it is a salve or bandage which suffering humanity has invented to ease its wounds. Undoubtedly, Mrs. Conklin was one who had so eased hers.

Her business (or call, if you wish) was running a mission. She was one of those peculiar beings who rent a store in a shabby street, install a small organ, a set of hymn books, some chairs, a desk or rostrum, some mottoes or quotations from the Bible, a picture of Christ or a map of Palestine, or both, and set up in religion for themselves. Yet not to any self-aggrandising or nefarious end. Her spirit was too generous and too pitiful for that. One could tell that from the signs or mottoes or quotations from the Bible, with which, in shabby frames or with mere blue paint hand-lettered on the bare

494

white walls of her barren mission, she set forth such thoughts or messages as she considered most useful or helpful to those who, like herself, were treading the lorn ways of defeat.

> "Take hold of shield and buckler, and stand up for mine help." Psalms 35: 2.

> "And ye, my flock, the flock of my pasture, are men, and I am your God, saith the Lord God." Ezekiel 34: 31.

> "O God, Thou knowest my foolishness, and my sins are not hid from Thee." Psalms 69: 5.

> "If ye have faith as a grain of mustard seed, ye shall say unto this mountain, Remove hence to yonder place; and it shall remove; and nothing shall be impossible unto you." Matthew 17: 20.

> "For there shall be no reward to the evil man." Proverbs 24: 20.

> "Look not thou upon the wine when it is red: it biteth like a serpent and stingeth like an adder." Proverbs 23: 31, 32.

Too little life, in the instance of the human, like too little sunlight in that of the plant, is thus humbling to the soul. Rob either of their natural flood of contact and they become pale, anæmic, humble, peculiar, and frequently spiritual. In fact, spirituality, according to the best of the religionists, consists in avoiding that which in the beginning, mayhap, they most desired—the earthly if mortal pleasures to which we are all subject. Hence, to be truly spiritual is not only to contemn but avoid whatsoever concerning earthly motives and impulses smacks of our strongest animal desires.

When you come to think of it, though, it is a very decent and respectable way to make a living, considering or providing you do not use it as a cloak to cover one or another nefarious and self-aggrandising scheme. Why not? Should only the great church organisations be permitted to monopolise a false and yet so profitable field? And on what ground? That God revealed to some individual somewhere the panacea or cure for all human ills? Or sent His only begotten son? Think of it! Ridiculous! That might do if there were only one religion and everyone accepted it, but when you think of the scores of great religions and the host of minor sects or schismatics, all taking toll as they go, why should not anyone be permitted to set up in religion for himself, and especially where it might serve to aid or comfort others as well as himself? The best interpretation of religion that I have ever heard is that to be found in St. James 1: 27—"Pure religion and undefiled before God and the Father is this: To visit the fatherless and widows in their affliction"—not when they are prosperous, mind you!—"and to keep himself unspotted from the world." And the best method of worshipping God—which is certainly an integral portion of religion—is found in St. John 4: 24—"God is a Spirit, and they that worship Him must worship Him in spirit and in truth!"—or let us say, sincerity.

Now if these two things mean anything and anyone is willing to take the Bible as a guide—which all professing Christians surely ought to be willing to do—forms and methods of procedure ought not to count for much. There is no precise ritual prescribed in the New Testament, and if there were, no word of God's or of Christ's would prevent one group of individuals from practising it as against another group. No, the method, outside of a certain generosity of soul—tenderness, charity, abstemiousness and the like—has usually been left to the individual. And it is only because powerful and wholly practical and political organisations have usurped the religious business, gone, wholesale, into the business of electing officers or heads, building churches, collecting money and using the same not merely as a means of bare subsistence but to erect and enjoy power and the panoply of the same, and to direct the masses as they will, that they have won to the point, in pride and strength, where they have become able to harry and destroy any lesser organisation or individual or group of individuals attempting for reasons or sufferings of their own to address God or Nature direct. For these smaller fry are but seeds that threaten to grow into sects or organisations that in time may rival and so invade the domain of these others. Hence, destruction! Anathema! The lesser religionist scorned and spit upon and ordered not to seek emotional ease or security from any save those who have set up to monopolise it. The newer and poorer adventurers in this realm are to be kept out, and even destroyed.

The Russians, like the French and English before them, made it a business of the state to monopolise religion and then to let it function as a monopoly, the lesser man being told that he was neither sufficiently wise nor clean nor fit to understand all this; that to understand God and practise religion requires a long and careful course of study; and that one must go to school and by a certain course of acts, thoughts, deeds and the like which have long since been arranged, catalogued, and—worse—ritualised, fit himself for the great work of not so much understanding as approaching God. And thus most people have come to believe. They have been told so.

Besides, and much better, they lack the money or the influence or the leisure to secure or go through the prescribed folderol which would cause them to feel spiritual and so fit to understand God and practise religion. Hence, lacking the natural gift of understanding, they are awed, afraid, ashamed to pretend to religiosity. More, they are dumbfounded by the great spectacle which the churches, such as those of the Greek Orthodox and the Catholic, make. Bell, book, incense, candle, robes, religious edifices, stained glass windows—all have tended to make religion a great, solid, material-seeming affair on which one can lay hands, feel, and cart off in wagons, for instance, like any other wood or stone. Fortunately, there are others who while practically admitting or believing all this, or at least the better part of it, are still inclined to think that they can start up in religion for themselves, and while not doing any real harm to the great institutions which they admire and sanction, still serve God, do him a good turn, as it were, by gathering up the forgotten straws and scattered grains in the Master's vineyard, quite as did Ruth. They think they can do this and at the same time serve themselves to this extent: that then, God, being pleased with their good work, will provide them with a living.

I am sorry to have seemingly digressed to this very great extent, but it has really been necessary to make clear Mrs.

Conklin's point of view. She believed that she was a good woman; that her intentions were always of the best; and that God should be served by man by eschewing all evil—drinking, smoking, swearing, evil women—and out of the profits of his abstemiousness setting aside a portion—say ten per cent.—of all his earnings for the worship of God. This money, if it fell into the hands of good Christians or religionists—as it probably would—would be used, after the manner of all good Christians, to the glory of God. That is, more churches or mission halls would be established, organs installed, hymn books and Bibles bought, and so the word of God read and His glory sung and all men made abstemious, honest, generous, and pure.

Now every practical work of this kind must have leaders, workers, helpers, and the labourer is surely worthy of his hire. The Bible says so. So Mrs. Conklin—as she once troubled to explain to me and as I could see—being frequently sent on errands to her—usually for something forgotten by Conklin—felt called upon to be, and justified herself in being, one such labourer. Only in times of prosperity, as she herself once told me, she felt herself entitled to desist from the arduous labours which called her into her mission almost all day and every evening and Sunday, since it was very wearing and her strength not too great. But when Asa failed, as he often did, or was doing poorly, as so recently he had been, it was her duty to undertake her mission work. For always she sought to do good, not ill. And God knew it! More, Asa had never been much, if any, help. By turns, as she once explained, he had been a grocer, a tea dealer, a sales agent, a laundryman, a farmer, and other things in his long life, and now he was going into the real estate business. And since she did not know as yet how he was coming out, and despite this financial windfall of theirs, she proposed to continue her mission, at least until he showed some signs of succeeding in his new venture.

I think she had little, if any, faith in his business ability at this late date. And I also doubt if she even liked, let alone admired, him. He was so wholly ridiculous and impossible as a man. But he was her husband. She had sworn to cherish, honour and obey him, and she accepted and perhaps even believed in that as a cross placed upon her by her Saviour.

Certainly, her pale, patient face and hands indicated as much. And personally, and regardless of her religious views, I liked her. I liked the courage, the patience, the soft voice; the firm, upstanding declarations of her belief in a Creator and Saviour. She was like the strong, moving quotations she had chosen for her mission.

"I tell you," she said to me one day, as we were discussing this matter of religion, "there *is* a God, and He will provide and help. I have tested it in my own life over and over. God has aided me when I had no one else to turn to. When I did not know where I was going to get the next meal, God has sent a man into this room with a loaf of bread under his arm, and that man has gone off and left it, and as I did not know where to find him, I was free to eat it. God has always sent money, or some ways or means, when I have not known which way to turn. He certainly expects us to provide for ourselves, to try, and be God-fearing in the trying, but when all else fails, He, spiritually, will manifest Himself and help us. He fed Elijah by sending the ravens to him; He fed the children of Israel by raining manna in the wilderness; He led them through the parted waters of the Red Sea. He has fed and kept me when I did not know which way to turn, and I will proclaim His mercy and glory to my dying day!"

There you are! Now what do you know about that?

CHAPTER LXXXI

NOW I do not care to enter into an explanation of the real estate business or pretend that I understand its various ramifications. But one thing I did see clearly after a very little while, and that was that if "A. Conklin, Real Estate, Insurance, Rentals, etc." was to obtain any business, I would have to create it. There was none—practically none —that came to us directly. Yet everywhere, on every hand, were stores, flats, houses and apartments to be leased or controlled or sold by agents, but to obtain this privilege and so earn the fee or commission paid for securing a tenant—usually ten or fifteen per cent. of the first month's rent or the sale— one had to see the owner and make an arrangement. This, Conklin either did not comprehend or could not do.

Having seen in other real estate office windows cards which described this or that piece of property as for sale or rent, I conceived the astoundingly original idea of getting similar cards from a near-by print shop and placing them in our window —a move which appeared to bring a caller or two. At least people occasionally did stop and look. Next an idea which Conklin had and which I urged should be followed up was that since any "For Sale" or "For Rent" sign anywhere meant that the owner or lessee of the property desired a customer, the same owner or lessee might be approached in regard to a double-listing. The only problem connected with that was to find the owner. Now it so happened that Conklin had a small mare and light buggy which when not in use by him he kept standing in front of the office in order to convey any possible customers to such stores or pieces of property as he might have listed. In consequence I immediately suggested that if he would let me have the horse and buggy, I would seek out such owners and see if we could not add to our "For Rent" and "For Sale" cards. And since he agreed, I at once set forth, inquiring here and there for owners of unrented or unsold property, until at last, and on the first day, I secured the privilege of listing some two or three places, and of hanging our sign in their windows. Other signs there were, to be sure, but these owners were dissatisfied and in consequence requested me to see what I could do. Five hundred paper signs were at once ordered, and with glue and my bills I immediately proceeded to these houses and posted our first advertisements.

It causes me to smile, but I really think that with a little better management behind me, I might easily have developed a very profitable renting agency here, for I liked the work, liked to talk to people, and appeared to make some friends— so much so that soon we had a really respectable list of offerings and, better, some rentals if not land sales. But Conklin was no land bargainer, no shrewd, magnetic realtor by any means, and I knew nothing about talking up the prospective values of land and the ensuing profits. I had had no least drilling in that phase of the work. Nevertheless, my house-renting success astonished me. And I had reason for so being. For up the street a few blocks was another real estate agency— Mosher & Co.—which seemed to have nearly all the houses and property hereabouts and which had erected quite expensive wooden signs—things which we could not afford as yet. Yet within two weeks, using Conklin's horse and buggy, I secured over forty houses and apartments and some ten pieces of land. More, I ran into such curious and interesting people—solid Irish or Germans, dull to all save the practicalities and materialities of this world, yet building houses or apartments in this vicinity and hoping, of course, to reap a splendid harvest out of rents. In fact, there was one buxom Irish woman of forty-five or thereabouts—solid, handsome, genial—who took an instantaneous liking for me, as she said, and who, owning a large apartment house in which she lived not far from our office, facing Ogden Avenue and Jackson Boulevard, made me a most peculiar and startling offer, as I now think of it.

For on my arrival one sunny June morning at about ten or eleven o'clock, she it was who personally chanced to open the door, and at first appeared inclined to close it on me. Another real estate agent, and a boy at that! Bah! But just the same, as I began rapidly to speak of our new firm and how anxious we were to get nice places, and that we would advertise them—I had heard Conklin say that if he made a little money he would do this—she opened the door wider, and finally smiled a broad, amused and not wholly complimentary (as I saw it) Irish smile.

"Will you be lookin' at him? And the likes o' him, runnin' around tryin' to build up a real estate business! Sure, and I can tell you're not long at this! You're too young and in-nocent-like! So you think you can rent my apartments for me, do you? Well, Mr. Mosher has them now, and he's done very well by me. But I don't like to discourage you either. You're too young and aisy-lookin'. You're not a Catholic, by any chance, are ye?"

Thinking that in all probability she desired me to be one and that it would help me to get the renting of her place, and that nominally I was still a Catholic, I said: "Yessem, I am."

"Well, now, that's fine!" she responded, warming up to me at once. "And you're such a bright lookin' boy, too. Well, now, I'll tell you what I'll do. Come inside! Come inside! It's not to be that ye're to put your signs up here yet—Mr. Mosher havin' the agreement with me—but you can keep track of these places in your office and if you rent any of them, I'll give you the commission just the same. Not only that, but I wish you'd call on me now and then. I'd like to find out more about you. I have a pretty daughter here with me, and if she should chance to like you, well, you never know what might come of it. She's a nice girl, and I don't want her run-nin' off and marryin' some good-for-nothin' that's no Catholic. If you're as nice as I think maybe you are, you might marry her some day, if she'd have you. You haven't any money of your own, have you?"

"Not a cent," I replied, defiantly and yet flushing a little.

"Well, if you're the right sort, money need never trouble you. I've money enough for the three of us, and I won't be livin' for ever." She smiled a sunny, friendly smile and finally let me go—as astonished as she was genial and liberal in her talk.

Now, wild as this may seem, I am transcribing the literal truth. The phraseology is by no means exact, but this is the substance of it, dramatised for the occasion in order to give it the interest and reality that it had for me at the time. In fact, I was so astonished that I could scarcely believe my ears. I even trembled in anticipatory delight of my approaching prosperity and the general turn for the better which apparently my affairs were taking. To be offered the courting, if not the hand, of a pretty and rich girl, Catholic or not! And on a first meeting with a quite good-looking woman, and at this, my work! At once, of course, my thoughts ran to the girl. What was she like? Was she really as pretty as she said. These mothers, you know! But then, on a return visit to obtain some keys, the daughter still not present, my hostess or prospective mother-in-law, or what you will, took me over to a mantel and showed me her daughter's picture, young, pudgy-faced, animal, but attractive. In addition, as I noted, and by the same process of reasoning, the furniture in these rooms seemed very grand to me and in the best of taste. There were bright, and no doubt cheap, rugs; airy summer draperies over the windows; a varnished hard-wood floor, and furniture that was intended to simulate cherry or mahogany. And all new! Ha! Romance at last! An inexperienced and rich girl to deal with—not one of those shrewd, experienced girls of O'Connor's and Levitt's. Might I not succeed with one such in some quiet, unsophisticated way? I wondered. Not the least thought at the moment as to possible character differences or the religious supervision that was sure to follow. All I was thinking of, you may be sure, was good clothes, food, entertainment, travel, and this buxom young girl in my arms —the delight of ravishing her and having all the other comforts added unto me.

Alas for me, though, things were not to turn out exactly as I fancied. And for the very novel reason, in my case, that I could not bring myself to believe that it would be a good thing for me. Believe that or not! For up to the time of my going to college, I had been more or less doubtful of the validity of Catholic dogma. Personalities such as those of Aaberg and Miss Fielding had made me feel that my suspicions in regard to the same were only too well grounded. By the end of my mooning college year, I was thoroughly satisfied that there was nothing in the Catholic or any other sectarian pretence to divine authority and very little substance to the Christ legend either. Aside from admiring it as an artistic spectacle,

I had already resolved to wash my hands of Catholicism. Instead of resenting my father's dogmatic insistence, I was beginning to smile, and, more, to urge the other members of the family to do likewise—to go through the motions and smile.

But having reached this state, and after a very little reflection on my part, the proposition of Mrs. O'Doris (I believe that was her name) became antipathetic. All of the extras I have described as moving me at first, and once I was out in the June sunshine again, left me cold. Because I resented the numbskull state of mind that faith in the Catholic Church represents—yes, just that—I began to feel differently about it. Besides, mentally I was like that—could take just such sudden and final, if not violent, turns. Rosabel O'Doris, according to her picture, was, no doubt, charming, and her mother obviously well-to-do, but what about my future? Was I breaking loose from the Church in one direction only to have it seize me in another? Never! In this instance, the matter of the assumed insurmountable barrier of my impotence seemed, for the time being, to be out of mind. To be sure, there was lurking about somewhere the old silly illusion that I could not satisfy any normal, healthy girl. None the less, I was not being affected by that in this conclusion. In short, I was beginning to think—so long and so variously had I meditated on this sex problem—that with some girls at least—the not too experienced or bold—I might easily carry on a charming flirtation up to the fatal resistance or non-resistance period, and so enjoy all the delights of caressing and fondling, and then, the fatal hour at hand, decamp. Or better—and this was always a co-extensive hope with me—I might in some very simple, loving relationship, achieve a natural recovery, since a medical work that I had recently encountered and consulted had said so. But still, and even so, I did not want Rosabel. She was a Catholic.

Just the same, at her mother's request, I did pay one call, presumably on business, yet of an evening—about nine o'clock —at which I was introduced—with an obvious lack of subtlety, it seemed to me—to Rosabel. And as her mother had said, she was attractive enough physically. Quite. More, she was not unfriendly—easy and homey with me—her mother having talked me up to her, no doubt. Just the same, lacking in the least trace of gallantry and feeling as I did about the Church, I saw no way of interesting her or of being interested without injury, and after an hour of my usual agony under such circumstances, departed, cursing myself for a dunce. You must remember that with me you are abroad in those mystic chambers of the brain where vagaries and fancies of all descriptions, and even the indescribable, abound, and that this illusion as to my condition was half the time crossed with forgetfulness as to whether I was in this condition or not.

There was another woman, though, also a widow and very well-to-do, who approached me in a very different manner. On my calling at her home to secure a listing of some property she owned, she greeted me most cordially. Would I not come in? I explained my mission, and she smiled most winsomely. Her face was not exactly homely and yet sufficiently so to alienate me. Youth and beauty were what I was after. At the same time, she had a pleasing figure and was handsomely gowned. "Yes, I have some property," she said. "A tract of thirty-five acres out on Douglas Boulevard that I want to divide and sell some day. Some clever real estate man is going to make a good thing out of it some time. Why don't you come around some evening and let me show you what I want to do about it? I haven't my maps here now. Or, better yet, come to-morrow for lunch. I haven't time to go into it right now."

I promised, enthusiastically, and departed, a little flustered by the calm, steady way in which she had looked into my eyes and the genial and sympathetic manner in which she clasped my hand. But excited by this news of an entire tract which we might handle or even develop, I drove swiftly back to the office and reported my find to Conklin. When excited, he had a habit of trotting up and down the office floor, slapping his hands behind his back and smacking his lips, if pleased, or if annoyed or distressed, muttering "Tchut! Tchut! Tchut!" To-day he did all of these, for a tract of land which could be sub-divided into lots and sold on commission was certainly an ideal real estate proposition. Personally I had vaguely sensed the import of it as Mrs. Woodward talked, but as he trotted and exclaimed here, I began to see it in its true light.

"This is a real find!" he said. "A real find! We mustn't

let this get out of our hands. If this goes through and I make any money, I'll give you five hundred dollars of it at once. You certainly deserve it. I'm sorry I can't pay you any more now, but I can't." (Thus far, in spite of my activity, I do not believe we had taken in a cent—rental commissions were slow.) "Perhaps you'd better let me go and see her. I am older and she might have more confidence in me." Then, after asking me various questions as to her manner and personality, he finally added: "No, now that you've started it, perhaps you'd better finish it. Apparently she has taken a fancy to you and thinks you are a bright boy."

He rambled on, declaring that if this thing went through —if some arrangement could be made whereby we could subdivide and advertise this as the Woodward or Conklin division —our fortunes would be made. He said he thought he knew a banker who would finance it. The mere thought of bankers and advertising and legal papers and bookkeeping was as confusing as Greek to me. I began to fear lest my inadequacy as a bookkeeper would hamper and finally destroy all.

The next day, though, I called, and to my surprise found Mrs. Woodward so richly—I will not say tastefully—arrayed as to be disconcerting. The dark, flowered morning gown of the day before had given place to a close-fitting street dress of light brown velvet, to which were added brown velvet shoes and an amplitude of gold ornaments which harmonised. Her cheeks and lips were rouged and her hair done in short curls about her forehead.

I realised at once that her object was by no means real estate alone. She was too genial and wooing, invited me into the drawing-room and sat down on the same settee with me and wanted to know how I had been, who I was, what I had been doing previous to this work, and so on. And through a doorway giving into the dining-room I could see a small table set for two and crowded with over-elaborate cut glass. I began to think that my situation was getting serious.

And I was by no means mistaken. For, to my distress, she laid an affectionate hand on my arm, and leaning very close, wanted to know if I had decided to work all the time like most young men or wouldn't I prefer now and then to rest and play. I think I explained, in an aloof and yet genial way, that I liked to play but that I didn't have either the means or the time. Whereupon she began talking of trips, the need of some people working, but not all. Only, since the arts of middle-aged women who seek to over-persuade young men are by no means a novelty, I will not dwell on hers. The principal thing was that she was a novelty to me, and interesting on that score, and that score only. For of course, by now, I was decidedly resentful of the fact that all the beautiful girls I had ever known had been either most aloof or, because of my cowardice, beyond my grasp. And now here was this homely, if well-dressed, and even semi-refined woman, trying to make me do what at the last test, even if I should overcome my objection to her rouge, her slight wrinkles and her none-too-handsome teeth, I might not, as I thought, be able to do. Unacquainted with the type, I was still conscious of a buccaneering spirit here—the particular phase of buccaneering in the realm of the affections that achieves—or seeks to—by surprise, over-persuasion, almost storm, that which it could not ordinarily and normally obtain. In this instance, however, the lady miscalculated as to my power of opposition, my private sex fears, and my extreme objection to anything less than beauty in the other sex, though if I had not been so doubtful of my own powers and she had not thrust herself upon me so obviously and forcefully, I might have succumbed. As it was, she pressed so close and breathed upon me so heavily that I was moved finally and desperately to exert myself, and rising, pretended to be interested in things outside the window.

She was not to be daunted, though. Fearing failure, she went to look after the lunch and invited me in. A maid served at first, but soon she sent her away and officiously helped me to everything I did not want. I began to feel that unless I acted very coldly I should not escape, and yet I was so much interested in the sub-division that I scarcely dared resist her. Yet since she bent over me much too close, when pouring more coffee, I almost had chills. At last I managed to ask about the property. She said calmly that the maps had not come yet; that she expected them at any moment; but if they did not come by two-thirty, I could come around any evening, the succeeding Friday preferably. Then she began again. Noting me look at a girl passing on the other side of the street, she exclaimed: "You like pretty girls, don't you?"

"Oh, yes," I replied, innocently enough, as though really I was quite a devil of a fellow when I wanted to be.

"Pretty legs, hasn't she? You like those, too?" Then she laughed ecstatically. "Oh, you men!" she declared. "You are regular young devils, every one of you, aren't you?"

I now solemnly cogitated as to whether I should summon my courage and attempt to feel her breasts—which showed very full under her dress—and to urge her to the sex relation with me, or flee. Her face was not attractive, but it was not by any means ugly either. And, I said to myself, her form may compensate me. Yet that fear as to my own potence or lasting power, plus uncertainty as to her, the tangle in which constant pursuit by her might involve me, all combined to restrain me. I spoke of my need of attending to other matters; that I should be glad to come Friday; that already I was late—a series of nervous excuses which made rather plain that either I was not interested or was frightened, the thirty-five acre real estate deal to the contrary notwithstanding.

"I see, Theodore," she said, familiarly, at the close of the interview, and when she saw that her assault would have to be continued on another occasion, "that I shall have to teach you a lot of things you don't know. You're too bashful. Will you come Friday?"

I promised her faithfully.

But I never went. And I can see her smiling winsomely, and possibly regretfully or resentfully, after me as I went down her front stairs.

CHAPTER LXXXII

BUT this real estate deal was another matter, and a very troublesome one, for once outside I realised that unless I returned and submitted to her blandishments—made myself into a gigolo or youthful prostitute—*no* real estate deal! And Conklin's hopes were already running so high. As a matter of fact, as I neared the office—the large plate-glass windows reaching from floor to ceiling—I could see him within as excited as when I had left, walking to and fro across the office floor and twiddling his fingers, his hands still folded across his back—a vacuous and hopeless old shell.

And now came the problem of how I was to explain to him, since he being a Christian business man might not relish the details which had led up to this uncertainty or disappointment. Should I or should I not tell him? I decided that since his hopes would be so completely dashed, if he knew, I would not lie exactly but say that she had kept me waiting for some maps and that incidentally she had provided me with lunch —a social kindness which he looked upon as promising—in fact, very promising. It cheered him up. But then there was the Friday engagement, which I did not even mention, but said rather that she had instructed me to come and see her a little later—which he interpreted to mean that the deal was practically closed and that the next time I went it might be well if he went along—a thought, if not a decision, which started me worrying. For most certainly nothing would come of that. She would see what a feather-brained dunce he was—and so . . .

I worried and worried until the following Monday morning —allowing the promised Friday evening call to slide—and then, out of a clear sky, a miracle—an Elijah descending (not ascending) and into our very office—the answer to all my woes in this connection, as I will herewith proceed to show. For blowing into the office with the morning breeze—and a fine sunlit morning breeze it was, too—one of the most fascinating and truly Dickensian types or characters that it has ever been my good fortune to meet—from the interpretive literary sense, purely, that is. (I forgot to say that following my announcement as to Mrs. Woodward's tract of land, Conklin had placed an advertisement in one of the local papers calling for a partner with means to finance a most important and sure to be profitable real estate deal—a brilliant opportunity for the right man.) On top of that appeared this Colonel Thomas Bundy, "Real Estate, Mines, Insurance," as his card read. I can see him yet—one of the most broad-chested, full-gutted and impressive bluffs I have ever known. Utterly delightful! Utterly! And it was I who received him in our impressively large but meagrely furnished office. Conklin, as it chanced, had not yet arrived or had gone on some small mission. But of what import as delay or deterrent was that to the Hon. Colonel Thomas Bundy? None at all! Just none at all! He was ready to begin impressing and infiltrating with his particular brand of gas and blarney quite any and everybody whom he chanced to encounter, and so, why not me?

Haven't you known people whose faces and chests—expansive, heavily modelled and forceful—suggest a kind of wonder of ability which borders on pure romance? There is, no doubt, a way of detecting the false from the real—gold from iron pyrites—but the most observant may sometimes be deceived. At this time, I was so young that mere bluff and swagger were impressive, and Bundy had so much more than that. He wore grey-striped trousers and a flowing frock-coat, a high hat and cane, polished shoes and even spats, and looked at me out of direct, narrowed, heavily-shaded eyes. Your commercial bombasto-furioso, you see?

"Mr. Conklin in?"

"He's out to lunch," I replied weakly. "He'll be back in an hour."

"You're in his employ, I presume?" he inquired.

"Yes, I work here," I replied.

"Good! Now I haven't much time. I saw this advertisement this morning. Is Mr. Conklin the sole owner of this concern?"

"Yes, sir."

"How long have you been in business?"

I told him.

"Let me see—is he an old or a young man? It seems to me I know A. Conklin."

I described Mr. Conklin.

"Oh, yes, exactly." He rubbed his chin impressively, Hamlet-wise, and thought. "Very good, I'll be back in an hour. By the way, what is the nature of this deal he is thinking of, if you know?"

Since the deal was my deal, if anyone's, I mildly hinted as to its character.

"Exactly! Exactly!" he exclaimed, brightening even beyond his natural brightness. "Something that would require at least forty-five or fifty thousand dollars to manipulate perhaps—trees, walks, water mains, some money to get the city to help you, a bonus to one of the car lines to run a line out to the property,"—he waved his hand in a rhythmic, inclusive way which somehow presented to my eyes a picture of a flourishing real estate development: houses going up, handsome macadam roads, gas lamps, trees growing in even rows.

"But Mr. Conklin is a novice, I can see that," he added, looking around our sparsely furnished office. "This office —you need rugs and more furniture. There ought to be a railing across here. This is a growing section. There's millions to be made out of real estate in Chicago. Millions! You're a bright young man, I can see that, but you need someone to direct you and back you up. Real estate is bound up with financial audacity, and I am not sure that you have that here as yet." He glowed and beamed, then saying he would return later, he walked out, leaving me enthralled as by a magician. Positively a spell had been cast over me— the spell of the utmost possibilities of the city itself. Because of his physical presence, aplomb, glow of mind, this, that, I had visions of a splendid salary, the best of clothes, myself hob-nobbing with successful people; theatres, restaurants, mansions, money, girls!

When Conklin returned, I was prepared to tell him of the wonderful future that awaited us if such a man as this could be secured. I described Bundy—his ability. And once more Conklin, like the little opera comique sailor that he was, trod the deck of romance, his hands clasped behind him.

"So the widow still wants you to come, does she? You're sure I wouldn't be better? Perhaps this Colonel Bundy . . ."

At once the thought of Colonel Bundy, Mrs. Woodward and her tract were joined in my imagination. Here was the man to take her and the tract in tow and rid me of her! I could not really interest myself in her the way she wanted. But Bundy! With that presence and finesse! God! How easy! I saw it all and said as much to Conklin. If only we had Bundy! If only we had Bundy! Ah, the euthanasiac gas of him, by which now I was completely filled and floating skyward! And so thoroughly did I impress Conklin with my own enthusiasm that by the time Bundy was about to return, he was fairly sweating lest he should not. To be so near a fortune and yet really not of it!

"He said he could raise fifty thousand dollars, did he?" Conklin said to me a number of times as he trotted regularly to and fro. "That is just what we need to finance this thing properly! It would be the making of us!" Once more he turned and trotted away and then back, up and down, up and down.

Late that afternoon, Colonel Bundy did return, and with that same broad, expansive, flourishing smile and manner. When he came into the room, it was as if a stirring, rosy glow were cast over all our hopes.

Ah, so this was Mr. Conklin—Mr. A. Conklin! This bright young clerk had been telling him of Mr. Conklin and his business. Well, this was Mr. Bundy—Colonel Thomas Bundy, of St. Paul, Minnesota.

"My brother is George H. Bundy, the publisher of the *Christian Age*, of St. Paul. Recently I have been out in Montana . . ." He went glibly on, explaining that recently he had been looking at mines and woodlands in the far west, but Chicago, growing so fast, had at last attracted him and he had decided to return here. He was thinking of entering the banking and real estate business once he straightened out his western affairs, which, owing to the fact that he had over-invested in a mine (which same he was now trying to close out) were a little involved. But a mere nothing, that! A mere nothing! A matter of a few weeks at the most! For the present, he could undertake a small real estate investment if it did not require more than forty or fifty thousand dollars. He might even raise sixty, but it would be difficult at this time. If Mr. Conklin had anything which was really sound . . .

Conklin had had many wild dreams in his time, no doubt, but I think one of his wildest was generated right here. As he saw it, Mr. Bundy had arrived on purpose to make the fortunes of all of us. We could rely on him. Immediate and free cash—a fortune, no less—was plainly in sight. When Bundy commented on me as being a most vivid youth, Conklin (who had been astonished at seeing his name pasted all over this area) joined in the praise. He recited all I had done, winding up with the disclosure that it was I who had found the widow with the tract of land. At once Colonel Bundy's eye lighted.

"So that is your proposition?" he said. "Who is the lady? Do you care to tell me who she is? Perhaps that, among other things, can be worked out."

Conklin hesitated. He found that his dreams were carrying him away. Still, without business ability himself, he knew he must find someone, and Mr. Bundy was such a striking and ingratiating creature.

I cannot possibly even more than suggest the opportunistic fluidity of a situation which was so compact of genial chicane, the hope of self-betterment, all the shining, treacherous surfaces of self-expression that make of life the crinkling, abysmal wonder that it is. Conklin, with his insipid, inefficient blue eyes and his yet very real imagination, seeking to better himself and to retain the lion's share of any future fortune which association with this stranger might bring. Bundy— but I will leave Bundy to the facts. Myself, a rooster-like phantasm of fancy, dancing gaily and inconsequentially about a too-solid world of fact. The three of us—unless perchance Bundy—knowing nothing of sound commercial procedure.

But Bundy, suave, dogmatic, managerial, talked of the ease with which he could manage this situation once he knew all about it. Certainly the necessary funds would be forthcoming. Never fear about that! Let him but once see this widow; let him get the details surrounding and the conditions governing this land! At last Conklin told him her name. Very shortly thereafter it was agreed between them that

Bundy was to become vice-president of the reorganised company of Conklin, Bundy & Company, with Theodore Dreiser secretary, no less! We were to deal in large properties and be almost instantaneously rich.

For a few days I walked on air. And the following Tuesday —Bundy saying that he required several days to close certain other matters—a large roll-top desk and chair arrived, consigned to Conklin, Bundy & Co. And soon thereafter Bundy in person. Only, and except for odd moments now and then —now on one day and now on another—we saw little enough of him. He took quarters in a near-by apartment in Adams Street, a very attractive apartment, by the way. Not only that, but within twenty-four hours he was sending me out for cigars, stationery, laundry he had left, saying I was to say they were for Mr. Bundy and they were to be charged. He ate at near-by restaurants—not always the same one—and once he invited me, saying to the cashier as we left that he would arrange it all by cheque soon and taking a handful of cigars into the bargain. Naturally enough, he borrowed Conklin's buggy for various ventures—indeed took charge of it and almost monopolised it. Incidentally, he also took charge of Mrs. Woodward, inducing her, as he told us, to take him to see the property and bringing back pencil maps which he redrew for us on his desk while we gazed, seeing as he talked a great and prosperous sub-division of the city grow up under our very eyes.

"A charming woman, Mrs. Woodward!" he exclaimed, grandiloquently. "A charming woman! A most charming woman! She has a sense of humour, too—a most pleasing sense of humour! We went all over the property yesterday. She gave me her idea in detail and I gave her ours. Here" —and he pointed to a central spot on his map—"we intend to put a small agency building as soon as the details are completed—right on the corner which is nearest the Ogden car line. Here I have persuaded Mrs. Woodward to build a house if things look favourable. It is always well to have the owner build a house, or seem to. It is a good thing to tell prospective purchasers, and it can be sold afterwards. And here I am going to try to induce the city authorities to build a school. There is no school building anywhere within a mile of this property. I may even give them a site or induce Mrs.

Woodward to do so. It's a mere bagatelle one way or the other, however you figure it. If the city decides to build or we give it a site, the price of the property rises and the gain is equal to eight or ten times the site. A mere detail! A mere detail!"

I can see him now, in those warm late June afternoon hours, a large cigar in his mouth and himself leaning back in his new chair before his new desk, a good dinner in sight, a comfortable suite of rooms awaiting him, possibly the endearing caresses of the widow later in the evening, and all by reason of our imaginative appreciation of his intense imagination. I cannot say that I seriously believe this man was dishonest. As I think of it now, I think he was a little crazy—a wandering gaberlunzie with magnificent ideas and no sense of proportion or current human relationship.

As to the long hours in which he was driving around in Conklin's buggy, I did not know what he was doing. Perhaps seeing downtown bankers or real estate speculators. One thing is sure: he was not paying his landlady nor the several restaurateurs who provided meals and cigars, nor the cigar man near by from whom he must have secured as much as fifteen dollars' worth of cigars, nor the shoe man who repaired his shoes, nor the tailor who pressed his suits, nor the laundryman—for all of these individuals appeared in due time, singly and separately, to inquire, to complain, to denounce. I really felt sorry for two little old ladies who conducted a very clean and neat restaurant near by. He owed them something like nineteen dollars, and they could ill afford to lose it. If he had had the least sense of responsibility or decency, he could not have done that. But Bundy was—well, Bundy—magnificent, ingratiating, cheering to one and all. And perhaps by reason of the wonderful optimistic dreams which he caused to spring in the minds of quite all whom he encountered, he paid in full for what he took. I am inclined to think so. Certainly, most certainly, he repaid me with the most glorious sense of imminent grandeur that ever up to that time had been mine.

But what of his relations with Mrs. Woodward? I never really discovered. I know he drove her about, for I saw them. But where? As time wore on, and in spite of his drivings, dinings, explanations, spoutings, map drawings and the like, Conklin began to worry. Rent day came around but some hitch in Mr. Bundy's affairs prevented him for the moment (the moment only, you understand) from paying that. Similarly, the bill for the desk, chair, rug, some new stationery and other items that had been added unto us and were now due. At the same time, though Conklin's religious and well-meaning nature bade him be very careful as to how he judged anyone, Mr. Bundy included, he was becoming troubled and a bit suspicious. For as yet Bundy had produced no agreement with Mrs. Woodward, although it was always near. As yet also he had made no arrangement to perfect the partnership, which required the filing of a certificate and the laying down of at least five hundred dollars as against Conklin's original five hundred for office expenses. The furniture company from which he had secured the excellent desk, a rug, and a handsome chair for patrons, sent bill after bill, finally serving notice on Conklin, Bundy & Co. that unless the bill were immediately paid the articles would be removed. Yet always the matter of extracting himself from those troublesome western mining deals stood in the way—not important—soon to be brushed away—but still delaying—and to Conklin and myself even agonising.

At last Conklin began to realise that something quite radical was amiss. That as yet not produced five hundred dollars which was the ground-stone of the agreement! The various bills in the vicinity! No tangible deal with Mrs. Woodward! Nothing!

"Why!" exclaimed Conklin to me one morning, reciting for God knows the what-th time, many, if not all, of the ills that were steadily gathering about us. "Either the man is a faker or he is a crook or worse. Sometimes I think he is a little crazy. Maybe he is. And to think I should have taken up with him in this way, without any investigation of any kind! And now," he added, pausing only to wring his hands, "the expenses we have piled up here, the time wasted!" He clucked with his tongue, then concluded: "Why, you did better than he has ever done. After all, as long as you were using the buggy, we did get some flats to rent and our sign was up everywhere. Of course, it hasn't done us much good, but the renting season isn't quite here either. We ought to do some business in August and September."

I agreed.

"And again, that Mrs. Woodward deal—that looks very suspicious to me. Why, you had her well in hand before ever he came here. She was going to arrange with you, or rather me through you. Now I suppose he has spoiled that or it has fallen through. I have about concluded that the man is a dead-beat, and I am going to go and see Mrs. Woodward myself and find out what she knows about him. Perhaps if she wouldn't come to terms with him, she will with me."

I had to smile as I looked at Conklin—thinking of Mrs. Woodward.

"I am going to talk to him this day," he finally exclaimed. "I'm going to lay down the law to him like a Dutch uncle! He's not going to fool around with me any longer. I don't believe he has any mines. I'm going to write to his brother and see what I can find out up there."

Suiting action to word, he first addressed a letter of inquiry to the brother and then started out to see Mrs. Woodward. Alas for our dreams of sudden real estate supremacy! His visit to the lady proved that there were no relations of any character existing between her and Bundy.

" 'That man!' " Conklin said she said to him. " 'Why, I think he is a bit crazy, and if you sanction his actions, you are not much better. He now owes me fifty dollars which I will never get—borrowed it because he was short one day at lunch. And of all things, he wanted me to furnish my land and let him mortgage it to put on the improvements which would make it saleable.'

"Oh, she was hopping mad, I tell you!" concluded Conklin. "I wouldn't be the least bit surprised but what she'll try to put Bundy in prison if she gets her hands on him."

In the meantime, Bundy had arrived in the office and extracted at least five dollars from me on the ground that he was a full partner and entitled to it. He had done this once before—for we were doing a small renting business which brought us in a few commissions of five or ten dollars each once or twice a week. The first time Conklin protested rather feebly, saying that he would prefer that the partnership papers be drawn up and Bundy's five hundred put in before any cash was extracted. On this day, though, Bundy chanced to be present when ten dollars in connection with a neighbourhood fire insurance policy was paid to me—two five-dollar bills.

He came over to my drawer, opened it, and with an ingratiating smile as well as an air of solid proprietorship, said, "I want to take five of this for a few minutes."

"But Mr. Conklin told me I was not to let you do that," I protested, having been solemnly warned by Conklin as to this.

"My boy," he replied, with an air of reproach and kindly supervision, "you mustn't be suspicious. You mustn't let Conklin make you so. He knows nothing about the real estate business, while I do. I am Colonel Thomas Bundy and I can buy and sell Asa Conklin a hundred times over. I merely want to go up here and pay the cigar man, because I haven't the change about me, but I'll draw a cheque when I come back and you can cash that."

When Conklin came back, he was furious. I never saw a weak little man—a wool-pated, blue-eyed, fat little man—more wrought up or more picturesquely futile. Between walking the floor, wringing his hands behind his back, exclaiming "Tchut! Tchut!" and scratching his head, he raved. "That scoundrel! That miserable windbag! Here I am just starting again in the world, not a single dollar more than I need, my wife depriving herself of really the necessaries of life to assist me, and this pretender comes in here and deceives me! He has deceived everybody else, too. And now Mrs. Woodward doesn't want anything more to do with us. He gets out of here to-day once and for all! I've had enough of him! He's a loafer, a regular tramp and cheat, I'm afraid." Then he suddenly paused, and added: "This is awful. I've been telling my wife our prospects were so bright." He trotted to and fro, commiserating himself while I pretended to keep books.

At last Bundy arrived. I think he realised that he was near his commercial end with us, but he came in with his usual swaggering air. "I have just been down in La Salle Street," he began, "talking to President So and So of Such and Such a Bank. He is certainly interested in this land scheme of ours. Of course, these are the dull summer months."

"Land scheme! Land scheme!" exclaimed Conklin, jumping up. "You haven't any land scheme, and you know it! You're a cheat, that's what you are! You're a swindler! I've just been over to see Mrs. Woodward and she says you owe her

518

fifty dollars and that she hasn't had anything to do with you for weeks and doesn't want anything to do with you. You've swindled me, that's what you've done! You've used my time and my buggy ..." (I forget all of the tirade, but it was extensive and vehement.) The last thing Conklin asseverated was: "And this morning you come in here and steal another five dollars from this boy—stole it—that's what you did—and I can have you arrested for it—that's what I can do!"

During this long outburst Bundy had stood just inside the railing, his arms akimbo, surveying Conklin in the most sympathetic and lofty way.

"What do you mean, stole?" he inquired, in an injured tone. "Ain't I a partner here?"

"No, you're not, and I want you to get out of here right now! You're a beat, a crook, that's what you are! If you don't go," he added, as a frown darkened Bundy's face, "I'm going to go out now and get an officer. I'll have the law on you. I want that five dollars, too, if you still have it."

"Oh, very well," replied Bundy, scornfully, completely ignoring the demand for the five. "If that's the way you feel about it! There was a real chance here for a business man with imagination, but if that's the attitude you take, I can't do anything."

He turned and strolled out, his broad shoulders erect, and went ... where? Actually I felt sorry for him. In the light of all that had happened, he seemed so inefficient, so frittering. Suppose he did impose upon a neighbourhood to the tune of a hundred dollars or so, what good would it do him? He would always be moving; he would have no real friends. One person after another would impugn, denounce, pursue him, and even have him arrested, perhaps. Socially he was an Ishmael, and as it looked to me, he craved human sympathy, for he was always coming so close and painting such human scenes in words.

But out he went, and that was the end. A letter from the man whom he claimed as a brother denounced him as an impostor and no relative at all. Tradesmen sought him at his rooms, but he had flown. They even threatened to sue Conklin as his partner, but he explained that there was no partnership, and so they went away crestfallen and despairing. As for myself, it was a clear illustration of the nature and ways

519

of the bluff and the faker, the imaginative, senseless, useless ne'er-do-well, the ninny, booby, loon, gaberlunzie. I have always wondered what became of Bundy, and whenever I think of him, I smile. And yet I cannot help feeling a little sad. *Why*, do you suppose?

CHAPTER LXXXIII

THE blow to our non-existent business was, obviously, nothing financially, but to our spirit—particularly Conklin's—it was staggering. He actually seemed broken. Bundy had been so impressive, so handsome, so presentable, so self-convinced in all his ways, thoughts and talks—and now there was no Bundy and no glorious dream of wealth to brighten and hearten each day—nothing save the rueful Conklin and me and the office, minus Bundy's grand furniture and rugs, which had also been taken away. The place was lorn without him. Indeed, in connection with the ending of this illusion, Conklin seemed to see the fading of his hopes in connection with himself, his wife, life, everything. In truth, he was face to face with his own utter futility and seemed derailed and wrecked. I never saw a more reduced and dreary specimen of a man—faded and ready to quit, to die even. (Actually, he did die the following spring, of pneumonia, though by then he had failed months before and I was elsewhere.)

And I, who had visioned myself seated at a rosewood desk, drawing at least twenty-five dollars a week—which at that time seemed a fortune—doing, I scarcely know what—checking up incoming payments, I presume—was so downcast I scarcely knew what to do. For at least nine or ten hours I moped, feeling I must quit and seek work elsewhere, then seeing Conklin said nothing about shutting up shop, I decided to hang on for a few weeks more, for I argued that since this was only August fifteenth and the true renting season did not begin until the middle of September, we could still make some money if we secured flats to rent. So I took Conklin's buggy and started out once more, driving in the delightful summer weather, returning whenever Conklin had an appointment to keep or in time to let him drive home to lunch and at five-thirty in the evening, while I stayed on until six and even six-thirty in the hope of a stray customer. During the next thirty days, I saw all sorts of people, secured a number of houses to list, drove all sorts of people to see all sorts of apartments, and wound up by earning my salary, the rent, gas bills, and whatever else "overhead" there was, but no more. For despite the growth and prosperity of the neighbourhood, rents and prices were low and hence possible profits not great. Many people rented their rooms, no doubt, to persons whom we sent to them, but denied it to save the fee. Also, through my activities, one or two lots were sold, but the commission was not great—fifty dollars in one instance, thirty-five or forty in another. And once Conklin sold a small business for a man—a stationery business for five hundred dollars, stock and goodwill. Out of that he cleared thirty-five dollars, but you would have thought, for a few hours, that he was on the high road to a sure fortune.

"Now, now," he exclaimed, warmly, "if we can just do two or three things like that every week, we won't need Mr. Bundy. After all, there is more money in these little things, if we can just get enough of them, than there is in big ones. If I just hadn't made the mistake of taking up with that scoundrel, we'd be much further along. As it is, we may do some business yet."

But we did no more business of that kind. Indeed, I verily believe that was the one bright moment in his whole real estate experience.

But I . . . how I hoped and dreamed through the wonderful September and October days! It mattered little that toward the middle of October my salary ceased, owing to slackness of income, and that I had to be content with promises that if business picked up, I would get it. I have only the vaguest idea now as to why I hung on, or what it was that I was hoping for, if anything. Perhaps it was because I had a buggy to ride in, a good horse to drive, a bright clean office, and I seemed to be working—whereas opposed to that was the dreariness, and even misery, of getting out and hunting for a new job—an approaching necessity which induced lassitude and even terror whenever I thought of it. More, I cannot in any wise explain now why it was that I did not look in related real estate offices for work of a similar character. Perhaps it was because I was always attributing my stay here to Conklin's inefficiency, holding the thought, as it were, that in any more businesslike office I could not possibly do as well. For instance, I was as much overawed by Mosher & Company and other real estate offices in this vicinity, as well as farther downtown, as though they were institutions of a much more complicated and even entirely different character, and hence thought I could not possibly succeed in these. Whatever the cause, I certainly did not look. Besides, here I was somebody—in charge at least of this, profitable or unprofitable—and so it was that I hung on. For what would I be in the next place? And when would I find the next place?

One of the things that did come out of this real estate fiasco was the sudden and, to me, fairly conclusive demonstration that the sexual ineffectiveness I was always worrying about was more of an illusion than a fact. Only I shall have to approach the proof in a roundabout way. It came about really through the existence at the back of our main office —which was triangular and lighted on its two sides by immense glass panes—of that second or store-room, much smaller and with only two small windows of glazed glass, one portion of which was partitioned off as a toilet, the major portion containing shelves, boxes (the abandoned property of the defunct cosmetic company previously mentioned and some of whose bottles and literature were still lying around), and most intriguing of all, in so far as this particular venture is concerned, a small iron and wire spring cot to which was attached an old thin mattress or cover no more than an inch or two thick. On it when I came were piled some boxes and papers. As Conklin was under the impression, as he said, that someone might still return for it, it was never disturbed. But as I observed it from time to time, it came to be identified in my mind with an entirely different idea. There was that constant and unsatisfied urge in me. And here was this room, shut off from the glare and noise of the street. And so often during this late summer, after the noble Bundy had gone and we were slowly but surely drifting toward failure, Conklin would go home as early as four or four-thirty, leaving me to stay on as late as I would, often until six or six-thirty. It being pleasant here—a broad view of two streets along which passed cars and pedestrians—I liked to sit and dream or read, only an occasional inquirer breaking the monotony.

And as I did so, either at night or before Conklin arrived in the morning—for I opened the office, swept it out and did whatever was to be done—I used to dream of . . . well . . . supposing some attractive girl should come in here some day and, of course, enter on a friendly and by degrees sensual conversation with me—and I should be able to persuade her, as I had that girl of O'Connor's, to do the same thing here. How convenient! And hence how easily achieved if only fate would now find the girl for me! And curiously enough, if you will believe it—for such is the communicative as well as effective power of desire—presently there was a young widow who worked in a branch post office in this same building, and who, after selling me stamps a few times, began to stop at my desk for a chat whenever she noted that Conklin was not there. And since she was really very attractive—blonde, neat, healthy, although at least seven or eight years older than myself—and very friendly and mildly provocative, I have always thought this could and would have passed quickly enough into something more intimate had it not been that I, as usual, was slow and dubious as to myself, and hence slow in prosecuting a quest which I was beginning to feel reasonably sure would end as I wished. For there was that room. And if not that, maybe she had a place of her own to which she would invite me.

At any rate, as she sat on the edge of my desk at different times, making those trivial remarks which have no value other than that of maintaining a physical contact, I even pondered on petting her hand or feeling her legs, but could not, my own silly physical fears being what they were. Yet eager, poised, tense, I was always on the verge, and perhaps it was that that interested and intrigued her.

And so, too, with a second woman of about thirty, who was nothing more nor less than a "kept" woman, or one who by the aid of various male friends and the services she rendered them maintained a quite luxuriously-furnished apartment directly over us, and could be seen from time to time emerging or returning and occasionally looking in our place as she did so, myself studying her and thinking such thoughts as usually troubled me in connection with one so well favoured and alive. For she was well formed and always very well, if somewhat enticingly, dressed.

But nothing came of that either, until one day she came in

to say that she would like to list her apartment, since she desired to move that fall, and having a lease would need to find a tenant. Also since she did not wish any sign hung in her window, it would be best, if I found any likely tenant, to bring him or her up. Meanwhile I was to come and look at the place myself—a visit which once it was made—the morning following—would surely have resulted in something more than it did had a better man been involved. For her rooms were so sensually enticing: a place of drapes, couches, pillows, in faint blues, pinks, creams and related shades. And she herself when I arrived, in some clinging morning thing which revealed so much of her flesh beneath that I felt moved to attempt contact of some kind. And so friendly. I saw that I was not unacceptable to her—quite the contrary—only unlike the troubled Mrs. Woodward, who had found her looks against her, this lady did not deem it necessary to exercise any particular arts or wiles. She was sufficiently attractive, as she well knew, to excite the male automatically and so provoke pursuit. Even I could see and feel that. Yet just the same, about her eyes and mouth as we talked about the renting details of the place, was a provoking smile. I felt as though she wanted me to say something, become more personal and intimate, at the same time that she waited exactly at that line, fingering at this drapery or that, and calling my attention at the last to some prints of nudes by Bouguereau, Boucher, Lancret and other French exquisites whose prints were amazingly popular in the America of that day.

But despite the proximity and suggestiveness of all that I saw, nothing, unless it was one thing of which I am now about to speak—a certain desperate conclusiveness in regard to any such future opportunities as might be vouchsafed me. For there and then, as I emerged from this place, defeated by my own fears, I resolved that come what might, I would try. True, in that first instance I had failed, but was it not possible to be calmer, to restrain in some way that intense excitement which had resulted in an immediate emotion and so left me incapable of doing anything more? Although I was not sure of it, the thought had arrived as a definite one, and to stay. And although nothing came of it immediately—no particular opportunity arising within the next week or ten days—nevertheless the thought grew in force and persuasiveness until at last I was convinced that if I would but struggle to keep my courage and my nerves in hand, I might come through with something which might pass as a proper relationship and so deceive a woman as well as relieve myself of the tense and unending torture of unsatisfied desire.

And true enough—and because of this decision as well as that providential store-room at the back of the office—my first real success in this field was achieved. I make so much of it because whether only partly successful or not, it made such a great difference to me in my own estimation of myself, my mental viewpoint and, relatively speaking, my mental peace. And yet at the same time, such a wholly incidental and passing thing.

For sitting one late afternoon—just after Conklin had gone for the day with his horse and buggy—I was watching the beginning or early drift of homeward-bound people, which, between five and six, gave Ogden Avenue a somewhat brisker air than ordinarily at other hours it wore. And thinking, as you may well guess, of adventure—something I would like to do—the one thing and nothing else at this time. And not a single attractive girl passing anywhere near but what I proceeded to build about her some romance which connected her with me in this way.

And then, as I was so day-dreaming, who should approach and pause, first before an outside board which carried our "For Rent" cards, and next—because, as she afterwards said, she saw me looking at her so interestedly—before one of the windows, but a young and decidedly attractive, if idle and somewhat reckless and adventuring-looking, Italian girl of not more than sixteen or seventeen. But with dark, liquid eyes and bushy, black, curly hair, not framed or shaped by any hat, merely bound above the ears by a red ribbon. Her clothes, cheap but seemingly clean, became her well enough, or if they did not, then her youth, prettiness and self-confidence based on the same caused them to seem becoming. At any rate, an idle and adventuring mood motivating her, she first looked at me, then at the billboard or window, and romance-hungry, I actually ventured to smile at her and she smiled in return. And as I have said, having fought with myself so long concerning my cowardice with girls and having come to the conclusion I had, and now being alone here—just she and myself facing each other—not even a stranger passing at the moment—I decided on a heroic course. I would beckon to her to come in. And to my astonishment she came in, not nervously or with any shyness or marked reticence, but rather with a laughing, independent, adventuring and most fearless look about her mouth and eyes, which caused me to feel that she was about to rag or tease me, and nothing more.

And that is exactly what she proceeded to do. And with one or more of those ironic and indifferent and purely make-believe inquiries such as: "What sort of a place is this, anyhow? Do you rent rooms here, too? Are you the only person working in here now? About where is that flat over on Monroe Street? . . ."

Since she was not at all frightened of me—so much at ease and even bold for her years—I decided that I should prove the gallant this time or never. And so proceeded. "Oh, it's a real estate office, all right. Certainly I'm the only person working here. Do you see anybody else? Do you really want to see that flat over on Monroe Street?" To which she replied, in her teasing, bland way: "Certainly! Why do you suppose I'd be asking?" In reply to which I explained that I had a horse and buggy—sent home for the day—but if she really wanted to see things like that and would come in the morning . . .

But before I had even gotten that far, her mind had glanced off to something else, just playing about, as she was, to see what authoritative things she could achieve here without being molested. I could feel that she felt that my admiration for her already put me at her mercy.

"What's in that room back there?" she finally inquired, after looking at almost everything else in the place—picture, calendars, my high-topped bookkeeper's desk, some real estate maps on the wall: things which had no least interest for her but served to prolong her stay. At the same time, and by reason of this bravado and sex-consciousness of hers which irradiated the entire room, I had gotten up and was following her about and by now had become excruciatingly conscious not only of her charm and my desire but something in her which was redolent of a related desire, whether wholly controlled or not I could not say. But her body was so trim, her gestures those of one who knew exactly how provoking she could be. A girl who was really madly over-sexed and daring in her search for adventure.

When she inquired concerning the rear room, it was exactly what I most desired. It was such a nervous delight to open the door, and once inside, looking at such things as were there, as she minced coquettishly here and there, I followed her about, seeking to intrigue her with myself, to magnetise her in some way so that she would be drawn to me. And fevered by such remarks as: "Oh, you have a couch here. Do you sleep on that?" a provoking half-laugh going with this which finally broke the tense restraint of myself. For answer I slipped my arm about her waist and sought to kiss her. And for answer to that there was mock opposition. "Now, listen! Say, what do you mean by this? If you are going to act this way, I'd better be going." But just the same, a kiss achieved, and then a second, and after a struggle during which she asserted that if I didn't let her go she would scream or not come again, still a conversation on the couch itself, with her bantering and begging, along with not too much struggling, until at last the actual contact was established.

But in this a mental determination not to be frightened, and more, to master my own fever sufficiently to achieve adequacy —an effort which so surprised and pleased me by its results that never after that was I again to feel the terror which had so persistently defeated me up to this hour. For once the contact was made, she relaxed, if not completely, at least sufficiently to permit an emotion to be achieved; and more, at the very last, to seize me convulsively and even affectionately —a gesture which, followed by a smiling calm, was proof in itself that I had achieved my first adequate and decisive relation—a fact so thrilling that it almost overshadowed the pleasure of the immediate relationship. Then I was not impotent! I *could* hold this relationship with a normal, healthy girl. No longer need I fear that sickening, reducing, really destroying sense of incompetence. Go where I would, allure what girl I might, or be allured by her, from henceforth I need not be harried by that!

And although this young stranger immediately after jumped up, saying that she was late and that she would need to get "clear" to Canal Street before six and that I must let her go —and sure, if I really wanted her to, she would come again or

I could find her—only not to speak but just signal—she couldn't receive any letter because of her father and mother —I was in no way depressed by her going. Attractive, to be sure. Not a nice girl mentally, or one sufficiently well placed socially or reserved enough physically, perhaps, to be as desirable as she might be, nor sufficiently cautious for her own good, either; going, no doubt, now with this one, now with that, in just this casual way, as I immediately decided. But still worth while, and valuable, if only she would see me. . . .

But apart from that also, as curious as it may seem, an utterly glorious feeling in regard to myself and girls in general—not this one girl or any one girl anywhere, but many. Regret, for instance, in connection with all those with whom I had failed. But cheer as well as hope in regard to all others with whom subsequently I might come into intimate and affectionate relationship—a grand programme.

None the less, and notwithstanding, one more slight blow in connection with all this. My young Italian-American, for all my prowess, never returned. And although she had given me her name as Lissitina Cella, and said her father was the owner of a fruit market in Canal Street near Adams, opposite the old Union Station there, I found no such market.

So (sadly) what was the matter? Had I been, after all, too brash, too aggressive, too unattractive, too this, too that, even too inefficient that way? Oh, had I, and after all my glorious satisfaction with myself, not been so satisfactory, or so such-a-much after all?

Oh, reducing thought!

Oh, cracked and flawed conclusion!

And yet, and just the same, and in spite of all this, I was not wholly ready to believe that I had not established myself as a competent male. And that in that field, if in no other, I might now reasonably hope to succeed. For there had been that last convulsive embrace. And a quite friendly, if not exactly affectionate, conversation afterwards. Only why in the devil hadn't she returned after all that? Now just why? I stand puzzled to this hour, even a little dismayed.

CHAPTER LXXXIV

IT was just about this time, though, that the first, and quite the most profound, psychologic shake-up I ever received, occurred. I had noticed, even before we came to Chicago, that my mother was tending to become more and more sedentary, inclined to sit around in a kind of dreamy stupor and meditate on the spectacle of life. Here in Chicago, owing to her weight, labours about the house, this and that, she went out scarcely more than once a month, and then to a theatre, if anywhere, with one or another of the girls. But now, early in August of this year, we all began to note something: a sort of brooding wistfulness in her mood. My brother Paul, who, as I have mentioned, had been home not so long before that —his first visit in several years—had observed to others that he did not think she was looking as well as she might, and could not more of the housework be done by the girls—all of it, in short—a hint which was subsequently made a reality, or nearly so. But after he left, and our state was really not so very much different from what it had ever been, she fell into her old mood and began to speculate—aloud at times—as to whether she was not going to be seriously ill.

I never saw a group of individuals more profoundly affected by the state of one person's health than was our family by hers. However much we might quarrel among ourselves, as I have previously indicated, our allegiance to her was direct and pathetic. I recall my sister Ruth's strange depression at the very first suggestion of something untoward. A haunting fear that settled in her eyes and on her face. Her beloved mother, her beloved mother—one could read it in her every look and word. Meeting her one morning in the upper hall as I was about to leave for the day, she looked at me in an earnest, perturbed way: "Have you noticed anything wrong with mother of late?" she asked.

"No," I replied. "What makes you ask?"

"She seems so dispirited. I wish you would take her riding in your buggy. Could you? It would do her so much good."

"Sure I can!" I replied at once. "To-day, if she wants to! But what makes you say that? She's all right, isn't she?"

"Oh, I don't know," she replied, and all of a sudden her lips trembled and tears rose to her eyes. And at sight of this my own heart half stopping. Mother! Illness! Could it be possible that after all these years with us, she might . . . she might . . . I went back to look at and talk with her, to ask her if she would like to go driving that same day, but feeling at the same time—I cannot describe it to you—weak, forlorn, as one who walks in shadows in the heart of an unpeopled and lorn waste. Mother, my mother! No! And thereafter a nervous contemplation of her always, as though my watching and reporting to any and all of us any change, might help to save her.

Yet there was no immediate or at least no notable change. She seemed to go on as before. And I began to think of Ruth's tears as mere nervous sensitiveness in regard to anything that related to her mother. And so once saying to her, "Ruth, don't be foolish! She'll be all right. She'll get better. I'm taking her out to-day again if she'll go, and I will any day she wants to go."

"I know," she replied, "but, oh, I can't help it. She looks all right at times, but she's so weak and quiet. I wish we could take her away to the country or somewhere." And then she went downstairs to where mother was sewing.

And as usual, I took mother for a drive that same day, pretending to Conklin that I had some business far out; but if she was at all depressed at that time, she said nothing about it to me. Later she grew more sedentary, not ailing exactly, but sickish. Calomel and physic were resorted to, but instead of better she grew worse. Still later, a doctor was called and she began to lie abed late of a morning and to retire early in the evening, even lying down during the day—something I had never noted in connection with her before. And all those heavy burdens which for years she had assumed and insisted on were, perforce, though willingly enough on her part now, lifted from her shoulders.

I have never seen a family more speedily united in mood, more affectionately drawn together for the time, than was ours by this impending danger. For where all were previously so individual, touchy, argumentative, even bitterly quarrelsome at times, now they were united in the quieting bond of sympathy for her, and not only sympathy but a heart-clutching fear. For might she not be fatally ill? Who could tell? The visiting doctor said not, but what did he know? Not that anyone really believed that she was about to die, but that each so feared that. And forthwith money from one source and another, to take her to the theatre: to McVickar's, where Mary Anderson was appearing in Shakespearean rôles; to Hooley's, where Nat Goodwin was amusing the public in "The Gold Mine"; and others. Her joy in these things was intense—I doubt whether before coming to Chicago she had ever been in a theatre. But just the same, lassitude, weariness, a preference for her bed and rest. (And why not, after such a life?) Regularly I took her for a drive at least twice a week, counting my job important, even though my salary was not paid, so long as it afforded my mother this pleasure.

A notable change in connection with all this was presented by my sister Eleanor. Often dogmatic, irritating, where the rest of us were concerned, she now, because of this threatening danger, became as nervous and reduced as one who borders on collapse. In fear of what she feared, she was about constantly, anxious to take charge of everything, but prevented in this instance by the pale and distrait authority of my sister Ruth, who less nervously anxious, was more the quiet, sacrificial devotee. I think I never saw a more lovely devotion. So moved by love and tenderness was she that her steps were noiseless, her eyes strained and full of fear, her face pale, her voice low, reduced almost to a whisper. And as for service, there was no limit to it or the time in which to perform it. For her there was no time, nor weariness.

As for the rest of us, the whole house was in a ferment of anxiety. Yet on the surface, hushed and solemn, in order that mother might not see or feel what was going on. I recall that my father sat around, strained and greatly distressed, often his eyes closed as though he were praying. And I am sure he was. Also that all his prayers were now offered for her recovery. Similarly, Al, Ed and myself, who had hitherto roamed about at nights seeking entertainment as best we might, now stayed at home and played games or read. I know that I, for one, had a keen desire to be near my mother and to make up to her in some sympathetic way for my past deficiencies as well as her past miseries, however little that could have meant then. At the same time, in a kind of bumptiousness of spirit, seeking to fit myself for any fate, to meet all impending ills with optimism, etc., I was for sitting around among the others and mouthing profound nonsense about the nothingness of everything and of spiritual peace being the great thing—thoughts which I had heard at college and the repetition of which flattered my sense of individuality. I also recall that my mother appeared to like some romantic pieces I managed to finger out on Al's guitar, in the hope of diverting her at times; at least she did not request me to cease. What she thought of my cheap stoicism, if she heard any of it, I can never know. I can readily tell you now, though, what she should have thought.

What damn' fools we really are, the most of us! Never, as I see myself now, was there a greater mountebank than myself at that age! Already imagining myself, because of my one year at college and the fact that one person and another had deemed me promising, a devil of a fellow! What, life top me? Difficulties and danger such as this destroy me? Impossible! I was passing into manhood now and should prove myself stoic, philosopher, patron to all members of the family —the white hope of the same, no less. Yet at the thought of losing mother I would become utterly helpless and bereft, a mere nothing, destined to suffer and mourn, scarcely able to go my way alone. The next moment—when she appeared to be feeling better—I was aloft with fine notions of personal distinction and future dominance, and getting out in the world, if need be, alone. I even condescended to sympathise with the others as not being as able as myself to take care of themselves.

Be that as it may, the days drifted by and she grew steadily worse. One day, in late October, when the leaves were turning, she asked me to take her for a drive, and as we rode along the handsome, new boulevards and park roads, she suddenly turned to me with an appealing, helpless look and said: "You know, I feel so strange these days. I hate to see the leaves turning. I'm afraid I won't see them again."

"Oh, ma, how you talk!" I replied. "You're just feeling

blue now because you're sick. You'll be all right again soon. Just wait and see! We'll get a good doctor for you, and he'll bring you around."

"You think so?" she sighed. "Well, maybe. But I have such strange dreams. Last night I dreamed my father and mother were near me and motioning me to come."

I fell into a deep depression at this, and urged my sisters to get another doctor at once, which they did. Yet he merely administered this and that nostrum the while a steadily weakening though intermittent fever reigned. Even then her condition did not seem so bad, but she could not move about as before. Instead she stayed in bed most of the time. "Change of life" was suspected and a general systematic derangement and possibly organic lesion. Finally there was a very pretentious and commercial-looking doctor who was called in consultation and who looked wise, and prescribed—guesses. At the same time, letters were sent to Paul, Rome (at some address he had left when he disappeared long before), Janet and Amy in New York. They were informed that mother's state was dubious, that she was seriously ill. As for Al, Ed, Trina and myself, we frequently grouped ourselves in conversation, wondering what we should do if she died, what would become of the home and our long and needful connection with it. The years that had gone! The happiness that had been! Was it all to end now, as surely, surely, it would, with the passing of her, the love mother, the binding mother, the one great tie between all of us?

And then at last the fatal blow fell. It was on one of those fine, November days which take one back to early September for crispness and warmth. The day before she had experienced periods of unconsciousness and her temperature was very high. Our regular, polite, whiskered and most carefully-tailored physician had been calling twice a day for a week, looking very solemn, writing out more prescriptions, and suggesting this, that and the other service. A few days before the end, he proposed that still a third physician be called in consultation—at ten dollars or more for that service. The latter, a heavy, pursy man, with side whiskers and a silk hat, looked very grave, talked in a low voice, and finally stated that he agreed with the first physician. No change in medicine was suggested. All that could be done had been done.

534

In one sense at this time there was one fortunate thing that befell us. During the week preceding my mother's death, my brother Paul arrived with his company and was able to spend these last few days with her—a phase of timeliness which he looked upon as providential, though he was moved to tears by the fact that being in fever she could not recognise him. With him, though, at this time was a stage beauty of his company—his latest flame—who because he refused to remain anywhere else but near his mother, came and took up her abode in one of the upper rooms of the house. She was a creature of rounded arms, oval face, blonde hair, and a velvety, tailored perfection which quite upset me, and talked much of her glowing affection for Paul, her sorrow because of his sorrow. In appreciation of the solemnity of the occasion, no doubt, she refused to have more than public and passing contact with him here, at least in so far as the eye could see. But the rings, ear-rings, brooches, pendent watch, bracelets, what not else! And the perfumes and powders! I can see her now, resembling an odalisque, most heavily redolent of perfume and quite obviously, and I might say solely, concerned with her beauty and her sexual interest in Paul, but pretending a deep, wide-eyed sympathy for his mother. As for Eleanor and Trina, they were inclined to hate her at once, the while I myself was wishing, sex-wise, that I might enjoy so beautiful a woman. But they were soon won over by presents and a show of affection on the part of this Miss Wood (I will call her that); thought she was "lovely," barring a few weaknesses and imperfections, while I had the supreme satisfaction of taking her for a drive once or twice.

Ruth—and alone of all of us, I think—clung unchangingly and slavishly to her mother, waiting on her night and day. If anyone said anything, offered to assist, replace her at odd hours or moments, it was as though we were meddling with some great duty she had in hand. No! No! Go! Leave her alone! Leave her with her mother! She would do all, all that could be done. And all this with white face, tense eyes, whispers. Verily, greater love hath no man than that he shall lay down his life for another! No hours of the night or day but what you would find her close by the bedside, half asleep perhaps but ready to jump up at the least stir or sigh. She it was who administered the last medicines, the baths, the hot and cold cloths for her head and feet. She assumed, as I have said, a kind of fierce and undivided control of the order of the household, its silence and cleanliness, the goings to and fro of restless feet. In me—and in the others, I am sure—she evoked a silent gratefulness as well as admiration and sympathy which gave her her will in everything. By her face one could see that she was suffering intensely because of feverish, frightened, eager, battling love.

Indeed, my father, most rampant of moralists and duty-demanders, in this instance was satisfied. "That Ruth," he said to me or someone one afternoon about the time of my mother's death, "she has a good heart. I wouldn't have thought it." And Eleanor, who had often quarrelled with her about this and that, now acknowledged as much, grudgingly at first, it is true. It was so with Trina, Al, and the rest. At the same time, she was not different from what she had been before or would be after. An idealist at bottom, passionately fond of life and passionately—almost more, I had said —fond of her mother, she illustrated for me something in this gross, fierce struggle for existence that is neither gross nor fierce but only tender and beautiful.

One morning, though, about twelve, I had stopped home for lunch and was in mother's room, permitted there by Ruth because mother said she was feeling much better. And Ruth, consoled by this, was seizing the moment to take a bath. "Now don't let her stir too much and don't talk to her," she cautioned me as she left the room.

I sat there looking at my mother. She seemed cheerful enough, tried to turn and sit up. I am wondering now, and for the first time in all these years, whether she might not have been in a dream, or slightly deranged, maybe. At any rate, she now said: "Help me up. I feel so much better. I want to use the stool. I'm strong enough."

"Do you think you'd better, ma?" I asked. "You heard what Ruth said."

"Yes, I know, but help me. I must . . . I'll be all right."

And because she was pulling at the covers, trying to throw them off, I sprang to her side and put my arms around her. With my aid, she sat up, and a moment later, after I had arranged or improvised the toilet and had gone back to her, she attempted to rise. As heavy as she was—weighing all

536

of two hundred pounds—she half rose, half slid to her feet, and even sought to move a step or two. But almost as immediately, and with a groan, drooped, and except for all my strength vigorously exerted, would have fallen. As it was, she slipped to the rug at the side of the bed, relaxed, very weak and pale, and then looked at me, at first with such sickly and weary eyes, a most exhausted and worn look. But in almost the same moment, as I noticed—in a trice, no more— a, to me, mystic thing appeared or took place. Her eyes cleared—that muggy yellowness that was in them before, gone, and as instantly and in its place a clear, intelligent, healthy light, quite remarkable and most arresting to me, even startling. For now it looked as though she were thinking or trying to say something to me, but through her eyes alone. But only for a second or two, and then, as suddenly, a heavy, grey dullness once more, almost fishy and unintelligent, and then complete blankness, no light or fire at all. And all was over.

"Mamma!" I called. "Mamma!" And as Ruth, hearing me cry, came running in, I called to her: "She's dying! She's dying!"

In an instant, Ruth was beside us on her knees, clasping her hands in a most agonised way, then rushing out of the room to send for the doctor. In her absence, though, my father came running. He had been reading downstairs. At sight of her dead on the floor, he got down on his knees beside her and began to blubber in a forlorn, exhausted, and uncontrollable way. To me at that moment he looked so old, so hopeless, so forsaken, so much in need of affection and care. And how is it that to any in such need, the heart goes forth madly and sadly?

"Mom! Mom!" he called. "You are not really dead! Not really! Oh, I should have gone first! I am so old! What is my life?"

The next I knew Eleanor and Ruth were leading him away. Then Eleanor returned, with hysterical cries. And later Ed, since it was noon and he was home for lunch. Of all in the city, only Al, Trina and Paul were absent. It was deemed best to let Paul complete his afternoon matinée before notifying him. Ed and myself started at once to get Al, but by some chance met him at the nearest corner, coming. For some reason Ed had refused to go in to see his mother thus far, but as he saw Al turn the corner near our home, he ran forward, and with a wild, agonised gesture, exclaimed: "She's dead! She's dead!"

"Who? Not mother!" exclaimed Al, his face twisting strangely.

"Yes, she died just now," returned Ed.

"No! . . . Well, that's the end of our home," he added, laconically, and hurried on before us, to see for himself.

CHAPTER LXXXV

I NEVER saw a house more shaken or disrupted than was ours by this event. It was as if an explosion had occurred and many had been killed or injured. We were beside ourselves with grief, worry, perhaps fear of new and worse disasters to follow. The mental shake-up it gave me was so profound as to seem for the time being not only destructive to my current happiness but to my future as well. For interesting as were my brothers and sisters, and a seeming reliance in a world where blood, at times, appears to be thicker than water, still now I saw very clearly, and as in a flash, that they could not be looked to for any really sustaining sympathy or interest. They had their own lives to look after and would soon go their own way. As for my father, he was too old to be of any service, and his mental grasp of anything really valuable was nil. He could offer no aid—merely needed it. My mother, as I now saw so clearly, had been the sustaining force here, the great comfort and strength, and now she was gone. Actually as I thought of this, I suffered as from a great weakness —a strong sustaining cord having broken—a floor on which I stood having fallen away. While I had not been looking to her to sustain me in any way in the future—quite the contrary —I now saw, as Al had seen at once, that this was the end of our home. Our youth and home were over. She was gone— collapsed and even vanishing as a cloud—and all that she had represented was so soon to go with her.

Never before, in this deep emotional sense, had I been confronted by that phase of death which is not only of one's blood and bone but the very essence of one's thought and spirit, one's days and experiences. For from what part of my life so far had my mother been absent; what phase of my needs and moods thus far had she not sensed and cherished? And now to see that fleshy something that had been eyes and tender hands and sympathetic and encouraging thought and mood, quite still, mere meat, but holding the form of my mother! Her worn hands! The tired face! The waxy flesh, stiffened and fallen slightly, but still suggesting her old sweetness! But where the life, the fever of the blood, the unsatisfied longings and dreams? Dissipated entirely? I could not, after all the palaver concerning souls and spirits, believe that, and yet, too, I could. For by then had come not a little knowledge of chemistry as well as physics and those troublesome meditations that relate to the endless and in most cases so slightly modified repetition of any given form from oyster to man, so that one could scarcely say: I am an individual and as such worthy of continuation; but rather: I am one of a type that shall be repeated and repeated and repeated! And yet here, and in the very face of this, was a part of my own life that had died, my earliest youth, my earliest happinesses and pains and dreams and illusions—here and now they had died with her. And I was no more to know her as that part of them that she was.

And yet my eyes were not wet. Far, far beyond tears are certain ills and moods. I could only look and feel her cold hands and cheeks, and think of that last look she had given me, and speculate as to where, if anywhere, but certainly nevermore here. . . . And in their place—but only for so little a time as that—dissolving elements—salts, acids, the watery ash of how many elements—and then even this cold form would be gone. No trace—no other suggestion of her anywhere ever.

That she might live for a time here—here!

And as curious as anything else, that night I felt, as I lay in my bed, that I was really under an alien roof. This was no home of mine any more, only a boarding house. Eleanor might be there for a time, of course, and possibly attempting to take charge, and Ruth quarrelling with her or leaving, or vice versa. My father, useless as a binding influence, would become a care, and what was to become of him? I troubled over that greatly. For while Al, Trina, Ed, Ruth, my father and myself might get along for a time, how long really would we hold together? For neither Trina and Ruth, nor Trina and Al, nor Al and Ruth, agreed very well. As for Ed, Al and myself, would not we, too, soon wish to go our separate ways? I feared so.

But if I suffered a profound emotional and philosophic shake-up, the others were, if anything, more wrought-up. For in unreasoning and very individual ways, they were drawn to their mother by these same mystic cords that had drawn me, the severing of which caused them as much pain. Only the one she grieved most over—Rome—was not there at the time. He, as I have said, had wandered off the year before and had not been heard from since. During her last days, as was characteristic of her, she had asked after him frequently, wishing that somehow he could be found, some word gotten to him.

As for the actual tragedy of the moment, Paul came home at nearly six o'clock from the matinée performance of his show, so stricken that he could scarcely say a word, or make even a sign. He merely stared at her body in silence, pressing his lips together and finally, unable to restrain himself, wiping away the few tears that ran down his cheeks. Then he left the room. And Al did the same, saying: "I can't cry. I don't know what's the matter with me, but I can't." When one of us went in to view the body—we had no friends or acquaintances in Chicago to speak of, so that the mourning was confined to the family—the others went along, for reason of that intense curiosity, no doubt, which runs as a binding thread through all our emotions, grave or gay. Each seemed desirous, apparently, of seeing—at first, at least—the effect of the actual sight of an ill upon another. Or could it have been that some aspect of our mood or grief, or the lack of it, was to be taken as a test of our humanity? I have often wondered. I know that I personally was purposely and after the first blow almost vainly calm and collected, in order to show how individual and forceful I now was, yet not, as I have said, merely seeking to conceal my suffering. For within me now was something else: a new sense of individuality which my mother's passing seemed suddenly to have completed. For now I was I. And alone. Her part—her strength and living, sustaining love—had gone from me. I could not have her any more to lean on or turn to. And so must now turn to myself—must. And that thought seemed actually to swell in me as a new strength—which most certainly it was. For apart from her I did not really desire anyone else so much—really wished only to be alone for the time being—as I was for many years thereafter—a lone barque on a lone sea.

On the other hand, as it seemed to me, neither Al, Ed, Ruth, Eleanor nor my father seemed to be thinking of anything save their loss. The various strands of built-up feeling and emotions and motives which constitute the cable of family life seemed so completely ripped as to end in numbness for all of them. They cried, or walked, or stood about dry-eyed. I recall finding Paul, late that same night after an unescapable performance at the theatre, standing outside the door of the room in which the body of his mother lay awaiting the arrival of the embalmer on the morrow, and saying to me or someone —possibly Ruth or Eleanor—"I can't go in again. I'll have to stay here a while." And so staying for minutes before he could collect himself sufficiently to enter. As for Al, I found him the following morning, which was Sunday, sitting on the edge of his bed, brooding. "It's a strange thing," he said at last, "I can't feel anything now. I'm going to feel bad after a while, I know that, but isn't it strange that I can't feel anything at all? It's just as though I was numb in my brain."

Sometimes I think it is just as well that we take life at its face value, for when you pry below the surface you get lost in its amazing and wholly confusing abstrusities—grow mind-weary and more befogged—even waste years and your very life pottering among the undecipherable plexi of its methods and faces. It is at times like lifting a man-hole cover in a street only to find below a world of complicated wires; or again, like flaying the skin from an animal to behold the network of muscles, nerves, bones, the *raison d'être* for which can only relatively be discovered anyhow. In our several actions under this stress of emotion, I personally was busy tracing out all sorts of secondary manifestations in myself and others— curiosity, vanity, selfish thoughts as to freedom from control in the future, and the like—but the great thing to note in this instance was that they were secondary only. For even though as I sat beside my mother's body once or twice, holding her dead hand, I found myself acting to myself, posing as a philosopher, emotionalist, this, that and the other, none the less, and all things considered, I *was* stricken, as I have said —heavy with grief because my mother, to me so beautiful, so patient, so tolerant, so long-suffering, was now like this or not here—or worse, not anywhere—ended, concluded, a dream that was encased only in the most lovely memories.

Followed several days of the usual proceedings in connection with death—embalming, coffining, arranging with the local Catholic priest for services. I recall that a great bitterness toward the Catholic Church was aroused in our family by the fact that the priest—my mother having neglected her duties of confession and communion for some time—was doubtful as to whether he should come to bless the body or whether she could be taken to the church at all, or buried in consecrated ground—that privilege which good Catholics value so highly and seem to think insures the peace of their fancied immortal spirits—she who had always pleaded with the rest of us to attend its services! The chief trouble, as it appeared, sprang from the fact that the dear father had not been called in during her last illness to hear her confession, administer communion and extreme unction, and so all this was now taken as proof by him of an innate and even deadly opposition to the Church, my father's slavish and pleading devotion to the contrary notwithstanding. But the real truth was that my sister Ruth, freed by reason of her affectional contact with the intellectual and pagan Davis from all belief in Romanistic dogma, had been opposed all along to the introduction of the Roman clergy in this final hour. Why a priest with his oils and crosses hovering about one who was ill and weary unto death and needed him not at all? Worse, my father, most anxious all along to have a priest called, had been deceived by Ruth and the others into delaying the invasion of the Church on the ground that mother was really not fatally ill, as, in fact, it had really seemed for a time. Ruth had been determined that mother was not to be disturbed or frightened by those preliminary religious rites which indicate mortal extremity. Anyhow, the priest had not been called, and now that my father was determined that he should come, there was the difficulty of explaining why these last rules of Holy Church had not been complied with.

I never saw a man more depressed by a spiritual complication. A poor, wind-blown straw in the hands of the religionists at all times, he was now quite beside himself with shame, grief, and religious terror, not only because of his own sinful connection with this lapse of duty but fear as to his wife's future life in the spirit world. You would have thought that the local parish priest, noting him as a regular communicant and one carrying all his spare pence to the collection box during these several years, would have taken these things into consideration and out of sympathy for him, as well as reverence for those signs and symbols wherewith the Church chooses to befog the brains of its weaklings and which, disregarded, mean either heaven or hell to the faithful, would not have tortured him with uncertainty as to whether the soul of his wife—the mother of his children—was destined to burn in hell or rest in heaven.

But not so. This low-browed, dogmatic little Bavarian, panoplied with the trashy authority of his Church, chose instead to come to our door, and disregarding the pleas of my father, if not the rest of us, show how savagely Mother Church would repay by stern denial of her hieratic pomp and meaningless formulas the spiritual lapses which it condemned. In short, as I recall him—and I was present at the time—his face was a distorted and dictatorial cloud of narrow, Teutonic, bigoted religion and authority. What? The wife and mother of this household dead? And was she a Catholic? The slavish reply of my father was that she had been, but since living in Chicago and being stout and old, the last several years had been marked by some lapses, to be sure, but that just the same, in former times her devotion to the Church had most certainly been thus and so.

But before he was anywhere near concluding, this authoritative clerical ignoramus and martinet was out with: "What? Then she has been allowed to die in mortal sin? She has not been to confession or communion in months? Why was not I called in while she was ill, then? Why did I not hear her last confession? Why was I not notified of all this before? What kind of religion is this? Have I ever seen her in my church? No! And now you call me here to bless the body! Or to perform the last rites of the Church in the church and permit her to be buried in consecrated ground! No, no, no! If that is the religion of this place, then let someone else attend her now. The Church keeps its services and its sacraments for those who deserve them—not for those who ignore them until it is too late! No, no, no!" And talking thus in German, he strutted up and down with the air of a supreme ruler, the corpse being stared at as if it were some very undesirable object. And my father the while turning his hands

544

within themselves, his eyes dark pools of misery. But myself boiling with a poorly-repressed rage. (How swiftly the Church was rising in my esteem!) And my sister Ruth the same, her spiritual type of beauty showing white and tense under stress of her emotions. God! My father's servile attitude, and born of complete and unreasoned religious prostration before such numbskulls as this!

But at last—and after this petty little beast had swept himself out and my father had begun with, "Oh, oh, now you see! And to think that she has died so!"—the pain and fury of this loving daughter at last found voice and burst forth with: "To think that that fat little beast of a priest should dare to come in here and talk and strut around like that! And after all you and mother have done for the Church—given land, money—and all of us kept in its schools until it was almost too late for us to learn anything!" She was white, tense, savage even. But then beginning to whimper, she added: "If ever there was a saint! Poor dear mother!" She went over and smoothed her face. "And *that* saying that she is not to be buried in consecrated ground! Well, it doesn't make any difference to her or anyone whether she is or not—but *his* attitude—as though it could make any difference to her!" Then she cried, bitterly.

But my father, following at the heels of the priest as does a dog at those of its master, was completely broken. What Holy Church said was the truth, and so the beginning and end of all things for the soul of his wife. Unless she was forgiven, blessed, buried from the church, let down into holy ground, what hope for her before the Great White Throne? And so a crawling pilgrimage after this priest. No doubt, tears as well as supplications. And after what belly-crawlings I know not, masses for the repose of her soul then and there arranged for, at the rate of two dollars per mass—all he could think of affording at the time. And so, while no further visit to the house, still, permission to bring the body to the church. (I think my brother Paul had something to do with that.) And further, permission also to bury her presently in St. Boniface Holy Roman Catholic Cemetery—laid out on a dreary waste on the North Side—lots so much per square foot.

And then, during two more days, the body embalmed and

laid out to view in the front parlour in which she had died, to await the arrival of my sisters Amy and Janet from New York—two who had departed so long ago, as it then seemed to me, but were now hurrying west. And on their arrival (Paul having been compelled to go south to St. Louis and Cincinnati with his company), I was witness to more of that binding influence which my mother had exercised. The spasms and whorls of grief unlocked by what memories—those same that had so moved and anguished me! Amy, as I noted on her arrival, was the same sensuous, nebulous girl she had always been, self-conscious but chastened by circumstance, living, no doubt, in a world of dreams and never thinking of seeking any serious constructive employment, but only of love, pleasure, romance. And Janet, slightly more sober because of marriage and children, clad in furs and silks and arriving in a carriage, weeping convulsively over the pale shell which meant to her—what? I sometimes envy the world its illusions of sorrow, its great foolish griefs which seem to attest the reality of something that is as fantastic and unreal as life. Indeed, life as I see it only takes its reality from these same tears, guffaws, hates, envies, desires. But remove these passing immaterial things, and where is it? Who has it? When we think, meditate, then does it vanish into thin air or confusion. I know that after years of absence my mother's death could not have been as crushing as it seemed to these two. Yet they wept as though they would never smile again.

Came now the funeral services at the church—a solemn, artistic, moving function to me—with the large black coffin set in the central aisle, tall candles at each end; and then the burial in the small new German graveyard out on the North Side, where stub willows and tall yellow grass interrupted a dreary, windy, prairie landscape. At the door of the house, when the body was being carried out, and again at the church door and before the vault (for we could not endure to see her put away so completely for ever as an earth grave would have doomed), there were scenes of such hysterical violence as to unnerve me completely. Ruth, Eleanor, Janet, Amy, Trina, Ed and my father were apparently inconsolable. They wept in a racking, agonising way. I looked at my father, clad in an old-fashioned cape coat, hanging limp about his thin shoulders, his derby hat carried respectfully in his hand,

546

while he covered his eyes with his big white handkerchief and cried. And then I cried with and for him—he seemed so helpless, so utterly forlorn. As he truly inquired, why could he not have gone first?

At the vault, in that sandy, windy place, we stood about in the raw weather, looking at the almost leafless trees and the low tomb. They put her on a shelf and shut the door, and then we continued to stand about, weeping and grieving, until the undertaker, considerate of his carriage charges as well as the length of time to be devoted to any funeral, made it plain that we must return. Then back to the gloomy house, my sister Janet returning to New York, while Amy, intrigued by this latest vision of Chicago, decided to remain for the present to seek work. And Eleanor and Ruth retiring to their respective rooms to mourn.

Nearly three weeks passed, and then the last touch in regard to all this, at least in so far as I was concerned. I was sitting in my office—the last frittering days of A. Conklin, Real Estate —one day late in November, when of a sudden, and much to my surprise, my brother Rome came bustling in, a strained look of fear, curiosity and excitement in his face. From some source—I forgot where—he had secured my address.

"How's mother?" he demanded, without stopping to greet me in any way or ask any other question. "Where is she?" Evidently our moving had upset him, for one thing.

"Why, Rome," I exclaimed, realising how he would feel the moment he heard the news, "don't you know? Where do you come from?" I looked at him nervously, trying to frame the news so that he would not take it very much to heart. At this his brows knitted and his face took on a hard, pained, angry look. Instead of replying, and with a pained, dramatic gesture he exclaimed: "I knew it! She's dead! She appeared to me on a black horse in a dream five weeks ago. I knew she was dead then or going to die." He began to cry.

"We tried to write you," I sympathised.

"And she asked me in the dream why I didn't come home," he continued. "That's why I'm here."

"Oh, Rome," I said, "I'm so sorry. She wanted to see you, too."

His heavy, guttural, Gargantuan weeping made me cry. "I knew it! I knew it! The only friend I ever had, the only friend. And she always wanted me to do better!" He sat down and buried his face in a handkerchief. After a time he added: "Where is she buried?" and learning that she was still in a vault in St. Boniface Cemetery, announced that he was going there at once—which he did, describing his impressions and reactions to us afterwards. He spent that afternoon in the vault alone with her, as he afterwards said.

Later came a period of drunkenness, then reform, then drunkenness, and so on—a long story. But his depression was very great and convincing. Although he often spoke of reforming on her account and for her sake, he never did, liquor and wandering remaining his two obsessions. Some mystery of temperament doomed him from the beginning. But is it not time we revised the list of senses and included that of telepathy or premonition? How is it that this is still denied—long-distance sensitivity to important occurrences?

CHAPTER LXXXVI

FOR two or three weeks after my mother's death, I mooned about the real estate office wondering what was to become of me and what I was to do next. The future of our family life seemed very uncertain. As far as my present work was concerned, Conklin was plainly on the verge of giving up. He had made his rent, but really nothing more. My salary had not been paid for six weeks or more. (The only reason I retained the place was because for a time I could use it to take mother for a drive.) I think Mrs. Conklin must have often commented on his foolishness in continuing this office, for daily he walked the floor there, the grey, busy life of November outside, striking his hands and commiserating himself and his future. "If just a little business would come in. Just a little!" But none did; at least no more than would pay the rent and incidentals.

And now my father, being the natural heir to control in our house, began to plead for those particularities in conduct and that prompt payment of weekly dues on the part of all which suited his idea of how life should be lived and morality expressed. Really, in his insistence on petty details, religious and otherwise, he could be at most times maddening. A number of debts having been contracted by my mother, or my sisters because of her—medicine, furniture, fruits and delicacies, and now, largest of all, funeral expenses (those amazing charges for paraphernalia which then as now were and are unloaded on the mourning living as necessary tributes to the departed, tokens of this and that, and all so profitable to those bandits now labelled "morticians"!)—their prompt and more than prompt payment became now his principal care, a first lien on and the joint duty of all of us, individually and collectively, to contribute as much as possible every week until they were cleared away. And there would not have been any great objection to this if only they had been reasonably fair debts which required immediate settlement, but they were not. Rather, they were nearly all those exaggerated "easy" or time payment affairs, contracted with the understanding that time was the essence of the contract and calculated to yield the creditors not a hundred but nearer a thousand per cent. profit. And yet my father insisting that they should be paid almost at once.

More, there were bills for services in connection with the church (masses for the repose of my mother's soul) which my father had contracted for and which had to be paid weekly or oftener at $2.50 per mass. His religious fears in regard to my mother's fate made him feel that this was necessary, as well as that no debts of any kind should be over his head or ours. The fact that the family would be compelled to undergo as much of that old-time hardship as ever (he actually seemed to relish poverty at times) was neither here nor there. To him it was a sin to be in debt. If one died owing money, heathen or Christian though he be, the flames of purgatory would have to purge him of the injustice. So horribly depressed by the errors my mother had committed in not being religious, in not giving heed to the exact religious duties required of her by the Church, in not having compelled or influenced (with his aid) the proper religious conduct of her children, he seemed to me and the others to be reasonably sure that her soul was not so very far from hell itself, in the nethermost depths of that most profitable religious pit: Purgatory. So the very least that could be done here was to have endless masses said as well as the debts paid, in order to lighten the long sentence. I thought he was losing his mind or passing into his dotage, and yet, and even so, having caught my ear with his long and passionate protests, I found him leaning mostly on me for sympathy and justification. I was such a good listener.

"When I think," he once exclaimed to me in a passionate, despairing way, "of all the pains and suffering that she may have to endure in the next world, I feel as though my life was a terrible failure! My children! My children! How they have carried on!"

Needless to say, neither I nor any of the others could share in this agonised conception of what the future held in store. His prayers and private tears, his daily and almost hourly visits to the church, his pleadings with us—particularly we four younger ones—to reform or at least be more diligent in our observation of religious duties, and above all, his pleading that we go nearly hungry and buy no clothes until these ridiculous debts were paid, were to us almost amazing. He seemed a little cracked or obsessed, running off in vague, insubstantial abstrusities which had no relation to real life.

But because of his general goodwill toward me always and because even before my mother's death my salary had ceased and Conklin was now owing me the sum of twenty-one dollars, I was the one to suffer after the first attack as to what should be done about these debts and what I should personally do. And this in the face of the fact that not only had I been irregularly paid—all I earned going for board and room money—but also that I really needed a fall suit and an overcoat. And yet I was hanging on to this job from sheer lack of courage to move, I presume, and he, of course, was anxious that I should get into something better and help him.

"This man must be a scoundrel!" my father insisted, speaking of poor old Conklin. "You are not earning as much as you should. Why don't you talk to him? Why don't you tell him? For a cent I would go to him myself." (Poor old Conklin!)

I explained to him that Conklin had only the kindliest feelings for me, and surely would pay me later if we made any money. But one day, unknown to me, he went to Conklin and, explaining his own situation, demanded to know why he did not pay me. Imagine! Only I wish I had been there, for it must have been amusing, to say the least. Conklin, as my father explained to me afterwards, recited all his joy in me—the wonderful, deserving youth I was—but that as true as that was, he could do nothing for me just then. Business was too awful. And he would think it natural and the part of wisdom on my part if I should leave him and seek something better. He was by no means sure he could go on, rather sure of the contrary as things were going. My father asked what about the twenty-one dollars due me. Could not something be done about that?

Poor old Conklin! I could vision him scratching his grey and empty head. Being a religious man like my father, he must have felt that he should do something, and so, possibly to avoid an accounting with his wife, he devised the idea—since he could not pay me anything in cash—of letting me use his credit at a certain clothing store for a suit and overcoat. Although this suggestion was a great blow—since my father was determined to get the cash—rather than see me kept out of my money indefinitely, he came round to the idea, urging me to get them at once and then leave.

These new clothes, as I recall them, were dizzy things—a coat and waistcoat of thick, cheap, blue cotton-wool chinchilla, as this particular weave was then known, and a pair of steel-grey striped trousers which I greatly admired, to say nothing of a black frieze overcoat which seemed wonderful. Whether they were of the customary side-street, store-shelf character I cannot recall, but I presume so. Anyhow, regardless of how they looked, they seemed satisfactory, and although I had no money, aroused in me all sorts of flaring ideas as to how easy it might be now, on account of my handsome appearance, to make further conquests among the girls.

Thus, once more, in late November, I struck out into the world to seek a new place. And once again, the same old trepidation, faltering before doors which I felt I ought to enter but, because of shame at being idle and this kind of a flotsam-jetsam job-seeker, held back. Now and then a man or woman standing at a window, or at a door, or waiting inside, or a too publicly-exposed general office, or a too severe-looking proprietor or manager or clerk at a desk, all and severally served to put me out of countenance with myself and cause me to slink away. Often I asked myself of what good had my schooling been to me; what my various other jobs? Always I thought of the boys or men, those usually seen at desks through a window, who were thus winning to a technical position or who had graduated with honours and gone into these high places of the world, whereas I . . . I . . . well, here I was tramping the streets again. Would I always be getting poor places and losing them? It seemed at times as though I could not bring myself to face people. Frequently I would walk away from a building, complaining to myself of my cowardice as I went, and then after going two or three blocks pull myself together and come back, only to find someone else at the door or some other hindrance, and so go away again. Casper Milquetoast!

I often wonder whether anyone who has been brought up in the bosom of a family, where means and connections guarantee at least an opening or start, can have the faintest idea of what it means to be compelled to search thus aimlessly hither and yon. It is so different where friends, a definite understanding, an aptitude for something within oneself, or a definite training of some kind, give one confidence enough to speak clearly for oneself and, as it were, compel a hearing. But to be, as I was, a nebulous dreamer, with no least understanding of what I wanted to be—it really was very trying.

This real estate business, it is true, had taught me something, as had the hardware business before it, and most definitely I felt that if someone would give me a chance and not be too hard on me at first, I would succeed, but being so poorly organised mentally from a practical point of view, I was not able to make that obviously necessary use of my knowledge: look, for instance, as though I really knew something. I could not bring myself to feel that I was really interested or that if I were given a place I would make that brilliant stir which I ought to make. Everyone else always seemed so much more alert, more practical, more experienced, more this and that, as no doubt they were, than was I. (And after all my success as a realtor!) In fact, I actually envied every dapper clerk I saw. I could not actually say to myself—so roving and uncertain was my mind in regard to almost everything—that this or that I would like to do and if I do it, it will be profitable for me as well as my employer. Ah, no! Instead I was really mooning over life in a nebulous, philosophic way, with here and there and now and then, as I now recall, a tendency to an artistic interpretation of some kind—a feeling that I would like to say this or that about it—picture it as might a painter, perhaps, but no more. And so principally wandering and thinking—enjoying the light, colour, movement of life more than any specific phase of it, any phase or labour relating to subsistence.

And yet at bottom I don't suppose I would have changed places with anyone, either. For, as earlier, certain books still fascinated me and I was reading at such times as I could. Besides, the artistry of any passing scene—a boat, a sail, a crowd, a tower, a flock of pigeons—was sufficient to hold me for moments or hours. I loved to tramp the streets, when I could forget that I was looking for work, and would stand for fifteen or twenty minutes at a time, occasionally much longer, where men were digging the foundations for a building or where dredges or scows were churning and cleaning the Chicago River, or where boats—large, sea-going, three- and four-masted, and steamers of the Great Lakes—were crowded about a draw; or where trains and engines made smoky and clamorous some immense and bewildering railroad yards. As I saw it here, I loved life. Its material facial texture—the lamps that glowed at evening in the stores; the cars that jingled; the cables—now already laid on the West Side—that clanged; the odours of cooking, baking, canning that came from one place and another; the sense of peace, content, happiness, enthusiasm for life which seemed to surround and fill those who had something to do—all shone and resounded in my ears as might a symphony.

And when night fell, and tired and hungry after a day of such brilliant life-pictures—but no work—I turned homewards, it was with the thought of all of the nice, comfortable homes that were being lighted and put in order to receive the day-workers of the world; of pretty women awaiting husbands and fathers and lovers with kisses; of well-laden tables set for them. What thousands of spirited youths would now dine and dress and then go out to see those girls whose pretty faces tortured me on every hand; what thousands of girls would now deck and primp to play around with these boys! And constantly now my mind ran forward to the time when I should be better placed, when with money jingling in my pocket and handsome clothes on my back, I should be going out, too. When was that time to come? Must my youth slip away and I have none of it? Eighteen years had thus far been frittered away in longing and mooning, and here I was, once more on the streets, no trade, no profession, no job, my year at college wasted—or so I told myself—and, all in all, my life a failure!

I recall a Chinese water-lily that I planted some years ago in a green bowl, with pebbles and water at the bottom to keep it upright, give its roots something to cling to and its veins life. This, in its growth and difficulty in finding itself, reminds me of myself at this time. It was a good enough lily, a long, slender bulb, but in its physiologic development it had been so convoluted, its prospective stalks so twisted and folded in the bulb, that it experienced great difficulty in getting its head out. For a long time, this was twisted under, only a whitish-green hoop showing above the stones. I began to despair of it. And at last I said of it, looking at it most ruefully: "That is myself, as I was in my youth (and many others also, I presume), all bent and twisted within myself, my thoughts convolute and interlaced, my head twisted under my arm or leg in some unconscionable way. I will name it Theodore and see what happens." And so I did.

Only it grew thus, and grew and grew. A great powerful hoop, it seemed to back itself out of a hole, determined to stand straight, yet no head. Finally, after many weeks, the hampering fibres were broken, split in twain, and the head began to rear itself upward. Only then I said: "It is too late. The thing has been injured for life. Its central portion has been twisted all out of shape. It will never stand up properly. It cannot." But slowly the thing did bring its head about and stood up, and finally became a really tall and rugged stem. And though there was no sunlight where it stood, it began to head and was about to bloom, when I was called away. But I took it as a sign that even under such wholly unpropitious circumstances, it would bloom, and I said: "Am I not, or was I not, like that, after a fashion? Intellectually my mind was twisted like that. I had just as difficult a time myself. But now I am straight, and shall hope eventually to bloom, just as will this lily." And though unable to continue the observation and so draw faith from its conclusion, nevertheless my faith was that it would and did bloom.

That symbolic lily which is myself I have not tended, I fear, with sufficient care!

CHAPTER LXXXVII

IN spite of all this, I soon found a job—not the kind I wanted, but a job. I had been figuring, ever since I left Conklin, that I was worthy of a clerkship of some kind, but it was not forthcoming. No one seemed to want me, and as I look back on myself, I can see why, for I was by no means the clerkly type. But one day I had a bright idea. I had seen various advertisements reading: "Wanted, driver on laundry wagon; man who can get business"; or: "man who knows West Side" or "South Side." Salary was always mentioned as eight or nine or ten dollars. After having gone so long on three dollars and not always getting it, the idea of eight or nine or ten seemed enormous. It spelled all the creature comforts which I could reasonably expect. Why not a job as a driver of a laundry wagon? I could drive. I had learned the West Side by driving Conklin's buggy over nearly every portion of it. I could certainly say I was experienced in that respect. So the next day I visited a laundry, and to my surprise, after explaining my experience, was accepted at eight dollars a week.

It appeared, as I thought it out afterwards, that this laundry, an old and well-established one, distrusted drivers who were well-experienced or well along in years and able to get trade, because these men, when they learned the routes and knew the patrons sufficiently well, would usually leave and go to new and less prosperous laundries, taking, or endeavouring to take, a portion of the trade with them. Hence, mere boys, who were not sufficiently businesslike to solicit patronage but who knew enough to drive, collect and deliver and make change, were preferred and invariably given the open places. The man who had had my route before me had gone to another laundry and was now attempting to secure the Munger business, but the foreman—a lean, gentle Iago—smiled as he told me about it. "He can't get the Munger trade," he explained. "Nobody can get it, really. We do good work and we're prompt. Our customers have no reason for changing."

And this was literally true. In fact, I never saw a better-conducted business of this kind. It was on Madison Street, only a little way from those apartments or flats in which we had lived when I first came to Chicago from Evansville. It occupied what would be the equivalent of three store-fronts of twenty-five feet each, and was all of sixty or seventy feet deep—a great, low-ceiled, almost square room, literally crowded with machinery, as was the basement underneath it. I never knew there were so many kinds of laundry machines until I saw these things. There were machines for ironing sheets, pillow-cases, towels and napkins—great long things of polished steel rolls, very hot and covered with clean linen, and in sizes to accommodate the various kinds of work. Then there were machines that ironed collars and cuffs, and machines that glossed them. There were also great barrel-like steel tanks and churn-like steel tubs in the basement; the first revolving, churning the great mass of clothes deposited therein, along with soap and hot water, in a slow, leisurely manner, the second spinning them so many hundreds of revolutions per minute or second, and so centrifugally throwing out all of the water, or nearly all. After that the drying was easy. There were machines, too, for laces and fine linens, and a number of single ironing-boards, where fancy laces, dress-shirt bosoms, difficult collars and the like, were ironed by hand. The laundry slip, printed red on white, showed a long list of articles, covering almost every possible requirement and all sorts of prices for the different work done. There was usually one girl to each machine, sometimes two or three, and they worked with a speed and energy which astonished me. They were so deft, intent, and withal so genial and sometimes talkative.

In the basement again, where the heavy washing was done, were to be found a number of gross-looking German, Irish or Polish women, who worked in a hot, steamy atmosphere which was like that of a Turkish bath. They were almost swinish as a rule, big-armed, red-faced, heavy-lipped women, wearing drabby skirts and close-fitting, sleeveless undershirts which outlined their great breasts almost disgustingly. Often

557

they walked about without shoes or stockings. Always on Monday, Tuesday and Wednesday mornings, in bringing in my load of clothes, I had to carry my bundles down into this cellar or basement, where checkers, washers, counters, etc., received them and after insuring their identity turned them over to these women. I never saw a steamier, meatier world.

Once when I spoke of this to our lean, genial foreman, he interrupted me with: "Don't talk to me about them! I know 'em! It's a tough job they have, but they're tough, too. Jesus, you ought to hear 'em swear when they get started among themselves. And drink! Like fish! They're regular sows in their home life—most of 'em—rushing the can and lying around drunk Sundays. That's why they look so glum Monday mornings. I have to let one or two of 'em go every now and then, when they get too bad, but we hate to discharge 'em because it's hard to get anybody to do that work. A woman with any refinement won't work down there. It's that sort or nothing. And they'd just as leave throw one another in the machines as not, when they get sore. Jesus, we've had some peaches here from time to time."

Upstairs, as I could see and as I learned later, the girls were different, and inclined to be clannish according to the kind of work they did. The rough-piece workers—towels, sheets, pillow-cases and the like—were, as a rule, of a dull or more solid and physically vigorous turn, and in addition, frequently with few inhibitions or restraints—sensual, immoral, and so avoided by the others, the more conventional or let us say, more clerkly, girls who worked at the front windows or near the door, in spruce dresses, ironing collars, cuffs, laces and the like. These were the aristocrats of the laundry and kept to themselves, usually ignoring even each other and hurrying out at six in the most tasteful clothing they could afford, some of it exaggerated enough for that day. Sometimes dapper youths in good clothes were waiting for them. I often wished that one of these maids would smile on me, but being a mere driver, wearing my oldest clothes, they scarcely noticed me.

Again, there were the expert piece workers—old maids or deserted married women or widows, all of them, and looking much alike—who could handle so many fancy shirt-bosoms, flouncy skirts or befrilled linen dresses in an hour. Some of these were speedy and some were slow, but all careful according to their tasks—but always they gave me the feeling of beaten and resigned creatures who had so little in their lives as to make them scarcely worth the living. Being especially good workers—and very likely poorly paid—they were—to make up to them in some inexpensive fashion—greeted most genially by the foreman as well as the manager, and even made way for respectfully, as becomes people who work hard and ask little. As a matter of fact, young Calverton, the assistant manager, who was up on economics and such, once said to me, in so many words, that it paid the company to be nice to them.

Again, there were eight or nine nondescript girls—pretty, mushy, sensuous, animal creatures—who did the intermediate simple work—socks, handkerchiefs, undershirts, drawers. One of the drivers—a red-headed tyke who was always chasing the girls, and who was so gay and smart that they all gave him nods and smiles, even the most exclusive of them—told me about them one night, out of the corner of his mouth, as we were checking up our loads.

"See that girl in the white waist over there. The one with the brown skirt? She does . . . you can have that for two dollars."

"See that little black-haired girl in the corner? The one with the red ribbon in her hair? One of the hottest in the place! Gee, they're all tough, that bunch over there! Love it! Say, they can't wait for six o'clock to come!"

And so he went on down the list. At once I fancied myself in a kind of Adamless paradise, where houri were to be had just for the asking. And I began to speculate as to how one or another of them might be induced to smile on me. The delights I conjured to myself at such moments made my head spin and my eyes almost blur as I checked up the load of laundry I was to deliver. One of these girls while I was there came subsequently to be connected with a scandal, but that can wait.

All told, though, it was an amazing three or four months I spent in this institution, though I was so poorly paid, as I subsequently came to think, that I was glad to leave. While these girls did not rush into my arms—as I half imagined they might—still I was in the proximity of a veritable garden of femininity not at all bad to look upon, and it gave me the feeling that with a little more daring I might have achieved what I desired. Several were astonishingly attractive, so much so that one wondered why they worked at all. Surely there were many men who would have married or "kept" them. Owing to the heat of the work, their charms were frequently most disturbingly displayed—arms bared to the shoulder, collars open to or slightly below the tops of their breasts, skirts tucked up above their calves—a daring effect for those days—in order to give them freedom of movement. In the heat, with pink cheeks, moist lips, and a certain enticing gaiety that most of them attempted whenever a man was near, such a temptation might have troubled even Saint Anthony!

But I, as I have said, was still without that very direct courage necessary for a speedy approach, and so, with one exception, my stay here was, in that sense, not so profitable. I will speak of that one later. Meanwhile, it was always a marvel to me to see with what an air of freedom, superiority, or genial sociability, so many youths approached so many girls. The patent-medicine manufacturer for whom Al worked, for instance, and his three sons, all of whom resided near here and were to be seen about this vicinity driving smart traps, wearing sporty clothes, were also masters of women in what was to me at that time a most enviable way. Al had pointed them out to me and told me about them, and the effect on me was the usual one. Ah, to have money, good clothes, to be able to walk up to a girl, lift your hat, smile and say some utterly inane but effective thing, then take her arm, walk off and entertain her for an hour or more! How did one do that? What did one say? I used to try to frame conversations that would carry me as long as say three or four minutes, but even when I was alone and amazingly courageous in my mind, it was a most difficult thing to do.

And yet, when evening came—particularly the evenings of the early spring, but more especially Saturday evening— and when I saw, as I always did, boys and girls strolling together here and there, laughing and talking, holding hands, drinking ice-cream sodas in a bright candy shop, I became almost wild. Spring madness! To have to work, to have to be financially as well as emotionally restrained as I was . . . ah! Yet under the pressure of all this, I think I achieved a poetic mood which was almost as wonderful as reality, though not quite—not as good as love in reality. The trees and the stars and the lights and the sounds of this breathing and tinkling world were so maddeningly sweet. A symphony! And I was the instrument through which all of this was achieving reality for me. It was I, and none other in so far as I myself was concerned, who was the horn through which this sweet blast was blown. But the tenderness! The colour! The wild delirium of these notes! Their vibrations stirring my soul even at this late date—vibrations that cannot die wholly, or utterly, save with me.

Behind the cashier's desk in this laundry there was a little Scotch girl—Presbyterian Scotch—who was at once pretty and, after her fashion, sensuous, but not as I saw or felt, as daring or as sensual as these others—just sweet. She had even white teeth; clever, twinkling grey eyes; hair not too lustreful or smartly arranged and yet plentiful—a demure type of girl, and say at least a year or two older than myself. She was not at all the type whom I would have picked out of a group of beauties, not the one I would have selected by preference out of this laundry force even, but the one, as circumstances proved, that I could win.

Let me by no means be unfair. She was not unattractive —far from it—for apart from her demureness and shyness— which I was not exactly seeking then—she was gay, good-natured, and quick at repartee—a good little business-girl, having the complete confidence of the resident manager of this branch, and by no means a prude, but embedded in a conservative and wholly religious family—Scotch Presbyterian. Withal that, though, she was passionate enough within her conventional tether, and so eager that before we were done I almost overran her good judgment.

How did I get in with her? I can scarcely recall. It came gradually—a smile, a bit of gossip concerning customers, complaints, mistakes in change or balances, which were calculated every night, and the like. At first she avoided me as I did her when I saw that she was demure, retiring, and, as I assumed, much too conservative. By degrees, though, and for lack of contact with one of the others, her charms came to be evident enough, her face, figure, arms, mouth, eyes, smile, all reasonably provocative. Had she been as lustful as these others or that little Italian girl, assuredly she would have enslaved me. Principally it was that she was not sufficiently coquettish or daring. The last to receive the cash returns of the day and to check up undelivered goods (the manager would trust no other, not even the foreman), it was necessary for her to remain quite late at times and to converse with the drivers, and there were five or six of us. And since frequently I came last, and so was alone with her in the office for a little while each night, we came to chat and laugh over this and that girl, driver, customer. Once it was raining and because she had no umbrella, I asked her if I might drive her home in my covered wagon. She accepted with such alacrity and genial, innocent gaiety that she put me quite at my ease, and we talked all the way, about the people in the place, without my being much more than polite.

Another time, though, she asked me to help check up the uncalled-for stock—it was around the first of the year and the foreman had asked her to get someone to help her. We did it after hours, and I felt so drawn to her at moments: she smiled so gaily; made me drop bundles, pretending to toss them and then withholding them for a second and then tossing them quickly. I could scarcely keep my hands off her. I did take hold of her hands once, holding them for a second too long perhaps, when the humour died out of her eyes and she became serious and businesslike. When I grew glum, she became very gay again, and teased me about being moody.

One night I helped her on with her coat; another night helped her hunt her parasol. Finally, when it was almost too plain that she liked me very much, I put my arms about her just outside the great clothes-locker where all the wraps were kept, and kissed her. She pretended to resist, but pretended only, and when I kissed her again and held her head back, she quit resisting and let her head lie on my shoulder. Her face, as I saw, was tense with emotion.

"Do you love me, Nellie?" I asked, foolishly, ecstatically, nervously.

"Go on with ye!" she said, imitating the Irish. "D'ye suppose me head would be here if I didn't?"

I kissed her again, passionately, and she put her arms tight about my neck.

"That'll be enough now for to-night," she said, laughing. "It's time ye were goin' home, and me, too."

And she went.

NELLIE MACPHERSON'S family, as I found when I was first permitted to call, consisted of a widowed mother, who did—I scarcely recall what—housework, I believe; a blind uncle, who had lost his sight from shock—falling through a ship's scupper, he being a captain's mate at the time; and a younger sister, Lilly. Scotch, Presbyterian, and all economical and conservative to the last degree, though the youngest, after the American fashion, later changed her ways completely after she turned to clerking in a great store.

Nellie, as I have said, was the elder and most practical and intelligent, though without an iota of that thing we call vision, which makes for artistic individuality. She would best be described as innocent, sweet, and pure-minded after the conservative and conventional formula, though I might term her "a case of arrested development," and be heartily damned for it, I presume.

Yet this home as a picture interested me, and I took pleasure in making myself a part of it. With the least encouragement from anyone, I was inclined always to assume a grand air of ability and superiority, for my courage rose as I was admired or received. And these people, much to my surprise, as you can guess, looked upon me not so much—not at all, in fact —as a playboy looking for romance but as a quite serious suitor for Nellie's hand in marriage—a development which did not enthuse me as much as it might have some. My mind was certainly not on marriage at nine dollars a week, and scarcely at any other conceivable salary as I see it now. Of course, they could not understand that I was an embryo historian, philosopher, and semi-scientific-minded experimentalist, blowing here and there in search of experience. But so I was. And in justice to myself, I can quite truly say I scarcely knew it either.

Be that as it may, they were simple and for all their

very humble means, very cheerful people. Mrs. MacPherson, Scotch of the "chares dirt" variety, seemed more of an amusing character than anything else to me—no real knowledge of anything save careful housekeeping and saving. The blind uncle, instead of appealing to my sympathies, as one would think he might under such circumstances, struck me as hard, and savage even, a cold, canny driving Scot. Rough enough as a mate on a boat in his day, I'll warrant, and looking and talking it, but now relying, and that rather irritably, on these much humbler relatives, whom previously, as Nellie told me, he had ignored. But they owned the little home they occupied, he had a little money, and between his board money and Mrs. MacPherson's and her daughter's work, they got along fairly well. No money, though, or very little, for clothes, ornaments, or pleasures of any kind, or only at times far removed from each other. Yet Nellie and Lilly, because they were young and attractive, seemed really charming and worth while to me. Of the two, once I saw them both, I preferred Lilly, though having chosen Nellie first, I had to abide by my choice, although Lilly, about sixteen at the time, began to manifest an interest on which her mother promptly frowned. Yet we met again in later years.

I remember now, though, how, on Wednesdays and Sundays (Wednesdays hurrying home and scarcely giving myself time to eat), I would shave, dress, powder my face, brush my hair in what I thought the most becoming manner, *à la* Pompadour, and adjusting my new fedora hat—price $1.50, I fancy—and carefully dusting my patent-leather shoes—which at last I had been able to purchase and now saved for such occasions —would sally forth to the MacPherson home, where I could pose and be made much of as a beau and prospective husband! Ha, ha! My spirit on these occasions, while engaged in part with the errand before me, was really much more broadly and thoroughly immersed in affairs of law and state and history, such as my constant reading—whenever I had a moment to spare—was causing me to become aware of: Richelieu, Voltaire, Peter the Great, Disraeli. And indeed at all times then and for the most part thereafter, I was no more the romantic ass than I was the thinker or perhaps—and better yet—the composer, who without instruments at hand to test the dream of melodies that assails his ear, still orchestrates great symphonies and hears them, each remotest flute and violin to the faintest division.

For unwittingly, in the technical mental sense, I was orchestrating as I walked or rode, the song that life was singing in my ears. Instead of thinking of my day's work or of any business I wished to undertake or perfect myself in, I was really immersed in the spectacle of living, and found myself constantly and spiritually present at all its secret scenes, from hidden murder and debauchery of the Cenci type to the inmost councils of state and the darkest avenues of chicane, *à la* Richelieu—any pleasure or revelry in which I might eventually participate, or some great acclaim which I might receive as an orator, statesman, general, or great organiser, never as a writer or poet. And as I walked and lived and created in the fashion here indicated, my mind naturally skipped all intermediate labour—studies, planning, scheming. In short, even then and there I was finding myself at the zenith of my days—wealthy, happy, famous, with some radiantly beautiful woman to share my happiness—the while I was preparing to call on Nellie MacPherson.

The pity of it was that in so far as Nellie was concerned, I was not as truly smitten with her as I was with crude, vigorous and yet beautiful sex, and was in reality looking for gratification in that field anywhere I could find it. And was actually seeing in her younger sister, who was more vigorous in that sense, something more of what I truly desired. Yet debarred there, continuing with Nellie. I think I must have been her first serious affair. The pity of it was that she had no understanding of the type of youth she was dealing with, any more than had I of myself, and soon believed in the gushing phrases I lavished upon her. Also she would sit in my lap, smooth my hair, look into my eyes, and let me whisper to her of the happy times we would have after marriage, always guarding herself, though, against those sly advances I was so anxious to make. At that, when aroused she was voluptuous enough, and at times, as I could see and feel, found it hard to resist, for her body would relax, her eyes mellow and grow moist and vague, her embraces urgent, only to be followed after a time by a white tenseness which marked her need of division between her almost savage embraces and kisses and her duty to her thus far enforced private convictions or early social and religious instruction. And once afterwards she told me how much her mother watched and cautioned her. But then it would be because I would press her breasts too tightly or seek the lines of her form too amorously, whereupon she would leap from my arms as from a dream and look at me at once nervously and defiantly and with not a little shame—although my pleadings and extended arms would usually bring her back. But sometimes she would stand by a window or door and make me talk to her so, or suggest that we walk. Yet I always lived in the hope of her yielding the next time, more fully at least, until . . .

My work for the Munger Company, in the meantime, was as interesting, from a character point of view, as any I have ever done, and contributed much to my understanding of people and life. It consisted of visiting on Mondays, Tuesdays and Wednesdays—each half-day being set aside for a separate trip or route—as many as sixty or seventy addresses—homes, apartments, flats—in a widely separated section of the West Side, and collecting the bundles of laundry, usually pinned, wrapped or tied, and waiting for me at the door or some stand just outside it. On Thursdays, Fridays and Saturdays, these routes were gone over again, this time to deliver the laundry so gathered.

These groups of people and the manner in which they paid their bills, delivered and received their laundry, constituted a lesson in human psychology which I have never forgotten. Thus, there were at that time two sections of the city— Washington and Ashland Boulevards and their allied side streets—from which, or in which, I collected from the rich or well-to-do. These regions have changed greatly since then, but at that time they were the best on the West Side. And their residents lived in spacious houses or in exclusive boarding or apartment or bachelor homes, where the air was one of ease, luxury and entertainment, coloured somewhat by the arts, and where I frequently saw those with whom I dealt. In those days money was being acquired with exceeding swiftness in this western city, and often on winter evenings (and I only worked for this company one winter), I was greeted between the hours of five and seven by men and women in that pinky perfection of dress which presages a dinner, a dance, a theatre party, or the opera. Chicago in these regions seemed—to me, at least—a very splendiferous and comfortable place to live. Servants in livery—the first I ever saw in America—were not at all unusual in Ashland Avenue. For the most part also, the men of these homes, precise and thoughtful as to their apparel, were yet careless as to their belongings and money, asking me to throw the laundry anywhere, or directing me to take the money from a chiffonier or bureau drawer while they went on shaving or reading a book, seeing me as merely a mechanical or lay figure. Occasionally, one or another of them—as for instance, the two young sons of George M. Pullman, of Pullman Car Company fame—manifested a slight trace of interest, as though they thought I might be human, though I was not so foolish as to expect anything of this kind.

"Snowing, eh?" one of these Pullman youths once observed to me, apropos of my appearance. "Won't you come over to the fire and warm up? Bad night driving around. Harry, here's your laundry! We'll have to take a closed carriage; it's snowing like blazes!" He offered me a cigar, then cigarettes, then a drink, and finding I wanted nothing, smiled, as he added: "Can't use 'em in your business? Well, I don't blame you." And out I went.

There was another man who has lingered in my memory as one of the most curious and individual of them all. He was tall and dark and tousled of hair, a Greek or Roman type, with a beard that grew so fast that although he apparently shaved every day and used much face-powder, his cheeks always looked dusty or black. His eyes, too, were black and round and stary, yet dreamy and forceful. When I called at his suite in Ashland Avenue, morning or evening, he was usually lying on a chaise-longue before a fire, or in bed propped up by pillows, a tabouret and tray with siphon and bottles on it, and cigarettes scattered about in profusion. Often he was reading, a cigarette in his mouth, his coloured silk pyjamas contrasting pleasingly with the coverlet and woodwork. Without moving, sometimes without looking up, he would direct me where to find his laundry or the money with which to pay myself. Always I had to do up his laundry myself, collecting it from drawers, suitcases, closets. For this he always offered to tip me, but that I refused. I was opposed to it as suggesting something that I was not, could not be:

568

menial. And once he said to me, quite apropos of nothing that I could think of at the moment, for he was not reading: "Did you ever read any of Huxley's Essays?" Having discussed Huxley with Sutcliffe and others at college, I claimed familiarity, and he made some additional comment which I forget. But what surprised and flattered me (for he had never spoken to me before save to ask me to get his laundry or pay myself or have a drink or smoke), was that he should assume an advanced mental interest on my part, and without any previous indication of the same.

For days I was thrilled by that and I wondered whether he would now begin to be friends with me. But he did not. I don't believe we ever had any other conversation of any duration or importance, but that one raised my estimate of myself in these very humble days.

And then, the type of self-sufficient, remote and somewhat disdainful woman customer in these houses or apartments! It is true that I rarely met or saw them, servants taking the bundle and handing me the money, but in some instances a woman appeared, giving me a passing glance and disappearing again—solid, aggressive, occasionally stately types, and some of them beautiful to me. Inclined as I was at that time to exaggerate or imagine what I did not see—create beauty, perhaps, where was only dowdy stuffiness and richness of texture—I was thrilled, and peering through a doorway, into boudoirs and reception rooms, I was inclined to imagine that I was seeing flashing touches of social superiority and social supremacy. Chicago seemed so splendid! Here, certainly, I thought, was the place to live! Ah, to succeed financially by marriage with some beautiful and wealthy girl, or otherwise attain to some such atmosphere as this! All my thoughts were of luxury such as I saw here—a petty and wholly material viewpoint, as I see it now. But so it was. And when I thought of Nellie MacPherson—I am sorry to have to confess this—she seemed a mere trifle. How quickly I would leave her for something better! And yet . . .

Was I a *parvenu*, a bounder, a snob? I presume so. Potentially, anyhow. But whether, assuming my wishes to have been granted, I would have done as I thought, I am not sure. I was never of the strutting type exactly—too much the observer and bystander. Just the same, at that time I could see myself in golden chambers, giving myself over to what luxuries and delights. But since I never achieved any such exotic luxuries—at least not until I was too old to make any particular use of them—perhaps I will be forgiven. At best, I fancy, they were only the giddy dreams of a boy driving a laundry wagon. Brought up in a conventional and successful world, I might have assumed that the rich had all of those virtues which the poor are too often assumed not to have—wisdom, refinement, ambition, sensitivity—whereas as it was, and per circumstances, the shoe was on the other foot. Being poor, I thought the poor were very much underestimated and underpaid and misunderstood—myself a shining illustration, as it were. At the same time, there was growing in me a fairly clear perception of the value of personality as distinct from either poverty or riches—Sutcliffe, for instance, and after (or perhaps before), my mother. Poverty had never altered her distinction for me. At the same time, and despite these to me two shining examples, I still gave way occasionally to the whining notion that if something were done for me —much—I would amount to a great deal—a whimper which had taken its rise out of my self-exaggerated deprivations. At the same time, as you will note, I was working and seeking ceaselessly. And which one of us is not anxious, or at least willing, to have things done for him?

CHAPTER LXXXIX

BUT if these more comfortable sections excited my avid fancy, the poorer ones—and we had our share of the middle class and poorer ones—aroused my curiosity and even profound sympathy. The great region of alien strangers, living under such troubled and befogged circumstances; the great region of the unemployed in South Clark, South State, East Harrison, and Twelfth Streets; the great region of the shop- and factory-poor, mile on mile, as I came to know.

There was one factory and tenement district which interested me because of the tall chimneys, lines and lines of windows where workers, men and women, were to be seen, at such unimaginative and routine tasks—machines, machines, machines, thundering over this or that—keys, cans, carpets, furniture, machinery itself. And the run-down homes built in an earlier day and for a better purpose or for the very poor in the first place, as was the case in some streets where one might see what were once large chambers or apartments, now divided into shabby cubbyholes and leased to Italians, Swedes, Danes, Irish, and a peculiar and to me often very offensive type of poor Americans—of which type more anon. This region, as I came to know, contained houses of convenience: "bed-houses," as the current phrase had it. From these we took immense bundles of laundry—sheets, pillowcases and towels. I was astonished one day when my friend "Reddy" Lasher, the young driver whom I have described as being so attractive to women, said to me: "Don't you ever collect laundry from Calverton's house?" (He was the lean, genial foreman I have described.)

"Sure," I said. "Why?"

"Well, aren't you on?" he inquired, with a cynical, informative grin, and when I indicated that I was not "on," went on to say: "Don't you get an awful big bundle of sheets and things from there?" His blue eyes twinkled wickedly.

"I don't know what you mean," I said, for I was always slow to get a point of this kind.

"Wake up! Wake up!" he said. "They keep a bed-house. She does. He says they rent furnished rooms, but that many sheets couldn't come from that sort of a place. They rent rooms to couples, don't you get that?"

I smiled, and coloured, for I wanted to appear wise and sophisticated in all such matters. Besides, already I had been interested by Mrs. Calverton, who was a short, stout, genial, black-haired woman of forty. She always came to the door and indicated a most amazingly large bundle of sheets, pillow-cases, towels and the like lying near at hand, or received the one I returned. But decidedly I had never connected her or Calverton with any such commercial mechanism as this. It evoked all sorts of exciting visions, and at once.

Yet Mrs. Calverton, so genial, industrious, and reserved. Was there no end to the subtlety and depravity of people? I could not add "depravity," though, because at bottom I did not really feel that this was so depraved—more human and necessary than otherwise. And Mr. Calverton. He too had seemed—still did—such a decent type—a little cynical at times but never rough or coarse, and working hard himself every day and always kindly and tolerant in not only his comments on but his actions toward those working under him. Apparently, though, this charge concerning their home business was true enough, and neither he nor she had any better sense than to send this immense bundle of laundry each week to this branch of the Munger Company, where all those associated with him as help or equals could see and surmise. If a certain Mr. Blackman, a very short, dark-haired, wiry man, who managed this branch so efficiently, knew of it, he blinked his eyes, probably because he was not without his own sex interests, as time was to prove.

But this house or apartment was but one of many of this kind in that district, I think, for I certainly gathered laundry from as many as four others. Again, there was the type of family that did not feel it beneath itself—its membership—to make friends with a working youth like myself, or to put it better, a laundry wagon-driver. There were girls in these families who flirted with me, or would have if I had had either the time, inclination or in some instances, skill, to take advantage of their advances; also wives—often stuffy, lumpish, meaty creatures—who were not above casual coition if the right type of youth came along. I could relate incident after incident where the purpose was plain, but where I, fearful in some instances of uncleanness, in others of contacts which could only prove troublesome or disagreeable—since I had to return regularly—or all too often because there was not sufficient charm—pretended not to be interested or not to understand.

But not always. For since my urge was what it was, and occasionally there appeared a woman or girl who was not too divorced from me in texture and mood as to be offensive, I did condescend—and that was exactly the mood in which I approached the matter—allowing myself to be drawn into the relationship then and there, which made it exceedingly brief, or when asked so to do, returning at night after hours, only to discover, and quite invariably, that there were such unæsthetic phases involved—not too clean clothing or bodies or beds or this or that, and almost invariably coupled with such wholly unæsthetic minds—as to make and leave me quite nauseated. And myself then and there deciding, and even swearing, to avoid any such shabby and meagre temptations as led to such disgusting results—and actually so doing over reasonably long periods, since it was of youth and beauty of almost unrivalled perfection that I was really thinking and dreaming.

The routes which seemed most normal and which contained the type of individual I understood best were those which concerned a rather hard-working, saving, managerial class —husbands who were floorwalkers, salesmen, theatre treasurers, brokers, musicians, grocers, police captains, politicians, contractors and the like. In this world I encountered, almost invariably, the housewives themselves. And here it was that I certainly saw American bourgeois virtue at its best. For here, and scarcely elsewhere, I would hear complaints as to torn shirts, missing or damaged collars, slowness in delivery and the like. And from these several varieties of peoples and neighbourhoods as well as from the condition of the bundle itself, I learned to judge whether the housewife was a slattern or whether she was cautious, courteous, liberal, sympathetic, or what not. You could nearly always tell after one look at a bundle or a patron. Straws showed—and usually the very first straw at that. A slattern would hand out a bundle without a paper or string or pins, and the laundry in such a filthy or shabby condition as to alienate you at once. The trim, cautious housewife would appear with a bundle usually small but wrapped and tied with the greatest care, and there would be a number of instructions, reproaches and demands. Again, there was the genial, comfy woman who would pin her bundle up at the last minute, stuffing in everything she could find without counting it, and handing it to you with a smile, usually sufficiently well financed to be able to do things in this way and suffer no harm from it.

"There you are! I guess that will do. Is it very bad out to-day?"

"Do you think that will hold? Perhaps I'd better stick in one more pin. Nice day, isn't it?"

"Aren't you cold, you poor thing? Don't you want to come in for a minute? I should think you'd freeze to death!"

As a matter of fact, I only suffered from the cold for the first few weeks, after which I began to enjoy it, since fresh air and exercise—the concomitants of this out-of-door employment —swiftly hardened me to weather and even brought a distaste for too much indoor life. Finally, only the rawest and fiercest days could make me feel cold, and this not for long. For I was in and out of same every other minute or so, and for the rest I was merely set up, as by a tonic, by cold winds and snow, and instead of growing weaker or more subject to cold rapidly grew stronger and more pleased with my health and work.

Lastly, to return to those types I was speaking of, there was the shrew or cheat, always intent on making trouble, never paying willingly, and frequently appearing at the office to complain of one thing or another and so winning a small rebate or a gift of a collar or a shirt. I could not say that I liked best either this class or the morally lower or socially higher. All were interesting. At very bottom, though, I am suré that at that time I preferred, first, the richer, because of the suggested ease and comfort; next, the lower, if not the lowest, because of what it not only suggested but even furnished betimes in the way of sex intimacies; while the middle class or region stood with me for those more stable virtues so persistently commended if not followed by all—order, care, restraint, economy, cleanliness and the like. But the most wealthy or well-placed, as I saw wealth and emplacement at the time, always appealed to me as those with whom I most properly belonged. Was I not intelligent, ambitious, observing, and by degrees, as I also saw, coming to make my way in connection with that one greatest necessity—sex satisfaction —which had so blocked and tortured me up to this time? I would have what I wanted—I would have what I wanted —was one of the thoughts that persistently drummed in my ears, even though now, as in Warsaw and elsewhere, I was set at naught or quite regularly defeated and so still tortured by some one girl somewhere who was exceptionally beautiful and, by reason of that, proud and indifferent. Ha, the searing power of her! The ashes to which all lesser acceptances were reduced!

My working hours were so lengthy at times as to seem intolerable; they left me such brief periods for play that I was almost inclined to weep. Since I had to get my horse and wagon out of the company barn and report at the door at seven a.m., it will be plain that I had to leave the house at six-thirty, or a little before. That meant rising at five-forty-five, for by now I was addicted to the cold bath habit and wanted a light breakfast in the bargain. At noontime, as a rule, I lunched wherever I happened to be, usually in a small outlying restaurant where I could get a meal for fifteen or twenty cents. At night, of course, I managed to get home to eat, but never before seven-thirty or seven-forty-five on weekdays—on Saturdays we were expected to work until midnight or even one o'clock, without extra pay, in order to clear away the extras and rush orders which came in on all routes late Friday night and early Saturday morning. Hence, a rather fagged Sunday, which none the less and because of these hard weekdays I enjoyed as one might a feast or rare holiday. But how some of the young drivers—and they were a healthy, friendly lot—used to swear as they contemplated the immense stacks of laundry which meant their last loads after six o'clock on Saturday!

"God damn the God damn bastardly laundry business!" young Lasher used to growl as he carried out load after load

575

to his wagon late Saturday night, the while others were presumably hurrying to this or that pleasure and the cars and sidewalks were crowded with Saturday night throngs out for a good time. "Look at 'em! Everybody can have a good time except you and me! What damned fools we are! I know I am! I wouldn'a taken this job if it hadn't been I lost my other one over to the furniture works. But I'll get outta this soon. By God, I will! I won't stand for it! Nine dollars, and all this work, and overtime!" (I was getting eight.) Yet finally he would crawl into his wagon, grumbling and yet with a genial determination to make the best of it. He received nine dollars, as he told me once, because he had been there six months longer than I had. But he soon left, and before I did.

With me, however, the novelty of the life helped a little, as well as the fact that I needed the money, which was more than I had ever received before. I liked the long, easy drives, the interesting city scenes, the individuals and the crowds. Life was fascinatingly displayed here, more fully than ever before under my eyes—a welter of the commonplace, the uniform, the ugly, the beautiful, the difficult, and yet promising all that was worth anything, as it seemed to me then and as it still seems—the ultimate agreeable union of one man with one woman, and vice versa. What other reason it had, if any, was not quite plain. Work for work's sake, study, improving the mind, hoarding means against want, being famous? Yes, but wherever one turned, here were those little nests, with lamps, rugs, cookstoves, curtains, and built out of and sustained by whatever energy or effort or thought there was; and resulting in children to be reared and trained to continue this. What else? Laws, rules, religion were nothing much save schemes to make these little homes reasonably secure. All the troubles, storms, dramas, arose out of things which militated against the peace of these or their component members. As for these homes themselves, apart from their social or evolutionary origin, I saw them as well suited to the average mind, my own included, only I always wondered how I was to resist the attractions of so many other women who might arrive on the scene later and who would smile or at least be too beautiful not to arouse emotions which the sanctity of the home would suggest ought not to be satisfied. And so, possibly result in the destruction of that home. Therein lay the puzzle for me. And it was a great puzzle.

Not long after I started working for the Munger Company, one of those little sex comedy-dramas occurred which illustrated exactly what I was thinking of. Our resident manager —an unattractive little man, it seemed to me, but clever enough—bald-headed, with thick, black shoe-brush whiskers and black, beady, birdlike eyes—was the kind of a man to whom I would have said no really attractive girl would have given a second glance. But that only showed how little I knew. For Blackman was not only married to a very attractive woman, who had had two children by him—he lived in the next street beyond ours in a house well suited to his conventional taste and good income—but he had an attractive sweetheart also, as I will show. Only he and his wife—to the outward eye at least—were the pink of conventional neighbourhood perfection, church-going, home-loving, and the like. I knew roughly in a way, because quite regularly I called there to collect and deliver laundry.

In the laundry, as I have indicated, were all sorts of girls— the lean, the fat, the pretty, the homely or nearly so, the dull, the bright, and so on. And among them was one who had often caught my eye—a short, plump but not too stout, girl of perhaps nineteen, whose face and arms suggested something—a geniality, warmth, sensuousness and so on, somehow a nebulous unmorality which made for wonder, the usual wonder. Often and long, when she was not looking, I had studied her. But to no result in so far as I could see. And for a very good reason. Her eyes were elsewhere. And on none other than Blackman, who, as all knew, was interested in her. It was my sweetheart, among others, who called my attention to the fact that he employed her in the front office close to his desk and at labour presumably above her capacity. At any rate, she sat on a stool adjoining his and checked up accounts with him.

"Gee, it's a cinch to be a manager," commented Lasher. "All you have to do is call 'em up to the office and sit 'em up on a high stool. Then you can do what you like." He smiled cynically.

"What do you mean?" I asked, eager to hear what he would say.

"Oh, he's getting what he wants from Kitty Ballion."
(That was her name.) "I see 'em now and then over in
Randolph Street." (This was the district in which the con-
venient houses were located.)

After that I studied this girl with fascinated eyes. According to my youthful standards, she was too young and attractive
to be wasting herself on so small and pinchbeck a specimen
as Blackman. Why not myself, and not wasting, either! I
did not then so clearly as later understand how many elements
may enter into a union of this kind—maternal as well as sensual
considerations, the value of a job or mere money, to say nothing
of real affection.

But this liaison was not of long duration, alas. (I am
speaking for Mr. Blackman, and Mr. Blackman only.) Someone—some moral or envious busybody in the office, I assume,
jealous of the favours extended this girl—wrote Mrs. Blackman,
giving her full information. At any rate, one day there she
was. And presto! One of those fierce domestic scenes
enacted in the front office which arrested the attention of
not only the laundry but the street, as I heard. I was not
present except at the very last, seeing Mrs. Blackman, a stocky,
vigorous, black-haired woman, leaving with her husband,
very pale and tense, looking as though he were about to
collapse from excitement. And according to my Nellie,
Mrs. Blackman had come in blazing angry, a clicking light in
her black eyes, and hurrying behind the counter and into
Blackman's small office, had there found her husband standing
behind the Ballion girl and had at once begun to upbraid and
even assault him, the while she ordered the offending girl
from the place. And instead of his asserting his authority as
manager of the place and compelling her to respect it or leave,
he allowed the girl to go and then sought to persuade his
wife to peace and silence. But not so. Girls came from
the general workroom to peer in through the doorway. Nellie,
as she told me, had been compelled to retreat to a discreet
distance, pretending not to see or hear. As for myself, when
I came in, I saw, and, such is my human frailty, almost rejoiced
in the tense excitement and terror. Ha, ha, my fine bird!
So he was caught, was he? Excellent! For why should he,
etc., etc., not being I, be allowed to get away with such things?
Never! I . . . I . . . well, in any case . . .

Just the same, this burst of marital rage had a marked effect on me. It roused all sorts of troublesome thoughts as to the security of marriage and whether a man had a right to be unfaithful to his wife. My father and the Catholic Church would emphatically say no. Sutcliffe, who was here in Chicago at this very time, working in a factory and visiting me betimes, would say that a man should not give vent to his lower or animal passions, that his mind should be fixed on superior or spiritual things. Personally, after due thought, I could not see it that way. I found myself siding with the individual and the passions which nature had created as opposed to the hard and fast rules of society. And why not? Was not life, and more life, and pleasure, the point of it all? I thought so—secretly, at least. Not that I did not respect society, or certain successful phases of it at least, and the care and rearing of children where I found them being well reared and cared for; but I could not help looking upon men and women as individuals, not teams, and in the face of the great passions which animate them, unaccountable.

For instance, it was useless for anyone to say to me "Thou shalt not commit adultery" and expect me not to do so if a beautiful woman offered herself to me, my desires being what they were. And again, it was useless to say "Thou shalt not lie"—a thing which at that time I imagined was one of the Ten Commandments, assuming "Thou shalt not bear false witness against thy neighbour" to be the same thing— when if I had committed adultery and did not lie, I would be open to the opposition of the whole community. My feeling was that here was one place at least where necessity compelled one unavoidably to part company with asserted moral law or permit asserted moral law to destroy one's delight in life. I, for one, did not propose that asserted moral law should interfere with my sharp human instincts, and the only thing to do then was to lie and pretend that I was moral, or at least avoid the subject so that I could not be put on record.

Among most men, as I also saw well enough, there was a tendency to condone lapses of this kind, while among women it was quite the other way about, and I could not figure that out. Why were women, especially married women, more moral than men—if they really were (and I assumed, because of the vast palaver on the subject, that they were)? And why were men at heart apparently varietists? I, for one, found myself damning infidelity and yet at the same time seeking to break the moral code for myself.

Similarly, I found myself growling at the rich for enjoying pleasures which I could not enjoy, while seeking eagerly to be wealthy myself so that I could do the same. Was not that shabby, I asked myself? In my own family, our boys and girls did, or certainly had done, as they pleased, without taking religion and ethics into too strong consideration. Still, being a thinker and having an inclination to unravel the mystery of human relationship, I was interested to see if I could justify myself as against the current conceptions of my community. I could not, really, for I was overawed by the number of persons who believed otherwise and who could and would visit their opposition on one. Again, the presence of a vast number, dominated like my father by fixed religious beliefs, tended to make one feel that there might be something in this moral code, whether I could justify it to myself or not. The voice or instincts of the people might be the voice of God, and the true instincts of the majority might be different from mine. I might be, as it were, a freak, a scoundrel, a villain. Still, when I saw the large number of persons about me who seemed to have no moral scruples, and when I read the papers crowded with crime or social lapses, or visited the streets where people lived in horrible ignorance and poverty, or saw the rows of immoral houses and realised that nightly thousands of men were secretly visiting them, and that thousands upon thousands of others were having intimate relations with women and girls outside these institutions, I could not help but feel that there was great confusion in the minds of many as to the authority of the asserted moral law; also that if there was a moral God, there certainly was a most powerful devil who busied himself building up an intense sex hunger in men like myself, and that if we erred it was because we were very hungry and because these passions had been built up in us quite outside our willing.

It is strange, I said to myself, how this world works—and then I would think of my father, and Blackman and his wife and his girl, and O'Connor, and Levitt, and all those who did or did not do as the moral code suggested. I was not ready to believe as yet that Christianity and religions in general use were wholly an illusion, or that Christ never really lived, or that all our theories as to justice, truth, mercy and the like sprang from a desire to establish an equation or balance among the millions who find themselves living on this earth. God was still some kind of entity somewhere—the devil another. There were powers of evil and good—not one vast turning of the same thing in many guises.

But enough! I was confused. And my sex desire was intense. And that was all—that and the lack of sufficient means and gratification—that was really ailing me.

CHAPTER XC

LIFE was not so bad, though, now that I had a girl, even though I could not afford any of the various pleasures— theatres, concerts and the like—that I wished to share with her, nor yet compel her to yield to my desires. For at least I had her as a companion, lovable and devoted. She seemed so sure that one day I would marry her, and even talked of how many children we were to have and where we would live— talks which on my part seemed so baldly hypocritical that at times afterwards I was ashamed of myself. For did I really want to marry her, or any girl? I knew I did not. And as for children—in my position and on my wages—nonsense! What I really wanted was one or more of those hoyden girls of the laundry, who never gave marriage a thought—some vivacious, daring creature like Lissitina Cella, who could play and not care. . . . Curses on her for not returning my smiles! Some other fellow was being preferred to me—that was plain!

Then there was a new and actual pleasure and pride which had come upon me since leaving college, and that was the knowledge that if I could not be anything else, I could be seriously intellectual if I chose—acquire a general if not extensive education, even though I had to work so industriously and long. For during the summer, as I have indicated, Sutcliffe had appeared on the scene, ready to take up the struggle for existence, but at the same time reading and philosophising as before. And he it was, plus Miss Fielding (who came over occasionally to look me up or invite me out to Irving Park—where she now taught—of a Sunday) who urged me to find myself and think high thoughts and not bother about material joys. And this thought, not so soundly gotten hold of by me before this, pleasure-loving as I was, now began to loom before me as an open door through which

I might pass to something really important. I reconcentrated on my reading: a little law, medicine, history, physiology, botany, philosophy, general literature, anything and everything I could lay my hands on.

I recall that it was in these and related days that I first encountered Robert Louis Stevenson and Mrs. Humphry Ward. (The books of the latter I could not abide but I also noticed, and almost for the first time critically, that they sold enormously.) But best of all up to then, Tolstoi in his novelistic phase: "The Kreutzer Sonata" and "The Death of Ivan Ilyitch." I recall it was Sutcliffe who suggested these, not as sociologic material but as stories which painted life truthfully and yet were creating a stir. I was so astounded and thrilled by the pictures of life they presented that it suddenly occurred to me—almost as a new thought—that it would be a wonderful thing to be a novelist. If a man could but write like Tolstoi and have all the world listen to him! I do not recall that even then it occurred to me to write. I had no adequate material or it was not solved, but the wish to obtain a related mental effect was certainly bubbling to the surface.

What I did definitely resolve to strive for eventually was intellectuality, whether profound or not. I would be informed! In this connection, the great Chicago papers, with their fund of literary, artistic, social, dramatic and scientific gossip, interested me. I came to take almost a student's interest in what was going on in these worlds. Again in Chicago, as I learned from Sutcliffe and Miss Fielding, there were four or five celebrated lecturers or preachers, the latter of no special denomination or religious tendency; among them, Professor David Swing, a really interesting thinker, and the Rev. Frank Gunsaulus, a rather pyrotechnic religious yet semi-liberal orator who rejoiced in presenting by way of illustration historic and biographic material in connection with the growth of the world. Gunsaulus lectured on Sunday evenings at Central Music Hall, then at Wabash and Randolph, I think. Again, there was a most delightful speaker and thinker, a learned, sympathetic and interpretive person, the Rev. H. W. Thomas, who, as I learned in due time, had been thrown out of the Methodist Church years before and who now spoke every Sunday morning at McVickar's

Theatre. I came to love him dearly for the charm and obvious generosity of his nature. He seemed so concerned to make people understand and think for themselves concerning life, not to urge or force any particular theory or dogma upon them.

Again, there was a celebrated rabbi on the South Side, one Emil G. Hirsch. He was really a Jewish H. W. Thomas, and commanded the love and attention of thousands. And at the Grand Theatre congregated what was known as the Ethical Culture Society, which every Sunday morning gathered to listen to one of its six or seven lecturers who found diversion in exchanging pulpits in various cities. Of all of these, one M. M. Mangasarian—an Armenian, I believe—interested me most. He was so obviously your poet and artist and philosopher turned lecturer, and thrilled me with the wealth and colour of his mental and emotional reactions to the world around him. I hold him in grateful and admiring memory as one of the most enlightening thinkers at whose feet I ever sat. And still again, far out on the South Side, was the Rev. Jenkins Lloyd Jones, a most positive and enthusiastic transcendentalist, who ran an independent church known as Lincoln Centre. In fact, quite every Sunday morning it was to one or another of these independent churches or thinkers that I hurried, sometimes with Sutcliffe, sometimes with Al (to whom as the most intellectual and liberal member of our family I immediately pointed out these mental treats), and occasionally with Nell, whenever I could manage it.

And now I sometimes wonder if men of this stamp ever fully realise the charm and inspiration they provide for thousands who will never equal them in ability. I know that from an intellectual, practical or scientific point of view, many of them seem insufficiently definite or conclusive, but on the other hand, I doubt whether the particular groups who followed the men I have mentioned could have been arrested by definiteness and conclusiveness. They were not sufficiently developed to understand better men—if there were any better men, really. On the other hand, these speakers were so fit to lead just such audiences and to help them; they were so sincere and inquiring. From an artistic standpoint, as seen from the point of view of the art involved in oratory and poetic thought, their value is, I think, very considerable, particularly in such workaday cities as London, Chicago, Philadelphia and others. I know, for instance, that in my case, aside from the theatre—of which I caught but fleeting glimpses, the prices being prohibitive—these very presentable men, seen against a background of considerable artistry— church or stage—and pouring forth thoughts on life, literature and world personalities, moved and enlightened me, and greatly. For here in Chicago—and especially for one like myself—there was so little other than this. Inspirationally, they were of far more importance than any or all of the professors I had heard at college. They had the faculty of suggesting the fullness and richness of life, its possibilities and opportunities for the cultivation of the intellect. Besides, it was such an intense relief, after a weak of dreary economic routine, or slavery even, to find men in pulpits, or their relative places, unshackled of dogma, trying to interpret life, from a pro-moralistic point of view, it is true, none the less suggesting much of the wonder and actuality of history, philosophy, science, that was not to be gained, as I knew, from more dogmatic sources.

You see, the thing that all along I had been seeking to escape was the intellectual dry-rot of the Middle Ages, the horrible charnel house of mediæval ideas, as represented by my father's Church. The things these men offered me were splendid intellectual suggestions, pro-moralistic at times, it is true, but also liberal, sympathetic, intelligent. They attacked the wrongs of politics, the narrowness of sectarian views, the clannish isolation of families and social cliques and layers, and offered as a substitute a love of literature, art, music, and a freer, gayer public life. Needless to say, I was greatly impressed. Once more, as in the days I first entered the Warsaw public school, I felt my soul expand. And ever since then I have identified the Chicago of that day—its rare, youthful, inspirational quality—with these men, and per contra, these men, their intellectual dreams of a happy, perfect world, with Chicago.

In the ensuing springtime—late April or early May, I believe—I was approached (the first time in my life up to then that a position sought me) by one of the members of a younger and less successful laundry concern—Barnhart Brothers' Troy Laundry—which had a place in Ogden Avenue near my home. As the foreman of the Munger Laundry Company had said to me, they were seeking drivers of older established laundries who could bring them business. But they were making a very definite mistake in selecting me. Yet so it was. A small, dusty, little Jew, in some ways an offensive type, in other ways not so much so, but always a most amusing person, called at our house one evening and after introducing himself, said: "You work for Munger?"

"Yes."

"Well, I and my brothers own the Troy Laundry over here. I suppose you know about it."

"I do," I replied.

"Well," he continued, "we know all about you." (Most astoundingly flattering, that!) "We know all the promising young men in the different laundries. We watch them. We are building up a fine business, which is going to be much bigger. Now it's against our policy to take any man away from any other laundry. If you were working for us and doing good work, we wouldn't want anyone to take you away. What I just came to say, though, is this: that if at any time for any reason you want to leave, we'll pay you ten dollars a week to begin with and a commission on any new business you get. You see it's this way"—he had a slight Jewish inflection which I cannot indicate here—"we don't expect you to try and take any of Munger's customers away from him, but being an experienced man, you know where the good neighbourhoods are and perhaps you know some people who are dissatisfied with Munger, and if we don't get them, somebody else will. In that case, it would be perfectly safe to ask them—not solicit exactly, you see, but ask." I saw but as carefully refrained from indicating what, or smiling either.

I remember so clearly the oily, ingratiating, slippery tone of this man's voice, his left eye screwed up as he surveyed me from his lesser height, and that velvety instability which causes one to feel that there is nothing stable or sure anywhere in the world. He was so mouse-like, so dusty, and withal so Hebraic.

"Yes," I said, my appetite sharpening at the thought of

586

two dollars more every week and a percentage on all new business. New business, as I knew by then, comes to almost every laundry driver. He is hailed by passing pedestrians, called in by housewives from windows on occasion. He went on to explain that they would allow me ten per cent., so ten dollars' worth of new business meant eleven dollars a week, and twenty, twelve dollars. Wonderful!

But equally joined with the thought of profit in change were the intolerably long hours exacted by Munger, the policy of raising salaries only once a year, if at all; the driving nature of the work, which kept one on the jump all week long and sent one to bed thoroughly weary on Saturday night. In connection with all this, though, I was overlooking the fact that because of this very driving out-door work I never felt better, that physically and mentally my state had improved by leaps and bounds, that I was sleeping soundly and my appetite was ravenous. My meals never tasted better. A dish of beans, a cup of coffee, and a few slices of bread, were as delicious as nightingales' tongues to an epicure. Besides, I had the pleasure of indulging to the full my tendency to ruminate and speculate as to the whyness and beauty of life.

Just the same, and notwithstanding, I there and then decided to leave the Munger Laundry, after having been with them for a period of six months. For the brothers Barnhart, as I already knew from the talk of some of our drivers, were an industrious trio who brought all of the Jewish aptitude for business to bear on their laundry. Their building in Ogden Avenue had large, glistening, white-lettered windows, plus entirely new machinery and three wagons, which were newer and smarter than even those of the Munger Company. So after considering and being once more called upon by this same man, I felt this to be a solidly-established and certain to be successful concern, and hence worthy of my efforts. Besides, the man who called on me, as it turned out, was an uncle of the three brothers—all of them plump, meaty and almost gaudily dressed youths—and he assured me that I would be well treated and promptly paid. "You won't be disappointed here; you'll like it," he said. And so I believed.

My experience with these brothers Barnhart covered a

period of slightly over three months, and proved, as it seemed at the time, one of the roughest and most disastrous of my early experiences. For no sooner had I made the change than I found that the conditions were radically different from those at Munger's. Here, instead of customers being close together —almost a house-to-house collection and delivery in certain streets—they were blocks and blocks apart. And owing to the large number of calls allotted each man, the work was, if anything, more arduous, requiring a greater hurry in driving, a swifter aptitude for making change, a greater skill in laying out routes—all of which was left to the driver. More, a part of their business, as I now found, was in the business heart of Chicago, the great downtown section where traffic was so congested as to spell hours of delay for an unskilful driver, which for all my driving I still really was.

And that same little uncle whom I have described, and whose first name was Isadore, was now my pilot for a week or two, and a more finicky, irritable, picayune little creature—now that I had become an employee instead of one sought as an employee—I had never known. He was always about with the most urgent and compelling orders as to speed, method, manner—in short, the technique which their much more difficult business required. And demanding that I pay the strictest attention and do exactly as he ordered in connection with labour which was all too severe without orders. Didn't I know more about harnessing a horse than to do this or that?—some little thing which, as he saw it, delayed the speed of my morning departure. And once at the laundry and carrying out bundles—didn't I know enough not to pile bundles in such a way as to waste space? There weren't to be any extra trips here! This wasn't Munger's! More, as to the streets and addresses, some of which were in sections which I had never visited—what did I mean by turning down in this direction when by going in a somewhat different way, I could have saved a block or two? Didn't I know Chicago better than that? I began to sense trouble here.

More, as to the three brothers within the laundry—one of whom was business manager; a second, the floor or technical manager; and the third, the bookkeeper and general helper, inside and out—I noticed that the geniality of their original conversations was a very thin veneer over something which now showed as a hard and almost from the first quite unpleasant insistence on new business, and this at a time when I was almost wholly unfamiliar with the old and its routes. They kept me racing to collect and deliver, let alone solicit—a work which as it stood would have required that I labour from seven in the morning until eight or ten at night, and every night, and this did not appeal to me at all. It was too much like slavery. Not only that, but as it soon appeared, if I did not begin to get new business, I could not expect to receive the extra large wage of ten dollars which, as the eldest brother explained, was paid solely and in order to get men who could get new business, not merely men who did work which any competent driver could do.

But by temperament I was no business solicitor, at least in this field. It did not appeal to me to ask people for their laundry business. Just why I cannot say. Sutcliffe had done it at college, and I had admired him for it there. But here, and particularly for this company, no! Besides, this little Uncle Isadore was getting on my nerves, and really disgusting me with my work, and that at the very beginning. How fearful he was of possible damage to the company's fine wagons! How careful and sparing of the horse at one moment, and the next, because of some bridge he desired to cross before it opened, lashing him into a sweat. Worse, he was for ever criticising my every little action: wanting to know why I was so slow, following me inside to hurry me, grabbing bundles out of my arms and stuffing them into the wagon in order to accelerate our speed, and so on, until, like the horse, I myself was in a lather.

Within two or three weeks I was accused of returning the wrong change to this and that person, who did not speak to me but called at the office and had it corrected—errors which brought about deductions of from one to three dollars from my salary and caused me to say that the customers ought to be made to speak to me—a comment which threw the elder Barnhart into an angry mood. Did I doubt the word of the laundry? Well, speak to the customer! I did so in one instance and found him to be a Jew in a very wretched flat. I would never have sought his trade. I began to think it queer. Besides, if true, it was wholly unconscious on my part, and certainly I found no extra change in my pocket. One man, though, whose bill was $1.35 and who, as I recalled, asked me to charge it, called at the office and asserted that he had paid me at the door. This enraged me greatly. I disputed the thing as a fact, which seemed to enrage the elder brother. His rule was, as he told me then and afterwards, that the customer was always right, and that if I wanted to get along with them I would have to be more careful.

"You don't work as fast as the others," he added. "We thought you were an experienced man and could get new business. The other men do."

I stood for this criticism, anxious not to be discharged so soon, seeing that I had boasted at home of making a great step upward, but my day here was not long. One hot day in August, as I was turning a corner in the downtown district, anxious to make as much speed as possible, I collided slantingly with a swift-moving truck coming in an opposite direction, which neatly and with great despatch removed a wheel. The front axletree was bent, the body of the beautiful wagon scraped. I was in a sweat of fear and shame as I thought of the rage and scorn of my employers. No doubt they would insist on my paying for it or discharge me, or even bring legal proceedings of some kind. I was so flustered that I quite forgot to take down the name of the truck which had destroyed me, and would have returned without it save that a methodical bystander called my attention to it. Also that the truck had been too near the curb on my side. Finally, with the aid of a policeman and several bystanders, a board which would sustain the front axle by adjusting it to the left shaft, was brought, and limping thus I sought a downtown smithy. Then I took a car and went out to the laundry.

I never saw three more enraged men in my life.

"That's a devil of a note!" exclaimed the eldest brother, whose name was Frank, fixing me with a hard and contemptuous eye. "Where is the horse? Why didn't you bring the horse back? Do you want him stolen? And all the laundry? I suppose that was spilled all over the street and lost. Was the body of the wagon smashed? Hey, Abe, come in here! Now he's gone and smashed the wagon down in La Salle Street, and left it somewhere, horse, laundry, everything! Of course, he couldn't send a message out here. Get Isadore! Have him jump a car and go right down there. This is awful! A brand new wagon, too!"

"Well, wha'd I tell you?" inquired Abe, a cool, dressy, clever-looking boy, who during his elder brother's harangue had been standing, his hands in his pockets, surveying me with supreme contempt and even derision. "You would keep him! I told you to drop him three weeks ago."

By now the two were joined by Isadore and the third brother, Samuel, still younger.

"Why didn't you find some street boy and send him out here with a note?" demanded Samuel, irritably.

"Was there much laundry?" This from Frank.

"Was the horse hurt?" This from Uncle Isadore.

I answered question after question, fired at me like bullets out of a gun, the while one or the other said to one or the other that I ought to be discharged at once; that I would have to pay for it, of course; that some case would have to be fixed up against the company to which the truck belonged, witnesses secured and the like. I was upbraided, heckled, cackled at, and finally compelled to return with Isadore and Samuel first to the smithy, where everything was found just as I had left it—the horse hitched to a post in the yard, the wagon in process of repair—and from thence to the corner of Randolph and La Salle where the accident occurred. At once Uncle Isadore and Samuel undertook to interrogate the big Irish policeman stationed there, but he seemed to be filled with a lofty contempt for them and me.

"Sure, I don't know which one ran into the other," he declared. "I wasn't there. You'll have to ask other people. I don't know anything about the other wagon. There was a truck—yes. Move along now. I haven't any more time." He turned his back to furnish directions to some inquiring pedestrian and left us.

But although I was instantly discharged—that was understood the moment I said the wagon was damaged—and although the small bit of salary due me on the week was retained—as was fit and proper, no doubt—and although I had been visited with the utmost contempt and contumely up to this point, when it finally appeared (owing to the discovery of a cigar man, in return for a consideration, I believe) that the truck was out of its proper course, their attitude toward me was modified somewhat.

"You will have to come along and tell them how badly they have damaged the wagon," said Uncle Isadore to me, unctuously and with a show of favour. "It appears that you weren't so much to blame after all. That driver was on the wrong side of the street. You should have been more careful, of course, but he had no business to be there. You owe it to us, you owe it to yourself. They have lost you your place. If we can get the cost out of them, we won't hold you responsible."

He rambled on about the wagon being worth nine hundred dollars and the horse being injured in the left hind leg—things which were not true at all. My contempt for these two—particularly Uncle Isadore—grew and grew as they talked. I resolved, since I had lost my place anyhow, that I would see only justice done—no more. Besides, it was possibly as much my fault as the other person's—I could not say—but decidedly they had harried and bullied me until I was resentful and desirous of leaving. And finally, at seven o'clock, I did so, but not until I drove the by then repaired wagon to their own back yard, where, except for the scratches on the side, it looked as sound as ever. Just the same, and before I left, I had to go over all of the details of the encounter again and again; check up the laundry and write out a description of what had happened.

Each time, though, I noticed they would frame sentences for me—such as: "You were well on your own side of the street, weren't you? You remember that, don't you? You saw the hind wheel of the truck hit the horse, didn't you? Some laundry rolled out in the street and was trampled on, wasn't it?"—to all of which, being overawed and somewhat afraid to defy them, I at first returned evasive answers and then agreed to get rid of them, resolved that if the thing came to trial I would tell the truth.

I went home that night sick of my own inefficiency and error, sick of the whole hurrying, driving, conniving face of trade. Jews, for the moment at least, were anathema to me, not so much because they were opposed to me in this instance —though that was not without its import—as that they appeared so sly or clever and withal conscienceless. The morals and trade fairness of the average Gentile as I saw them then —race prejudice, possibly—appeared so much better. Jews, as I then pictured them to myself, were opportunists, with a fine eye for the immediate loophole, regardless of shame, pride, dignity, fairness, anything you will. I was not then aware, as I am to-day, of the possible beauty of the individual soul in any race, Jew as well as Gentile.

THE character of the life in the Barnhart Laundry—
the girls as well as these brothers and their inter-
relations was another thing which had interested and troubled
me, stirring up thoughts and desires which in such a world as
this I had neither the time nor the opportunity even to seek
to satisfy. Just the same, as I noted through my troubled,
hurried hours, this place was a veritable hotbed of sex, presenting far more flagrantly than even Munger's a case of commercial licence—work, for instance, in exchange for almost
compulsory concubinage. For, as anyone could see, all three
of these brothers as well as Uncle Isadore, were so lustful, so
urgent, domineering and insistent in regard to sex that any
good-looking girl who accepted a place here practically contributed her body along with her work. These brothers—all
three of them good-looking—were not to be escaped. More,
as anyone could see, the place had been selectively filled with
the most sensuous types of girls available, selected absolutely
as much for their looks as for their ability to do the work,
yet made to work by day and then, in most instances, play by
night. For these three brothers seemed to prey at will among
them, and there were three girls—as this same Uncle Isadore
later told me, and you will see why—whom they maintained
openly as mistresses in a house not far from the laundry.
(I also got this from another driver as discontented as myself.)
Here they lived—*en famille*, as it were—and it was to the
rear yard of this place that the damaged wagon was taken.

That I am fairly well justified in what I am saying will
appear from what follows. For not only did my own observations as well as those of the driver I have mentioned bear this
out, but Uncle Isadore coming, some two months after I had
left, to a grand falling-out with his nephews, came to me one
morning with a long and excited catalogue of wrongs in order
to get me to recall certain conversations and statements

(which I had never heard) in regard to a fourth interest which he said had been promised him, and in my presence, but now denied him! And after first trying to convince me that I would have to appear at some possible trial to testify that they had not only broken their faith with him but had, in addition, broken all sorts of agreements and promises to me, and after declaring that they had mulcted the wholesale grocery firm that had presumably damaged the wagon, he launched into a glowing account of their immoral life, repeating what the driver told me.

"They live right over there all together in that house now," he declared. "Frank is a regular devil. He has ruined six or seven girls. And Sam is no better. The scoundrels! I'm going to look up the parents of those girls. The police ought to be notified!"

He went away swearing vengeance, but I noticed the Barnhart Brothers' Laundry still continued in business, no scandal flamed in the papers, and after a time, passing there one evening, I saw Uncle Isadore inside as usual, conversing with his shameless nephews. And all appearing as sleek and cheerful and companionable as ever.

But my passing thoughts at the time in regard to the sex delights in connection with this house were as paradoxical as they were exciting and painful. For one thing, I resented the ability of these three men to take such attractive girls and as a part of their privileges as employers, debauch them, and at the same time I envied them this privilege. For was not I here, and unable to conquer such exceedingly attractive specimens? And, at the same time, as you will note, only to think that these girls should be so low as to lend themselves to men of this calibre! If they were determined on being low, why couldn't they be low and vile with me? (Only I did not really think they were low or vile, but lovely, delightful.)

The mental and physical appetites of man alone explain him. He is, regardless of ideals or dreams or material equipment, an eating, savage animal, and in youth, and often in age, his greatest appetite, sex. And from that, as I have always said, and still stand prepared to maintain, arises all that we know —implements and the industries for the manufacture of them: houses, temples, arts, travels and dreams of the world, its literature and its seekings. There is no other direct first cause for man. Beyond that, to be sure, may lie other things—electro-physical forces in endless combinations and varieties—but evoking what more than is seen here, and where? And who is to say, on what grounds testify? I am waiting to hear. As for myself at this time—sensing subconsciously much if not all of this—I was miserable. Life was so obviously cruel and partial; myself so hungry and inefficient. Its tortures, via the joys and beauties to which sex gave rise, so exquisite. If one could not win to these, here and now, then what was there anywhere else? I could see nothing then and can see nothing now. *Væ Victus!* Or if there is, no super-force that we know of troubles to whisper of it. Either man must help himself here or depart unsatisfied. A grim thought! Some break through at times, it is true, and like an unleashed avalanche, rage and tear over the fields they most crave. But what of those who seek and seek and yearn helplessly, and turn their thoughts into fiery flowers or deeds of other kinds? Does it repay? Is it sufficient? Does anything really repay those sensitive to desire, for its defeat? Answer, Dante! Answer, Abelard! Answer, Francesco! Romeo! Shakespeare! Goethe! Answer, all you tense-faced company of failures in love! Will you not say how agonising it is?

So to the streets again, and it was again fall, or nearly so. But then a wonderful thing. One morning, as I was preparing to start out in search of a job—this time at the doors of other laundry companies—I received a letter. It was from the Lovell Manufacturing Company, Frank Nesbit, Manager, and it stated that if I was open to consider a position as collector at a salary of fourteen dollars to begin with, I should call at the office, 65 East Lake Street. I could scarcely believe my eyes, could not understand why anybody, out of a clear sky, should offer me a job just as I was starting out to seek one, and after just having been discharged, and left for the place at once.

When I arrived I found a somewhat large and gloomy store loft situated on the second floor of a mid-block business building in East Lake Street, lighted only from the front, but its somewhat dark interior crowded with clocks, rugs, lamps, albums, and furniture of the most gaudy and junky character. After a few moments' conversation, though, it appeared that the Lovell Manufacturing Company was really a branch agency

596

of a very large factory in Pennsylvania. The salesmen of this particular branch were scarcely more than street peddlers, taking these rugs, clocks, albums, etc.—each the thing he most felt himself able to sell (all of them if he chose)—and hieing themselves to one or another portion of the city (the honest working-class regions preferred), where on salary or commission, or both, they sold these things. Most of the articles were priced at from twelve to eighteen dollars, the payments being distributed over a year or more by the simple process of collecting only thirty-five cents a week on each article. And that was where I was to come in. But why? Well, I will now tell you why.

The person who secured me this very interesting position was none other than Mr. Nesbit's wife, a woman on whom I had regularly called for laundry while I was with the Munger concern, but never once, in so far as I could recall, addressing her in any particularly personal or extra-friendly way. In short, and at the time I learned of this, I could do little more than recall her as a stout, middle-aged woman, who had greeted me cordially enough, but certainly not more so than many of my industrious female customers. But like the wife of the assistant manager of Munger's, as I had suspected at the time, she was the keeper of one of those interesting houses of convenience for unmarried couples, which seemed so common in the Chicago of that day. When Mr. Nesbit explained that his wife had suggested me for the job, I recalled her immediately, although he did not know that I knew the nature of their home business. He explained that his wife had noted my diligence as a laundry driver, and believing that I was as honest as I was energetic—and that on my looks, if you please!—(I call your attention to this, O, reader)—had recommended me to his attention, and now that he saw me, well, if I chose, he was willing to try me for a time anyhow. Now how is that? I began to wonder what it was that Mrs. Nesbit saw that I did not quite as clearly see for myself. Was I as good as all that! Gee!

The job was an easy one, very—just calling on so many people per day—as Mr. Nesbit explained. The great thing was to be honest—a quality which he usually guaranteed to himself by exacting a bond or money deposit in advance. But in my case, and on account of his wife's judgment, he was going to waive this. My hours were to be from eight-thirty or nine in the morning until such time in the afternoon as I could complete the calls on a packet of bills which he would give me, at the end of which time, but never later than five o'clock, I was to report at the office and turn in my cash. He would then listen to my explanations concerning delinquents, "moveds," "refusals," "sicks" and the like and decide what to do. In the vast majority of cases, as he told me a little later, nothing was done, even though the purchaser brazenly refused to pay for the goods and also would not give them up.

"The expense of proceeding is too great," he said. "The goods are not worth it. It's cheaper to ding-dong at them. Sometimes we can nag them into paying. Anyhow, we can keep fairly good track of them in this way and not sell them anything else."

Some salesmen, as he also explained to me at this time, had the habit or trickiness of selling to anyone, even though they knew the person was dishonest and would never pay. The first deposit they received was theirs, and the custom of the company being so, the moment a purchaser acknowledged receipt of an article and had signed an agreement to pay, these salesmen were paid their full commission in advance. This made very clear the necessity for the firm's dealing with honest people, and Mr. Nesbit made it his business to steer as clear of all others as possible. He showed me a map of Chicago, on which certain areas were marked in red, and in these areas, as he said, no sales would be accepted.

The articles to be sold, as I soon learned—and from Mr. Nesbit himself, if you please—were worth only from one-sixth to one-tenth of their face value—no more. They were sold on these terms because they were the terms which most appealed to the poor and ignorant. They were gotten up to make the greatest possible show for the least expenditure of money, material and workmanship, and certainly they were the most gaudy fakes I have ever laid eyes upon. I had not been there a week before I was marvelling that hard-earned money could be taken in exchange for such things. But so it was. These roving peddlers or "salesmen" were little more than hypnotic, mind-reading crooks who could select and influence a victim about as easily as a man could take candy from a child, yet always well within the limits of the law. And always, as I have indicated, they took to the streets of the poorer sections of the city—the poor but honest regions—a bright red or blue rug over one shoulder, a clock, vase or lamp in one hand, and ambling to and fro, knocked here and there at such likely doors as promised a cleanly, saving housewife with a hard-working husband, whereupon they would flash these gaudy baubles before her eyes, explaining how easy it was to pay for them and how willing they were to trust her. And lo, a sale!

And there were such large areas here in Chicago crowded with just these poor, small, pathetic, unpainted one or two-story cottages, set low on the wet, flat prairie and dominated by towering manufacturing structures, great gas tanks, huge Catholic churches; and in every pathetic "parlour" you would find either an album, a lamp, a rug, a clock, a settee or a chair —sometimes all—bought on this basis. In most cases, they were—as I could also sense—the bright particular jewels of these households. I haven't the slightest doubt that from one point of view they were well worth the price asked to these poor drudges of people, who had neither imagination nor skill for searching, and since they gave so much joy to those who had about as much sound artistic understanding as an animal, they probably were reasonable enough.

"My, my, my!" I can still hear these seamed-faced, gaunt-eyed, worn-handed women, in black shawls and shabby dresses, exclaim as they stood before a yellow plush album or imitation stone clock (poplar or pine weighted with lead was what they were made of), or pink or green or yellow "Smyrna" rug, newly delivered, and so happy because it had been. "Now isn't that be-yoo-ti-ful!" And the sharks conducting the Pennsylvania factory as well as those managers like Nesbit in Chicago, and hundreds of others of such kidney in every manufacturing city in the country, aided by these clever, genial, lynx-eyed "salesmen" and such numbskull collectors as myself, joined in this flim-flam game, the profits of which were sufficient to make more of those trashy millionaires who have at last made America the economic bedlam as well as robbers' roost that it is! For, as Nesbit once confided (for he soon took a real fancy to me): "I make fifty per cent. on my cost; the company makes fifty per cent. on theirs, and the salesman makes thirty-five on his, so you can figure for yourself what the articles cost and how much the people have to pay."

"But we have to do it," he added another time, in a spirit of self-justification. "These things aren't so bad, and they're what most of the people want. They wouldn't appreciate anything better. And the percentage of loss to me is very high. There are whole neighbourhoods in which I can't sell anything at all"—and he showed me these on an office map—"because anything sold in them is like something thrown in the lake. They're all thieves and whores and burglars. In the next place, in the good neighbourhoods there is always a percentage of people who are dishonest, twenty-five or thirty per cent. anyhow. They move away or say they didn't get the goods or change their names, so the honest people have to pay for all of these. Again, there's a certain amount of waste in the goods themselves. People buy them, use them for a while, find they can't pay for them and return them. Once they've been used, they're no good to us or anyone else. We have to take them out and sell them for what we can get, which is very little. So you see . . ." and he beamed on me with a most proprietary and unctuous beam . . . "there isn't much in this business after all." (He had forgotten that he had just told me that he was clearing fifty per cent.)

But I noticed that I collected from fifty to sixty dollars daily for Mr. Nesbit, as did six or seven other collectors, and that as I turned over the greenbacks and silver, he fingered them tenderly, really with a kind of miserly affection, as though he were moved voluptuously to the very core of his being. Ah, money, money, money! And of all that he took in, fifty per cent. was his. And so, who knows, one day he might be rich! Ah!

As for the poor, shifty, drunken "salesmen," I sometimes felt sorry for them, too. They made good money when they worked and when they had a novelty, but they did not always have a novelty, and they could not always work—rainy days interfered with their luck, they drank in their hours of freedom, perhaps to forget their shabby task, and there were girls who preyed on them as they preyed on their customers. All in all, they did not earn as much as they should have earned.

"Most of these fellows are nice enough men," said Nesbit one evening as he was going over his gold, "but they haven't any real business instinct, no power to save, and they drink. Very few of them have either wife or children. They run around with loose women and like to drift around the world, and they're always broke. Sometimes I have to make 'em a loan in advance in order to get 'em started to work, and then they stop when they please, because they can, you see. They're not reliable, and this is the only business they could get along in, for it's kinda like unskilled labour, only better paid, and that's the only kind of labour they can do."

He beamed on me at the very same time that he shook his head solemnly over their lot, because obviously it was just such wastrels as these that he needed to earn for him his very comfortable income. And as I could see and feel, he felt himself to be skilled, and so, safe. Oh, yes! He knew how to save his money and hire others. I can see him now, in his little wire cage—a small, dapper, oily, slightly bald man, whose voice was as soft as a woman's. Indeed, he was somewhat like a woman, and somehow catlike, too, wetting his fingers as he sorted the bills and scratching or touching his ears, and all but purring betimes. In truth, I liked him. Greedy or not, shrewd or not, he was such an ardent lover of money, and of life in such lights as he saw it.

ONCE I had taken this position, though—and I did it most joyfully and thankfully—I found myself in one of the most interesting and easy-going worlds it has ever been my lot to share. In the parlance of a later day, this work was "a cinch"—a pleasant, healthful, daily open-air walk between the hours of nine and one or two, after which I could go home and read or visit the Art Institute or the Public Library, and remain until a quarter to five, when I went to the office. You see, I was a good walker, loved it, if albeit a gabby and sociable collector, and so made my way much better than at first I had anticipated.

And such a world as it was to view from a philosophic and romantic point of view! Such bizarre neighbourhoods! Such types and characters! Although I had been drilled in variety in the laundry and real estate businesses, here I found new phases—the open houses of prostitution, for instance, Negro and white, in the newer and stranger neighbourhoods where these worthless objects were occasionally sold and where I collected from dancing or singing, or even naked or doped, whores and their paramours. Also, as I have indicated, there were the characterful sections of Poles and Huns, crowded with a hard-working, thrifty and yet volatile people, whose very eyes and gestures spelled vivacity and life and whose names, aspects, dialects—all—were intriguing to me because all so strange. And oh, how fine to be abroad these days seeing and sensing these people and their lives, their petty ambitions and eager dreams! I think of them all unto this day with so much interest. They were so separate socially as well as regionally. Swedes, Danes, Germans, Italians, Irish!

One thing I noticed at once. Although there were large areas of Jews and Negroes, we never sold anything to the Jews and little to the Negroes: the Jews because they were too clever to buy such trash; the Negroes because, in the main, they were too poor and shiftless. There were sections, though, as I have said, holding as in a tether the most degraded Americans I have ever seen—horrible, scummy, soggy, animal types, joined in with thieves, panhandlers, hoboes, barrel-house bums—regions in which the smoking of opium and the eating of cocaine, morphine and the allied soporifics were common, where nothing was sold and where unless some poor customer from another region chanced to move there, I never entered —regions in which strumpets and semi-insane wastrels were to be encountered walking in the streets or asleep at the saloon doors, and often actually surveying one with bleary or malicious eyes and seeming to threaten some horrible fate either by act or the more remote processes of contagion!

In truth, I have never seen more picturesque or more terrible neighbourhoods than Chicago contained at that time. The city had grown so fast and assembled such vast hordes of rovers and loafers and crooks and God knows what—the rakings of the slums of the world, I truly believe. More, it had been so flimsily built in the first place that great areas of the shabbiest frame houses had already, after only a few years, fallen into the most appalling decay. Streets were still unpaved, or paved so badly with broken-down cedar blocks that they would better not have been paved at all. Sidewalks were still of wood, raised all of six feet above the original prairie level on none too well-made trestles, which in their turn had sagged or at least been crushed flat to the ground, making walking in places really dangerous. In addition, there was present a quite general and strong smell of sour beer or stale whiskey or uric acid or sewer gas out of broken mains, or poisonous vapours from some distant paint factory or glue works, but always one or the other or all in combination. More, here were pasty-faced, matted-haired children, with garments that were worn and grimy and eyes that seemed bleared or diseased, at eight, ten, twelve years of age. And literally sows of women and degenerate men lolling about saloon doorsteps or in alleys, either "rushing the can" or vegetating in slimy, rancid indifference. You have perhaps seen Hogarth's drawings of London in the time of Charles II (The Rake's Progress). Chicago, between Madison Street on the north, Twelfth Street on the south, Halstead Street on the west, and the Chicago River on the east, was like that.

Those were the days, though, in which the city was growing most fascinatingly. Certain streets, like Archer, Blue Island, and Cottage Grove Avenues, were already, to me, amazing thoroughfares, providing long vistas of vehicles and pedestrians which smacked of the life of a middle or lower stratum. On some of my walks I caught imposing views of enormous railroad yards, crossed by viaducts, or towering Catholic churches dominating regions of low, rain-sodden cottages, or amazing residence sections, like Grand, Michigan and Drexel Boulevards, where new and immense mansions were either present or in process of construction. In the downtown heart, to which I returned every evening at five, were immense skyscrapers, the earliest to be reared in America. New theatres and splendid hotels—the Auditorium, for one, with its solemn Florentine tower and heavy buttressed arches. The city, as I viewed it then, seemed like a lithe young giant, unkempt in the main and befogged with the unintelligence of youth, but smooth-limbed, erect, powerful, hopeful. There was actually—and as I so often noted for myself—a note of not only hope but faith—yet in gold only, I fear. A small elevated road, newly completed—and largely because New York had one (for New York, then as now, was the envy as well as the Mecca of all America)—ran from Congress to 61st Street on the South Side. There were also immense department stores gracing State Street—The Fair, Mandel Brothers; Siegel, Cooper's; The Boston Store, Marshall Field's. And all of the principal street car lines, which formerly had been drawn by horses, were now pulled by cables and threaded the downtown thoroughfares in clanking rows. The very sight of them envisioned always the far-flung suburbs of the city. In short, the city then appeared to give promise of becoming one of the foremost in the world, and it was something to walk its streets, ponder over its youth, wealth and power, and wish that one might share in some way in its happy and halcyon future.

But as to my individual customers . . . allow me! What varied types indeed! I recall, for instance, one group of firemen and engineers, who were embedded, as it seemed to me, in the centre of a great railroad yard, where stood an enormous round-house, smoking, hissing and glowing with immense engines, the smoke of them rose-tinted in the sky above. To reach this place I had to make my way across a network of tracks alive with trains. These men, inveigled by some oily and "hail fellow" salesman, had invested in these silly rugs, clocks, lamps and the like to a ridiculous amount when considered in toto. When I found them—and after endless pains in locating and identifying them—they one and all told me to call on the first of the month, pay-day. God, I thought, surely here is a bad investment! These men are in and out of the city all the time! How is one ever to locate them on the exact day they have money?

As it turned out, though, this was by no means the case. On the contrary, when I reached the round-house on the particular afternoon indicated, here they were—nearly all—ranged about the side walls. They explained that they were really waiting for me. Those who could not be present had left the money with the others, and many of them being flush and having decided that they did not care to bother with so picayune a transaction as a dollar a month payment on a six-dollar album or a fourteen-dollar clock, paid me out of hand and took a receipt. I never did such a fine day's business again while I worked in this line. I believe I took in as much as one hundred and sixteen dollars from this one group. This so surprised my employer that he could scarcely believe it. I think he fancied for the moment that he had found a veritable treasure in me, that I must be amazingly honest not to have taken this goodly sum and decamped.

Be that as it may, there were other groups or sections, as you may well believe, neither so prosperous nor so honest. Some would lock the door, post a guard, and refuse to pay a cent on what they must have looked on as booty. Now and then, too, I would find someone who would assure me that so and so (and one I wanted) had moved away, or that such and such a person (the debtor) had never lived there at all. Sometimes I was met with curses, jeers, laughter, sometimes actually pushed out and the door slammed in my face. In contrast to this somewhat rough procedure, now and then would appear behind a shutter-crack or window curtain a mysterious and nearly always disconcerting eye, which would survey me solemnly and, as it seemed to me, derisively. If I pounded, called, or made too great an uproar, neighbours might appear —horrible slatterns, sometimes—who would proceed to make fun of me. Or betimes a grimy, dangerous-looking individual of the Bill Sikes variety, suddenly opening the door on me, and with an ugly leer exclaiming: "What the hell do you want?" or "Who the hell are you lookin' fer, anyway?" When I would explain, he would add irritably, and even threateningly: "Ain't no such person here now. Cut it, see, and don't come round no more either!"

When a man looked as though he would draw a knife and slit my throat, is it any wonder that waiving the amazing sum of fourteen dollars to be collected at the rate of twenty-five cents a week, I would write: "No answer" on my slip and give that place a wide berth.

The most amusing and contentious were the Irish and Polish saloon-keepers, who almost invariably selected clocks and who as invariably raised a row and refused to pay after they had paid two-thirds or three-fourths of their bill, because the clocks could never be made to keep exact time. They used the clocks as bar ornaments, and when they learned, as they did in most cases, that these clocks were made of the cheapest of wood and that it was almost impossible to regulate them, they would want me to do so or exchange them for new clocks—a thing which Nesbit would not do. The most he ever did was to show me how to move a little bar in the face of the clock which was supposed to make it run fast or slow, but I could never see that it made any difference. And so as a rule, the clocks were never fully paid for.

Then I recall an old Irish woman, who had bought an immense piano lamp, with a gaudy pink shade, which she kept standing by the piano, unlighted, for the simple reason that the ceiling was so low she could not light it. And indeed, it was not the light that she wanted, but the beauty of the pink shade, which glowed like an orchid in the dusty little room. Again, there was another woman who had bought two clocks, one for the front room and one for the back, so that she could always see one or the other as she worked and hear them strike their wiry, gong-y strike. Her husband was the driver of an ice wagon.

The thing that came home to me at this time, dimly enough, I am sure—since at that age my eyes and ears were scarcely attuned to anything save sound and colour—was the pathos of blundering humanity seeking in its purblind way a few crumbs from the magnificent banquet which art has spread for its devotees. For what would you call this fumbling love of colour and form, lacking as it was in any appreciation of textures or workmanship or pure and relatively exact art forms? Darwin, I believe, recorded the case of a crow that attempted to ornament its nest with bits of blue and red glass and stone; and another naturalist—whose name I have forgotten—describes a dog that brought home bits of yellow string, blue glass, white door knobs and the like, to make a collection which he kept in a secret corner of the yard. Why? For the same reason, it seems to me, that these people bought the clocks, lamps, albums, rugs and their ilk, or that a savage sticks bright feathers and beads about his head and smears his features with coloured paints. Art! The first weak impulse of the organised cell to do more than feed and maintain itself in life.

In many cases where death or non-employment interfered with the completion of an agreement, it seemed to me a shame to take the money, to come week after week and collect with threats or sour looks for something which had been amply paid for by the first seven or eight payments. Still, so I did. For behind me, as behind them, was compulsion. I, too, was needing things—a new suit, shoes, shirts, etc. And dreaming of getting them soon. And so, while I sympathised, I demanded, and where at last I closed an account, I went off gaily enough, glad to be rid of the struggle that had finally closed it. And in some cases, even these pathetic messes of neighbourhoods came to seem so hopeless or unimportant that worry was useless. Why worry over anything which was, in toto, beyond the aid of any single individual? The relinquishing of these claims would, I argued, have only permitted these people to plunge into some new folly, and after all, our follies are our life and what we are most willing to pay for. Yes, yes, yes! A thousand times yes! By our sanities and foresights and savings, we manage sometimes—not always—to keep ourselves in countenance and health. By our follies, though, and inanities, we come to know what the sting of existence really means. For what is the hoarding of wealth, after all, but an illusion? At its best or worst or last, it is a really lunatic assumption that in masses of potential freedom and usage—which gold is—lie sure freedom and sure usage. But what an illusion! For over every stack of gold or bonds or buildings

607

or promises to pay, hover no more than the dreams and illusions and frailties of one single individual. And only note daily what time and chance do to those! How frail and evanescent is not only wealth but the power and strength to use it! How death, changes of mood, changes in life itself, destroy or alter or sicken all original values so that all, all that is left is distaste, a destroying sickness of the heart and of the flesh! One might well say: Take it away—every hoard—substitute necessity and energy for security and sloth and live!

Yet I am one who still believes that something can be done by an intelligent organisation, or, in other words, government. The men at the top, if they chance to be reasonably wise and will trouble to give thought to the matter, can think out economic as well as social policies that without hoarding or oppressing will certainly prove beneficial to all, just as a scientist can discover a cure or utility which will make lighter the burden of every man. Christ said: "Feed my sheep; feed my lambs." And I say, as a breeder can control and improve the condition of his stock, so wise men in high places can think out improvements and control not only follies and errors but those who prey on them, the sharp and tricky individualists whose one aim is gross satisfaction at whatever cost to any.

For wise men—whom nature on occasion seems accidentally, if not willingly, to produce—might reasonably look to it that the grosser and more self-centred and wholly unsocial individualists be not permitted to prey too mercilessly upon those who are less intelligent or less avaricious. Not that I decry individualism. I hold myself to be a fair example of it. What I do decry is immense and wholly unreasonable rewards allotted to individuals. They ask too much, waste too much, gorge too much, strut and lord it too unnecessarily and often too cruelly for what little they do in return. True, life is an eating game, and unopposed by force within itself, appears to be willing to fill the world with weeds, to make a tropic terror. Yet opposed by thought, as it sometimes is, it can take on a much more pleasing aspect and does kindly by millions. Therefore, although I am by no means of the opinion that we are born either free or equal—not even equal before any law—still I am in favour of those mental and educational processes and palliations of any system by which an equation between the too weak and the too strong may be reached. Life, by and large, certainly organised society, depends on and therefore demands this. It all depends on whether organised society as we know it is worth something or nothing. If it is worth nothing, then obviously we accept the jungle. But do we? And if not, then that is what education means—shaping man for organised society. That, and nothing more and nothing less. And true democracy is to me a highly organised and pleasure-producing association of persons—not a jungle of extremes of outrage and brutality.

What I truly believe is that law and all other governing devices and systems can be so calculated, where careful thought is taken, as to achieve the greatest possible latitude for all, consistent with the greatest possible peace and comfort, and each according to his talents. Nature, either necessarily or because spiritually it desires it (and I think the former is the case), is seeking an equation between extremes which would otherwise clash in enormous contests for dominance, the one to the exclusion of the other through æons of time.

CHAPTER XCIII

MY days with Mr. Nesbit were six months all told, when for no less a delinquency than withholding twenty-five dollars—though I held the intention of repaying the same soon—I was discharged.

This lapse on my part I lay to my opportunistic and pagan disposition. But I offer in extenuation that here I was daily faced with evidences of the carelessness and senselessness of some persons in the disposition of their meagre funds and the cleverness of others in devising a method to trick money out of the dull or unsophisticated. (I am not really offering this as an excuse; I do not even feel that I need any. I am merely trying to elucidate the psychologic effect of certain conditions on me.) And also by now, I should say, I had become enamoured of a larger measure of existence. By no means can I indicate the varied and foolish ways in which this was manifesting itself. Suffice it to say that I had indulged in a better suit, more shoes, shirts, ties and hats than I had ever previously possessed, but as yet no really good overcoat. Rather, an old thing made over the year before by a neighbourhood tailor from a discarded coat left by my brother Paul at the time 'of my mother's death, and much worn since by me. And since now I had Nell and these women whom I occasionally encountered on my rounds, and was hoping for more and better love affairs—to be a man with a way where girls were concerned—well, judge for yourself!

The fact was, though, that after I had paid my board and room rent at home, I had as much as five or six dollars to spend on myself, and while this did not permit of any too grandiose improvements—not a really smart suit and overcoat (for these, as I found, cost not a little even then)—still I was beginning to think of myself as attractive if not handsome—having a girl to tell me so—and hence desirous of various things that might make me more so. And all the more so since a new brisk winter was near at hand, with all sorts of public entertainments listed on various billboards and in the newspapers—theatres, opera, to say nothing of that assortment of non-sectarian ministers whom I so much admired, as well as other things constantly swimming into my ken—books, magazines, newspapers, galleries of art, libraries—a whole world of things that to a youth of my temperament most strongly appealed.

But how to enter on all, or even a portion, of these things without more money! It was a puzzle. For, in a cautious way I was also venturing to reconnoitre the lobbies of some of the new and more important hotels and observing the panorama of life displayed there. And because of my now somewhat increased means, I desired to venture—and did —with Nell at times on my arm—into various theatres—Hooley's, McVickar's, and the Chicago Opera House, paying as much as a dollar and a half or two dollars each for seats, less for the balcony. The Haymarket, the Olympic, or H. R. Jacobs' were frequently visited by Al, Ed and myself in company. My sisters, busy about affairs of their own, were not sufficiently a part of my world to cause me even to think of them as companions in this sense. They were, for me at least, too remote temperamentally as well as idealistically.

Then, too, the restaurants. Alone at times, and really in an experimental sense—so curious was I about all things—I began to venture into what seemed to me at the time amazingly expensive restaurants, in which the prices soared as high as fifty and sixty cents for meat dishes. When I ate in one of these places—usually at the noon hour—I felt as though I were embarking upon a reckless and hence dangerous career which could end only in want—the downward path, as it were. At the same time, I began thinking of myself as at last tasting luxury, my ridiculous youthful goal, and in consequence my brain was fairly bubbling with ideas of still greater grandeur to come; in short, how I might climb and climb until even the best hotels would not be beyond me and I could walk unashamed and untroubled into the best theatres, etc., money in my pocket, a sense of real ability and fitness to live enfolding me as a cloak.

I have to smile. Poor, cocky, hungry, without the faintest notion of the deeps on deeps of luxury, expenditure, control, taste, here I was, assuming that I was reasonably near if not well within the gate! And at the same time, nervous as to the impending ills of a rake! In short, a nibbling ass, afraid of his own shadow, tiptoeing around, hoping that life might give him, for longing, that which he had neither the subtlety nor the courage as yet to attain. Once more I laugh.

But this matter of the twenty-five dollars was a rueful affair, which sprang from my desire for a really good-looking overcoat and hat. I saw such fascinating coats in the windows of the great stores—those perfect things hung with cards and set under lights that bring out every least detail of the fabric. My thought was that if I could once secure such a coat, with a handsome satin lining, and also a pair of good gloves and a cane, I would be practically irresistible. Some one of those beautiful girls upon whom I was always gazing with Dante-esque solemnity would look at me and say: "Isn't he handsome?" And, having such fine clothes, I would be able to talk. And there you are!

But the reverse of the picture was that I could not satisfy my dreams on fourteen dollars a week. I had to take them out in longing or devise some way of raising the money. Well . . . every day at five I had all of fifty or sixty dollars in my pocket—indeed, my pocket was always bulging with loose silver and bills, the mere handling of which was an intense satisfaction, and even delight. And every evening at five-thirty or there-abouts I did not have it—just my car-fare and a little loose change. And then the next day people would pay me more money, and so it went. Every now and then someone—usually a hard-working Danish or Swedish woman—would pay up the whole of some bill at once. And my state being what it was—and my desire—and my knowledge of how this very loose profit-taking business was conducted—Mr. Nesbit assuring me that he never made less than fifty per cent.—what more natural, really, than that it should occur to me to with-hold twenty-five or thirty dollars from the total of various such payments? The thought was interesting, the plan feasible. And although I did not act at once, still the weather growing colder and my desire stronger, finally one day someone handing me three or four dollars in complete settlement of a bill, I said to myself: Now why should I not hold this and a few more sums like it up to twenty-five dollars and get my coat and the other little things I want? Then as I go along,

I can repay it at the rate of thirty-five cents a week on each bill until these various bills are paid out!

And so thinking, I acted, and got the coat, determined to pay back each week a portion of what I took. But alas for this conclusion, as in so many such cases in life, one could not guarantee that no accident would happen. And in my case one did. For although all things went well for quite some time, at least a month or six weeks, nevertheless and none the less one day—and near the accursed Christmas holidays, too —the days of expectancy and giving—one of the women whose money I had retained, called at the office to complain that her clock was defective. She stated, of course, that she had paid the full bill, whereas my lease (all things were leased—not sold outright) on which all payments and charges were entered, showed, when then and there examined, that there was still a certain amount due. Mr. Nesbit, shrewd but pacific— quite your Robespierre in some ways—was waiting for me when I returned at five. And very gentle and sad he was, too, for he liked me and I liked him. But then, and out of a clear sky, a most devastating bolt. For with the gentlest of expressions he began: "Theodore, there is a little matter here which seems to be mixed up somewhat." And then the bill itself—and my red, shamed face, my flustered eyes and trembling hands and knees. (God, I have never taken a dime since!) I think I lost my voice completely and answered in a whisper. I know that I flushed, turned white and suffered cold chills up and down my spine. The roots of my hair hurt. "Are there any more like this?" he asked, contemplating me solemnly.

"Two or three," I admitted, weakly, believing that I might be arrested at once.

He went on counting the money I had turned in, checking up the bills according to my notations, and when he had finished turned to me in the most kindly mood, apparently, and said: "Theodore, I'm dreadfully sorry about this. You're a bright boy, and I don't think you're naturally dishonest. My wife picked you on your looks alone. But if you're going to begin anything like this, you know, you're on the straight road to hell, and I can't keep you." He paused as though he expected me to say something, but so troubled was I that I could not. This one lease showed a peculation of no more than three or four dollars, but what would he say or do if I admitted there and then to having taken twenty-five? It seemed enormous, then. But no word coming from me, he went on. "This is the dullest season of year, anyhow, Theodore, and I'll have to let two or three men go. But when things pick up again, if your accounts are no worse than I think they are, I may take you back again. Anyhow, I won't stand in the way of your getting anything else. But whatever you do, please don't begin that. Don't! It will be the finish of you as sure as hell!"

I waited, not knowing what to say, afraid to go for fear he might detain me, wretched in staying because I could not really continue to face him. I think I said I thought so, too. Finally he said: "Well, you go now. You needn't come to-morrow. There isn't enough for you to do, anyhow." And out I went.

But my thoughts as to him and his general kindness to me! And his wife and her good thoughts of me! And now she would hear of this! And worse, into the streets again—mine ancient bugaboo. And this was just about ten days before Christmas. And with the added terror that at any moment Nesbit, finding that my defalcation was larger than he anticipated—I had mentioned two or three items, but there were really six or seven—enough to amount to twenty-five dollars—would call me back or have me arrested. And, as if consonant with this fear, in a day or two a letter saying that he had discovered that what I had taken totalled twenty-five dollars, and asking me to state if there was any more and to remit the full amount as soon as possible.

Terrorised by the thought of arrest and exposure, I sat down and composed a most pleading and to me painful letter, in which I explained clearly how I had come to take the money, insisting that what he had discovered was all, and asking him to wait until I secured another job. Also that this had been a great lesson to me; that if he would not interfere with my chances of getting something else, I would behave myself. No answer to this letter, and he did nothing, not even so much as to ask for the money again or interfere in any way with my taking a place with a rival concern, to which I applied presently —after my fears had calmed somewhat—and for which, in answer to an application which I had to file stating that I had been employed by the Lovell Manufacturing Company, I was called to go to work.

But one of the hardest things I had to face was explaining to my father that first night that I was laid off on account of poor business, and that I might not get anything else until after the first of the year. Those debts—my mother's funeral expenses, to say nothing of masses for her soul, furniture accounts and the like—were still hanging over us. And he worried so and sometimes wept over them. My greatest fear, though, was that, as in the case of Conklin, he would go to the Lovell Company and inquire why so industrious a youth had been so summarily dropped. And then . . . But he did not. Only I was kept waiting in that tortured state until the second day of the new year, when, as stated, being called by the John Corbin Company, a concern of identically the same character, I went to work there.

But with this, as I have always thought, ended my true youth.

CHAPTER XCIV

IN considering all I have written here, I suddenly become
deeply aware of the fact that educationally speaking,
where any sensitive and properly interpretive mind is concerned, experience is the only true teacher—that education,
which is little more than a selective presentation of certain
stored or canned phases of experience, is at best an elucidative,
or at its poorest, a polishing process offered to experience which
is always basic.

For in looking over my own life as well as that of many
others, what do I find? In my case, principally observation
and deduction preceded in my youth, at least, by the stored
dogmas and conclusions of haywire religionists, all wholly
wrong, and yet determined upon inculcating the same, and
befuddling the natural force of my own observation. And
as for others, how many have confessed themselves to me as
deluded by conventions, baseless theories, religions and otherwise, and so, such sanities as by direct observation and intention
they might have achieved, nullified. In my case, books and
the helpful thoughts of teachers and their hints of a limited
number of working technicalia which I might or might not
use or need, helped to weed out nonsense.

Yet even without the religionists, there were the moralists
as well as the conventionalists all serving to betray me into
notions or moods which later I found to be mere clamps or
bonds which had to be broken—in short, data intended to
make me conform rather more than less to passing acceptance
which I have been struggling ever since to get rid of. In
fact, at the present time, I am strongly of the conviction that,
apart from the three Rs and the world's libraries which can
be examined at one's leisure anywhere, the formal general
education so called, supplied by the public schools and colleges
merely supplements (and, in most instances, how little) the
natural precepts and creative flares of the sensitive and creative

mind. We need only refer to such instances as those of Newton, Watt, Harvey, Franklin with his lightning kite, Fulton with his steamboat, Morse with his telegraph code, Bell with his telephone, and the more or less informed but conventionally uneducated Wright Brothers. In short, it has been the naturally sensitive as well as the highly gifted who, drawing more from casual or necessitous experience than from storehouses of education and training and their agents, have advanced and very often electrified the lockstep students of the known and the printed.

In short, in so far as education is concerned to-day, my first personal inquiry and concern would not be as to how much concentration on stored data was advisable, but rather what type of mind and character or both was attempting the concentration or studying. For from that and that alone can come any valuable changes or results. The rest? Mere page turning and thought marking. And as for morals or religion or convention in education—while I am willing to admit that nothing comes without some organisation and that, for that reason alone, certain methods must be worked out, and hence rules established and instruction in regard to the same applied, still, it is much more necessary that youth be left to free experience and those natural deductions which must follow. For, in the case of supersensitive minds, these so often give rise to advances in many fields, or are at least likely to. As for the taboos or rules of organised society, they are most often for the dumb, and one need scarcely trouble as to those. They will remain dumb and useless.

For as I see life, while I am one who believes that it is certainly advisable to try to organise life—since nothing appears without it—and to the utmost in any direction in which it shows the greatest artistic as well as practical and, therefore, comfort-giving possibilities, still I am not one who now deems this visible scheme of things as enormously important. What, cooking, eating, coition, job holding, growing, ageing, losing, winning, in so changeful and passing a scene as this, important? Bunk! It is some form of titillating illusion with about as much import to the superior forces that bring it all about as the functions and gyrations of a fly. No more. And maybe less. For these forces! ! And how little we know about them. Peeking and peering through telescopes and microscopes—like cats at mouse-holes, but bringing away what? Understanding? The answer? Any solvent for our real and continuous and unescapable ills? Yes? And since when?

For I take no meaning from life other than the picture it presents to the eye—the pleasure and pain it gives to the body. But can these be of universal interest or import? And if not —and I cannot feel that they are—they are certainly not worth preserving for any other state. I cannot feel, for instance, that a greater knowledge of chemistry or physics or mathematics is to solve anything in so far as the totality of the universe is concerned, and, personally, I do not care very much. Am I interested to know? Yes! But only curiously so. But is *all* Nature? Or the Creator? I wonder. Hence as for speculations, developments, the science of this and the art of that, to me they are only partially valuable, and at that only as passing curios or toys, useful to man as stimuli to his curiosity (sometimes—not always), and apart from that, mere phantoms of the eternal unrest which seeks apparently to entertain itself in diverse ways. For only think of eating here or drinking, or dressing, or parading, or making a name for oneself here, as meaning anything anywhere else. Tush! Life, lust, vanity, greed here merely make it seem so. But elsewhere? Tra la! Tra la!

But let me elucidate still further. For instance, I cannot see or feel that a greater knowledge of history or geology or social economics, any more than a knowledge of archery or hawking or the Greek mysteries, is to render man anything more than a temporary service here, something whereby he may comfort or entertain himself in dull hours and so escape boredom. But as for anything more than that, well, certainly, an entirely different form of intelligence (so called), based on forces and motives of which we now know nothing, may arise. Spirits of the air, or fire, or this, or that. But would they, for instance, find our architecture or our mechanics or our history, or even geology, as we know them, significant? I doubt it. A physicist will tell you, for instance, that our glorious sunsets are accidents of dust, and a geologist will report that all scenery, as we know it, is chance, never to appear perhaps anywhere again. Well, then, what of geology or scenery, or the minds that rejoice in them? Of what import, other than knowing